www.wadsworth.com

wadsworth.com is the World Wide Web site for Wadsworth and is your direct source to dozens of online resources.

At *wadsworth.com* you can find out about supplements, demonstration software, and student resources. You can also send email to many of our authors and preview new publications and exciting new technologies.

wadsworth.com
Changing the way the world learns®

CRIMINOLOGY
The Core

Larry J. Siegel, Ph.D.
University of Massachusetts—Lowell

WADSWORTH
™
THOMSON LEARNING

Australia • Canada • Mexico • Singapore • Spain • United Kingdom • United States

WADSWORTH

THOMSON LEARNING

Executive Editor, Criminal Justice: Sabra Horne
Development Editor: Terri Edwards
Assistant Editor: Dawn Mesa
Editorial Assistant: Lee McCracken
Marketing Manager: Jennifer Somerville
Marketing Assistant: Karyl Davis
Project Manager, Editorial Production: Jennie Redwitz
Print/Media Buyer: Mary Noel
Technology Project Manager: Susan DeVanna
Permissions Editor: Bob Kauser
Production Service: Cecile Joyner/The Cooper Company

Text Designer: Harry Voigt
Indexer: Kay Banning
Photo Researcher: Linda Rill
Copy Editor: Peggy Tropp
Illustrator: Robert Voigts/Wordsworth Design
Cover Designer: Yvo Riezebos
Cover Image: Collage by Noah Woods
Cover Printer: R. R. Donnelley/Roanoke
Compositor: R&S Book Composition
Printer: R. R. Donnelley/Roanoke
Photo credits: See last page of book

Printed in the United States of America
1 2 3 4 5 6 7 05 04 03 02 01

Library of Congress Cataloging-in-Publication Data
Siegel, Larry J.
    Criminology: the core/Larry J. Siegel
        p.   cm.
    Includes bibliographical references and index.
    ISBN 0-534-51942-3
    Instructor's Edition ISBN: 0-534-51953-9
1. Criminology. 2. Crime—United States.   I. Title.
HV6025.S48 2002
364—dc21   2001026060

Wadsworth/Thomson Learning
10 Davis Drive
Belmont, CA 94002-3098
USA

For more information about our products, contact us:
Thomson Learning Academic Resource Center
1-800-423-0563
http://www.wadsworth.com

International Headquarters
Thomson Learning
International Division
290 Harbor Drive, 2nd Floor
Stamford, CT 06902-7477
USA

UK/Europe/Middle East/South Africa
Thomson Learning
Berkshire House
168-173 High Holborn
London WC1V 7AA
United Kingdom

Asia
Thomson Learning
60 Albert Street, #15-01
Albert Complex
Singapore 189969

Canada
Nelson Thomson Learning
1120 Birchmount Road
Toronto, Ontario M1K 5G4
Canada

This book is dedicated to my children, Julie, Andrew, and Eric Siegel and Rachel Macy, to my wife, Therese J. Libby, and to my new son-in-law, Jason Macy, aka "Mace Danger"

Brief Contents

Contents

A. C. Cooper Ltd.; by permission of The Inner Temple, London

**Policy and Practice
in Criminology**
Exotic Defenses 20

2   Theories of Crime Causation   67

AP/Wide World Photos

Race, Culture, Gender, and Criminology
Deterring Domestic Violence   84

The Criminological Enterprise
The Nature Assumption   94

The Criminological Enterprise
Are You What You Eat? 97

Chapter 6 Social Structure Theory: Because They're Poor   117

Race, Culture, Gender, and Criminology
When Work Disappears   120

Chapter 7 Social Process Theories: Socialized to Crime   145

Policy and Practice in Criminology

Policy and Practice in Criminology

Race, Culture, Gender, and Criminology

© Esbin-Anderson/The Image Works

The Criminological Enterprise

The Criminological Enterprise

3 Crime Typologies   217

AP/Wide World Photos

4 The Criminal Justice System 329

**Policy and Practice
in Criminology**
Penal Harm: The No-Frills Movement 348

**Race, Culture, Gender,
and Criminology**
Race and Sentencing 352

Preface

Michael McDermott walked into his place of employment, an Internet consulting company in suburban Wakefield, Massachusetts, on December 26, 2000, and shot and killed seven of his coworkers. As is typical of such cases, investigators learned that McDermott was a troubled man who had been hospitalized at least three times for severe depression. Yet, despite this history of instability, he was able to obtain and keep a state firearms identification card and legally buy at stores in Massachusetts at least three of the four guns he used. He was able to buy the guns despite the fact that state law prohibits people who have been involuntarily confined to a mental institution from obtaining a license to buy any type of firearm and federal law prohibits them from buying a handgun. His parents have said Mr. McDermott was still under the care of a psychiatrist and taking antidepressant medication at the time of the shooting. Should people such as McDermott be prohibited from owning guns? Or does this restrict the right to bear arms?

Events such as the Wakefield shootings remind us of the great impact crime, law, and justice have on the American psyche. The media seem incapable of ever losing interest in notorious killers, serial murderers, drug lords, and sex criminals. It is not surprising, then, that many Americans are more concerned about crime than almost any other social problem. Most of us are worried about becoming the victims of violent crime, having our houses broken into or our cars stolen. We alter our behaviors to limit the risk of victimization and question whether legal punishment alone can control criminal offenders. We watch movies about law firms, clients, fugitives, and stone-cold killers. We are shocked at graphic accounts of drive-by shootings, police brutality, and prison riots.

I, too, have had a life-long interest in crime, law, and justice. Why do people behave the way they do? What causes one person to become violent and anti-social, while another channels his or her energy into work, school, and family? Why are some adolescents able to resist the "temptation of the streets" and become law-abiding citizens, while others join gangs and enter a criminal career? Conversely, what accounts for the behavior of the multimillionaire who cheats on his or her taxes or engages in fraudulent schemes? The former has nothing yet is able to resist crime; the latter has everything and falls prey to crime's lure.

I have been able to channel this interest into a career as a teacher of criminology. My goal in writing this text is to help students generate the same interest in criminology that has sustained me during my thirty years in college teaching. What could be more important or fascinating than a field of study that deals with such wide-ranging topics as the motivation for mass murder, the effects of violent media on young people, drug abuse, and organized crime? Criminology is a dynamic field, changing constantly with the release of major research studies, Supreme Court rulings, and governmental policy. Its dynamism and diversity make it an important and engrossing area of study.

One reason that the study of criminology is so important is that debates continue over the nature and extent of crime and the causes and prevention of criminality. Some view criminals as society's victims who are forced to violate the law because of poverty and the lack of opportunity. Others view aggressive, antisocial behavior as a product of mental and physical abnormalities, present at birth or soon after, which are stable over the life course. Still another view is that crime is a function of the rational choice of greedy, selfish people who can only be deterred though the threat of harsh punishments.

Because interest in crime and justice is so great and so timely, this text is designed to review these ongoing issues and cover the field of criminology in an organized and comprehensive manner. It is meant as a broad overview of the field, designed to whet the reader's appetite and encourage further and more in-depth exploration.

Goals and Objectives

Criminology: The Core has been carefully structured to cover relevant material in a comprehensive, balanced, and objective fashion. Every attempt has been made to make the presentation of material interesting and contemporary. No single political or theoretical position dominates the text; instead, the many diverse views that are contained within criminology and characterize its interdisciplinary nature are presented. While the text includes analysis of the most important scholarly works and scientific research reports, it also includes a great deal of topical information on recent cases and events, such as the brutal dragging death of James Byrd by white supremacists in Jasper, Texas, as well as the case of Thomas Junta, a 42-year-old truck driver who on July 5, 2000, beat his son's hockey coach to death after they had a disagreement about the coach's ability to control the game.

My primary goals in writing this text are as follows:

1. To provide students with a thorough knowledge of criminology in a brief format
2. To be as thorough and up to date as possible
3. To be objective and unbiased
4. To describe current theories, crime types, and methods of social control, and analyze their strengths and weaknesses

Topic Areas

Criminology: The Core is a concise yet thorough introduction to this fascinating field. It is divided into four main sections or topic areas.

Part 1 provides a framework for studying criminology. The first chapter defines the field and discusses its most basic concepts: the definition of crime, the component areas of criminology, the history of criminology, criminological research methods, the concept of criminal law, and the ethical issues that confront the field. Chapter 2 covers the nature, extent, and patterns of crime. Chapter 3 is devoted to the concept of victimization, including the nature of victims, theories of victimization, and programs designed to help crime victims.

Part 2 contains six chapters that cover criminological theory: Why do people behave the way they do? These views include choice (Chapter 4), biology and psychology (Chapter 5), structure and culture (Chapter 6), social process and socialization (Chapter 7), social conflict (Chapter 8), and latent trait and human development (Chapter 9).

Part 3 is devoted to the major forms of criminal behavior. The chapters in this section cover violent crime (Chapter 10), common theft offenses (Chapter 11), white-collar and organized crimes (Chapter12), and public order crimes, including sex offenses and substance abuse (Chapter 13).

Part 4 contains a single chapter that describes the criminal justice system (Chapter 14). This chapter provides an overview of the entire justice system, including the process of justice, the major organizations that make up the justice system, and concepts and perspectives of justice.

Key Features

This text contains a full array of pedagogical features and boxes (accompanied by critical thinking questions and links to *InfoTrac College Edition*) that help students analyze material in greater depth.

- **The Criminological Enterprise** reviews important issues in criminology. For example, in Chapter 2, a box titled "Explaining Crime Trends" discusses the social and political factors that cause crime rates to rise and fall.

- **Policy and Practice in Criminology** shows how criminological ideas and research can be put into action. For example, in Chapter 8, the box titled "Restorative Justice in the Community" discusses how humanistic measures are now being used to reduce criminality.

- **Race, Culture, Gender, and Criminology** examines diversity issues. In Chapter 14, for example, there is an in-depth discussion on how race influences sentencing in criminal courts.

- **Connections** help link the material to other areas covered in the book. For example, a Connections box in Chapter 11 shows how efforts to control theft offenses are linked to the choice theory of crime discussed in Chapter 4.

- **Checkpoints** are concept summaries appearing at strategic points throughout each chapter that continually reinforce learning.

- **Find It on InfoTrac College Edition** gives students added experience using the Internet and doing Web-based research.

- A **running glossary** in the margins ensures that students understand words and concepts as they are introduced.

- **Thinking Like a Criminologist,** at the end of each chapter, presents a challenging question or issue that students must use their criminological knowledge to answer or confront. Applying the information learned in the text will help students begin to "think like criminologists."

Supplements

A number of supplements are provided by Wadsworth to help instructors use *Criminology: The Core* in their courses and to aid students in preparing for exams. These include:

Instructor's Manual

The manual includes lecture outlines, discussion topics, student activities, Internet connections, media resources, and testing suggestions that will help time-pressed teachers more effectively communicate with their students and also strengthen the coverage of course material. Each chapter has multiple-choice and true/false test items, as well as sample essay questions.

Student Study Guide

An extensive student study guide has been developed for this edition. Because students learn in different ways, a variety of pedagogical aids are included in the guide to help them. Each chapter is outlined, major terms are defined, and summaries and sample tests are provided.

Criminology 2002: A Microsoft® PowerPoint® Presentation Tool

This one-stop presentation tool—designed to make it easy to assemble, edit, publish, and present custom lectures for your course—features hundreds of slides from the textbook.

Criminology Transparency Acetates

To help bring key concepts of the text to the classroom, 50 full-color transparency masters for overhead projection are available in our Criminology transparency package. These transparencies help instructors to fully discuss concepts and research findings with students.

ExamView®   This computerized testing software helps instructors create and customize exams in minutes. Instructors can easily edit and import their own questions and graphics, change test layouts, and reorganize questions. This software also offers the ability to test and grade online. It is available for both Windows and Macintosh.

Web Tutor™ on WebCT and Blackboard   Designed specifically for *Criminology: The Core,* Web Tutor is an online resource that gives both instructors and students a virtual environment that is rich with study and communication tools. For instructors, Web Tutor can provide virtual office hours, post syllabi, set up threaded discussions, and track student progress. Web Tutor can also be customized in a variety of ways, such as uploading images and other resources and adding Web links to create customized practice materials. For students, Web Tutor offers real-time access to many study aids, including flash cards, practice quizzes, online tutorials, and Web links.

Web Site for *Criminology: The Core*   This text-specific Web site, located at *http://cj.wadsworth.com,* offers a variety of online resources for students and instructors. Students can enhance their learning experience with book-specific and chapter-based resources. Web links, periodicals, and InfoTrac College Edition offer valuable and reliable sources for researching specific topics. Projects and quizzing activities provide immediate feedback and can be emailed to instructors. Online homework assignments integrate Web site research with textbook activities. Student study tips provide a well-developed guide to encourage student success. Instructor downloads and Web links for professionals offer an array of resources for curriculum development.

CNN Today Videos: Criminology, Vol. I, Criminology, Vol. II, Criminology, Vol. III, Criminology, Vol. IV   Exclusively from Wadsworth/Thomson Learning, the *CNN Today Video Series* offers compelling videos that feature current news footage from the Cable News Network's comprehensive archives. Criminology Volumes I through IV each provide a collection of two- to eight-minute clips on hot topics in criminology such as children who murder, the insanity defense, hate crimes, cyber terrorism, and much more. Available to qualified adopters, these videotapes are great lecture launchers as well as classroom discussion pieces.

The Wadsworth Criminal Justice Video Library   The Wadsworth Criminal Justice Video Library offers an exciting collection of videos to enrich lectures. Qualified adopters may select from a wide variety of professionally prepared videos covering various aspects of policing, corrections, and other areas of the criminal justice system. The selections include videos from *Films for the Humanities & Sciences, Court TV* videos that feature provocative one-hour court cases to illustrate seminal and high-profile cases in depth, *A&E American Justice Series* videos, *National Institute of Justice: Crime File* videos, *ABC News* videos, and *MPI Home Videos.*

InfoTrac® College Edition   Students receive four months of real-time access to InfoTrac College Edition's online database of continuously updated, full-length articles from hundreds of journals and periodicals. By doing a simple keyword search, users can quickly generate a list of related articles, then select relevant articles to explore and print out for reference or further study.

Crime Scenes: An Interactive Criminal Justice CD-ROM

This highly visual and interactive program casts students as the decision makers in various roles as they explore all aspects of the criminal justice system. Exciting videos and supporting documents put students in the midst of a juvenile murder trial, a prostitution case that turns into manslaughter, and several other scenarios. This product received the gold medal in higher education and silver medal for video interface from *NewMedia Magazine's Invision Awards*.

Mind of a Killer CD-ROM

Based on Eric Hickey's book *Serial Murderers and Their Victims*, this award-winning CD-ROM offers viewers a look at the psyches of the world's most notorious killers. Students can view confessions of and interviews with serial killers, and they can examine famous cases through original video documentaries and news footage. Included are 3-D profiling simulations, which are extensive mapping systems that seek to find out what motivates these killers.

Careers in Criminal Justice Interactive CD-ROM

This engaging self-exploration CD-ROM provides an interactive discovery of the wide range of careers in criminal justice. The self-assessment helps steer students to suitable careers based on their personal profile. Students can gather information on various careers from the job descriptions, salaries, employment requirements, sample tests, and video profiles of criminal justice professionals presented on this valuable tool.

Seeking Employment in Criminal Justice and Related Fields

Written by J. Scott Harr and Kären Hess, this practical book, now in its Third Edition, helps students develop a search strategy to find employment in criminal justice and related fields. Each chapter includes "insiders' views," written by individuals in the field and addressing promotions and career planning.

Guide to Careers in Criminal Justice

This concise 60-page booklet provides a brief introduction to the exciting and diverse field of criminal justice. Students can learn about opportunities in law enforcement, courts, and corrections and how they can go about getting these jobs.

Criminal Justice Internet Investigator III

This handy brochure lists the most useful criminal justice links on the World Wide Web. It includes the most popular criminal justice and criminology sites featuring online newsletters, grants and funding information, statistics, and more.

Internet Guide for Criminal Justice

Developed by Daniel Kurland and Christina Polsenberg, this easy reference text helps newcomers as well as experienced Web surfers use the Internet for criminal justice research.

Internet Activities for Criminal Justice

This 60-page booklet shows how to best utilize the Internet for research via searches and activities.

Criminology: An Introduction Using MicroCase ExplorIt, Fourth Edition

This book features real data to help students examine major criminological theories such as social disorganization, deviant associations, and others. It has 12 one-hour exercises and five independent projects in all, covering dozens of topic areas and offering an exciting view of criminological research.

Acknowledgments

My colleagues at Wadsworth Publishing did their typically outstanding job of aiding me in the preparation of the text and putting up with my seasonal angst. Sabra Horne, my wonderful editor, is always there with encouragement, enthusiasm, and advice; Terri Edwards is a terrific developmental editor who has become a good friend. Linda Rill did her usual thorough, professional job in photo research (she is almost a member of the family) and Cecile Joyner, the book's production editor, is a joy to work with (that is, she never gets mad at me no matter how I screw things up!). The sensational Jennie Redwitz somehow pulls everything together as production manager, and Jen Somerville, the marvelous marketing manager and my dear friend, helps explain to people what the book is all about. Assistant Editor Dawn Mesa was invaluable in developing the supplemental package; Technology Project Manager Susan DeVanna was invaluable in developing the text-specific Web site. And, while Dan Alpert did not work on this book (he is now Education Editor), it's reassuring to know that he is there when needed for advice and comfort (that's what a mensch is supposed to do).

Finally, I would like to thank the following reviewers for their valuable comments: John Broderick, Stonehill College; Dana C. De Witt, Chadron State College; Sandra Emory, University of New Mexico; Dorothy M. Goldsborough, Chaminade University; Robert G. Hewitt, Edison Community College; Ronald Sopenoff, Brookdale Community College; Mark A. Stelter, Montgomery College; Tom Tomlinson, Western Illinois University; and Matt Vetter, Saint Mary's University.

Larry Siegel
Bedford, New Hampshire

Part 1

Concepts of Crime, Law, and Criminology

How is crime defined? How much crime is there, and what are the trends and patterns in the crime rate? How many people fall victim to crime, and who is likely to become a crime victim? How did our system of criminal law develop, and what are the basic elements of crimes? What is the science of criminology all about? These are some of the core issues that will be addressed in the first three chapters of this text.

Chapter 1 introduces students to the field of criminology: its nature, area of study, methodologies, and historical development. Concern about crime and justice has been an important part of the human condition for more than 5,000 years, since the first criminal codes were set down in the Middle East. And, while the scientific study of crime—criminology—is considered a modern science, it has existed for more than 200 years. Chapter 1 also introduces students to one of the key components of criminology—the development of criminal law. It discusses the social history of law, the purpose of law, and how law defines crime, and it briefly examines criminal defenses and reform of the law.

The last two chapters of this section review the various sources of crime data to derive a picture of crime in the United States. Chapter 2 focuses on the nature and extent of crime, while Chapter 3 is devoted to victims and victimization. Important, stable patterns in the rates of crime and victimization indicate that these are not random events. The way crime and victimization are organized and patterned profoundly influences how criminologists view the causes of crime.

A. C. Cooper Ltd., by permission of The Inner Temple, London

1 Crime and Criminology

INTRODUCTION

Nathaniel Abraham sits in a Michigan courtroom during his trial on murder charges. How can the violent behavior of an 11-year-old child be explained? Is it a function of his environment? Upbringing? Personality? Or a combination of many different social, economic, and psychological traits and conditions?

criminology

The scientific study of the nature, extent, cause, and control of criminal behavior.

interdisciplinary

Involving two or more academic fields.

At the age of 11, Nathaniel Abraham was the youngest person to be charged with murder as an adult in the state of Michigan.[1] The boy was 11 when, on October 29, 1997, he fired a shot from a .22-caliber rifle, fatally wounding 18-year-old Ronnie Lee Greene Jr., who was standing 288 feet away. As his trial began, Nathaniel's defense attorney told jurors in his opening statement that the shooting was a "very tragic, tragic accident" and that Nathaniel had the developmental abilities of a boy 6 to 8 years old at the time of the killing. He argued that Nathaniel, one of the youngest people ever to face murder charges as an adult in the United States, was not capable of forming the intent to kill, as is required for a first-degree murder conviction. However, the prosecutor retorted that Nathaniel later bragged to friends about the killing. Prosecutors noted that Nathaniel had had 22 scrapes with police and that his mother had tried to have him ruled incorrigible in juvenile court.

After his conviction for murder, prosecutors sought a blended sentence of incarceration in a juvenile facility until age 21 followed by imprisonment in an adult facility. However, the sentencing judge ordered him to be held in juvenile detention until age 21, and then released. "While there is no guarantee Nathaniel will be rehabilitated at 21, it is clear 10 years is enough to accomplish this goal," said Judge Eugene Moore at the sentencing hearing. If society is committed to preventing future criminal behavior, Moore went on, rehabilitation through the juvenile system is the answer. "You clearly need to learn to think before you act. You have probably done the worst thing that can be done . . . you are going to have to come to terms with this," Moore told the boy.[2]

The Nathaniel Abraham case, while certainly extreme, is representative of the problems and issues that face criminologists and shape their field of study. How can we explain the violent behavior of such a young child? Was it his environment? Or was it the way he was raised and socialized? What should be done with dangerous young offenders such as Nathaniel? Offer him rehabilitative treatment, or lock him up for the rest of his life?

Such questions about crime and its control have spurred the development of **criminology**, an academic discipline that makes use of scientific methods to study the nature, extent, cause, and control of criminal behavior. Unlike political figures and media commentators, whose opinions about crime may be colored by personal experiences, biases, and election concerns, criminologists remain objective as they study crime and its consequences. For example, some politicians have sought to capitalize on public fear by advocating restrictive immigration laws. However, criminologists John Hagan and Alberto Palloni have conducted objective, scientific research that shows that immigrants are actually less involved in crime than citizens and by many measures of personal well-being do better than citizens![3]

Criminology is an **interdisciplinary** science. Criminologists hold degrees in a variety of diverse fields, most commonly sociology, but also criminal justice, political science, psychology, economics, and the natural sciences. For most of the twentieth century, criminology's primary orientation was sociological, but today it can be viewed as an integrated approach to the study of criminal behavior.

3

A Brief History of Criminology

The scientific study of crime and criminality is a relatively recent development.

During the Middle Ages (1200–1600), people who violated social norms or religious practices were believed to be witches or possessed by demons.[4] It was common practice to use cruel torture to extract confessions. Those convicted of violent or theft crimes suffered extremely harsh penalties, including whipping, branding, maiming, and execution. For example, between 1575 and 1590, Nicholas Remy, head of the Inquisition in the French province of Lorraine, ordered 900 sorcerers and witches burned to death. An estimated 100,000 people were prosecuted throughout Europe for witchcraft during the sixteenth and seventeenth centuries.

Classical Criminology

By the mid-eighteenth century, social philosophers began to argue for a more rational approach to punishment. They sought to eliminate cruel public executions, which were designed to frighten people into obedience. Reformers stressed that the relationship between crime and punishment should be balanced and fair. This more moderate view of criminal sanctions can be traced to the writings of an Italian scholar, Cesare Beccaria (1738–1794), who was one of the first scholars to develop a systematic understanding of why people committed crime.

Beccaria believed in the concept of **utilitarianism**: In their behavior choices, people want to achieve pleasure and avoid pain. Crimes occur when the potential pleasure and reward from illegal acts outweigh the likely pains of punishment. To deter crime, punishment must be sufficient—no more, no less—to counterbalance criminal gain. Beccaria's famous theorem was that in order for punishment to be effective it must be public, prompt, necessary, the least possible in the given circumstances, proportionate, and dictated by law.[5]

The writings of Beccaria and his followers form the core of what today is referred to as **classical criminology**. As originally conceived in the eighteenth century, classical criminology theory had several basic elements:

1. In every society, people have free will to choose criminal or lawful solutions to meet their needs or settle their problems.

2. Criminal solutions may be more attractive than lawful ones because they usually require less work for a greater payoff.

3. A person's choice of criminal solutions may be controlled by his or her fear of punishment.

4. The more severe, certain, and swift the punishment, the better able it is to control criminal behavior.

This classical perspective influenced judicial philosophy, and sentences were geared to be proportionate to the seriousness of the crime. Executions were still widely used but gradually came to be employed for only the most serious crimes. The catch phrase was "let the punishment fit the crime."

utilitarianism

The view that people's behavior is motivated by the pursuit of pleasure and the avoidance of pain.

classical criminology

The theoretical perspective suggesting that (1) people have free will to choose criminal or conventional behaviors; (2) people choose to commit crime for reasons of greed or personal need; and (3) crime can be controlled only by the fear of criminal sanctions.

Positivist Criminology

During the nineteenth century, a new vision of the world challenged the validity of classical theory and presented an innovative way of looking at the causes of crime. The scientific method was beginning to take hold in Europe and North America. Scientists were using careful observation and analysis of natural phenomena to explain how the world worked. New discoveries were being made in biology, astronomy, and chemistry. If the scientific method could be applied to the study of nature, then why not use it to study human behavior?

Auguste Comte (1798–1857), considered the founder of sociology, argued that societies pass through stages that can be grouped on the basis of how

positivism

The branch of social science that uses the scientific method of the natural sciences and suggests that human behavior is a product of social, biological, psychological, or economic forces.

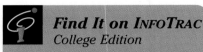

Find It on INFOTRAC
College Edition

Positivism can be used as an orientation in shaping the content of the law. To read about this perspective, look up Claire Finkelstein, "Positivism and the Notion of an Offense," *California Law Review,* March 2000 v88 i2 p335

people try to understand the world in which they live. People in primitive societies believe that inanimate objects have life (for example, the sun is a god); in later social stages, people embrace a rational, scientific view of the world. Comte called this the positive stage, and those who followed his writings became known as positivists.

Positivism has two main elements:

1. Positivists see human behavior as a function of external forces that are often beyond individual control. Some are social, such as wealth and class; others are political and historical, such as war and famine. Personal factors, such as an individual's brain structure and biological makeup or mental ability, also influence human behavior.

2. Positivists rely on the scientific method. They would agree that an abstract concept such as "intelligence" exists because it can be measured by an IQ test. They would challenge a concept such as the "soul" because it cannot be verified by the scientific method.

Early Positivism The earliest "scientific" studies examining human behavior now seem quaint and primitive. Physiognomists, such as J. K. Lavater (1741–1801), studied the facial features of criminals and found that the shape of ears, nose, and eyes and the distances between them were associated with antisocial behavior. Phrenologists, such as Franz Joseph Gall (1758–1828) and Johann K. Spurzheim (1776–1832), studied the shape of the skull and bumps on the head and concluded that these physical attributes were linked to criminal behavior.

By the early nineteenth century, abnormality in the human mind was being linked to criminal behavior patterns. Phillipe Pinel, one of the founders of French psychiatry, coined the phrase *manie sans delire* to denote what eventually was referred to as a psychopathic personality. In 1812 an American, Benjamin Rush, described patients with an "innate preternatural moral depravity."[6] English physician Henry Maudsley (1835–1918) believed that insanity and criminal behavior were strongly linked.[7] These early research efforts shifted attention to brain functioning and personality as the key to criminal behavior.

Biological Determinism In Italy Cesare Lombroso (1835–1909), known as the "father of criminology," began to study the cadavers of executed criminals in an effort to determine scientifically how criminals differed from noncriminals.

His research soon convinced Lombroso that serious and violent offenders had inherited criminal traits. These "born criminals" suffered from "atavistic anomalies"; physically, they were throwbacks to more primitive times when people were savages and were believed to have the enormous jaws and strong canine teeth common to carnivores and savages who devour raw flesh. Lombroso's version of criminal anthropology was brought to the United States via articles and textbooks that adopted his ideas.[8] By the beginning of the twentieth century, American authors were discussing "the science of penology" and "the science of criminology."[9]

Although Lombroso's version of strict biological determinism is no longer taken seriously, some criminologists have

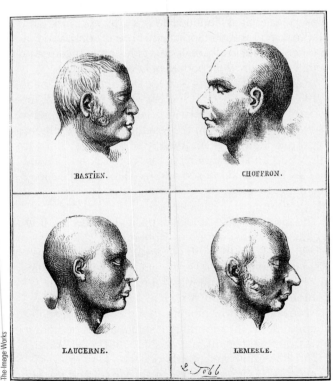

BASTIEN.   CHOFFRON.

LAUCERNE.   LEMESLE.

La *Phrénologie* criminelle.

Early positivists believed that the shape of the skull was a key determinant of behavior. These drawings from the nineteenth century illustrated "typical" criminally shaped heads.

biosocial theory

Approach to criminology that focuses on the interaction between biological and social factors as they relate to crime.

Sociological Criminology

sociological criminology

Approach to criminology, based on the work of Quertelet and Durkheim, that focuses on the relationship between social factors and crime.

anomie

A lack of norms or clear social standards. Because of rapidly shifting moral values, the individual has few guides to what is socially acceptable.

Chicago School

Group of urban sociologists who studied the relationship between environmental conditions and crime.

recently linked crime and biological traits. Because they believe that social and environmental conditions also influence human behavior, the term **biosocial theory** has been coined to reflect the assumed link between physical and social traits and their influence on behavior.

At the same time that biological views were dominating criminology, another group of positivists was developing the field of sociology to study scientifically the major social changes that were taking place in nineteenth-century society. The foundations of **sociological criminology** can be traced to the work of pioneering sociologists L.A.J. (Adolphe) Quetelet (1796–1874) and (David) Emile Durkheim (1858–1917).[10]

Quetelet was a Belgian mathematician who (along with a Frenchman, Andre-Michel Guerry) used social statistics that were just being developed in Europe to investigate the influence of social factors on the propensity to commit crime. In addition to finding a strong influence of age and sex on crime, Quetelet uncovered evidence that season, climate, population composition, and poverty were also related to criminality.[11] He was one of the first criminologists to link crime rates to alcohol consumption.[12]

According to Emile Durkheim's vision of social positivism, crime is normal because it is virtually impossible to imagine a society in which criminal behavior is totally absent.[13] Durkheim believed that crime is inevitable because people are so different from one another and use such a variety of methods and forms of behavior to meet their needs. Even if "real" crimes were eliminated, human weaknesses and petty vices would be elevated to the status of crimes. Durkheim suggested that crime can be useful and occasionally even healthful for society because it paves the way for social change. To illustrate this concept, Durkheim offered the example of the Greek philosopher Socrates, who was considered a criminal and put to death for corrupting the morals of youth simply because he expressed ideas that were different from what people believed at that time.

In his famous book *The Division of Labor in Society*, Durkheim described the consequences of the shift from a small, rural society, which he labeled "mechanical," to the more modern "organic" society with a large urban population, division of labor, and personal isolation.[14] From the resulting structural changes flowed **anomie**, or norm and role confusion. An anomic society is in chaos, experiencing moral uncertainty and an accompanying loss of traditional values. People who suffer anomie may become confused and rebellious. Might the dawning of the "Internet age" create anomie in our own culture?

The Chicago School The primacy of sociological positivism was secured by research begun in the early twentieth century by Robert Ezra Park (1864–1944), Ernest W. Burgess (1886–1966), Louis Wirth (1897–1952), and their colleagues in the sociology department at the University of Chicago. The scholars who taught at this program created what is still referred to as the **Chicago School** in honor of their unique style of doing research.

These urban sociologists examined how neighborhood conditions, such as poverty levels, influenced crime rates. They found that social forces operating in urban areas created a crime-promoting environment; some neighborhoods were "natural areas" for crime.[15] In urban neighborhoods with high levels of poverty, the fabric of critical social institutions, such as the school and the family, became undone. Their traditional ability to control behavior was undermined, and the outcome was a high crime rate.

Chicago School sociologists argued that crime was not a function of personal traits or characteristics, but rather a reaction to an environment that was inadequate for proper human relations and development. Thus, they challenged the widely held belief that criminals were biologically or psychologically

Find It on INFOTRAC
College Edition

**To learn more about how so-
cialization affects human development, use "socialization" as
a keyword on InfoTrac College
Edition. To learn how TV affects
socialization, you may want to
look at the following article:**
Susan D. Witt, "The Influence of Television
on Children's Gender Role Socialization,"
Childhood Education, Midsummer 2000 v76 i5
p322

impaired or morally inferior. Instead, crime was a social phenomenon and could
be eradicated by improving social and economic conditions.

Socialization Views During the 1930s and 1940s, another group of sociologists began conducting research that linked criminal behavior to the quality of an
individual's relationship to important social processes, such as education, family
life, and peer relations. They found that children who grew up in homes wracked
by conflict, attended inadequate schools, or associated with deviant peers became exposed to procrime forces. One position, championed by the preeminent
American criminologist Edwin Sutherland, was that people learn criminal attitudes from older, more experienced law violators. Another view, developed by
Chicago School sociologist Walter Reckless, was that crime occurs when children
develop an inadequate self-image, which renders them incapable of controlling
their own misbehavior. Both of these views linked criminality to the failure of **socialization**—the interactions people have with the various individuals, organizations, institutions, and processes of society that help them mature and develop.

Conflict Criminology

socialization

Process of human development and enculturation. Socialization is influenced by key
social processes and institutions.

While most criminologists embraced either the ecological view or the socialization view of crime, the writings of another social thinker, Karl Marx (1818–1883),
had sown the seeds for a new approach in criminology.[16]

In his *Communist Manifesto* and other writings, Marx described the oppressive labor conditions prevalent during the rise of industrial capitalism. Marx was
convinced that the character of every civilization is determined by its mode of
production—the way its people develop and produce material goods. The most
important relationship in industrial culture is between the owners of the means
of production, the capitalist bourgeoisie, and the people who do the actual
labor, the proletariat. The economic system controls all facets of human life;
consequently, people's lives revolve around the means of production. The exploitation of the working class, he believed, would eventually lead to class conflict and the end of the capitalist system.

conflict theory

The view that human behavior is shaped by
interpersonal conflict and that those who
maintain social power will use it to further
their own ends.

Although these writings laid the foundation for a Marxist criminology, it was
not until the social and political upheaval of the 1960s, fueled by the Vietnam
War, the development of an antiestablishment counterculture movement, the
civil rights movement, and the women's movement, that **conflict theory** took
hold. Young sociologists, interested in applying Marxist principles to the study of
crime, began to analyze the social conditions in the United States that promoted class conflict and crime. What emerged from this intellectual ferment
was a Marxist-based radical criminology that indicted the economic system as
producing the conditions that support a high crime rate. The Marxist tradition
has played a significant role in criminology ever since.

Contemporary Criminology

rational choice theory

The view that crime is a function of a
decision-making process in which the potential offender weighs the potential costs
and benefits of an illegal act.

These various schools of criminology, developed over 200 years, have been constantly evolving. Classical theory has evolved into modern **rational choice
theory**, which argues that criminals are rational decision makers. They use
available information to choose criminal or conventional behaviors, and their
choice is structured by the fear of punishment. Lombrosian theory has evolved
into contemporary biosocial and psychological views. Criminologists no longer
believe that a single trait or inherited characteristic can explain crime, but some
are convinced that biological and psychological traits interact with environmental factors to influence all human behavior, including criminality. Biological
and psychological theorists study the association between criminal behavior
and such factors as diet, hormonal makeup, personality, and intelligence.

social structure theory

The view that disadvantaged economic
class position is a primary cause of crime.

The original Chicago School vision has been updated in **social structure
theory**, which maintains that the social environment directly controls criminal

Figure 1.1

Criminology Perspectives

The major perspectives of criminology focus on *individual* (biological, psychological, and choice theories), *social* (structural and process theories), *political and economic* (conflict), and *multiple* (integrated) factors.

CLASSICAL/CHOICE PERSPECTIVE	**Situational forces** Crime is a function of free will and personal choice. Punishment is a deterrent to crime.
BIOLOGICAL/PSYCHOLOGICAL PERSPECTIVE	**Internal forces** Crime is a function of chemical, neurological, genetic, personality, intelligence, or mental traits.
STRUCTURAL PERSPECTIVE	**Ecological forces** Crime rates are a function of neighborhood conditions, cultural forces, and norm conflict.
PROCESS PERSPECTIVE	**Socialization forces** Crime is a function of upbringing, learning, and control. Peers, parents, and teachers influence behavior.
CONFLICT PERSPECTIVE	**Economic and political forces** Crime is a function of competition for limited resources and power. Class conflict produces crime.
INTEGRATED PERSPECTIVE	**Multiple forces** Biological, social-psychological, economic, and political forces may combine to produce crime.

CONNECTIONS

Criminologists have sought to reconcile the differences among these visions of crime by combining or integrating them into unified but complex theories of criminality. At their core, these integrated theories suggest that as people develop over the life course, a variety of factors—some social, others personal—shape their behavior patterns. What these factors are and the influence they have on human behavior will be discussed in Chapter 9.

behavior. According to this view, people at the bottom of the social structure, who cannot achieve success through conventional means, experience anomie, strain, failure, and frustration; they are the most likely to turn to criminal solutions to their problems. The social process view is also still prominent. Some theorists believe that children learn to commit crime by interacting with and modeling their behavior after others they admire; others find that criminal offenders are people whose life experiences have shattered their social bonds to society.

The writings of Marx and his followers continue to be influential. Many criminologists still view social and political conflict as the root cause of crime. The inherently unfair economic structure of the United States and other advanced capitalist countries is the engine that drives the high crime rate. Some contemporary criminologists are now combining elements from each of these views into complex integrated theories of criminal career development.

Each of the major perspectives is summarized in Figure 1.1.

What Criminologists Do: The Criminological Enterprise

Regardless of their background or training, criminologists are primarily interested in studying crime and criminal behavior. Their professional training, occupational role, and income are derived from a scientific approach to the study and analysis of crime and criminal behavior.[17]

Several subareas exist within the broader arena of criminology. Taken together, these subareas make up the criminological enterprise. Criminologists may specialize in a subarea in the same way that psychologists might specialize in a subfield of psychology, such as child development, perception, personality, psychopathology, or sexuality. Some of the more important criminological specialties are described in the following sections and summarized in Figure 1.2.

Figure 1.2

The Criminological Enterprise

These subareas constitute the field/discipline of criminology.

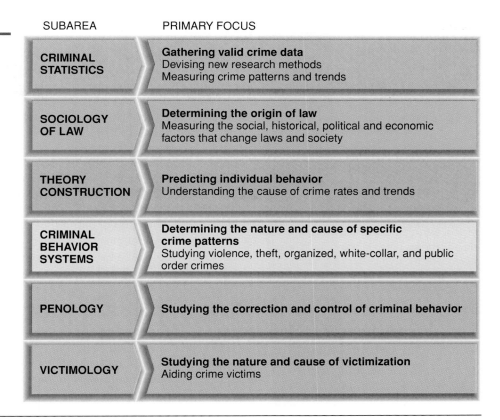

SUBAREA	PRIMARY FOCUS
CRIMINAL STATISTICS	**Gathering valid crime data** Devising new research methods Measuring crime patterns and trends
SOCIOLOGY OF LAW	**Determining the origin of law** Measuring the social, historical, political and economic factors that change laws and society
THEORY CONSTRUCTION	**Predicting individual behavior** Understanding the cause of crime rates and trends
CRIMINAL BEHAVIOR SYSTEMS	**Determining the nature and cause of specific crime patterns** Studying violence, theft, organized, white-collar, and public order crimes
PENOLOGY	**Studying the correction and control of criminal behavior**
VICTIMOLOGY	**Studying the nature and cause of victimization** Aiding crime victims

Criminal Statistics

valid

Actually measuring what one intends to measure; relevant.

reliable

Producing consistent results from one measurement to another.

The subarea of criminal statistics involves measuring the amount and trends of criminal activity. How much crime occurs annually? Who commits it? When and where does it occur? Which crimes are the most serious?

Criminologists interested in criminal statistics try to create **valid** and **reliable** measurements of criminal behavior. For example, they create techniques to analyze the records of police and court agencies. They develop methods such as questionnaires to measure the percentage of people who actually commit crimes but who escape detection by the justice system. They also develop techniques to identify the victims of crime: how many people are victims of crime and what percentage report crime to police. The study of criminal statistics is one of the most crucial aspects of the criminological enterprise because without valid and reliable data sources, efforts to conduct research on crime and create criminological theories would be futile.

Sociology of Law

CONNECTIONS

For the criminological view on the relationship between media and violence, see Chapter 5. For more on the relationship between pornography and crime, see Chapter 13.

The sociology of law is a subarea of criminology concerned with the role social forces play in shaping criminal law and the role of criminal law in shaping society. Criminologists study the history of legal thought in an effort to understand how criminal acts, such as theft, rape, and murder, evolved into their present form.

Often criminologists are asked to join the debate when a new law is proposed to outlaw or control a particular behavior. For example, across the United States a debate has been raging over the legality of artworks, films, photographs, and even music that some people find offensive and lewd and others consider harmless. Criminologists help determine the role that the law will play in curbing public access to controversial media. They may be called upon to help answer relevant questions: Do children exposed to pornography experience psychological harm? Will they later go on to commit violent crime? The answers

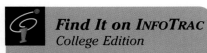

Find It on INFOTRAC
College Edition

To learn more about the sociology of law, use "sociological jurisprudence" as a subject guide. You may also want to look at the following paper:
George P. Fletcher, "The Nature and Function of Criminal Theory," *California Law Review*, May 2000 v88 i3 p687

white-collar crime

Illegal acts that capitalize on a person's status in the marketplace. White-collar crimes may include theft, embezzlement, fraud, market manipulation, restraint of trade, and false advertising.

penology

Subarea of criminology that focuses on the correction and control of criminal offenders.

rehabilitation

Treatment of criminal offenders aimed at preventing future criminal behavior.

capital punishment

The execution of criminal offenders; the death penalty.

to these question may one day shape the direction of legislation controlling Internet content.

Criminologists also participate actively in updating the content of criminal law, helping lawmakers respond to changing times and conditions. For example, computer fraud, airplane hijacking, theft from automatic teller machines, Internet scams, and illegal tapping of television cable lines are behaviors that did not exist when criminal law was originally conceived. The law must be constantly revised to reflect cultural, societal, and technological adaptations of common acts. For example, Dr. Jack Kevorkian made headlines by helping people to kill themselves using his "suicide machine." Many supporters considered Dr. Kevorkian's actions as humane. The tide turned when Michigan passed legislation making it a felony to help anyone commit suicide.[18] Nonetheless, numerous attempts to convict Kevorkian failed. Then, on March 26, 1999, Dr. Kevorkian was convicted of murder for helping a man suffering from ALS (Lou Gehrig's disease) commit suicide. His conviction may be an indication that the public's view of physician-assisted suicide has undergone change. Criminologists can help make the determination when a law should be changed, updated, or eliminated.

Developing Theories of Crime Causation

From the beginning, criminologists have wondered why people engage in criminal acts even though their behavior may result in harsh punishment and social disapproval. Some criminologists with a psychological orientation view crime as a function of personality, development, social learning, or cognition. Others investigate the biological correlates of antisocial behavior and study the biochemical, genetic, and neurological linkages to crime. Sociologists look at the social forces producing criminal behavior, including neighborhood conditions, poverty, socialization, and group interaction.

Understanding the true cause of crime remains a difficult problem. Criminologists are still unsure why, given similar conditions, some people choose criminal solutions to their problems while others conform to accepted social rules of behavior.

Understanding and Describing Criminal Behavior

Another subarea of criminology involves research on specific criminal types and patterns: violent crime, theft crime, public order crime, organized crime, and so on. Numerous attempts have been made to describe and understand particular crime types. Marvin Wolfgang's famous 1958 study, *Patterns in Criminal Homicide,* is considered a landmark analysis of the nature of homicide and the relationship between victim and offender.[19] Edwin Sutherland's analysis of business-related offenses helped coin a new phrase, **white-collar crime**, to describe economic crime activities of the affluent.

Penology

The study of **penology** involves the correction and control of known criminal offenders. Some criminologists are advocates of **rehabilitation**; they direct their efforts at identifying effective treatment strategies for individuals convicted of law violations. Others argue that crime can be prevented only through a strict policy of social control; they advocate such measures as **capital punishment** and **mandatory sentences**. Criminologists also help evaluate correctional initiatives to determine if they are effective and how they impact people's lives.

Victimology

Criminologists recognize the critical role of the victim in the criminal process and that the victim's behavior is often a key determinant of crime.[20] **Victimology** includes the following areas of interest:

mandatory sentences

A statutory requirement that a certain penalty shall be carried out in all cases of conviction for a specified offense or series of offenses.

victimology

The study of the victim's role in criminal events.

- Using victim surveys to measure the nature and extent of criminal behavior and calculate the actual costs of crime to victims
- Calculating probabilities of victimization risk
- Studying victim culpability in the precipitation of crime
- Designing services for crime victims, such as counseling and compensation programs

Victimology has taken on greater importance as more criminologists focus attention on the victim's role in the criminal event.

Deviant or Criminal? How Criminologists Define Crime

deviance

Behavior that departs from the social norm but is not necessarily criminal.

crime

An act, deemed socially harmful or dangerous, that is specifically defined, prohibited, and punished under the criminal law.

Criminologists devote themselves to measuring, understanding, and controlling crime and deviance. How are these behaviors defined, and how do we distinguish between them?

Criminologists view deviant behavior as any action that departs from the social norms of society.[21] **Deviance** thus includes a broad spectrum of behaviors, ranging from the most socially harmful, such as rape and murder, to the relatively inoffensive, such as joining a religious cult or cross-dressing. A deviant act becomes a **crime** when it is deemed socially harmful or dangerous; it then will be specifically defined, prohibited, and punished under the criminal law.

Crime and deviance are often confused because not all crimes are deviant and not all deviant acts are illegal or criminal. For example, recreational drug use such as smoking marijuana may be a crime, but is it deviant? A significant percentage of the population has used recreational drugs (including some well-known politicians). To argue that all crimes are behaviors that depart from the norms of society is probably erroneous. Similarly, many deviant acts are not criminal, even though they may be shocking or depraved. For example, a passerby who observes a person drowning is not required to jump in and render aid. Although the general public would probably condemn the person's behavior as callous, immoral, and deviant, no legal action could be taken because citizens are not required by law to effect rescues. In sum, many criminal acts, but not all, fall within the concept of deviance. Similarly, some deviant acts, but not all, are considered crimes.

Criminologists are often concerned with the concept of deviance and its relationship to criminality. The shifting definition of deviant behavior is closely associated with our concepts of crime: Where should society draw the line between behavior that is merely considered deviant and unusual, and behavior that is considered dangerous and criminal? For example, when does sexually oriented material stop being merely erotic and suggestive (deviant) and become obscene and pornographic (criminal)? Can a clear line be drawn separating sexually oriented materials into two groups, one that is legally acceptable and a second that is considered depraved or obscene? And if such a line can be drawn, who gets to draw it? If an illegal act, such as viewing Internet pornography, becomes a norm, should society reevaluate its criminal status and let it become merely an unusual or deviant act? Conversely, if scientists show that a normative act, such as smoking or drinking, poses a serious health hazard, should it be made criminal?

© Scott Houston/Corbis Sygma

Possessing marijuana may be illegal, but is it deviant? High school students who smoke "pot" may not see themselves as socially deviant but rather as cool kids who have the courage to flaunt the rules laid down by adults. Are they criminals? Are they deviant?

Though crimes may be defined as acts that are socially harmful or dangerous, criminologists still differ over what acts are truly "harmful" and who decides that they are "dangerous." As you may recall, professional criminologists usually align themselves with one of several schools of thought or perspectives. Each of these perspectives maintains its own view of what constitutes criminal behavior and what causes people to engage in criminality. A criminologist's choice of orientation or perspective thus depends, in part, on his or her definition of crime. The three most common concepts of crime used by criminologists are the consensus view, the conflict view, and the interactionist view.

The Consensus View of Crime

consensus view

The belief that the majority of citizens in a society share common values and agree on what behaviors should be defined as criminal.

criminal law

The written code that defines crimes and their punishments.

According to the **consensus view**, crimes are behaviors that all elements of society consider to be repugnant. The rich and powerful as well as the poor and indigent are believed to agree on which behaviors are so repugnant that they should be outlawed and criminalized. Therefore, the **criminal law**—the written code that defines crimes and their punishments—reflects the values, beliefs, and opinions of society's mainstream. The term *consensus* implies general agreement among a majority of citizens on what behaviors should be prohibited by criminal law and hence be viewed as crimes.[22]

This approach to crime implies that it is a function of the beliefs, morality, and rules that are inherent in Western civilization. Ideally, the laws apply equally to all members of society and their effects are not restricted to any single element of society. Whereas laws banning burglary and robbery are directed at controlling the neediest members of society, laws banning insider trading, embezzlement, and corporate price-fixing are aimed at controlling the wealthiest.

The Conflict View of Crime

conflict view

The belief that criminal behavior is defined by those in a position of power to protect and advance their own self-interest.

Although most practicing criminologists accept the consensus model of crime, others take a more political orientation toward its content. The **conflict view** depicts society as a collection of diverse groups—such as owners, workers, professionals, and students—who are in constant and continuing conflict. Groups able to assert their political power use the law and the criminal justice system to advance their economic and social position. Criminal laws, therefore, are viewed as acts created to protect the haves from the have-nots. Conflict criminologists often contrast the harsh penalties exacted on the poor for their "street crimes" (burglary, robbery, and larceny) with the minor penalties the wealthy receive for their white-collar crimes (securities violations and other illegal business practices). Whereas the poor go to prison for minor law violations, the wealthy are given lenient sentences for even the most serious breaches of law.

According to the conflict view, the definition of crime is controlled by wealth, power, and position and not by moral consensus or the fear of social disruption.[23] Crime, according to this definition, is a political concept designed to protect the power and position of the upper classes at the expense of the poor. Even laws prohibiting violent acts, such as armed robbery, rape, and murder, may have political undertones. Banning violent acts ensures domestic tranquillity and guarantees that the anger of the poor and disenfranchised classes will not be directed at their wealthy capitalist exploiters. Rape may be inspired by the capitalist system's devaluation of women, which may increase their vulnerability to sexual assault. The conflict view of crime, then, includes the following in a comprehensive list of "real" crimes:

- Violations of human rights due to racism, sexism, and imperialism
- Unsafe working conditions
- Inadequate child care

- Inadequate opportunities for employment and education and substandard housing and medical care
- Crimes of economic and political domination
- Pollution of the environment
- Price-fixing
- Police brutality
- Assassinations and warmaking
- Violations of human dignity
- Denial of physical needs and necessities, and impediments to self-determination
- Deprivation of adequate food and blocked opportunities to participate in political decision making [24]

The Interactionist View of Crime

interactionist view

The belief that those with social power are able to impose their values on society as a whole, and these values then define criminal behavior.

According to the **interactionist view** the definition of crime reflects the preferences and opinions of people who hold social power in a particular legal jurisdiction. These people use their influence to impose their definition of right and wrong on the rest of the population. Criminals are individuals that society labels as outcasts or deviants because they have violated social rules. In a classic statement, sociologist Howard Becker argued, "The deviant is one to whom that label has successfully been applied; deviant behavior is behavior people so label."[25] Crimes are outlawed behaviors because society defines them that way, not because they are inherently evil or immoral acts.

The interactionist view of crime is similar to the conflict perspective in that behavior is outlawed when it offends those with sufficient social, economic, and political power to make the law conform to their interests or needs. However, unlike the conflict view, the interactionist perspective does not attribute capitalist economic and political motives to the process of defining crime. Instead, interactionists see criminal law as conforming to the beliefs of "moral crusaders" or moral entrepreneurs, who use their influence to shape the legal process as they see fit.[26] Laws against pornography, prostitution, and drugs are believed to be motivated more by moral crusades than by capitalist sensibilities. Consequently, interactionists are concerned with shifting moral and legal standards.

A Definition of Crime

Because of their diverse perspectives, criminologists have taken a variety of approaches in explaining crime's causes and suggesting methods for its control (see Figure 1.3). Considering these differences, we can take elements from each school of thought to formulate an integrated definition of crime such as the following:

> Crime is a violation of societal rules of behavior as interpreted and expressed by the criminal law, which reflects public opinion, traditional values, and the viewpoint of people currently holding social and political power. Individuals who violate these rules are subject to sanctions by state authority, social stigma, and loss of status.

This definition combines the consensus view that the criminal law defines crimes, the conflict perspective's emphasis on political power and control, and the interactionist concept of stigma. Thus, crime as defined here is a political, social, and economic function of modern life.

No matter which definition of crime we embrace, criminal behavior is tied to the criminal law. It is therefore important for all criminologists to have some understanding of the development of criminal law, its objectives, its elements, and how it evolves.

Figure 1.3

The Definition of Crime

The definition of crime affects how criminologists view the cause and control of illegal behavior and shapes their research orientation.

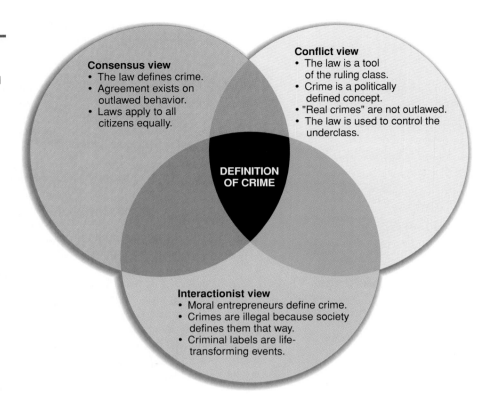

Consensus view
- The law defines crime.
- Agreement exists on outlawed behavior.
- Laws apply to all citizens equally.

Conflict view
- The law is a tool of the ruling class.
- Crime is a politically defined concept.
- "Real crimes" are not outlawed.
- The law is used to control the underclass.

DEFINITION OF CRIME

Interactionist view
- Moral entrepreneurs define crime.
- Crimes are illegal because society defines them that way.
- Criminal labels are life-transforming events.

Crime and the Criminal Law

Code of Hammurabi

The first written criminal code, developed in Babylonia about 2000 B.C.

Mosaic Code

The laws of the ancient Israelites, found in the Old Testament of the Judeo-Christian Bible.

Find It on INFOTRAC
College Edition

Did you know that the ancient Romans had laws governing the behavior of women at parties? To learn more about these and other ancient laws, use "Greek law" and "Roman law" as InfoTrac College Edition subject guides.

The concept of criminal law has been recognized for more than 3,000 years. Hammurabi (1792–1750 B.C.), the sixth king of Babylon, created the most famous set of written laws of the ancient world, known today as the **Code of Hammurabi**. Preserved on basalt rock columns, the code established a system of crime and punishment based on physical retaliation ("an eye for an eye"). The severity of punishment depended on class standing: If convicted of an unprovoked assault, a slave would be killed, whereas a freeman might lose a limb.

More familiar is the **Mosaic Code** of the Israelites (1200 B.C.). According to tradition, God entered into a covenant or contract with the tribes of Israel in which they agreed to obey his law (the 613 laws of the Old Testament, including the Ten Commandments), as presented to them by Moses, in return for God's special care and protection. The Mosaic Code is not only the foundation of Judeo-Christian moral teachings but also a basis for the U.S. legal system. Prohibitions against murder, theft, perjury, and adultery preceded, by several thousand years, the same laws found in the modern United States.

Though ancient formal legal codes were lost during the Dark Ages, early German and Anglo-Saxon societies developed legal systems featuring monetary compensation for criminal violations. Guilt was determined by two methods. One was compurgation, in which the accused person swore an oath of innocence with the backing of 12 to 25 oathhelpers, who would attest to his or her character and claims of innocence. The second was trial by ordeal, which was based on the principle that divine forces would not allow an innocent person to be harmed. It involved such measures as having the accused place his or her hand in boiling water or hold a hot iron. If the wound healed, the person was found innocent; if the wound did not heal, the accused was deemed guilty. Another version, trial by combat, allowed the accused to challenge his accuser to a duel, with the outcome determining the legitimacy of the accusation. Punishments included public flogging, branding, beheading, and burning.

Common Law

After the Norman conquest of England in 1066, royal judges began to travel throughout the land, holding court in each county several times a year. When court was in session, the royal administrator, or judge, would summon a number of citizens who would, on their oath, tell of the crimes and serious breaches of the peace that had occurred since the judge's last visit. The royal judge would then decide what to do in each case, using local custom and rules of conduct as his guide. Courts were bound to follow the law established in previous cases unless a higher authority, such as the king or the pope, overruled the law.

The present English system of law came into existence during the reign of Henry II (1154–1189), when royal judges began to publish their decisions in local cases. Judges began to use these written decisions as a basis for their decision making, and eventually a fixed body of legal rules and principles was established. If a new rule was successfully applied in a number of different cases, it would become a **precedent**. These precedents would then be commonly applied in all similar cases—hence the term **common law**. Crimes such as murder, burglary, arson, and rape are common-law crimes whose elements were initially defined by judges. They are referred to as *mala in se,* or inherently evil and depraved. When the situation required, the English Parliament enacted legislation to supplement the judge-made common law. Crimes defined by Parliament, which reflected existing social conditions, were referred to as *mala prohibitum,* or **statutory crimes**.

Before the American Revolution, the colonies, then under British rule, were subject to the common law. After the colonies acquired their independence, state legislatures standardized common-law crimes such as murder, burglary, arson, and rape by putting them into statutory form in criminal codes. As in England, whenever common law proved inadequate to deal with changing social and moral issues, the states and Congress supplemented it with legislative statutes, creating new elements in the various state and federal legal codes. Table 1.1 lists a number of crimes that were first defined in common law.

precedent

A rule derived from previous judicial decisions and applied to future cases; the basis of common law.

common law

Early English law, developed by judges, that became the standardized law of the land in England and eventually formed the basis of the criminal law in the United States.

statutory crimes

Crimes defined by legislative bodies in response to changing social conditions, public opinion, and custom.

Contemporary Criminal Law

Criminal laws are now divided into felonies and misdemeanors. The distinction is based on seriousness: A **felony** is a serious offense; a **misdemeanor** is a minor or petty crime. Crimes such as murder, rape, and burglary are felonies; they are punished with long prison sentences or even death. Crimes such as unarmed assault and battery, petty larceny, and disturbing the peace are misdemeanors; they are punished with a fine or a period of incarceration in a county jail.

Regardless of their classification, acts prohibited by the criminal law constitute behaviors considered unacceptable and impermissible by those in power. People who engage in these acts are eligible for severe sanctions. By outlawing these behaviors, the government expects to achieve a number of social goals:

■ *Enforcing social control.* Those who hold political power rely on criminal law to formally prohibit behaviors believed to threaten societal well-being or to challenge their authority. For example, U.S. criminal law incorporates centuries-old prohibitions against the following behaviors harmful to others: taking another person's possessions, physically harming another person, damaging another person's property, and cheating another person out of his or her possessions. Similarly, the law prevents actions that challenge the legitimacy of the government, such as planning its overthrow, collaborating with its enemies, and so on.

felony

A serious offense that carries a penalty of imprisonment, usually for one year or more, and may entail loss of political rights.

misdemeanor

A minor crime usually punished by a short jail term and/or a fine.

Table 1.1 Common-Law Crimes

CRIMES	EXAMPLES
Crimes Against the Person	
First-degree murder. Unlawful killing of another human being with malice aforethought and with premeditation and deliberation.	A woman buys some poison and pours it into a cup of coffee her husband is drinking, intending to kill him. The motive—to get the insurance benefits of the victim.
Voluntary manslaughter. Intentional killing committed under extenuating circumstances that mitigate the killing, such as killing in the heat of passion after being provoked.	A husband coming home early from work finds his wife in bed with another man. The husband goes into a rage and shoots and kills both lovers with a gun he keeps by his bedside.
Battery. Unlawful touching of another with intent to cause injury.	A man seeing a stranger sitting in his favorite seat in a cafeteria goes up to that person and pushes him out of the seat.
Assault. Intentional placing of another in fear of receiving an immediate battery.	A student aims an unloaded gun at her professor, who believes the gun is loaded. She says she is going to shoot.
Rape. Unlawful sexual intercourse with a female without her consent.	After a party, a man offers to drive a young female acquaintance home. He takes her to a wooded area and, despite her protests, forces her to have sexual relations with him.
Robbery. Wrongful taking and carrying away of personal property from a person by violence or intimidation.	A man armed with a loaded gun approaches another man on a deserted street and demands his wallet.
Inchoate (Incomplete) Offenses	
Attempt. An intentional act for the purpose of committing a crime that is more than mere preparation or planning of the crime. The crime is not completed, however.	A person intending to kill another person places a bomb in the intended victim's car so that it will detonate when the ignition key is used. The bomb is discovered before the car is started. Attempted murder has been committed.
Conspiracy. Voluntary agreement between two or more persons to achieve an unlawful object or to achieve a lawful object using means forbidden by law.	A drug company sells larger-than-normal quantities of drugs to a doctor, knowing that the doctor is distributing the drugs illegally. The drug company is guilty of conspiracy.
Crimes Against Property	
Burglary. Breaking and entering of a dwelling house of another in the nighttime with the intent to commit a felony.	Intending to steal some jewelry and silver, a young man breaks a window and enters another's house at 10 P.M.
Arson. Intentional burning of a dwelling house of another.	A secretary, angry that her boss did not give her a raise, goes to her boss's house and sets fire to it.
Larceny. Taking and carrying away the personal property of another with the intent to keep and possess the property.	While a woman is shopping, she sees a diamond ring displayed at the jewelry counter. When no one is looking, the woman takes the ring and walks out of the store.

SOURCE: Developed by Therese J. Libby, J.D.

■ *Discouraging revenge.* By punishing people who infringe on the rights, property, and freedom of others, the law shifts the burden of revenge from the individual to the state. As Oliver Wendell Holmes stated, this prevents "the greater evil of private retribution."[27] Although state retaliation may offend the sensibilities of many citizens, it is greatly preferable to a system in which people would have to seek justice for themselves.

■ *Expressing public opinion and morality.* Criminal law reflects constantly changing public opinions and moral values. *Mala in se* crimes, such as murder and forcible rape, are almost universally prohibited; however, the prohibition of legislatively created *mala prohibitum* crimes, such as traffic offenses and gambling violations, changes according to social conditions and attitudes. Criminal law is used to codify these changes.

■ *Deterring criminal behavior.* Criminal law has a social control function. It can control, restrain, and direct human behavior through its sanctioning power. The threat of punishment associated with violating the law is designed to prevent crimes before they occur. During the Middle Ages, public executions drove this point home. Today criminal law's impact is felt through news accounts of long prison sentences and an occasional execution.

■ *Punishing wrongdoing.* The deterrent power of criminal law is tied to the authority it gives the state to sanction or punish offenders. Those who violate criminal law are subject to physical coercion and punishment.

■ *Maintaining social order.* All legal systems are designed to support and maintain the boundaries of the social system they serve. In medieval England, the law protected the feudal system by defining an orderly system of property transfer and ownership. Laws in some socialist nations protect the primacy of the state by strictly curtailing profiteering and individual enterprise. Our own capitalist system is also supported and sustained by criminal law. In a sense, the content of criminal law is more a reflection of the needs of those who control the existing economic and political system than a representation of some idealized moral code.

The Elements of a Crime

actus reus

An illegal or "guilty" act. It may be an affirmative act, such as killing, or a failure to act when legally required to do so.

mens rea

A "guilty mind"; the intent to commit a criminal act.

In order for a crime to occur, the state must show that the accused committed the guilty act, or *actus reus*, and had the *mens rea*, or criminal intent, to commit the act. The *actus reus* may be an aggressive act, such as taking someone's money, burning a building, or shooting someone; or it may be a failure to act when there is a legal duty to do so, such as a parent's neglecting to seek medical attention for a sick child. The *mens rea* (guilty mind) refers to an individual's state of mind at the time of the act or, more specifically, the person's intent to commit the crime.

For most crimes, both the *actus reus* and the *mens rea* must be present for the act to be considered a crime. For example, if George decides to kill Bob and then takes a gun and shoots Bob, George can be convicted of the crime of murder, because both elements are present. George's shooting of Bob is the *actus reus*; his decision to kill Bob is the *mens rea*. However, if George only thinks about shooting Bob but does nothing about it, the element of *actus reus* is absent, and no crime has been committed. Thoughts of committing an act do not, in themselves, constitute a crime. Let us now look more closely at these issues.

Actus Reus To satisfy the requirements of *actus reus*, guilty actions must be voluntary. Even though an act may cause harm or damage, it is not considered a crime if it was done by accident or was an involuntary act. For example, it would not be a crime if a motorist obeying all the traffic laws hit a child who had ran into the street. If the same motorist were drinking or speeding, then his action would be considered a vehicular crime because it was a product of negligence. Similarly, it would not be considered a crime if a baby-sitter accidentally dropped a child and the child died. However, it would be considered manslaughter if the sitter threw the child down in anger or frustration and the blow caused the child's death. In some circumstances of *actus reus*, the use of words is considered criminal. In the crime of sedition, the words of disloyalty constitute the *actus reus*. If a person falsely yells "fire" in a crowded theater and people are injured in the rush to exit, that person is held responsible for the injuries, because the use of the word in that situation constitutes an illegal act.

Typically, the law does not require people to aid people in distress, such as entering a burning building to rescue people trapped by a fire. However, failure to act is considered a crime in certain instances:

AP/Wide World Photos

The law requires that a mother obtain medical attention for a sick child. Failure to do so can result in criminal charges. Here, Rebecca Corneau is escorted out of Bristol County District Court by two police officers in Attleboro, Massachusetts. Corneau, who is pregnant and is suspected of covering up the death of her last child, was ordered into custody after she refused to submit to a court-ordered medical exam. Corneau is a member of a fundamentalist religious sect that rejects conventional medical treatment, and prosecutors are looking into whether Corneau's last baby and another infant in the sect died because they did not receive needed care.

1. *Relationship of the parties based on status.* Some people are bound by relationship to give aid. These relationships include parent–child and husband–wife. If a husband finds his wife unconscious because she took an overdose of sleeping pills, he is obligated to save her life by seeking medical aid. If he fails to do so and she dies, he can be held responsible for her death.

2. *Imposition by statute.* Some states have passed laws requiring people to give aid. For example, a person who observes a broken-down automobile in the desert but fails to stop and help the other parties involved may be committing a crime.

3. *Contractual relationships.* These relationships include life-guard and swimmer, doctor and patient, and baby-sitter or au pair and child. Because lifeguards have been hired to ensure the safety of swimmers, they have a legal duty to come to the aid of drowning persons. If a lifeguard knows a swimmer is in danger and does nothing about it and the swimmer drowns, the lifeguard is legally responsible for the swimmer's death.

Mens Rea In most situations, for an act to constitute a crime, it must be done with criminal intent, or *mens rea.* Intent, in the legal sense, can mean carrying out an act intentionally, knowingly, and willingly. However, the definition also encompasses situations in which recklessness or negligence establishes the required criminal intent.

Criminal intent also exists if the results of an action, although originally unintended, are certain to occur. For example, when Timothy McVeigh planted a bomb in front of the Murrah Federal Building in Oklahoma City, he did not intend to kill any particular person in the building. Yet the law would hold that McVeigh or any other person would be substantially certain that people in the building would be killed in the blast, and McVeigh therefore had the criminal intent to commit murder.

Strict Liability Though common-law crimes require that both the *actus reus* and the *mens rea* must be present before a person can be convicted of a crime, several crimes defined by statute do not require *mens rea.* In these cases, the person accused is guilty simply by doing what the statute prohibits; intent does not enter the picture. These **strict liability crimes**, or public welfare offenses, include violations of health and safety regulations, traffic laws, and narcotic control laws.

For example, a person stopped for speeding is guilty of breaking the traffic laws regardless of whether he or she intended to go over the speed limit or did it by accident. The underlying purpose of these laws is to protect the public; therefore, intent is not required.[28]

Criminal Defenses

strict liability crimes

Illegal acts in which guilt does not depend on intent. They are usually acts that endanger the public welfare, such as violations of health and safety regulations.

When people defend themselves against criminal charges, they must refute one or more of the elements of the crime of which they have been accused. A number of different approaches can be taken to create this defense.

First, defendants may deny the *actus reus* by arguing that they were falsely accused and that the real culprit has yet to be identified. Second, defendants may claim that although they engaged in the criminal act of which they are accused, they lacked the *mens rea* (intent) needed to be found guilty of the crime.

excuse defense

Criminal defense based on a lack of criminal intent (*mens rea*). Excuse defenses include insanity, intoxication, and ignorance.

justification defense

Criminal defense that claims an illegal action was justified by circumstances and therefore not criminal. Justification defenses include necessity, duress, self-defense, and entrapment.

If a person whose mental state is impaired commits a criminal act, it is possible for the person to excuse his or her criminal actions by claiming that he or she lacked the capacity to form sufficient intent to be held criminally responsible. Insanity, intoxication, and ignorance are types of **excuse defenses**. Another type of defense is justification. Here the individual usually admits committing the criminal act but maintains that he or she should not be held criminally liable because the act was justified. Among the **justification defenses** are necessity, duress, self-defense, and entrapment.

Persons standing trial for criminal offenses may thus defend themselves by claiming that they did not commit the act in question, that their actions were justified under the circumstances, or that their behavior can be excused by their lack of *mens rea*. If either the physical or mental elements of a crime cannot be proven, then the defendant cannot be convicted.

In recent years, some defense attorneys have tried to devise innovative or "exotic" defenses to prove that their clients did not have the mental capacity to commit the crimes with which they have been charged. The accompanying Policy and Practice in Criminology box discusses these defenses in some detail.

The Evolution of Criminal Law

appellate court

Court that reviews trial court procedures to determine whether they have complied with accepted rules and constitutional doctrines.

The criminal law is constantly evolving in an effort to reflect social and economic conditions. For example, physician-assisted suicide became the subject of national debate when Dr. Jack Kevorkian began practicing what he called obitiatry, helping people take their own lives.[29] In an attempt to stop Kevorkian, Michigan banned assisted suicide, reflecting what lawmakers believed to be prevailing public opinion; Kevorkian was convicted under the new law and sent to prison.[30] Similarly, the Brady Handgun Control Law of 1993, requiring a five-business-day waiting period before an individual can buy a handgun, reflects concern with gun violence and easy access to handguns.

Sometimes legal changes are prompted by highly publicized cases that generate fear and concern. For example, a number of highly publicized cases of celebrity stalking, including Robert John Bardo's fatal shooting of actress Rebecca Schaeffer on July 18, 1989, prompted more than 25 U.S. states to enact stalking statutes. Such laws prohibit "the willful, malicious, and repeated following and harassing of another person."[31] Similarly, after 7-year-old Megan Kanka of Hamilton Township, New Jersey, was killed in 1994 by a repeat sexual offender who had moved into her neighborhood, the federal government passed legislation requiring that the general public be notified of local pedophiles (sexual offenders who target children).[32] California's sexual predator law, which took effect on January 1, 1996, allows people convicted of sexually violent crimes against two or more victims to be committed to a mental institution after their prison terms have been served. This law has already been upheld by **appellate court** judges in the state.[33]

The future direction of U.S. criminal law remains unclear. Certain actions, such as crimes by corporations and political corruption, will be labeled as criminal and given more attention. Other offenses, such as recreational drug use, may be reduced in importance or removed entirely from the criminal law system. In addition, changing technology and its ever-increasing global and local roles in our lives will require modifications in criminal law. For example, such technologies as automatic teller machines and cellular phones have already spawned a new generation of criminal acts such as theft of access numbers and software piracy. As the information highway sprawls toward new expanses, the nation's computer network advances, and biotechnology produces new substances, criminal law will be forced to address threats to the public safety that today are unknown. ✔ **Checkpoints**

✔ Checkpoints

✔ The American legal system is a direct descendant of the British common law.

✔ The criminal law has a number of different goals, including social control, punishment, retribution, deterrence, and the representation of morality.

✔ Each crime has both a physical and a mental element.

✔ Persons accused of crimes can defend themselves either by denying the criminal act or by presenting an excuse or justification for their actions.

✔ The criminal law is constantly changing in an effort to reflect social values and contemporary issues and problems.

Exotic Defenses

Virginia Kelly, 35, of Jacksonville, Florida, claimed that she shot and killed her husband because he had abused her. However, her use of the "battered woman's defense" was pierced by prosecutors, who told jurors that she had actually left her husband at one point and moved to South Carolina but wrote him a letter asking him to contact her. When Virginia Kelly returned to Jacksonville, she found that her husband was involved with another woman and shot him in a jealous rage. She was convicted of second-degree murder on January 9, 1998, and sentenced to 25 years in prison.

Although Kelly was convicted, it has become common for defense attorneys to defend their clients by raising a variety of new exotic defenses based on preexisting conditions or syndromes with which their clients were afflicted. Examples include battered woman syndrome, Vietnam syndrome, child sexual abuse syndrome, Holocaust survivor syndrome, and adopted child syndrome. In using these defenses, attorneys either ask judges to recognize a new excuse for crime or seek to fit these conditions within preexisting defenses. For example, a person who used lethal violence in self-defense might argue that the trauma of serving in Vietnam caused him to overreact to provocation. Or a victim of child abuse may use that experience to mitigate culpability in a crime, asking a jury to consider her background when making a death penalty decision. In one prominent case, the Menendez brothers, on trial for killing their parents, claimed that their actions were the product of earlier sex-

ual and physical abuse. This defense tactic led to a hung jury, although upon retrial the brothers were convicted.

Some exotic criminal defenses have been gender-specific. Attorneys have argued that female clients' behavior was a result of premenstrual syndrome (PMS) and that male clients were aggressive because of unbalanced testosterone levels. These defenses have achieved relatively little success in the United States. Some commentators contend that prosecuting attorneys can turn the tables and use these defenses against the defendant. For example, some have suggested that courts will ultimately view PMS as an aggravating condition in a crime, prompting harsher penalties.

A good deal of debate rages over the application of self-defense to a woman who is battered by her husband and then kills him, often referred to as the "battered wife syndrome." In one highly publicized case, Lorena Bobbitt convinced a jury that physical and sexual abuse removed her responsibility for the sexual mutilation of her husband. Alan Dershowitz, the well-known Harvard Law School professor, dubs such defenses the "abuse excuses." Dershowitz argues that the abuse excuse not only undermines the legal system, but also means that individuals, ethnic groups, and even nations are unwilling to take responsibility for their actions. Dershowitz has identified more than 40 "syndromes" that have been used as excuses for crime, including adopted child syndrome, black rage syndrome (used by the killer on the Long Island Railroad), Holocaust sur-

vivor syndrome, Super Bowl Sunday syndrome, and UFO survivor syndrome. Dershowitz argues that these defenses open the doors to vigilante justice and anarchy. Yet they remain popular because some are "politically correct."

Critical Thinking

1. Is it fair to reduce people's criminal responsibility simply because they had a tough childhood or were emotionally and/or physically abused? If that is the case, wouldn't almost all crime be excused because few criminals actually had happy, successful childhoods?

2. Would it be fair to punish someone suffering from severe emotional trauma who committed a murder in the same manner as someone who killed for money? Should motive influence punishment?

 InfoTrac College Edition Research

To learn more about "criminal defenses," use it as a subject guide in InfoTrac College Edition. To focus more on exotic defenses, use "battered woman defense" as a key term.

SOURCES: Vivian Wakefield, "Woman Gets 25 Years for Killing Husband," *Jacksonville Times-Union,* 10 January 1998; Deborah W. Denno, "Gender, Crime, and the Criminal Law Defenses," *Journal of Criminal Law and Criminology* 85 (Summer 1994): 80–180; Stephanie Goldberg, "Fault Lines," *American Bar Association Journal* 80 (1994): 40–46; Alan M. Dershowitz, *The Abuse Excuse and Other Cop-Outs: Sob Stories and Evasions of Responsibility* (New York: Little, Brown, 1994).

Criminological Research Methods

Criminologists use a wide variety of research techniques to measure the nature and extent of criminal behavior. To understand and evaluate theories and patterns of criminal behavior, it is important to understand how these data are collected. This understanding also shows how professional criminologists approach various problems and questions in their field.

Survey Research

Survey research can measure the attitudes, beliefs, values, personality traits, and behavior of participants. A great deal of crime measurement is based on analy-

sampling

Selecting a limited number of people for study as representative of a larger group.

population

All people who share a particular characteristic, such as all high school students or all police officers.

cross-sectional research

Interviewing or questioning a diverse sample of subjects, representing a cross-section of a community, at the same point in time.

sis of survey data, which are gathered using techniques such as self-report surveys and interviews. Both types of surveys involve **sampling**, the process of selecting for study a limited number of subjects to represent a larger group, called a **population**. For example, a criminologist might interview a sample of 3,000 prison inmates drawn from the population of more than 1 million inmates in the United States; in this case, the sample represents the entire population of U.S. inmates. The characteristics of people or events in a randomly selected sample should be quite similar to those of the population at large.

One common type of survey simultaneously interviews or questions a diverse sample of subjects, representing a cross-section of a community, about research topics under consideration. This method is referred to as **cross-sectional research**. For example, all youths in the tenth grade in a public high school can be surveyed about their substance abuse. If most youths in this community attend public school, the survey will contain a sample that represents a cross-section of the community: rich and poor, males and females, users and nonusers, and so on.

Self-report surveys may ask participants to describe in detail their recent and lifetime criminal activities. Victimization surveys seek information from people who have been victims of crime. Attitude surveys measure the attitudes, beliefs, and values of different groups, such as prostitutes, students, drug addicts, police officers, judges, or juvenile delinquents.

Statistical analysis of data gathered from randomly drawn samples enables researchers to generalize their findings from small groups to large populations. Although cross-sectional research measures subjects at a single point in time, survey questions can elicit information on subjects' prior behavior as well as their future goals and aspirations.[34]

Cohort Research

longitudinal research

Tracking the development of the same group of subjects over time.

cohort

A group of subjects that is studied over time.

Longitudinal research involves observing a group of people who share some common characteristic over a period of time. Such a group is known as a **cohort**. For example, researchers might select all girls born in Albany, New York, in 1980 and then follow their behavior patterns for 20 years. The research data might include their school experiences, arrests, hospitalizations, and information about their family life (such as divorces or parental relations). The subjects might be given repeated intelligence and physical exams, and their diets might be monitored. Data can be collected directly from the subjects, or without their knowledge from schools, police, and other sources. If the research is carefully conducted, it may be possible to determine which life experiences, such as growing up in a troubled home or failing at school, typically preceded the onset of crime and delinquency.

Record Data

Uniform Crime Report (UCR)

Large database, compiled by the Federal Bureau of Investigation (FBI), of crimes reported and arrests made each year throughout the United States.

Aggregate record data can tell us about the effects of social trends and patterns on the crime rate. Criminologists use large government agency and research foundation databases, such as those from the U.S. Census Bureau, Labor Department, and state correctional departments. The most important of these sources is the **Uniform Crime Report (UCR)**, compiled by the Federal Bureau of Investigation (FBI).[35] The UCR collects records of the number of crimes reported by citizens to local police departments and the number of arrests made by police agencies in a given year.

Record data can be used to focus on the social forces that affect crime. For example, to study the relationship between crime and poverty, criminologists can use Census Bureau data to obtain information about income, the number of people on welfare, and single-parent families in a given urban area. They can then cross-reference this information with police records from the same locality.

Experimental Research

experimental research

Manipulating or intervening in the lives of subjects to observe the outcome or effect of a specific intervention. True experiments usually include (1) random selection of subjects, (2) a control or comparison group, and (3) an experimental condition.

CONNECTIONS

The FBI's Uniform Crime Report remains the most important source of official crime statistics and is discussed more completely in Chapter 2.

Sometimes criminologists want to study the direct effect of one factor on another. For example, they may wish to test whether watching a violent TV show will cause viewers to act aggressively. Answering this type of question requires **experimental research**—manipulating or intervening in the lives of subjects to observe the outcome or effect of a specific intervention. True experiments usually have three elements: (1) random selection of subjects, (2) a control or comparison group, and (3) an experimental condition.

To study the effects of violent TV, a criminologist might have one group of randomly chosen subjects watch an extremely violent and gory film (such as *Scream* or *Psycho*) while another randomly selected group views something more mellow (like *Babe* or *The Parent Trap*). The behavior of both groups would be monitored, and if the subjects who had watched the violent film were significantly more aggressive than those who had watched the nonviolent film, an association between media content and behavior would be supported. The fact that both groups were randomly selected would prevent some preexisting condition from invalidating the results of the experiment.

When it is impossible to select subjects randomly or manipulate conditions, a different type of experiment is used. For example, a criminologist may want to measure the change in driving fatalities and drunk driving arrests brought about by a new state law that mandates jail sentences for persons convicted of driving while intoxicated (DWI). Because police cannot randomly arrest drunk drivers, criminologists need to find an alternative strategy, such as comparing the state's DWI arrest and fatality trends with those of nearby states that have more lenient DWI statutes. Although not a true experiment, this approach would give some indication of the effectiveness of mandatory sentences because the states are comparable except for their drunk driving legislation.

Observational and Interview Research

✔ Checkpoints

✔ Criminologists use a wide variety of research methods.

✔ Surveys employ samples of subjects who are asked about their behavior and attitudes.

✔ Cohort research follows a group of people who share some characteristic.

✔ Record studies use large databases collected by institutions such as police and correctional agencies, schools, and hospitals.

✔ Experimental research involves introducing a stimulus to determine the effect of the intervention.

✔ Observational studies focus on the daily lives and activities of particular individuals or groups.

Sometimes criminologists focus their research on relatively few subjects, interviewing them in depth or observing them as they go about their activities. This research often results in the kind of in-depth data absent in large surveys. For example, a recent study by Claire Sterk focused on the lives of middle-class female drug abusers.[36] The 34 interviews she conducted provide insight into a group whose behavior might not be captured in a large survey. Sterk found that these women were introduced to cocaine at first "just for fun." One 34-year-old lawyer told her, "I do drugs because I like the feeling. I would never let drugs take over my life."[37] Unfortunately, many of these subjects succumbed to the power of drugs and suffered both emotional and financial stress.

Another common criminological method is to observe criminals firsthand in order to gain insight into their motives and activities. This may involve going into the field and participating in group activities, as was done in sociologist William Whyte's famous study of a Boston gang, *Street Corner Society*.[38] Other observers conduct field studies but remain in the background, observing but not being part of the ongoing activity.[39]

Still another type of observation involves bringing subjects into a structured laboratory setting and observing how they react to a predetermined condition or stimulus. This approach is common in experimental studies testing the effect of observational learning on aggressive behavior. For example, the experiment described previously, in which subjects view violent films and their subsequent behavior is monitored, would typically be conducted in a laboratory setting.[40]

Criminology, then, relies on many of the basic research methods common to other fields, including sociology, psychology, and political science. Multiple methods are needed to achieve the goals of criminological inquiry. ✔ Checkpoints

Ethical Issues in Criminology

A critical issue facing criminology students involves recognizing the field's political and social consequences. All too often criminologists forget the social responsibility they bear as experts in the area of crime and justice. When government agencies request their views of issues, their pronouncements and opinions may become the basis for sweeping social policy.

The lives of millions of people can be influenced by criminological research data. Debates over gun control, capital punishment, and mandatory sentences are ongoing and contentious. Some criminologists have argued successfully for social service, treatment, and rehabilitation programs to reduce the crime rate; others consider these a waste of time, suggesting instead that a massive prison construction program coupled with tough criminal sentences can bring the crime rate down. By accepting their roles as experts on law-violating behavior, criminologists place themselves in a position of power. The potential consequences of their actions are enormous. Therefore, they must be both aware of the ethics of their profession and prepared to defend their work in the light of public scrutiny. Major ethical issues include what to study, whom to study, and how to conduct those studies.

■ *What to study.* Criminologists must be concerned about the topics they study. It is important that their research not be directed by the sources of funding on which research projects rely. The objectivity of research may be questioned if studies are funded by organizations that have a vested interest in the outcome of the research. For example, a study on the effectiveness of the defensive use of handguns to stop crime may be tainted if the funding for the project comes from a gun manufacturer whose sales may be affected by the research findings.

■ *Whom to study.* Another ethical issue in criminology concerns selection of research subjects. Too often criminologists focus their attention on the poor and minorities while ignoring middle-class white-collar crime, organized crime, and government crime. For example, a few social scientists have suggested that criminals have lower intelligence quotients than the average citizen and that because the average IQ score is lower among some minority groups, their crime rates are high.[41] This was the conclusion reached in *The Bell Curve,* a popular but highly controversial book written by Richard Herrnstein and Charles Murray.[42] Although such research is often methodologically unsound, it brings to light the tendency of criminologists to focus on one element of the community while ignoring others.

■ *How to study.* A third area of concern involves the methods used in conducting research. One issue is whether subjects are fully informed about the purpose of research. For example, when European American and African American youngsters are asked to participate in a survey of their behavior or to take an IQ test, are they told in advance that the data they provide may later be used to demonstrate racial differences in their self-reported crime rates? Criminologists must also be careful to keep records and information confidential in order to maintain the privacy of research participants. In studies that involve experimentation and treatment, care must be taken to protect those subjects who have been chosen for experimental and control groups. For example, is it ethical to provide a special program for one group while depriving others of the same opportunity just so they can later be compared? Conversely, criminologists must be careful to protect subjects from experiments that may actually cause harm. An examination of the highly publicized "Scared Straight" program, which brings youngsters into contact with hard-core felons in a prison setting, found that participants may have been harmed by their experience. Rather than being frightened into conformity, subjects actually increased their criminal behavior.[43] Finally, criminologists must take extreme care to ensure that research subjects are selected in a random and unbiased manner.[44]

Summary

Criminology is the scientific approach to the study of criminal behavior and society's reaction to law violations and violators. It is essentially an interdisciplinary field; many of its practitioners were originally trained as sociologists, psychologists, economists, political scientists, historians, and natural scientists.

Criminology has a rich history, with roots in the utilitarian philosophy of Beccaria, the biological positivism of Lombroso, the social theory of Durkheim, and the political philosophy of Marx.

The criminological enterprise includes subareas such as criminal statistics, the sociology of law, theory construction, criminal behavior systems, penology, and victimology.

Criminologists believe in one of three perspectives: the consensus view, the conflict view, or the interactionist view. The consensus view holds that criminal behavior is defined by laws that reflect the values and morals of a majority of citizens. The conflict view states that criminal behavior is defined in such a way that economically powerful groups can retain their control over society. The interactionist view portrays criminal behavior as a relativistic, constantly changing concept that reflects society's current moral values. According to the interactionist view, behavior is labeled as criminal by those in power; criminals are people society chooses to label as outsiders or deviants.

The criminal law is a set of rules that specify the behaviors society has outlawed. The criminal law serves several important purposes: It represents public opinion and moral values, it enforces social controls, it deters criminal behavior and wrongdoing, it punishes transgressors, and it banishes private retribution.

The criminal law used in U.S. jurisdictions traces its origin to the English common law. In the U.S. legal system, lawmakers have codified common-law crimes into state and federal penal codes. Every crime has specific elements. In most instances, these elements include both the *actus reus* (guilty act) and the *mens rea* (guilty mind)—the person's state of mind or criminal intent.

At trial, a defendant may claim to have lacked *mens rea* and, therefore, not to be responsible for a criminal action. One type of defense is excuse for mental reasons, such as insanity, intoxication, necessity, or duress. Another type of defense is justification by reason of self-defense or entrapment.

The criminal law is undergoing constant reform. Some acts are being decriminalized—their penalties are being reduced—while penalties for others are becoming more severe.

Criminologists use various research methods to gather information that will shed light on criminal behavior. These methods include surveys, longitudinal studies, record studies, experiments, and observations. Ethical issues arise when information-gathering methods appear biased or exclusionary. These issues may cause serious consequences because research findings can significantly impact individuals and groups.

For additional chapter links, discussions, and quizzes, see the book-specific Web site at http://www.wadsworth.com/product/0534519423s.

Thinking Like a Criminologist

You have been experimenting with various techniques in order to identify a surefire method for predicting violent behavior in delinquents. Your procedure involves brain scans, DNA testing, and blood analysis. Used with samples of incarcerated adolescents, your procedure has been able to distinguish with 80 percent accuracy between youths with a history of violence and those who are exclusively property offenders. Your research indicates that if all youths were tested with your techniques, potentially violence-prone career criminals could be easily identified for special treatment. For example, children in the local school system could be tested, and those identified as violence-prone could be carefully monitored by teachers.

Those at risk for future violence could be put into special programs as a precaution.

Some of your colleagues argue that this type of testing is unconstitutional because it violates the subjects' Fifth Amendment right against self-incrimination. There is also the problem of error: Some children may be falsely labeled as violence-prone.

How would you answer your critics? Is it fair or ethical to label people as potentially criminal and violent even though they have not yet exhibited any antisocial behavior? Do the risks of such a procedure outweigh its benefits?

Key Terms

criminology	penology	felony
interdisciplinary	rehabilitation	misdemeanor
utilitarianism	capital punishment	*actus reus*
classical criminology	mandatory sentences	*mens rea*
positivism	victimology	strict liability crimes
biosocial theory	deviance	excuse defense
sociological criminology	crime	justification defense
anomie	consensus view	appellate court
Chicago School	criminal law	sampling
socialization	conflict view	population
conflict theory	interactionist view	cross-sectional research
rational choice theory	Code of Hammurabi	longitudinal research
social structure theory	Mosaic Code	cohort
valid	precedent	Uniform Crime Report (UCR)
reliable	common law	experimental research
white-collar crime	statutory crimes	

Discussion Questions

1. What are the specific aims and purposes of the criminal law? To what extent does the criminal law control behavior? Do you believe that the law is too restrictive? Not restrictive enough?

2. If you ran the world, which acts, now legal, would you make criminal? Which criminal acts would you legalize? What would be the likely consequences of your actions?

3. Beccaria argued that the threat of punishment controls crime. Are there other forms of social control? Aside from the threat of legal punishment, what else controls your own behavior?

4. What research method would you employ if you wanted to study drug and alcohol abuse at your own school?

5. Would it be ethical for a criminologist to observe a teenage gang by hanging with them, drinking, and watching as they steal cars? Should the criminologist report that behavior to the police?

2 The Nature and Extent of Crime

INTRODUCTION

Thomas Junta, shown here at a court appearance, stands accused of killing a hockey referee in a fit of "sports rage." What do such outbursts say about American culture? Can such violent acts be prevented or controlled?

On July 5, 2000, Thomas Junta, a 42-year-old truck driver with no previous criminal record, assaulted Michael Costin at a hockey rink in Reading, Massachusetts, a town north of Boston. The beating followed a pickup hockey game, refereed by Costin, in which Junta's 10-year-old son was playing alongside Costin's own child. As the game came to a close, an argument ensued over Costin's ability to control the game. Junta, who is 6-foot-2 and 275 pounds, assaulted Costin, 5-foot-11 and 170 pounds, as he left the ice. After being ordered out by a rink manager, Junta returned and slammed Costin to the ground beside a soda machine. The blow caused immediate brain death. Nonetheless, Junta pushed his knee into Costin's chest and continued to beat and punch his head until he was virtually unrecognizable.[1]

S tories such as this help convince most Americans that we live in a violent society. Are Americans justified in their fear of violent crime? Should they, in fact, barricade themselves behind armed guards? Are crime rates actually rising or falling? Where do most crimes occur? To answer these and similar questions, criminologists have devised elaborate methods of crime data collection and analysis. Without accurate data on the nature and extent of crime, it would not be possible to formulate theories that explain the onset of crime or to devise social policies that facilitate its control or elimination.

In this chapter, we review how data are collected on criminal offenders and offenses and what this information tells us about crime patterns and trends. We also examine the concept of criminal careers and discover what available crime data can tell us about the onset, continuation, and termination of criminality. We begin with a discussion of the most important sources of crime data.

The Uniform Crime Report

Uniform Crime Report (UCR)

Large database, compiled by the Federal Bureau of Investigation (FBI), of crimes reported and arrests made each year throughout the United States.

index crimes

The eight most serious offenses included in the UCR: murder, rape, assault, robbery, burglary, arson, larceny, and motor vehicle theft.

The Federal Bureau of Investigation's **Uniform Crime Report (UCR)** is the best-known and most widely cited source of aggregate criminal statistics.[2] The FBI receives and compiles records from more than 17,000 police departments serving a majority of the U.S. population. Table 2.1 defines the eight most serious offenses, or **index crimes**, included in the UCR. The FBI tallies and annually publishes the number of reported offenses by city, county, standard metropolitan statistical area, and geographical division of the United States. In addition to these statistics, the UCR shows the number and characteristics (age, race, and gender) of individuals who have been arrested for these and all other crimes, except traffic violations.

The UCR uses three methods to express crime data. First, the number of crimes reported to the police and arrests made are expressed as raw figures (for example, 15,553 murders occurred in 1999). Second, crime rates per 100,000 people are computed. That is, when the UCR indicates that the murder rate was 5.7 in 1999, it means that about 6 people in every 100,000 were murdered between January 1 and December 31 of 1999. This is the equation used:

$$\frac{\text{Number of reported crimes}}{\text{Total U.S. population}} \times 100{,}000 = \text{Rate per 100,000}$$

Third, the FBI computes changes in the number and rate of crime over time. For example, murder rates declined 9.3 percent between 1997 and 1999.

The accuracy of the UCR is somewhat suspect. Surveys indicate that fewer than half of all crime victims report incidents to police. Nonreporters may

Table 2.1 Uniform Crime Report: Index Crimes

CRIME	DESCRIPTION
Criminal homicide	a. Murder and nonnegligent manslaughter: the willful (nonnegligent) killing of one human being by another. Deaths caused by negligence, attempts to kill, assaults to kill, suicides, accidental deaths, and justifiable homicides are excluded. Justifiable homicides are limited to (1) the killing of a felon by a law enforcement officer in the line of duty and (2) the killing of a felon, during the commission of a felony, by a private citizen. b. Manslaughter by negligence: the killing of another person through gross negligence. Traffic fatalities are excluded.
Forcible rape	The carnal knowledge of a female forcibly and against her will. Included are rapes by force and attempts or assaults to rape. Statutory offenses (no force used—victim under age of consent) are excluded.
Robbery	The taking or attempting to take anything of value from the care, custody, or control of a person or persons by force or threat of force or violence and/or by putting the victim in fear.
Aggravated assault	An unlawful attack by one person upon another for the purpose of inflicting severe or aggravated bodily injury. This type of assault usually is accompanied by the use of a weapon or by means likely to produce death or great bodily harm. Simple assaults are excluded.
Burglary/breaking and entering	The unlawful entry of a structure to commit a felony or a theft. Attempted forcible entry is included.
Larceny/theft (except motor vehicle theft)	The unlawful taking, carrying, leading, or riding away of property from the possession or constructive possession of another. Examples are thefts of bicycles or automobile accessories, shoplifting, pocket picking, or the stealing of any property or article that is not taken by force and violence or by fraud. Attempted larcenies are included. Embezzlement, con games, forgery, worthless checks, and so on are excluded.
Motor vehicle theft	The theft or attempted theft of a motor vehicle. A motor vehicle is self-propelled and runs on the surface and not on rails. Specifically excluded from this category are motorboats, construction equipment, airplanes, and farming equipment.
Arson	Any willful or malicious burning or attempt to burn, with or without intent to defraud, a dwelling house, public building, motor vehicle or aircraft, personal property of another, or the like.

SOURCE: FBI, Uniform Crime Report, 1999.

Find It on INFOTRAC
College Edition

Did you know that a sports team will reflect the personality of its coach? If the coach is baiting and taunting the officials, players will pick up on that and do the same thing. To research the effects of coaching on team violence, use "sports violence" as keywords on InfoTrac College Edition. You may want to read

Edgar Shields, "Intimidation and Violence by Males in High School Athletics," *Adolescence*, Fall 1999 v34 i135 p503

believe that the victimization was "a private matter," that "nothing could be done," or that the victimization was "not important enough."[3]

There is also evidence that local law enforcement agencies make errors in their reporting practices. Some departments may define crimes loosely—for example, reporting an assault on a woman as an attempted rape—whereas others pay strict attention to FBI guidelines.[4] Some local police departments make unintentional but systematic errors in UCR reporting, and others may deliberately alter reported crimes to improve their department's public image. Police administrators interested in lowering the crime rate may falsify crime reports by, for example, classifying a burglary as a nonreportable trespass.[5] Ironically, what appears to be a rising crime rate may be simply an artifact of improved police record-keeping ability.[6]

Methodological issues also contribute to questions regarding the UCR's validity. The complex scoring procedure used by the FBI means that many serious crimes are not counted. For example, during an armed bank robbery, the offender strikes a teller with the butt of a handgun. The robber runs from the bank and steals an automobile at the curb. Although the offender has technically committed robbery, aggravated assault, and motor vehicle theft, because robbery is the most serious offense, it would be the only one recorded in the

---

Table 2.2 Factors Affecting the Validity of the Uniform Crime Reports

1. No federal crimes are reported.

2. Reports are voluntary and vary in accuracy and completeness.

3. Not all police departments submit reports.

4. The FBI uses estimates in its total crime projections.

5. If an offender commits multiple crimes, only the most serious is recorded. Thus, if a narcotics addict rapes, robs, and murders a victim, only the murder is recorded. Consequently, many lesser crimes go unreported.

6. Each act is listed as a single offense for some crimes but not for others. If a man robbed six people in a bar, the offense would be listed as one robbery; but if he assaulted or murdered them, it would be listed as six assaults or six murders.

7. Incomplete acts are lumped together with completed ones.

8. Important differences exist between the FBI's definition of certain crimes and those used in a number of states.

9. Victimless crimes often go undetected.

10. Many cases of child abuse and family violence are unreported.

SOURCE: Leonard Savitz, "Official Statistics," in *Contemporary Criminology*, ed. Leonard Savitz and Norman Johnston (New York: John Wiley, 1982), pp. 3–15; updated 2000.

UCR.[7] The most common issues affecting the validity of the UCR are summarized in Table 2.2.

Victim Surveys

The second source of crime data is surveys that ask crime victims about their encounters with criminals. Because many victims do not report their experiences to the police, victim surveys are considered a method of getting at the unknown figures of crime. The **National Crime Victimization Survey (NCVS)** is the current method of assessing victimization in the United States.

The NCVS is conducted by the U.S. Bureau of the Census in cooperation with the Bureau of Justice Statistics of the U.S. Department of Justice.[8] Each year, data are obtained from a nationally representative sample of roughly 45,000 households, including more than 94,000 persons. People are asked to report their victimization experiences with such crimes as rape, sexual assault, robbery, assault, theft, household burglary, and motor vehicle theft. Because of the care with which the samples are drawn and the high completion rate, NCVS data are considered a relatively unbiased, valid estimate of all victimizations for the target crimes included in the survey.

National Crime Victimization Survey (NCVS)

The ongoing victimization study conducted jointly by the Justice Department and the U.S. Census Bureau that surveys victims about their experiences with law violation.

NCVS Findings

The number of crimes accounted for by the NCVS (about 31 million) is considerably larger than the number of crimes reported to the FBI. For example, whereas the UCR shows that about 410,000 robberies occurred in 1999, the NCVS estimates that about 810,000 actually occurred. The reason for such discrepancies is that fewer than half of violent crimes, fewer than one-third of personal theft crimes (such as pocket picking), and fewer than half of household thefts are reported to police. Victims seem to report to the police only crimes that involve considerable loss or injury. If we are to believe NCVS findings, the official UCR statistics do not provide an accurate picture of the crime problem because many crimes go unreported to the police.

Validity of the NCVS

Like the UCR, the NCVS may also suffer from some methodological problems. As a result, its findings must be interpreted with caution. Among the potential problems are the following:

- Overreporting due to victims' misinterpretation of events. For example, a lost wallet may be reported as stolen, or an open door may be viewed as a burglary attempt.
- Underreporting due to the embarrassment of reporting crime to interviewers, fear of getting in trouble, or simply forgetting an incident.
- Inability to record the personal criminal activity of those interviewed, such as drug use or gambling; murder is also not included, for obvious reasons.
- Sampling errors, which produce a group of respondents who do not represent the nation as a whole.
- Inadequate question format that invalidates responses. Some groups, such as adolescents, may be particularly susceptible to error because of question format.[9]

CONNECTIONS

Victim surveys provide information not only about criminal incidents that have occurred, but also about the individuals who are most at risk of falling victim to crime, and where and when they are most likely to become victimized. Data from recent NCVS surveys will be used in Chapter 3 to draw a portrait of the nature and extent of victimization in the United States.

Self-Report Surveys

Self-report surveys ask people to reveal information about their own law violations. Most often, self-report surveys are administered to groups of subjects through a mass distribution of questionnaires. The basic assumption of self-report studies is that the assurance of anonymity and confidentiality will encourage people to describe their illegal activities accurately. Self-reports are viewed as a mechanism to get at the "dark figures of crime," the figures missed by official statistics. Figure 2.1 illustrates some typical self-report items.

Most self-report studies have focused on juvenile delinquency and youth crime, for three reasons.[10] First, the school setting makes it convenient to test thousands of subjects simultaneously because they all have the means to re-

self-report surveys

A research approach that requires subjects to reveal their own participation in delinquent or criminal acts.

Figure 2.1

Self-Report Survey Questions

PLEASE INDICATE HOW OFTEN IN THE PAST 12 MONTHS YOU DID EACH ACT. (CHECK THE BEST ANSWER.)	Never did act	One time	2-5 times	6-9 times	10+ times
Stole something worth less than $50					
Stole something worth more than $50					
Used cocaine					
Been in a fistfight					
Carried a weapon such as a gun or knife					
Fought someone using a weapon					

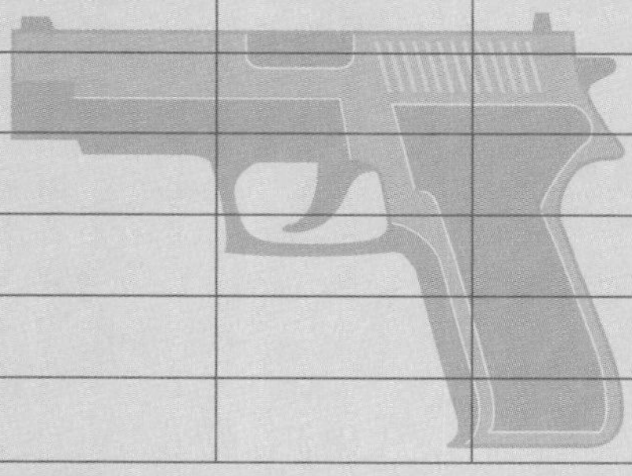

spond to a research questionnaire (pens, desks, and time). Second, because school attendance is universal, a school-based self-report survey represents a cross-section of the community. Finally, juveniles have the highest reported crime rates; measuring delinquent behavior, therefore, is a key to understanding the nature and extent of crime.

Self-reports are not restricted to youth crime, however. They are also used to examine the offense histories of prison inmates, drug users, and other segments of the population. Also, because most self-report instruments contain items measuring subjects' attitudes, values, personal characteristics, and behaviors, the data obtained from them can be used for various purposes, including testing theories, measuring attitudes toward crime, and computing the association between crime and important social variables, such as family relations, educational attainment, and income.[11]

Self-Report Findings

In general, self-reports, like victimization surveys, indicate that the number of people who break the law is far greater than the number projected by official statistics. Almost everyone questioned is found to have violated some law at some time.[12] Furthermore, self-reports dispute the notion that criminals and delinquents specialize in one type of crime or another; offenders seem to engage in a "mixed bag" of crime and deviance.[13]

Self-report studies indicate that the most common offenses are truancy, alcohol abuse, use of a false ID, shoplifting or larceny under $50, fighting, marijuana use, and damage to the property of others. What is surprising is the consistency of these findings in samples taken around the United States. Table 2.3 contains data from a self-report study called Monitoring the Future, which researchers at the University of Michigan Institute for Social Research (ISR) conduct annually. This national survey of more than 2,500 high school seniors, one of the most important sources of self-report data, shows a widespread yet stable pattern of youth crime since 1978.[14]

As Table 2.3 shows, young people self-report a great deal of crime: about 40 percent of high school seniors report stealing in the past 12 months; almost 20 percent were involved in a gang fight; more than 10 percent injured someone so badly that the victim had to see a doctor; almost 30 percent shoplifted; and almost one-quarter engaged in breaking and entering. The fact that so many—at least one-third—of all U.S. high school students engaged in theft and about 20 percent committed a serious violent act during the past year suggests that criminal activity is widespread and is not restricted to a few "bad apples."

Table 2.3 Self-Reported Delinquent Activity During the Past 12 Months Among High School Seniors, 1999

CRIME CATEGORY	PERCENTAGE ENGAGING IN OFFENSES	
	AT LEAST ONE OFFENSE	MULTIPLE OFFENSES
Serious fight	9%	6%
Gang fight	11%	8%
Hurt someone badly	8%	6%
Used a weapon to steal	2%	2%
Stole less than $50	13%	18%
Stole more than $50	5%	6%
Shoplifted	11%	16%
Did breaking and entering	11%	13%
Committed arson	1%	2%
Damaged school property	6%	7%

SOURCE: *Monitoring the Future, 1999* (Ann Arbor, MI: Institute for Social Research, 2000).

Accuracy of Self-Reports

Although self-report data have profoundly affected criminological inquiry, some important methodological issues have been raised about their accuracy. Critics of self-report studies frequently suggest that it is unreasonable to expect people to candidly admit illegal acts. This is especially true of those with official records, who may be engaging in the most criminality. At the same time, some people may exaggerate their criminal acts, forget some of them, or be confused about what is being asked. Some surveys contain an overabundance of trivial offenses, such as shoplifting small items or using false identification, often lumped together with serious crimes to form a total crime index. Consequently, comparisons between groups can be highly misleading.

The "missing cases" phenomenon is also a concern. Even if 90 percent of a school population voluntarily participate in a self-report study, researchers can never be sure whether the few who refuse to participate or are absent that day comprise a significant portion of the school's population of persistent high-rate offenders. Research indicates that offenders with the most extensive prior criminality are also the most likely to "be poor historians of their own crime commission rates."[15] It is also unlikely that the most serious chronic offenders in the teenage population are the most willing to cooperate with university-based criminologists administering self-report tests.[16] Institutionalized youths, who are not generally represented in the self-report surveys, are not only more delinquent than the general youth population, but are also considerably more misbehaving than the most delinquent youths identified in the typical self-report survey.[17] Consequently, self-reports may measure only nonserious, occasional delinquents while ignoring hard-core chronic offenders who may be institutionalized and unavailable for self-reports.

Evaluating Crime Data

Each source of crime data has strengths and weaknesses. The FBI survey is carefully tallied and contains data on the number of murders and people arrested, information that the other data sources lack. However, this survey omits the many crimes victims choose not to report to police, and it is subject to the reporting caprices of individual police departments.

The NCVS includes unreported crime and important information on the personal characteristics of victims. However, the data consist of estimates made from relatively limited samples of the total U.S. population, so that even narrow fluctuations in the rates of some crimes can have a major impact on findings. It also relies on personal recollections that may be inaccurate. The NCVS does not include data on important crime patterns, including murder and drug abuse.

Self-report surveys can provide information on the personal characteristics of offenders, such as their attitudes, values, beliefs, and psychological profiles, that is unavailable from any other source. Yet, at their core, self-reports rely on the honesty of criminal offenders and drug abusers, a population not generally known for accuracy and integrity.

Although their tallies of crimes are certainly not in synch, the crime patterns and trends they record are often quite similar.[18] For example, all three sources generally agree about the personal characteristics of serious criminals (such as age and gender) and where and when crime occurs (such as urban areas, nighttime, and summer months). In addition, the problems inherent in each source are consistent over time. Therefore, even if the data sources are incapable of providing a precise and valid count of crime at any given time, they are reliable indicators of changes and fluctuations in yearly crime rates.

What do these data sources tell us about crime trends and patterns?

Crime Trends

Crime is not new to this century.[19] Studies have indicated that a gradual increase in the crime rate, especially in violent crime, occurred from 1830 to 1860. Following the Civil War, this rate increased significantly for about 15 years. Then, from 1880 up to the time of the First World War, with the possible exception of the years immediately preceding and following the war, the number of reported crimes decreased. After

Figure 2.2

Crime Rate Trends

After years of steady increase, crime rates declined between 1993 and 1998.

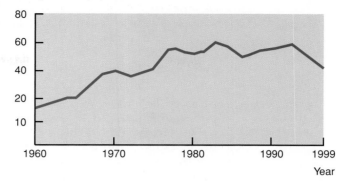

Rate per 1,000 population

SOURCE: FBI, Uniform Crime Report, 1999.

a period of readjustment, the crime rate steadily declined until the Depression (about 1930), when another crime wave was recorded. Crime rates increased gradually from the 1930s until the 1960s, when the growth rate became much greater. The homicide rate, which had actually declined from the 1930s to the 1960s, also began a sharp increase that continued through the 1970s and 1980s.

In 1991, police recorded about 14.6 million crimes. Both the number and rate of crimes have been declining ever since. For example, between 1995 and 1999, the crime rate declined by 16 percent. In 1999, about 11.6 million crimes were reported to the police, a decrease of more than 7 percent from the preceding year. The number of reported crimes has declined by about 3 million from the 1991 peak (see Figure 2.2). Even teenage criminality, a source of national concern, has been in decline during this period, decreasing by about one-third over the past 20 years. The teen murder rate, which had remained stubbornly high, has also declined during the past few years.[20] The factors that help explain the upward and downward movement in crime rates are discussed in the accompanying Criminological Enterprise box.

Trends in Violent Crime

The violent crimes reported by the FBI include murder, rape, assault, and robbery. In 1999, about 1.4 million violent crimes were reported to police, a rate of around 600 per 100,000 Americans. According to the UCR, violence in the United States has decreased significantly during the past decade, reversing a long trend of skyrocketing increases. The total number of violent crimes declined about 20 percent between 1994 and 1999, and the violence rate dropped more than 20 percent.

Particularly encouraging has been the decrease in the number and rate of murders. The murder statistics are generally regarded as the most accurate aspect of the UCR. Figure 2.3, on page 37, illustrates homicide rate trends since 1900. Note that the rate peaked around 1930, then fell, rose dramatically in the 1960s and 1970s, and peaked once again in 1991, when the number of murders topped 24,000 for the first time in the nation's history. Since 1994 the murder rate has declined by more than 30 percent. The decline in the violence rate has been both unexpected and welcome. Some major cities, such as New York, report a decline of more than 50 percent in their murder rates through the 1990s.

Explaining Crime Trends

Criminologists have identified a variety of social, economic, personal, and demographic factors that influence crime rate trends. Some of the most important factors are discussed here.

Age

Criminologists view change in the population age distribution as having the greatest influence on crime trends. As a general rule, the crime rate follows the proportion of young males in the population. With the "graying" of society in the 1980s and a decline in the birth rate, it is not surprising that the overall crime rate declined between 1990 and 1999. As the teen population increases during the next decade, so too may crime rates.

Economy

There is still some debate over the effects the economy has on crime rates. Some criminologists believe that a poor economy actually helps to lower crime rates because unemployed parents are at home to supervise children and guard their possessions. Because there is less to spend, a poor economy reduces the number of valuables worth stealing. Also, it seems unlikely that law-abiding, middle-aged workers will suddenly turn to a life of crime if they are laid off during an economic downturn.

Although a poor economy may lower crime rates in the short run, its long-term effects may prove the opposite. Crime rates rise during prolonged periods of economic weakness and unemployment. A long-term economic recession, such as the one that occurred in the late 1980s, may produce a climate of hopelessness in the nation's largest cities, which helps increase crime rates. Then, when the economy turned around in the 1990s, it coincided with a decade-long drop in the crime rate. Cities such as New York, which experienced an economic boom and rapid increase in real estate prices, also saw a dramatic decline in crime.

Social Problems

As the level of social problems—such as racial conflict, dropout rates, teen pregnancies, and single-parent families—increases, so too do crime rates. There is a positive correlation between the homicide rate of a particular age group (such as 17-year-olds) and the percentage of its members born to unwed mothers. Recently, the number of births to unwed single mothers has been in decline, and so too have crime rates.

Racial conflict may also increase crime rates. Areas undergoing racial change, especially those experiencing an in-migration of minorities into predominantly white neighborhoods, seem prone to significant increases in their crime rate. Whites in these areas may be using violence to protect what they view as their home turf. Racially motivated crimes actually diminish as neighborhoods become more integrated and power struggles diminish.

Abortion

In a controversial study, John J. Donohue III and Steven D. Levitt found empirical evidence that the recent drop in the crime rate may be attributable to the availability of legalized abortion. In 1973, *Roe* v. *Wade* legalized abortion nationwide. Within a few years, more than 1 million abortions were being performed annually, or roughly one abortion for every three live births. Donohue and Levitt suggest that the crime rate drop that began approximately 18 years later (1991) can be tied to the fact that at that point the first groups of potential offenders affected by the abortion decision began reaching the peak age of criminal activity. They found that states that legalized abortion before the rest of the nation were the first to experience decreasing crime and that states with higher abortion rates have seen a greater fall in crime since 1985. The abortion-related reduction in crime is predominantly attributable to a decrease in crime per capita among the young. It is possible that the link between crime rates and abortion is the result of two mechanisms: (1) selective abortion on the part of women most at risk to have children who would engage in criminal activity, and (2) improved child-rearing or environmental circumstances caused by better maternal, familial, or fetal circumstances because women are having fewer children. If abortion were illegal, they conclude, crime rates might be 10–20 percent higher than they currently are. If these estimates are correct, legalized abortion can explain about half of the recent fall in crime. All else being equal, Donohue and Levitt predict that crime rates will continue to fall slowly for an additional 15–20 years as the full effects of legalized abortion are gradually felt.

Gun Availability

The availability of firearms may influence the crime rate, especially the proliferation of weapons in the hands of

Trends in Property Crime

The property crimes reported in the UCR include larceny, motor vehicle theft, and arson. In 1999, about 10 million property crimes were reported, a rate of about 3,700 per 100,000 population. Property crime rates have declined in recent years, though the drop has not been as dramatic as that experienced by the violent crime rate. Between 1998 and 1999, property crime rates declined about 8 percent, including a drop of 11 percent for burglary and 9 percent for auto theft.

teens. There is evidence that more guns than ever before are finding their way into the hands of young people. Surveys of high school students indicate that between 6 and 10 percent carry guns at least some of the time. Guns also cause escalation in the seriousness of crime. As the number of gun-toting students increases, so too will the seriousness of violent crime as, for example, a schoolyard fight turns into murder.

Gangs

The explosive growth in teenage gangs may have increased crime rates in the 1980s. Surveys indicate that there may be between 500,000 and 700,000 gang members in the United States. Boys who are members of gangs are far more likely to possess guns than non–gang members; criminal activity increases when kids join gangs.

The recent decline in the crime rate may be tied to changing gang values. Some streetwise kids have told researchers that they now avoid gangs because of the "younger brother syndrome"—they have watched their older siblings or parents caught in gangs or drugs and want to avoid the same fate.

Drug Use

Some experts tie increases in the violent crime rate between 1980 and 1990 to the crack cocaine epidemic, which swept the nation's largest cities, and drug-trafficking gangs, which fought over drug turf. These well-armed gangs did not hesitate to use violence to control territory, intimidate rivals, and increase market share. As the crack epidemic has subsided, so too has the violence in cities such as New York and other metropolitan areas where the crack epidemic was rampant.

Justice Policy

Some law enforcement experts have suggested that a reduction in crime rates may be attributable to aggressive police practices that target "quality of life" crimes such as panhandling, graffiti, petty drug dealing, and loitering. By showing that even the smallest infractions will be dealt with seriously, aggressive police departments may be able to discourage potential criminals from committing more serious crimes.

It is also possible that tough laws targeting drug dealing and repeat offenders with lengthy prison terms can affect crime rates. The fear of punishment may inhibit some would-be criminals. Lengthy sentences also help boost the nation's prison population. Placing a significant number of potentially high-rate offenders behind bars may help stabilize crime rates. Some ex-criminals have told researchers that they stopped committing crime because they perceived higher levels of street enforcement and incarceration rates.

Critical Thinking

1. What social policies might be most effective in getting the crime rate down?

2. Can you identify recent social changes that may be responsible for a decline in crime rates?

 InfoTrac College Edition Research

Gang activity may have a big impact on crime rates. To read about why kids join gangs, see
Benjamin B. Lahey, Rachel A. Gordon, Rolf Loeber, Magda Stouthamer-Loeber, and David P. Farrington, "Boys Who Join Gangs: A Prospective Study of Pre-

dictors of First Gang Entry," *Journal of Abnormal Child Psychology,* August 1999 v27 i4 p261

SOURCES: John J. Donohue III and Steven D. Levitt, "Legalized Abortion and Crime" (unpublished paper, University of Chicago, June 24, 1999); Donald Green, Dara Strolovitch, and Janelle Wong, "Defended Neighborhoods, Integration, and Racially Motivated Crime," *American Journal of Sociology* 104 (1998): 372–403; Robert O'Brien, Jean Stockard, and Lynne Isaacson, "The Enduring Effects of Cohort Characteristics on Age-Specific Homicide Rates, 1960–1995," *American Journal of Sociology* 104 (1999): 1061–1095; Darrell Steffensmeier and Miles Harer, "Making Sense of Recent U.S. Crime Trends, 1980 to 1996/1998: Age Composition Effects and Other Explanations," *Journal of Research in Crime and Delinquency* 36 (1999): 235–274; Desmond Ellis and Lori Wright, "Estrangement, Interventions, and Male Violence Toward Female Partners," *Violence and Victims* 12 (1997): 51–68; Richard Rosenfeld, "Changing Relationships Between Men and Women: A Note on the Decline in Intimate Partner Homicide," *Homicide Studies* 1 (1997): 72–83; Bruce Johnson, Andrew Golub, and Jeffrey Fagan, "Careers in Crack, Drug Use, Drug Distribution, and Nondrug Criminality," *Crime and Delinquency* 41 (1995): 275–295; Alfred Blumstein, "Violence by Young People: Why the Deadly Nexus," *National Institute of Justice Journal* 229 (1995): 2–9; Joseph Sheley and James Wright, *In the Line of Fire: Youth, Guns, and Violence in Urban America* (New York: Aldine de Gruyter, 1995); Alan Lizotte, Gregory Howard, Marvin Krohn, and Terence Thornberry, "Patterns of Illegal Gun Carrying Among Young Urban Males," *Valparaiso University Law Review* 31 (1997): 376–394; and Rosemary Gartner, "Family Structure, Welfare Spending, and Child Homicide in Developed Democracies," *Journal of Marriage and the Family* 53 (1991): 231–240.

Trends in Self-Reports and Victimization

Self-report results appear to be more stable than the UCR. When the results of recent self-report surveys are compared with various studies conducted over a 20-year period, a uniform pattern emerges. The use of drugs and alcohol increased markedly in the 1970s, leveled off in the 1980s, and then began to increase in the mid-1990s until 1997, when drug use began to decline. Theft, violence, and damage-related crimes seem more stable. Although a self-reported crime wave has not occurred, neither has there been any visible reduction in self-reported criminality.

Even though the official crime data tell us that the violence rate is in steep decline, highly publicized cases such as the shootings at Columbine High School in Colorado help convince the general public that U.S. society is extremely violent. Politicians seize on these tragedies to advocate a quick fix for teen violence: ban violent TV; encourage school prayers; prohibit rap music with offensive lyrics. Can such measures possibly deter violent outbursts such as Columbine?

According to the most recently available NCVS data (1999), about 30 million personal crimes occur each year. Like the UCR, the NCVS also shows that crime rates have undergone a major decline in the 1990s. For example, between 1993 and 1999, violent crime rates fell about 30 percent, while property crime decreased about 35 percent. Figure 2.4 shows trends in the NCVS over the past decades. Note that victim trends parallel the crime trends recorded by the UCR.

What the Future Holds   It is always risky to speculate about the future of crime trends because current conditions can change rapidly. But some criminologists have tried to predict future patterns.

Criminologist James A. Fox predicts a significant increase in teen violence if current trends persist. The United States has approximately 50 million school-age children, many of them under age 10. Although many come from stable homes, others lack stable families and adequate supervision. These children will soon enter their prime crime years. As a result, Fox predicts a wave of youth violence.[21]

Fox's predictions may be valid: It appears that the reduction in crime rate may be slowing. According to preliminary Uniform Crime Reports (released 12/18/2000) for the first six months of 2000 (the most recent data available), crime decreased by only 0.3 percent compared to the year before. Both violent crime and property crime declined by 0.3 percent when compared with the data from the same period in 1999. Some crimes (larceny and motor-vehicle theft) actually increased. Do these data portend an end to the declining crime rate?

Figure 2.3

Homicide Rate Trends, 1900–1999

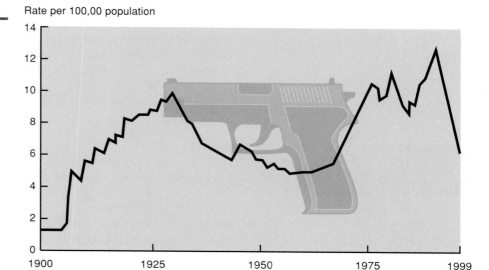

Rate per 100,00 population

SOURCE: Bureau of Justice Statistics, *Violent Crime in the United States* (Washington, DC: Bureau of Justice Statistics, 1992; updated 1999).

Figure 2.4

Victimization Rate Trends, 1973–1999

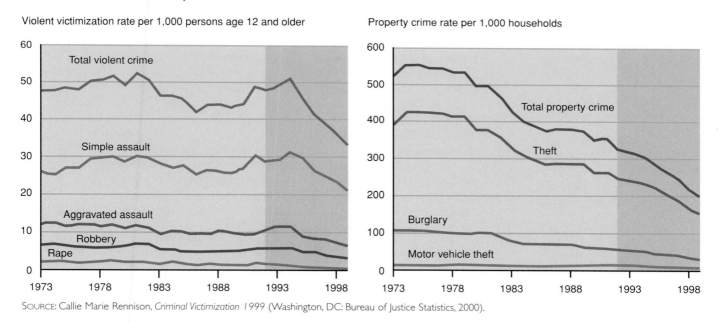

Violent victimization rate per 1,000 persons age 12 and older

Property crime rate per 1,000 households

SOURCE: Callie Marie Rennison, *Criminal Victimization 1999* (Washington, DC: Bureau of Justice Statistics, 2000).

Although Fox's predictions are persuasive, not all criminologists believe that we are in for an age-driven crime wave. Steven Levitt, for example, does not believe that the population's age makeup contributes as much to the crime rate as Fox and others suggest.[22] He argues that even if teens do commit more crime in the future, their contribution may be offset by the aging of the population, which will produce a large number of senior citizens and elderly in the population, a group with a relatively low crime rate.

Although such prognostication may be reassuring, there is no way of telling what future changes may influence crime rates. Technological developments such as the rapid expansion of e-commerce have created new classes of crime. Concern about the environment in rural areas may produce a rapid upswing in environmental crimes ranging from vandalism to violence.[23] So, while crime rates have trended downward, it is too early to predict that this trend will continue into the foreseeable future. ✔ **Checkpoints on page 39**

Crime Patterns

To gain insight into the nature of crime, criminologists look for stable crime rate patterns. If crime rates are consistently higher at certain times, in certain areas, and among certain groups, this knowledge might help explain the onset or cause of crime. For example, if criminal statistics show that crime rates are consistently higher in poor neighborhoods in large urban areas, then crime may be a function of poverty and neighborhood decline. If, in contrast, crime rates were spread evenly across the social structure, this would provide little evidence that crime has an economic basis; instead, crime might be linked to socialization, personality, intelligence, or some other trait unrelated to class position or income. In this section we examine traits and patterns that may influence the crime rate.

The Ecology of Crime

Most reported crimes occur during the warm summer months of July and August. During the summer, teenagers, who usually have the highest crime levels, are out of school and have greater opportunity to commit crime. People also spend more time outdoors, making them easier targets. Two exceptions to this trend are murders and robberies, which occur frequently in December and January (although rates are also high during the summer). Robbery rates increase in the winter partly because the Christmas shopping season means more money in the cash registers of potential targets.[24]

Crime rates also may be higher on the first day of the month than at any other time. Government welfare and Social Security checks arrive at this time, and with them come increases in such activities as breaking into mailboxes and accosting recipients on the streets. Also, people may have more disposable income at this time, and the availability of extra money may relate to behaviors associated with crime, such as partying, drinking, and gambling.[25]

Weather effects, such as temperature swings, may also affect violent crime rates. Crime rates increase with rising temperatures up to a point (about 85 degrees), but then begin to decline, perhaps because it becomes too hot for physical exertion.[26] However, the rates of some crimes, such as domestic assault, continue to increase as temperatures rise.[27]

Large urban areas have by far the highest violence rates; rural areas have the lowest per capita crime rates.

Use of Firearms

Firearms play a dominant role in criminal activity. According to the NCVS, firearms are typically involved in about 20 percent of robberies, 10 percent of assaults, and 6 percent of rapes. In 1999, the UCR reported that almost 70 percent of all murders involved firearms; most of these weapons were handguns.

According to international criminologists Franklin Zimring and Gordon Hawkins, the proliferation of handguns and the high rate of lethal violence they cause is the single most significant factor separating the crime problem in the United States from the rest of the developed world.[28] Differences between the United States and Europe in nonlethal crimes are only modest at best.[29] Because this issue is so important, the Policy and Practice in Criminology feature on pages 40–41 discusses gun control issues.

Social Class and Crime

instrumental crimes

Offenses designed to improve the financial or social position of the criminal.

expressive crimes

Offenses committed not for profit or gain but to vent rage, anger, or frustration.

✔ Checkpoints

✔ The FBI's Uniform Crime Report is an annual tally of crime reported to local police departments. It is the nation's official crime database.

✔ The National Crime Victimization Survey (NCVS) samples more than 50,000 people annually in order to estimate the total number of criminal incidents, including those not reported to police.

✔ Self-report surveys ask respondents about their own criminal activity. They are useful in measuring crimes rarely reported to police, such as drug usage.

✔ Crime rates peaked in the early 1990s and have been in sharp decline ever since. The murder rate has undergone a particularly steep decline.

✔ A number of factors influence crime rate trends, including the economy, drug use, gun availability, and crime control policies.

✔ It is difficult to gauge future trends. Some experts forecast an increase in crime, while others foresee a long-term decline in the crime rate.

Traditionally crime has been thought of as a lower-class phenomenon. After all, people at the lowest rungs of the social structure have the greatest incentive to commit crimes. Those unable to obtain desired goods and services through conventional means may resort to theft and other illegal activities—such as selling narcotics—to obtain them. These activities are referred to as **instrumental crimes**. Those living in poverty are also believed to engage in disproportionate numbers of **expressive crimes**, such as rape and assault, as a means of expressing their rage, frustration, and anger against society. Alcohol and drug abuse, common in impoverished areas, helps fuel violent episodes.[30]

Official statistics indicate that victimization rates for both males and females in inner-city, high-poverty areas are generally higher than those in suburban or wealthier areas.[31] Studies using aggregate police statistics (arrest records) have consistently shown that crime rates in lower-class areas exceed those in wealthier neighborhoods. Another "official" indicator of a class–crime relationship comes from surveys of prison inmates, which consistently show that prisoners were members of the lower class and unemployed or underemployed in the years before their incarceration.

An alternative explanation for these findings is that the relationship between official crime and social class is a function of law enforcement practices, not actual criminal behavior patterns. Police may devote more resources to poor areas, and consequently apprehension rates may be higher there. Similarly, police may be more likely to formally arrest and prosecute lower-class citizens than those in the middle and upper classes, which may account for the lower class's overrepresentation in official statistics and the prison population.

Class and Self-Reports Self-report data have been used extensively to test the class–crime relationship. If people in all social classes self-report similar crime patterns, but only those in the lower class are formally arrested, that would explain higher crime rates in lower-class neighborhoods. However, if lower-class people report greater criminal activity than their middle- and upper-class peers, it would indicate that official statistics accurately represent the crime problem.

Surprisingly, self-report studies generally do not find a direct relationship between social class and youth crime.[32] Socioeconomic class is related to official processing by police, courts, and correctional agencies, but not to the actual commission of crimes. While lower- and middle-class youths self-report equal amounts of crime, the lower-class youths have a greater chance of getting arrested, convicted, and incarcerated and becoming official delinquents.[33] More than 20 years ago, Charles Tittle, Wayne Villemez, and Douglas Smith concluded that little if any support exists for the contention that crime is primarily a lower-class phenomenon. They argued that official statistics probably reflect class bias in processing lower-class offenders.[34]

Weighing the Evidence for a Class–Crime Relationship Tittle's research has sparked significant debate. Many self-report instruments include trivial offenses such as using a false ID or drinking alcohol. Their inclusion may obscure the true class–crime relationship because affluent youths frequently engage in trivial offenses such as petty larceny, using drugs, and simple assault. Those who support a class–crime relationship suggest that if only serious felony offenses are considered, a significant association can be observed.[35] Studies showing middle- and lower-class youths to be equally delinquent rely on measures weighted toward minor crimes (for example, using a false ID or skipping school); when serious crimes, such as burglary and assault, are compared, lower-class youths are significantly more delinquent.[36] There is also debate over the most appropriate measure of class. Should it be income? Occupation? Educational attainment? Findings may be skewed if the measurement of class used

Policy and Practice in Criminology

Gun Control Issues

More than 200 million guns are in private hands in the United States; half of all U.S. households possess a gun. An estimated 50 million of these guns are illegal. Handguns are linked to many violent crimes, including 20 percent of all injury deaths (second to autos) and 60 percent of all homicides and suicides. They are also responsible for the deaths of about two-thirds of all police officers who are killed in the line of duty. The association between guns and crime has spurred many Americans to advocate controlling the sale of handguns and banning the cheap mass-produced handguns known as "Saturday night specials." In contrast, gun advocates view control as a threat to personal liberty and call for severe punishment of criminals rather than control of handguns. They argue that the Second Amendment of the U.S. Constitution protects the right to bear arms.

Efforts to control handguns have taken many forms. The states and many local jurisdictions have laws banning or restricting the sale or possession of guns; some regulate dealers who sell guns. The Federal Gun Control Act of 1968, which is still in effect, re-

quires that all dealers be licensed, fill out forms detailing each trade, and avoid selling to people prohibited from owning guns such as minors, ex-felons, and drug users.

On November 30, 1993, the Brady Handgun Violence Prevention Act (named after former Press Secretary James Brady, who was severely wounded in the 1981 attempted assassination of President Ronald Reagan) was enacted. The **Brady law** imposes a waiting period of five days before a licensed importer, manufacturer, or dealer may sell, deliver, or transfer a handgun to an unlicensed individual. The Brady law provides an instant check on whether a prospective buyer is prohibited from purchasing a weapon. Federal law bans gun purchases by people convicted of or under indictment for felony charges, fugitives, the mentally ill, those with dishonorable military discharges, those who have renounced U.S. citizenship, illegal aliens, illegal drug users, and those convicted of domestic violence misdemeanors or who are under domestic violence restraining orders; individual state laws may create other restrictions.

In addition to federal law, some state jurisdictions have tried to reduce gun violence by adding extra punishment, such as a mandatory prison sentence, for any crime involving a handgun. California's "10-20-life" law requires an additional 10 years in prison for carrying a gun while committing a violent felony, 20 years if the gun is fired, and if someone is injured, from 25 years to life in prison.

Although gun control advocates see this legislation as a good first step, the government's ability to control guns is problematic, and some question whether any gun control measures will ultimately curb gun violence. For example, when Jens Ludwig and Philip Cook compared two sets of states—32 that installed the Brady law in 1994, and 18 states plus the District of Columbia that already had similar laws prior to 1994—they found no evidence that the Brady law contributed to a reduction in homicide.

What problems face gun control efforts? Private citizens can still sell, barter, or trade handguns. Unregulated gun fairs and auctions are common throughout the United States; many gun deals are made at gun shows with

Brady law

Federal law that imposes a five-day waiting period for gun purchases and provides an instant check on whether a prospective buyer is prohibited from purchasing a weapon.

is inappropriate or invalid. Finally, research shows that class affects crime rates for nonwhites more than it does for whites.[37]

Like so many other criminological controversies, the debate over the true relationship between class and crime will most likely persist. The weight of recent evidence seems to suggest that serious, official crime is more prevalent among the lower classes, whereas less serious, self-reported crime is spread more evenly throughout the social structure.[38] Income inequality, poverty, and resource deprivation are all associated with the most serious violent crimes, including homicide and assault.[39] Communities that lack economic and social opportunities also produce high levels of frustration; their residents believe that they are relatively more deprived than residents of more affluent areas and may turn to criminal behavior to relieve their frustration.[40] Family life is disrupted and law-violating youth groups thrive in a climate that undermines adult supervision.[41] Conversely, when the poor are provided with economic opportunities via welfare and public assistance, crime rates drop.[42]

Nonetheless, although crime rates may be higher in lower-class areas, poverty alone cannot explain why a particular individual becomes a chronic violent criminal; if it did, the crime problem would be much worse than it is now.[43]

few questions asked. Regulating dealers is difficult, and tighter controls on them would only encourage private sales and bartering. Corrupt dealers can circumvent the law by ignoring state registration requirements or making unrecorded or misrecorded sales to individuals and unlicensed dealers. Even a few corrupt dealers can supply tens of thousands of illegal handguns.

Not all experts are convinced that strict gun control is a good thing. Criminologist Gary Kleck argues that guns may actually inhibit violence because they allow criminals to scare their victims, who are unlikely to fight back and be injured when facing the threat of a gun. Victims can back down without losing face because is socially acceptable to retreat from an armed assailant. Conversely, arming people may help reduce crime because criminals are afraid of gun-toting victims. When John R. Lott, Jr., analyzed the crime trends in 23 states that made it easier for citizens to arm themselves by carrying concealed weapons, he found a significant yearly drop in crimes such as murder and rape.

While these arguments are persuasive, the recent spate of gun violence makes a powerful statement against gun ownership. Studies show that many people who want to buy guns legally and/or purchase licenses to carry concealed weapons have prior criminal records and engage in patterns of heavy drinking. Strict control of gun purchases by this high-risk group may help reduce the rate of violent crimes.

Critical Thinking

1. Should the sale and possession of handguns be banned?

2. Which of the gun control methods discussed do you feel would be most effective in deterring crime?

 InfoTrac College Edition Research

Conservatives are adamant about keeping their guns, charging that "liberals" spread false stories about gun violence. To check out this perspective, read
Dave Kopel, "An Army of Gun Lies: How the Other Side Plays," *National Review,* 17 April 2000 v52 i7 pNA
For an opposing, more liberal view, see Michael Warfel, "Why Gun Control? An Individual's Right to Own and Bear Arms Must Be Balanced by the Greater Social Needs of a Society," *America,* 15 April 2000 v182 i13 p18

SOURCES: Jens Ludwig and Philip Cook, "Homicide and Suicide Rates Associated with the Implementation of the Brady Violence Prevention Act," *Journal of the American Medical Association* 284 (2000): 585–591; John R. Lott, Jr., *More Guns, Less Crime: Understanding Crime and Gun-Control Laws* (Chicago: University of Chicago Press, 1998); Julius Wachtel, "Sources of Crime Guns in Los Angeles, California," *Policing* 21 (1998): 220–239; Gary Kleck and Michael Hogan, "National Case-Control Study of Homicide Offending and Gun Ownership," *Social Problems* 46 (1999): 275–293; Garen Wintemute, Mora Wright, Carrie Parham, Christina Drake, and James Beaumont, "Denial of Handgun Purchase: A Description of the Affected Population and a Controlled Study of Their Handgun Preferences," *Journal of Criminal Justice* 27 (1999): 21–31; Shawn Schwaner, L. Allen Furr, Cynthia Negrey, and Rachelle Seger, "Who Wants a Gun License," *Journal of Criminal Justice* 27 (1999): 1-10; "Gun Crime Mandatory Sentences Take Effect in California," *Criminal Justice Newsletter* 28 (15 December 1997); Gary Kleck and Marc Gertz, "Armed Resistance to Crime: The Prevalence and Nature of Self-Defense with a Gun," *Journal of Criminal Law and Criminology* 86 (1995): 150–187; Gary Kleck, "The Incidence of Gun Violence Among Young People," *Public Perspective* 4 (1993): 3–6.

Age and Crime

There is general agreement that age is inversely related to criminality.[44] Regardless of economic status, marital status, race, sex, or other factors, younger people commit crime more often than their older peers. Research indicates this relationship has been stable across time periods ranging from 1935 to the present.[45]

Official statistics tell us that young people are arrested at a disproportionate rate to their numbers in the population; victim surveys generate similar findings for crimes in which assailant age can be determined. Whereas youths ages 13 to 17 collectively make up about 6 percent of the total U.S. population, they account for about 25 percent of index crime arrests and 17 percent of arrests for all crimes. As a general rule, the peak age for property crime is believed to be 16, and for violence, 18 (see Figure 2.5). In contrast, adults 45 and over, who make up more than 30 percent of the population, account for less than 10 percent of index crime arrests.

The elderly are particularly resistant to the temptations of crime; they make up more than 12 percent of the population and less than 1 percent of arrests. Elderly males 65 and over are arrested predominantly for alcohol-related matters (public drunkenness and drunk driving) and elderly females for larceny (shoplifting). The elderly crime rate has remained stable for the past 20 years.[46]

CONNECTIONS

If class and crime are unrelated, then the causes of crime must be found in factors experienced by members of all social classes—psychological impairment, family conflict, peer pressure, school failure, and so on. Theories that view crime as a function of problems experienced by members of all social classes are reviewed in Chapter 7.

Figure 2.5

The Relationship Between Age and Serious Violent Crime

Violent crime rates peak in the late teens and then decline rapidly.

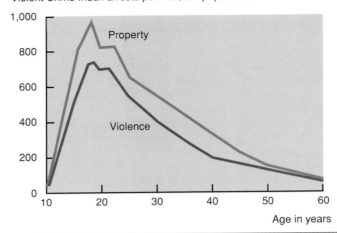

Violent Crime Index arrests per 100,000 population

aging out (desistance)

The fact that people commit less crime as they mature.

The fact that people commit less crime as they mature is referred to as **aging out or desistance: aging out (desistance).**

Why does aging out occur? One view is that there is a direct relationship between aging and crime. Psychologists note that young people, especially the indigent and antisocial, tend to discount the future.[47] They are impatient, and, because their future is uncertain, they are unwilling or unable to delay gratification. As they mature, troubled youths are able to develop a long-term life view and resist the need for immediate gratification.[48] Kids may view crime as fun, a risky but exciting social activity. As they grow older, life patterns such as job and marriage become inconsistent with criminality; people literally grow out of crime.[49]

James Q. Wilson and Richard Herrnstein argue that aging out is a function of the natural history of the human life cycle.[50] Deviance in adolescence is fueled by the need for conventionally unobtainable money and sex and reinforced by close relationships with peers who defy conventional morality. At the same time, teenagers are becoming independent from parents and other adults who enforce conventional standards. They have a new sense of energy and strength and are involved with peers who are similarly vigorous and frustrated. Adults, on the other hand, develop the ability to delay gratification and forgo the immediate gains that law violations bring. They also start wanting to take responsibility for their behavior and to adhere to conventional mores, such as establishing long-term relationships and starting a family.[51] Research shows that young people may turn to crime as a way to solve the problems of adolescence, including loneliness, frustration, and fear of peer rejection. As they mature, conventional means of problem solving become available and their life experience helps them seek out nondestructive solutions to their personal travails.[52]

Although most people age out of crime, some do pursue a criminal career. Yet even career criminals eventually slow down as they age. Crime is too dangerous, physically taxing, and unrewarding (and punishments too harsh and long-lasting) to become a long-term way of life for most people.[53] By middle age, even the most chronic offenders terminate criminal behavior.

CONNECTIONS

A discussion of how life events influence behavioral choices is presented in more depth in Chapter 9.

Gender and Crime

All three data-gathering criminal statistics tools support the theory that male crime rates are much higher than those of females. Victims report that their assailant was male in more than 80 percent of all violent personal crimes. The Uniform Crime Report arrest statistics indicate that the overall male–female arrest ratio is about 3.5 male offenders to 1 female offender; for serious violent crimes, the ratio is closer to 5 males to 1 female; murder arrests are 8 males to 1 female. Recent self-report data collected by the Institute for Social Research at the University of Michigan also show that males commit more serious crimes, such as robbery, assault, and burglary, than females. However, although the patterns in self-reports parallel official data, the ratios seem smaller. In other words, males self-report more criminal behavior than females, but not to the degree suggested by official data.

Why are there gender differences in the crime rate? Early criminologists pointed to emotional, physical, and psychological differences between males and females to explain the differences in crime rates. They maintained that because females were weaker and more passive, they were less likely to commit crimes. Cesare Lombroso argued that a small group of female criminals lacked "typical" female traits of "piety, maternity, undeveloped intelligence, and weakness."[54] Lombroso's theory became known as the **masculinity hypothesis**; in essence, a few "masculine" females were responsible for the handful of crimes that women commit.[55]

Although these early writings are no longer taken seriously, some criminologists still consider trait differences a key determinant of crime rate differences. For example, some criminologists link antisocial behavior to hormonal influences by arguing that male sex hormones (androgens) account for more aggressive male behavior; thus, gender-related hormonal differences can explain the gender gap in the crime rate.[56]

By the mid-twentieth century, criminologists commonly portrayed gender differences in the crime rate as a function of socialization. Female criminals were described as troubled individuals, alienated at home, who pursued crime as a means of compensating for their disrupted personal lives.[57] The streets became a "second home" to girls whose physical and emotional adjustment was hampered by a strained home life marked by such conditions as absent fathers or overly competitive mothers. The relatively few females who commit violent crimes report having home and family relationships that are more troubled than those experienced by males.[58]

In the 1970s, liberal feminists focused their attention on the social and economic role of women in society and its relationship to female crime rates.[59] They suggested that the traditionally lower crime rate for women could be

masculinity hypothesis

The view that women who commit crimes have biological and psychological traits similar to those of men.

CONNECTIONS

Gender differences in the crime rate may be a function of androgen levels; these hormones cause areas of the brain to become less sensitive to environmental stimuli, making males more likely to seek high levels of stimulation and to tolerate more pain in the process. Chapter 5 discusses the biosocial causes of crime and reviews this issue in greater detail.

Rates of female violence are rising faster than rates for males. One reason may be that growing numbers of young girls are joining gangs. Here, one gang member attacks another on the streets of Los Angeles.

© Deborah Copaken/Liaison Agency

CONNECTIONS

Critical criminologists view gender inequality as stemming from the unequal power of men and women in a capitalist society and the exploitation of females by fathers and husbands. This perspective, along with radical feminism, is considered more fully in Chapter 8.

explained by their "second-class" economic and social position. They predicted that as women's social roles changed and their lifestyles became more like those of men, their crime rates would converge.[60]

Although arrest rates are still considerably higher for males than for females, female arrest rates seem to be increasing at a faster pace. For example, between 1990 and 1999, male arrests actually decreased 5 percent, while female arrests increased almost 18 percent. During this period, female violent crime arrests rose 37 percent, while male violent crime arrests declined 15 percent. The increase in arrests of teenage girls during this period was triple the increase in male teenage arrests, suggesting that young females are increasing their offense rates at a pace even greater than their older sisters.[61]

Race and Crime

Official crime data indicate that minority group members are involved in a disproportionate share of criminal activity. According to UCR reports, African Americans make up about 12 percent of the general population, yet they account for about 42 percent of violent crime arrests and 27 percent of property crime arrests.

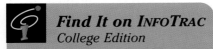

Find It on INFOTRAC
College Edition

Many explanations have been offered for the gender difference in crime rates. To research this topic on InfoTrac College Edition, use "gender and crime" as keywords.

Self-Reports and Race Another approach to examining this issue is to compare the racial differences in self-report data with those found in official delinquency records. Charges of racial discrimination in the arrest process would be supported if racial differences in self-report data were insignificant.

Nationwide studies of youth have found few racial differences in crime rates, although black youths were much more likely to be arrested and taken into custody.[62] These self-report studies seem to indicate that the criminal behavior rates of black and white teenagers are generally similar and that differences in arrest statistics may indicate a differential selection policy by police.[63]

Causes of Racial Disparity Racial differences in the crime rate remain an extremely sensitive issue. Although official arrest records indicate that African Americans are arrested at a higher rate than members of other racial groups, some question whether this is a function of crime rate differences, racism by police, or faulty data collection.[64] Research shows that suspects who are poor, minority, and male are more likely to be formally arrested than suspects who are white, affluent, and female.[65] Some critics charge that police officers routinely use "racial profiling" to stop African Americans and search their cars without probable cause or reasonable suspicion. Some cynics have gone so far as to suggest that police officers have created a new form of traffic offense called DWB—driving while black.[66]

While the UCR may reflect discriminatory police practices, African Americans are arrested for a disproportionate amount of violent crime, such as robbery and murder, and it is improbable that police discretion alone could account for these proportions. It is doubtful that police routinely ignore white killers, robbers, and rapists while arresting violent black offenders. Many criminologists today concede that recorded differences in the black and white violent crime arrest rates cannot be explained away solely by racism or differential treatment within the criminal justice system.[67] To do so would be to ignore the social problems that exist in the nation's inner cities.

CONNECTIONS

According to some criminologists, racism has created isolated subcultures that espouse violence as a way of coping with conflict situations. Exasperation and frustration among minority group members who feel powerless to fit within middle-class society are manifested in aggression. This view is discussed further in Chapter 10's review of the subculture of violence theory.

Racism and Crime How, then, can racial patterns be explained? Most explanations focus on the impact of economic deprivation, social disorganization, subcultural adaptations, and the legacy of racism and discrimination on personality and behavior.[68] That U.S. culture influences African American crime rates is underscored by the fact that black violence rates are much lower in other nations—both those that are predominantly white, such as Canada, and those that are predominantly black, such as Nigeria.[69]

African Americans have suffered through a long history of racism in the United States that has left long-lasting emotional scars.[70] Racism is still an element of daily life in the African American community, undermining faith in social and political institutions and weakening confidence in the justice system. Such fears are supported by empirical evidence that, in at least some jurisdictions, young African American males are treated more harshly by the criminal justice system than members of any other group.[71] There is also evidence that in some legal jurisdictions African Americans, especially those who are indigent or unemployed, receive longer prison sentences than European Americans. It is possible that some judges view poor blacks as "social dynamite," considering them more dangerous and likely to recidivate than white offenders.[72] Yet black victims of crime receive less public concern and media attention than white victims.[73]

Is Convergence Possible? Considering these overwhelming social problems, is it possible that racial crime rates will soon converge? One argument is that if economic conditions improve in the minority community, then differences in crime rates will eventually disappear.[74] A trend toward residential integration, under way since 1980, may also help reduce race-based crime rate differentials.[75] Despite economic disparity, there are actually few racial differences in attitudes toward crime and justice today. Convergence in crime rates will occur if economic and social obstacles can be removed.

In sum, the weight of the evidence shows that although there is little difference in self-reported overall crime rates by race, African Americans are more likely to be arrested for serious violent crimes. The causes of minority crime have been linked to poverty, racism, hopelessness, lack of opportunity, and urban problems experienced by all too many African Americans. ✔ **Checkpoints**

The Chronic Offender

chronic offenders

A small group of persistent offenders who account for a majority of all criminal offenses.

Crime data show that most offenders commit a single criminal act and, upon arrest, discontinue their antisocial activity. Others commit a few, less serious crimes. Finally, a small group of persistent offenders accounts for a majority of all criminal offenses. These persistent offenders are referred to as career criminals or **chronic offenders**.

The concept of the chronic or career offender is most closely associated with the research efforts of Marvin Wolfgang, Robert Figlio, and Thorsten Sellin.[76] In their landmark 1972 study, *Delinquency in a Birth Cohort,* they used official records to follow the criminal careers of a cohort of 9,945 boys born in Philadelphia in 1945, from the time of their birth until they reached 18 years of age in 1963. Official police records were used to identify delinquents. About one-third of the boys (3,475) had some police contact. The remaining two-thirds (6,470) had none. The best-known discovery of Wolfgang and his associates was the phenomenon of the chronic offender. They identified a group of 627 boys who had been arrested five times or more. This group was responsible for a total of 5,305 offenses, or 51.9 percent of all the offenses committed by the cohort. Even more striking was their involvement in serious criminal acts. Though comprising only about 6 percent of the entire sample, they committed 71 percent of the homicides, 73 percent of the rapes, 82 percent of the robberies, and 69 percent of the aggravated assaults.

Wolfgang and his associates found that arrests and court experience did little to deter the chronic offender. In fact, punishment was inversely related to chronic offending: The more stringent the sanction chronic offenders received, the more likely they were to engage in repeated criminal behavior.

Wolfgang's pioneering effort to identify the chronic career offender has since been replicated by a number of other researchers in a variety of locations in the United States and abroad.[77]

The findings of the cohort studies and the discovery of the chronic offender have revitalized criminological theory. If relatively few offenders become chronic, persistent criminals, then perhaps they possess some individual trait that is responsible for their behavior. Most people exposed to troublesome social conditions, such as poverty, do not become chronic offenders, so it is unlikely that social conditions alone can cause chronic offending.

Traditional theories of criminal behavior failed to distinguish between chronic and occasional offenders. They concentrated more on explaining why people begin to commit crime and paid scant attention to why people stop offending. The discovery of the chronic offender 25 years ago forced criminologists to consider such issues as persistence and desistance in their explanations of crime; more recent theories account for not only the onset of criminality but also its termination.

Summary

There are three primary sources of crime statistics: the Uniform Crime Reports, based on police data accumulated by the FBI; self-reports from criminal behavior surveys; and victim surveys. They tell us that there is quite a bit of crime in the United States, although the amount of violent crime is decreasing. Each data source has its strengths and weaknesses, and, although quite different from one another, they actually agree on the nature of criminal behavior.

The data sources show stable patterns in the crime rate. Ecological patterns show that crime varies by season and by urban versus rural environment. There is also evidence of gender and age gaps in the crime rate: Men commit more crime than women, and young people commit more crime than the elderly. Crime data show that people commit less crime as they age, but the significance and cause of this pattern are still not completely understood.

Similarly, racial and class patterns appear in the crime rate. However, it is still unclear whether these are true differences or a function of discriminatory law enforcement.

One of the most important findings in the crime statistics is the existence of the chronic offender, a repeat criminal responsible for a significant amount of all law violations. Chronic offenders begin their careers early in life and, rather than aging out of crime, persist into adulthood. The discovery of the chronic offender has led to the study of developmental criminology—why people persist, desist, terminate, or escalate their deviant behavior.

For additional chapter links, discussions, and quizzes, see the book-specific Web site at http://www.wadsworth.com/product/0534519423s.

Thinking Like a Criminologist

The planning director for the State Department of Juvenile Justice has asked for your advice on how to reduce the threat of chronic offenders. Some of the more conservative members of her staff seem to believe that these young offenders need a strict dose of rough justice if they are to be turned away from a life of crime. They believe that juvenile delinquents who are punished harshly are less likely to recidivate than youths who receive lesser punishments, such as community corrections or probation. In addition, they believe that hard-core, violent offenders deserve to be punished; excessive concern for offenders and not their acts ignores the rights of victims and society in general.

The planning director is unsure whether such an approach can reduce the threat of chronic offending. Can tough punishment produce deviant identities that lock young offenders into a criminal way of life? She is concerned that a strategy stressing punishment will have relatively little impact on chronic offenders and, if anything, may cause escalation in serious criminal behaviors.

She has asked you for your professional advice. On the one hand, the system must be sensitive to the adverse effects of stigma and labeling. On the other hand, the need for control and deterrence must not be ignored. Is it possible to reconcile these two opposing views?

Key Terms

Uniform Crime Report (UCR)	self-report surveys	aging out (desistance)
index crimes	instrumental crimes	masculinity hypothesis
National Crime Victimization Survey (NCVS)	expressive crimes	chronic offenders
	Brady law	

Discussion Questions

1. Would you answer honestly if a national crime survey asked you about your criminal behavior, including drinking and drug use? If not, why?

2. How would you explain gender differences in the crime rate? That is, why do you think males are more violent than females?

3. Assuming that males are more violent than females, does that mean that crime has a biological rather than a social basis (because males and females share a similar environment)?

4. The UCR tells us that crime rates are higher in large cities than in small villages. What does that tell us about the effect of TV, films, and music on teenage behavior?

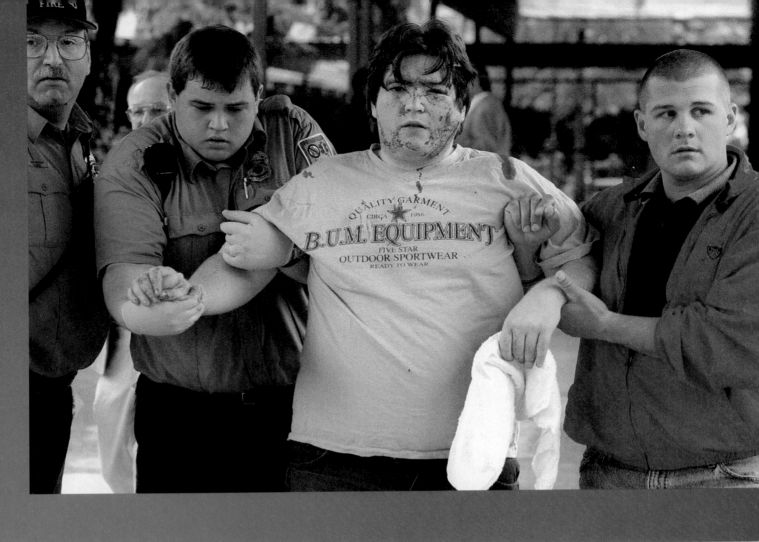

© The Register Guard/Corbis Sygma

3 Victims and Victimization

INTRODUCTION

Brandon Wilson, killer of nine-year-old Matthew Cecchi, is shown at his arraignment in a California courtroom. Is it possible to protect children from such irrational acts, or is victimization a random event that can happen to anyone at any time?

victimology

The study of the victim's role in criminal events.

victimologists

Criminologists who focus on the victims of crime.

In 1998, Brandon Wilson, 21, slashed the throat of Matthew Cecchi, a nine-year-old California boy, then stabbed him in the back and left him to bleed to death. After his conviction on murder charges, Wilson told the jury that he would "do it again in a second if I had the chance." When the jury later met to consider the death penalty, Wilson told them, "My whole purpose in life is to help destroy your society. You people are here as representatives of that society. As such, you should do everything in your power to rid the world of me—execute me." Granting him his wish, the jury foreman told reporters, "if there was ever a case that deserved the death penalty, this one fit."[1]

The horrific acts of a seemingly demented child killer such as Brandon Wilson illustrate the terrible impact crime can have on victims, their families, and society in general. Why do people become targets of predatory criminals? Is victimization a matter of chance, or can a victim somehow deflect or avoid criminal behavior? What can be done to protect victims, and, failing that, what can be done to help them in the aftermath of crime?

For many years, crime victims were not considered an important topic for criminological study. Victims were viewed as the passive recipients of a criminal's anger, greed, or frustration; they were considered to be people "in the wrong place at the wrong time." In the late 1960s, a number of pioneering studies found that, contrary to popular belief, the victim's own behavior is important in the crime process. Victims were found to influence criminal behavior by playing an active role in a criminal incident, as when an assault victim initially provokes an eventual attacker. Victims can also play an indirect role in a criminal incident, as when a woman adopts a lifestyle that continually brings her into high-crime areas.

The discovery that victims play an important role in the crime process has prompted the scientific study of victims, or **victimology**. Criminologists who focus their attention on crime victims refer to themselves as **victimologists**.

In this chapter, we examine victims and their relationship to the criminal process. First, using available victim data, we analyze the nature and extent of victimization. We then discuss the relationship between victims and criminal offenders. In this context, we look at various theories of victimization that attempt to explain the victim's role in the crime problem. Finally, we examine how society has responded to the needs of victims and consider what special problems they still face.

Problems of Crime Victims

The National Crime Victimization Survey (NCVS) indicates that the annual number of victimizations in the United States is about 30 million incidents. Being the target or victim of a rape, robbery, or assault is a terrible burden that can have considerable long-term consequences. In this section we explore some of the effects of these incidents.

Economic Loss

Based on estimates of property taken during larcenies, burglaries, and other reported crimes, the FBI estimates that victims lose about $11 billion per year. Of that amount, after the crime has been cleared, they recover about $4 billion of their losses.[2] When added to productivity losses caused by injury, pain and emotional trauma, the cost of victimization is estimated to be more than $100 billion.

Table 3.1 Costs per Victimization

CRIME	TANGIBLE COSTS	INTANGIBLE COSTS	TOTAL COSTS
Murder	$1,030,000	$1,910,000	$2,940,000
Rape/sexual assault	5,100	81,400	86,500
Robbery/attempt with injury	5,200	13,800	19,000
Assault or attempt	1,550	7,800	9,350
Burglary or attempt	1,100	300	1,400

SOURCE: Ted Miller, Mark Cohen, and Brian Wiersema, *The Extent and Costs of Crime Victimization: A New Look* (Washington, DC: National Institute of Justice, 1996), p. 2.

If the cost of long-term suffering, trauma, and risk of death is included, the total loss due to crime amounts to $450 billion annually, or about $1,800 per U.S. citizen[3] (see Table 3.1). Crime also produces social costs that must be paid by nonvictims as well. For example, each heroin addict is estimated to cost society more than $135,000 per year (see Figure 3.1); an estimated half-million addicts cost society about $68 billion per year.[4]

In addition to these societal costs, victims may suffer long-term losses in earnings and occupational attainment. Research by Ross Macmillan shows that Americans who suffer a violent victimization during adolescence earn about $82,000 less than nonvictims; Canadian victims earn $237,000 less. Macmillan reasons that victims bear psychological and physical ills that inhibit first their academic achievement and later their economic and professional success.[5]

System Abuse

The suffering endured by crime victims does not end when their attacker leaves the scene of the crime. They may suffer more victimization by the justice system.

While the crime is still fresh in their minds, victims may find that the police interrogation following the crime is handled callously, with innuendos or insinuations that they were somehow at fault. They have difficulty learning what is going on in the case; property is often kept for a long time as evidence and may never be returned. Some rape victims report that the treatment they receive from legal, medical, and mental health services is so destructive that they can't help feeling "re-raped."[6] Victims may also suffer economic hardship because of wages lost while they testify in court and find that authorities are indifferent to their fear of retaliation if they cooperate in the offenders' prosecution.[7]

Long-Term Stress

Victims may suffer stress and anxiety long after the incident is over and the justice process has been forgotten. For example, girls who were psychologically, sexually, or physically abused as children are more likely to have lower self-esteem and be more suicidal as adults than those who were not abused.[8] Chil-

Figure 3.1

The Costs of Heroin Addiction

Each heroin addict incurs the following losses annually:

Lost employment earnings	$11,918.12
Value of premature death	$6,909.59
Crime costs	$56,974.91
Costs to the criminal justice system	$30,000.00
Cost of spreading addiction to other users	$29,624.73
Total	**$135,427.35**

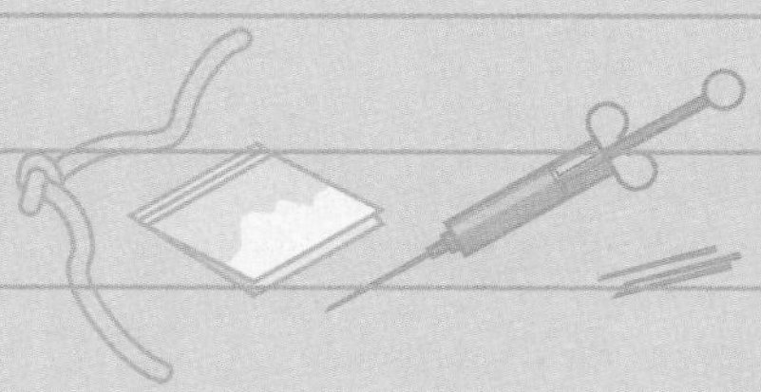

SOURCE: George Rengert, *The Geography of Illegal Drugs* (Boulder, CO: Westview Press, 1996), p. 5.

dren who are victimized in the home are more likely to run away to escape their environment, which puts them at risk for juvenile arrest and involvement with the justice system.[9]

Stress does not end in childhood. Spousal abuse victims suffer an extremely high prevalence of depression, **posttraumatic stress disorder** (an emotional disturbance following exposure to stresses outside the range of normal human experience), anxiety disorder, and obsessive-compulsive disorder (an extreme preoccupation with certain thoughts and compulsive performance of certain behaviors).[10] One reason may be that abusive spouses are as likely to abuse their victims psychologically with threats and intimidation as they are to use physical force; psychological abuse can lead to depression and other long-term disabilities.[11]

Some victims are physically disabled as a result of serious wounds sustained during episodes of random violence, including a growing number that suffer paralyzing spinal cord injuries. And if victims have no insurance, the long-term effects of the crime may have devastating financial as well as the emotional and physical consequences.[12]

Fear

People who have suffered crime victimization remain fearful long after their wounds have healed. Even if they have escaped attack themselves, hearing about another's victimization may make people timid and cautious. For example, a recent effort to reduce gang crime and drug dealing in some of Chicago's most troubled housing projects failed to meet its objectives because residents feared retaliation from gang boys and possible loss of relationships; joining an effort to organize against crime placed them at extreme risk.[13]

Victims of violent crime are the most deeply affected, fearing a repeat of their attack. There may be a spillover effect in which victims become fearful of other forms of crime they have not yet experienced; people who have been assaulted develop fears that their house will be burglarized.[14] Many go through a fundamental life change, viewing the world more suspiciously and less as a safe, controllable, and meaningful place. These people are more likely to suffer psychological stress for extended periods of time.[15]

posttraumatic stress disorder

Psychological reaction to a highly stressful event; symptoms may include depression, anxiety, flashbacks, and recurring nightmares.

Communities may live in fear when news of a violent incident grips the neighborhood. Sometimes local incidents become national news. The shooting of Amadou Diallo by New York City police officers was a graphic example of urban violence that can put an entire city in fear. Here, Vickie Smith of the Capital Region Justice for Diallo Committee stands in front of the Albany County (New York) Courthouse near a door painted with a body and bullet holes to symbolize the fatal wounds of Amadou Diallo.

© Albany Times Union/The Image Works

Figure 3.2

Percentage of Male High School Students (Grades 9–12) Reporting Smoking, Drinking, or Using Drugs, by Physical/Sexual Abuse Status

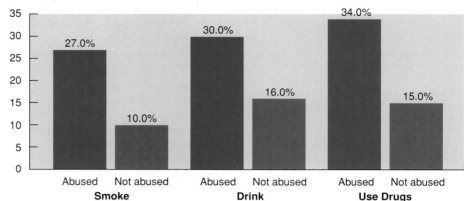

Notes: Smoke: smoked at least several cigarettes in the past week; Drink: drank at least once a month; Use drugs: used illegal drugs at least once in the past month. The survey was an in-class questionnaire completed by 3,162 boys in grades 5–12 at a nationally representative sample of 265 public, private, and parochial schools from December 1996 to June 1997. The survey included roughly equal samples of adolescent boys in grades 5–8 and 9–12. All responses were weighted to reflect grade, region, race and ethnicity, and gender.

SOURCE: Cathy Schoen et al., *The Health of Adolescent Boys: Commonwealth Fund Survey Findings* (New York: Commonwealth Fund, 1998). Figure prepared by The Center for Substance Abuse Research, University of Maryland, College Park.

Antisocial Behavior

There is growing evidence that crime victims are more likely to commit crime themselves. Being abused or neglected as a child increases the odds of being arrested, both as a juvenile and as an adult.[16] People, especially young males, who were physically or sexually abused are much more likely to smoke, drink, and take drugs than are nonabused youth (see Figure 3.2). Incarcerated offenders report significant amounts of posttraumatic stress disorder as a result of prior victimization, which may in part explain their violent and criminal behaviors.[17]

cycle of violence

Victims of crime, especially childhood abuse, are more likely to commit crime themselves.

The abuse–crime phenomenon is referred to as the **cycle of violence**.[18] Research shows that both boys and girls are more likely to engage in violent behavior if they were (1) the target of physical abuse and (2) exposed to violent behavior among adults they know or live with, or exposed to weapons.[19]

✓ **Checkpoints on page 53**

The Nature of Victimization

How many crime victims are there in the United States, and what are the trends and patterns in victimization? According to the NCVS, an estimated 28.8 million criminal events occurred during 1999.[20] As you may recall from Chapter 2, the NCVS, like the Uniform Crime Report, finds that crime rates have been declining. For example, between 1993 and 1999, the violent crime victimization rate fell 34 percent and the personal theft rate dropped from 2.3 to 0.9 per 1,000 people.

Patterns in the victimization survey findings are stable and repetitive, suggesting that victimization is not random but a function of personal and ecological factors. The stability of these patterns allows judgments to be made about the nature of victimization; policies can then be created in an effort to reduce the victimization rate. Who are victims? Where does victimization take place? What is the relationship between victims and criminals? The following sections discuss some of the most important victimization patterns and trends.

The Social Ecology of Victimization

The NCVS shows that violent crimes are slightly more likely to take place in an open, public area, such as a street, a park, or a field, in a school building, or at a commercial establishment such as a tavern, during the daytime or early evening

CONNECTIONS

As we saw in Chapter 2, the NCVS is currently the leading source of information on the nature and extent of victimization. It uses a sophisticated sampling methodology to collect data; statistical techniques then estimate victimization rates, trends, and patterns for the entire U.S. population.

hours than in a private home during the morning or late evening hours. The more serious violent crimes, such as rape and aggravated assault, typically take place after 6 P.M. Approximately two-thirds of rapes and sexual assaults occur at night—6 P.M. to 6 A.M. Less serious forms of violence, such as unarmed robberies and personal larcenies like purse snatching, are more likely to occur during the daytime.

Neighborhood characteristics affect the chances of victimization. Those living in the central city have significantly higher rates of theft and violence than suburbanites; people living in nonmetropolitan, rural areas have a victimization rate almost half that of city dwellers. The risk of murder for both men and women is significantly higher in disorganized inner-city areas where gangs flourish and drug trafficking is commonplace.

The Victim's Household

The NCVS tells us that within the United States, larger, higher-income, African American, Western, and urban homes are the most vulnerable to crime. In contrast, poor, rural, European American homes in the Northeast are the least likely to contain crime victims or be the target of theft offenses, such as burglary or larceny. People who own their homes are less vulnerable than renters.

Recent population movement and changes may account for recent decreases in crime victimization. U.S. residents have become extremely mobile, moving from urban areas to suburban and rural areas. In addition, family size has been reduced; more people than ever before are living in single-person homes (about 25 percent of households). It is possible that the decline in household victimization rates during the past 15 years can be explained by the fact that smaller households in less populated areas have a lower victimization risk.

Victim Characteristics

Social and demographic characteristics also distinguish victims and nonvictims. The most important of these factors are gender, age, social status, and race.

Gender As Figure 3.3 shows, gender affects victimization risk: Except for the crimes of rape and sexual assault, males are much more likely than females to be the victims of violent crime. Men are almost twice as likely as women to experience aggravated assault and robbery. Women, however, are seven times more likely than men to be victims of rape or sexual assault. For all crimes, males are 22 percent more likely to be victimized than females. When men are the victims of violent crime, the perpetrator is described as a stranger; women are much more likely to be attacked by a relative than are men. About two-thirds of all attacks against women are committed by a husband, boyfriend, family member, or acquaintance.[21] In two-thirds of sexual assaults, the victim knew or was acquainted with her or his attacker.

Age Victim data reveal that young people face a much greater victimization risk than do older persons. As Figure 3.4 shows, victim risk diminishes rapidly after age 25. The elderly, who are thought of as the helpless targets of predatory criminals, are actually much safer than their grandchildren. People over 65, who make up about 15 percent of the population, account for only 1 percent of violent victimizations; teens 12–19, who also make up 15 percent of the population, typically account for more than 30 percent of victimizations. For example, teens are 35 times more likely to be raped or sexually assaulted than people ages 50–64.

Social Status The poorest Americans are also the most likely victims of violent crime. This association occurs across all gender, age, and racial groups (see Figure 3.5). Although the poor are more likely to suffer violent crimes, the

✔ Checkpoints

✔ Victimology is the branch of criminology that examines the nature and extent of crime victimization.

✔ The total economic loss from crime victimization amounts to hundreds of billions of dollars annually.

✔ Victims may suffer long-term trauma, including posttraumatic stress disorder.

✔ Many victims become fearful and go through a fundamental life change.

✔ People who are victims may be more likely to engage in antisocial acts themselves.

Find It on INFOTRAC
College Edition

Did you know that a great deal of victimization occurs in school buildings? Though school violence may be declining, about one-third of all students are injured in a physical altercation each year. To learn more about this phenomenon, read

"Violence Decreasing in U.S. High Schools," *The Brown University Child and Adolescent Behavior Letter,* December 1999 v15 i12 p3

wealthy are more likely targets of personal theft crimes such as pocket picking and purse snatching. Perhaps the affluent, who sport more expensive attire and drive better cars, attract the attention of thieves.

Marital Status Marital status also influences victimization risk. Never-married males and females are victimized more often than married people. Widows and widowers have the lowest victimization risk. This association between marital status and victimization is probably influenced by age, gender, and lifestyle:

1. Many young people, who have the highest victim risk, are actually too young to have been married.

2. Young single people also go out in public more often and sometimes interact with high-risk peers, increasing their exposure to victimization.

3. Widows and widowers suffer much lower victimization rates because they are older, interact with older people, and are more likely to stay home at night and to avoid public places.

Race and Ethnicity African Americans are more likely than European Americans to be victims of violent crime: African Americans are three times more likely to be the victims of robbery and twice as likely to experience aggravated assault. Young black males face a murder risk four or five times greater than that of young black females, five to eight times higher than that of young white males, and 16 to 22 times higher than that of young white females.[22]

Other ethnic minorities also have a high risk of victimization. For example, Hispanics are much more likely than non-Hispanics to fall victim to robbery and aggravated assault. Hispanics are also more likely to suffer completed violent crimes than are non-Hispanics.

Figure 3.3

Rate of Victimization per 1,000 Persons Age 12 or Older in 1999

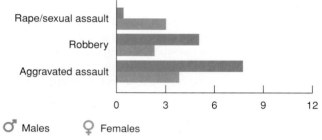

♂ Males   ♀ Females

SOURCE: Callie Marie Rennison, *Criminal Victimization 1999: Changes* (Washington, DC: Bureau of Justice Statistics, 2000), p. 6.

Figure 3.4

Correlation Between Age and Victimization

Rate of violent victimization by age (rape, robbery, assault, or personal theft) in 1999 per 1,000 persons age 12 or older

Age of victim

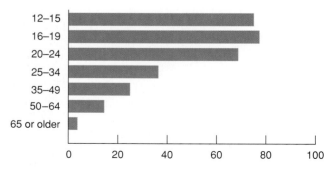

SOURCE: Callie Marie Rennison, *Criminal Victimization 1999: Changes* (Washington, DC: Bureau of Justice Statistics, 2000), p. 7.

Figure 3.5

Victimization by Income and Status

Rate of victimization from crimes of violence (rape, robbery, assault, and personal theft) by household income per 1,000 persons age 12 or older in 1999

Annual household income

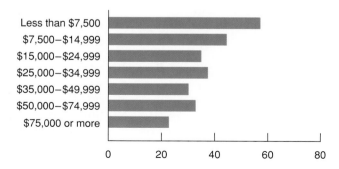

SOURCE: Callie Marie Rennison, *Criminal Victimization 1999: Changes* (Washington, DC: Bureau of Justice Statistics, 2000), p. 6.

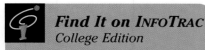

CONNECTIONS

The association between age and victimization is undoubtedly tied to lifestyle: Adolescents often stay out late at night, go to public places, and hang out with other young people who have a high risk of criminal involvement. Teens also face a high victimization risk because they spend a great deal of time in the most dangerous building in the community: the local school!

Why do these discrepancies exist? Because of income inequality, racial and ethnic minority group members are often forced to live in deteriorated urban areas beset by alcohol and drug abuse, poverty, racial discrimination, and violence. Consequently, their lifestyle places them in the most "at risk" population group.

Repeat Victimization Does prior victimization enhance or reduce the chances of future victimization? Individuals who have been crime victims have a significantly higher chance of future victimization than people who have remained nonvictims.[23] Households that have experienced victimization in the past are the ones most likely to experience it again in the future.[24]

What factors predict chronic victimization? Most repeat victimizations occur soon after a previous crime has occurred, suggesting that repeat victims share some personal characteristic that makes them a magnet for predators.[25] For example, children who are shy, physically weak, or socially isolated may be prone to being bullied in the schoolyard.[26] David Finkelhor and Nancy Asigian have found that three specific types of characteristics increase the potential for victimization:

1. *Target vulnerability.* The victims' physical weakness or psychological distress renders them incapable of resisting or deterring crime and makes them easy targets.

2. *Target gratifiability.* Some victims have some quality, possession, skill, or attribute that an offender wants to obtain, use, have access to, or manipulate. Having attractive possessions such as a leather coat may make one vulnerable to predatory crime.

3. *Target antagonism.* Some characteristics increase risk because they arouse anger, jealousy, or destructive impulses in potential offenders. Being gay or effeminate, for example, may bring on undeserved attacks in the street; being argumentative and alcoholic may provoke barroom assault.[27]

Repeat victimization may occur when the victim does not take defensive action. For example, if an abusive husband finds out that his battered wife will not call police, he repeatedly victimizes her; or if a hate crime is committed and the police do not respond to reported offenses, the perpetrators learn they have little to fear from the law.[28]

The Victims and Their Criminals

The victim data also tell us something about the relationship between victims and criminals.

Victims report that most crimes were committed by a single offender over age 20. Crime tends to be intraracial: African American offenders victimize blacks, and European Americans victimize whites. However, because the country's population is predominantly white, it stands to reason that criminals of all races will be more likely to target white victims. Victims report that substance abuse was involved in about one-third of violent crime incidents.[29]

Although many violent crimes are committed by strangers, a surprising number of violent crimes are committed by relatives or acquaintances of the victims. In fact, more than half of all nonfatal personal crimes are committed by people who are described as being known to the victim. For example, one-fourth of all rapes/sexual assaults are committed by nonrelatives well known to the victim. Victimization commonly occurs within families, involving parents, children, and extended family. ✓ **Checkpoints on page 56**

Theories of Victimization

For many years criminological theory focused on the actions of the criminal offender; the role of the victim was virtually ignored. More than 50 years ago scholars began to realize that the victim was not simply a passive target in crime, but someone whose behavior can influence his or her own fate, who "shapes and molds the criminal."[30]

These early works helped focus attention on the role of the victim in the crime problem and led to further research efforts that have sharpened the image of the crime victim. Today a number of different theories attempt to explain the causes of victimization.

Victim Precipitation Theory

According to **victim precipitation theory**, some people may actually initiate the confrontation that eventually leads to their injury or death. Victim precipitation can be either active or passive.

Active precipitation occurs when victims act provocatively, use threats or fighting words, or even attack first.[31] In 1971, Menachem Amir suggested that female rape victims often contribute to their attacks by dressing provocatively or pursuing a relationship with the rapist.[32] Although Amir's findings are controversial, courts have continued to return not guilty verdicts in rape cases if a victim's actions can in any way be construed as consenting to sexual intimacy.[33]

In contrast, **passive precipitation** occurs when the victim exhibits some personal characteristic that unknowingly either threatens or encourages the attacker. The crime can occur because of personal conflict—for example, when two people compete over a job, promotion, love interest, or some other scarce and coveted commodity. For example, a woman may become the target of intimate violence when she improves her job status and her success results in a backlash from a jealous spouse or partner.[34] In other situations, although the victim may never have met the attacker or even known of his or her existence, the attacker feels menaced and acts accordingly.[35]

Passive precipitation may also occur when the victim belongs to a group whose mere presence threatens the attacker's reputation, status, or economic well-being. For example, hate crime violence may be precipitated by immigrant group members' arriving in the community to compete for jobs and housing. Research indicates that passive precipitation is related to power: If the target group can establish themselves economically or gain political power in the community, their vulnerability will diminish. They are still a potential threat, but they become too formidable a target to attack; they are no longer passive precipitators.[36] By implication, economic power reduces victimization risk.

Lifestyle Theories

Some criminologists believe that people may become crime victims because their lifestyles increase their exposure to criminal offenders. Victimization risk is increased by such behaviors as associating with young men, going out in public places late at night, and living in an urban area. Conversely, one's chances of victimization can be reduced by staying home at night, moving to a rural area, staying out of public places, earning more money, and getting married. The basis of such **lifestyle theories** is that crime is not a random occurrence, but rather a function of the victim's lifestyle.

High-Risk Lifestyles People who have high-risk lifestyles have a much greater chance of victimization. For example, young runaways are at high risk for victimization; the more time they are exposed to street life, the greater their risk of becoming crime victims.[37]

✔ Checkpoints

✔ Males are more often the victims of crime than females; women are more likely than men to be attacked by a relative.

✔ The indigent are much more likely than the affluent to be the victims of violent crime; the wealthy are more likely to be the targets of personal theft.

✔ Younger, single people are more often targets than older, married people.

✔ Rates of violent victimization are much higher for African Americans than for European Americans. Crime victimization tends to be intraracial.

✔ Some people and places are targets of repeat victimization.

---

victim precipitation theory

The view that victims may initiate, either actively or passively, the confrontation that leads to their victimization.

active precipitation

Aggressive or provocative behavior of victims that results in their victimization.

Because almost every American will one day become a crime victim, more than 2,000 victim–witness asistance programs have been developed throughout the United States. Representatives help victims deal with the stress they may endure when a family member becomes a crime victim. Here, Margaret Ensley, president of Mothers Against Violence in Schools, stands with a photo of her son Michael, a victim of gun violence in 1993, during a 1999 news conference in Los Angeles. A group of California cities and counties, led by Los Angeles and San Francisco, have sued handgun makers, hoping to force the weapons industry to pay for gun-related injuries and deaths.

AP/Wide World Photos

passive precipitation

Personal or social characteristics of victims that make them "attractive" targets for criminals; such victims may unknowingly either threaten or encourage their attackers.

lifestyle theories

The view that people become crime victims because of lifestyles that increase their exposure to criminal offenders.

deviant place theory

The view that victimization is primarily a function of where people live.

Teenage males have an extremely high victimization risk because their lifestyle places them at risk both at school and once they leave the school grounds.[38] They spend a great deal of time hanging out with their friends and pursuing recreational fun.[39] Their friends may give them a false ID so they can go drinking in the neighborhood bar. They may hang out in taverns at night, which places them at risk because many fights and assaults occur in places that serve liquor. Those who have a history of engaging in serious delinquency, getting involved in gangs, carrying guns, and selling drugs have an increased chance of being shot and killed.[40]

Lifestyle risks continue into young adulthood. College students who spend several nights each week partying and who take recreational drugs are much more likely to be victims of violent crime than those who avoid such risky academic lifestyles.[41]

Deviant Place Theory According to **deviant place theory**, victims do not encourage crime, but are victim prone because they reside in socially disorganized high-crime areas where they have the greatest risk of coming into contact with criminal offenders, irrespective of their own behavior or lifestyle.[42] Consequently, there may be little reason for residents in lower-class areas to alter their lifestyle or take safety precautions because personal behavior choices do not influence the likelihood of victimization.[43] Neighborhood crime levels may be more important for determining the chances of victimization than individual characteristics.

Deviant places are poor, densely populated, highly transient neighborhoods in which commercial and residential properties exist side by side.[44] The commercial establishments provide criminals with easy targets for theft crimes, such as shoplifting and larceny. Successful people stay out of these stigmatized areas. They are home to "demoralized kinds of people" who are easy targets for crime: the homeless, the addicted, the retarded, and the elderly poor.[45]

People who live in more affluent areas and take safety precautions significantly lower their chances of becoming crime victims; the effect of safety precautions is less pronounced in poor areas. Residents of poor areas have a much greater risk of becoming victims because they live in areas with many motivated offenders; to protect themselves, they have to try harder to be safe than do the more affluent.[46]

Routine Activities Theory

routine activities theory

The view that victimization results from the interaction of three everyday factors: the availability of suitable targets, the absence of capable guardians, and the presence of motivated offenders.

suitable targets

Objects of crime (persons or property) that are attractive and readily available.

capable guardians

Effective deterrents to crime, such as police or watchful neighbors.

motivated offenders

People willing and able to commit crimes.

Routine activities theory was first articulated in a series of papers by Lawrence Cohen and Marcus Felson.[47]

Cohen and Felson assume that both the motivation to commit crime and the supply of offenders are constant.[48] Every society will always have some people who are willing to break the law for revenge, greed, or some other motive. The volume and distribution of predatory crime (violent crimes against a person and crimes in which an offender attempts to steal an object directly) are closely related to the interaction of three variables that reflect the routine activities of the typical American lifestyle:

1. The availability of **suitable targets**, such as homes containing easily salable goods

2. The absence of **capable guardians**, such as police, homeowners, neighbors, friends, and relatives

3. The presence of **motivated offenders**, such as a large number of unemployed teenagers

The presence of these components increases the likelihood that a predatory crime will take place. Targets are more likely to be victimized if they are poorly guarded and exposed to a large group of motivated offenders such as teenage boys.[49] The interacting components of routine activities theory are illustrated in Figure 3.6.

Cohen and Felson argue that crime rates increased between 1960 and 1980 because the number of adult caretakers at home during the day (guardians) decreased as a result of increased female participation in the workforce. While mothers are at work and children in day care, homes are left unguarded. Similarly, with the growth of suburbia and the decline of the traditional neighborhood, the number of such familiar guardians as family, neighbors, and friends diminished. At the same time, the volume of easily transportable wealth increased, creating a greater number of available targets.[50] Skyrocketing drug use in the 1980s created an excess of motivated offenders, and the rates of some crimes, such as robbery, increased dramatically. Falling crime rates in the 1990s would be explained by a robust economy, which decreases the pool of motivated offenders, and the growing number of police officers, which increases guardianship.

Figure 3.6

Routine Activities Theory

Crime and victimization involve the interaction of three factors.

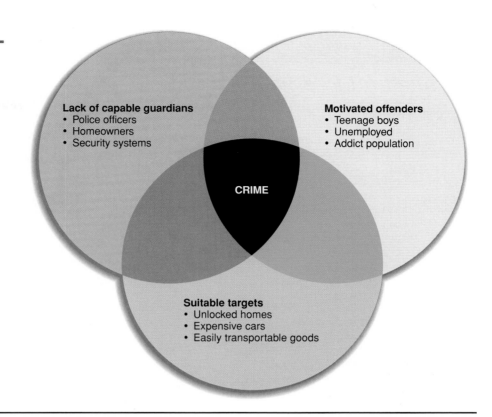

Lack of capable guardians
- Police officers
- Homeowners
- Security systems

Motivated offenders
- Teenage boys
- Unemployed
- Addict population

CRIME

Suitable targets
- Unlocked homes
- Expensive cars
- Easily transportable goods

Routine Activities and Lifestyle

Routine activities theory and the lifestyle approach have a number of similarities. They both assume that a person's living arrangements can affect victim risk and that people who live in unguarded areas are at the mercy of motivated offenders. These two theories both rely on four basic concepts: (1) proximity to criminals, (2) time of exposure to criminals, (3) target attractiveness, and (4) guardianship.[51]

Based on the same basic concepts, these theories share the following predictions: People increase their victimization risk if they (1) live in high-crime areas, (2) go out late at night, (3) carry valuables such as an expensive watch, (4) engage in risky behavior such as drinking alcohol, and (5) are without friends or family to watch or help them.[52] For example, young women who drink to excess in bars and fraternity houses may elevate their risk of date rape because (1) they are easy targets and (2) their attackers can rationalize raping them because they are intoxicated ("she's loose and immoral so I didn't think she'd care"). Intoxication is sometimes seen as making the victim culpable for the crime.[53] Conversely, people can reduce their chances of repeat victimization if they change their lifestyle and adopt crime-suppressing routines such as getting married, having children, or moving to a small town.[54]

The accompanying Criminological Enterprise box on crime in everyday life shows how these relationships can be influenced by cultural and structural change. ✔ Checkpoints

The Criminological Enterprise

Crime and Everyday Life

A core premise of routine activities theory is that, all things being equal, the greater the *opportunity* to commit crime, the higher the crime and victimization rates. Marcus Felson elaborates on this thesis in his classic book *Crime and Everyday Life.* Using a routine activities perspective, Felson shows why he believes American crime rates are so high and why U.S. citizens suffer such high rates of victimization.

According to Felson, there are always impulsive, motivated offenders who are willing to take the chance, if conditions are right, of committing crime for profit. Therefore, crime rates are a function of changing social conditions. Crime increased in the United States as the country changed from a nation of small villages and towns to one of large urban environments. In a village, not only could a thief be easily recognized, but the items that were stolen could be identified long after the crime occurred. Cities provided a critical population mass, allowing predatory criminals to hide and evade apprehension. After the crime, criminals could blend into the crowd, disperse their loot, and make a quick escape using the public transportation system.

The modern-day equivalent of the urban center is the shopping mall. Here, strangers converge in large numbers and youths "hang out." The interior is filled with people, so drug deals can be concealed in the pedestrian flow. Stores have attractively displayed goods, encouraging shoplifting and employee pilferage. Substantial numbers of cars are parked in areas that make larceny and car theft virtually undetectable. Cars that carry away stolen merchandise have an undistinguished appearance: Who notices people placing items in a car in a shopping mall lot? Also, shoppers can be attacked in parking lots as they walk in isolation to and from their cars.

As American suburbs grew in importance, labor and family life began to scatter away from the household, decreasing guardianship. Microwave ovens, automatic dishwashers, and fast-food meals have freed adolescents from common household chores. Rather than help prepare the family dinner and wash dishes afterward, adolescents are free to meet with their peers and avoid parental control. As car ownership increases, teens have greater access to transportation outside parental control. Greater mobility and access to transportation makes it impossible for neighbors to know if a teen belongs in an area or is an intruder planning to commit a crime. As schools become larger and more complex, they provide ideal sites for crime. The many hallways and corridors prevent teachers from knowing who belongs where; spacious school grounds reduce teacher supervision.

Felson finds that these changes in the structure and function of society have been responsible for changes in the crime rates. He concludes that, rather than trying to change people, crime prevention strategies must reduce the opportunity to commit crime.

Critical Thinking

1. What recent technological changes have influenced crime rates? The Internet? Video and computer games? Paging systems? Fax machines? Automatic teller systems?

2. Would increased family contact decrease adolescent crime rates, or would it increase the opportunity for child abuse?

 InfoTrac College Edition Research

To see how the routine activities approach is used to explain violent victimizations, see Thoroddur Bjarnason, Thordis J. Sigurdardottir, and Thorolfur Thorlindsson, "Human Agency, Capable Guardians, and Structural Constraints: A Lifestyle Approach to the Study of Violent Victimization," *Journal of Youth and Adolescence,* February 1999 v28 i1 p105(1)

SOURCE: Marcus Felson, *Crime and Everyday Life: Insights and Implications for Society* (Thousand Oaks, CA: Pine Forge Press, 1994; 2nd edition, 1998).

Caring for the Victim

National victim surveys indicate that almost every American age 12 and over will one day become the victim of a common-law crime, such as larceny or burglary, and in the aftermath suffer financial problems, mental stress, and physical hardship.[55] Surveys show that upward of 75 percent of the general public have been victimized by crime at least once in their lives. As many as 25 percent of the victims develop post-traumatic stress syndrome, with symptoms that last for more than a decade after the crime occurred.[56]

Helping the victim to cope is the responsibility of all of society. Law enforcement agencies, courts, and correctional and human service systems have come to realize that due process and human rights exist not only for the criminal defendant but also for the victim of criminal behavior.

Antonio Jorge, center, sits next to his wife, Laura Jorge, while being comforted by Elaine Rendine, director of the Victim's Assistance Program, as the jury announces on February 13, 1998, that it has found Charles Smith guilty of first-degree murder in the death of his 16-year-old stepdaughter, Kristen M. Jorge.

AP/Wide World Photos

Find It on INFOTRAC
College Edition

The National Center for Victims of Crime (NCVC) in Arlington, Virginia, conducts research on the effectiveness of state constitutional amendments and other laws designed to protect victims. To read more about its work, go to InfoTrac College Edition and read

Julie Brienza, "Crime Victim Laws Sometimes Ignored," *Trial*, May 1999 v35 i5 p103

Because of public concern over violent personal crime, President Ronald Reagan created a Task Force on Victims of Crime in 1982.[57] This group suggested that a balance be achieved between recognizing the victim's rights and providing the defendant with due process. Recommendations included providing witnesses and victims with protection from intimidation, requiring restitution in criminal cases, developing guidelines for fair treatment of crime victims and witnesses, and expanding programs of victim compensation.[58]

As a result, Congress passed the Omnibus Victim and Witness Protection Act, requiring the use of victim impact statements at sentencing in federal criminal cases, greater protection for witnesses, more stringent bail laws, and the use of restitution in criminal cases. In 1984, the Comprehensive Crime Control Act and the Victims of Crime Act authorized federal funding for state victim compensation and assistance projects.[59] With these acts, the federal government recognized the plight of the victim and made victim assistance an even greater concern of the public and the justice system.

Victim Service Programs

victim–witness assistance programs

Government programs that help crime victims and witnesses; may include compensation, court services, and/or crisis intervention.

compensation

Financial aid awarded to crime victims to repay them for their loss and injuries; may cover medical bills, loss of wages, loss of future earnings, and/or counseling.

An estimated 2,000 **victim–witness assistance programs** have been developed throughout the United States.[60] These programs are organized on a variety of government levels and serve a variety of clients. We will look briefly at some prominent forms of victim assistance operating in the United States.[61]

Victim Compensation One of the primary goals of victim advocates has been to lobby for legislation creating crime victim **compensation** programs.[62] As a result of such legislation, the victim ordinarily receives compensation from the state to pay for damages associated with the crime. Rarely are two compensation schemes alike, however, and many state programs suffer from a lack of both adequate funding and proper organization within the criminal justice system. Compensation may be provided for medical bills, loss of wages, loss of future earnings, and counseling. In the case of death, the victim's survivors may receive burial expenses and aid for loss of support.[63] Awards typically range from $100 to $15,000. Occasionally, programs will provide emergency assistance to indigent victims until compensation is available. Emergency assistance may come in the form of food vouchers or replacement of prescription medicines.

Court Services A common victim program service helps victims deal with the criminal justice system. One approach is to prepare victims and witnesses by explaining court procedures: how to be a witness, how bail works, and what to do if the defendant makes a threat. Lack of such knowledge can cause confusion and fear, making some victims reluctant to testify in court procedures. Many victim programs also provide transportation to and from court and counselors who remain in the courtroom during hearings to explain procedures and provide support. Court escorts are particularly important for elderly and disabled victims, victims of child abuse and assault, and victims who have been intimidated by friends or relatives of the defendant.

Public Education More than half of all victim programs include public education programs that help familiarize the general public with their services and with other agencies that help crime victims. In some instances, these are primary prevention programs, which teach methods of dealing with conflict without resorting to violence. For example, school-based programs present information on spousal and dating abuse, followed by discussions of how to reduce violent incidents.[64]

Crisis Intervention Most victim programs refer victims to specific services to help them recover from their ordeal. Clients are commonly referred to the local network of public and private social service agencies that can provide emergency and long-term assistance with transportation, medical care, shelter, food, and clothing. In addition, more than half of all victim programs provide **crisis intervention** for victims who feel isolated, vulnerable, and in need of immediate services. Some programs counsel at their offices, while others visit victims in their homes, at the crime scene, or in the hospital.

Victim–Offender Reconciliation Program (VORP) **Victim–offender reconciliation programs** use mediators to facilitate face-to-face encounters between victims and their attackers. The aim is to engage in direct negotiations that lead to restitution agreements and, possibly, reconciliation between the two parties involved.[65] More than 120 reconciliation programs currently in operation handle an estimated 16,000 cases per year. Designed at first to handle routine misdemeanors such as petty theft and vandalism, programs now commonly hammer out restitution agreements in more serious incidents such as residential burglary and even attempted murder.

Victims' Rights

Legal scholar Frank Carrington suggests that crime victims have legal rights that should assure them basic services from the government.[66] According to Carrington, just as the defendant has the right to counsel and a fair trial, society is also obliged to ensure basic rights for law-abiding citizens. These rights range from adequate protection from violent crimes to victim compensation and assistance from the criminal justice system. Some suggested changes that might enhance the relationship between the victim and the criminal justice system are listed in Table 3.2.

About 14 states have actually incorporated language similar to Table 3.2 within their legal codes as a "Victims' Bill of Rights." Victims are now entitled to find out about the progress of their cases in 22 states and to be present at sentencing hearings in 37 and at parole hearings in 36.[67]

Assuring victims' rights may involve an eclectic mix of advocacy groups—some independent, others government-sponsored, and some self-help. Advo-

---

CONNECTIONS

Reconciliation programs are based on the concept of restorative justice, which rejects punitive correctional measures and instead suggests that crimes of violence and theft should be viewed as interpersonal conflicts that need to be settled in the community through noncoercive means. See Chapter 8 for more on this approach.

---

crisis intervention

Emergency counseling for crime victims.

victim–offender reconciliation programs

Mediated face-to-face encounters between victims and their attackers, designed to produce restitution agreements and, if possible, reconciliation.

preventive detention

The practice of holding dangerous suspects before trial without bail.

Table 3.2 Proposals to Ensure the Rights of Victims
• Use **preventive detention** (pretrial jailing without the right to bail) for dangerous criminals awaiting trial
• Eliminate delays between the arrest and the initial hearing and between the hearing and the trial, thus limiting the offender's opportunity to intimidate victims or witnesses
• Eliminate plea bargaining, or if that proves impossible, allow victims to participate in the plea negotiations
• Control defense attorneys' cross-examination of victims
• Allow hearsay testimony of police at the preliminary hearing instead of requiring the victim to appear
• Abolish the exclusionary rule, which allows the guilty to go free on technicalities
• Allow victims to participate in sentencing
• Establish minimum mandatory sentences for crimes
• Prohibit murderers given life sentences from being freed on parole
• Make criminals serve time for each crime they are convicted of and reduce the use of concurrent sentences (serving time for multiple crimes simultaneously)
• Tighten the granting of parole and allow victims to participate in parole hearings
• Provide full restitution or compensation to victims in all crimes
SOURCE: Frank Carrington, "Victim's Rights Litigation: A Wave of the Future," in *Perspectives on Crime Victims*, ed. Burt Galaway and Joe Hudson (St. Louis: C.V. Mosby Co., 1981).

cates can be especially helpful when victims need to interact with the agencies of justice. For example, advocates can lobby police departments to keep investigations open as well as request the return of recovered stolen property. They can demand that prosecutors and judges provide protection from harassment and reprisals by, for example, making "no contact" a condition of bail. They can help victims make statements during sentencing hearings as well as probation and parole revocation procedures. Victim advocates can also interact with news media, making sure that reporting is accurate and that victim privacy is not violated. Victim advocates can be part of an independent agency similar to a legal aid society. If successful, top-notch advocates may eventually open private offices, similar to attorneys, private investigators, or jury consultants.[68]

Self-Protection

Although the general public mostly approves of the police, fear of crime and concern about community safety have prompted many people to become their own "police force," taking an active role in community protection and citizen crime control groups.[69] The more crime in an area, the greater the amount of fear, and the more likely residents will be to engage in self-protective measures.[70] Research indicates that a significant number of crimes may not be reported to police simply because victims prefer to take matters into their own hands.[71]

target hardening

Making one's home or business crime-proof through the use of locks, bars, alarms, and other devices.

One manifestation of this trend is the concept of **target hardening**, or making one's home and business crime-proof through the use of locks, bars, alarms, and other devices.[72] Commonly used crime prevention techniques include a fence or barricade at the entrance; a doorkeeper, guard, or receptionist in an apartment building; an intercom or phone to gain access to the building; surveillance cameras; window bars; warning signs; and dogs chosen for their ability to guard property. The use of these measures is inversely proportional to perception of neighborhood safety: People who fear crime are more likely to use crime prevention techniques.

Although the true relationship is still unclear, there is mounting evidence that people who protect their homes are less likely to be victimized by property crimes.[73] One study conducted in the Philadelphia area found that people who install burglar alarms are less likely to suffer burglary than those who forgo similar preventive measures.[74]

Community Organization

Some communities have organized on the neighborhood level against crime. Citizens have been working independently and in cooperation with local police agencies in neighborhood patrol and block watch programs. These programs organize local citizens in urban areas to patrol neighborhoods, watch for suspicious people, help secure the neighborhood, lobby for improvements (such as increased lighting), report crime to police, put out community newsletters, conduct home security surveys, and serve as a source for crime information or tips.[75]

Although such programs are welcome additions to police services, there is little evidence that they appreciably affect the crime rate. There is also concern that their effectiveness is spottier in low-income, high-crime areas, which need the most crime prevention assistance.[76] Block watches and neighborhood patrols seem more successful when they are part of general-purpose or multi-issue community groups, rather than when they focus directly on crime problems.[77]

Summary

Criminologists now consider victims and victimization a major focus of study. About 30 million U.S. citizens are victims of crime each year, and the social and economic costs of crime are in the billions of dollars. Like crime, victimization has stable patterns and trends. Violent crime victims tend to be young, poor, single males living in large cities, although victims come in all ages, sizes, races, and genders. Many victimizations occur in the home, and many victims are the target of relatives and loved ones.

There are a number of theories of victimization. One view, called victim precipitation, is that victims provoke criminals. More common are lifestyle theories that suggest that victims put themselves in danger by engaging in high-risk activities, such as going out late at night, living in a high-crime area, and associating with high-risk peers. Deviant place theory argues that victimization risk is related to neighborhood crime rates. The routine activities theory maintains that a pool of motivated offenders exists and that these offenders will take advantage of unguarded, suitable targets. The major theories of victimization are summarized in Table 3.3.

Numerous programs help victims by providing court services, economic compensation, public education, and crisis intervention. Some people suggest that the U.S. Constitution should be amended to include protection of victims' rights. Rather than depend on the justice system, some victims have attempted to help themselves through community organization for self-protection.

For additional chapter links, discussions, and quizzes, see the book-specific Web site at http://www.wadsworth.com/product/0534519423s.

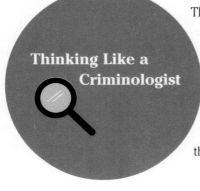

Thinking Like a Criminologist

The director of the state's department of human services has asked you to evaluate a self-report survey of adolescents ages 10 to 18. She has provided you with the following information on physical abuse.

Adolescents experiencing abuse or violence are at high risk of immediate and lasting negative effects on health and well-being. Of the high school students surveyed, an alarming one in five (21 percent) said they had been physically abused. Of the older students, ages 15 to 18, 29 percent said they had been physically abused. Younger students also reported significant rates of abuse: 17 percent responded "yes" when questioned whether they had been physically abused. Although girls were far less likely to report

Table 3.3 Victimization Theories

THEORY	MAJOR PREMISE	STRENGTHS
Victim precipitation	Victims trigger criminal acts by their provocative behavior. Active precipitation involves fighting words or gestures. Passive precipitation occurs when victims unknowingly threaten their attacker.	Explains multiple victimizations. If people precipitate crime, it follows that they will become repeat victims if their behavior persists over time.
Lifestyle	Victimization risk is increased when people have a high-risk lifestyle. Placing oneself at risk by going out to dangerous places results in increased victimization.	Explains victimization patterns in the social structure. Males, young people, and the poor have high victimization rates because they have a higher-risk lifestyle than females, the elderly, and the affluent.
Deviant places	People who live in deviant places are at high risk for crime. Victim behavior has little influence over the criminal act.	Places the focus of crime on deviant places. Shows why people with conventional lifestyles become crime victims.
Routine activities	Crime rates can be explained by the availability of suitable targets, the absence of capable guardians, and the presence of motivated offenders.	Can explain crime rates and trends. Shows how victim behavior can influence criminal opportunity. Suggests that victimization risk can be reduced by increasing guardianship and/or reducing target vulnerability.

abuse than boys, 12 percent said they had been physically abused. Most abuse occurs at home; it occurs more than once; and the abuser is usually a family member. More than half of those physically abused had tried alcohol and drugs, and 60 percent had admitted to a violent act. Nonabused children were significantly less likely to abuse substances, and only 30 percent indicated they had committed a violent act.

How would you interpret these data? What factors might influence their validity? What is your interpretation of the association between abuse and delinquency?

Key Terms

victimology
victimologists
posttraumatic stress disorder
cycle of violence
victim precipitation theory
active precipitation
passive precipitation

lifestyle theories
deviant place theory
routine activities theory
suitable targets
capable guardians
motivated offenders
victim–witness assistance programs

compensation
crisis intervention
victim–offender reconciliation
  programs
preventive detention
target hardening

Discussion Questions

1. Considering what you have learned in this chapter about crime victimization, what measures can you take to better protect yourself from crime?

2. Do you agree with the assessment that a school is one of the most dangerous locations in the community? Did you find your high school to be a dangerous environment?

3. Do people bear some of the responsibility for their victimization if they maintain a lifestyle that contributes to the chances of becoming a crime victim? That is, should we "blame the victim"?

4. Have you ever experienced someone "precipitating" crime? If so, did you do anything to help the situation?

Part 2

Theories of Crime Causation

An important goal of the criminological enterprise is to generate valid and accurate theories of crime causation. Social scientists have defined theory as sets of statements that explain why and how several concepts are related. For a set of statements to qualify as a theory, we must be able to deduce some conclusions from it that are subject to empirical verification; that is, theories must predict or prohibit certain observable events or conditions.*

Criminologists have sought to collect vital facts about crime and interpret them in a scientifically meaningful fashion. By developing empirically verifiable statements, or hypotheses, and organizing them into theories of crime causation, they hope to identify the causes of crime.

Since the late nineteenth century, criminological theory has pointed to various underlying causes of crime. The earliest theories generally attributed crime to a single underlying cause: atypical body build, genetic abnormality, insanity, physical anomalies, or poverty. Later theories attributed crime causation to multiple factors: poverty, peer influence, school problems, and family dysfunction.

In this section, theories of crime causation are grouped into six chapters. Chapters 4 and 5 focus on theories based on individual traits. These theories hold that crime is either a free-will choice made by an individual, a function of personal psychological or biological abnormality, or both. Chapters 6 through 8 investigate theories based in sociology and political economy. These theories portray crime as a function of the structure, process, and conflicts of social living. Chapter 9 is devoted to theories that combine or integrate these various concepts into a cohesive, complex view of crime.

*Rodney Stark, *Sociology*, 2nd ed. (Belmont, CA: Wadsworth, 1987), 618.

4 Choice Theory: Because They Want To

INTRODUCTION

In 1999, after a two-year criminal investigation, investigators in Italy turned up evidence that Russian organized-crime figures had funneled millions of dollars through the Bank of New York in a massive money-laundering scheme.[1] Italian prosecutors found that Russian mobsters were raising money in Italy by extorting money from immigrants from the former Soviet Union. In one of many schemes, legitimate Russian businessmen were forced to hand over invoices for goods they bought in Italy and then shipped back home to Russia. The mobsters then used the invoices to get millions of dollars in reimbursement on the taxes paid on goods shipped out of the country. The illegal funds were then routed first to Moscow and then to New York and finally rerouted back to Italian bank accounts. Between 1996 and 1999, the Russian mob is believed to have moved at least $7.5 billion through the Bank of New York.

The complex intrigues of the Russian international money laundering scheme suggest that the decision to commit crime can involve rational and detailed planning and decision making, designed to maximize personal gain and avoid capture and punishment. Some criminologists go as far as suggesting that any criminal violation—committing a robbery, selling drugs, attacking a rival, or filing a false tax return—is based on rational decision making. Such a decision may be motivated by a variety of personal reasons, including greed, revenge, need, anger, lust, jealousy, thrill-seeking, or vanity. But if it is made after weighing the potential benefits and consequences, then the illegal act is a **rational choice**. This view of crime is referred to here as **choice theory**.

In this chapter, we review the philosophical underpinnings of choice theory—the view that criminals rationally choose crime. We then turn to theories of crime prevention and control that flow from the concept of choice: situational crime control, general deterrence theory, specific deterrence theory, and incapacitation. Finally, we take a brief look at how choice theory has influenced criminal justice policy.

rational choice

The view that crime is a function of a decision-making process in which the potential offender weighs the potential costs and benefits of an illegal act.

choice theory

The school of thought holding that people choose to engage in delinquent and criminal behavior after weighing the consequences and benefits of their actions.

The Development of Rational Choice Theory

Rational choice theory has its roots in the classical school of criminology developed by the Italian social thinker Cesare Beccaria, whose utilitarian approach powerfully influenced the criminal justice system and was widely accepted throughout Europe and the United States.[2] It seemed more rational to let the "punishment fit the crime" than to punish criminals in a cruel and capricious manner. Beccaria's vision was influential in the move away from torture and physical punishment in the nineteenth century toward prison sentences geared to fit the severity of crime. These practices were the cornerstone of what is today known as **classical criminology**, a view that remained popular for a century.

By the end of the nineteenth century, the popularity of the classical approach began to decline, and, by the middle of the twentieth century, the perspective was neglected by mainstream criminologists. During this period, positivist criminologists focused on internal and external factors—poverty, IQ, education—rather than personal choice and decision making.

Beginning in the late 1970s, a number of criminologists began to revisit classical ideas, producing books and monographs expounding the theme that

classical criminology

The theoretical perspective suggesting that (1) people have free will to choose criminal or conventional behaviors; (2) people choose to commit crime for reasons of greed or personal need; and (3) crime can be controlled only by the fear of criminal sanctions.

C O N N E C T I O N S
- - - - - - - - - - - - - - - -
As you may recall from Chapter 1, Beccaria believed that criminals weighed the benefits and conseqences of crime before choosing to violate the law. They would be unlikely to choose crime if punishment was swift, certain, and severe.

criminals are rational actors who plan their crimes, could be controlled by the fear of punishment, and deserve to be penalized for their misdeeds. In *Thinking About Crime,* political scientist James Q. Wilson observed that people who are likely to commit crime are unafraid of breaking the law because they value the excitement and thrills of crime, have a low stake in conformity, and are willing to take greater chances than the average person. If they could be convinced that their actions would bring severe punishment, only the totally irrational would be willing to engage in crime.[3]

From these roots has evolved a more contemporary version of classical theory, based on intelligent thought processes and criminal decision making; today this is referred to as the rational choice approach to crime causation.[4]

The Concepts of Rational Choice

According to the rational choice approach, law-violating behavior is the product of careful thought and planning. Offenders choose crime after considering both personal needs—money, revenge, thrills, entertainment—and situational factors, such as how well a target is protected and the efficiency of the local police force. The reasoning criminal evaluates the risk of apprehension, the seriousness of expected punishment, the potential value of the criminal enterprise, and his or her immediate need for criminal gain.

The decision to commit a specific type of crime, then, is a matter of personal choice made after weighing and evaluating available information. Conversely, the decision to forgo crime may be based on the criminal's perception that the potential rewards of the criminal act are not worth the risk of apprehension. For example, burglars may choose not to commit crime if they believe that a neighborhood is well patrolled by police.[5] In fact, when police concentrate patrols in a particular area of the city, crime rates tend to increase in adjacent areas because calculating criminals view them as being safer.[6]

Offense and Offender Specifications

offense-specific

The idea that offenders react selectively to the characteristics of particular crimes.

offender-specific

The idea that offenders evaluate their skills, motives, needs, and fears before deciding to commit crime.

Rational choice theorists view crime as both offense- and offender-specific.[7] Crime is said to be **offense-specific** because offenders react selectively to the characteristics of particular crimes. Deciding to commit a particular burglary, for example, might involve evaluating the target's likely cash yield, the availability of resources such as a getaway car, and the probability of capture by police.[8]

Crime is **offender-specific** because criminals are not simply driven people who, for one reason or another, engage in random antisocial acts. Before deciding to commit crime, they analyze whether they have what it takes to be successful; they carefully evaluate their skills, motives, needs, and fears. A criminal act might be ruled out, for example, if potential offenders perceive that they can reach a desired personal goal through legitimate means, such as a part-time job or borrowing money from a relative.

Note the distinction made here between crime and criminality.[9] Crime is an event; criminality is a personal trait. Criminals do not commit crime all the time; conversely, even the most honest citizens may, on occasion, violate the law. On the one hand, some high-risk people lacking opportunity may never commit crime; on the other hand, given enough provocation or opportunity, a low-risk, law-abiding person may commit crime.

Structuring Criminality

A number of personal factors condition people to choose criminality. Offenders are likely to desist from crime if they believe (1) that their future criminal earnings will be relatively low and (2) that attractive and legal opportunities to generate income are available.[10] In contrast, criminals may be motivated when they know people who have made "big scores" and are quite successful at crime. Though the prevailing wisdom is that "crime does not pay," a small but significant subset of criminals actually enjoy earnings of close to $50,000 per year from crime, and their success may help motivate other would-be offenders.[11] In this sense, rational choice is a function of a person's perception of conventional alternatives and opportunities.

Learning and experience may be important elements in structuring criminality.[12] Career criminals may learn the limitations of their powers; they know when to take a chance and when to be cautious. Experienced criminals may turn from a life of crime when they develop a belief that the risk of crime is greater than its potential profit.[13]

Personality and lifestyle also affect criminal choices. Criminals appear to be more impulsive and have less self-control than other people; they seem unaffected by fear of criminal punishment.[14] They are typically under stress or facing some serious personal problem or condition that forces them to choose risky behavior.[15]

Structuring Crime

According to the rational choice approach, the decision to commit crime, regardless of its substance, is structured by (1) where it occurs, (2) the characteristics of the target, and (3) available means.

Choosing the Place Criminals carefully choose where they will commit their crime. Criminologist Bruce Jacobs's interviews with 40 active crack cocaine street dealers in a Midwestern city showed that dealers carefully evaluate the desirability of their sales area before setting up shop.[16] Dealers consider the middle of a long block the best choice because they can see everything in both directions; police raids can be spotted before they occur.[17] Another tactic is to entice new buyers into spaces between apartment buildings or into back lots. Although the dealers may lose the tactical edge of being on a public street, they gain a measure of protection because their colleagues can watch over the operation and come to the rescue if the buyer tries to "pull something."[18]

Choosing Targets Evidence of rational choice may also be found in the way criminals locate their targets. Victimization data indicate that while the affluent are rarely the victims of violent crimes, high-income households are the most likely targets of burglary.[19] Interviews with burglars find that they check to make sure that no one is home before they enter a residence. Some call ahead, whereas others ring the doorbell, preparing to claim they had the wrong address if someone answers. Some find out which families have star high school athletes because those that do are sure to be at the weekend football game, leaving their houses unguarded.[20] Others seek unlocked doors and avoid the ones with deadbolts; houses with dogs are usually considered off-limits.[21] Burglars also report being sensitive to the activities of their victims. They note that homemakers often develop predictable behavior patterns, which helps them plan their crimes.[22] Burglars seem to prefer "working" between 9 A.M. and 11 A.M. and in midafternoon, when parents are either working or dropping off or picking up children at school. Burglars appear to monitor car and pedestrian traffic and avoid selecting targets on heavily traveled streets.[23] It does not seem surprising that well-organized communities that restrict traffic and limit neighborhood entrance and exit routes have experienced significant declines in property crime.[24]

CONNECTIONS

Rational choice theory dovetails with routine activities theory, which you learned about in Chapter 3. Although not identical, these approaches both claim that crime rates are a product of criminal opportunity. They suggest that increasing the number of guardians, decreasing the suitability of targets, or reducing the offender population should lower crime rates. Conversely, increased opportunity and reduced guardianship will increase crime rates.

Table 4.1 Female Crack Dealers' Arrest Avoidance Techniques

Projected Self-Image
Female crack dealers learn the art of conveying a sense of normalcy and ordinariness in their demeanor and physical appearance to avoid attention. Female crack dealers avoid typical male behavior. They refuse to dress provocatively and wear flashy jewelry but instead dress down, wearing blue jeans and sweat pants to look like a "resident." Some affect the attire of crack users, figuring the police will not think them worth the trouble of an arrest.

Stashing
Female crack dealers learn how to hide drugs on their person, in the street, or at home. One dealer told how she hid drugs in the empty shaft of a curtain rod; another wore hollow ear muffs to hide crack. Knowing that a female officer has to do body cavity searches gives the dealers time to get rid of their drugs before they get to the station house. Dealers are aware of legal definitions of possession. One said she stashed her drugs 250 feet from her home because that was beyond the distance (150 feet) police considered a person legally to be in "constructive possession" of drugs.

Selling Hours
The women are aware of the danger of dealing at the wrong time of day. For example, it would be impossible to tell police you were out shopping at 3 A.M. If liquor stores are open, a plausible story could be concocted: I was out buying beer for a party. Dealers who sell from their homes cultivate positive relations with neighbors who might otherwise be tempted to tip off police. Some had barbecues and even sent over plates of ribs and pork to those who did not show up for dinner.

Routine Activities/Staged Performances
Dealers camouflage their activities within the bustle of their daily lives. They sell crack while hanging out in a park or shooting hoops in a playground. They meet their customers in a lounge and try to act normal, having a good time, anything not to draw attention to themselves and their business. They use props to disguise drug deals.

SOURCE: Bruce Jacobs and Jody Miller, "Crack Dealing, Gender, and Arrest Avoidance," *Social Problems* 45 (1998): 550–566.

✔ Checkpoints

✔ Choice theory can be traced to Beccaria's view that crime is rational and can be prevented by punishment that is swift, severe, and certain.

✔ Crime is said to be offense-specific because criminals evaluate the characteristics of targets to determine their suitability.

✔ Crime is offender-specific because criminals evaluate their skills, motivations, and needs before committing a specific crime.

✔ Criminal choice involves such actions as choosing the place of crime, selecting targets, and learning criminal techniques.

Learning Criminal Techniques Criminals report learning techniques of crime to help them avoid detection (see Table 4.1). Research conducted by Leanne Fiftal Alarid and her partners found that women drawn into dealing drugs learn the trade in a businesslike manner. One young dealer told Alarid how she learned the techniques of the trade from an older male partner: "He taught me how to 'recon' [reconstitute] cocaine, cutting and repacking a brick from 91 proof to 50 proof, just like a business. He treats me like an equal partner, and many of the friends are business associates. I am a catalyst. . . . I even get guys turned on to drugs."[25] Note the business terminology used. This coke dealer could be talking about taking a computer training course at a major corporation! If criminal acts are treated as business decisions, in which profit and loss potential must be carefully calculated, then crime must indeed be a rational event.

In sum, rational choice involves both shaping criminality and structuring crime. Personality, age, status, risk, and opportunity seem to influence the decision to become a criminal; place, target, and techniques help to structure crime.[26] ✔ Checkpoints

Is Crime Rational?

It is relatively easy to show that some crimes are the product of rational, objective thought, especially when they involve an ongoing criminal conspiracy centered on economic gain. For example, when prominent bankers in the savings and loan industry were indicted for criminal fraud, their elaborate financial schemes not only showed signs of rationality but exhibited brilliant, though flawed, financial expertise.[27] Similarly, the drug dealings of organized crime bosses demonstrate a reasoned analysis of market conditions, interests, and risks. But what about crimes that are immediate rather than ongoing? Do they show signs of rationality?

Are Street Crimes Rational?

There is evidence that even seemingly "unplanned" street crimes may also be the product of careful risk assessment, including environmental, social, and structural factors. Target selection seems highly rational. Ronald Clarke and Patricia Harris found that auto thieves are very selective in their choice of targets. Vehicle selection seems to be based on attractiveness and suitability for a particular purpose; for example, German cars are selected for stripping because they usually have high-quality audio equipment that has good value on the second-hand market.[28]

There are also signs of rationality in the choices made by armed robbers. They generally choose targets close to their homes or in areas which they routinely travel. Familiarity with the area gives them ready knowledge of escape routes; this is referred to as their "awareness space."[29] Robbers may be wary of people who are watching the community for signs of trouble: research by Paul Bellair shows that robbery levels are relatively low in neighborhoods where residents keep a watchful eye on their neighbors' property.[30] Many robbers avoid freestanding buildings because they can more easily be surrounded by police; others select targets that are known to do a primarily cash business, such as bars, supermarkets, and restaurants.[31]

Is Drug Use Rational?

© John T. Barr/Liaison Agency

Is drug use rational? If so, how can persistent abuse by such well-known celebrities as Robert Downey, Jr., shown here in court during a hearing on charges of drug possession, be explained? After all, they have everything to lose and nothing to gain from their behavior.

Did actor Robert Downey, Jr., make an objective, rational choice to abuse drugs and potentially sabotage his career? Did comedian Chris Farley make a rational choice when he abused alcohol and other drugs to the point that it killed him? Is it possible that drug users and dealers, a group not usually associated with clear thinking, make rational choices? Research does in fact show that at its onset, drug use is controlled by rational decision making. Users report that they begin taking drugs when they believe that the benefits of substance abuse outweigh its costs: They believe that drugs will provide a fun, exciting, thrilling experience. They choose what they consider safe sites to buy and sell drugs.[32] Their entry into substance abuse is facilitated by their perception that valued friends and family members endorse and encourage drug use and abuse substances themselves.[33]

Drug dealers approach their profession in a businesslike fashion. According to criminologist George Rengert's study of drug markets, drug dealers face many of the same problems as legitimate retailers. If they are too successful in one location, rivals will be attracted to the area, and stiff competition may drive down prices and cut profits. The dealer can fight back by discounting the cost of drugs or increasing quality, as long as it doesn't reduce profit margins.[34] In other words, drug dealers face many of the same problems as legitimate businesspeople. Bruce Jacobs found that dealers use specific techniques to avoid being apprehended by police. They play what they call the "peep game" before dealing drugs, scoping out the territory to make sure the turf is free from anything out of place that may be a potential threat (such as police officers or rival gang members).[35] One crack dealer told Jacobs,

There was this red Pontiac sittin' on the corner one day with two white guys inside. They was just sittin' there for an hour, not doin' nothin.' Another day, diff'rent people be walkin' up and down the street you don't really recognize. You think they might be kin of someone but then you be askin' around and they (neighbors) ain't never seen them before neither. When ya' see strange things like that, you think somethin' be goin' on (and you don't deal).[36]

Can Violence Be Rational?

Is it possible that violent acts, through which the offender gains little material benefit, are the product of reasoned decision making?

Evidence confirms that even violent criminals select suitable targets by picking people who are vulnerable and lack adequate defenses.[37] For example, when Richard Wright and Scott Decker interviewed active street robbers in St. Louis, Missouri, their subjects expressed a considerable amount of rational thought before choosing a robbery, which may involve violence, over a burglary, which involves stealth and cunning.[38] One told them why he chose to be a robber:

> I feel more safer doing a robbery because doing a burglary, I got a fear of breaking into somebody's house not knowing who might be up in there. . . . On robbery I can select my victims, I can select my place of business. I can watch and see who all work in there or I can rob a person and pull them around in the alley or push them up in a doorway and rob them.[39]

edgework

The excitement or exhilaration of successfully executing illegal activities in dangerous situations.

seductions of crime

The situational inducements or immediate benefits that draw offenders into law violations.

Violent offenders avoid victims who may be armed and dangerous.[40]

Even in apparently senseless killings among strangers, the conscious motive is typically revenge for a prior dispute or disagreement among the parties involved or their families.[41] Many homicides are motivated by the offenders' desire to avoid retaliation from a victim they assaulted or to avoid future prosecutions by getting rid of witnesses.[42] Although some killings are the result of anger and aggression, others are the result of rational planning.

Why Do People Commit Crime?

Assuming that crime is rational, why—knowing its often unpleasant consequences—do people choose to commit crime? Rational choice theorists believe the answer is both simple and obvious. For many people, crime is a more attractive alternative than law-abiding behavior. It brings rewards, excitement, prestige, or other desirable outcomes without lengthy work or effort. Whether it is violent or profit-oriented, crime has an allure that some people cannot resist. Crime may produce a natural "high" and other positive sensations that are instrumental in maintaining and reinforcing criminal behavior.[43] Some law violators describe the "adrenaline rush" that comes from successfully executing illegal activities in dangerous situations. This has been termed **edgework**: the "exhilarating, momentary integration of danger, risk, and skill" that motivates people to try a variety of dangerous criminal and noncriminal behavior.[44]

Sociologist Jack Katz argues that there are, in fact, immediate benefits to criminality. These situational inducements, which he labels the **seductions of crime**,[45] directly precede the commission of crime and draw offenders into law violations. For example, someone challenges their authority or moral position, and they vanquish their opponent with a beating; or they want to do something exciting, so they break into and vandalize a school building.

According to Katz, choosing crime can help satisfy personal needs. For some people, shoplifting and vandalism are attractive because getting away with crime is a thrilling demonstration of personal competence (Katz calls this "sneaky thrills"). Even murder can have an emotional payoff: Killers behave like

✔ Checkpoints

✔ Theft crimes appear rational because thieves and burglars typically choose targets that present little risk and they plan their attacks carefully.

✔ Robbers report that they select vulnerable targets who are unlikely to fight back. They avoid armed victims.

✔ Drug users and dealers use elaborate ploys to avoid detection. They employ businesslike practices in their commercial enterprises.

(continued)

the avenging gods of mythology, choosing to have life-or-death control over their victims.[46]

If committing crime is a rational choice, it follows that crime can be controlled or eradicated by convincing potential offenders that crime is a poor choice—that it will bring them not rewards, but pain, hardship, and deprivation. Evidence shows that jurisdictions with relatively low incarceration rates also experience the highest crime rates.[47] As we have seen, according to rational choice theory, street-smart offenders know which areas offer the least threat and plan their crimes accordingly. A number of potential strategies flow from this premise. The following sections discuss each of these crime reduction or control strategies based on the rationality of criminal behavior. ✔ Checkpoints

Situational Crime Prevention

situational crime prevention

A method of crime prevention that seeks to eliminate or reduce particular crimes in narrow settings.

defensible space

The principle that crime can be prevented or displaced by modifying the physical environment to reduce the opportunity individuals have to commit crime.

Rational choice theory suggests that because criminal activity is offense-specific, crime prevention, or at least crime reduction, can be achieved through policies that convince potential criminals to desist from criminal activities, delay their actions, or avoid a particular target. Criminal acts will be avoided if (1) potential targets are carefully guarded, (2) the means to commit crime are controlled, and (3) potential offenders are carefully monitored. Desperate people may contemplate crime, but only the truly irrational will attack a well-defended, inaccessible target and risk strict punishment.

One way of preventing crime, then, is to reduce the opportunities people have to commit particular crimes. This approach is known as **situational crime prevention**. It was first popularized in the United States in the early 1970s by Oscar Newman, who coined the term **defensible space**. The idea is that crime can be prevented or displaced through the use of residential designs that reduce criminal opportunity, such as well-lit housing projects that maximize surveillance.[48]

Crime Prevention Strategies

Situational crime prevention involves developing tactics to reduce or eliminate a specific crime problem (such as shoplifting in an urban mall or street-level drug dealing). According to criminologists Ronald Clarke and Ross Homel, crime prevention tactics used today generally fall into one of four categories:

- Increase the effort needed to commit crime.
- Increase the risks of committing crime.
- Reduce the rewards for committing crime.
- Induce guilt or shame for committing crime.

Find It on INFOTRAC
College Edition

Evidence suggests that the design of a property has a considerable impact on building security. The configuration of doors, hallways, exits, and other parts of a building can lower the incidence of crime rates. To find out more, use "crime prevention" and "architectural designs" as keywords on InfoTrac College Edition.

These basic techniques and some specific methods that can be used to achieve them are summarized in Table 4.2.

Some of the tactics to increase effort include target-hardening techniques such as putting unbreakable glass on storefronts, locking gates, and fencing yards. Even simple prevention measures can work. Removing signs from store windows, installing brighter lights, and instituting a pay-first policy have helped reduce thefts from gas stations and convenience stores.[49]

Technological advances can also make it more difficult for would-be offenders to commit crimes; for example, having an owner's photo on credit cards should reduce the use of stolen cards. New security products such as steering locks on cars have reduced the incidence of theft.[50] Similarly, installing a locking device on cars that prevents drunken drivers from starting the vehicle significantly reduces drunk-driving rates.[51]

Table 4.2 Sixteen Techniques of Situational Prevention

INCREASING PERCEIVED EFFORT	INCREASING PERCEIVED RISKS	REDUCING ANTICIPATED REWARDS	INDUCING GUILT OR SHAME
1. *Target hardening* Slug rejector devices Steering locks Bandit screens	5. *Entry/exit screening* Automatic ticket gates Baggage screening Merchandise tags	9. *Target removal* Removable car radio Women's refuges Phone card	13. *Rule setting* Harassment codes Customs declaration Hotel registrations
2. *Access control* Parking lot barriers Fenced yards Entry phones	6. *Formal surveillance* Burglar alarms Speed cameras Security guards	10. *Identifying property* Property marking Vehicle licensing Cattle branding	14. *Strengthening moral condemnation* "Shoplifting is stealing" Roadside speedometers "Bloody idiots drink and drive"
3. *Deflecting offenders* Bus stop placement Tavern location Street closures	7. *Surveillance by employees* Pay phone location Park attendants Closed-circuit TV systems	11. *Reducing temptation* Gender-neutral phone lists Off-street parking	15. *Controlling disinhibitors* Drinking age laws Ignition interlock Server intervention
4. *Controlling facilitators* Credit card photo Caller ID Gun controls	8. *Natural surveillance* Defensible space Street lighting Cab driver ID	12. *Denying benefits* Ink merchandise tags PIN for car radios Graffiti cleaning	16. *Facilitating compliance* Improved library checkout Public lavatories Trash bins

SOURCE: Ronald Clarke and Ross Homel, "A Revised Classification of Situational Crime Prevention Techniques," in *Crime Prevention at a Crossroads*, ed. Steven Lab (Cincinnati: Anderson, 1997), p. 4.

Find It on INFOTRAC
College Edition

Use "shoplifting" as a keyword to find out how retail establishments are using situational crime prevention techniques to prevent retail theft.

Target reduction strategies are designed to reduce the value of crime to the potential criminal. These include making car radios removable so they can be kept at home at night, marking property so that it is more difficult to sell when stolen, and having gender-neutral phone listings to discourage obscene phone calls. Tracking systems, such as those made by the Lojack Corporation, help police locate and return stolen vehicles.

Inducing guilt or shame might include such techniques as setting strict rules to embarrass offenders. For example, publishing "John lists" in the newspaper punishes those arrested for soliciting prostitutes. Facilitating compliance by providing trash bins might shame chronic litterers into using them. Ronald Clarke found that caller ID in New Jersey resulted in significant reductions in the number of obscene phone calls, presumably because of the shame presented by the threat of exposure.[52]

Displacement, Extinction, Discouragement, and Diffusion

displacement

An effect of crime prevention efforts in which efforts to control crime in one area shift illegal activities to another.

extinction

The phenomenon in which a crime prevention effort has an immediate impact that then dissipates as criminals adjust to new conditions.

Situational crime prevention efforts, however, may produce unforeseen and unwanted consequences. Preventing crime in one location does not address or deter criminal motivation. People who desire the benefits of crime may choose alternative targets, so that crime is not prevented but deflected or displaced.[53] For example, beefed-up police patrols in one area may shift crimes to a more vulnerable neighborhood.[54] Although crime **displacement** certainly does not solve the general problem of crime, it has been shown to reduce the frequency of crime or produce less serious offense patterns.[55]

There is also the problem of **extinction**: Crime reduction programs may produce a short-term positive effect, but benefits dissipate as criminals adjust to new conditions. They learn to dismantle alarms or avoid patrols. They may also try new offenses they had previously avoided. For example, if every residence in a neighborhood has a foolproof burglar alarm system, motivated offenders may turn to armed robbery, a riskier and more violent crime.

diffusion of benefits

An effect that occurs when efforts to prevent one crime unintentionally prevent another, or when crime control efforts in one locale reduce crime in other nontarget areas.

discouragement

An effect that occurs when limiting access to one target reduces other types of crime as well.

Although displacement and extinction may create problems, there may also be advantages.[56] **Diffusion of benefits** occurs (1) when efforts to prevent one crime unintentionally prevent another and/or (2) when crime control efforts in one locale reduce crime in other nontarget areas. What causes diffusion? First, crime prevention efforts may produce a generalized fear of apprehension. For example, video cameras set up in a mall to reduce shoplifting can also reduce property damage because would-be vandals fear they will be caught on camera. Or intensive police patrol efforts targeting neighborhood drug dealers may convince prostitutes that it is too dangerous to ply their trade in that area.[57]

Situational crime prevention efforts may also produce **discouragement**: Limiting access to one target convinces would-be lawbreakers that crime no longer pays in general. For example, evaluations of the Lojack auto protection system, which uses hidden radio transmitters to track stolen cars, have found that the device helps lower car theft rates. Not only does Lojack deter auto thieves, it also seems to disrupt the operation of "chop shops," where stolen vehicles are taken apart for the resale of parts. Stolen car buyers cannot be sure if a stolen vehicle they purchase contains Lojack, which the police can trace to their base of operations.[58] Thus, a device designed to protect cars from theft also has the benefit of disrupting the sale of stolen car parts.

General Deterrence

general deterrence

A crime control policy that depends on the fear of criminal penalties, convincing the potential law violator that the pains associated with crime outweigh its benefits.

According to the rational choice view, motivated people will violate the law if left free and unrestricted. The concept of **general deterrence** is that, conversely, the decision to commit crime can be controlled by the threat of criminal punishment. If people fear being apprehended and punished, they will not risk breaking the law. An inverse relationship should exist between crime rates and the severity, certainty, and speed of legal sanctions. If, for example, the punishment for a crime is increased and the effectiveness and efficiency of the criminal justice system are improved, then the number of people engaging in that crime should decline.

The factors of severity, certainty, and speed of punishment may also be interactive. For example, if a crime—say, robbery—is punished severely, but few robbers are ever caught or punished, the severity of punishment for robbery will probably not deter people from robbing. On the other hand, if the certainty of apprehension and conviction is increased by modern technology, more efficient police work, or some other factor, then even minor punishment might deter the potential robber.

Do these factors actually affect the decision to commit crime and, consequently, general crime rates?

Certainty of Punishment

According to deterrence theory, if the certainty of arrest, conviction, and sanctioning increases, crime rates should decline. Rational offenders will soon realize that the increased likelihood of punishment outweighs any benefit they perceive from committing crimes. According to this view, crime persists because most criminals believe (1) that there is only a small chance they will get arrested for committing a particular crime, (2) that police officers are sometimes reluctant to make arrests even if they are aware of crime, and (3) that even if apprehended there is a good chance of receiving a lenient punishment.[59]

Although this view seems logical enough, the relationship between certainty of punishment and crime rates is far from settled. While a few research efforts do show a direct relationship between crime rates and the certainty of punishment,[60] a great deal of contradictory evidence indicates that the likelihood of being arrested or imprisoned has little effect on crime.[61]

One reason for this ambivalent finding is that the association between certainty of punishment and crime may be time-, crime-, and group-specific. For example, research shows that when the number of arrests increases, the number of index crimes reported to police declines the next day.[62] It is possible that news of increased and aggressive police activity is rapidly diffused through the population and has an immediate impact, but that the effect erodes over time.

Research also finds that the certainty of punishment may be race-specific. African American arrests probability influence only African American offense rates, whereas European American arrests probability affect European American offending patterns. In large cities, the threat of arrest may be communicated within neighborhoods, many of which are racially segregated. This threat affects residents of each racial grouping independently.[63]

Some research efforts have found a crime-specific deterrent effect. For example, using national data sets measuring crime and arrest rates, criminologist Edwin Zedlewski found that an increased probability of arrest may help lower the burglary rate, whereas larceny rates remain unaffected by law enforcement efforts.[64]

Level of Police Activity

If certainty of apprehension and punishment deters criminal behavior, then increasing the number of police officers on the street should cut the crime rate. Moreover, if these police officers are active, aggressive crime fighters, would-be criminals should be convinced that the risk of apprehension outweighs the benefits they can gain from crime. However, the evidence that adding police leads to reduced crime rates is spotty.[65] Numerous studies have failed to show that increasing the number of police officers in a community can, by itself, lower crime rates.[66]

It is possible that while adding police may not work, adding more effective police could reduce crime. Research indicates that if police could make an arrest in at least 30 percent of all reported crimes, the crime rate would decline significantly.[67] But how can that figure be achieved, considering that arrest rates today hover at 20 percent?

To lower crime rates, some police departments have instituted **crackdowns**—sudden changes in police activity designed to increase the communicated threat or actual certainty of punishment. For example, a police task force might target street-level narcotics dealers by using undercover agents and surveillance cameras in known drug-dealing locales. These efforts have not proven to be successful mechanisms for lowering crime rates.[68] An analysis of 18 police crackdowns by Lawrence Sherman found that while they initially deterred crime, crime rates resumed earlier levels once the crackdown ended.[69] Although these results contradict the deterrence concept, research shows that more focused efforts may reduce crime levels. Crime rates are reduced when police officers use aggressive problem-solving and community improvement techniques, such as increasing lighting and cleaning vacant lots, to fight particular crimes in selected places.[70] For example, a recent initiative by the Dallas Police Department to aggressively pursue truancy and curfew enforcement resulted in lower rates of gang violence.[71]

crackdown

The concentration of police resources on a particular problem area to eradicate or displace criminal activity.

Severity of Punishment

The introduction or threat of severe punishment should also bring the crime rate down. Although some studies have found that increasing sanction levels can control common criminal behaviors, there is little consensus that strict punishments alone can reduce criminal activities.[72] Because the likelihood of getting caught for some crimes is relatively low, the impact of deterrent measures is negligible over the long term.[73] For example, laws that provide expanded or mandatory sentences for felonies committed with guns have received mixed re-

This historical woodcut depicts the execution of King Charles I of England in 1649. Severe punishments have traditionally been used to deter criminal offenses. The execution of as great a personage as England's king must certainly have had a dramatic impact on the common person. Would severe and public punishment have a similar effect in contemporary society?

The Granger Collection, New York, NY

views. While some experts believe that these laws can lower crime rates, others question their deterrent effect. In sum, there is little empirical evidence that they have worked as planned.[74]

Capital Punishment

It stands to reason that if severity of punishment can deter crime, then fear of the death penalty, the ultimate legal deterrent, should significantly reduce murder rates. Because no one denies its emotional impact, failure of the death penalty to deter violent crime jeopardizes the validity of the entire deterrence concept.

Various studies have tested the assumption that capital punishment deters violent crime. The research can be divided into three types: immediate impact studies, comparative research, and time-series analysis.

Immediate Impact If capital punishment is a deterrent, the reasoning goes, then its impact should be greatest after a well-publicized execution. Robert Dann began testing this assumption in 1935, when he chose five highly publicized executions of convicted murderers in different years and determined the number of homicides in the 60 days before and after each execution.[75] Each 120-day period had approximately the same number of homicides, as well as the same number of days on which homicides occurred. Dann's study revealed that an average of 4.4 more homicides occurred during the 60 days following an execution than during those preceding it, suggesting that the overall impact of executions might actually be to increase the incidence of homicide.

The fact that executions may actually increase the likelihood of murders' being committed is a consequence referred to as the **brutalization effect**. The basis of this theory is that potential criminals may begin to model their behavior after state authorities: If the government can kill its enemies, so can they.[76] The brutalization effect means that after an execution murders may increase, causing even more deaths of innocent victims.[77]

brutalization effect

The belief that capital punishment creates an atmosphere of brutality that enhances rather than deters the level of violence in society.

Although many criminologists question the utility of capital punishment, claiming that it causes more harm than it prevents, others believe that in the short run, executing criminals can bring the murder rate down.[78] Steven Stack's analysis of 16 well-publicized executions concluded that they may have saved 480 lives by immediately deterring potential murderers.[79] In sum, a number of criminologists find that executions actually increase murder rates, whereas others argue that their immediate impact is to lower murder rates.

Comparative Research Another type of research compares the murder rates in jurisdictions that have abolished the death penalty with the rates in those that employ the death penalty.[80] Two pioneering studies, one by Thorsten Sellin (1959) and the other by Walter Reckless (1969), showed little difference in the murder rates of adjacent states, regardless of their use of the death penalty; capital punishment did not appear to influence the reported rate of homicide.[81] More recent research gives little reason to believe that executions deter homicide.[82] Studies have compared murder rates in jurisdictions having a death penalty statute with those that don't, and have also taken into account the number of people actually executed. These comparisons indicate that the death penalty—whether on the books or actually used—does not deter violent crime.[83]

The failure to show a deterrent effect of the death penalty is not limited to comparisons among U.S. states. Research conducted in 14 nations around the world found little evidence that countries with a death penalty have lower violence rates than those without. In fact, homicide rates decline after capital punishment is abolished, a direct contradiction to its supposed deterrent effect.[84]

Time-Series Analysis Statistical analysis has allowed researchers to gauge whether the murder rate changes when death penalty statutes are created or eliminated. The most widely cited study is Isaac Ehrlich's 1975 work, in which he used national crime and execution data to reach the conclusion that each execution in the United States would save seven or eight people from being murdered.[85] Ehrlich's research has been widely cited by advocates of the death penalty as empirical proof of the deterrent effect of capital punishment. However, subsequent research that attempted to replicate Ehrlich's analysis showed that his approach was flawed and that capital punishment is no more effective as a deterrent than life imprisonment.[86] For example, a recent test of the deterrent effect of the death penalty during the years 1984–1997 in Texas found no association between the frequency of execution and murder rates.[87]

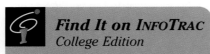

Find It on INFOTRAC
College Edition

Some advocates of the death penalty believe that the punishment's deterrent effect would increase if people actually watched executions on televsion. Could such a strategy actually work, or would it have unforeseen consequences? Read

Don Corrigan, "Viewing Executions: Does the Public Have a Right to See?" *St. Louis Journalism Review*, March 1999 v29 i14 p1(2)

Why Capital Punishment Fails In sum, studies that have attempted to show the deterrent effect of capital punishment on the murder rate indicate that executing convicted criminals has relatively little influence on behavior.[88] Although it is still uncertain why the threat of capital punishment has failed as a deterrent, the cause may lie in the nature of homicide itself. Murder is often an expressive "crime of passion" involving people who know each other and who may be under the influence of drugs or alcohol. Murder is also a by-product of the criminal activity of people who suffer from the burdens of poverty and income inequality.[89] These factors may either prevent or inhibit rational evaluation of the long-term consequences of an immediate violent act.

The failure of the "ultimate deterrent" to deter the "ultimate crime" has been used by critics to question the validity of the general deterrence hypothesis that severe punishment will lower crime rates. In general, there is little direct evidence that severity of punishment alone can reduce or eliminate crime.

Swiftness of Punishment

A core element of general deterrence theory is that people who believe that they will be swiftly punished if they break the law will abstain from crime.[90] Again, the evidence on the association between perceived punishment risk and crime has been mixed. Some research efforts have found a relationship,[91] while others have not.[92]

The threat of swift retaliation seems to work best when would-be criminals believe they will be subjected to very harsh punishments.[93] However, even this fear may be negated or overcome by the belief that a crime gives them a significant chance for large profit. When interviewed by criminologists Alex Piquero and George Rengert, active burglars reported that fear of a quick capture was in fact a deterrent, but one that could be overcome by the promise of a "big score." In short, greed overcomes fear![94]

Informal Sanctions

informal sanctions

Disapproval, stigma, or anger directed toward an offender by significant others (parents, peers, neighbors, teachers), resulting in shame, embarrassment, and loss of respect.

Although the threat of even the most severe punishment may not have a deterrent effect, evidence is accumulating that the fear of informal sanctions may in fact reduce crime.[95] **Informal sanctions** occur when significant others—such as parents, peers, neighbors, and teachers—direct their disapproval, stigma, anger, and indignation toward an offender. If this happens, law violators run the risk of feeling shame, being embarrassed, and suffering a loss of respect.[96] Can the fear of public humiliation deter crime?

Research efforts have in fact established that the threat of informal sanctions can be a more effective deterrent than the threat of formal sanctions.[97] Fear of shame and embarrassment can be a powerful deterrent to crime. Those who fear being rejected by family and peers are reluctant to engage in deviant behavior.[98] These factors manifest themselves in two ways: (1) personal shame over violating the law and (2) the fear of public humiliation if the deviant behavior becomes public knowledge. People who say that their involvement in crime would cause them to feel ashamed are less likely to commit theft, fraud, motor vehicular, and other offenses than people who report they would not feel ashamed.[99]

Anticrime campaigns have been designed to play on this fear of shame. They are most effective when they convince the general public that being accused of crime will make them feel ashamed or embarrassed.[100] For example, spouse abusers report they are more afraid of the social costs of crime (loss of friends and family disapproval) than they are of legal punishment (going to jail). Women are more likely to fear shame and embarrassment than men, a finding that may help explain gender differences in the crime rate.[101]

The effect of informal sanctions may vary according to the cohesiveness of community structure and the type of crime. Not surprisingly, informal sanctions may be most effective in highly unified areas where everyone knows one another and the crime cannot be hidden from public view.[102]

Critique of General Deterrence

Some experts believe that the purpose of the law and justice system is to create a "threat system."[103] The threat of legal punishment should, on the face of it, deter lawbreakers through fear. Nonetheless, the relationship between crime rates and deterrent measures is far less than choice theorists might expect. Despite efforts to punish criminals and make them fear crime, there is little evidence that the fear of apprehension and punishment alone can reduce crime rates. How can this discrepancy be explained?

Rationality Deterrence theory assumes a rational offender who weighs the costs and benefits of a criminal act before deciding on a course of action. Criminals may be desperate people who choose crime because they believe there is no reasonable alternative. Some may suffer from personality disorders that impair their judgment and render them incapable of making truly rational decisions. Psychologists believe that chronic offenders suffer from an emotional state that renders them both incapable of fearing punishment and less likely to appreciate the consequences of crime.[104] For example, research on repeat sex offenders finds that they suffer from an elevated emotional state that negates the deterrent effect of the law.[105]

Certainty, Severity, and Speed As Beccaria's famous equation tells us, the threat of punishment involves not only its severity, but its certainty and speed. The American legal system is not very effective. Only 10 percent of all serious offenses result in apprehension. Half of these crimes go unreported, and police make arrests in only about 20 percent of reported crimes. Even when offenders are detected, police officers may choose to warn rather than arrest.[106] The odds of receiving a prison term are less than 20 per 1000 crimes committed. As a result, some offenders believe that they will not be severely punished for their acts and consequently have little regard for the law's deterrent power. Even those accused of murder are often convicted of lesser offenses and spend relatively short amounts of time behind bars.[107] In making their "rational choice," offenders may be aware that the deterrent effect of the law is minimal.

Choice Among some groups of high-risk offenders, such as teens living in economically depressed neighborhoods, the threat of formal sanctions is irrelevant. Young people in these areas have little to lose if arrested, because their opportunities are few and they have little attachment to social institutions such as school or family. Even if they truly fear the consequences of the law, they must commit crime to survive in a hostile environment.

Summary Studies measuring the perception of punishment agree with studies using aggregate criminal justice data that the certainty of punishment has a greater deterrent effect than its severity. Nonetheless, neither the perception nor the reality of punishment can deter most crimes.

Specific Deterrence

specific deterrence

The view that criminal sanctions should be so powerful that offenders will never repeat their criminal acts.

The theory of **specific deterrence** (also called special or particular deterrence) holds that criminal sanctions should be so powerful that known criminals will never repeat their criminal acts. According to this view, the drunk driver whose sentence is a substantial fine and a week in the county jail should be convinced that the price to be paid for drinking and driving is too great to consider future violations. Similarly, burglars who spend five years in a tough, maximum-security prison should find their enthusiasm for theft dampened.[108] In principle, punishment works if a connection can be established between the planned action and memories of its consequence; if these recollections are adequately intense, the action will be unlikely to occur again.[109]

Does Specific Deterrence Deter Crime?

incarceration

Confinement in jail or prison.

recidivism

Repetition of criminal behavior.

At first glance, specific deterrence does not seem to work, because a majority of known criminals are not deterred by their punishment. Research on chronic offenders indicates that arrest and punishment seem to have little effect on experienced criminals and may even increase the likelihood that first-time offenders will commit new crimes.[110] About two-thirds of all convicted felons are rearrested within three years of their release from prison, and those who have been punished in the past are the most likely to commit a new offense.[111] **Incarceration** may sometimes slow down or delay **recidivism** in the short term, but the overall probability of rearrest does not change following incarceration.[112] Nor does leniency seem to help. Offenders receiving community sentences, such as

probation

The conditional release of a convicted offender into the community under the supervision of a probation officer and subject to certain conditions.

probation, have rates of recidivism similar to those who are sentenced to prison.[113]

Some research efforts have shown that, rather than reducing the frequency of crime, severe punishment actually increases reoffending rates.[114] Punishment may bring defiance rather than deterrence, while the stigma of apprehension may help lock offenders into a criminal career. The effects of specific deterrence in preventing domestic violence are discussed in the accompanying Race, Culture, Gender, and Criminology feature.

Stigmatization versus Reintegrative Shaming

In his book *Crime, Shame, and Reintegration*, John Braithwaite helps explain why specific deterrence measures may be doomed to failure.[115] In the United States, punishment stigmatizes offenders and sets them, resentful, outside the mainstream. Law violators view themselves as victims of the justice system, punished by strangers, such as police and judges, who are being paid to act. In contrast, Braithwaite notes that countries such as Japan, in which conviction for crimes brings an inordinate amount of personal shame, have extremely low crime rates.

stigmatization

Ongoing degradation or humiliation, in which the offender is branded as an evil person and cast out of society.

Braithwaite divides the concept of shame into two distinct types. In American society, shaming typically involves **stigmatization**—an ongoing process of degradation in which the offender is branded as an evil person and cast out of society. Shaming can occur at a school disciplinary hearing or a criminal court trial. As a specific deterrent, stigma is doomed to failure. People who suffer humiliation at the hands of the justice system "reject their rejectors" by joining a deviant subculture of like-minded people who collectively resist social control. Despite these dangers, there has been an ongoing effort to brand offenders and make their "shame" both public and permanent. For example, most states have passed sex offender registry and notification laws that make public the names of those convicted of sex offenses and warn neighbors of their presence in the community.[116]

reintegrative shaming

Brief and controlled shaming that is followed by forgiveness, apology, repentance, and reconnection with the community.

Braithwaite argues that crime control can be better achieved through a policy of **reintegrative shaming**. In this approach, the offenders' evil deeds are condemned while, at the same time, efforts are made to reconnect them to their neighbors, friends, and family. A critical element of reintegrative shaming is an effort to help offenders understand and recognize their wrongdoing and feel ashamed of their actions. To be reintegrative, shaming must be brief and controlled and then followed by ceremonies of forgiveness, apology, and repentance.

An important part of reintegrative shaming are efforts to bring offenders together with victims so that the offenders can learn to understand the impact of their actions. Close family members and peers are also present to help the offender reintegrate back into society. Efforts like these can humanize a system of justice that today relies on repression, rather than forgiveness, as the basis of specific deterrence.

CONNECTIONS

The concept of reintegrative shaming is a key component of the restorative justice movement, which seeks to eliminate coercive punishment in the justice system. This humanistic perspective is discussed further in Chapter 14.

Incapacitation

It stands to reason that if more criminals are sent to prison, the crime rate should go down. Because most people age out of crime, the duration of a criminal career is limited. Placing offenders behind bars during their prime crime years should lessen their lifetime opportunity to commit crime. The shorter the span of opportunity, the fewer offenses they can commit during their lives; hence crime is reduced. This theory, known as the **incapacitation effect**, seems logical, but does it work?

incapacitation effect

The idea that keeping offenders in confinement will eliminate the risk of their committing further offenses.

The past 20 years have witnessed significant growth in the number and percentage of the population held in prisons and jails. Today more than 2 million Americans are incarcerated. Advocates of incapacitation suggest that this effort

Race, Culture, Gender, and Criminology

Deterring Domestic Violence

Is it possible to use a specific deterrence strategy to control domestic violence? Would the memory of a formal police arrest reduce the incidence of spousal abuse? Despite the fact that domestic violence is a prevalent, serious crime, police departments have been accused of rarely arresting suspected perpetrators. Lack of forceful action may contribute to chronic episodes of violence, which obviously is of great concern to women's advocacy groups. Is it possible that prompt, formal action by police agencies might prevent the reoccurrence of this serious crime that threatens and even kills so many women?

In their famous Minneapolis domestic violence study, Lawrence Sherman and Richard Berk had police officers randomly assign one of three treatments to the domestic assault cases they encountered on their beats. One approach was to give some sort of advice and mediation; another was to send the assailant out of the home for a period of eight hours; and the third was to arrest the assailant. They found that when police took formal action (arrest), the chance of recidivism was

substantially less than with less punitive measures, such as warning offenders or ordering offenders out of the house for a cooling-off period. A six-month follow-up found that only 10 percent of those who had been arrested repeated their violent behavior, while 19 percent of those advised and 24 percent of those sent away repeated their offenses. Sherman and Berk demonstrated that arrests were somewhat effective in controlling domestic assaults: 19 percent of the women whose attackers had been arrested reported that their mates had assaulted them again; in contrast, 37 percent of those whose mates were advised and 33 percent of those whose mates were sent away reported further assaults. Sherman and Berk concluded that a formal arrest was the most effective means of controlling domestic violence, regardless of what happened to the offender in court.

The Minneapolis experiment deeply affected police operations around the nation. Atlanta, Chicago, Dallas, Denver, Detroit, New York, Miami, San Francisco, and Seattle, among other large cities, adopted policies encouraging arrests

in domestic violence cases. A number of states adopted legislation mandating that police either take formal action in domestic abuse cases or explain in writing their failure to act.

Although the findings of the Minneapolis experiment received quick acceptance, government-funded research replicating the experimental design in other locales, including Omaha, Nebraska, and Charlotte, North Carolina, failed to duplicate the original results. In these locales, formal arrest was not a greater deterrent to domestic abuse than warning or advising the assailant. There are also indications that police officers in Minneapolis failed to assign cases randomly, which altered the experimental findings.

In another study, Sherman and his associates found that the duration of custody influenced recidivism. A short-term arrest (custody lasting about three hours) was found to have a different impact, and may actually have been more effective, than an arrest followed by a longer period of detention. However, while a short-term arrest served initially as a deterrent, this effect quickly decayed; the long-run ef-

---

has been responsible for the decade-long decline in crime rates. However, critics counter that what appears to be an incapacitation effect may actually reflect the effect of some other legal or social phenomenon. The economy has improved, police may be more effective, and the crack cocaine epidemic has waned. Crime rates may be dropping simply because potential criminals now recognize and fear the tough new sentencing laws that provide long mandatory prison sentences for drug and violent crimes. What appears to be an incapacitation effect may actually be an effect of general deterrence.[117]

Can Incapacitation Reduce Crime?

Research on the direct benefits of incapacitation has been inconclusive. A number of studies have set out to measure the precise effect of incarceration rates on crime rates, and the results have not supported a strict incarceration policy.[118] It has been estimated that if the prison population were cut in half, the crime rate would most likely go up only 4 percent; if prisons were entirely eliminated, crime might increase 8 percent.[119] Looking at this relationship from another perspective, if the average prison sentence were increased 50 percent, the crime rate might be reduced only 4 percent.[120]

While these findings are problematic, a few studies have found an inverse relationship between incarceration rates and crime rates. In a frequently cited fect may be an escalation in the frequency of repeat domestic violence.

Explaining why the initial deterrent effect of arrest decays over time is difficult. It is possible that offenders who are arrested initially fear punishment, but eventually, when their cases do not result in severe punishment, fear is replaced with anger and violent intent toward their mates. Many repeat abusers do not fear arrest, believing that formal police action will not cause them harm. They may be aware that police are reluctant to make arrests in domestic violence cases unless there is a significant chance of injury to the victim, such as when a weapon is used.

A stronger response, perhaps including mandatory jail time, might be necessary before the threat of arrest can deter domestic violence. However, the association between severity of postconviction punishment and repeat domestic violence is equally ambivalent. Men are just as likely to recidivate if their case is dismissed, if they are given probation, or even if they are sent to jail. In sum, domestic violence research indicates that the association between specific deterrence measures and criminality is tenuous at best.

Critical Thinking

1. Why do arrests seem to have little effect on future domestic violence? Could it be that getting arrested increases feelings of strain and hostility and does little to reduce the problems that led to domestic conflict in the first place? Explain how you think this works.

2. What policies would you suggest to reduce the reoccurrence of domestic violence?

 InfoTrac College Edition Research

Would police be more efficient in combating domestic violence if they feared lawsuits from victims? To find out, read

Lisa Gelhaus, "Civil Suits Against Police Change Domestic Violence Response," *Trial,* September 1999 v35 p103

SOURCES: Robert Kane, "Patterns of Arrest in Domestic Violence Encounters: Identifying a Police Decision-Making Model," *Journal of Criminal Justice* 27 (1999): 65–79; Dana Jones and Joanne Belknap, "Police Responses to Battering in a Progressive Pro-Arrest Jurisdiction," *Justice Quarterly* 16 (1999): 249–273; Robert Davis, Barbara Smith, and Laura Nickles, "The Deterrent Ef-

fect of Prosecuting Domestic Violence Misdemeanors," *Crime and Delinquency* 44 (1998): 434–442; Amy Thistlethwaite, John Wooldredge, and David Gibbs, "Severity of Dispositions and Domestic Violence Recidivism," *Crime and Delinquency* 44 (1998): 388–398; J. David Hirschel, Ira Hutchison, and Charles Dean, "The Failure of Arrest to Deter Spouse Abuse," *Journal of Research in Crime and Delinquency* 29 (1992): 7–33; Franklyn Dunford, David Huizinga, and Delbert Elliott, "The Role of Arrest in Domestic Assault: The Omaha Experiment," *Criminology* 28 (1990): 183–206; Lawrence Sherman, Janell Schmidt, Dennis Rogan, Patrick Gartin, Ellen Cohn, Dean Collins, and Anthony Bacich, "From Initial Deterrence to Long-Term Escalation: Short-Custody Arrest for Domestic Violence," *Criminology* 29 (1991): 821–850; Lawrence Sherman and Richard Berk, "The Specific Deterrent Effects of Arrest for Domestic Assault," *American Sociological Review* 49 (1984): 261–272; Michael Steinman, "Lowering Recidivism Among Men Who Batter Women," *Journal of Police Science and Administration* 17 (1990): 124–131; Susan Miller and Leeann Iovanni, "Determinants of Perceived Risk of Formal Sanction for Courtship Violence," *Justice Quarterly* 11 (1994): 282–312.

study, Reuel Shinnar and Shlomo Shinnar's research on incapacitation in New York led them to conclude that mandatory prison sentences of five years for violent crime and three for property offenses could reduce the reported crime rate by a factor of four or five.[121] Other research studies also claim that a strict incarceration policy can reduce the level of violent crime.[122]

The Logic Behind Incarceration

Considering that the criminals are unable to continue their illegal activities while housed in a prison or jail, incapacitation should in fact be an excellent crime control strategy. For example, a recent study of 201 heroin abusers in New York City found that, if given a one-year jail sentence, they would not have been able to commit their yearly haul of crimes: 1,000 robberies, 4,000 burglaries, 10,000 shopliftings, and more than 3,000 other property crimes.[123]

Nonetheless, evaluations of incarceration strategies reveal that their impact is less than expected. For one thing, there is little evidence that incapacitating criminals will deter them from future criminality and even more reason to believe that they may be more inclined to commit crimes upon release. Prison has few specific deterrent effects: The more prior incarceration experiences inmates have, the more likely they are to recidivate (and return to prison) within 12 months of their release.[124] The short-term crime reduction effect of

AP/Wide World Photos

Simply put, if dangerous criminals were incapacitated, they would never have the opportunity to prey upon others. One of the most dramatic examples of the utility of incapacitation is the case of Lawrence Singleton, who in 1978 raped a young California girl, Mary Vincent, and then chopped off her arms with an axe. He served eight years in prison for this vile crime. Upon his release, he moved to Florida, where in 1997 he killed a woman, Roxanne Hayes. Vincent is shown here as she testified at the penalty phase of Singleton's trial; he was sentenced to death. Should a dangerous predator such as Singleton ever be released from incapacitation? Is rehabilitation even a remote possibility?

incapacitating criminals is negated if the prison experience has the long-term effect of escalating the frequency of criminal behavior upon release. By its nature, the prison experience exposes young, first-time offenders to higher-risk, more experienced inmates who can influence their lifestyle and help shape their attitudes. Novice inmates also run an increased risk of becoming infected with AIDS and other health hazards, and that exposure reduces their life chances after release.[125]

Furthermore, the economics of crime suggest that if money can be made from criminal activity, there will always be someone to take the place of the incarcerated offender. New criminals will be recruited and trained, offsetting any benefit accrued by incarceration. Imprisoning established offenders may likewise open new opportunities for competitors who were suppressed by the more experienced criminals. For example, incarcerating organized crime members may open drug markets to new gangs. The flow of narcotics into the country may actually increase after the more experienced organized crime leaders are imprisoned, because newcomers are willing to take greater risks.

Another reason that incarceration may not work is that most criminal offenses are committed by teens and very young adult offenders, who are unlikely to be sent to prison for a single felony conviction. At the same time, many incarcerated criminals, aging behind bars, are already past the age when they are likely to commit crime. As a result, a strict incarceration policy may keep people in prison beyond the time they are a threat to society while a new cohort of high-risk adolescents is on the street. It is possible that the most serious criminals are already behind bars and that adding less dangerous offenders to the population will have little appreciable effect while adding tremendous costs to the correctional system.[126]

An incapacitation strategy is terribly expensive. The prison system costs billions of dollars each year. Even if incarceration could reduce the crime rate, the costs would be enormous. Are U.S. taxpayers willing to spend billions more on new prison construction and annual maintenance fees? A strict incarceration policy would result in a growing number of elderly inmates whose maintenance costs, estimated at $69,000 per year, are three times higher than those of younger inmates. In 2001 there will be more than 125,000 of these elderly inmates, and by 2005 about 16 percent of the prison population will be over 50.[127]

Three Strikes and You're Out

Some experts maintain that incapacitation can work if it is focused on the most serious chronic offenders. For example, the **three strikes and you're out** policy, giving people convicted of three felony offenses a mandatory life sentence, has received widespread publicity. Many states already employ habitual offender laws that provide long (or life) sentences for repeat offenders. Criminologists retort that although such strategies are politically compelling, they will not work, for several reasons:

three strikes and you're out

Policy whereby people convicted of three felony offenses receive a mandatory life sentence.

just desert

The principle that those who violate the rights of others deserve punishment commensurate with the seriousness of the crime, without regard to their personal characteristics or circumstances.

- Most three-time losers are at the verge of aging out of crime anyway.
- Current sentences for violent crimes are already quite severe.
- An expanding prison population will drive up already high prison costs.
- There would be racial disparity in sentencing.
- The police would be in danger because two-time offenders would violently resist a third arrest, knowing they face a life sentence.[128]
- The prison population probably already contains the highest-frequency criminals.

Those who support a selective incapacitation strategy argue that criminals who are already in prison (high-rate offenders) commit significantly more crimes each year than the average criminal who is on the outside (low-rate offenders). If a broad policy of incarceration were employed, requiring mandatory prison sentences for all those convicted of crimes, more low-rate criminals would be placed behind bars.[129] It would be both costly and nonproductive to incarcerate large groups of people who commit relatively few crimes. It makes more economic sense to focus incarceration efforts on known high-rate offenders by lengthening their sentences. **✔ Checkpoints**

Policy Implications of Choice Theory

From the origins of classical theory to the development of modern rational choice views, the belief that criminals choose to commit crime has influenced the relationship among law, punishment, and crime. Although research on the core principles of choice theory and deterrence theories has produced mixed results, these models have had an important impact on crime prevention strategies.

When police patrol in well-marked cars, it is assumed that their presence will deter would-be criminals. When the harsh realities of prison life are portrayed in movies and TV shows, the lesson is not lost on potential criminals. Nowhere is the idea that the threat of punishment can control crime more evident than in the implementation of tough mandatory criminal sentences to control violent crime and drug trafficking.

Despite its questionable deterrent effect, some advocates argue that the death penalty can effectively restrict criminality; at least it ensures that convicted criminals never again get the opportunity to kill. Many observers are dismayed because people who are convicted of murder sometimes kill again when released on parole. One study of 52,000 incarcerated murderers found that 810 had been previously convicted of murder and had killed 821 people following their previous release from prison.[130] About 9 percent of all inmates on death row have had prior convictions for homicide. Death penalty advocates argue that if these criminals had been executed for their first offenses, hundreds of people would be alive today.[131]

The concept of criminal choice has also prompted the development of justice policies that treat all offenders equally, without regard for their background or personal characteristics. This is referred to as the concept of **just desert**. The just desert position has been most clearly spelled out by criminologist Andrew Von Hirsch in his book *Doing Justice*.[132] Von Hirsch argues that while punishment is needed to preserve the social equity disturbed by crime, it should be commensurate with the seriousness of the crime.[133] Von Hirsch's views can be summarized as follows:

1. Those who violate others' rights deserve to be punished.
2. We should not deliberately add to human suffering; punishment makes those punished suffer.

✔ Checkpoints

✔ Situational crime prevention efforts are designed to reduce or redirect crime by making it more difficult to profit from illegal acts.

✔ General deterrence models are based on the fear of punishment that is severe, swift, and certain.

✔ Specific deterrence aims at reducing crime through the application of severe punishments. Once offenders experience these punishments, they will be unwilling to repeat their criminal activities.

✔ Incapacitation strategies are designed to reduce crime by taking known criminals out of circulation, preventing them from having the opportunity to commit further offenses.

3. Punishment may prevent more misery than it inflicts, which justifies the need for desert-based punishment.[134]

Desert theory is also concerned with the rights of the accused. It alleges that the rights of the person being punished should not be unduly sacrificed for the good of others (as with deterrence). The offender should not be treated as more (or less) blameworthy than is warranted by the character of his or her offense. For example, Von Hirsch asks the following question: If two crimes, A and B, are equally serious, but if severe penalties are shown to have a deterrent effect only with respect to A, would it be fair to punish the person who has committed crime A more harshly simply to deter others from committing the crime? Conversely, it is unfair for a merciful judge to impose a light sentence on a teenage criminal, because in so doing he arbitrarily makes the younger offender less blameworthy than an older criminal who commits the same act. All offenders must be treated the same on the basis of what they did, not who they are.

In sum, the just desert model suggests that retribution justifies punishment because people deserve what they get for past deeds. Punishment based on deterrence or incapacitation is wrong because it involves an offender's future actions, which cannot be accurately predicted. Punishment should be the same for all people who commit the same crime. Criminal sentences based on individual needs or characteristics are inherently unfair because all people are equally blameworthy for their misdeeds. The influence of Von Hirsch's views can be seen in mandatory sentencing models that give the same punishment to all people who commit the same type of crime.

Summary

Choice theories assume that criminals carefully choose whether to commit criminal acts. These theories are summarized in Table 4.3. People are influenced by their fear of the criminal penalties associated with being caught and convicted for law violations. The more severe, certain, and swift the punishment, the more likely it is to control crime. The choice approach is rooted in the classical criminology of Cesare Beccaria, who argued that punishment should be certain, swift, and severe enough to deter crime.

Today, choice theorists view crime as offense- and offender-specific. Research shows that offenders consider their targets carefully before deciding on a course of action. By implication, crime can be prevented or displaced by convincing potential criminals that the risks of violating the law exceed the benefits.

Deterrence theory holds that if criminals are indeed rational, an inverse relationship should exist between punishment and crime. However, a number of factors confound the relationship. For example, if people do not believe they will be caught, even harsh punishment may not deter crime. Deterrence theory has been criticized on the grounds that it wrongfully assumes that criminals make a rational choice before committing crimes, it ignores the intricacies of the criminal justice system, and it does not take into account the social and psychological factors that may influence criminality. Research designed to test the validity of the deterrence concept has not indicated that deterrent measures actually reduce the crime rate.

Specific deterrence theory holds that the crime rate can be reduced if known offenders are punished so severely that they never commit crimes again. However, there is little evidence that harsh punishment actually reduces the crime rate. Incapacitation theory maintains that if deterrence does not work, the best course of action is to incarcerate known offenders for long periods so that they lack criminal opportunity. Research efforts, however, have not proved that

Table 4.3 Choice Theories

THEORY	MAJOR PREMISE	STRENGTHS
Rational choice	Law-violating behavior occurs after offenders weigh information on their personal needs and the situational factors involved in the difficulty and risk of committing a crime.	Explains why high-risk youths do not constantly engage in delinquency. Relates theory to delinquency control policy. It is not limited by class or other social variables.
Routine activities	Crime and delinquency are functions of the presence of motivated offenders, the availability of suitable targets, and the absence of capable guardians.	Can explain fluctuations in crime and delinquency rates. Shows how victim behavior influences criminal choice.
General deterrence	People will commit crime and delinquency if they perceive that the benefits outweigh the risks. Crime is a function of the severity, certainty, and speed of punishment.	Shows the relationship between crime and punishment. Suggests a real solution to crime.
Specific deterrence	If punishment is severe enough, criminals will not repeat their illegal acts.	Provides a strategy to reduce crime.
Incapacitation	Keeping known criminals out of circulation will reduce crime rates.	Recognizes the role that opportunity plays in criminal behavior. Provides a solution to chronic offending.

increasing the number of people in prison—and increasing prison sentences—will reduce crime rates.

Choice theory has been influential in shaping public policy. Criminal law is designed to deter potential criminals and fairly punish those who have been caught in illegal acts. Some courts have changed sentencing policies to adapt to classical principles, and the U.S. correctional system seems geared toward incapacitation and specific deterrence. The just desert view is that criminal sanctions should be geared precisely to the seriousness of the crime. People should be punished on the basis of whether they deserve to be punished for what they did, and not because punishment may affect or deter their future behavior.

For additional chapter links, discussions, and quizzes, see the book-specific Web site at http://www.wadsworth.com/product/0534519423s.

Thinking Like a Criminologist

The attorney general has recently funded a national survey of state sentencing practices. The table below provides the most important findings from the survey.

TYPE OF OFFENSE	AVERAGE SENTENCE	AVERAGE SENTENCE SERVED BEFORE RELEASE	AVERAGE PERCENTAGE OF SENTENCE SERVED
All violent	89 months	43 months	48%
Homicide	149 months	71 months	48%
Rape	117 months	65 months	56%
Kidnapping	104 months	52 months	50%
Robbery	95 months	44 months	46%
Sexual assault	72 months	35 months	49%
Assault	61 months	29 months	48%
Other	60 months	28 months	47%

The attorney general wants you to make some recommendations about criminal punishment. Is it possible, she asks, that both the length of criminal sentences and the way they are served can impact crime rates? What could be gained by either increasing punishment or requiring inmates to spend more time behind bars before their release? Are we being too lenient or too punitive? As someone who has studied choice theory, how would you interpret these data, and what do they tell you about sentencing patterns? How might crime rates be affected if the way we punished offenders were radically changed?

Key Terms

rational choice	displacement	incarceration
choice theory	extinction	recidivism
classical criminology	diffusion of benefits	probation
offense-specific	discouragement	stigmatization
offender-specific	general deterrence	reintegrative shaming
edgework	crackdown	incapacitation effect
seductions of crime	brutalization effect	three strikes and you're out
situational crime prevention	informal sanctions	just desert
defensible space	specific deterrence	

Discussion Questions

1. Are criminals rational decision makers, or are they motivated by noncontrollable psychological and emotional drives?

2. Would you want to live in a society where crime rates are quite low because they are controlled by extremely harsh punishments, such as flogging for vandalism?

3. Which would you be more afraid of if you were caught by the police while shoplifting: receiving criminal punishment or having to face your friends or relatives?

4. Is it possible to create a method of capital punishment that would actually deter murder—for example, by televising executions? What might be some of the negative consequences of such a policy?

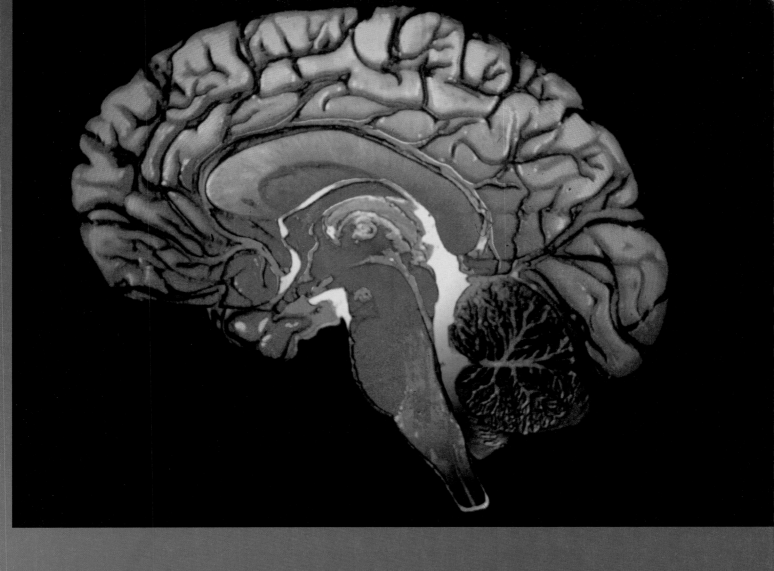

5 Trait Theory: It's in Their Blood

INTRODUCTION

Russell Eugene Weston's violent shooting spree in the U.S. Capitol seemed to be the product of a deranged mind. Can people such as Weston who go on murderous rampages ever be considered "normal" or "sane"?

trait theory

The view that criminality is a product of abnormal biological and/or psychological traits.

Russell Eugene Weston, Jr., 41, was a quiet loner who drifted back and forth between a cabin in the Montana mountains and a modest house in rural Illinois.[1] He became an increasingly troubled figure and was hospitalized in 1996 after he wrote threatening letters to government officials. On July 25, 1998, Weston entered the U.S. Capitol building and went on a shooting rampage. Two capitol police officers were slain, and a female tourist was wounded. After his arrest, his parents told officials that their son had been diagnosed by a medical professional as a paranoid schizophrenic. His neighbors portrayed Weston as a withdrawn, introverted loner who had grown increasingly angry and alienated over the years. When invitations to a 20-year reunion went out to the 63 members of his 1974 graduating class at Valmeyer High School, his came back scrawled with obscenities and a warning never to contact him again. "When he was on his medication, he was fine, he would wave and talk," said a neighbor who knew Weston during his youth. "When he was off the medication, he was paranoid; you just didn't know."

Weston's case provides the public with an image of the criminal offender as a deeply disturbed individual who suffers from a variety of mental and physical abnormalities (Weston was found to be mentally ill and incompetent to stand trial). The image of a disturbed, mentally ill offender seems plausible because a generation of Americans has grown up on films and TV shows that portray violent criminals as mentally deranged and physically abnormal. Beginning with Alfred Hitchcock's film *Psycho,* producers have made millions depicting the ghoulish acts of people who at first seem normal and even friendly but turn out to be demented and dangerous. Lurking out there are deranged roommates (*Single White Female*); abnormal girlfriends (*Fatal Attraction*) and boyfriends (*Fear*); lunatic high school friends (*Scream*) who evolve into even crazier college classmates (*Scream II*) and then grow up to become nutsy young adults (*Scream III*). No one is safe when the psychologists and psychiatrists who are hired to treat these disturbed people turn out to be demonic murderers themselves (*Silence of the Lambs; Hannibal*). Is it any wonder that we respond to a particularly horrible crime by saying of the perpetrator, "That guy must be crazy" or "She is a monster"?

This chapter reviews those criminological theories that suggest that criminality is a matter of abnormal human traits. These **trait theories** can be subdivided into two major categories: one stressing biological makeup and the other stressing psychological functioning. Although these views often overlap (for example, brain function may have a biological basis), each branch has its unique characteristics and will be discussed separately.

The Development of Trait Theory

The view that criminals have physical or mental traits that make them different and abnormal is not restricted to movie viewers, but began with the Italian physician and criminologist Cesare Lombroso.

The early research of Lombroso and his contemporaries is today regarded as historical curiosity, not scientific fact. The research methodology they used was slipshod, and many of the traits they as-

AP/Wide World Photos

sociobiology

View that human behavior is motivated by inborn biological urges to survive and preserve the species.

C O N N E C T I O N S

As you may recall (Chapter 1), Lombroso's work on the born criminal was a direct offshoot of applying the scientific method to the study of crime. His identification of primitive, atavistic anomalies was based on what he believed to be sound empirical research using established scientific methods.

Contemporary Trait Theory

equipotentiality

The view that all humans are born with equal potential to learn and achieve.

Find It on INFOTRAC
College Edition

Sociobiologists suggest that when males desire younger females, they are engaging in a procreation strategy that will maximize the chance of producing healthy offspring. Females prefer older males because the survival of their offspring will be enhanced by someone with greater prestige and wealth. To learn more, use "sociobiology" as a subject guide in InfoTrac College Edition.

sumed to be inherited are not really genetically determined but caused by environment and diet. As criticism of their work mounted, biological explanations of crime fell out of favor and were abandoned in the early twentieth century.[2]

In the early 1970s, spurred by the publication of *Sociobiology* by Edmund O. Wilson, biological explanations of crime once again emerged.[3] **Sociobiology** differs from earlier theories of behavior in that it stresses that biological and genetic conditions affect how social behaviors are learned and perceived. It suggests that both animal and human behavior is determined in part by the need to ensure survival of offspring and replenishment of the gene pool. These perceptions, in turn, are linked to existing environmental structures.

Sociobiologists view biology, environment, and learning as mutually interdependent factors. These views revived interest in finding a biological and/or psychological basis for crime and delinquency. It prompted some criminologists to conclude that personal traits must separate the deviant members of society from the nondeviant. Possessing these traits may help explain why, when faced with the same life situations, one person commits crime, whereas another obeys the law. Put another way, living in a disadvantaged neighborhood will not cause a well-adjusted person to commit crime; living in an affluent area will not stop a maladapted person from offending.[4] All people may be aware of and even fear the sanctioning power of the law, but some are unable to control their urges and passions.

Contemporary trait theorists do not suggest that a single biological or psychological attribute adequately explains all criminality. Rather, each offender is considered physically and mentally unique; consequently, there must be different explanations for each person's behavior. Some may have inherited criminal tendencies; others may be suffering from neurological problems; still others may have blood chemistry disorders that heighten their antisocial activity. Criminologists who focus on the individual see many explanations for crime because, in fact, there are many differences among criminal offenders.

Contemporary trait theorists focus on basic human behavior and drives that are linked to antisocial behavior patterns. Because not all humans are born with equal potential to learn and achieve (**equipotentiality**), the combination of physical traits and the environment produces individual behavior patterns. There is a significant link between behavior patterns and physical or chemical changes in the brain, autonomic nervous system, and central nervous system. Furthermore, most human behavior is a learned response to environmental stimulus, and learning is influenced by instinctual drives developed over the course of human history. For example, rape and other sex crimes may be linked to a primitive instinctual drive that males have to possess and control females.[5]

Trait theorists today recognize that having a particular physical characteristic does not, in itself, produce criminality. Crime-producing interactions involve both personal traits (such as defective intelligence, impulsive personality, and abnormal brain chemistry) and environmental factors (such as family life, educational attainment, socioeconomic status, and neighborhood conditions). People may develop physical or mental traits at birth or soon after that affect their social functioning over the life course and influence their behavior choices. For example, low-birth-weight babies have been found to suffer poor educational achievement later in life; academic deficiency, in turn, has been linked to delinquency and drug abuse.[6] A condition present at birth or soon after can thus affect behavior across the life span.

Although some people may have a predisposition toward aggression, that does not mean that they will necessarily or automatically engage in violent behaviors; environmental stimuli can either suppress or trigger antisocial acts.[7]

The Criminological Enterprise

The Nature Assumption

In her book *The Nature Assumption,* psychologist Judith Rich Harris questions the cherished belief that parents play an important, if not the most important, role in a child's upbringing. Instead of family influence, Harris claims that genetics and environment determine, to a large extent, how a child turns out. Children's own temperament and peer relations shape their behavior and modify the characteristics they were born with; their interpersonal relations determine the kind of people they will be when they mature.

Harris reasons that parenting skills may be irrelevant to children's future success. Most parents don't have a single child-rearing style and may treat each child in the family independently. They are more permissive with their mild-mannered children and stricter and more punitive with those who are temperamental or defiant. Even if every child were treated the same in a family, this would not explain why siblings raised in the same family under relatively similar conditions turn out so differently. Those sent to day care are quite similar to those who remain at home; having working parents seems to have little long-term effect. Family structure also does not seem to matter: Adults who grew up in one-parent homes are as likely to be successful as those who were raised in two-parent households.

Harris also questions the abuse–delinquency link. Despite some experts' findings that abused children are more likely to behave antisocially, others have found that most children growing up in troubled or abusive households are noncriminal and do not suffer lasting psychological damage. Conversely, many children who are raised in nurturing homes by caring parents take drugs, join gangs, and are continually involved in antisocial behavior.

If parenting has little direct influence on children's long-term development, what does? While Harris believes that genetics play the most important role in behavior, the child's total social environment is the other key influence that helps shape behavior. Children who act one way at home may be totally different at school or with their peers. Some who are mild-mannered around the house are hell-raisers in the schoolyard, whereas others who bully their siblings are docile with friends. Children may conform to parental expectations at home but leave them behind in their own social environment.

In their own world, the need to conform to peer group values replaces parental influence as the key determinant of behavior. Children know that the peer group is quick to scapegoat anyone who is different, who has different interests, clothes, or accent. Children can be heartless in abusing a child who is different; conforming thus becomes a matter of survival. Children develop their own culture with unique traditions, words, rules, and activities, which often conflict with parental and adult values. What parents encourage their children to pierce their bodies or get tattoos? Parents encourage their children to do the things that will make them successful adults, but children are more concerned with becoming successful children! And that often means not behaving like adults. Parents and peers share many social values, such as honesty and loyalty; but when these values clash, the peer group wins.

Peer influence, then, is more important than family environment. When peer influence is considered, family factors are not significant. There are exceptions to this pattern. Harris concedes that some children are square pegs. Some have special skills or an especially close bond to their parents, which enables them to resist peer pressure. But as a general rule, children are more oriented to their peers than to their parents. If parents are close to their children, Harris claims, it should be because they want to be their companions and friends and not because it will help their life chances.

Critical Thinking

1. Harris's views are quite provocative. She suggests that parents should not blame themselves if their children "go bad," nor should they take much credit for their parenting skills if their offspring are overachievers. Is it possible that children growing up with cold, distant parents who show them little interest have the same life chances as children whose parents are warm, loving, and involved?

2. Do you feel that you are a product of your parents, peers, environment, or all three? Can you trace any specific characteristics to your parents? If so, what are they?

InfoTrac College Edition Research

Can parents control their children's behavior? Some commentators believe so. To learn more, read B. K. Eakman, "The Seven Deadly Sins of Parental Irresponsibility," *Insight on the News,* 7 August 2000 v16 i29 p45

SOURCE: Judith Rich Harris, *The Nature Assumption: Why Children Turn Out the Way They Do* (New York: Free Press, 1998).

The combined influence of heredity and environment is the topic of the accompanying Criminological Enterprise feature.

Trait theories have gained prominence recently because of what is now known about chronic recidivism and the development of criminal careers. If only a few offenders become persistent repeaters, then what sets them apart from the rest of the criminal population may be an abnormal biochemical makeup, brain structure, genetic constitution, or some other human trait.[8] Even if crime is a choice, the fact that some people make that choice repeatedly could be linked to their physical and mental makeup. According to this view, biological makeup contributes significantly to human behavior.

✓ Checkpoints on page 96

Biological Trait Theories

One branch of contemporary trait theory focuses on the biological conditions that control human behavior. Criminologists who work in this area typically refer to themselves as biocriminologists, biosocial criminologists, or biologically oriented criminologists; the terms are used here interchangeably.

The following sections examine some important subareas within biological criminology (see Figure 5.1). First we review the biochemical factors that are believed to affect how proper behavior patterns are learned. Then we consider the relationship between brain function and crime. Next we analyze current ideas about the association between genetic factors and crime. Finally, we evaluate evolutionary views of crime causation.

Biochemical Conditions and Crime

Some trait theorists believe that biochemical conditions, including both those that are genetically predetermined and those that are acquired through diet and environment, influence antisocial behavior. This view of crime received national attention in 1979 when Dan White, who confessed to killing San Francisco Mayor George Moscone and City Councilman Harvey Milk, claimed that his behavior was precipitated by an addiction to sugar-laden junk foods.[9] White's successful "Twinkie defense" prompted a California jury to find him guilty of the lesser offense of diminished-capacity manslaughter rather than first-degree murder. (White committed suicide after serving his prison sentence.) Some of the biochemical factors that have been linked to criminality are set out in detail here.

Figure 5.1

Biosocial Perspectives on Criminality

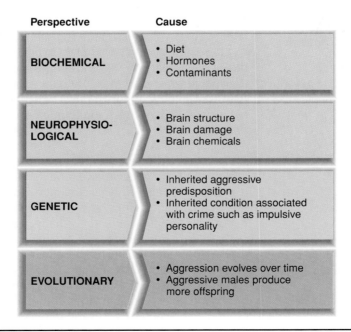

hypoglycemia

A condition that occurs when glucose (sugar) in the blood falls below levels necessary for normal and efficient brain functioning.

Chemical and Mineral Influences Biocriminologists maintain that minimal levels of minerals and chemicals are needed for normal brain functioning and growth, especially in the early years of life.

Research conducted over the past decade shows that dietary inadequacy of certain chemicals and minerals, including sodium, potassium, calcium, amino acids, monoamines, and peptides, can lead to depression, mania, cognitive problems, memory loss, and abnormal sexual activity.[10] Research studies examining the relationship between crime and vitamin deficiency and dependency have identified a close link between antisocial behavior and insufficient quantities of some B vitamins and vitamin C. In addition, studies have purported to show that a major proportion of all schizophrenics and children with learning and behavior disorders have abnormal levels of vitamins B3 and B6.[11]

Another suspected nutritional influence on aggressive behavior is a diet especially high in carbohydrates and sugar.[12] Experiments have altered children's diets so that sweet drinks were replaced with fruit juices, table sugar was replaced with honey, and so on. Results indicate that these changes can reduce aggression levels.[13]

Although these results are impressive, some recent research efforts have failed to find a link between sugar consumption and violence.[14] In one important study, a group of researchers had 25 preschool children and 23 school-age children described as sensitive to sugar follow a different diet for three consecutive three-week periods. One diet was high in sucrose, the second substituted aspartame (Nutrasweet) as a sweetener, and the third relied on saccharin. Careful measurement of the subjects found little evidence of cognitive or behavioral differences that could be linked to diet. If anything, sugar seemed to calm the children.[15] In some cases, in fact, sugar intake has been found to possibly reduce or curtail violent tendencies.[16]

While this research damages the suspected link between diet and aggression, some recent research indicates that it may be premature to dismiss the suspected association between the two factors. This issue is explored further in the accompanying Criminological Enterprise box.

Glucose Metabolism Research shows that persistent abnormality in the way the brain metabolizes glucose can be linked to substance abuse.[17] **Hypoglycemia** occurs when blood glucose (sugar) falls below levels necessary for normal and efficient brain functioning. Symptoms of hypoglycemia include irritability, anxiety, depression, crying spells, headaches, and confusion.

Research studies have linked hypoglycemia to outbursts of antisocial behavior and violence.[18] Several studies have related assaults and sexual offenses to hypoglycemic reactions.[19] Studies of jail and prison inmate populations have found a higher than normal level of hypoglycemia.[20] High levels of reactive hypoglycemia have been found in groups of habitually violent and impulsive offenders.[21]

Hormonal Influences Biosocial theorists note that males are biologically and naturally more aggressive than females, whereas women are more nurturing toward the young.[22] This discrepency has been linked to gender-based hormonal differences. Hormones cause areas of the brain to become less sensitive to environmental stimuli. Abnormally high hormone levels require people to seek excess stimulation and to be willing to tolerate pain in their quest for thrills. Hormones are linked to brain seizures that, under stressful conditions, can result in emotional volatility. They also affect the brain structure itself: They influence the left hemisphere of the neocortex, the part of the brain that controls sympathetic feelings toward others.[23] These effects promote violence and other serious crimes by causing people to seek greater levels of environmental

The Criminological Enterprise

Are You What You Eat?

Stephen Schoenthaler, a well-known biocriminologist, has conducted a number of studies that indicate a significant association between diet and aggressive behavior patterns. In some cases, the relationship is direct; in others, a poor diet may compromise individual functioning, which in turn produces aggressive behavior responses. For example, a poor diet may inhibit school performance, and children who fail at school are at risk for delinquent behavior and criminality.

In one study of 803 New York City public schools, Schoenthaler found that the academic performance of 1.1 million schoolchildren rose 16 percent after their diets were modified. The number of "learning disabled" children fell from 125,000 to 74,000 in one year. No other changes in school programs for the learning disabled were initiated that year. In a similar experiment conducted in a correctional institution, violent and nonviolent antisocial behavior fell an average of 48 percent among 8,047 offenders after dietary changes were implemented. In both these studies, the improvements in behavior and academic performance were attributed to diets containing more vitamins and minerals as compared with the old diets. The greater amounts of these essential nutrients in the new diets were believed to have corrected impaired brain function caused by poor nutrition.

More recently, Schoenthaler conducted three randomized controlled studies in which 66 elementary school children, 62 confined teenage delinquents, and 402 confined adult felons received dietary supplements—the equivalent of a diet providing more fruits, vegetables, and whole grains. In order to remove experimental bias, neither subjects nor researchers knew who received the supplement and who received a placebo. In each study, the subjects receiving the dietary supple-ment demonstrated significantly less violent and nonviolent antisocial behavior when compared to the control subjects who received placebos. The carefully collected data verified that a very good diet, as defined by the World Health Organization, has significant behavioral benefits beyond its health effects.

Schoenthaler and his associates have also evaluated the relationship between nutrition and intelligence. These studies involved 1,753 children and young adults in California, Arizona, Oklahoma, Missouri, England, Wales, Scotland, and Belgium. In each study, subjects who were poorly nourished and who were given dietary supplements showed a greater increase in IQ—an average of 16 points—than did those in the placebo group. (Overall, IQ rose more than 3 points.) The differences in IQ could be attributed to about 20 percent of the children who were presumably inadequately nourished prior to supplementation. The IQ research was expanded to include academic performance in two studies of more than 300 schoolchildren ages 6 to 14 years in Arizona and California. In both studies, children who received daily supplements at school for three months achieved significantly higher gains in grade level compared to the matched control group taking placebos. The children taking a supplement improved academically at twice the rate of the children who took placebos.

Schoenthaler concludes that parents with a child who behaves badly, or does poorly in school, may benefit from having the child take a blood test to determine if concentrations of certain nutrients are below the reference norms; if so, a dietary supplement may correct the child's conduct and performance. There is evidence that 19 nutrients may be critical; low levels appear to adversely affect brain function, aca-demic performance, intelligence, and conduct. When attempting to improve IQ or conduct, it is critical to assess all these nutrients, and correct deficiencies as needed. If blood nutrient concentrations are consistently in the normal range, physicians and parents should consider looking elsewhere for the cause of a child's difficulties.

Though more research is needed before the scientific community reaches a consensus on how low is "too low," Schoenthaler finds evidence that vitamins, minerals, chemicals, and other nutrients from a diet rich in fruits, vegetables, and whole grains can improve brain function, basic intelligence, and academic performance. These are all variables that have been linked to antisocial behavior.

Critical Thinking

1. If Schoenthaler is correct in his assumptions, should schools be required to provide a proper lunch for all children?
2. How would Schoenthaler explain the "aging out" process? Hint: Do people eat better as they mature? What about after they get married?

 InfoTrac College Edition Research

To read more about the relationship between nutrition and behavior, use "nutrition and behavior" as key terms in InfoTrac College Edition.

SOURCE: Stephen Schoenthaler, "Intelligence, Academic Performance, and Brain Function," California State University, Stanislaus, 2000. See also S. Schoenthaler and I. Bier, "The Effect of Vitamin–Mineral Supplementation on Juvenile Delinquency Among American Schoolchildren: A Randomized Double-Blind Placebo-Controlled Trial," *Journal of Alternative and Complementary Medicine: Research on Paradigm, Practice, and Policy* 6 (2000): 7–18.

androgens

Male sex hormones.

testosterone

The principal male hormone.

Find It on INFOTRAC
College Edition

Some biologists have claimed that the only difference between men and women is a hormonal system that renders men more aggressive. To research this phemonenon further, use "testosterone" and "violence" as keywords in Info-Trac College Edition.

premenstrual syndrome (PMS)

The idea that several days prior to and during menstruation, excessive amounts of female sex hormones stimulate antisocial, aggressive behavior.

stimulation and to tolerate more punishment, and by increasing impulsivity, emotional volatility, and antisocial emotions.[24]

Biosocial research has found that abnormal levels of male sex hormones (**androgens**) do in fact produce aggressive behavior.[25] Other androgen-related male traits include sensation seeking, impulsivity, dominance, and reduced verbal skills; all of these androgen-related traits are also related to antisocial behavior.[26] A growing body of evidence suggests that hormonal changes are also related to mood and behavior. Adolescents experience more intense mood swings, anxiety, and restlessness than their elders, explaining in part the high violence rates found among teenage males.[27]

Testosterone, the most abundant androgen, which controls secondary sex characteristics such as facial hair and voice timbre, has been linked to criminality.[28] Research conducted on both human and animal subjects has found that prenatal exposure to unnaturally high levels of testosterone permanently alters behavior. Girls who were unintentionally exposed to elevated amounts of testosterone during their fetal development display an unusually high, long-term tendency toward aggression. Conversely, boys who were prenatally exposed to steroids that decrease testosterone levels display decreased aggressiveness.[29] Gender differences in the crime rate, therefore, may be explained by the relative difference in testosterone and other androgens between the two sexes. Females may be biologically protected from deviant behavior in the same way they are immune from some diseases that strike males.[30] Hormone levels also help explain the aging-out process. Levels of testosterone decline during the life cycle, which may explain why violence rates diminish over time.[31]

Premenstrual Syndrome The suspicion has long existed that the onset of the menstrual cycle triggers excessive amounts of the female sex hormones, which stimulate antisocial, aggressive behavior. This condition is commonly referred to as **premenstrual syndrome (PMS)**.[32] The link between PMS and delinquency was first popularized more than 30 years ago by Katharina Dalton, whose studies of English women indicated that females are more likely to commit suicide and to be aggressive and otherwise antisocial just before or during menstruation.[33]

Although the Dalton research is often cited as evidence of the link between PMS and crime, methodological problems make it impossible to accept her findings at face value. There is still significant debate over any link between PMS and aggression. Some doubters argue that the relationship is spurious; it is equally likely that the psychological and physical stress of aggression brings on menstruation and not vice versa.[34] However, Diana Fishbein, a noted expert on biosocial theory, concludes that there is in fact an association between elevated levels of female aggression and menstruation. Research efforts, she argues, show that (1) a significant number of incarcerated females committed their crimes during the premenstrual phase and (2) at least a small percentage of women appear vulnerable to cyclical hormonal changes that make them more prone to anxiety and hostility.[35]

The debate is ongoing, but the overwhelming majority of females who suffer anxiety and hostility before and during menstruation do not engage in violent criminal behavior. Thus, any link between PMS and crime is tenuous at best.[36]

Environmental Contaminants Dangerous amounts of copper, cadmium, mercury, and inorganic gases, such as chlorine and nitrogen dioxide, are found in the ecosystem. Research indicates that these environmental contaminants can influence behavior. At high levels, these substances can cause severe illness or death; at more moderate levels, they have been linked to emotional and behavioral disorders.[37] Some studies have linked the ingestion of food dyes and artificial colors and flavors to hostile, impulsive, and otherwise antisocial behavior in youths.[38] Lighting may be another important environmental influence on antisocial behavior. Research projects have suggested that radiation from artificial light sources, such as fluorescent tubes and television sets, may produce antisocial, aggressive behavior.[39]

A number of recent research studies have linked lead ingestion to problem behavior. Ingestion of lead may help explain why hyperactive children manifest conduct problems and antisocial behavior.[40] Criminologist Deborah Denno investigated the behavior of more than 900 African American youths and found that lead poisoning was one of the most significant predictors of male delinquency and persistent adult criminality.[41]

Neurophysiological Conditions and Crime

neurophysiology

The study of brain activity.

Some researchers focus their attention on **neurophysiology**, or the study of brain activity.[42] They believe that neurological and physical abnormalities, acquired as early as the fetal or perinatal stage or through birth delivery trauma, control behavior throughout the life span.[43]

The relationship between neurological dysfunction and crime first received a great deal of attention in 1968 following a tragic incident in Texas. Charles Whitman killed his wife and mother, then barricaded himself in a tower at the University of Texas with a high-powered rifle; he killed 14 people and wounded 24 others before he was killed by police. An autopsy revealed that Whitman suffered from a malignant infiltrating brain tumor. He had previously experienced uncontrollable urges to kill and had gone to a psychiatrist seeking help for his problems. He kept careful notes documenting his feelings and his inability to control his homicidal urges, and he left instructions for his estate to be given to a mental health foundation to study mental problems such as his own.[44]

Since the Whitman case, a great deal of attention has been focused on the association between neurological impairment and crime. Studies conducted in the United States and elsewhere have shown a significant relationship between impairment in executive brain functions (such as abstract reasoning, problem solving, and motor skills) and aggressive behavior.[45] Research using memorization and visual awareness tests, short-term auditory memory tests, and verbal IQ tests indicates that this relationship can be detected quite early and that children who suffer measurable neurological deficits at birth or in adolescence are more likely to become criminals later in life.[46]

Studies using an electroencephalograph (EEG)—a device that records electrical impulses in the brain—have found far higher levels of abnormal EEG recordings in violent criminals than in nonviolent or one-time offenders.[47] Although about 5 percent of the general population show abnormal EEG readings, about 50 to 60 percent of adolescents with known behavior disorders display abnormal recordings.[48] Behaviors highly correlated with abnormal EEG readings include poor impulse control, inadequate social adaptation, hostility, temper tantrums, and destructiveness.[49]

Newer brain-scanning techniques using electronic imaging, such as positron emission tomography (PET), brain electrical activity mapping (BEAM), and superconducting interference device (SQUID), have made it possible to assess which areas of the brain are directly linked to antisocial behavior.[50] Both violent criminals and substance abusers have been found to have impairment in the prefrontal lobes, thalamus, medial temporal lobe, and superior parietal and left angular gyrus areas of the brain.[51] Chronic violent criminals have far higher levels of brain dysfunction than the general population; murderers exhibit brain pathology at a rate 32 times greater than in the general population.[52]

minimal brain dysfunction (MBD)

An abruptly appearing, maladaptive behavior, such as episodic periods of explosive rage.

Minimal Brain Dysfunction (MBD)

Minimal Brain Dysfunction (MBD) Related to abnormal cerebral structure, **minimal brain dysfunction (MBD)** has been defined as an abruptly appearing, maladaptive behavior that interrupts an individual's lifestyle and life

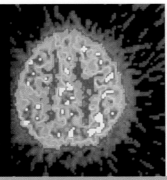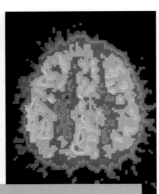

This scan compares a normal brain (left) and an ADHD brain (right). Areas of orange and white demonstrate a higher rate of metabolism, while areas of blue and green represent an abnormally low metabolic rate. Why is ADHD so prevalent in the United States today? Some experts believe that our immigrant forebears, risk takers who impulsively left their homelands for life in a new world, may have brought with them a genetic predisposition for ADHD.

attention deficit/hyperactivity disorder (ADHD)

A developmentally inappropriate lack of attention, along with impulsivity and hyperactivity.

neurotransmitters

Chemical compounds that influence or activate brain functions.

flow. One type of minimal brain dysfunction is manifested in episodic periods of explosive rage. This form of the disorder is considered an important cause of behaviors such as spouse and child abuse, suicide, aggressiveness, and motiveless homicide. One perplexing feature of this syndrome is that people who are afflicted with it often maintain warm, pleasant personalities between episodes of violence. Studies measuring the presence of minimal brain dysfunction in offender populations have found that up to 60 percent exhibit brain dysfunction on psychological tests.[53] More sophisticated brain-scanning techniques, such as PET, have also shown that brain abnormality is linked to violent crime.[54]

Attention Deficit/Hyperactivity Disorder (ADHD)

Many parents have noticed that their children do not pay attention to them—they run around and do things in their own way. Sometimes this inattention is a function of age; in other instances it is a symptom of **attention deficit/ hyperactivity disorder (ADHD)**, in which a child shows a developmentally inappropriate lack of attention, impulsivity, and hyperactivity. The various symptoms of ADHD are listed in Table 5.1. About 3 percent of U.S. children, most often boys, are believed to suffer from this disorder, and it is the most common reason children are referred to mental health clinics. The condition has been associated with poor school performance, grade retention, placement in special needs classes, bullying, stubbornness, and lack of response to discipline.[55] Although the origin of ADHD is still unknown, suspected causes include neurological damage, prenatal stress, and even reactions to food additives and chemical allergies. Recent research has suggested a genetic link.[56] There are also links to family turmoil: mothers of ADHD children are more likely to be divorced or separated, and ADHD children are much more likely to move to new locales than non-ADHD children.[57] It may be possible that emotional turmoil either produces symptoms of ADHD or, if they already exist, causes them to intensify.

Research studies now link ADHD to the onset and maintenance of a delinquent career.[58] Children diagnosed as having ADHD are more likely to be suspended from school and to engage in criminal behavior as adults. This ADHD–crime association is important because symptoms of ADHD seem stable through adolescence into adulthood.[59] Early diagnosis and treatment of children with ADHD may enhance their life chances. Today the most typical treatment is doses of stimulants, such as Ritalin, which ironically help control emotional and behavioral outbursts. The relationship between chronic delinquency and attention disorders may also be mediated by school performance. Children who are poor readers are the most prone to antisocial behavior; many poor readers also have attention problems.[60] Early school-based intervention programs may thus benefit children with ADHD.

Brain Chemistry

Neurotransmitters are chemical compounds that influence or activate brain functions. Those studied in relation to aggression include dopamine, norepinephrine, serotonin, monoamine oxidase, and GABA.[61] Evidence exists that abnormal levels of these chemicals are associated with aggression. Recent studies of habitually violent Finnish criminals show that low serotonin (5-hydroxytryptamine; 5-HT) levels are associated with poor impulse control and hyperactivity. In addition, a relatively low concentration of

Table 5.1 Symptoms of Attention Deficit/Hyperactivity Disorder

Lack of Attention
Frequently fails to finish projects
Does not seem to pay attention
Does not sustain interest in play activities
Cannot sustain concentration on schoolwork or related tasks
Is easily distracted

Impulsivity
Frequently acts without thinking
Often "calls out" in class
Does not want to wait his or her turn in lines or games
Shifts from activity to activity
Cannot organize tasks or work
Requires constant supervision

Hyperactivity
Constantly runs around and climbs on things
Shows excessive motor activity while asleep
Cannot sit still; is constantly fidgeting
Does not remain in his or her seat in class
Is constantly on the go like a "motor"

SOURCE: Adapted from American Psychiatric Association, *Diagnostic and Statistical Manual of Mental Disorders,* 4th ed. (Washington, DC: American Psychiatric Press, 1994).

arousal theory

The view that people seek to maintain a preferred level of arousal, but vary in how they process sensory input. A need for high levels of environmental stimulation may lead to aggressive, violent behavior patterns.

5-hydroxyindoleacetic acid (5-HIAA) predicts increased irritability, sensation seeking, and impaired impulse control.[62]

What is the link between brain chemistry and crime? Prenatal exposure of the brain to high levels of androgens can result in a brain structure that is less sensitive to environmental inputs. Affected individuals seek more intense and varied stimulation and are willing to tolerate more adverse consequences than individuals not so affected.[63] It has also been suggested that individuals with a low supply of the enzyme monoamine oxidase (MAO) engage in behaviors linked with violence and property crime, including defiance of punishment, impulsivity, hyperactivity, poor academic performance, sensation seeking and risk taking, and recreational drug use. Abnormal MAO levels may explain both individual and group differences in the crime rate. For example, females have higher MAO levels than males, which may explain gender differences in the crime rate.[64]

Because this linkage has been found, it is not uncommon for violence-prone people to be treated with antipsychotic drugs, such as Haldol, Stelazine, Prolixin, and Risperdal. These drugs, which help control levels of neurotransmitters (such as serotonin or dopamine), are sometimes referred to as chemical restraints or chemical straitjackets.

Arousal Theory According to **arousal theory**, for a variety of genetic and environmental reasons, people's brains function differently in response to environmental stimuli. All of us seek to maintain a preferred or optimal level of arousal: too much stimulation leaves us anxious and stressed, whereas too little makes us feel bored and weary. However, people vary in the way their brains process sensory input. Some nearly always feel comfortable with little stimulation, whereas others require a high degree of environmental input to feel comfortable. The latter group of "sensation seekers" look for stimulating activities, which may include aggressive, violent behavior patterns.[65]

Although the factors that determine a person's level of arousal are not fully understood, suspected sources include brain chemistry (such as serotonin levels) and brain structure. Some brains have many more nerve cells with receptor sites for neurotransmitters than others. Another view is that people with low heart rates are more likely to commit crime because they seek stimulation to increase their arousal to normal levels.[66]

Genetics and Crime

Another biosocial theme is that the human traits associated with criminality have a genetic basis.[67] This line of reasoning was spotlighted in the 1970s when genetic testing of Richard Speck, the convicted killer of eight Chicago nurses, allegedly found that he had an abnormal XYY chromosomal structure (XY is normal in males). There was much public concern that all people with XYY chromosomes were potential killers and should be closely controlled. Civil libertarians expressed fear that all XYY males could be labeled dangerous and violent regardless of whether they had engaged in violent activities.[68] When it was disclosed that neither Speck nor most violent offenders actually had an extra Y chromosome, interest in the XYY theory dissipated.[69] However, the Speck case drew researchers' attention to looking for a genetic basis of crime.

Researchers have carefully explored the heritability of criminal tendencies by looking at a variety of factors. Some of the most important are described here.

Parental Deviance   If criminal tendencies are inherited, then the children of criminal parents should be more likely to become law violators than the offspring of conventional parents. A number of studies have found that parental criminality and deviance do, in fact, powerfully influence delinquent behavior.[70] Some of the most important data on parental deviance were gathered by Donald J. West and David P. Farrington as part of the long-term Cambridge Youth Survey. These cohort data indicate that a significant number of delinquent youths have criminal fathers.[71] Whereas 8.4 percent of the sons of noncriminal fathers eventually became chronic offenders, about 37 percent of youths with criminal fathers were multiple offenders.[72] In another important analysis, Farrington found that one type of parental deviance, schoolyard aggression or bullying, may be both inter- and intragenerational. Bullies have children who bully others, and these second-generation bullies grow up to father children who are also bullies, in a never-ending cycle.[73]

Although there is no certainty about the relationship between parental and child deviance, recent evidence indicates that at least part of the association is genetic.[74]

Twin Behavior   If, in fact, inherited traits cause criminal behavior, we might expect that twins would be quite similar in their antisocial activities. However, because twins are usually brought up in the same household and exposed to the same social conditions, determining whether their behavior is a result of biological, sociological, or psychological conditions is difficult. Trait theorists have tried to overcome this dilemma by comparing identical, **monozygotic (MZ) twins** with fraternal, **dizygotic (DZ) twins**.[75] MZ twins are genetically identical, whereas DZ twins have only half their genes in common. If heredity determines criminal behavior, we should expect that MZ twins would be much more similar in their antisocial activities than DZ twins.

The earliest studies conducted on twin behavior detected a significant relationship between the criminal activities of MZ twins and a much lower association between those of DZ twins. A review of relevant studies found that 60 percent of MZ twins shared criminal behavior patterns (if one twin was criminal, so was the other), whereas only 30 percent of DZ twins were similarly related.[76] These findings may be viewed as powerful evidence of a genetic basis for criminality. Similarly, criminologists David Rowe and D. Wayne Osgood analyzed the factors that influence self-reported delinquency in a sample of twin pairs and concluded that genetic influences have significant explanatory power.[77] Genetic effects significantly predict problem behaviors in children as young as 3 years old.[78] Although the behavior of some twin pairs seems to be influenced by their environment, others display behavior disturbances that can be explained only by their genetic similarity.[79]

Not all research efforts have found that MZ twin pairs are more closely related in their criminal behavior than DZ or ordinary sibling pairs, and some have found an association that is at best modest.[80] On the other hand, some experts conclude that individuals who share genes are alike in personality regardless of how they are reared; environment, they argue, induces little or no personality resemblance in twin pairs.[81]

Adoption Studies   It seems logical that if the behavior of adopted children is more closely aligned to that of their biological parents than to that of their adoptive parents, then the idea of a genetic basis for criminality would be supported. If, on the other hand, adoptees' behavior is more closely aligned to the

monozygotic (MZ) twins

Identical twins.

dizygotic (DZ) twins

Fraternal (nonidentical) twins.

Find It on INFOTRAC
College Edition

Twin studies show that some traits, such as bulimia, are environmental, whereas schizophrenia, autism, and bipolar (manic-depressive) disorder seem to be genetic. To learn more about this phenomenon, go to Infotrac College Edition and read
Peter McGuffin and Martin Neilson, "Behaviour and Genes," *British Medical Journal*, 3 July 1999 v319 i7201 p37

behavior of their adoptive parents than of their biological parents, an environmental basis for crime would seem more valid.

Several studies indicate that some relationship exists between biological parents' behavior and the behavior of their children, even when they have had no contact.[82] In what is considered the most significant study in this area, Barry Hutchings and Sarnoff Mednick analyzed 1,145 male adoptees born in Copenhagen, Denmark, between 1927 and 1941. Of these, 185 had criminal records.[83] After following up on 143 of the criminal adoptees and matching them with a control group of 143 noncriminal adoptees, Hutchings and Mednick found that the biological father's criminality strongly predicted the child's criminal behavior. When both the biological and the adoptive fathers were criminal, the probability that the youth would engage in criminal behavior greatly increased. Of the boys whose adoptive and biological fathers were both criminals, 24.5 percent had been convicted of a criminal law violation. Only 13.5 percent of those whose biological and adoptive fathers were not criminals had similar conviction records.[84]

The findings of the twin and adoption studies tentatively support a genetic basis for criminality. However, those who dispute the genes–crime relationship point to inadequate research designs and weak methodologies in the supporting research. Newer, better-designed research studies, critics charge, provide less support than earlier, less methodologically sound studies.[85]

Evolutionary Views of Crime

Some criminologists believe that the human traits that produce violence and aggression have been advanced by the long process of human evolution.[86] According to this evolutionary view, the competition for scarce resources has influenced and shaped the human species.[87] Over the course of human existence, people whose personal characteristics allowed them to accumulate more than others were the most likely to breed and dominate the species. People have been shaped to engage in actions that promote their well-being and ensure the survival and reproduction of their genetic line. Males who are impulsive risk takers may be able to father more children because they are reckless in their social relationships and have sexual encounters with numerous partners. If, according to evolutionary theories, such behavior patterns are inherited, impulsive behavior becomes intergenerational, passed down from parents to children. It is therefore not surprising that human history has been marked by war, violence, and aggression.

The Evolution of Gender and Crime

Evolutionary concepts that have been linked to gender differences in violence rates are based loosely on mammalian mating patterns. To ensure survival of the gene pool (and the species), it is beneficial for a male of any species to mate with as many suitable females as possible, because each can bear his offspring. In contrast, because of the long period of gestation, females require a secure home and a single, stable, nurturing partner to ensure their survival. Because of these differences in mating patterns, the most aggressive males mate most often and have the greatest number of offspring. Therefore, over the history of the human species, aggressive males have had the greatest impact on the gene pool. The descendants of these aggressive males now account for the disproportionate amount of male aggression and violence.[88]

Crime rate differences between the genders, then, may be less a matter of socialization than of inherent differences in mating patterns that have developed over time.[89] Among young men, reckless, life-threatening risk proneness is especially likely to evolve in cultures that force them to find suitable mates to ensure their ability to reproduce. Unless they are aggressive with potential mates and potential rivals for those suitable mates, they will remain childless.[90]

CONNECTIONS

The relationship between evolutionary factors and crime has just begun to be studied. Criminologists are now exploring how social organizations and institutions interact with biological traits to influence personal decision making, including criminal strategies. See the discussion of latent trait theories in Chapter 9 for more about the integration of biological and environmental factors.

cheater theory

A theory suggesting that a subpopulation of men has evolved with genes that incline them toward extremely low parental involvement. Sexually aggressive, they use deceit for sexual conquest of as many females as possible.

CONNECTIONS

Biosocial theory focuses on the violent crimes of the lower classes while ignoring the white-collar crimes of the upper and middle classes. That is, although it may seem logical to believe there is a biological basis to aggression and violence, it is more difficult to explain how insider trading and fraud are biologically related. For the causes of white-collar crime, see Chapter 12.

Evaluation of the Biological Branch of Trait Theory

✔ Checkpoints

✔ Brain chemistry and hormonal differences are related to aggression and violence.

✔ Most evidence suggests that there is no relationship between sugar intake and crime.

✔ The male hormone testosterone is linked to criminality.

✔ Neurological impairments have been linked to crime.

✔ Genetic theory holds that violence-producing traits are passed on from generation to generation.

✔ According to evolutionary theory, instinctual drives control

(continued)

High rates of spouse abuse in modern society may be a function of aggressive men seeking to control and possess mates. Men who feel most threatened over the potential of losing mates to rivals are the most likely to engage in sexual violence. Research shows that women in common-law marriages, especially those who are much younger than their husbands, are at greater risk of abuse than older, married women. Abusive males may fear the potential loss of their younger mates, especially if they are not bound by a marriage contract, and may use force for purposes of control and possession.[91]

"Cheater" Theory According to **cheater theory**, a subpopulation of men has evolved with genes that incline them toward extremely low parental involvement. They are sexually aggressive and use cunning to achieve sexual conquest of as many females as possible. Because females would not willingly choose them as mates, they use stealth to gain sexual access, including such tactics as mimicking the behavior of more stable males. They use devious, illegal means to acquire resources they need for sexual domination. These deceptive reproductive tactics spill over into other endeavors, where their irresponsible, opportunistic behavior supports their antisocial activities. Deceptive reproductive strategies, then, are linked to a deceitful lifestyle.[92]

Psychologist Byron Roth notes that cheater-type males may be especially attractive to younger, less intelligent women who begin having children at a very early age. State-sponsored welfare, claims Roth, removes the need for potential mates to have the resources required of stable providers and family caretakers.[93] With the state meeting their financial needs, these women are drawn to men who are physically attractive and flamboyant. Their fleeting courtship produces children with low IQ scores, aggressive personalities, and little chance of proper socialization in father-absent families. Because the criminal justice system treats them leniently, argues Roth, sexually irresponsible men are free to prey upon young girls. Over time, their offspring will make up an ever-expanding supply of cheaters who are both antisocial and sexually aggressive.

Biosocial perspectives on crime have raised some challenging questions. Critics find some of these theories racist and dysfunctional. If there are biological explanations for street crimes such as assault, murder, or rape, the argument goes, and if, as official crime statistics suggest, the poor and minority-group members commit a disproportionate number of such acts, then by implication, biological theory says that members of these groups are biologically different, flawed, or inferior.

Biological explanations for the geographic, social, and temporal patterns in the crime rate are also problematic. Is it possible that more people are genetically predisposed to crime in the South and the West than in New England and the Midwest? Furthermore, biological theory seems to divide people into criminals and noncriminals on the basis of their genetic and physical makeup, ignoring self-reports that indicate almost everyone has engaged in some type of illegal activity.

Biosocial theorists counter that their views should not be confused with Lombrosian, deterministic biology. Rather than suggesting that there are born criminals and noncriminals, they maintain that some people carry the potential to be violent or antisocial and that environmental conditions can sometimes trigger antisocial responses.[94] This would explain why some otherwise law-abiding citizens perform a single, seemingly unexplainable antisocial act and, conversely, why some people with long criminal careers often behave conventionally. It also explains geographic and temporal patterns in the crime rate: People who are predisposed to crime may simply have more opportunities to

✔ **Checkpoints**

behavior. The urge to procreate influences male violence.

✔ Biological explanations fail to account for the geographic, social, and temporal patterns in the crime rate; critics question the methodology used.

commit illegal acts in the summer in Los Angeles and Atlanta than in the winter in Bedford, New Hampshire, and Minot, North Dakota.

The most significant criticism of biosocial theory has been the lack of adequate empirical testing. Most research samples are relatively small and nonrepresentative. A great deal of biosocial research is conducted with samples of adjudicated offenders who have been placed in clinical treatment settings. Methodological problems make it impossible to determine whether findings apply only to offenders who have been convicted of crimes and placed in treatment or to all criminals.[95] More research is needed to clarify the relationships proposed by biosocial researchers and to silence critics. ✔ Checkpoints

Psychological Trait Theories

The second branch of trait theory focuses on the psychological aspects of crime, including the associations among intelligence, personality, learning, and criminal behavior. This view has a long history, and psychologists, psychiatrists, and other mental health professionals have long played an active role in formulating criminological theory.

Among nineteenth-century pioneers in this area were Charles Goring (1870–1919) and Gabriel Tarde (1843–1904). Goring studied 3,000 English convicts and found little difference in the physical characteristics of criminals and noncriminals. However, he uncovered a significant relationship between crime and a condition he referred to as "defective intelligence," which involved such traits as feeblemindedness, epilepsy, insanity, and defective social instinct.[96] Tarde was the forerunner of modern learning theorists, who hold that people learn from one another through imitation.[97]

In their quest to understand and treat all varieties of abnormal mental conditions, psychologists have encountered clients whose behavior falls within the categories that society has labeled as criminal, deviant, violent, and antisocial. A number of different psychological views have been associated with criminal behavior causation (see Figure 5.2). The most important of these perspectives are discussed in the following sections.

CONNECTIONS

Chapter I discussed how some of the early founders of psychiatry tried to understand the criminal mind. Early theories suggested that mental illness and insanity were inherited and that deviants were inherently mentally damaged by their inferior genetic makeup.

Psychodynamic Perspective

Psychodynamic (or **psychoanalytic**) psychology was originated by Viennese psychiatrist Sigmund Freud (1856–1939) and has remained a prominent segment of psychological theory ever since.[98] Freud believed that we all carry with us residue of the most significant emotional attachments of our childhood, which then guides our future interpersonal relationships.

According to Freud's version of psychodynamic theory, the human personality has a three-part structure. The **id** is the primitive part of people's mental makeup, present at birth, that represents unconscious biological drives for food, sex, and other life-sustaining necessities. The id seeks instant gratification without concern for the rights of others. The **ego** develops early in life, when a child begins to learn that his or her wishes cannot be instantly gratified. The ego is the part of the personality that compensates for the demands of the id by helping the individual guide his or her actions to remain within the boundaries of social convention. The **superego** develops as a result of incorporating within the personality the moral standards and values of parents, community, and significant others. It is the moral aspect of people's personalities; it judges their behavior.

psychodynamic (psychoanalytic)

Theory originated by Freud that the human personality is controlled by unconscious mental processes developed early in childhood, involving the interaction of id, ego, and superego.

id

The primitive part of people's mental makeup, present at birth, that represents unconscious biological drives for food, sex, and other life-sustaining necessities. The id seeks instant gratification without concern for the rights of others.

Psychodynamics of Abnormal Behavior Psychodynamic theory originally used the term **neurotic** to refer to people who experienced feelings of mental anguish and feared that they were losing control of their personalities. People who had completely lost control and who were dominated by their primitive id were referred to as **psychotic**. Today these terms have, for the most

Figure 5.2

Psychological Perspectives on Criminality

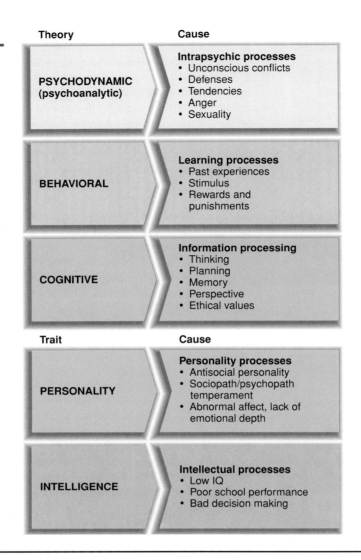

Theory	Cause
PSYCHODYNAMIC (psychoanalytic)	**Intrapsychic processes** • Unconscious conflicts • Defenses • Tendencies • Anger • Sexuality
BEHAVIORAL	**Learning processes** • Past experiences • Stimulus • Rewards and punishments
COGNITIVE	**Information processing** • Thinking • Planning • Memory • Perspective • Ethical values

Trait	Cause
PERSONALITY	**Personality processes** • Antisocial personality • Sociopath/psychopath temperament • Abnormal affect, lack of emotional depth
INTELLIGENCE	**Intellectual processes** • Low IQ • Poor school performance • Bad decision making

ego

The part of the personality, developed in early childhood, that helps control the id and keep people's actions within the boundaries of social convention.

superego

Incorporation within the personality of the moral standards and values of parents, community, and significant others.

neurotic

In Freudian psychology, a personality marked by mental anguish and feared loss of control.

part, been replaced by the term **disorder**, as in anxiety disorders, mood disorders, and conduct disorders. The most serious disorder is **schizophrenia**, marked by hearing nonexistent voices, seeing hallucinations, and exhibiting inappropriate responses.

Schizophrenics have illogical, incoherent thought processes and lack insight into their behavior. They may experience delusions and hallucinate. For example, they may see themselves as agents of the devil, avenging angels, or the recipients of messages from animals and plants. Serial killer David Berkowitz, dubbed "Son of Sam" or the "44-calibre killer," claimed that his 1976–1977 killing spree began after he received messages from a neighbor's dog. Paranoid schizophrenics, such as U.S. Capitol slayer Russell Eugene Weston, suffer complex behavioral delusions involving wrongdoing or persecution—they think everyone is out to get them.

Psychodynamics of Criminal Behavior Since Freud's original research, psychoanalysts have continued to view criminals as id-dominated persons who suffer from one or more disorders that render them incapable of controlling impulsive, pleasure-seeking drives.[99] The psychoanalyst whose work is most closely associated with criminality is August Aichorn.[100] After examining

psychotic

In Freudian psychology, a personality marked by complete loss of control over the id, characterized by delusions, hallucinations, and sudden mood shifts.

disorder

Any type of psychological problem (formerly labeled neurotic or psychotic), such as anxiety disorders, mood disorders, and conduct disorders.

schizophrenia

A severe disorder marked by hearing nonexistent voices, seeing hallucinations, and exhibiting inappropriate responses.

latent delinquency

A psychological predisposition to commit antisocial acts because of an id-dominated personality that renders an individual incapable of controlling impulsive, pleasure-seeking drives.

bipolar disorder

An emotional disturbance in which moods alternate between periods of wild elation and deep depression.

many delinquent youths, Aichorn concluded that societal stress, though damaging, could not in itself cause a life of crime unless a predisposition existed that psychologically prepared youths for antisocial acts. This mental state, which he labeled **latent delinquency**, is found in youngsters whose personality requires them to

- Seek immediate gratification (act impulsively)
- Consider satisfying their personal needs to be more important than relating to others
- Satisfy instinctual urges without considering right and wrong (that is, they lack guilt)

The psychodynamic model of the criminal offender depicts an aggressive, frustrated person dominated by events that occurred early in childhood. Perhaps as a result of unhappy experiences in childhood or families that could not provide proper love and care, criminals suffer from weak or damaged egos that make them unable to cope with conventional society. Weak egos are associated with immaturity, poor social skills, and excessive dependence on others. People with weak egos may be easily led into crime by antisocial peers and drug abuse. Some offenders have underdeveloped superegos and consequently lack internalized representations of those behaviors that are punished in conventional society. They commit crimes because they have difficulty understanding the consequences of their actions.[101]

Offenders, then, have various mood and behavior disorders. They may be histrionic, depressed, antisocial, or narcissistic.[102] They may exhibit conduct disorders (long histories of antisocial behavior) or mood disorders (disturbance in expressed emotions). Among the latter is **bipolar disorder**, in which moods alternate between periods of wild elation and deep depression.[103] Some offenders are driven by an unconscious desire to be punished for prior sins, either real or imaginary. They may violate the law to gain attention or punish their parents.

From this perspective, then, crime is a manifestation of feelings of oppression and people's inability to develop the proper psychological defenses and rationales to keep these feelings under control. Criminality allows troubled people to survive by producing positive psychic results: It helps them feel free and independent, and it gives them the possibility of excitement and the chance to use their skills and imagination. In addition, it allows them to blame others for their predicament (for example, the police), and it gives them a chance to rationalize their sense of failure ("If I hadn't gotten into trouble, I could have been a success").[104]

Crime and Mental Illness Psychodynamic theory suggests a linkage between mental illness and crime. Although the association appears clear-cut, empirical evidence has been contradictory.

Many early research efforts found that offenders who engage in serious, violent crimes suffer from some sort of mental disturbance. Studies of adolescent males accused of murder found that 75 percent could be classified as having some mental illness, including schizophrenia.[105] Abusive mothers have been found to have mood and personality disorders and a history of psychiatric diagnoses.[106] The diagnosed mentally ill appear in arrest and court statistics at a rate disproportionate to their presence in the population.[107]

Despite this evidence, questions remain as to whether the mentally ill population has a greater inclination toward criminal behavior than the mentally sound. The mentally ill may in fact be more likely to withdraw or harm themselves than to act aggressively toward others.[108] Research shows that after release, prisoners with prior histories of hospitalization for mental disorders are

Sometimes a sensational case in which a mentally challenged person commits a terrible crime gives the public the false impression that the mentally ill have a much higher crime rate than the mentally sound. In one notorious case, Andrew Goldstein, shown here being escorted by police officers, pushed a young woman under a train in a New York City subway station. Goldstein was under psychiatric care at the time and had been institutionalized many times. Despite such highly charged incidents, most people who suffer from mental illness are not criminals.

AP/Wide World Photos

less likely to be rearrested than those who have never been hospitalized.[109] Even research that finds a mental illness–crime association indicates that the great majority of known criminals are not mentally ill and that the relationship is modest at best. And if there is a statistically significant association between mental illness and crime, the fact remains that most mentally ill people are not criminals.

Although research efforts only tentatively support the proposition that mental disturbance or illness can cause violent crime, it is still possible that some link exists. Existing data suggest that certain symptoms of mental illness are connected to violence: for example, the feeling that others wish the person harm, or that the person's mind is dominated by forces beyond his or her control, or that thoughts are being put into the person's head by others.[110] Currently, major assessments and research studies are ongoing; results should soon determine the true link between mental illness and crime.[111]

Behavioral Perspective: Social Learning Theory

behavior theory

The view that all human behavior is learned through a process of social reinforcement (rewards and punishment).

social learning theory

The view that people learn to be aggressive by observing others acting aggressively to achieve some goal or being rewarded for violent acts.

Behavior theory maintains that human actions are developed through learning experiences. The major premise of behavior theory is that people alter their behavior according to the reactions it receives from others: Behavior is supported by rewards and extinguished by negative reactions or punishments. The behaviorist views crimes, especially violent acts, as learned responses to life situations that do not necessarily represent abnormality or moral immaturity.

The branch of behavior theory most relevant to criminology is **social learning theory**.[112] Social learning theorists, most notably Albert Bandura, argue that people are not actually born with the ability to act violently, but that they learn to be aggressive through their life experiences. These experiences include personally observing others acting aggressively to achieve some goal or watching people being rewarded for violent acts on television or in movies. People learn to act aggressively when, as children, they model their behavior after the violent acts of adults. Later in life, these violent behavior patterns persist in social relationships. For example, the boy who sees his father repeatedly strike his mother with impunity is likely to become a battering parent and husband.

Although social learning theorists agree that mental or physical traits may predispose a person toward violence, they believe that a person's violent tendencies are activated by factors in the environment. The specific form of aggressive behavior, the frequency with which it is expressed, the situations in which it is displayed, and the specific targets selected for attack are largely determined by social learning. However, people are also self-aware and engage in purposeful learning. Their interpretations of behavior outcomes and situations influence the way they learn from experiences. One adolescent who spends a weekend in jail for drunk driving may find it the most awful experience of her life—one that teaches her never to drink and drive again. Another person, however, may find it an exciting experience about which he can brag to his friends.

Social learning theorists view violence as something learned through a process called **behavior modeling**. In modern society, aggressive acts are usually modeled after three principal sources:

1. *Family interaction.* Studies of family life show that aggressive children have parents who use similar tactics when dealing with others.

2. *Environmental experiences.* People who reside in areas where violence occurs daily are more likely to act violently than those who dwell in low-crime areas whose norms stress conventional behavior.

3. *Mass media.* Films and television shows commonly depict violence graphically. Moreover, violence is often portrayed as acceptable, especially for heroes who never have to face legal consequences for their actions.[113] Viewing violence is believed to influence behavior in a number of ways, summarized in Table 5.2.

behavior modeling

Process of learning behavior (notably aggression) by observing others. Aggressive models may be parents, criminals in the neighborhood, or characters on television or in movies.

Table 5.2 How the Media Influence Violence

- Media violence can provide aggressive scripts that children store in memory. Repeated exposure to these scripts can increase their retention and change attitudes.
- Children learn from what they observe. In the same way they learn cognitive and social skills from their parents and friends, children learn to be violent by watching television.
- Television violence increases the arousal levels of viewers and makes them more prone to act aggressively. Studies measuring the galvanic skin response of subjects—a physical indication of arousal based on the amount of electricity conducted across the palm of the hand—show that viewing violent television shows increases arousal levels in young children.
- Watching television violence promotes negative attitudes such as suspiciousness and the expectation that the viewer will become involved in violence. Those who watch television frequently view aggression and violence as common, socially acceptable behavior.
- Television violence allows aggressive youths to justify their behavior. Rather than causing violence, television may help violent youths rationalize their behavior as socially acceptable.
- Television violence may disinhibit aggressive behavior, which is normally controlled by other learning processes. Disinhibition takes place when adults are viewed as being rewarded for violence and when violence is seen as socially acceptable. This contradicts previous learning experiences in which violent behavior was viewed as wrong.

Sources: UCLA Center for Communication Policy, *Television Violence Monitoring Project* (Los Angeles, 1995); Jonathan Freedman, "Television Violence and Aggression: A Rejoinder," *Psychological Bulletin* 100 (1986): 372–378; Wendy Wood, Frank Wong, and J. Gregory Chachere, "Effects of Media Violence on Viewers' Aggression in Unconstrained Social Interaction," *Psychological Bulletin* 109 (1991): 371–383.

Social learning theorists have tried to determine what triggers violent acts. One position is that a direct, pain-producing, physical assault will usually trigger a violent response. Yet the relationship between painful attacks and aggressive responses has been found to be inconsistent. Whether people counterattack depends, in part, on their fighting skill and their perception of the strength of their attackers. Verbal taunts and insults have also been linked to aggressive responses. People who are predisposed to aggression by their learning experiences are likely to view insults from others as a challenge to their social status and to react violently.

Still another violence-triggering mechanism is a perceived reduction in one's life conditions. Prime examples of this phenomenon are riots and demonstrations in poverty-stricken inner-city areas. Studies have shown that discontent also produces aggression in the more successful members of lower-class groups, who have been led to believe they can succeed but then have been thwarted in their aspirations. Although it is still uncertain how this relationship is constructed, it is apparently complex. No matter how deprived some individuals are, they will not resort to violence. People's perceptions of their relative deprivation have different effects on their aggressive responses.

In summary, social learning theorists suggest that the following four factors may contribute to violent or aggressive behavior:

1. An event that heightens arousal—such as a person's frustrating or provoking another through physical assault or verbal abuse.

2. Aggressive skills—learned aggressive responses picked up from observing others, either personally or through the media.

3. Expected outcomes—the belief that aggression will somehow be rewarded. Rewards can come in the form of reducing tension or anger, gaining some financial reward, building self-esteem, or gaining the praise of others.

4. Consistency of behavior with values—the belief, gained from observing others, that aggression is justified and appropriate, given the circumstances of the current situation.

Cognitive Theory

cognitive theory

Psychological perspective that focuses on mental processes: how people perceive and mentally represent the world around them and solve problems.

information-processing theory

Theory that focuses on how people process, store, encode, retrieve, and manipulate information to make decisions and solve problems.

One area of psychology that has received increasing recognition in recent years is **cognitive theory**. Psychologists with a cognitive perspective focus on mental processes—how people perceive and mentally represent the world around them and solve problems. The pioneers of this school were Wilhelm Wundt (1832–1920), Edward Titchener (1867–1927), and William James (1842–1920). Today the cognitive area includes several subdisciplines. The moral development branch is concerned with how people morally represent and reason about the world. Humanistic psychology stresses self-awareness and getting in touch with feelings. **Information-processing theory** focuses on how people process, store, encode, retrieve, and manipulate information to make decisions and solve problems.

When cognitive theorists who study information processing try to explain antisocial behavior, they do so in terms of mental perception and how people use information to understand their environment. When people make decisions, they engage in a sequence of cognitive thought processes:

1. First, they encode information so that it can be interpreted.

2. Next, they search for a proper response and decide on the most appropriate action.

3. Finally, they act on their decision.[114]

According to this cognitive approach, people who use information properly, who are better conditioned to make reasoned judgments, and who can make quick and reasoned decisions when facing emotion-laden events are best able to avoid antisocial behavior choices.[115] In contrast, violence-prone people may use information incorrectly when they make decisions. One reason is that they may be relying on mental scripts learned in childhood that tell them how to interpret events, what to expect, how they should react, and what the outcome of the interaction should be.[116] Hostile children may have learned improper scripts by observing how others react to events; their own parents' aggressive, inappropriate behavior would have considerable impact. Some may have had early, prolonged exposure to violence (such as child abuse), which increases their sensitivity to slights and maltreatment. Oversensitivity to rejection by their peers is a continuation of sensitivity to rejection by their parents.[117] Violence becomes a stable behavior because the scripts that emphasize aggressive responses are repeatedly rehearsed as the child matures.

Information-processing theory has been used to explain the occurrence of date rape. Sexually violent males believe that when their dates refuse sexual advances, the women are really playing games and actually want to be taken forcefully.[118]

Personality and Crime

personality

The reasonably stable patterns of behavior, including thoughts and emotions, that distinguish one person from another.

Personality can be defined as the reasonably stable patterns of behavior, including thoughts and emotions, that distinguish one person from another.[119] One's personality reflects a characteristic way of adapting to life's demands and problems. The way we behave is a function of how our personality enables us to interpret life events and make appropriate behavioral choices. Can the cause of crime be linked to personality?

Several research efforts have attempted to identify criminal personality traits.[120] Suspected traits include impulsivity, hostility, and aggression.[121] For example, Hans Eysenck associates two personality traits with antisocial behavior: extraversion-introversion and stability-instability. Extreme introverts are overaroused and avoid sources of stimulation; extreme extroverts are underaroused and seek sensation. Introverts are slow to learn and be conditioned; extroverts are impulsive individuals who lack the ability to examine their own motives and behaviors. Those who are unstable, a condition that Eysenck calls neuroticism, are anxious, tense, and emotionally unstable.[122] People who are both neurotic and extroverted lack self-insight and are impulsive and emotionally unstable; they are unlikely to have reasoned judgments of life events. Whereas extroverted neurotics may act self-destructively, for example, by abusing drugs, more stable people will be able to reason that such behavior is ultimately harmful. Eysenck believes that personality is controlled by genetic factors and is heritable.

A number of other personality deficits have been identified in the criminal population. A common theme is that criminals are hyperactive, impulsive individuals with short attention spans (attention deficit disorder), conduct disorders, anxiety disorders, and depression.[123] They lack affect, cannot empathize with others, and are short-sighted and hedonistic. These traits make them prone to problems ranging from psychopathology to drug abuse, sexual promiscuity, and violence.[124] As a group, people who share these traits are believed to have a character defect referred to as sociopathic, psychopathic, or **antisocial personality**. Although these terms are often used interchangeably, some psychologists distinguish between sociopaths and psychopaths by suggesting that the former are a product of a destructive home environment, whereas the latter are a product of a defect or aberration within themselves.[125]

Studies of the antisocial personality have been conducted worldwide.[126] There is evidence that offenders with an antisocial personality are crime-prone,

antisocial personality

Combination of traits, such as hyperactivity, impulsivity, hedonism, and inability to empathize with others, that make a person prone to deviant behavior and violence; also referred to as sociopathic or psychopathic personality.

Find It on INFOTRAC
College Edition

Some psychologists believe that the psychopath's extreme lack of empathy is caused by an impaired ability to process emotion-rich information in the brain. To research this issue, use "psychopath" as a subject guide in InfoTrac College Edition.

respond to frustrating events with strong negative emotions, feel stressed and harassed, and are adversarial in their interpersonal relationships. They maintain "negative emotionality"—a tendency to experience aversive affective states such as anger, anxiety, and irritability. They also are predisposed to weak personal constraints and have difficulty controlling impulsive behavior urges. Because they are both impulsive and aggressive, crime-prone people are quick to act against perceived threats.

Evidence that personality traits predict crime and violence suggests that the root cause of crime can be found in the forces that influence early human development. If these results are valid, rather than focus on job creation and neighborhood improvement, crime control efforts might be better focused on helping families raise reasoned, reflective children who enjoy a safe environment.

Intelligence and Crime

Early criminologists maintained that many delinquents and criminals have below-average intelligence and that low IQ causes their criminality. Criminals were believed to have inherently substandard intelligence and thus seemed naturally inclined to commit more crimes than more intelligent persons. Furthermore, it was thought that if authorities could determine which individuals had low IQs, they might identify potential criminals before they committed socially harmful acts. These ideas led to the nature-versus-nurture controversy that continues to rage today.

nature theory

The view that intelligence is largely determined genetically and that low intelligence is linked to criminal behavior.

Nature Theory Proponents of **nature theory** argue that intelligence is largely determined genetically, that ancestry determines IQ, and that low intelligence, as demonstrated by low IQ, is linked to criminal behavior. When newly developed IQ tests were administered to inmates of prisons and juvenile training schools in the first decades of the twentieth century, the nature position gained support because most of the inmates scored low on the tests.[127] In 1926, William Healy and Augusta Bronner tested groups of delinquent boys in Chicago and Boston and found that 37 percent were subnormal in intelligence. They concluded that delinquents were 5 to 10 times more likely to be mentally deficient than normal boys.[128] These and other early studies were embraced as proof that low IQ scores indicated potentially delinquent children and that a correlation existed between innate low intelligence and deviant behavior. IQ tests were believed to measure the inborn genetic makeup of individuals, and many criminologists accepted the idea that individuals with substandard IQs were predisposed toward delinquency and adult criminality.

nurture theory

The view that intelligence is not inherited, but is largely a product of environment. Low IQ scores do not cause crime, but may result from the same environmental factors.

Nurture Theory Proponents of **nurture theory** argue that intelligence is not inherited and that low-IQ parents do not necessarily produce low-IQ children.[129] Intelligence must be viewed as partly biological but primarily sociological. Nurture theorists discredit the notion that persons commit crimes because they have low IQs. Instead, they postulate that environmental stimulation from parents, relatives, social contacts, schools, peer groups, and innumerable others account for a child's IQ level and that low IQs may result from an environment that also encourages delinquent and criminal behavior. Thus, if low IQ scores are recorded among criminals, these scores may reflect the criminals' cultural background, not their mental ability.

In 1931, Edwin Sutherland evaluated IQ studies of criminals and delinquents and questioned whether criminals in fact have low IQs.[130] Sutherland's research all but put an end to the belief that crime was caused by feeblemindedness; the IQ–crime link was almost forgotten in criminological literature.

IQ and Criminality Although the alleged IQ–crime link was dismissed by mainstream criminologists, it once again became an important area of study when respected criminologists Travis Hirschi and Michael Hindelang published a widely read 1977 article linking the two variables.[131] They proposed the idea that low IQ increases the likelihood of criminal behavior through its effect on school performance. That is, youths with low IQs do poorly in school, and school failure and academic incompetence are highly related to delinquency and later to adult criminality.

Hirschi and Hindelang's inferences have been supported by both U.S. and international research.[132] In their influential book *Crime and Human Nature*, James Q. Wilson and Richard Herrnstein also agreed that the IQ–crime link is indirect: Low intelligence leads to poor school performance, which enhances the chances of criminality.[133] They conclude, "A child who chronically loses standing in the competition of the classroom may feel justified in settling the score outside, by violence, theft, and other forms of defiant illegality."[134]

IQ and Crime Reconsidered In their controversial 1994 book, *The Bell Curve*, Richard Herrnstein and Charles Murray firmly advocate an IQ–crime link. Their extensive review of the available literature shows that adolescents with low IQs are more likely to commit crime, get caught, and be sent to prison. Conversely, at-risk kids with higher IQs seem to be protected from becoming criminals by their superior ability to succeed in school and in social relationships. Herrnstein and Murray conclude that criminal offenders have an average IQ of 92, about 8 points below the mean; chronic offenders score even lower than the average criminal. To those who suggest that the IQ–crime relationship can be explained by the fact that only low-IQ criminals get caught, they counter with data showing little difference in IQ scores between self-reported and official criminals.[135] This means that even criminals whose activities go undetected have lower IQs than the general public; the IQ–crime relationship cannot be explained away by the fact that slow-witted criminals are the ones most likely to be apprehended.

Although Herrnstein and Murray's review of the literature was extensive, a number of recent studies have found that IQ has negligible influence on criminal behavior.[136] Also, a recent evaluation of research on intelligence conducted by the American Psychological Association concludes that the strength of an IQ–crime link is "very low."[137]

It is unlikely that the IQ–criminality debate will be settled soon. Measurement is beset by many methodological problems. The well-documented criticisms suggesting that IQ tests are race- and class-biased would certainly influence the testing of the criminal population, which is besieged with a multitude of social and economic problems. Even if it can be shown that known offenders have lower IQs than the general population, it is difficult to explain many patterns in the crime rate: Why are there more male than female criminals? Why do crime rates vary by region, time of year, and even weather patterns? Why does aging out occur? IQ does not increase with age, so why should crime rates fall? ✔ Checkpoints

✔ Checkpoints

✔ According to psychodynamic theory, unconscious motivations developed early in childhood propel some people into destructive or illegal behavior.

✔ Behaviorists view aggression as a learned behavior.

✔ Learning may be either direct and experiential or observational, such as watching TV and movies.

✔ Cognitive theory stresses knowing and perception. Some people have a warped view of the world.

✔ There is evidence that people with abnormal or antisocial personalities are crime-prone.

✔ While some criminologists find a link between intelligence and crime, others dispute any linkage between IQ level and law-violating behaviors.

Social Policy Implications

For most of the twentieth century, biological and psychological views of criminality have influenced crime control and prevention policy. The result has been front-end or **primary prevention programs** that seek to treat personal problems before they manifest themselves as crime. To this end, thousands of family therapy organizations, substance abuse clinics, and mental health associations operate throughout the United States. Teachers, employers, courts, welfare agencies, and others make referrals to these facilities. These services are based on the premise that if

primary prevention programs

Programs, such as substance abuse clinics and mental health associations, that seek to treat personal problems before they manifest themselves as crime.

secondary prevention programs

Programs that provide treatment such as psychological counseling to youths and adults after they have violated the law.

a person's problems can be treated before they become overwhelming, some future crimes will be prevented. **Secondary prevention programs** provide treatment such as psychological counseling to youths and adults after they have violated the law. Attendance at such programs may be a requirement of a probation order, part of a diversionary sentence, or aftercare at the end of a prison sentence.

Biologically oriented therapy is also being used in the criminal justice system. Programs have altered diets, changed lighting, compensated for learning disabilities, treated allergies, and so on.[138] More controversial has been the use of mood-altering chemicals, such as lithium, pemoline, imipramine, phenytoin, and benzodiazepines, to control behavior. Another practice that has elicited concern is the use of psychosurgery (brain surgery) to control antisocial behavior. Surgical procedures have been used to alter the brain structure of convicted sex offenders in an effort to eliminate or control their sex drives. Results are still preliminary, but some critics argue that these procedures are without scientific merit.[139]

Numerous psychologically based treatment methods range from individual counseling to behavior modification. For example, treatment based on how people process information takes into account that people are more likely to respond aggressively to provocation if thoughts intensify the insult or otherwise stir feelings of anger. Cognitive therapists attempt to teach explosive people to control aggressive impulses by viewing social provocations as problems demanding a solution rather than retaliation. Programs are aimed at teaching problem-solving skills that may include self-disclosure, role-playing, listening, following instructions, joining in, and using self-control.[140] Therapeutic interventions designed to make people better problem solvers may involve measures that enhance

- Coping and problem-solving skills
- Relationships with peers, parents, and other adults
- Conflict resolution and communication skills, and methods for resisting peer pressure related to drug use and violence
- Consequential thinking and decision-making abilities
- Prosocial behaviors, including cooperation with others, self-responsibility, respecting others, and public speaking efficacy
- Empathy[141]

Summary

The earliest positivist criminologists were biologists. Led by Cesare Lombroso, these early researchers believed that some people manifested primitive traits that made them born criminals. Today their research is debunked because of poor methodology, testing, and logic.

Biological views fell out of favor in the early twentieth century. In the 1970s, spurred by the publication of Edmund O. Wilson's *Sociobiology,* several criminologists again turned to study of the biological basis of criminality. For the most part, the effort has focused on the cause of violent crime. Interest has centered on several areas: (1) biochemical factors, such as diet, allergies, hormonal imbalances, and environmental contaminants (such as lead); (2) neurophysiological factors, such as brain disorders, EEG abnormalities, tumors, and head injuries; and (3) genetic factors, such as the XYY syndrome and inherited traits. An evolutionary branch holds that changes in the human condition, which have taken millions of years to evolve, may help explain crime rate differences.

Table 5.3 Biological and Psychological Theories

THEORY	MAJOR PREMISE	STRENGTHS
Biosocial		
Biochemical	Crime, especially violence, is a function of diet, vitamin intake, hormonal imbalance, or food allergies.	Explains irrational violence. Shows how the environment interacts with personal traits to influence behavior.
Neurological	Criminals and delinquents often suffer brain impairment, as measured by the EEG. Attention deficit/hyperactivity disorder and minimal brain dysfunction are related to antisocial behavior.	Explains irrational violence. Shows how the environment interacts with personal traits to influence behavior.
Genetic	Criminal traits and predispositions are inherited. The criminality of parents can predict the delinquency of children.	Explains why only a small percentage of youth in a high-crime area become chronic offenders.
Evolutionary	As the human race evolved, traits and characteristics have become ingrained. Some of these traits make people aggressive and predisposed to commit crime.	Explains high violence rates and aggregate gender differences in the crime rate.
Psychological		
Psychodynamic	The development of the unconscious personality early in childhood influences behavior for the rest of a person's life. Criminals have weak egos and damaged personalities.	Explains the onset of crime and why crime and drug abuse cut across class lines.
Behavioral	People commit crime when they model their behavior after others they see being rewarded for the same acts. Behavior is reinforced by rewards and extinguished by punishment.	Explains the role of significant others in the crime process. Shows how family life and media can influence crime and violence.
Cognitive	Individual reasoning processes influence behavior. Reasoning is influenced by the way people perceive their environment.	Shows why criminal behavior patterns change over time as people mature and develop their reasoning powers. May explain the aging-out process.

Psychological attempts to explain criminal behavior have historical roots in the concept that all criminals are insane or mentally damaged. This position is no longer accepted. Today there are three main psychological perspectives: the psychodynamic view, the cognitive view, and the social learning perspective. The psychodynamic view, developed by Sigmund Freud, links aggressive behavior to personality conflicts arising from childhood. According to some psychoanalysts, psychotics are aggressive, unstable people who can easily become involved in crime. Cognitive psychology is concerned with human development and how people perceive the world. Criminality is viewed as a function of improper information processing. Behavioral and social learning theorists see criminality as a learned behavior. Children who are exposed to violence and see it rewarded may become violent as adults.

Psychological traits such as personality and intelligence have been linked to criminality. One important area of study has been the antisocial personality, a person who lacks emotion and concern for others. The controversial issue of the relationship of IQ to criminality has been resurrected once again with the publication of research studies purporting to show that criminals have lower IQs than noncriminals.

Table 5.3 summarizes the biological and psychological trait theories discussed in this chapter.

For additional chapter links, discussions, and quizzes, see the book-specific Web site at http://www.wadsworth.com/product/0534519423s.

Thinking Like a Criminologist

The American Psychiatric Association believes that a person should not be held legally responsible for a crime if the person's behavior meets the following standard developed by legal expert Richard Bonnie:

> A person charged with a criminal offense should be found not guilty by reason of insanity if it is shown that as a result of mental disease or mental retardation he was unable to appreciate the wrongfulness of his conduct at the time of the offense.
>
> As used in this standard, the terms *mental disease* or *mental retardation* include only those severely abnormal mental conditions that grossly and demonstrably impair a person's perception or understanding of reality and that are not attributable primarily to the voluntary ingestion of alcohol or other psychoactive substances.

As a criminologist who has expertise in trait theories of crime, do you agree with Bonnie's standard? What modifications, if any, might you make in order to include other categories of offenders who are not excused by this definition?

Key Terms

trait theory	monozygotic (MZ) twins	behavior theory
sociobiology	dizygotic (DZ) twins	social learning theory
equipotentiality	cheater theory	behavior modeling
hypoglycemia	psychodynamic (psychoanalytic)	cognitive theory
androgens	id	information-processing theory
testosterone	ego	personality
premenstrual syndrome (PMS)	superego	antisocial personality
neurophysiology	neurotic	nature theory
minimal brain dysfunction (MBD)	psychotic	nurture theory
attention deficit/hyperactivity disorder (ADHD)	disorder	primary prevention programs
	schizophrenia	secondary prevention programs
neurotransmitters	latent delinquincy	
arousal theory	bipolar disorder	

Discussion Questions

1. If research could show that the tendency to commit crime is inherited, what should be done with the young children of violence-prone criminals?

2. Would you recommend that young children be forbidden to view films with violent content?

3. Knowing what you do about trends and patterns in crime, how would you counteract the assertion that people who commit crime are physically or mentally abnormal?

4. Aside from becoming a criminal, what other career paths are open to psychopaths?

6 Social Structure Theory: Because They're Poor

On December 2, 2000, London police officers arrested three people who had been accused of stabbing to death a 10-year-old schoolboy named Damilola Taylor. The murder created a tremendous uproar in England, not only because of the age of the victim but also because two of those accused of the crime were 13 years old.

Taylor had immigrated from Nigeria with his mother and siblings in order to get medical care for his sister. The family was housed by local authorities in a run-down housing estate in Peckham, South London, which has been described as one of the toughest areas in Europe. London authorities attributed the violence to decades of underinvestment in housing, local government mismanagement, and a failure to confront bullying in schools. Local newspapers ran editorials claiming that immigrants to Britain often face worse racism and live in areas with social disintegration as dangerous as anything they may have left behind.[1]

The killing of Damilola Taylor substantiates the belief of many criminologists that crime and violence are endemic in poor, deteriorated neighborhoods. Because these neighborhoods have substantially higher crime rates than more affluent areas, the majority of criminologists believe it would be a mistake to ignore social and environmental factors in trying to understand the cause of criminal behavior.[2] Most criminals are indigent and desperate, not calculating or evil. Many were raised in deteriorated parts of town and lack the social support and economic resources familiar to more affluent members of society. Understanding criminal behavior, then, requires analyzing the influence of these destructive social forces on human behavior.

Criminologists have long attempted to discover why certain neighborhoods and geographic locations are more prone to criminal activity than others. Explanations of crime as an individual-level phenomenon, with its locus in either destructive personal choices or deviant traits, fail to account for these consistent crime rate patterns. If violence, as some criminologists suggest, is related to chemical or chromosome abnormality, then how can ecological differences in crime rates be explained? It is unlikely that all people with physical anomalies live in one section of town or in one area of the country. There has been a heated national debate over the effects of violent TV shows on adolescent aggression. Yet adolescents in cities and towns with widely disparate crime rates may all watch the same shows and movies; so how can crime rate differences in these areas be explained? If violence has a biological or psychological origin, should it not be distributed more evenly throughout the social structure rather than concentrated in certain areas?

Because of these issues, many criminologists believe that understanding the dynamics of interactions between individuals and important social institutions, such as families, peers, schools, jobs, and criminal justice agencies, is important for understanding the cause of crime.[3] The relationship of one social class or group to another or to the power structure that controls the nation's legal and economic system may also be closely related to criminality. It seems logical that people on the lowest rung of the economic ladder will have the greatest incentive to commit crime. They may be either enraged by their lack of economic success or simply financially desperate and disillusioned. In either case, crime, despite its inherent dangers, may be an attractive alternative to a life of indigence.

CONNECTIONS

Concern about the ecological distribution of crime, the effect of social change, and the interactive nature of crime itself has made sociology the foundation of modern criminology. This chapter reviews sociological theories that emphasize the relationship between social status and criminal behavior. In Chapter 7 the focus shifts to theories that emphasize socialization and its influence on crime and deviance; Chapter 8 covers theories based on the concept of social conflict.

Economic Structure and Crime

stratified

Grouped according to economic or social class; characterized by the unequal distribution of wealth, power, and prestige.

social class

Segment of the population whose members are at a relatively similar economic level and who share attitudes, values, norms, and an identifiable lifestyle.

People in the United States live in a **stratified** society. Social strata are created by unequal distribution of wealth, power, and prestige. **Social classes** are segments of the population whose members have a relatively similar portion of desirable things and who share attitudes, values, norms, and an identifiable lifestyle. In U.S. society, it is common to identify people as upper, middle, or lower class, with a broad range of economic variations within each group. The upper-upper class consists of a small number of exceptionally well-to-do families who control enormous financial and social resources. In contrast, the indigent have scant, if any, resources and suffer socially and economically as a result. Although the proportion of indigent Americans has been declining, about 13.3 percent, or 30 million people, still live below the poverty line, defined as a little more than $16,000 annually for a family of four and $12,800 for a family of three. Moreover, the government's definition of poverty seems understated. A more realistic figure of $18,000 annually for a family of three would mean that more than 50 million U.S. citizens live in poverty.[4]

Children are hit especially hard by poverty. Hundreds of studies have documented the association between family poverty and children's health, achievement, and behavior impairments.[5] Children who grow up in low-income homes are less likely to achieve in school and are less likely to complete their schooling than children with more affluent parents.[6] Poor children are also more likely to suffer from health problems and to receive inadequate health care. The number of U.S. children covered by health insurance is declining and will continue to do so for the foreseeable future.[7] Without health benefits or the means to afford medical care, these children are likely to have health problems that impede their long-term development. Children who live in extreme poverty or who remain poor for multiple years appear to suffer the worst outcomes. The timing of poverty also seems to be relevant. Findings suggest that poverty during early childhood may have a more severe impact than poverty during adolescence.[8]

Besides their increased chance of physical illness, poor children are much more likely than wealthy children to suffer various social and physical ills, ranging from low birth weight to a limited chance of earning a college degree. The social problems found in lower-class slum areas have been described as an "epidemic" that spreads like a contagious disease, destroying the inner workings that enable neighborhoods to survive; they become "hollowed out."[9] As neighborhood quality decreases, the probability that residents will develop problems sharply increases. Adolescents in the worst neighborhoods have the greatest risks of dropping out of school and of becoming teenage parents.

The rates of child poverty in the United States vary significantly by race and ethnicity. Hispanic and African American children are more than twice as likely to be poor as Asian and European American children.

Lower-Class Culture

Lower-class areas are scenes of inadequate housing and health care, disrupted family lives, underemployment, and despair. Members of the lower class also suffer in other ways. They are more prone to depression, less likely to have achievement motivation, and less likely to put off immediate gratification for future gain. For example, they may be less willing to stay in school because the rewards for educational achievement are in the distant future. Some are driven to desperate measures to cope with their economic plight.

Members of the lower class are constantly bombarded by advertisements linking material possessions to self-worth, but they are often unable to attain desired goods and services through conventional means. Although they are members of a society that extols material success above any other form, they are unable to satisfactorily compete for such success with members of the

Race, Culture, Gender, and Criminology

When Work Disappears

In 1987, William Julius Wilson provided a description of the plight of the lowest levels of the underclass, which he labeled the **truly disadvantaged**. Wilson portrayed members of this group as socially isolated people who dwell in urban inner cities, occupy the bottom rung of the social ladder, and are the victims of discrimination. They live in areas in which the basic institutions of society—family, school, housing—have long since declined. Their decline triggers similar breakdowns in the strengths of inner-city areas, including a loss of community cohesion and the ability of people living in the area to control the flow of drugs and criminal activity. For example, in a more affluent area, neighbors might complain to parents that their children were acting out. In distressed areas, this element of informal social control may be absent because parents are under stress or all too often absent. These effects magnify the isolation of the underclass from mainstream society and promote a ghetto culture and behavior.

Since the truly disadvantaged rarely come into contact with the actual source of their oppression, they direct their anger and aggression at those with whom they are in close and intimate contact, such as neighbors, businesspeople, and landlords. Members of this group, plagued by under- or unemployment, begin to lose self-confidence, a feeling supported by the plight of kin and friendship groups who also experience extreme economic marginality. Self-doubt is a neighborhood norm, overwhelming those forced to live in areas of concentrated poverty.

In one of his more recent works, *When Work Disappears,* Wilson assesses the effect of joblessness and underemployment on residents of poor neighborhoods on Chicago's South Side. He reports that at the end of the twentieth century, most adults in inner-city ghetto neighborhoods are not working during a typical week. He finds inner-city life only marginally affected by the surge in the nation's economy, which has been

brought about by new industrial growth connected with technological development. Poverty in these inner-city areas is eternal and unchanging and, if anything, worsening as residents are further shut out of the economic mainstream.

Wilson focuses on the plight of the African American community, which had enjoyed periods of relative prosperity in the 1950s and 1960s. He suggests that as difficult as life was in the 1940s and 1950s for African Americans, they at least had a reasonable hope of steady work. Now, because of the globalization of the economy, those opportunities have evaporated. Though in the past racial segregation had limited opportunity, growth in the manufacturing sector fueled upward mobility and provided the foundation for today's African American middle class. Those opportunities no longer exist, as manufacturing plants have moved to nonaccessible rural and overseas locations where the cost of doing business is lower. With manufacturing opportuni-

---

truly disadvantaged

The lowest level of the underclass; urban, inner-city, socially isolated people who occupy the bottom rung of the social ladder and are the victims of discrimination.

culture of poverty

A separate lower-class culture, characterized by apathy, cynicism, helplessness, and mistrust of social institutions such as schools, government agencies, and the police, that is passed from one generation to the next.

underclass

The lowest social stratum in any country, whose members lack the education and skills needed to function successfully in modern society.

upper classes. As a result, they may turn to illegal solutions to their economic plight. They may deal drugs for profit or steal cars and sell them to chop shops; they may even commit armed robberies for desperately needed funds. They may become so depressed that they take alcohol and drugs as a form of self-tranquilization; because of their poverty, they acquire the drugs and alcohol through illegal channels.

In 1966 sociologist Oscar Lewis argued that the crushing lifestyle of slum areas produces a **culture of poverty** passed from one generation to the next.[10] Apathy, cynicism, helplessness, and mistrust of social institutions, such as schools, government agencies, and the police, mark the culture of poverty. This mistrust prevents slum-dwellers from taking advantage of the meager opportunities available to them. Lewis's work was the first of a group of studies that described the plight of at-risk children and adults. In 1970 Swedish economist Gunnar Myrdal described a worldwide **underclass** that was cut off from society, its members lacking the education and skills needed to function successfully in modern society.[11]

The burdens of underclass life are most often felt by minority group members. Although poverty has actually been declining faster among minorities than among European Americans, about 26 percent of African Americans and 27 percent of Hispanic Americans still live in poverty, compared to about 9 percent of European Americans. According to the U.S. Census Bureau, the median family income of Hispanic and African Americans is only two-thirds that of European Americans.[12]

ties all but obsolete in the United States, service and retail establishments that depended on blue-collar spending have similarly disappeared, leaving behind an economy based on welfare and government supports. In less than 20 years, formerly active African American communities have become crime-infested slums.

The hardships faced by residents of Chicago's South Side are not unique to that community. Beyond sustaining inner-city poverty, the absence of employment opportunities has torn at the social fabric of the nation's inner-city neighborhoods. Work helps socialize young people into the wider society, instilling in them such desirable values as hard work, caring, and respect for others. When work becomes scarce, however, the discipline and structure it provides are absent. Community-wide underemployment destroys social cohesion, increasing the presence of neighborhood social problems ranging from drug use to educational failure. Schools in these areas are unable to teach basic skills. Because desirable employment is lacking, few adult role

models are available. In contrast to more affluent suburban households, where daily life is organized around job and career demands, children in inner-city areas are not socialized in the workings of the mainstream economy.

Wilson is not optimistic about the job prospects of lower-class African American males; neither white nor black employers seem particularly inclined to hire poor black men. He is skeptical that private employers will hire the poor as child care providers or in other service tasks even if given tax incentives to do so. Instead, Wilson believes that only a nationwide effort to improve schools, provide day care, and enhance public transportation can turn the inner-city around. A public works program modeled after those of the Great Depression may be needed to reverse the damage of inner-city unemployment. People want to work; they must be given the opportunity for legitimate and sustaining employment.

Critical Thinking

1. Is it unrealistic to assume that a government-sponsored public works

program can provide needed jobs in this era of budget cutbacks?

2. What are some of the hidden costs of unemployment in a community setting?

3. How would a biocriminologist explain Wilson's findings?

 InfoTrac College Edition Research

For more on Wilson's view of poverty, unemployment, and crime, check out Gunnar Almgren, Avery Guest, George Immerwahr, and Michael Spittel, "Joblessness, Family Disruption, and Violent Death in Chicago, 1970–90," *Social Forces* June 1998 v76 n4 p1465 William Julius Wilson, "Inner-City Dislocations," *Society,* January–February 1998 v35 n2 p270

SOURCES: William Julius Wilson, *The Truly Disadvantaged* (Chicago: University of Chicago Press, 1987); *When Work Disappears: The World of the Urban Poor* (New York: Alfred Knopf, 1996).

 Find It on INFOTRAC
College Edition

Did you know that although income per capita in the United States is among the world's highest, so is its rate of child poverty? To read more about this, use "poverty" and "children" as keywords in InfoTrac College Edition.

Economic disparity continually haunts members of the underclass and their children. Even if they value education and other middle-class norms, their desperate life circumstances (including high unemployment and nontraditional family structures) may prevent them from developing the skills, habits, and styles that lead first to educational success and later to success in the workplace. Both of these factors have been linked to crime and drug abuse.[13] These problems are exacerbated by the fact that in some jurisdictions, a significant portion—up to half—of all minority males are under criminal justice system control. The costs of crime, such as paying for lawyers and court costs, perpetuate poverty by depriving families and children of this money.[14]

Community effects may particularly damage children. Adolescents residing in areas of concentrated poverty are more likely to suffer in their cognitive development, sexual understanding, school attendance habits, and transition to employment.[15] Lack of education and family instability make them poor candidates for employment or for the eventual formation of their own cohesive families. These findings suggest that the poor of inner-city ghettos confront obstacles far greater than the mere lack of financial resources. The social problems faced by the poor render them unprepared to take advantage of employment opportunities even in tight labor markets.[16] The fact that many of the underclass are African American children who can expect to spend all their lives in poverty may be the single most important problem facing the United States today.[17] This issue is discussed further in the accompanying Race, Culture, Gender, and Criminology feature.

Social Structure Theories

social structure theory

The view that disadvantaged economic class position is a primary cause of crime.

social disorganization theory

Branch of social structure theory that focuses on the breakdown of institutions such as the family, school, and employment in inner-city neighborhoods.

strain theory

Branch of social structure theory that sees crime as a function of the conflict between people's goals and the means available to obtain them.

strain

The anger, frustration, and resentment experienced by people who believe they cannot achieve their goals through legitimate means.

cultural deviance theory

Branch of social structure theory that sees strain and social disorganization together resulting in a unique lower-class culture that conflicts with conventional social norms.

Many criminologists view disadvantaged economic class position as a primary cause of crime. This view is referred to as **social structure theory**. As a group, social structure theories suggest that social and economic forces operating in deteriorated lower-class areas push many of their residents into criminal behavior patterns. These theories consider the existence of unsupervised teenage gangs, high crime rates, and social disorder in slum areas as major social problems.

Lower-class crime is often the violent, destructive product of youth gangs and marginally employed or underemployed young adults. Underemployment means that many working adults earn relatively low wages and have few benefits such as health insurance and retirement programs. Their ability to accumulate capital for home ownership is restricted and so, consequently, is their stake in society.

Although members of the middle and upper classes also engage in crime, social structure theorists view middle-class and white-collar crime as being of relatively lower frequency, seriousness, and danger to the general public. The real crime problem is essentially a lower-class phenomenon that breeds criminal behavior, begins in youth, and continues into young adulthood. Because crime rates are higher in lower-class urban centers than in middle-class suburbs, social forces must influence or control behavior.[18] We will examine some specific structure theories that support this perspective.

The social structure perspective encompasses three independent yet overlapping branches: social disorganization theory, strain theory, and cultural deviance theory. These three branches are summarized in Figure 6.1.

Social disorganization theory focuses on the urban conditions that affect crime rates. A disorganized area is one in which institutions of social control, such as the family, commercial establishments, and schools, have broken down and can no longer perform their expected or stated functions. Indicators of social disorganization include high unemployment and school dropout rates, deteriorated housing, low income levels, and large numbers of single-parent households. Residents in these areas experience conflict and despair, and, as a result, antisocial behavior flourishes.

Strain theory holds that crime is a function of the conflict between people's goals and the means they can use to obtain them. Strain theorists argue that although social and economic goals are common to people in all

Figure 6.1

The Three Branches of Social Structure Theory

Social disorganization theory focuses on conditions in the environment:
- Deteriorated neighborhoods
- Inadequate social control
- Law-violating gangs and groups
- Conflicting social values

Strain theory focuses on conflict between goals and means:
- Unequal distribution of wealth and power
- Frustration
- Alternative methods of achievement

Cultural deviance theory combines the other two:
- Development of subcultures as a result of disorganization and stress
- Subcultural values in opposition to conventional values

CRIME

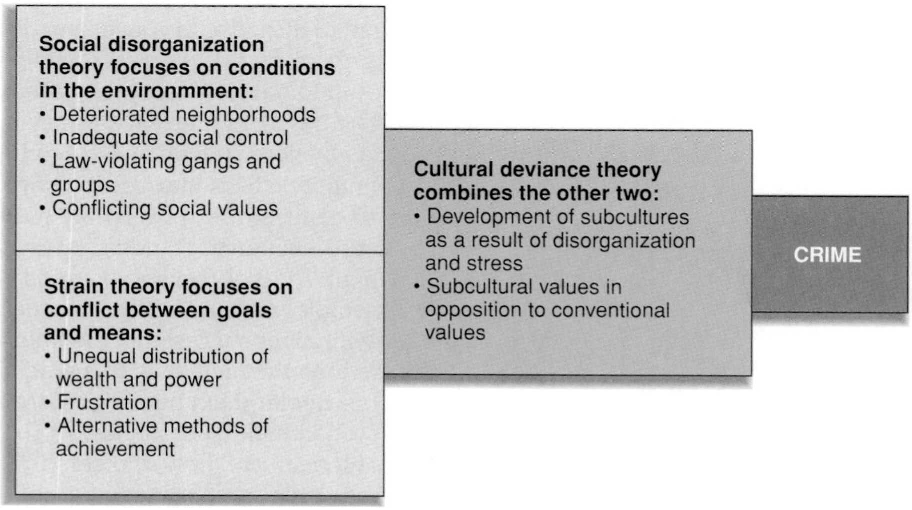

economic strata, the ability to obtain these goals is class-dependent. Most people in the United States desire wealth, material possessions, power, prestige, and other life comforts. Members of the lower class are unable to achieve these symbols of success through conventional means. Consequently, they feel anger, frustration, and resentment, referred to collectively as **strain**. Lower-class citizens can either accept their condition and live as socially responsible if unrewarded citizens, or they can choose an alternative means of achieving success, such as theft, violence, or drug trafficking.

Cultural deviance theory combines elements of both strain and social disorganization theories. According to this view, because of strain and social isolation, a unique lower-class culture develops in disorganized neighborhoods. These independent **subcultures** maintain unique values and beliefs that conflict with conventional social norms. Criminal behavior is an expression of conformity to lower-class subcultural values and traditions, not a rebellion from conventional society. Subcultural values are handed down from one generation to the next in a process called **cultural transmission**.

Although each of these theories is distinct in critical aspects, each approach has at its core the view that socially isolated people, living in disorganized neighborhoods, are likely to experience crime-producing social forces. In the remainder of this chapter, each branch of social structure theory will be discussed in some detail. ✔ Checkpoints

Social Disorganization Theory

subculture

A set of values, beliefs, and traditions unique to a particular social class or group within a larger society.

cultural transmission

Process whereby values, beliefs, and traditions are handed down from one generation to the next.

Social disorganization theory links crime rates to neighborhood ecological characteristics. Crime rates are elevated in highly transient, mixed-use (where residential and commercial property exist side by side), and changing neighborhoods in which the fabric of social life has become frayed. These localities are unable to provide essential services, such as education, health care, and proper housing, and, as a result, they experience significant levels of unemployment, single-parent families, and families on welfare.

Social disorganization theory views crime-ridden neighborhoods as those in which residents are trying to leave at the earliest opportunity. Residents are uninterested in community matters, so the common sources of control—the family, school, business community, social service agencies—are weak and disorganized. Personal relationships are strained because neighbors are constantly moving. Constant resident turnover weakens communications and blocks attempts at solving neighborhood problems or establishing common goals (see Figure 6.2).[19]

The Work of Shaw and McKay

transitional neighborhood

An area undergoing a shift in population and structure, usually from middle-class residential to lower-class mixed use.

Social disorganization theory was popularized by the work of two Chicago sociologists, Clifford R. Shaw and Henry McKay, who linked life in transitional slum areas to the inclination to commit crime. Shaw and McKay began their pioneering work on Chicago crime during the early 1920s while working as researchers for a state-supported social service agency.[20]

Shaw and McKay explained crime and delinquency within the context of the changing urban environment and ecological development of the city. They saw that Chicago had developed into distinct neighborhoods (natural areas), some affluent and others wracked by extreme poverty. These poverty-ridden **transitional neighborhoods** suffered high rates of population turnover and were incapable of inducing residents to remain and defend the neighborhoods against criminal groups.

In transitional areas, successive changes in the population composition, the disintegration of the traditional cultures, the diffusion of divergent cultural

Figure 6.2

Social Disorganization Theory

Poverty
- Development of isolated slums
- Lack of conventional social opportunities
- Racial and ethnic discrimination

Social disorganization
- Breakdown of social institutions and organizations such as school and family
- Lack of informal social control

Breakdown of social control
- Development of gangs, groups
- Peer group replaces family and social institutions

Criminal areas
- Neighborhood becomes crime-prone
- Stable pockets of delinquency develop
- Lack of external support and investment

Cultural transmission
Older youths pass norms (focal concerns) to younger generation, creating stable slum culture.

Criminal careers
Most youths "age out" of delinquency, marry, and raise families, but some remain in life of crime.

standards, and the gradual industrialization of the area dissolve neighborhood culture and organization. The continuity of conventional neighborhood traditions and institutions is broken, leaving children feeling displaced and without a strong or definitive set of values.

Concentric Zones Shaw and McKay identified the areas in Chicago that had excessive crime rates. They noted that distinct ecological areas had developed in the city, forming a series of nine concentric circles, or zones, and that there were stable and significant interzone differences in crime rates (see Figure 6.3). The areas of heaviest crime concentration appeared to be the transitional inner-city zones, where large numbers of foreign-born citizens had recently settled.[21] The zones farthest from the city's center had correspondingly lower crime rates.

Analysis of these data indicated a surprisingly stable pattern of criminal activity in the nine ecological zones over 65 years. Shaw and McKay concluded that in the transitional neighborhoods, multiple cultures and diverse values, both conventional and deviant, coexist. Children growing up in the street culture often find that adults who have adopted a deviant lifestyle (gamblers, pimps, drug dealers) are the most financially successful people in the neighborhood. Forced to choose between conventional and deviant lifestyles, many

Figure 6.3

Shaw and McKay's Concentric Zones Map of Chicago

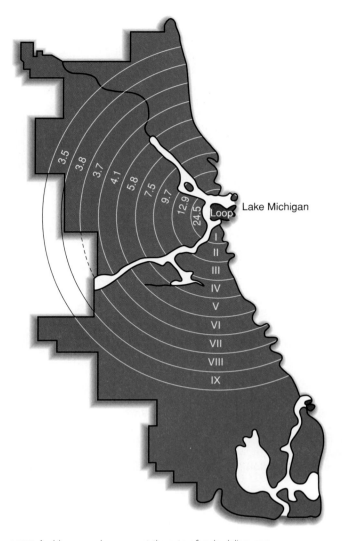

NOTE: Arabic numerals represent the rate of male delinquency.

SOURCE: Clifford R. Shaw et al., *Delinquency Areas* (Chicago: University of Chicago Press, 1929), p. 99. Reprinted with permission. Copyright 1929 by the University of Chicago. All rights reserved.

slum kids opt for the latter. They join other like-minded youths and form law-violating gangs and cliques. The development of teenage law-violating groups is an essential element of youthful misbehavior in slum areas. The values that slum youths adopt often conflict with existing middle-class norms, which demand strict obedience to the legal code. Consequently, a value conflict further separates the delinquent youth and his or her peer group from conventional society; the result is a more solid embrace of deviant goals and behavior. To further justify their choice of goals, these youths seek support for their choice by recruiting new members and passing on the delinquent tradition.

Shaw and McKay's statistical analysis confirmed that even though crime rates changed, the highest rates were always in zones I and II (the central city and a transitional area). The areas with the highest crime rates retained high rates even when their ethnic composition changed (the areas Shaw and McKay examined shifted from German and Irish to Italian and Polish).[22]

The Legacy of Shaw and McKay Social disorganization concepts articulated by Shaw and McKay have remained prominent within criminology for

When neighborhoods are under stress, people are reluctant to cooperate with the police, who they believe have little chance of controlling neighborhood disorder. Police may find it difficult to be effective crime fighters without community cooperation. Here, Chicago police officer Litty Mays hands out a flier in Chicago's greater Roseland neighborhood with a sketch of a suspect being sought in connection with a string of recent homicides on the city's South Side. The bodies of six women had been found in abandoned buildings in greater Roseland, leading police to fear a serial killer was at work in the neighborhood and prompting them to seek cooperation from local residents.

AP/Wide World Photos

more than 75 years. The most important of Shaw and McKay's findings were that crime rates correspond to neighborhood structure and that crime is created by the destructive ecological conditions in urban slums. They contended that criminals are not, as some criminologists of the time believed, biologically inferior, intellectually impaired, or psychologically damaged. Their research supported their belief that crime is a constant fixture in areas of poverty, regardless of residents' racial or ethnic identity. Because the basis of their theory was that neighborhood disintegration and slum conditions are the primary causes of criminal behavior, Shaw and McKay paved the way for many community action and treatment programs developed in the last half-century.

The Social Ecology School

During the 1970s, criminologists were influenced by several critical analyses of social disorganization theory that challenged its validity.[23] The criminological literature of the period was dominated by theories with a social-psychological orientation, stressing offender socialization within the family, school, and peer group.

In the 1980s, a group of criminologists continued studying ecological conditions, reviving concern about the effects of social disorganization.[24] These contemporary social ecologists developed a purer form of structural theory that emphasizes the association of community deterioration and economic decline with criminality but places less emphasis on value conflict. The following sections discuss some of the more recent social ecological research.

Community Disorganization Crime rates and the need for police services are associated with community deterioration: disorder, poverty, alienation, disassociation, and fear of crime.[25] Even in rural areas, which normally have low crime rates, increased levels of crime and violence are associated with indicators of social disorganization such as residential instability (a large number of people moving in and out), family disruption, and changing ethnic composition.[26]

In larger cities, neighborhoods with a high percentage of deserted houses and apartments experience high crime rates; abandoned buildings serve as a "magnet for crime."[27] Areas in which houses are in poor repair, boarded up, and burned out, whose owners are best described as slumlords, are also the location of the highest violence rates and gun crime.[28] These neighborhoods, in which retail establishments often go bankrupt, are abandoned and deteriorate physically.[29]

Poverty and Unemployment The percentage of people living in poverty and the percentage of broken homes are strongly related to neighborhood crime rates.[30] Violent crime rates are associated with such variables as the percentage of the neighborhood living below the poverty line, the lack of mortgage investment in a neighborhood, the unemployment rate, and the influx of new immigrants; these factors are usually found in disorganized areas.[31] The influence of these economic disadvantages is felt by both male and female residents. Though female crime rates may be lower than male rates, women living in deteriorated areas also feel the effects of poverty.[32]

Shaw and McKay claimed that areas continually wracked by poverty also experience social disorganization.[33] Research indicates that neighborhoods with few employment opportunities for youth and adults are the most vulnerable to predatory crime such as armed robbery and mugging.[34] Unemployment destabilizes households, and unstable families are likely to breed children who use violence and aggression to deal with limited opportunity. This lack of opportunity perpetuates higher crime rates, especially when large groups or cohorts of people of the same age compete for relatively scant resources.[35]

Limited employment opportunities also reduce the stabilizing influence of parents and other adults, who may once have counteracted the allure of youth gangs. Sociologist Elijah Anderson's analysis of Philadelphia neighborhood life found that "old heads" (respected neighborhood residents), who at one time played an important role in socializing youth, have been displaced by younger street hustlers and drug dealers. Although the old heads may complain that these newcomers have not earned or worked for their fortunes in the old-fashioned way, the old heads admire and envy these young people whose gold chains and luxury cars advertise their wealth amid poverty.[36] So while the old heads may disdain the violent manner in which they are acquired, they admire the fruits of crime.

Community Fear Disorganized neighborhoods suffer social and physical incivilities—rowdy youth, trash and litter, graffiti, abandoned storefronts, burned-out buildings, littered lots, strangers, drunks, vagabonds, loiterers, prostitutes, noise, congestion, angry words, dirt, and stench. The presence of such incivilities makes residents of disorganized areas believe that their neighborhood is dangerous and that they face a considerable chance of becoming crime victims. Therefore, when crime rates are actually high in these disorganized areas, fear levels increase dramatically.[37] Perceptions of crime and victimization produce neighborhood fear.[38]

Fear can be contagious. People tell others when they have been victimized, thus spreading the word that the neighborhood is getting dangerous and that the chance of future victimization is high.[39] As a result, people dread leaving their homes at night and withdraw from community life. Not surprisingly, people

CONNECTIONS

If social disorganization causes crime, why are most low-income people law-abiding? To explain this anomaly, some sociologists have devised theoretical models suggesting that individual socialization experiences mediate environmental influences. These theories will be discussed in Chapter 7.

who have already been victimized fear the future more than those who have escaped crime.[40]

Fear is a powerful influence. When it grips a neighborhood, business conditions begin to deteriorate, population mobility increases, and a "criminal element" begins to drift into the area.[41] In essence, the presence of fear incites more crime, increasing the chances of victimization and producing even more fear in a never-ending loop.[42]

Community Change Communities undergoing rapid structural changes in racial and economic composition also seem to experience the greatest change in crime rates. Recent studies recognize that change, not stability, is the hallmark of inner-city areas. A neighborhood's residents, wealth, density, and purpose are constantly evolving. Even disorganized neighborhoods acquire new identifying features. Some may become multiracial, while others become racially homogeneous. Some areas become stable and family-oriented, while in others, mobile, never-married people predominate.[43]

As areas decline, residents flee to safer, more stable locales. Those who cannot afford to leave for more affluent communities face an increased risk of victimization. Because of racial differences in economic well-being, those left behind are often minority citizens.[44] Those who cannot move find themselves surrounded by new residents. High population turnover can devastate community culture because it thwarts communication and information flow.[45] In response to this turnover, a culture may develop that dictates to neighborhood youth standards of dress, language, and behavior that are opposite to those of conventional society. All these factors are likely to increase crime rates.[46]

As communities change, neighborhood deterioration precedes increasing rates of crime and delinquency.[47] Neighborhoods most at risk for increased crime contain large numbers of single-parent families and unrelated people living together, have changed from owner-occupied to renter-occupied units, and have lost semiskilled and unskilled jobs (indicating a growing residue of discouraged workers who are no longer seeking employment).[48] These ecological disruptions strain existing social control mechanisms and inhibit their ability to control crime and delinquency.

Poverty Concentration One aspect of community change may be the concentration of poverty in deteriorated neighborhoods. William Julius Wilson describes how working- and middle-class families flee inner-city poverty areas, resulting in a **concentration effect** in which the most disadvantaged population is consolidated in urban ghettos. As the working and middle classes move out, they take with them their financial and institutional resources and support. Businesses are disinclined to locate in poor areas; banks become reluctant to lend money for new housing or businesses.[49] Areas marked by concentrated poverty become isolated and insulated from the social mainstream and more prone to criminal activity. Ethnically and racially isolated areas maintain the highest crime rates.[50] Minority group members living in these areas also suffer race-based inequality, including income inequality and institutional racism.[51] Gangs also concentrate in these areas, bringing with them a significant increase in criminal activity.[52]

Collective Efficacy Cohesive communities with high levels of social control develop **collective efficacy**: mutual trust, a willingness to intervene in the supervision of children, and the maintenance of public order.[53] In contrast, socially disorganized neighborhoods find that efforts at social control are weak and attenuated. When community social control efforts are blunted, crime rates increase, further weakening neighborhood cohesiveness.

CONNECTIONS

The concentration effect contradicts, in some measure, Shaw and McKay's position, discussed earlier in this chapter, that crime rates increase in transitional neighborhoods. Today the most crime-prone areas may be stable, homogeneous areas whose residents are trapped in public housing and urban ghettos.

concentration effect

As working- and middle-class families flee inner-city poverty areas, the most disadvantaged population is consolidated in urban ghettos.

collective efficacy

Social control exerted by cohesive communities, based on mutual trust, including intervention in the supervision of children and maintenance of public order.

When poverty begins to concentrate, neighborhoods crumble and businesses flee to more affluent areas. Residents become hopeless and bewildered, relying on the government for help. Here, Emma Gaither and David Gloss talk about the pile of rubble behind them that was once a house in their neighborhood. They are just two of the many people trying to get the City of Harrisburg, Pennsylvania, to clean up their neighborhoods.

AP/Wide World Photos

Neighborhoods maintain a variety of agencies and institutions of social control. Some operate on the primary or private level, involving the control placed on people by their peers and families. These sources exert informal control by either awarding or withholding approval, respect, and admiration. Informal control mechanisms include direct criticism, ridicule, ostracism, desertion, or physical punishment.[54] For example, families may exert control by corporal punishment, withholding privileges, or ridiculing lazy or disrespectful children. Communities also use internal networks and local institutions to control crime. Sources of institutional social control include businesses, schools, churches, and social service and volunteer organizations.[55]

Stable neighborhoods can arrange for external sources of social control. The level of policing, an important source of neighborhood stability, may vary among neighborhoods. Police officers patrolling in stable, low-crime areas may have the resources and motivation to respond vigorously to crime, preventing criminal groups from gaining a toehold in the neighborhood.[56] Community organizations and local leaders may have sufficient political clout to get funding for additional law enforcement personnel. The presence of police sends a message that the area will not tolerate deviant behavior. Criminals and drug dealers avoid such areas and relocate to easier and more appealing targets.[57] In more disorganized areas, police officers are less motivated, and their resources are stretched more tightly. These communities cannot mount an effective social control effort because as neighborhood disadvantage increases, informal social control decreases.[58]

The ramifications of having adequate controls are critical. In areas where collective efficacy remains high, children are less likely to become involved with deviant peers and engage in problem behaviors.[59] In disorganized areas, however, the population is transient, so interpersonal relationships remain superficial. Social institutions like schools and churches cannot work effectively in a climate of alienation and mistrust. In these areas, the absence of political power brokers limits access to external funding and protection; without outside money, the neighborhood cannot get back on its feet.[60] Children who live in these neighborhoods find that involvement with conventional social institutions, such as schools and afternoon programs, is blocked; they are instead at

social altruism

Voluntary mutual support systems, such as neighborhood associations and self-help groups, that reinforce moral and social obligations.

risk for recruitment into gangs.[61] These problems are stubborn and difficult to overcome. And even when an attempt is made to revitalize a disorganized neighborhood by creating institutional support programs such as community centers and better schools, the effort may be countered by the ongoing drain of deep-rooted economic and social deprivation.[62]

Social Support/Altruism Neighborhoods that provide strong social supports for their members help young people cope with life's stressors. Sometimes this support is organized on the block level, where neighbors meet face to face to deal with problems. Crime rates may be lower on blocks where people preserve their immediate environment by confronting destabilizing forces such as teen gangs and encourage others to do so also.[63] By helping neighbors become more resilient and self-confident, adults in these areas can provide external support systems that enable youths to desist from crime. For example, residents can teach one another that they have moral and social obligations to their fellow citizens; children can learn to be sensitive to the rights of others and respect differences. Residents may form neighborhood associations and self-help groups. In contrast, less altruistic areas stress individualism and self-interest.

The government can encourage **social altruism** by providing economic and social support through publicly funded social support and welfare programs. Although conservative politicians often criticize welfare programs as government handouts, there is a significant negative association between the amount of welfare money people receive and crime rates.[64] Government assistance can help people improve their social status by providing them with the financial resources to clothe, feed, and educate their children while at the same time reducing stress, frustration, and anger.

According to the social ecology school, then, social disorganization produces criminality. The quality of community life, including levels of change, fear, incivility, poverty, and deterioration, directly influences an area's crime rate. It is not some individual property or trait that causes some people to commit crime, but rather the quality and ambience of the community in which they live. Conversely, in socially altruistic areas, crime rates decrease no matter what the economic situation. ✔ **Checkpoints**

Strain Theories

Inhabitants of a disorganized inner-city area feel isolated, frustrated, ostracized from the economic mainstream, hopeless, and eventually angry. How do these feelings affect criminal activities?

Strain theorists view crime as a direct result of lower-class frustration and anger. They believe that although most people share similar values and goals, the ability to achieve personal goals is stratified by socioeconomic class. Strain is limited in affluent areas because educational and vocational opportunities are available. In disorganized areas, strain occurs because legitimate avenues for success are all but closed. To relieve strain, indigent people may achieve their goals through deviant methods, such as theft or drug trafficking, or they may reject socially accepted goals and substitute more deviant goals such as being tough and aggressive (see Figure 6.4).

anomie

A lack of norms or clear social standards. Because of rapidly shifting moral values, the individual has few guides to what is socially acceptable.

Theory of Anomie

Sociologist Robert Merton applied the sociological concepts first identified by Emile Durkheim to criminology in his theory of **anomie**.[65]

He found that two elements of culture interact to produce potentially anomic conditions: culturally defined goals and socially approved means for obtaining them. For example, U.S. society stresses the goals of acquiring wealth, success, and power. Socially permissible means include hard work, education, and thrift.

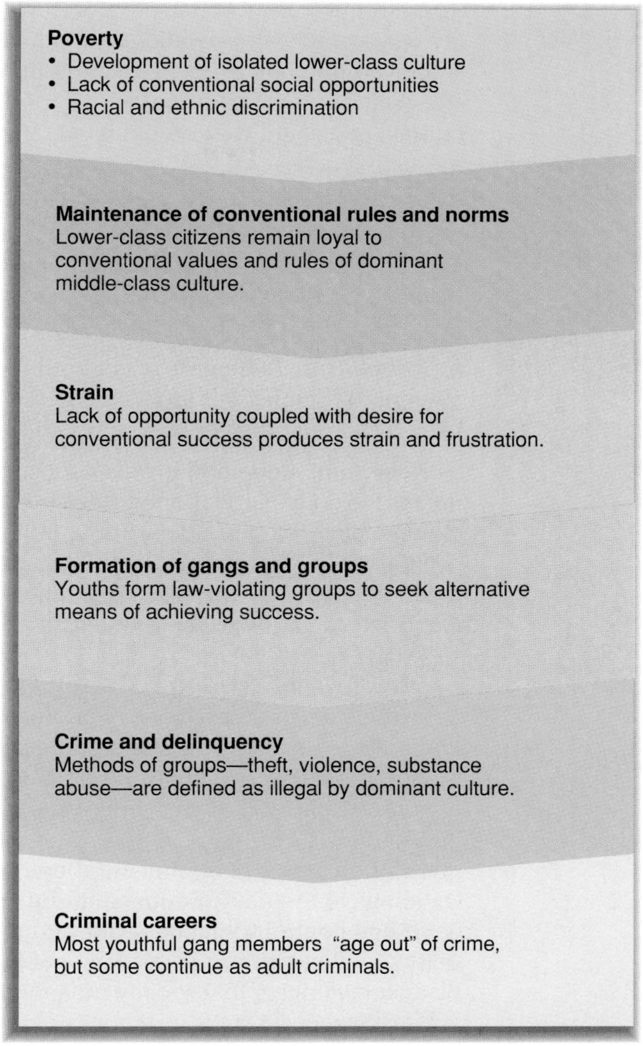

Figure 6.4

The Basic Compounds of Strain Theory

Poverty
- Development of isolated lower-class culture
- Lack of conventional social opportunities
- Racial and ethnic discrimination

Maintenance of conventional rules and norms
Lower-class citizens remain loyal to conventional values and rules of dominant middle-class culture.

Strain
Lack of opportunity coupled with desire for conventional success produces strain and frustration.

Formation of gangs and groups
Youths form law-violating groups to seek alternative means of achieving success.

Crime and delinquency
Methods of groups—theft, violence, substance abuse—are defined as illegal by dominant culture.

Criminal careers
Most youthful gang members "age out" of crime, but some continue as adult criminals.

CONNECTIONS

As you may recall (Chapter 1), the roots of strain theories can be traced to Emile Durkheim's notion of anomie (from the Greek *a nomos*, without norms). According to Durkheim, an anomic society is one in which rules of behavior—norms—have broken down or become inoperative during periods of rapid social change or social crisis such as war or famine.

Merton argues that in the United States, legitimate means to acquire wealth are stratified across class and status lines. Those with little formal education and few economic resources soon find that they are denied the ability to legally acquire wealth—the preeminent success symbol. When socially mandated goals are uniform throughout society and access to legitimate means is bound by class and status, the resulting strain produces anomie among those who are locked out of the legitimate opportunity structure. Consequently, they may develop criminal or delinquent solutions to the problem of attaining goals.

Social Adaptations Merton argues that each person has his or her own concept of society's goals and means to attain them. Some people have inadequate means of attaining success; others who have the means reject societal goals. The result is a variety of social adaptations.

1. *Conformity*. Conformity occurs when individuals embrace conventional social goals and also have the means to attain them. They remain law-abiding.

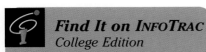

Find It on InfoTrac
College Edition

Anomie theory suggests that American culture prescribes material success as the prime goal while at the same time maintaining social structural arrangements that preclude many people from realistic access to means for legitimately achieving that goal. So says sociologist Richard I. Wark. Do you agree? To read what he and others have to say, use "anomie" as a keyword in Info-Trac College Edition.

anomie theory

View that anomie results when socially defined goals (such as wealth and power) are universally mandated but access to legitimate means (such as education and job opportunities) is stratified by class and status.

2. *Innovation.* Innovation occurs when an individual accepts the goals of society but is unable or unwilling to attain them through legitimate means. The resulting conflict forces them to adopt innovative solutions to their dilemma: they steal, sell drugs, or extort money. Of the five adaptations, innovation is most closely associated with criminal behavior.

3. *Ritualism.* Ritualists gain pleasure from practicing traditional ceremonies, regardless of whether they have a real purpose or a goal. The strict customs in religious orders, feudal societies, clubs, and college fraternities encourage and appeal to ritualists. Ritualists should have the lowest level of criminal behavior because they have abandoned the success goal, which is at the root of criminal activity.

4. *Retreatism.* Retreatists reject both the goals and the means of society. They attempt to escape their lack of success by withdrawing, either mentally or physically, by taking drugs or becoming drifters.

5. *Rebellion.* Rebellion involves substituting an alternative set of goals and means for conventional ones. Revolutionaries who wish to promote radical change in the existing social structure and who call for alternative lifestyles, goals, and beliefs are engaging in rebellion. Rebellion may be a reaction against a corrupt, hated government or an effort to create alternative opportunities and lifestyles within the existing system.

Evaluation of Anomie Theory According to **anomie theory**, social inequality leads to perceptions of anomie. To resolve the goals–means conflict and relieve their sense of strain, some people innovate by stealing or extorting money; others retreat into drugs and alcohol; some rebel by joining revolutionary groups; and still others get involved in ritualistic behavior by joining a religious cult.

Merton's view of anomie has been one of the most enduring and influential sociological theories of criminality. By linking deviant behavior to the success goals that control social behavior, anomie theory attempts to pinpoint the cause of the conflict that produces personal frustration and consequent criminality. By acknowledging that society unfairly distributes the legitimate means to achieving success, anomie theory helps explain the existence of high-crime areas and the apparent predominance of delinquent and criminal behavior in the lower class. By suggesting that social conditions, not individual personalities, produce crime, Merton greatly influenced the directions taken to reduce and control criminality during the latter half of the twentieth century.

A number of questions are left unanswered by anomie theory.[66] Merton does not explain why people choose to commit certain types of crime. For example, why does one anomic person become a mugger while another deals drugs? Anomie may explain differences in crime rates, but it cannot explain why most young criminals desist from crime as adults. Does this mean that perceptions of anomie dwindle with age? Is anomie short-lived?

Institutional Anomie Theory

institutional anomie theory

The view that anomie pervades U.S. culture because the drive for material wealth dominates and undermines social and community values.

Steven Messner and Richard Rosenfeld's **institutional anomie theory** is an updating of Merton's work.[67]

Messner and Rosenfeld agree with Merton that the success goal is pervasive in American culture. For them, the **American Dream** refers to both a goal and a process. As a goal, the American Dream involves accumulating material goods and wealth via open individual competition. As a process, it involves both being socialized to pursue material success and believing that prosperity is achievable in American culture. Anomic conditions arise because the desire to succeed at any cost drives people apart, weakens the collective sense of com-

American Dream

The goal of accumulating material goods and wealth through individual competition; the process of being socialized to pursue material success and to believe it is achievable.

munity, fosters ambition, and restricts the desire to achieve anything other than material wealth. Achieving respect, for example, is not sufficient.

Why does anomie pervade American culture? According to Messner and Rosenfeld, it is because institutions that might otherwise control the exaggerated emphasis on financial success, such as religious or charitable institutions, have been rendered powerless or obsolete. These social institutions have been undermined in three ways:

1. Noneconomic functions and roles have been devalued. Performance in other institutional settings—the family, school, or community—is assigned a lower priority than the goal of financial success.

2. When conflicts emerge, noneconomic roles become subordinate to and must accommodate economic roles. The schedules, routines, and demands of the workplace take priority over those of the home, the school, the community, and other aspects of social life.

3. Economic language, standards, and norms penetrate into noneconomic realms. Economic terms become part of the common vernacular: People want to get to the "bottom line." Spouses view themselves as "partners" who "manage" the household. Retired people say they want to "downsize" their household. We "outsource" home repairs instead of doing them ourselves. Corporate leaders run for public office promising to "run the country like a business."

According to Messner and Rosenfeld, the relatively high American crime rates can be explained by the interrelationship between culture and institutions. At the cultural level, the dominance of the American Dream mythology ensures that many people will develop desires for material goods that cannot be satisfied by legitimate means. Anomie becomes a norm, and extralegal means become a strategy for attaining material wealth. At the institutional level, the dominance of economic concerns weakens the informal social control exerted by family, church, and school. These institutions have lost their ability to regulate behavior and have instead become a conduit for promoting material success. For example, schools are evaluated not for imparting knowledge but for their ability to train students to get high-paying jobs. Social conditions reinforce each other: Culture determines institutions, and institutional change influences culture. Crime rates may rise in a healthy economy because national prosperity heightens the attractiveness of monetary rewards, encouraging people to gain financial success by any means possible, including illegal ones. In this culture of competition, self-interest prevails and generates amorality, acceptance of inequality, and disdain for the less fortunate.[68]

Find It on INFOTRAC
College Edition

Did you know that poverty among the poorest Americans has increased significantly in the 1990s and is reaching an all-time high? As a result, relative deprivation has increased among the poorest of the poor. To read more about this, go to InfoTrac College Edition and use "relative deprivation" as a subject guide. Then go to John A. Bishop, John P. Formby, and Buhong Zheng, "Extent of Material Hardship and Poverty in the United States: Comment," *Review of Social Economy*, September 1999 v57 i3 p388(1)

Relative Deprivation Theory

Criminologists have long assumed that income inequality increases both strain and crime rates. Sharp divisions between rich and poor create envy and mistrust. Societies in which income inequality flourishes are especially demeaning to the poor. Criminal motivation is fueled by both perceived humiliation and the perceived right to humiliate a victim in return.[69] Psychologists warn that under these circumstances, young males will fear and envy "winners" who are doing well at their expense. If they fail to use risky, aggressive tactics, they are surely going to lose out in social competition and have little chance of future success.[70] This perception is referred to as **relative deprivation**.

The concept of relative deprivation was proposed by sociologists Judith Blau and Peter Blau, who combined concepts from anomie theory with those found in social disorganization models.[71] According to the Blaus, lower-class people may feel both deprived and embittered when they compare their life circumstances to those of the more affluent. People who feel deprived because

relative deprivation

Envy, mistrust, and aggression resulting from perceptions of economic and social inequality.

CONNECTIONS

Can relative deprivation concepts can be applied to white-collar crime? Perhaps some of the individuals involved in the savings and loan scandals or Wall Street stock fraud cases felt relatively deprived and socially frustrated when they compared the paltry few millions they had already accumulated with the hundreds of millions held by wealthier people whom they envied. For more on this issue, see discussions of the savings and loan scandal and the causes of white-collar crime in Chapter 12.

of their race or economic class eventually develop a sense of injustice and discontent. The less fortunate begin to distrust the society that has nurtured social inequality and obstructed their chances of progressing by legitimate means. The constant frustration that results from these feelings of inadequacy produces pent-up aggression and hostility, eventually leading to violence and crime. The effect of inequality may be greatest when the impoverished believe that they are becoming less able to compete in a society whose balance of economic and social power is shifting further toward the already affluent. Under these conditions, the relatively poor are increasingly likely to choose illegitimate life-enhancing activities. Crime rates may then spiral upward even if the relative size of the poor population does not increase.[72]

Relative deprivation is felt most acutely by African American youths because they consistently suffer racial discrimination and economic deprivation that place them in a lower status than other urban residents.[73] Wage inequality may motivate young African American males to enter the drug trade, an enterprise that increases the likelihood they will become involved in violent crimes.[74]

In sum, according to the relative deprivation concept, people who perceive themselves as economically deprived relative to people they know, as well as to society in general, may begin to form negative self-feelings and hostility, which motivate them to engage in deviant and criminal behaviors.[75]

General Strain Theory (GST)

general strain theory (GST)

The view that multiple sources of strain interact with an individual's emotional traits and responses to produce criminality.

CONNECTIONS

The GST is not solely a cultural deviance theory since it recognizes non-class-related sources of strain. In this regard it is similar to the social process theories discussed in Chapter 7. It is included here because it incorporates the view that social class position can be an important source of strain, thus following in the tradition of Merton's theory of anomie.

negative affective states

Anger, frustration, and adverse emotions produced by a variety of sources of strain.

Sociologist Robert Agnew's **general strain theory (GST)** helps identify the micro- or individual-level influences of strain. Whereas Merton and Messner and Rosenfeld try to explain social class differences in the crime rate, Agnew tries to explain why individuals who feel stress and strain are likely to commit crimes. Agnew also attempts to offer a more general explanation of criminal activity among all elements of society rather than restrict his views to lower-class crime.[76]

Multiple Sources of Strain Agnew suggests that criminality is the direct result of **negative affective states**—the anger, frustration, and adverse emotions that emerge in the wake of destructive social relationships. He finds that negative affective states are produced by a variety of sources of strain (see Figure 6.5):

- *Failure to achieve positively valued goals.* This cause of strain, similar to what Merton speaks of in his theory of anomie, is a result of the disjunction between aspirations and expectations. This type of strain occurs when a youth aspires to wealth and fame but, lacking financial and educational resources, assumes that such goals are impossible to achieve; he then turns to crime and drug dealing.

- *Disjunction of expectations and achievements.* Strain can also be produced by a disjunction between expectations and achievements. When people compare themselves to peers who seem to be doing a lot better financially or socially (such as making more money or getting better grades), even those doing relatively well feel strain. For example, when a high school senior is accepted at a good college but not a prestige school, like some of her friends, she will feel strain. Perhaps she is not being treated fairly because the playing field is tilted against her: "Other kids have connections," she may say. Perceptions of inequity may result in many adverse reactions, ranging from running away from its source to lowering others' benefits through physical attacks or property vandalism.

Figure 6.5

Elements of General Strain Theory (GST)

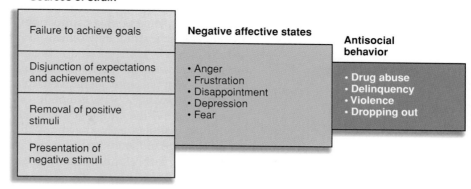

Sources of strain

Failure to achieve goals

Disjunction of expectations and achievements

Removal of positive stimuli

Presentation of negative stimuli

Negative affective states

- Anger
- Frustration
- Disappointment
- Depression
- Fear

Antisocial behavior

- **Drug abuse**
- **Delinquency**
- **Violence**
- **Dropping out**

■ *Removal of positively valued stimuli.* Strain may occur because of the actual or anticipated loss of positively valued stimuli.[77] For example, the loss of a girl- or boyfriend can produce strain, as can the death of a loved one, moving to a new neighborhood or school, or the divorce or separation of parents. The loss of positive stimuli may lead to delinquency as the adolescent tries to prevent the loss, retrieve what has been lost, obtain substitutes, or seek revenge against those responsible for the loss.

■ *Presentation of negative stimuli.* Strain may also be caused by negative or noxious stimuli, such as child abuse or neglect, crime victimization, physical punishment, family or peer conflict, school failure, or stressful life events ranging from verbal threats to air pollution. For example, adolescent delinquency has been linked to maltreatment through the rage and anger it generates. Children who are abused at home may take out their rage on younger children at school or become involved in violent delinquency.[78]

Although these sources of strain are independent of one another, they may overlap. For example, if a teacher insults a student, it may be viewed as an unfair application of negative stimuli that interferes with a student's academic aspirations. The greater the intensity and frequency of strain experiences, the greater their impact and the more likely they are to cause delinquency.

According to Agnew, each type of strain increases the likelihood of experiencing such negative emotions as disappointment, depression, fear, and most important, anger. Anger increases perceptions of injury and of being wronged. It produces a desire for revenge, energizes individuals to take action, and lowers inhibitions. Violence and aggression seem justified if you have been wronged and are righteously angry. Because it produces these emotions, chronic, repetitive strain can be considered a predisposing factor for delinquency when it creates a hostile, suspicious, aggressive attitude. Individual strain episodes may trigger delinquency, such as when a particularly stressful event ignites a violent reaction.

Coping with Strain   Not all people who experience strain eventually resort to criminality. Some are able to marshal their emotional, mental, and behavioral resources to cope with the anger and frustration produced by strain. Some individuals may be able to rationalize frustrating circumstances: Getting a good job is "just not that important"; they may be poor, but the "next guy is worse off"; if things didn't work out, they "got what they deserved." Others seek behavioral solutions, running away from adverse conditions or seeking revenge against those who caused the strain. Some try to regain emotional equilibrium with techniques ranging from physical exercise to drug abuse.

However, some people cannot cope with strain because they have traits that make them particularly sensitive to strain. These include an explosive temperament, low tolerance for adversity, poor problem-solving skills, and being overly sensitive or emotional. Although these traits, which are linked to aggressive, antisocial behavior, seem to be stable over the life cycle, they may peak during adolescence.[79] This is a period of social stress caused by weakening parental supervision and the development of relationships with a diverse peer group. Many adolescents going through the trauma of family breakup and frequent changes in family structure feel a high degree of strain. They may react by becoming involved in precocious sexuality or by turning to substance abuse to mask the strain.[80]

As children mature, their expectations increase. Some are unable to meet academic and social demands. Adolescents are very concerned about their standing with peers. Teenagers who are deficient in these areas may find they are social outcasts, another source of strain. In adulthood, crime rates may drop because these sources of strain are reduced. New sources of self-esteem emerge, and adults seem more likely to align their goals with reality.

Evaluating GST Agnew's important work both clarifies the concept of strain and directs future research agendas. It also adds to the body of literature describing how social and life history events influence offending patterns. Because sources of strain vary over the life course, so too do crime rates.

There is also empirical support for GST.[81] Some research efforts have shown that indicators of strain—family breakup, unemployment, moving, feelings of dissatisfaction with friends and school, dropping out of school—are positively related to criminality.[82]

As predicted by GST, people who report feelings of stress and anger are more likely to interact with delinquent peers and to engage in criminal behaviors.[83] Lashing out at others may reduce feelings of strain, as may stealing or vandalizing property.[84] There is also evidence that, as predicted by the GST, people who fail to meet success goals are more likely to engage in criminal activities.[85] ✔Checkpoints

---

✔ Checkpoints

✔ Strain theories hold that economic deprivation causes frustration, which leads to crime.

✔ According to Merton's anomie theory, many people who desire material goods and other forms of economic success lack the means to achieve their goals. Some may turn to crime.

✔ Messner and Rosenfeld's institutional anomie theory argues that the goal of success at all costs has invaded every aspect of American life.

✔ Agnew's general theory of strain suggests that there is more than one source of anomie.

Cultural Deviance Theory

The third branch of social structure theory combines the effects of social disorganization and strain to explain how people living in deteriorated neighborhoods react to social isolation and economic deprivation. Because their lifestyle is draining, frustrating, and dispiriting, members of the lower class create an independent subculture with its own set of rules and values. Whereas middle-class culture stresses hard work, delayed gratification, formal education, and being cautious, the lower-class subculture stresses excitement, toughness, taking risks, fearlessness, immediate gratification, and street smarts.

The lower-class subculture is an attractive alternative because the urban poor find it impossible to meet the behavioral demands of middle-class society. However, subcultural norms often clash with conventional values. Urban dwellers are forced to violate the law because they obey the rules of the deviant culture with which they are in immediate contact (see Figure 6.6).

More than 40 years ago, sociologist Walter Miller identified the unique conduct norms that help define lower-class culture.[86] Miller referred to them as **focal concerns**, values that have evolved specifically to fit conditions in lower-class environments. The major lower-class focal concerns are set out in Table 6.1.[87]

focal concerns

Values, such as toughness and street smarts, that have evolved specifically to fit conditions in lower-class environments.

Figure 6.6

Elements of Cultural Deviance Theory

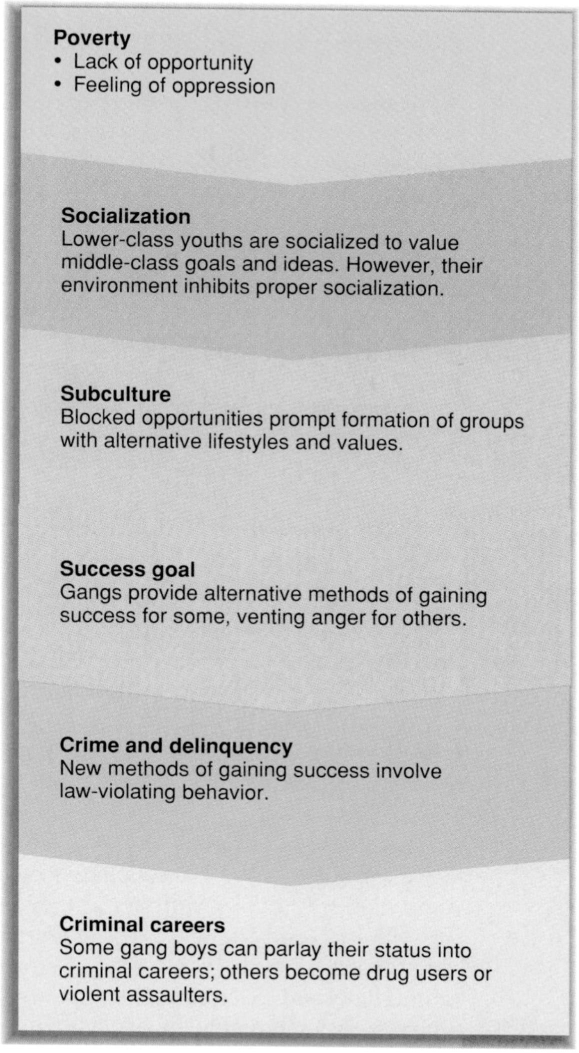

Poverty
• Lack of opportunity
• Feeling of oppression

Socialization
Lower-class youths are socialized to value middle-class goals and ideas. However, their environment inhibits proper socialization.

Subculture
Blocked opportunities prompt formation of groups with alternative lifestyles and values.

Success goal
Gangs provide alternative methods of gaining success for some, venting anger for others.

Crime and delinquency
New methods of gaining success involve law-violating behavior.

Criminal careers
Some gang boys can parlay their status into criminal careers; others become drug users or violent assaulters.

According to Miller, clinging to lower-class focal concerns promotes illegal or violent behavior. Toughness may mean displaying fighting prowess; street smarts may lead to drug deals; excitement may result in drinking, gambling, or drug abuse.[88] To illustrate, consider a recent study of violent young men in New York, conducted by sociologist Jeffrey Fagan. He found that the most compelling function that violence served was to develop status as a "tough," an identity that helps young men acquire social power while at the same time insulating them from becoming victims. Violence was also seen as a means to acquire the trappings of wealth (such as nice clothes, flashy cars, or access to clubs), control or humiliate another person, defy authority, settle drug-related disputes, attain retribution, satisfy the need for thrills or risk taking, and respond to challenges to one's manhood.[89] Lower-class focal concerns seem as relevant today as when they were first identified by Miller more than 40 years ago!

delinquent subculture

A value system adopted by lower-class youths that is directly opposed to that of the larger society.

Theory of Delinquent Subcultures

Albert Cohen first articulated the theory of **delinquent subcultures** in his classic 1955 book, *Delinquent Boys*.[90] Cohen's central position was that delinquent behavior of lower-class youths is actually a protest against the norms and values

Table 6.1 Miller's Lower-Class Focal Concerns

Trouble In lower-class communities, people are evaluated by their actual or potential involvement in making trouble. Getting into trouble includes such behaviors as fighting, drinking, and sexual misconduct. Dealing with trouble can confer prestige—for example, when a man establishes a reputation for being able to handle himself well in a fight. Not being able to handle trouble, and having to pay the consequences, can make a person look foolish and incompetent.

Toughness Lower-class males want local recognition of their physical and spiritual toughness. They refuse to be sentimental or soft and instead value physical strength, fighting ability, and athletic skill. Those who cannot meet these standards risk getting a reputation for being weak, inept, and effeminate.

Smartness Members of the lower-class culture want to maintain an image of being streetwise and savvy, using their street smarts, and having the ability to outfox and out-con the opponent. Although formal education is not admired, knowing essential survival techniques, such as gambling, conning, and outsmarting the law, is a requirement.

Excitement Members of the lower class search for fun and excitement to enliven an otherwise drab existence. The search for excitement may lead to gambling, fighting, getting drunk, and sexual adventures. In between, the lower-class citizen may simply "hang out" and "be cool."

Fate Lower-class citizens believe their lives are in the hands of strong spiritual forces that guide their destinies. Getting lucky, finding good fortune, and hitting the jackpot are all slum-dwellers' daily dreams.

Autonomy Being independent of authority figures, such as the police, teachers, and parents, is required; losing control is an unacceptable weakness, incompatible with toughness.

SOURCE: Walter Miller, "Lower-Class Culture as a Generating Milieu of Gang Delinquency," *Journal of Social Issues* 14 (1958): 5–19.

---

of middle-class U.S. culture. Because social conditions prevent them from achieving success legitimately, lower-class youths experience a form of culture conflict that Cohen labels **status frustration**.[91] As a result, many of them join gangs and engage in behavior that is "non-utilitarian, malicious, and negativistic."[92]

Cohen viewed the delinquent gang as a separate subculture, possessing a value system directly opposed to that of the larger society. He described the subculture as one that "takes its norms from the larger culture, but turns them upside down. The delinquent's conduct is right by the standards of his subculture precisely because it is wrong by the norms of the larger culture."[93]

According to Cohen, the development of the delinquent subculture is a consequence of socialization practices in lower-class environments. Here children lack the basic skills necessary to achieve social and economic success, including a proper education, which renders them incapable of developing the skills to succeed in society. Lower-class parents are incapable of teaching children the necessary techniques for entering the dominant middle-class culture. The consequences of this deprivation include developmental handicaps, poor speech and communication skills, and inability to delay gratification.

Middle-Class Measuring Rods One significant handicap that lower-class children face is the inability to positively impress authority figures, such as teachers, employers, or supervisors. In U.S. society, these positions tend to be held by members of the middle class, who have difficulty relating to the lower-class youngster. Cohen calls the standards set by these authority figures **middle-class measuring rods.**

status frustration

A form of culture conflict experienced by lower-class youths because social conditions prevent them from achieving success as defined by the larger society.

middle-class measuring rods

The standards by which authority figures, such as teachers and employers, evaluate lower-class youngsters and often prejudge them negatively.

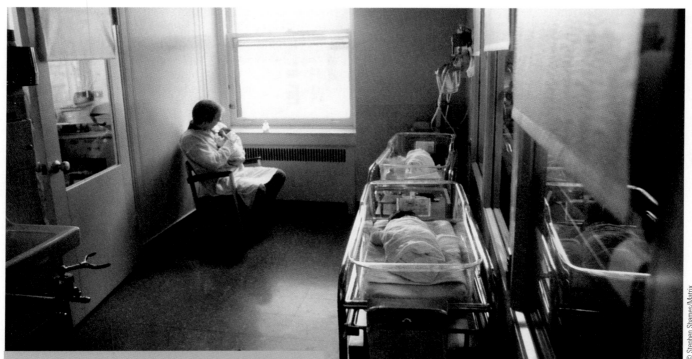

Deviant subcultures feature social problems that are handed down from one generation to the next. Thousands of drug-addicted babies are born each year, and many are soon abandoned by their parents. Here, a volunteer helps comfort a crack-addicted baby in an urban hospital ward.

The conflict and frustration lower-class youths experience when they fail to meet these standards is a primary cause of delinquency. They may find themselves prejudged by others and not measuring up in the final analysis. Negative evaluations become part of a permanent file that follows an individual for the rest of his or her life. When he or she wants to improve, evidence of prior failures is used to discourage advancement.

The Formation of Deviant Subcultures Cohen believes that lower-class boys rejected by middle-class decision makers usually join one of three existing subcultures: the corner boy, the college boy, or the delinquent boy.

The corner boy role is the most common response to middle-class rejection. The corner boy is not a chronic delinquent but may be a truant who engages in petty or status offenses, such as precocious sex and recreational drug abuse. His main loyalty is to his peer group, on which he depends for support, motivation, and interest. His values, therefore, are those of the group with which he is in close contact. The corner boy, well aware of his failure to achieve the standards of the American Dream, retreats into the comforting world of his lower-class peers and eventually becomes a stable member of his neighborhood, holding a menial job, marrying, and remaining in the community.

The college boy embraces the cultural and social values of the middle class. Rather than scorning middle-class measuring rods, he actively strives to succeed by those standards. Cohen views this type of youth as one who is embarking on an almost hopeless path because he is ill-equipped academically, socially, and linguistically to achieve the rewards of middle-class life.

The delinquent boy adopts a set of norms and principles that directly oppose middle-class values. He engages in *short-run hedonism,* living for today and letting "tomorrow take care of itself."[94] Delinquent boys strive for group autonomy. They resist efforts by family, school, or other sources of authority to control their behavior. Frustrated by their inability to succeed, these boys resort to a

reaction formation

Irrational hostility evidenced by young delinquents, who adopt norms directly opposed to middle-class goals and standards that seem impossible to achieve.

process Cohen calls **reaction formation**, including overly intense responses that seem disproportionate to the stimuli that trigger them. For the delinquent boy, this takes the form of irrational, malicious, and unaccountable hostility to the enemy, which in this case is "the norms of respectable middle-class society."[95]

Cohen's approach skillfully integrates strain and social disorganization theories and has become an enduring element of criminological literature.

Theory of Differential Opportunity

differential opportunity

The view that lower-class youths, whose legitimate opportunities are limited, join gangs and pursue criminal careers as alternative means to achieve universal success goals.

In their classic work *Delinquency and Opportunity,* written more than 40 years ago, Richard Cloward and Lloyd Ohlin combined strain and social disorganization principles to portray a gang-sustaining criminal subculture.[96]

The centerpiece of the Cloward and Ohlin theory is the concept of **differential opportunity**. According to this concept, people in all strata of society share the same success goals; however, those in the lower class have limited means of achieving them. People who perceive themselves as failures within conventional society will seek alternative or innovative ways to succeed. People who conclude that there is little hope for legitimate advancement may join like-minded peers to form a gang, which can provide them with emotional support. The youth who is considered a failure at school and is qualified for only a menial job at a minimum wage can earn thousands of dollars plus the respect of his or her peers by joining a gang and engaging in drug deals or armed robberies.

Cloward and Ohlin recognize that the opportunity for success in both conventional and criminal careers is limited. In stable areas, adolescents may be recruited by professional criminals, drug traffickers, or organized crime groups. Unstable areas, however, cannot support flourishing criminal opportunities. In these socially disorganized neighborhoods, adult role models are absent, and young criminals have few opportunities to join established gangs or learn the fine points of professional crime. Their most important finding, then, is that all opportunities for success, both illegal and conventional, are closed for the most disadvantaged youths.

Because of differential opportunity, young people are likely to join one of three types of gangs.

1. *Criminal gangs.* Criminal gangs exist in stable neighborhoods where close connections among adolescent, young adult, and adult offenders create an environment for successful criminal enterprise.[97] Youths are recruited into established criminal gangs that provide training for a successful criminal career. Gang membership is a learning experience in which the knowledge and skills needed for success in crime are acquired. During this apprenticeship, older, more experienced members of the criminal subculture hold youthful trainees on tight reins, limiting activities that might jeopardize the gang's profits (for example, engaging in nonfunctional, irrational violence).

2. *Conflict gangs.* Conflict gangs develop in communities unable to provide either legitimate or illegitimate opportunities.[98] These gangs attract tough adolescents who fight with weapons to win respect from rivals and engage in unpredictable and destructive assaults on people and property. Conflict gang members must be ready to fight to protect their own and their gang's integrity and honor. By doing so, they acquire a "rep," which gains admiration from their peers and consequently helps them develop their self-image.

3. *Retreatist gangs.* Retreatists are double failures, unable to gain success through legitimate means and unwilling to do so through illegal ones. Members of the retreatist subculture constantly search for ways of getting

high—alcohol, pot, heroin, unusual sexual experiences, music. To feed their habits, retreatists develop a "hustle"—pimping, conning, selling drugs, or committing petty crimes. Personal status in the retreatist subculture is derived from peer approval.

Cloward and Ohlin's theory integrates cultural deviance and social disorganization variables and recognizes different modes of criminal adaptation. The fact that criminal cultures can be supportive, rational, and profitable seems to more realistically reflect the actual world of the delinquent than Cohen's original view of purely negativistic, destructive delinquent youths who oppose all social values.

Social Structure Theory and Social Policy

Social structure theory has significantly influenced social policy. If the cause of criminality is viewed as a schism between lower-class individuals and conventional goals, norms, and rules, it seems logical that alternatives to criminal behavior can be provided by giving inner-city youth opportunities to share in the rewards of conventional society.

One approach is to give indigent people direct financial aid through public assistance or welfare. Although welfare has been curtailed under the Federal Welfare Reform Act of 1996, research shows that crime rates decrease when families receive supplemental income through public assistance payments.[99]

Efforts have also been made to reduce crime by improving the community structure in inner-city high-crime areas. Crime prevention efforts based on social structure precepts can be traced back to the Chicago Area Project supervised by Clifford R. Shaw. This program attempted to organize existing community structures to develop social stability in otherwise disorganized slums. The project sponsored recreation programs for neighborhood children, including summer camping. It campaigned for community improvements in such areas as education, sanitation, traffic safety, resource conservation, and law enforcement. Project members also worked with police and court agencies to supervise and treat gang youth and adult offenders.

Social structure concepts, especially Cloward and Ohlin's views, were a critical ingredient in the Kennedy and Johnson administrations' War on Poverty, begun in the early 1960s. War on Poverty programs—Head Start, Neighborhood Legal Services, and the Community Action Program—have continued to help people.

Summary

Sociology has been the main orientation of criminologists because they know that crime rates vary among elements of the social structure, that society goes through changes that affect crime, and that social interaction relates to criminality. Social structure theories suggest that people's places in the socioeconomic structure influence their chances of becoming a criminal. Poor people are more likely to commit crimes because they are unable to achieve monetary or social success in any other way. Social structure theory includes three schools of thought: social disorganization, strain, and cultural deviance theories (summarized in Table 6.2).

Social disorganization theory suggests that slum-dwellers violate the law because they live in areas in which social control has broken down. The origin of social disorganization theory can be traced to the work of Clifford R. Shaw and Henry D. McKay. Shaw and McKay concluded that disorganized areas, marked by divergent values and transitional populations, produce criminality. Modern social ecology theory looks at such issues as community fear, unemployment, and deterioration.

Table 6.2 Social Structure Theories

THEORY	MAJOR PREMISE	STRENGTHS
Social Disorganization Theory		
Shaw and McKay's concentric zone theory	Crime is a product of transitional neighborhoods that manifest social disorganization and value conflict.	Identifies why crime rates are highest in slum areas. Points out the factors that produce crime. Suggests programs to help reduce crime.
Social ecology theory	The conflicts and problems of urban social life and communities, including fear, unemployment, deterioration, and siege mentality, influence crime rates.	Accounts for urban crime rates and trends.
Strain Theory		
Anomie theory	People who adopt the goals of society but lack the means to attain them seek alternatives, such as crime.	Points out how competition for success creates conflict and crime. Suggests that social conditions and not personality can account for crime. Can explain middle- and upper-class crime.
Institutional anomie theory	Material goals pervade all aspects of American life.	Explains why crime rates are so high in American culture.
Relative deprivation theory	Crime occurs when the wealthy and poor live close to one another.	Explains high crime rates in deteriorated inner-city areas located near more affluent neighborhoods.
General strain theory	Strain has a variety of sources. Strain causes crime in the absence of adequate coping mechanisms.	Identifies the complexities of strain in modern society. Expands on anomie theory. Shows the influence of social events on behavior over the life course.
Cultural Deviance Theory		
Miller's focal concern theory	Citizens who obey the street rules of lower-class life (focal concerns) find themselves in conflict with the dominant culture.	Identifies the core values of lower-class culture and shows their association to crime.
Cohen's theory of delinquent gangs	Status frustration of lower-class boys, created by their failure to achieve middle-class success, causes them to join gangs.	Shows how the conditions of lower-class life produce crime. Explains violence and destructive acts. Identifies conflict of lower class with middle class.
Cloward and Ohlin's theory of opportunity	Blockage of conventional opportunities causes lower-class youths to join criminal, conflict, or retreatist gangs.	Shows that even illegal opportunities are structured in society. Indicates why people become involved in a particular type of criminal activity. Presents a way of preventing crime.

Strain theories view crime as resulting from the anger people experience over their inability to achieve legitimate social and economic success. Strain theories hold that most people share common values and beliefs, but the ability to achieve them is differentiated by the social structure. The best-known strain theory is Robert Merton's theory of anomie, which describes what happens when people have inadequate means to satisfy their goals. Steven Messner and Richard Rosenfeld show that American culture produces strain, and Robert Agnew suggests that strain has multiple sources.

Cultural deviance theories hold that a unique value system develops in lower-class areas. Lower-class values approve of behaviors such as being tough, never showing fear, and defying authority. People perceiving strain will bond together in their own groups or subcultures for support and recognition. Albert

Cohen links the formation of subcultures to the failure of lower-class citizens to achieve recognition from middle-class decision makers, such as teachers, employers, and police officers. Richard Cloward and Lloyd Ohlin have argued that crime results from lower-class people's perception that their opportunity for success is limited. Consequently, youths in low-income areas may join criminal, conflict, or retreatist gangs.

For additional chapter links, discussions, and quizzes, see the book-specific web site at http://www.wadsworth.com/product/0534519423s.

Thinking Like a Criminologist

You have accepted a position in Washington as an assistant to the undersecretary of urban affairs. The secretary informs you that he wants to initiate a demonstration project in a major city to show that government can reduce poverty, crime, and drug abuse.

The area he has chosen is a large inner-city neighborhood in a Midwestern city of more than 3 million people. It suffers disorganized community structure, poverty, and hopelessness. Predatory delinquent gangs run free, terrorizing local merchants and citizens. The school system has failed to provide opportunities and educational experiences sufficient to dampen enthusiasm for gang recruitment. Stores, homes, and public buildings are deteriorated and decayed. Commercial enterprise has fled the area, and civil servants are reluctant to enter the neighborhood. There is an uneasy truce among the varied ethnic and racial groups that populate the area. Residents feel that little can be done to bring the neighborhood back to life. Merchants are afraid to open stores, and there is little outside development from major retailers or manufacturers. People who want to start their own businesses find that banks will not lend them money.

One of the biggest problems has been the large housing projects that were developed in the 1960s. These are now overcrowded and deteriorated. Police are actually afraid to enter the buildings unless they arrive with a SWAT team. Each building is controlled by a gang whose members demand tribute from the residents.

You are asked to propose an urban redevelopment program to revitalize the area and eventually bring down the crime rate. You can bring any public or private element to bear on this overwhelming problem. You can also ask private industry to help in the struggle, promising them tax breaks for their participation. What programs would you recommend to break the cycle of urban poverty?

Key Terms

stratified	subculture	relative deprivation
social class	cultural transmission	general strain theory (GST)
truly disadvantaged	transitional neighborhood	negative affective states
culture of poverty	concentration effect	focal concerns
underclass	collective efficacy	delinquent subculture
social structure theory	social altruism	status frustration
social disorganization theory	anomie	middle-class measuring rods
strain theory	anomie theory	reaction formation
strain	institutional anomie theory	differential opportunity
cultural deviance theory	American Dream	

Discussion Questions

1. Is there a "transitional" area in your town or city? Does the crime rate remain constant there, regardless of who moves in or out?

2. Is it possible that a distinct lower-class culture exists? Do you know anyone who has the focal concerns Miller talks about? Were there "focal concerns" in your high school or college experience?

3. Have you ever perceived anomie? What causes anomie? Is there more than one cause of strain?

4. How would Merton explain middle-class crime? How would Agnew?

5. Could "relative deprivation" produce crime among college-educated white-collar workers?

© Anthony P. Gutierez/Liaison Agency

7 Social Process Theories: Socialized to Crime

Socialization and Crime

socialization

Process of human development and enculturation. Socialization is influenced by key social processes and institutions.

social process theory

The view that criminality is a function of people's interactions with various organizations, institutions, and processes in society.

Some criminologists focus their attention on social-psychological processes and interactions common to people in all segments of the social structure, not just the lower class. They believe that criminality is a function of individual **socialization** and the interactions people have with various organizations, institutions, and processes of society.

Most people are influenced by their family relationships, peer group associations, educational experiences, and interactions with authority figures, including teachers, employers, and agents of the justice system. If these relationships are positive and supportive, people can succeed within the rules of society; if these relationships are dysfunctional and destructive, conventional success may be impossible, and criminal solutions may become a feasible alternative. Taken together, this view of crime is referred to as **social process theory**.

Social process theories share one basic concept: All people, regardless of their race, class, or gender, have the potential to become delinquents or criminals. Although members of the lower class may have the added burdens of poverty, racism, poor schools, and disrupted family lives, these social forces can be counteracted by positive peer relations, a supportive family, and educational success. In contrast, even the most affluent members of society may turn to antisocial behavior if their life experiences are intolerable or destructive.

Social process theories have endured because the relationship between social class and crime is still uncertain. Most residents of inner-city areas refrain from criminal activity, and few of those that commit crimes persist into adulthood. If poverty were the sole cause of crime, then indigent adults would be as criminal as indigent teenagers. But we know that, regardless of class position, most people age out of crime. The association between economic status and crime is problematic because class position alone cannot explain crime rates.[1]

Criminologists have long studied the critical elements of socialization to determine how they contribute to a burgeoning criminal career. Prominent among these elements are family, peer group, school, and church.

Family Relations

Family relationships are considered a major determinant of behavior.[2] In fact, parenting factors, such as the ability to communicate and provide proper discipline, may play a critical role in determining whether people misbehave as children and even later as adults. This is one of the most replicated findings in the criminological literature.[3]

Youths who grow up in a household characterized by conflict and tension, where parents are absent or separated, or where there is a lack of familial love and support are susceptible to crime-promoting forces in the environment.[4] Even children living in high-crime areas will be better able to resist the temptations of the streets if they receive fair discipline, care, and support from parents who provide them with strong, positive role models.[5] Nonetheless, living in a disadvantaged neighborhood places terrific strain on family functioning, especially in single-parent families that are socially isolated from relatives, friends, and neighbors. Children raised within such distressed families are at risk for delinquency.[6]

At one time, growing up in a single-parent home was considered a primary cause of criminal behavior. However, many criminologists today discount the association between family structure and the onset of criminality, claiming that family conflict and discord determine behavior more than family structure.[7] Not all experts, though, discount the effects of family structure on crime. Even if single parents can make up for the loss of a second parent, the argument goes, it is simply more difficult to do so, and the chances of failure increase.[8] Single parents may find it difficult to provide adequate supervision, and children who live with single parents receive less encouragement and less help with school-

C O N N E C T I O N S

Chapter 2's analysis of the class–crime relationship showed why this relationship is still a hotly debated topic. Although serious criminals may be found disproportionately in lower-class areas, self-report studies show that criminality cuts across class lines. The discussion of drug use in Chapter 13, which shows that members of the middle class use and abuse recreational substances, suggests that law violators are not necessarily economically motivated.

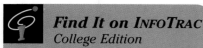

Find It on INFOTRAC
College Edition

Parents who assign their children chores allow them to experience responsibility. Independence and self-sufficiency in life are tied, ultimately, to mastery of two types of responsibility: personal responsibility and social responsibility. To read more about family relations and youthful behavior, go to InfoTrac College Edition and use "child rearing" as a keyword. You may want to read Rowland P. Barrett, "Assigned Chores Help Teach Social, Personal Responsibility," *Brown University Child and Adolescent Behavior Letter,* June 2000 v16 i6 p1

work. Poor school achievement and limited educational aspirations have been associated with delinquent behavior. Also, because they are receiving less attention as a result of having just one parent, these children may be more prone to rebellious acts, such as running away and truancy.[9] Children in two-parent households are more likely to want to attend college than those raised in single-parent homes.[10]

Other family factors that have predictive value include the following:

1. Inconsistent discipline, poor supervision, and the lack of a warm, loving, supportive parent–child relationship are all associated with delinquency.[11] Children who grow up in homes where parents use severe discipline yet lack warmth and involvement in their lives are prone to antisocial behavior.[12]

2. Children who have affectionate ties to their parents report greater levels of self-esteem beginning in adolescence and extending into adulthood; high self-esteem is inversely related to criminal behavior.[13]

3. Children growing up in homes where a parent suffers mental impairment are also at risk for delinquency.[14]

4. Children as young as 2 whose parents are drug abusers exhibit personality defects such as excessive anger and negativity.[15] These children, as well as older children of drug abusers, are more likely to become persistent substance abusers than the children of nonabusers.[16]

5. Children who experience abuse, neglect, or sexual abuse are believed to be more crime prone.[17] Links have been found among corporal punishment, delinquency, anger, spousal abuse, depression, and adult crime.[18]

Educational Experience

The educational process and adolescent school achievement have been linked to criminality. Children who do poorly in school, lack educational motivation, and feel alienated are the most likely to engage in criminal acts.[19] Children who fail in school offend more frequently than those who succeed. These children commit more serious and violent offenses and persist in crime into adulthood.[20]

Schools contribute to criminality by labeling problem youths, which sets them apart from conventional society. One way in which they perpetuate this stigmatization is through the track system, which identifies some students as college-bound and others as academic underachievers or potential dropouts.[21] Research findings over the past two decades indicate that many school dropouts, especially those who have been expelled, face a significant chance of entering a criminal career.[22]

Peer Relations

Psychologists have long recognized that peer groups powerfully affect human conduct and can dramatically influence decision making and behavior choices.[23] Children who are rejected by their peers are more likely to display aggressive behavior and disrupt group activities through bickering, bullying, or other antisocial behavior.[24] Research shows that adolescents who report inadequate or strained peer relations, and who say they are not popular with the opposite sex, are most likely to become delinquent.[25]

Delinquent peers often exert tremendous influence on behavior, attitudes, and beliefs.[26] In every level of the social structure, youths who fall in with a bad crowd become more susceptible to criminal behavior patterns.[27] Deviant peers provide friendship networks that support delinquency and drug use.[28] Activities such as riding around, staying out late, and partying with deviant peers give these youths the opportunity to commit deviant acts.[29] Because delinquent

social learning theory

The view that people learn to be aggressive by observing others acting aggressively to achieve some goal or being rewarded for violent acts.

Institutional Involvement and Belief

social control theory

The view that people commit crime when the forces that bind them to society are weakened or broken.

social reaction theory (labeling theory)

The view that people become criminals when labeled as such and they accept the label as a personal identity.

The Effects of Socialization on Crime

✔ Checkpoints

✔ Social process theories say that the way people are socialized controls their behavior choices.

✔ There is strong evidence that social relations influence behavior.

✔ Children growing up with conflict, abuse, and neglect are at risk for crime and delinquency.

✔ Educational failure has been linked to criminality.

✔ Adolescents who associate with deviant peers are more likely to engage in crime than those who maintain conventional peer group relations.

✔ Some criminologists maintain that crime is a learned behavior.

✔ Other criminologists view criminals as people whose behavior has not been controlled.

✔ Some view criminality as a function of labeling and stigma.

friends tend to be, as criminologist Mark Warr puts it, "sticky" (once acquired, they are not easily lost), peer influence may continue through the life span.[30] The more antisocial the peer group, the more likely its members are to engage in delinquency. Nondelinquent friends help to moderate delinquency.[31]

As children grow and move forward, friends influence their behavior, and their behavior influences their friends.[32] Antisocial friends guide delinquent careers so they withstand the aging-out process.[33] Chronic offenders surround themselves with peers who share their antisocial activities, and these relationships seem quite stable over time. People who maintain close relations with antisocial peers will sustain their own criminal behavior into adulthood. If peer influence diminishes, so too does criminal activity.[34]

Logic would dictate that people who hold high moral values and beliefs, who have learned to distinguish right from wrong, and who regularly attend religious services should also eschew crime and other antisocial behaviors. Religion binds people together and forces them to confront the consequences of their behavior. Committing crimes would violate the principles of all organized religions.

An often-cited study by sociologists Travis Hirschi and Rodney Stark found that, contrary to expectations, the association between religious attendance or belief and delinquent behavior patterns was negligible.[35] However, some recent research efforts have reached an opposing conclusion: Attending religious services significantly reduces crime. Interestingly, this type of participation seems to inhibit crime more than merely having religious beliefs and values.[36] Cross-national research shows that countries with high rates of church membership and attendance have lower crime rates.[37]

According to the social process view, people living in even the most deteriorated urban areas can successfully resist inducements to crime if they have a positive self-image, strong moral values, and support from their parents, peers, teachers, and neighbors. The girl with a positive self-image who is chosen for a college scholarship, has the warm, loving support of her parents, and is viewed as someone "going places" by friends and neighbors is less likely to adopt a criminal way of life than another young woman who is abused at home, who lives with criminal parents, and whose bond to her school and peer group is shattered because she is labeled a "troublemaker." The more social problems encountered during the socialization process, the greater the likelihood that youths will encounter difficulties and obstacles as they mature, such as being unemployed or becoming teenage parents.

The social process approach has several independent branches (see Figure 7.1). The first branch, **social learning theory**, suggests that people learn the techniques and attitudes of crime from close relationships with criminal peers: Crime is a learned behavior. The second branch, **social control theory**, maintains that everyone has the potential to become a criminal, but most people are controlled by their bonds to society. Crime occurs when the forces that bind people to society are weakened or broken. The third branch, **social reaction theory (labeling theory)**, says that people become criminals when significant members of society label them as such and they accept those labels as a personal identity.

Put another way, social learning theories assume that people are born good and learn to be bad; social control theory assumes that people are born bad and must be controlled in order to be good; and social reaction theory assumes that whether good or bad, people are controlled by the evaluations of others. Each of these independent branches will be discussed separately.

✔ Checkpoints

Figure 7.1

The Complex Web of Social Processes That Controls Human Behavior

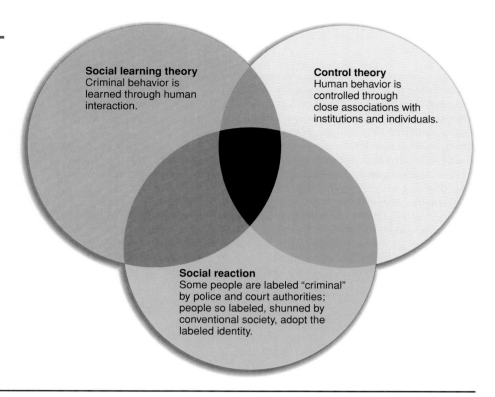

Social learning theory
Criminal behavior is learned through human interaction.

Control theory
Human behavior is controlled through close associations with institutions and individuals.

Social reaction
Some people are labeled "criminal" by police and court authorities; people so labeled, shunned by conventional society, adopt the labeled identity.

Social Learning Theories

Social learning theorists believe that crime is a product of learning the norms, values, and behaviors associated with criminal activity. Social learning can involve the actual techniques of crime (how to hot-wire a car or roll a joint) as well as the psychological aspects of criminality (how to deal with the guilt or shame associated with illegal activities). This section briefly reviews two of the most prominent forms of social learning theory: differential association theory and neutralization theory.

Differential Association Theory

differential association theory

The view that people commit crime when their social learning leads them to perceive more definitions favoring crime than favoring conventional behavior.

One of the most prominent social learning theories is Edwin H. Sutherland's **differential association theory**. Often considered the preeminent U.S. criminologist, Sutherland first put forth his theory in 1939 in his text *Principles of Criminology*.[38] The final version of the theory appeared in 1947. When Sutherland died in 1950, his longtime associate Donald Cressey continued his work. Cressey was so successful in explaining and popularizing his mentor's efforts that differential association theory remains one of the most enduring explanations of criminal behavior.

Sutherland's research on white-collar crime, professional theft, and intelligence led him to dispute the notion that crime was a function of the inadequacy of people in the lower classes.[39] He believed crime was a function of a learning process that could affect any individual in any culture. Acquiring a behavior is a socialization process, not a political or legal process. Skills and motives conducive to crime are learned as a result of contact with procrime values, attitudes, and definitions and other patterns of criminal behavior.

Principles of Differential Association Sutherland and Cressey explain the basic principles of differential association as follows:[40]

According to differential association theory, becoming a criminal is a learning process. Conversely, it may be possible to help troubled youth forgo criminality if they are taught prosocial behavior and attitudes. Here, brothers Hans (with daughter Jamile) and Ivan Hageman are shown outside the East Harlem School at Exodus House. The brothers gave up lucrative careers to run the school at the site of a former drug rehabilitation center. It has been described as a "nugget of hope within a neighborhood of despair."

AP/Wide World Photos

1. *Criminal behavior is learned.* This statement differentiates Sutherland's theory from prior attempts to classify criminal behavior as an inherent characteristic of criminals. Sutherland implies that criminality is learned in the same manner as any other learned behavior, such as writing, painting, or reading.

2. *Criminal behavior is learned as a by-product of interacting with others.* An individual does not start violating the law simply by living in a crimogenic environment or by manifesting personal characteristics, such as low IQ or family problems, associated with criminality. People actively learn as they are socialized and interact with other individuals who serve as teachers and guides to crime. Thus, criminality cannot occur without the aid of others.

3. *Learning criminal behavior occurs within intimate personal groups.* People's contacts with their most intimate social companions—family, friends, peers—have the greatest influence on their deviant behavior and attitude development. Relationships with these influential individuals color and control the way individuals interpret everyday events. For example, children who grow up in homes where parents abuse alcohol are more likely to view drinking as socially and physically beneficial.[41]

4. *Learning criminal behavior involves assimilating the techniques of committing crime, including motives, drives, rationalizations, and attitudes.* Young delinquents learn from their associates the proper way to pick a lock, shoplift, and obtain and use narcotics. In addition, novice criminals learn the proper terminology for their acts and acquire approved reactions to law violations. Criminals must learn how to react properly to their illegal acts, such as when to defend them, rationalize them, or show remorse for them.

5. *The specific direction of motives and drives is learned from perceptions of various aspects of the legal code as favorable or unfavorable.* Because the reaction to social rules and laws is not uniform across society, people constantly meet others who hold different views on the utility of obeying the legal code. Some people they admire may openly disdain or flout the law or ignore its substance. People experience what Sutherland calls **culture conflict** when they are exposed to opposing attitudes toward right and wrong or moral and immoral. The conflict of social attitudes and cultural norms is the basis for the concept of differential association.

culture conflict

Result of exposure to opposing norms, attitudes, and definitions of right and wrong, moral and immoral.

6. *A person becomes a criminal when he or she perceives more favorable than unfavorable consequences to violating the law.* According to Sutherland's theory, individuals become law violators when they are in contact with persons, groups, or events that produce an excess of definitions favorable toward criminality and are isolated from counteracting forces (see Figure 7.2). A definition favorable toward criminality occurs, for example, when a person hears friends talking about the virtues of getting high on drugs. A definition unfavorable toward crime occurs when friends or parents demonstrate their disapproval of crime.

7. *Differential associations may vary in frequency, duration, priority, and intensity.* Whether a person learns to obey the law or to disregard it is influenced by the quality of social interactions. Those of lasting duration have greater influence than those that are brief. Similarly, frequent contacts have greater effect than rare, haphazard contacts. *Priority* means the age of children when they first encounter definitions of criminality. Contacts made early in life probably have more influence than those developed later on. Finally, *intensity* is generally interpreted to mean the importance and prestige attributed to the individual or groups from whom the definitions are learned. For example, the influence of a father, mother, or trusted friend far outweighs the effect of more socially distant figures.

8. *The process of learning criminal behavior by association with criminal and anticriminal patterns involves all of the mechanisms that are involved in any other learning process.* Learning criminal behavior patterns is similar to learning nearly all other patterns and is not a matter of mere imitation.

9. *Although criminal behavior expresses general needs and values, it is not excused by those general needs and values because noncriminal behavior also expresses the same needs and values.* This principle suggests that the

Figure 7.2

Differential Associations

Differential association theory suggests that criminal behavior will occur when the definitions favorable toward crime outweigh the unfavorable definitions.

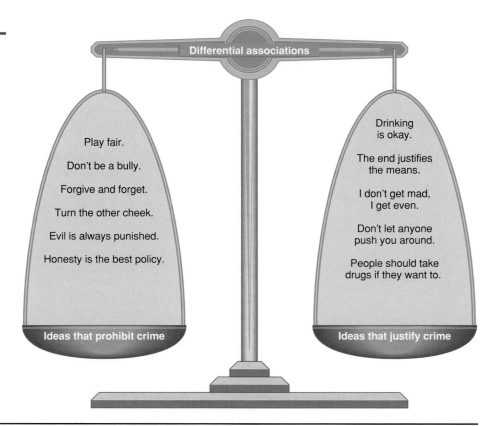

Differential associations

Play fair.

Don't be a bully.

Forgive and forget.

Turn the other cheek.

Evil is always punished.

Honesty is the best policy.

Drinking is okay.

The end justifies the means.

I don't get mad, I get even.

Don't let anyone push you around.

People should take drugs if they want to.

Ideas that prohibit crime

Ideas that justify crime

motives for criminal behavior cannot logically be the same as those for conventional behavior. Sutherland rules out such motives as desire to accumulate money or social status, personal frustration, or low self-concept as causes of crime because they are just as likely to produce noncriminal behavior, such as getting a better education or working harder on a job. Only the learning of deviant norms through contact with an excess of definitions favorable toward criminality produces illegal behavior.

In sum, differential association theory holds that people learn criminal attitudes and behavior during their adolescence from close, trusted friends or relatives. A criminal career develops if learned antisocial values and behaviors are not matched or exceeded by conventional attitudes and behaviors. Criminal behavior, then, is learned in a process that is similar to learning any other human behavior.

Testing Differential Association Theory Despite the importance of differential association theory, research devoted to testing its assumptions has been relatively sparse. It has proven difficult to conceptualize the principles of the theory in a way that can be tested empirically. For example, social scientists find it difficult to evaluate such vague concepts as "definition favorable toward criminality." It is also difficult to follow people over time, establish precisely when definitions favorable toward criminality begin to outweigh prosocial definitions, and determine if this imbalance produces criminal behavior.

Despite these limitations, several notable research efforts have supported the core principles of this theory. For example, Leanne Fiftal Alarid and her associates found that measures of differential association were a significant predictor of violent behavior in a sample of more than 1,000 convicted adult felons.[42] Differential association measures have also been associated with the onset of substance abuse and a career in the drug trade, which require learning proper techniques and attitudes from an experienced user or dealer.[43] Adolescent drug users are likely to have intimate relationships with a peer friendship network that supports their substance abuse and teaches them how to deal with the drug world.[44]

As predicted by differential association theory, having delinquent friends who support criminal attitudes and behavior is strongly related to developing criminal careers.[45] Criminologist Mark Warr found that delinquent peers interfere with the natural process of aging out of crime.[46]

Analysis of Differential Association Theory Differential association theory is important because it does not specify that criminals come from a disorganized area or are members of the lower class. Outwardly law-abiding, middle-class parents can encourage delinquent behavior by their own drinking, drug use, or family violence. The influence of differential associations is affected by social class; deviant learning experiences can affect youths in all classes.[47]

There are, however, a number of valid criticisms of Sutherland's work.[48] It fails to account for the origin of criminal definitions. How did the first "teacher" learn criminal attitudes and definitions in order to pass them on? Another criticism of differential association theory is that it assumes criminal and delinquent acts to be rational and systematic. This ignores spontaneous, wanton acts of violence and damage that appear to have little utility or purpose, such as the isolated psychopathic killing that is virtually unsolvable because of the killer's anonymity and lack of delinquent associations.

The most serious criticism of differential association theory concerns the vagueness of its terms, which makes its assumptions difficult to test. What constitutes an excess of definitions favorable toward criminality? How can we de-

Find It on INFOTRAC
College Edition

Use "differential association" as a subject guide in InfoTrac College Edition to review some of the latest studies that test Sutherland's basic assumptions about human nature.

CONNECTIONS

As you may recall from Chapter 2, most juveniles age out of crime and do not become adult offenders. Having delinquent friends may help to retard this process.

termine whether an individual actually has a crime-supporting imbalance of these deviant or antisocial definitions? Must we assume that, by definition, all criminals have experienced a majority of definitions toward crime and all non-criminals, a minority of them? Unless the theory's terms can be defined more precisely, its validity remains a matter of guesswork.

Neutralization Theory

neutralization theory

The view that law violators learn to neutralize conventional values and attitudes, enabling them to drift back and forth between criminal and conventional behavior.

drift

Movement in and out of delinquency, shifting between conventional and deviant values.

neutralization techniques

Methods of rationalizing deviant behavior, such as denying responsibility or blaming the victim.

Neutralization theory is identified with the writings of David Matza and his associate Gresham Sykes.[49] These criminologists also view the process of becoming a criminal as a learning experience. They theorize that law violators must learn and master techniques that enable them to neutralize conventional values and attitudes, thus allowing them to drift back and forth between illegitimate and conventional behavior.

Neutralization theory points out that even the most committed criminals and delinquents are not involved in criminality all the time; they also attend schools, family functions, and religious services. Thus, their behavior falls along a continuum between total freedom and total restraint. This process of **drift**, or movement from one extreme to another, produces behavior that is sometimes unconventional or deviant and at other times constrained and sober.[50] Learning **neutralization techniques** allows a person to temporarily drift away from conventional behavior and become involved in antisocial behaviors, including crime and drug abuse.[51]

Neutralization Techniques Sykes and Matza suggest that people develop a distinct set of justifications for their law-violating behavior. They base their theoretical model on several observations:[52]

1. *Criminals sometimes voice guilt over their illegal acts.* If they truly embraced criminal or antisocial values, criminals would probably not exhibit remorse for their acts, other than regret at being apprehended.

2. *Offenders frequently respect and admire honest, law-abiding persons.* Those admired may include entertainers, sports figures, priests and other clergy, parents, teachers, and neighbors.

3. *Criminals define whom they can victimize.* Members of similar ethnic groups, churches, or neighborhoods are often off-limits. This practice implies that criminals are aware of the wrongfulness of their acts.

4. *Criminals are not immune to the demands of conformity.* Most criminals frequently participate in the same social functions as law-abiding people—for example, school, church, and family activities.

Sykes and Matza conclude that criminals must first neutralize accepted social values before they are free to commit crimes; they do so by learning a set of techniques that allow them to counteract the moral dilemmas posed by illegal behavior.[53]

Through their research, Sykes and Matza have identified the following techniques of neutralization:

■ *Denial of responsibility.* Young offenders sometimes claim that their unlawful acts are not their fault—that they result from forces beyond their control or are accidents.

■ *Denial of injury.* By denying the injury caused by their acts, criminals neutralize illegal behavior. For example, stealing is viewed as borrowing; vandalism is considered mischief that has gotten out of hand. Offenders may find that their parents and friends support their denial of injury. In fact, they may claim that

CONNECTIONS

Denial of the victim may help explain hate crimes, in which people are victimized simply because they belong to the "wrong" race, religion, or ethnic group or because of their sexual orientation. Hate crimes are discussed in Chapter 10.

the behavior was merely a prank, helping affirm the offender's perception that crime can be socially acceptable.

■ *Denial of the victim.* Criminals sometimes neutralize wrongdoing by maintaining that the crime victim "had it coming." Vandalism may be directed against a disliked teacher or neighbor, or a gang may beat up homosexuals because their behavior is considered offensive.

■ *Condemnation of the condemners.* An offender views the world as a corrupt place with a dog-eat-dog code. Because police and judges are on the take, teachers show favoritism, and parents take out their frustrations on their children, offenders claim it is ironic and unfair for these authorities to condemn criminal misconduct. By shifting the blame to others, criminals repress the feeling that their own acts are wrong.

■ *Appeal to higher loyalties.* Novice criminals often argue that they are caught in the dilemma of being loyal to their peer group while attempting to abide by the rules of society. The needs of the group take precedence because group demands are immediate and localized (see Figure 7.3).

In sum, neutralization theory states that people neutralize conventional norms and values by using excuses that allow them to drift into crime.

Testing Neutralization Theory Attempts have been made to verify neutralization theory empirically, but the results have been inconclusive.[54] One area of research has been directed at determining whether law violators really need to neutralize moral constraints. The thinking behind this research is that if

Figure 7.3

Techniques of Neutralization

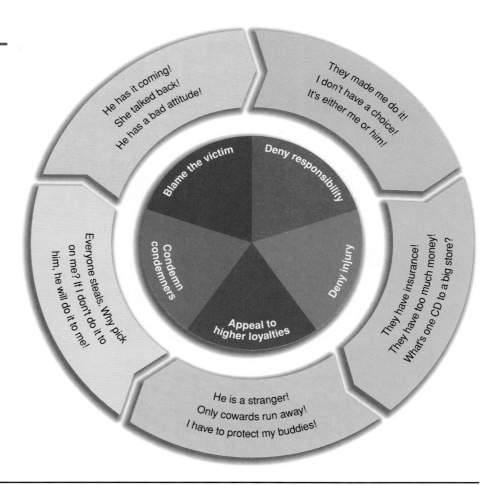

criminals hold values in opposition to accepted social norms, then there is really no need to neutralize. So far, the evidence is mixed. Some studies show that law violators approve of criminal behavior such as theft and violence, whereas others find evidence that even though they may be active participants themselves, criminals voice disapproval of illegal behavior.[55] Some studies indicate that law violators approve of social values such as honesty and fairness; others come to the opposite conclusion.[56]

Although the existing research findings are ambiguous, the weight of the evidence shows that most adolescents generally disapprove of deviant behaviors such as violence, and that neutralizations do in fact enable youths to engage in socially disapproved behavior.[57] And, as Matza predicted, people seem to drift in and out of antisocial behavior rather than being committed solely to a criminal way of life.[58]

Are Learning Theories Valid?

Learning theories contribute significantly to our understanding of the onset of criminal behavior. Nonetheless, the general learning model has been criticized. One complaint is that learning theorists fail to account for the origin of criminal definitions. How did the first criminal learn the necessary techniques and definitions? Who came up with the original neutralization technique?

Learning theories imply that people systematically learn techniques that allow them to be active, successful criminals. However, they fail to adequately explain spontaneous, wanton acts of violence, damage, and other expressive crimes that appear to have little utility or purpose. Although principles of differential association can easily explain shoplifting, is it possible that a random shooting is caused by excessive deviant definitions? It is estimated that about 70 percent of all arrestees were under the influence of drugs and alcohol when they committed their crime. Do "crack heads" pause to neutralize their moral inhibitions before mugging a victim? Do drug-involved kids stop to consider what they have learned about moral values?[59]

Little evidence exists that people learn the techniques that enable them to become criminals before they actually commit criminal acts. It is equally plausible that people who are already deviant seek others with similar lifestyles to learn from. Early onset of deviant behavior is now considered a key determinant of criminal careers. It is difficult to see how extremely young children have had the opportunity to learn criminal behavior and attitudes within a peer group setting.

Despite these criticisms, learning theories have an important place in the study of delinquent and criminal behavior. Unlike social structure theories, these theories are not limited to explaining a single facet of antisocial activity; they explain criminality across all class structures. Even corporate executives may be exposed to procriminal definitions and learn to neutralize moral constraints. Learning theories can thus be applied to a wide assortment of criminal activity.

Social Control Theory

Social control theorists maintain that all people have the potential to violate the law and that modern society presents many opportunities for illegal activity. Criminal activities, such as drug abuse and car theft, are often exciting pastimes that hold the promise of immediate reward and gratification.

Considering the attractions of crime, social control theorists question why people obey the rules of society. They argue that people obey the law because behavior and passions are controlled by internal and external forces. Some individuals have **self-control**—a strong moral sense that renders them incapable of hurting others and violating social norms. Other people have been

self-control

A strong moral sense that renders a person incapable of hurting others or violating social norms.

commitment to conformity

A strong personal investment in conventional institutions, individuals, and processes that prevents people from engaging in behavior that might jeopardize their reputation and achievements.

socialized to have a **commitment to conformity**. They have developed a real, present, and logical reason to obey the rules of society, and they instinctively avoid behavior that will jeopardize their reputation and achievements.[60] The stronger people's commitment to conventional institutions, individuals, and processes, the less likely they are to commit crime. If that commitment is absent, there is little to lose, and people are free to violate the law.[61]

Self-Concept and Crime

Early versions of control theory speculated that criminality was a product of weak self-concept and poor self-esteem. Youths who are socialized to feel good about themselves and maintain a positive attitude are able to resist the temptations of the streets.

As early as 1951, sociologist Albert Reiss described delinquents as having weak egos and lacking the self-control to produce conforming behavior.[62] Scott Briar and Irving Piliavin noted that youths who believe that criminal activity will damage their self-image and their relationships with others are likely to conform to social rules; in contrast, those less concerned about their social standing are free to violate the law.[63] Pioneering control theorist Walter Reckless argued that a strong self-image insulates a youth from the pressures of crimogenic influences in the environment.[64] In studies conducted within the school setting, Reckless and his colleagues found that students who were able to maintain a positive self-image were insulated from delinquency.[65]

These early works suggested that people who have a weak self-image and damaged ego are crime prone. They are immune from efforts to apply social control: Why obey the rules of society when you have no stake in the future and little to lose?

Contemporary Social Control Theory

social bond

The ties that bind people to society, including relationships with friends, family, neighbors, teachers, and employers. Elements of the social bond include commitment, attachment, involvement, and belief.

The version of control theory articulated by Travis Hirschi in his influential 1969 book *Causes of Delinquency,* is today the dominant version of control theories.[66] Hirschi links the onset of criminality to the weakening of the ties that bind people to society. He assumes that all individuals are potential law violators, but most are kept under control because they fear that illegal behavior will damage their relationships with friends, family, neighbors, teachers, and employers. Without these **social bonds** or ties, a person is free to commit criminal acts. Among all ethnic, religious, racial, and social groups, people whose bond to society is weak may fall prey to crimogenic behavior patterns.

Hirschi argues that the social bond a person maintains with society is divided into four main elements: attachment, commitment, involvement, and belief (see Figure 7.4).

1. *Attachment.* Attachment refers to a person's sensitivity to and interest in others.[67] Hirschi views parents, peers, and schools as the important social institutions with which a person should maintain ties. Attachment to parents is the most important. Even if a family is shattered by divorce or separation, a child must retain a strong attachment to one or both parents. Without this attachment, it is unlikely that respect for other authorities will develop.

2. *Commitment.* Commitment involves the time, energy, and effort expended in conventional actions such as getting an education and saving money for the future. If people build a strong commitment to conventional society, they will be less likely to engage in acts that jeopardize their hard-won position. Conversely, the lack of commitment to conventional values may foreshadow a condition in which risk-taking behavior, such as crime, becomes a reasonable behavior alternative.

Figure 7.4

Elements of the Social Bond

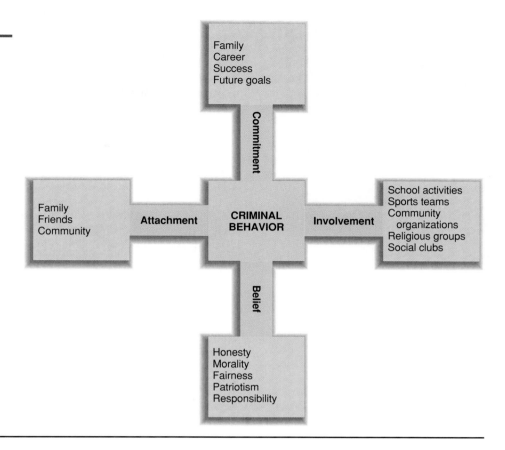

3. *Involvement.* Heavy involvement in conventional activities leaves little time for illegal behavior. Hirschi believes that involvement in school, recreation, and family insulates people from the potential lure of criminal behavior. Idleness, on the other hand, enhances that lure.

4. *Belief.* People who live in the same social setting often share common moral beliefs; they may adhere to such values as sharing, sensitivity to the rights of others, and admiration for the legal code. If these beliefs are absent or weakened, individuals are more likely to participate in antisocial or illegal acts.

Hirschi further suggests that the interrelationship of social bond elements controls subsequent behavior. For example, people who feel kinship and sensitivity to parents and friends should be more likely to adopt and work toward legitimate goals. On the other hand, a person who rejects such social relationships is more likely to lack commitment to conventional goals. Similarly, people who are highly committed to conventional acts and beliefs are more likely to be involved in conventional activities.

Testing Social Control Theory

One of Hirschi's most significant contributions was his attempt to test the principal hypotheses of social control theory. He administered a detailed self-report survey to a sample of more than 4,000 junior and senior high school students in Contra Costa County, California.[68] In a detailed analysis of the data, Hirschi found considerable evidence to support the control theory model. Among Hirschi's more important findings are the following:

CONNECTIONS

Although his work has achieved a prominent place in criminological literature, Hirschi, along with Michael Gottfredson, has restructured his concept of control by integrating biosocial, psychological, and rational choice theory ideas into a general theory of crime. Because this theory is essentially integrated, it will be discussed more fully in Chapter 9.

- Youths who were strongly attached to their parents were less likely to commit criminal acts.
- Youths involved in conventional activity, such as homework, were less likely to engage in criminal behavior.
- Youths involved in unconventional behavior, such as smoking and drinking, were more prone to delinquency.
- Youths who maintained weak, distant relationships with people tended toward delinquency.
- Those who shunned unconventional acts were attached to their peers.
- Delinquents and nondelinquents shared similar beliefs about society.

Hirschi's data gave important support to the validity of social control theory. Even when the statistical significance of his findings was less than he expected, the direction of his research data was notably consistent. Only rarely did his findings contradict the theory's most critical assumptions.

Supporting Research Hirschi's version of social control theory has been corroborated by numerous research studies showing that delinquent youths often feel detached from society.[69] Supporting research indicates that both male and female delinquents experience attachments to the family, peer group, and school that are strained and weakened.[70] In contrast, positive attachments help control delinquency.[71] For example, youths who fail at school and are detached from the educational experience are at risk of criminality; those who do well and are committed to school are less likely to engage in delinquent acts.[72]

Opposing Views More than 70 published attempts have been made to corroborate social control theory by replicating Hirschi's original survey techniques.[73] Though providing significant empirical support for Hirschi's work, these studies have also raised a number of questions.

Hirschi maintains that delinquents are not attached to their peers. Even if adolescents join together to form criminal gangs, within-group relationships are actually strained and remote. Here, girl gang members engage in a violent initiation ceremony. Can such violent youths have warm personal relationships?

■ *Friendship.* One significant criticism concerns Hirschi's contention that delinquents are detached loners whose bond to family and friends has been broken. In fact, delinquents seem not to be "lone wolves" whose only personal relationships are exploitative; their friendship patterns seem quite close to those of conventional youth.[74] Some types of offenders, such as drug abusers, may maintain even more intimate relations with their peers than nonabusers.[75]

■ *Failure to achieve.* Hirschi argues that commitment to career and economic advancement reduces criminal involvement. However, research indicates that people who are committed to success but fail to achieve it may be crime prone.[76]

■ *Involvement negates supervision.* Adolescents who report high levels of involvement, which Hirschi suggests should reduce delinquency, actually report high levels of criminal behavior. Perhaps adolescents who are involved in activities outside the home have less contact with parental supervision and greater opportunity to commit crime.[77]

■ *Deviant peers and parents.* Hirschi's conclusion that any form of social attachment is beneficial, even to deviant peers and parents, has also been disputed. Rather than deter delinquency, attachment to deviant peers may support and nurture antisocial behavior.[78] A number of research efforts have found that youths attached to drug-abusing parents are more likely to use drugs themselves.[79] Attachment to deviant family members, peers, and associates may help motivate youths to commit crime and facilitate their antisocial acts.[80]

■ Hirschi's theory proposes that a weakened bond leads to delinquency, but Robert Agnew suggests that the chain of events may flow in the opposite direction: Perhaps youngsters who break the law find that their bonds to parents, schools, and society eventually become weak. Other studies have also found that criminal behavior weakens social bonds and not vice versa.[81]

While these criticisms are important, Hirschi's views still constitute one of the preeminent theories in criminology.[82] Many criminologists consider social control theory the most important way of understanding the onset of youthful misbehavior. ✔ **Checkpoints**

✔ Checkpoints

✔ Social control theories maintain that behavior is a function of the attachment that people feel toward society. People who have a weak commitment to conformity are free to commit crime.

✔ A strong self-image may insulate people from crime.

✔ According to Hirschi, social control is measured by a person's attachment, commitment, involvement, and belief.

Social Reaction (Labeling) Theory

Social reaction theory, or labeling theory (the two terms are used interchangeably here), explains criminal careers in terms of destructive social interactions and stigma-producing encounters.

According to this view, people are given a variety of symbolic labels that help define not just one trait, but the whole person. Valued labels, such as "smart," "honest," and "hardworking," suggest overall competence. Sometimes the labels are symbolic, such as being named "most likely to succeed" or class valedictorian. People who hold these titles are automatically assumed to be leaders who are well on their way to success. Without meeting them, we know that they are hardworking, industrious, and bright. These positive labels can improve self-image and social standing. Research shows that people who are labeled with one positive trait, such as being physically attractive, are assumed to have other positive traits, such as being intelligent and competent.[83]

In contrast, some people are given negative labels, such as "troublemaker," "mentally ill," and "stupid," that **stigmatize** them and reduce their self-image. For example, people labeled "insane" are also assumed to be dangerous, dishonest, unstable, violent, strange, and otherwise unsound.

Both positive and negative labels involve subjective interpretation of behavior: A "troublemaker" is merely someone whom people label as "troublesome." There need not be any objective proof or measure indicating that the person is

stigmatize

To apply negative labeling with enduring effects on a person's self-image and social interactions.

The Scary Guy (now his legal name) is covered from head to toe in tattoos. What do you think he is like? What are his personality traits? Would you want him to meet your family? Are you labeling him?

AP/Wide World Photos

actually a troublemaker. Although a label may be a function of rumor, innuendo, or unfounded suspicion, its adverse impact can be immense.

If a devalued status is conferred by a significant other—teacher, police officer, parent, or valued peer—the negative label may permanently harm the target. The degree to which a person is perceived as a social deviant may affect his or her treatment at home, at work, at school, and in other social situations. Children may find that their parents consider them a bad influence on younger brothers and sisters. School officials may limit them to classes reserved for people with behavioral problems. Likewise, when adults are labeled as "criminal," "ex-con," or "drug addict," they may find their eligibility for employment severely restricted. If the label is bestowed as the result of conviction for a criminal offense, the labeled person may also be subjected to official sanctions ranging from a mild reprimand to incarceration. The simultaneous effects of labels and sanctions reinforce feelings of isolation and detachment.

According to labeling theory, depending on the visibility of the label and the manner and severity with which it is applied, negatively labeled individuals will become increasingly commited to a deviant career. They may be watched, suspected, and excluded more and more from legitimate opportunities.[84] Labeled persons may find themselves turning to others similarly stigmatized for support and companionship. Isolated from conventional society, they may identify themselves as members of an outcast group and become locked into deviance. Figure 7.5 illustrates this process.

Because the process of becoming stigmatized is essentially interactive, labeling theorists blame the establishment of criminal careers on the social agencies originally designed for crime control, such as police, courts, and correctional agencies. It is these institutions, labeling theorists claim, that produce the stigma that harms the people they are trying to help, treat, or correct. As a result, they actually help to maintain and amplify criminal behavior.

Crime and Labeling Theory

According to the social reaction approach, crime and deviance are defined by the social audience's reaction to people and their behavior and the subsequent effects of that reaction; they are not defined by the moral content of the illegal act itself. In a famous statement, Howard Becker sums up the importance of the audience's reaction:

> Social groups create deviance by making rules whose infractions constitute deviance, and by applying those rules to particular people and labeling them as outsiders. From this point of view, deviance is not a quality of the act a person commits, but rather a consequence of the application by others of rules and sanctions to an "offender." The deviant is one to whom the label has successfully been applied; deviant behavior is behavior that people so label.[85]

In its purest form, social reaction theory argues that even such crimes as murder, rape, and assault are only bad or evil because people label them as such. After all, the difference between an excusable act and a criminal one is often a matter of changing legal definition. Acts such as performing an abortion, using marijuana, possessing a handgun, and gambling have been legal at some times and places and illegal at others.

Even if some acts are labeled as bad or evil, those who participate in them can be spared a negative label. For example, it is possible to take another person's life but not be considered a "murderer" because the killing was considered self-defense or even an accident. Acts have negative consequences only when they are labeled wrong or evil by others.

A social reaction theorist views crime as a subjective concept whose definition depends entirely on the viewing audience. An act that is considered criminal by one person may be perfectly acceptable behavior to another. Because crime is defined by those in power, the shape of criminal law is defined by the values of those who rule, not an objective standard of moral conduct. Howard Becker refers to people who create rules as **moral entrepreneurs**. An example of a moral entrepreneur today might be a member of an ultra-orthodox religious group who targets the gay lifestyle and campaigns to prevent gays from adopting children or marrying their same-sex partners.[86]

moral entrepreneur

A person who creates moral rules, which thus reflect the values of those in power rather than any objective, universal standards of right and wrong.

Differential Enforcement

An important principle of social reaction theory is that the law is differentially applied, benefiting those who hold economic and social power and penalizing the powerless. The probability of being brought under the control of legal authority is a function of a person's race, wealth, gender, and social standing. A core concept of social reaction theory is that police officers are more likely to formally arrest males, minority group members, and those in the lower class, and to use their discretionary powers to give beneficial treatment to more favored groups.[87] Minorities and the poor are more likely to be prosecuted for criminal offenses and receive harsher punishment when convicted.[88] Judges may sympathize with white defendants and help them avoid criminal labels, especially if they seem to come from "good families," whereas minority youths are not afforded that luxury.[89] This helps to explain why there are significant racial and economic differences in the crime rate.

In sum, a major premise of social reaction theory is that the law is differentially constructed and applied, depending on the offender. It favors powerful members of society, who direct its content, and penalizes people whose actions threaten those in control, such as minority group members and the poor who demand equal rights.[90]

Consequences of Labeling

Negative labels stigmatize people and alter their self-image. The labeled person is transformed into a social outcast who is prevented from enjoying higher education, well-paying jobs, and other social benefits.

Public denunciation plays an important part in the labeling process. Condemnation is often carried out in "ceremonies" in which the individual's identity is officially transformed. Examples of such reidentification ceremonies are a competency hearing in which a person is declared to be "mentally ill" or a public trial in which a person is found to be a "rapist" or "child molester." During the process, a permanent record is produced, such as an arrest or conviction record, so that the denounced person is ritually separated from a place in the legitimate order and placed outside the world occupied by citizens of good standing. Harold Garfinkle has called transactions that produce irreversible, permanent labels "successful degradation ceremonies."[91]

Changing Self-Image Successful labeling produces a reevaluation of the self that reflects actual or perceived appraisals made by others. Children who view themselves as delinquents after being labeled as such are giving an inner voice to their perceptions of how parents, teachers, peers, and neighbors view them. When they believe that others view them as antisocial or troublemakers, they take on attitudes and roles that reflect this assumption. They expect to become suspects and then to be rejected.[92]

Tempering or enhancing the effect of this **reflective role-taking** are the people and institutions with whom the labeled person comes in contact. For example, an understanding teacher can help overcome the negative label of low-track student and encourage an adolescent to excel in school. However, when these groups are dysfunctional, such as when parents use drugs, they encourage rather than control antisocial behavior.[93]

Joining Deviant Cliques People who are labeled as deviant may join with similarly outcast peers who facilitate their behavior. Eventually, antisocial behavior becomes habitual and automatic.[94] The desire to join deviant cliques and groups may stem from self-rejecting attitudes ("At times, I think I am no good at all") that eventually weaken commitment to conventional values and behaviors. In turn, stigmatized individuals may acquire motives to deviate from social norms because they now share a common bond with similarly labeled social outcasts.[95] They may join cliques like the "Trenchcoat Mafia" whose members were involved in the 1999 Littleton, Colorado, school massacre. Membership in a deviant subculture often involves conforming to group norms that conflict with those of conventional society, further enhancing the effects of the labeling process.

Retrospective Reading Beyond any immediate results, labels tend to redefine the whole person. For example, the label "ex-con" may create in people's imaginations a whole series of behavior descriptions—tough, mean, dangerous, aggressive, dishonest, sneaky—that may or may not apply to a person who has been in prison. People react to the label description and what it signifies, instead of reacting to the actual behavior of the person who bears it. The labeled person's past is reviewed and reevaluated to fit his or her current status—a process known as **retrospective reading**. For example, boyhood friends of an

Figure 7.5

The Labeling Process

Initial criminal act
People commit crimes for a number of reasons.

Detection by the justice system
Arrest is influenced by racial, economic, and power relations.

Decision to label
Some are labeled "official" criminals by police and court authorities.

Creation of a new identity
Those labeled are known as troublemakers, criminals, etc., and shunned by conventional society.

Acceptance of labels
Labeled people begin to see themselves as outsiders (secondary deviance, self-labeling).

Deviance amplification
Stigmatized offenders are now locked into criminal careers.

reflective role-taking

Assuming an identity based on the actual or perceived appraisals of others.

retrospective reading

The reassessment of a person's past to fit a current generalized label.

assassin or serial killer, interviewed by the media, report that the suspect was withdrawn, suspicious, and negativistic as a youth; they were always suspicious but never thought to report their concerns to the authorities. According to this retrospective reading, we can now understand what prompted his current behavior; therefore, the label must be accurate.[96]

Labels, then, become the basis of personal identity. As the negative feedback of law enforcement agencies, parents, friends, teachers, and other figures amplifies the force of the original label, stigmatized offenders may begin to reevaluate their own identities. If they are not really evil or bad, they may ask themselves, why is everyone making such a fuss? This process has been referred to as the "dramatization of evil."[97]

Primary and Secondary Deviance

One of the better-known views of the labeling process is Edwin Lemert's concept of primary deviance and secondary deviance.[98] According to Lemert, **primary deviance** involves norm violations or crimes that have little influence on the actor and can be quickly forgotten. For example, a college student successfully steals a textbook at the campus bookstore, gets an A in the course, graduates, is admitted to law school, and later becomes a famous judge. Because his shoplifting goes unnoticed, it is a relatively unimportant event that has little bearing on his future life.

primary deviance

A norm violation or crime with little or no long-term influence on the violator.

In contrast, **secondary deviance** occurs when a deviant event comes to the attention of significant others or social control agents, who apply a negative label. The newly labeled offender then reorganizes his or her behavior and personality around the consequences of the deviant act. The shoplifting student is caught by a security guard and expelled from college. With his law school dreams dashed and future cloudy, his options are limited; people say he lacks character, and he begins to share their opinion. He eventually becomes a drug dealer and winds up in prison (see Figure 7.6).

secondary deviance

A norm violation or crime that comes to the attention of significant others or social control agents, who apply a negative label with long-term consequences for the violator's self-identity and social interactions.

Secondary deviance involves resocialization into a deviant role. The labeled person is transformed into one who, according to Lemert, "employs his behavior or a role based upon it as a means of defense, attack, or adjustment to

Figure 7.6

Primary and Secondary Deviance

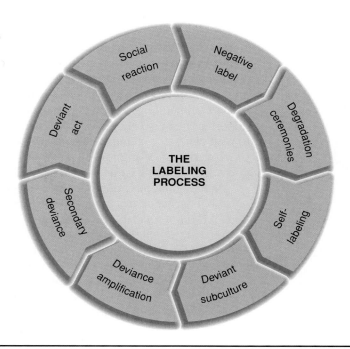

deviance amplification

Process whereby secondary deviance pushes offenders out of mainstream of society and locks them into an escalating cycle of deviance, apprehension, labeling, and criminal self-identity.

the overt and covert problems created by the consequent social reaction to him."[99] Secondary deviance produces a **deviance amplification** effect: Offenders feel isolated from the mainstream of society and become locked within their deviant role. They may seek others similarly labeled to form deviant groups. Ever more firmly enmeshed in their deviant role, they are trapped in an escalating cycle of deviance, apprehension, more powerful labels, and identity transformation. Lemert's concept of secondary deviance expresses the core of social reaction theory: Deviance is a process in which one's identity is transformed. Efforts to control offenders, whether by treatment or punishment, simply help to lock them in their deviant role.

Research on Social Reaction Theory

Research on social reaction theory can be classified into two distinct categories. The first focuses on the characteristics of those offenders who are chosen for labeling. The theory predicts that they will be relatively powerless people who are unable to defend themselves against the negative labeling. The second type of research attempts to discover the effects of being labeled. Labeling theorists predict that people who are negatively labeled will view themselves as deviant and commit increasing amounts of crime.

Victims of Labeling There is evidence that, as predicted by labeling theory, poor and powerless people are victimized by the law and justice system. Labels are not equally distributed across class and racial lines. From the police officer's decision on whom to arrest, to the prosecutor's decisions on whom to charge and how many and what kinds of charges to bring, to the court's decision on whom to release or grant bail, to the grand jury's decision on indictment, to the judge's decision on sentence length, discretion works to the detriment of minorities.[100] Sometimes the effects are subtle and hard to detect. Samuel Walker, Cassia Spohn, and Miriam DeLone identify what they call **contextual discrimination**, a practice in which African Americans receive harsher punishments in some instances (as when they victimize whites) but not in others (as when they victimize other blacks).[101] Judges may also be more likely to impose prison sentences on racial minorities in borderline cases for which whites get probation. According to Walker, Spohn, and DeLone, racism is hard to detect but still influences the distribution of criminal sanctions.

contextual discrimination

A practice in which African Americans receive harsher punishments in some instances (as when they victimize whites) but not in others (as when they victimize other blacks).

Effects of Labeling Empirical evidence shows that negative labels dramatically influence the self-image of offenders. Considerable evidence indicates that social sanctions lead to self-labeling and deviance amplification.[102] For example, children negatively labeled by their parents routinely suffer a variety of problems, including antisocial behavior and school failure.[103] This process is important because once they are labeled as troublemakers, adolescents begin to reassess their self-image. Parents who label their children as troublemakers promote deviance amplification. Labeling alienates parents from their children, and negative labels reduce children's self-image and increase delinquency.[104]

As they mature, children are in danger of receiving repeated, intensive, official labeling, which has been shown to produce self-labeling and damage identities.[105] Youngsters labeled as troublemakers in school are the most likely to drop out; dropping out has been linked to delinquent behavior.[106] Even in adults, the labeling process can take its toll. Male drug users labeled as addicts by social control agencies eventually become self-labeled and increase their drug use.[107] People arrested in domestic violence cases, especially those with a low stake in conformity (for example, those who are jobless and unmarried) increase offending after being given official labels.[108]

Empirical evidence supports the view that labeling plays an important role in persistent offending.[109] Although labels may not cause adolescents to initiate

CONNECTIONS

Fear of stigma has prompted efforts to reduce the impact of criminal labels through such programs as pretrial diversion and community treatment. In addition, some criminologists have called for noncoercive "peacemaking" solutions to interpersonal conflict. This peacemaking or restorative justice movement is reviewed in Chapter 8.

criminal behaviors, experienced delinquents are significantly more likely to continue offending if they believe that their parents and peers view them in a negative light.[110] Labeling, then, may help sustain criminality over time.

Is Labeling Theory Valid?

Criminologists Raymond Paternoster and Leeann Iovanni have identified features of the labeling perspective that are important contributions to the study of criminality:[111]

- The labeling perspective identifies the role played by social control agents in crime causation. Criminal behavior cannot be fully understood if the agencies and individuals empowered to control and treat it are neglected.
- Labeling theory recognizes that criminality is not a disease or pathological behavior. It focuses attention on the social interactions and reactions that shape individuals and their behavior.
- Labeling theory distinguishes between criminal acts (primary deviance) and criminal careers (secondary deviance) and shows that these concepts must be interpreted and treated differently.

Labeling theory is also important because of its focus on interaction as well as the situation surrounding the crime. Rather than viewing the criminal as a robotlike creature whose actions are predetermined, it recognizes that crime often results from complex interactions and processes. The decision to commit crime involves actions of a variety of people, including peers, victim, police, and other key characters. Labels may foster crime by guiding the actions of all parties involved in these criminal interactions. Actions deemed innocent when performed by one person are considered provocative when engaged in by someone who has been labeled as deviant. Similarly, labeled people may be quick to judge, take offense, or misinterpret others' behavior because of past experience. ✔ **Checkpoints**

✔ Checkpoints

✔ According to labeling theory, stigma helps lock people into a deviant career.

✔ Labels amplify deviant behavior rather than deter future criminality.

✔ Primary deviants view themselves as good people who have done a bad thing; secondary deviants accept a negative label as an identity.

✔ Labels are bestowed in a biased fashion. The poor and minority group members are more likely to receive labels.

An Evaluation of Social Process Theory

The branches of social process theory—social learning, social control, and social reaction—are compatible because they all suggest that criminal behavior is part of the socialization process. Criminals are people whose interactions with critically important social institutions and processes—the family, schools, the justice system, peer groups, employers, and neighbors—are troubled. Although some disagree about the relative importance of those influences and the form they take, there is little question that social interactions shape the behavior, beliefs, values, and self-image of the offender. People who have learned deviant social values, find themselves detached from conventional social relationships, or are the subject of stigma and labels from significant others are the most likely to commit crime. These negative influences can influence anyone, beginning in youth and continuing through adulthood. The major strength of the social process view is the vast body of empirical data showing that delinquents and criminals are people who grew up in dysfunctional families, who had troubled childhoods, and who failed at school, at work, and in marriage. Prison data show that these characteristics are typical of inmates.

Although persuasive, these theories do not always account for some of the patterns and fluctuations in the crime rate. If social process theories are valid, for example, people in the West and South must be socialized differently than those in the Midwest and New England, where crime rates are lower. How can seasonal crime rate variations be explained if crime is a function of learning or control? How can social processes explain why criminals escalate their activity or why they desist from crime? Once a social bond is broken, how can it be reattached? Once crime is learned, how can it be unlearned? These are questions that must still be answered by social process theorists.

Social Process Theory and Social Policy

Social process theories have had a major influence on social policies since the 1950s. Learning theories have greatly influenced the way criminal offenders are treated. The effect of these theories has been felt mainly by young offenders, who are viewed as being more salvageable than hardened criminals. Advocates of the social learning approach argue that if people become criminal by learning definitions and attitudes favoring criminality, they can unlearn them by being exposed to definitions favoring conventional behavior.

This philosophy has been used in numerous treatment facilities based in part on two early, pioneering efforts: the Highfields Project in New Jersey and the Silverlake Program in Los Angeles. These were residential treatment programs, geared toward young male offenders, that used group interaction sessions to attack criminal behavior orientations while promoting conventional lines of behavior. It is common today for residential and nonresidential programs to offer similar treatment, teaching children and adolescents to refuse drugs, to forgo delinquent behavior, and to stay in school. It is even common for celebrities to return to their old neighborhoods to urge young people to stay in school or off drugs. If learning did not affect behavior, such exercises would be futile.

Control theories have also influenced criminal justice and other social policies. Programs have been developed to increase people's commitment to conventional lines of action. Some work at creating and strengthening bonds early in life before the onset of criminality. The educational system has hosted numerous programs designed to improve basic skills and create an atmosphere in which youths will develop a bond to their schools. The accompanying Policy and Practice in Criminology discusses the Head Start program, perhaps the largest and most successful attempt to solidify social bonds.

Control theory's focus on the family has played a key role in programs designed to strengthen the bond between parent and child. Others attempt to repair bonds that have been broken and frayed. Examples of this approach are the career, work furlough, and educational opportunity programs being developed in the nation's prisons. These programs are designed to help inmates maintain a stake in society so they will be less willing to resort to criminal activity after their release.

Labeling theorists caution against too much intervention. Rather than ask social agencies to attempt to rehabilitate people having problems with the law, they argue, less is better. Put another way, the more institutions try to help people, the more these people will be stigmatized and labeled. For example, a special education program designed to help problem readers may cause them to label themselves and others as slow or stupid. Similarly, a mental health rehabilitation program created with the best intentions may cause clients to be labeled as crazy or dangerous.

The influence of labeling theory can be seen in diversion and restitution programs. **Diversion programs** remove both juvenile and adult offenders from the normal channels of the criminal justice process by placing them in rehabilitation programs. For example, a college student whose drunken driving hurts a pedestrian may, before trial, be placed for six months in an alcohol treatment program. If he successfully completes the program, charges against him will be dismissed; thus he avoids the stigma of a criminal label. Such programs are common throughout the United States. Often they offer counseling, medical advice, and vocational, educational, and family services.

diversion programs

Programs of rehabilitation that remove offenders from the normal channels of the criminal justice process, thus avoiding the stigma of a criminal label.

restitution

Permitting an offender to repay the victim or do useful work in the community rather than face the stigma of a formal trial and a court-ordered sentence.

Social process theories suggest that people can be helped by social programs that help them become committed and attached to society. Here, Head Start children in Illinois rally with their parents and care providers for improved day-care legislation. Participation in programs such as Head Start helps youngsters develop a commitment to society.

AP/Wide World Photos

Another popular label-avoiding innovation is **restitution**. Rather than face the stigma of a formal trial, an offender is asked either to pay back the victim of the crime for any loss incurred or to do some useful work in the community, in lieu of receiving a court-ordered sentence.

Despite their good intentions, stigma-reducing programs have not met with great success. Critics charge that they substitute one kind of stigma for another—for instance, attending a mental health program in lieu of a criminal trial. In addition, diversion and restitution programs usually screen out violent and repeat offenders. Finally, there is little hard evidence that these alternative programs improve recidivism rates.

Summary

Social process theories view criminality as a function of people's interaction with various organizations, institutions, and processes in society. People in all walks of life have the potential to become criminals if they maintain destructive social relationships. Social process theory has three main branches: Social learning theory stresses that people learn how to commit crimes. Social control theory analyzes the failure of society

Policy and Practice in Criminology

Head Start

Head Start is probably the best-known effort to help young children achieve proper socialization and, in so doing, reduce their potential for future criminality. Head Start programs were instituted in the 1960s as part of President Lyndon Johnson's War on Poverty. In the beginning, Head Start was a two-month summer program for children who were about to enter school. Aimed at embracing the "whole child," it offered comprehensive programming designed to enhance physical health, mental processes, social and emotional development, self-image, and interpersonal relationships. Preschoolers were provided with an enriched educational environment to develop their learning and cognitive skills. They were given the opportunity to use pegs and pegboards, puzzles, toy animals, dolls, letters and numbers, and other materials that middle-class children take for granted. These opportunities provided these children a leg up in the educational process.

Head Start teachers strive to provide a variety of learning experiences appropriate to the child's age and development. These experiences allow children to read books, to understand cultural diversity, to express feelings, and to play with and relate to their peers in an appropriate fashion. Students are guided in developing gross and fine motor skills and self-confidence. Health care is also an issue, and most children enrolled in the program receive comprehensive health screenings, physical and dental examinations, and appropriate follow-up. Many programs provide meals, helping children receive proper nourishment.

Head Start programs now serve parents in addition to their preschoolers. Some programs allow parents to enroll in classes, which cover parenting, literacy, nutrition/weight loss, domestic violence prevention, and other social issues; social services, health, nutrition, and education services are also available.

Considerable controversy has surrounded the success of the Head Start program. In 1970, the Westinghouse Learning Corporation issued a definitive evaluation of the Head Start effort and concluded that there was no evidence of lasting cognitive gains on the part of the participating children. Initial gains seemed to evaporate during the elementary school years, and by the third grade, the performance of the Head Start children was no different from that of their peers. Though disappointing, this evaluation focused on IQ levels and gave short shrift to improvement in social competence and other survival skills.

More recent research has produced dramatically different results. One report found that by age 5, children who had experienced the enriched day care offered by Head Start averaged more than 10 points higher on their IQ scores than their peers who did not participate in the program. Other research that carefully compared Head Start children to similar children who did not attend the program found that the former made significant intellectual gains. Head Start children were less likely to have been retained in a grade or placed in classes for slow learners; they outperformed peers on achievement tests; and they were more likely to graduate from high school.

Head Start children have also made strides in nonacademic areas. They appear to have better health, higher immunization rates, improved nutrition, and enhanced emotional characteristics after leaving the program. Research also shows that the Head Start program can have important psychological benefits for the mothers of participants, such as decreasing depression and anxiety and increasing feelings of life satisfaction. While findings in some areas may be tentative, they are all in the same direction: Head Start enhances school readiness and has enduring effects on social competence.

If, as many experts believe, there is a close link between school performance, family life, and crime, programs such as Head Start can help some potentially criminal young people avoid problems with the law. By implication, their success indicates that programs that help socialize youngsters can be used to combat urban criminality. Although some problems have been identified in individual centers, the government has shown its faith in Head Start as a socialization agent. The current budget of more than $4.2 billion is used to serve more than 820,000 children.

Critical Thinking

1. Does a program like Head Start substitute one type of negative label (special-needs child) for another (slow starter)?

2. What do you think are some benefits that children who participate in Head Start will carry with them throughout their childhood and adolescence?

InfoTrac College Edition Research

What can be done to improve educational achievement in America? Check out the following articles on InfoTrac College Edition:
Robert E. Slavin, "Can Education Reduce Social Inequity?" *Educational Leadership,* December 1997 v55 n4 p6
David Bennett, "Entrepreneurship: The Road to Salvation for Public Schools," *Educational Leadership,* September 1994 v52 n1 p76

SOURCES: Personal contact, Head Start Program, 2000; Edward Zigler and Sally Styfco, "Head Start: Criticisms in a Constructive Context," *American Psychologist* 49 (1994): 127–132; Nancy Kassebaum, "Head Start: Only the Best for America's Children," *American Psychologist* 49 (1994): 123–126; Faith Lamb Parker, Chaya Piorkowski, and Lenore Peay, "Head Start as Social Support for Mothers: The Psychological Benefits of Involvement," *American Journal of Orthopsychiatry* 57 (1987): 220–233.

Table 7.1 Social Process Theories

THEORY	MAJOR PREMISE	STRENGTH
Social Learning Theories		
Differential association theory	People learn to commit crime from exposure to antisocial definitions.	Explains onset of criminality. Explains the presence of crime in all elements of social structure. Explains why some people in high-crime areas refrain from criminality. Can apply to adults and juveniles.
Neutralization theory	Youths learn ways of neutralizing moral restraints and periodically drift in and out of criminal behavior patterns.	Explains why many delinquents do not become adult criminals. Explains why youthful law violators can participate in conventional behavior.
Social Control Theory		
Hirschi's control theory	A person's bond to society prevents him or her from violating social rules. If the bond weakens, the person is free to commit crime.	Explains the onset of crime; can apply to both middle- and lower-class crime. Explains its theoretical constructs adequately so they can be measured. Has been empirically tested.
Social Reaction Theory		
Labeling theory	People enter into law-violating careers when they are labeled for their acts and organize their personalities around the labels.	Explains the role of society in creating deviance. Explains why some juvenile offenders do not become adult criminals. Develops concepts of criminal careers.

to control criminal tendencies. Labeling theory maintains that negative labels produce criminal careers. These theories are summarized in Table 7.1.

Social learning theory suggests that people learn criminal behaviors much as they learn conventional behavior. Differential association theory, formulated by Edwin Sutherland, holds that criminality is a result of a person's perceiving an excess of definitions in favor of crime over definitions that uphold conventional values. Sykes and Matza's theory of neutralization stresses that youths learn behavior rationalizations that enable them to overcome societal values and norms and break the law.

Control theory maintains that all people have the potential to become criminals, but their bonds to conventional society prevent them from violating the law. This view suggests that a person's self-concept aids his or her commitment to conventional action. Travis Hirschi describes the social bond as containing elements of attachment, commitment, involvement, and belief. Weakened bonds allow youths to behave antisocially.

Social reaction or labeling theory holds that criminality is promoted by becoming negatively labeled by significant others. Such labels as "criminal," "ex-con," and "junkie" isolate people from society and lock them into lives of crime. Labels create expectations that the labeled person will act in a certain way; labeled people are always watched and suspected. Eventually these people begin to accept their labels as personal identities, locking them further into lives of crime and deviance. Edwin Lemert suggests that people who accept labels are involved in secondary deviance. Unfortunately, research on labeling has not supported its major premises. Consequently, critics have charged that it lacks credibility as a description of crime causation.

Social process theories have greatly influenced social policy. They have controlled treatment orientations as well as community action policies.

For additional chapter links, discussions, and quizzes, see the book-specific Web site at http://www.wadsworth.com/product/0534519423s.

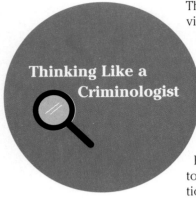

Thinking Like a Criminologist

The state legislature is considering a bill that requires the names of people convicted of certain offenses, such as vandalism, soliciting a prostitute, or nonpayment of child support, to be posted in local newspapers under the heading "The Rogues Gallery." Those who favor the bill cite similar practices elsewhere: In Boston, men arrested for soliciting prostitutes are forced to clean streets. In Dallas, shoplifters are made to stand outside stores with signs stating their misdeeds.

Members of the state Civil Liberties Union have opposed the bill, stating, "It's simply needless humiliation of the individual." They argue that public shaming is inhumane and further alienates criminals who already have little stake in society, further ostracizing them from the mainstream. According to civil liberties attorneys, shaming helps criminals acquire a damaged reputation, which further locks them into criminal behavior patterns.

This "liberal" position is challenged by those who believe that convicted lawbreakers have no right to conceal their crimes from the public. Shaming penalties seem attractive as cost-effective alternatives to imprisonment. These critics ask what could be wrong with requiring a teenage vandal to personally apologize at the school he or she defaced and wear a shirt with a big "V" on it while cleaning up the mess. If you do something wrong, they argue, you should have to face the consequences.

You have been asked to address a legislative committee on the issue of whether shaming could deter crime. What would you say?

Key Terms

socialization	neutralization theory	reflective role-taking
social process theory	drift	retrospective reading
social learning theory	neutralization techniques	primary deviance
social control theory	self-control	secondary deviance
social reaction theory (labeling theory)	commitment to conformity	deviance amplification
differential association theory	social bond	contextual discrimination
culture conflict	stigmatize	diversion programs
	moral entrepreneur	restitution

Discussion Questions

1. If criminal behavior is learned, who taught the first criminal? Are such behaviors as vandalism and bullying actually learned?

2. Children who do well in school are less likely to commit criminal acts than those who are school failures. Which element of Hirschi's theory is supported by the school failure–delinquency link?

3. Have you ever been given a negative label, and, if so, did it cause you social harm? How did you lose the label, or did it become a permanent marker that still troubles you today?

4. If negative labels are damaging, do positive ones help insulate children from crime-producing forces in their environment?

5. How would a social process theorist explain the fact that many children begin offending at an early age and then desist as they mature?

8 Social Conflict Theory: It's a Dog-Eat-Dog World

I t would be unusual to pick up the morning paper and not see headlines loudly proclaiming renewed strife between the United States and its overseas adversaries, between union negotiators and management attorneys, between citizens and police authorities, or between feminists and reactionary males protecting their turf. The world is filled with conflict. Conflict can be destructive when it leads to war, violence, and death; it can be functional when it results in positive social change.

Criminologists who view crime as a function of social conflict and economic rivalry are aligned with a number of schools of thought. These are referred to as conflict, critical, Marxist, or radical schools of criminology. Among their affiliated branches are peacemaking, left realism, radical feminism, and postmodernism (also called deconstructionism).

Social conflict theory tries to explain crime within economic and social contexts and to express the connection between social class, crime, and social control.[1] Conflict theorists are concerned with issues such as

- The role that government plays in creating a crimogenic environment
- The relationship between personal or group power and the shaping of criminal law
- The prevalence of bias in justice system operations
- The relationship between a capitalist, free enterprise economy and crime rates

Conflict promotes crime by creating a social atmosphere in which the law is a mechanism for controlling dissatisfied, have-not members of society while the wealthy maintain their power. This is why crimes that are the province of the wealthy, such as illegal corporate activities, are sanctioned much more leniently than those, such as burglary, that are considered lower-class activities. As you may recall (Chapter 1), Karl Marx identified the economic structures in society that control all human relations. In so doing, he planted the seeds of social conflict theory.

Those criminologists who gain their inspiration from Marx reject the notion that law is designed to maintain a tranquil, fair society and that criminals are malevolent people who wish to trample the rights of others. Conflict theorists consider acts of racism, sexism, imperialism, unsafe working conditions, inadequate child care, substandard housing, pollution of the environment, and war-making as a tool of foreign policy to be "true crimes." The crimes of the helpless—burglary, robbery, and assault—are more expressions of rage over unjust conditions than actual crimes.[2] By focusing on how the capitalist state uses law to control the lower classes, Marxist thought serves as the basis for all social conflict theory.

This chapter reviews criminological theories that allege that criminal behavior is a function of conflict, a reaction to the unfair distribution of wealth and power in society. The social conflict perspective has several independent branches. One, generally referred to as "pure" conflict theory, maintains that intergroup conflict and rivalry cause crime in any society, regardless of its economic structure. A second branch focuses on the crime-producing traits of capitalist society; included here are critical, radical, and Marxist criminology.[3] In general, the terms **radical criminology** and **Marxist criminology** will be used interchangeably; where appropriate, distinctions will be made between the various schools of thought they contain. Finally, emerging forms of social conflict theory include feminist, new realist, peacemaking, and postmodern thought (see Figure 8.1).

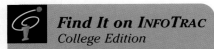

Figure 8.1

The Branches of Social Conflict Theory

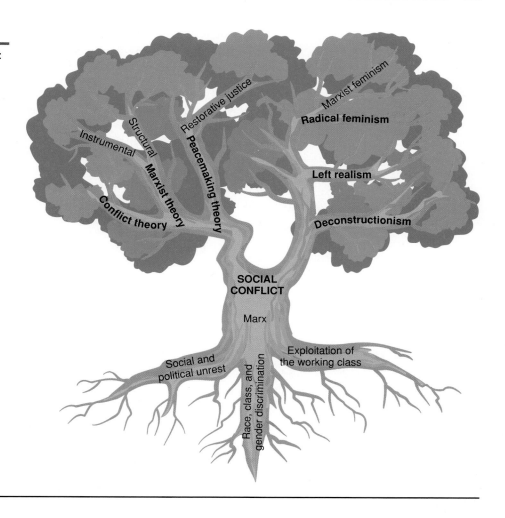

The Conflict Theory of Crime

Conflict theory came into criminological prominence during the 1960s, when self-report studies began to yield data suggesting that the class–crime correlation found in official crime data was spurious. The self-reports showed that crime and delinquency were distributed much more evenly through the social structure than indicated by official statistics, which reported more crime in lower-class environments.[4] If these self-reports were accurate, middle-class participation in crime was going unrecorded while the lower class was subjected to discriminatory law enforcement practices.[5]

The theme that dominated much of this scholarship was the contention that criminal legislation was determined by the relative power of groups determined to use criminal law to advance their own special interests or to impose their own moral preferences on others.[6] This movement was aided by the widespread social and political upheaval of the late 1960s and early 1970s. These social forces included anti–Vietnam War demonstrations, counterculture movements, and various forms of political protest. Conflict theory flourished within this framework because it provided a systematic basis for challenging the legitimacy of the government's creation and application of law. The federal government's crackdown on political dissidents and prosecution of draft resisters seemed designed to maintain control in the hands of political power brokers.

As conflict theory began to influence criminological study, several influential scholars embraced its ideas. William Chambliss and Robert Seidman wrote the well-respected treatise *Law, Order and Power,* which documented how the justice system protects the rich and powerful. After closely observing its operations, Chambliss and Seidman concluded,

> In America, it is frequently argued that to have "freedom" is to have a system which allows one group to make a profit over another. To maintain the existing legal system requires a choice. That choice is between maintaining a legal system that serves to support the existing economic system with its power structure and developing an equitable legal system accompanied by the loss of "personal freedom." But the old question comes back to plague us: Freedom for whom? Is the black man who provides such a ready source of cases for the welfare workers, the mental hospitals, and the prisons "free"? Are the slum dwellers who are arrested night after night for "loitering," "drunkenness," or being "suspicious" free? The freedom protected by the system of law is the freedom of those who can afford it. The law serves their interests, but they are not "society"; they are one element of society. They may in some complex societies even be a majority (though this is very rare), but the myth that the law serves the interests of "society" misrepresents the facts.[7]

Some common objectives of conflict criminology that appear in Chambliss and Seidman's writing include

- Describing how control of the political and economic system affects the way criminal justice is administered
- Showing how definitions of crime favor those who control the justice system
- Analyzing the role of conflict in contemporary society

Their scholarship also reflects another major objective of conflict theory: to show how U.S. justice is skewed. Those who deserve the most severe sanctions (wealthy white-collar criminals whose crimes cost society millions of dollars) are actually punished the least, whereas those whose relatively minor crimes are committed out of economic necessity (petty thieves and drug dealers) receive stricter penalites.[8]

CONNECTIONS

The enforcement of laws against illegal business activities such as price fixing, restraint of trade, environmental crimes, and false advertising is discussed in Chapter 12. Although some people are sent to prison for these white-collar offenses, many offenders are still punished with a fine or economic sanction.

Power Relations

power

The ability of persons and groups to control the behavior of others, to shape public opinion, and to define deviance.

According to the conflict view, crime is defined by those in power. **Power** refers to the ability of persons and groups to determine and control the behavior of others and to shape public opinion to meet their personal interests. Unequal distribution of power produces conflict, and conflict is rooted in the competition for power.

Nowhere is this relationship more evident than in the racism that pervades the justice process. Poor inner-city youths are driven to commit crimes out of economic desperation. Racial discrimination then results in discretionary decisions by law enforcement officers, who charge them with felonies, not misdemeanors, and send them to criminal courts, not diversion programs. Busy public defenders often pressure their clients into plea bargains that ensure early criminal records. Health-care workers and teachers are quick to report suspected violent acts to the police; this results in frequent, early arrests of minority youths and adults. Police routinely search, question, and detain all African American males in an area if a violent criminal has been described as "looking or sounding black"; this is called "racial profiling." By creating the image of pervasive African American criminality and coupling it with unfair treatment, those in power further alienate this population from the mainstream, perpetuating a class- and race-divided society. Surveys show that African Americans are much more likely to perceive criminal injustice than European Americans.[9]

Conflict theory views power as the ability to shape social relations to meet personal needs. The New Yorkers shown here are protesting the shooting of Amadou Diallo by city police officers. Although the officers were found not guilty at trial, protests such as this one attempt to shape social action through collective strength.

The Social Reality of Crime

social reality of crime

The main purpose of criminology is to promote a peaceful, just society.

Richard Quinney, one of the more influential conflict theorists of the time, integrated these beliefs about power, society, and criminality into a theory he referred to as the **social reality of crime**. According to Quinney, criminal definitions (law) represent the interests of those who hold power in society. Where there is conflict between social groups—for example, the wealthy and the poor—those who hold power create laws that benefit themselves and hold rivals in check.

According to Quinney, law is not an abstract body of rules that represents an absolute moral code; rather, law is an integral part of society, a force that represents a way of life and a method of doing things. Crime is a function of power relations and an inevitable result of social conflict. Criminals are not simply social misfits, but people who have come up short in the struggle for success and are seeking alternative means of achieving wealth, status, or even survival.[10] Consequently, law violations can be viewed as political or even quasi-revolutionary acts.[11]

Research on Conflict Theory

Conflict theorists maintain that social inequality forces people to commit some crimes, such as burglary and larceny, as a means of social and economic survival, whereas other crimes, such as assault, homicide, and drug use, are a means of expressing rage, frustration, and anger. Data show that crime rates vary according to indicators of poverty and need. For example, infant mortality rates have been associated with homicide rates, which shows that a society that cannot care for its young is also prone to social unrest and violence.[12] Crime rates seem strongly related to measures of social inequality such as income level, deteriorated living conditions, and relative economic deprivation.[13]

Another area of conflict-oriented research involves examining the criminal justice system to see if it operates as an instrument of class oppression or as a fair, even-handed social control agency. Some conflict researchers have found evidence of class bias. Legal jurisdictions with significant levels of economic disparity are also the most likely to have large numbers of people killed by police officers. Police may act more forcefully in areas where class conflict creates the perception that extreme forms of social control are needed to maintain

CONNECTIONS
- - - - - - - - - - - - - - - -

Quinney, a highly respected criminologist, has changed his outlook over his long and distinguished career. He now leads the Zen-inspired peacemaking movement, which seeks to remove violence and coercion from the criminal justice system and promotes healing, or restorative justice. See the section on peacemaking later in this chapter.

Find It on INFOTRAC
College Edition

Research shows that African Americans are sent to prison on drug charges at 27 to 50 times the rate of European Americans. To read more about the effects of racial discrimination, use the term "race discrimination" as a subject guide in InfoTrac College Edition.

order.[14] It is not surprising to conflict theorists that police brutality complaints are highest in minority neighborhoods, especially those that experience relative deprivation (African American residents earn significantly less money than the European American majority).[15]

Criminal courts are also more likely to punish members of powerless, disenfranchised groups.[16] When criminals are convicted, both white and black offenders have been found to receive stricter sentences if their personal characteristics (single, young, urban, male) show them to be members of the "dangerous classes."[17] The unemployed, especially racial minorities, may be perceived as "social dynamite" who present a real threat to society and must be controlled and incapacitated.[18]

Conflict theorists also point to studies showing that the criminal justice system is quick to act when a crime victim is wealthy, white, and male but is disinterested when the victim is poor, black, and female.[19] Analysis of national population trends and imprisonment rates shows that as the percentage of minority group members increases in a population, the imprisonment rate does likewise.[20] As minority populations increase, the majority may become less tolerant or feel more threatened.

One reason for such displays of discrimination may be the overt or covert racist attitudes of decision makers. Justice professionals who express racist values (such as stating that race-based trait differences actually exist) are also more punitive, believe that courts should be stricter and that the death penalty is an effective deterrent, and are likely to let race affect their judgments.[21] Critical theorists argue that there must be a thorough rethinking of the role and purpose of the criminal justice system, giving the powerless a greater voice to express their needs and concerns, if these inequities are to be addressed.[22] ✔ **Checkpoints**

Radical Criminology

The writings of Karl Marx and Friedrich Engels greatly influenced the development of social conflict thinking. Although Marx himself did not write much on the topic of crime, his views on the relationship between the economic structure and social behavior deeply influenced other thinkers.

In the 1960s, theories that focused on the relationship between crime and conflict in any society began to be supplanted by more radical, Marxist-oriented theories that examined the specific role of capitalism in law and criminality.

In 1968, a group of British sociologists formed the National Deviancy Conference (NDC). With about 300 members, this organization sponsored several national symposiums and dialogues. Members came from all walks of life, but at its core was a group of academics who were critical of the positivist criminology being taught in British and American universities. More specifically, they rejected the conservative stance of criminologists and their close financial relationship with government funding agencies.

The NDC was not conceived as a Marxist-oriented group; rather, it investigated the concept of deviance from a labeling perspective. It called attention to ways in which social control might actually cause deviance rather than just respond to antisocial behavior. Many conference members became concerned about the political nature of social control. In time, a schism developed within the NDC, with one group clinging to the interactionist/labeling perspective, while the second embraced Marxist thought.

In 1973, radical theory was given a powerful academic boost when British scholars Ian Taylor, Paul Walton, and Jock Young published *The New Criminology*.[23] This brilliant, thorough, and well-constructed critique of existing concepts in criminology called for the development of new methods of criminological

✔ **Checkpoints**

✔ Social conflict theory is aimed at identifying "real" crimes in U.S. society, such as profiteering, sexism, and racism.

✔ It seeks to evaluate how criminal law is used as a mechanism of social control.

✔ It describes how power relations create inequities in U.S. society.

✔ The idea of the social reality of crime is that those who hold power in society define those who oppose their values as criminals.

✔ Racism and classism pervade the U.S. justice system and shape crime rates.

analysis and critique. *The New Criminology* became the standard resource for scholars critical of both the field of criminology and the existing legal process.

During the same period, a small group of scholars in the United States also began to follow a new, radical approach to criminology. The locus of the radical school was the criminology program at the University of California at Berkeley. The most noted Marxist scholars at that institution were Anthony Platt, Paul Takagi, Herman Schwendinger, and Julia Schwendinger. Radical scholars at other U.S. academic institutions included Richard Quinney, William Chambliss, Steven Spitzer, and Barry Krisberg.

The U.S. radicals were influenced by the widespread social ferment during the late 1960s and early 1970s. The war in Vietnam, prison struggles, and the civil rights and feminist movements produced a climate in which criticism of the ruling class seemed a natural by-product. Mainstream, positivist criminology was criticized as being overtly conservative, progovernment, and antihuman. Critical criminologists scoffed when their fellow scholars used statistical analysis of computerized data to describe criminal and delinquent behavior.

Barry Krisberg, writing in 1975, lamented the social inadequacies of earlier criminologists: "Many of our scientific heroes of the past, upon rereading, turned out to be racists or, more generally, apologists for social injustice." In response to widespread protests on campuses and throughout society, many of the contemporary giants of social science emerged as defenders of the status quo and vocally dismissed the claims of the oppressed for social justice.[24]

Marxists did not enjoy widespread approval at major universities. Rumors that professors were being fired for their political beliefs were common during the 1970s, and the criminology school at Berkeley was eventually closed for what many believe were political reasons. Even today, conflict exists between critical thinkers and mainstream academics. Prestigious Harvard Law School and other law centers have seen conflict, tenure denials, and charges of purges because some professors held critical views of law and society. Although some isolated radicals are tolerated, the majority have been heavily victimized by what has been referred to as "academic McCarthyism."[25]

In the following years, new branches of a radical criminology developed in the United States and abroad. In the early 1980s, the left realism school was started by scholars affiliated with the Middlesex Polytechnic and the University of Edinburgh in Great Britain. In the United States, scholars influenced in part by the pioneering work of Dennis Sullivan and Larry Tifft laid the foundation for what eventually became known as the peacemaking movement, which calls for a humanist vision of justice.[26] At the same time, feminist scholars began to critically analyze the relationship between gender, power, and criminality. These movements have coalesced into a rich and complex criminological tradition.

Find It on INFOTRAC
College Edition

Are radical criminologists really "radical"? Or should that term be applied to people generally considered "conservative"? To find out, read
Elliott Currie, "Radical Criminology or Just Criminology—Then and Now," *Social Justice,* Summer 1999 v26 i2 p16

Fundamentals of Marxist Criminology

Above all, Marxism is a critique of capitalism.[27] Marxist criminologists view crime as a function of the capitalist mode of production. Capitalism produces haves and have-nots, each engaging in a particular branch of criminality.[28] The mode of production shapes social life. Because economic competitiveness is the essence of capitalism, conflict increases and eventually destabilizes social institutions and the individuals within them.[29]

In a capitalist society, those with economic and political power control the definition of crime and the manner in which the criminal justice system enforces the law.[30] Consequently, the only crimes available to the poor, or proletariat, are the severely sanctioned "street crimes": rape, murder, theft, and mugging. Members of the middle class, or petite bourgeoisie, cheat on their taxes and engage in petty corporate crime (employee theft), acts that generate social disapproval but are rarely punished severely. The wealthy bourgeoisie are involved in acts that should be described as crimes but are not, such as racism, sexism, and profiteering. Although regulatory laws control illegal business activities, these are rarely enforced, and violations are lightly punished. Laws regulating corporate crime are actually designed to impress the working class with how fair the justice system is. In reality, the justice system is the equivalent of an army that defends the owners of property in their ongoing struggle against the workers.[31]

The rich are insulated from street crimes because they live in areas far removed from crime. Those in power use the fear of crime as a tool to maintain their control over society. The poor are controlled through incarceration, and the middle class is diverted from caring about the crimes of the powerful by their fear of the crimes of the powerless.[32] Ironically, they may have more to lose from the economic crimes committed by the rich than the street crimes of the poor. Stock market swindles and savings and loan scams cost the public billions of dollars but are typically settled with fines and probationary sentences.

Because private ownership of property is the true measure of success in capitalism (as opposed to, being say, a worthy person), the state becomes an ally of the wealthy in protecting their property interests. As a result, theft-related crimes are often punished more severely than are acts of violence because while the former may be interclass, the latter are typically intraclass.

Defining Crime Marxists use the conflict definition of crime: Crime is a political concept designed to protect the power and position of the upper classes at the expense of the poor. Some, but not all, Marxists would include in a list of "real" crimes such acts as violations of human rights due to racism, sexism, and imperialism and other violations of human dignity and physical needs and necessities. Part of the radical agenda, argues criminologist Robert Bohm, is to make the public aware that these behaviors "are crimes just as much as burglary and robbery."[33]

The nature of a society controls the direction of its criminality; criminals are not social misfits, but products of the society and its economic system. "Capitalism," claims Bohm, "as a mode of production, has always produced a relatively high level of crime and violence."[34] According to Michael Lynch and W. Byron Groves, three implications follow from this view:

1. Each society produces its own types and amounts of crime.
2. Each society has its own distinctive ways of dealing with criminal behavior.
3. Each society gets the amount and type of crime that it deserves.[35]

This analysis tells us that criminals are not a group of outsiders who can be controlled by increased law enforcement. Criminality, instead, is a function of social and economic organization. To control crime and reduce criminality is to end the social conditions that promote crime.

Economic Structure and Surplus Value Although no single view or theory defines Marxist criminology today, its general theme is the relationship between crime and the ownership and control of private property in a capitalist society.[36] That ownership and control is the principal basis of power in U.S. society.[37] Social conflict is fundamentally related to the historical and social distribution of productive private property. Destructive social conflicts inherent within the capitalist system cannot be resolved unless that system is destroyed or ended.

One important aspect of the capitalist economic system is the effect of **surplus value**—the profits produced by the laboring classes that are accrued by business owners. Surplus value can be either reinvested or used to enrich the owners. To increase the rate of surplus value, workers can be made to work harder for less pay, be made more efficient, or be replaced by machines or tech-

surplus value

The difference between what workers produce and what they are paid, which goes to business owners as profits.

Social conflict is fundamentally related to the distribution of private property, a process that historically has been unfair, biased, and discriminatory. Here, protesters demonstrate against a meeting of the Fortune 500 in Austin, Texas. Protesters held signs against corporate domination of the American political system, the growing gap between rich and poor, and the militarization of the police.

marginalization

Displacement of workers, pushing them outside the economic and social mainstream.

Figure 8.2

Surplus Value and Crime

nology. Therefore, economic growth does not benefit all elements of the population, and in the long run it may produce the same effect as a depression or recession.

As the rate of surplus value increases, more people are displaced from productive relationships, and the size of the marginal population swells. As corporations downsize to increase profits, high-paying labor and managerial jobs are lost to computer-driven machinery. Displaced workers are forced into service jobs at minimum wage. Many become temporary employees without benefits or a secure position.

As more people are thrust outside the economic mainstream, a condition referred to as **marginalization**, a larger portion of the population is forced to live in areas conducive to crime. Once people are marginalized, commitment to the system declines, producing another crimogenic force: a weakened bond to society.[38] This process is illustrated in Figure 8.2.

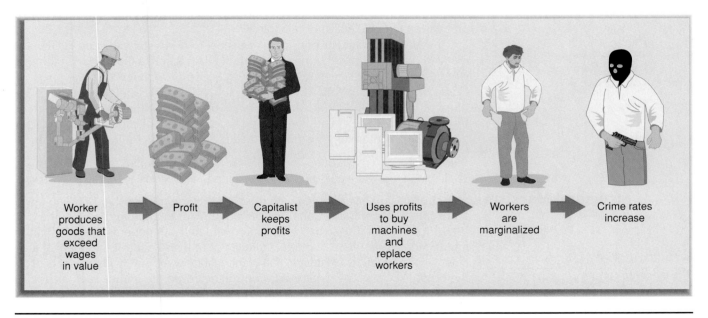

Worker produces goods that exceed wages in value → Profit → Capitalist keeps profits → Uses profits to buy machines and replace workers → Workers are marginalized → Crime rates increase

The government may be quick to respond during periods of economic decline because those in power assume that poor economic conditions breed crime and social disorder. When unemployment is increasing, public officials assume the worst and devote greater attention to the criminal justice system, perhaps building new prisons to prepare for the coming "crime wave."[39] Empirical research confirms that economic downturns are indeed linked to both crime rate increases and government activities such as passing anticrime legislation.[40] For example, as the level of surplus value increases, so too do police expenditures, most likely because of the perceived or real need for the state to control those on the economic margin.[41]

Although these themes can be found throughout Marxist writing, a number of different schools of thought have arisen within the radical literature. Among these various approaches are instrumental Marxism and structural Marxism.

Instrumental Marxism

instrumental Marxist

One who sees criminal law and the criminal justice system as capitalist instruments for controlling the lower class.

Instrumental Marxists view criminal law and the criminal justice system solely as instruments for controlling the poor, have-not members of society. They see the state as the tool of capitalists.

According to the instrumental view, capitalist justice serves the powerful and rich and enables them to impose their morality and standards of behavior on the entire society. Under capitalism, those who wield economic power are able to extend their self-serving definition of illegal or criminal behavior to encompass those who might threaten the status quo or interfere with their quest for ever-increasing profits.[42] For example, the concentration of economic assets in the nation's largest industrial firms translates into the political power needed to control tax laws to limit the firms' tax liabilities.[43] Some have the economic clout to hire top attorneys to defend themselves against antitrust actions, making them almost immune to regulation.

The poor, according to this branch of Marxist theory, may or may not commit more crimes than the rich, but they certainly are arrested and punished more often. Under the capitalist system, the poor are driven to crime because a natural frustration exists in a society in which affluence is well publicized but unattainable. When class conflict becomes unbearable, frustration can spill out in riots, such as the one that occurred in Los Angeles on April 29, 1992, which was described as a "class rebellion of the underprivileged against the privileged."[44] Because of class conflict, a deep-rooted hostility is generated among members of the lower class toward a social order they are not allowed to shape and whose benefits are unobtainable.[45]

demystify

To unmask the true purpose of law, justice, or other social institutions.

Instrumental Marxists consider it essential to **demystify** law and justice— that is, to unmask its true purpose. Criminological theories that focus on family structure, intelligence, peer relations, and school performance keep the lower classes servile by showing why they are more criminal, less intelligent, and more prone to school failure and family problems than the middle class. Demystification involves identifying the destructive intent of capitalist-inspired and -funded criminology. Instrumental Marxists' goal for criminology is to show how capitalist law preserves ruling-class power.[46]

Structural Marxism

structural Marxist

One who sees criminal law and the criminal justice system as means of defending and preserving the capitalist system.

Structural Marxists disagree with the view that the relationship between law and capitalism is unidirectional, always working for the rich and against the poor.[47] Law is not the exclusive domain of the rich, but rather is used to maintain the long-term interests of the capitalist system and control members of any class who threaten its existence. If law and justice were purely instruments of the capitalist class, why would laws controlling corporate crimes, such as price-fixing, false advertising, and illegal restraint of trade, have been created and enforced?

To a structuralist, the law is designed to keep the capitalist system operating efficiently, and anyone, capitalist or proletarian, who rocks the boat is targeted for sanction. For example, antitrust legislation is designed to prevent any single capitalist from dominating the system. If the capitalist system is to function, no single person can become too powerful at the expense of the economic system as a whole. Structuralists would regard the efforts of the U.S. government to break up Microsoft as an example of capitialists controlling capitalists to keep the system on an even keel.

Research on Marxist Criminology

Marxist criminologists rarely use standard social science methodologies to test their views because many believe the traditional approach of measuring research subjects is antihuman and insensitive.[48] Marxists believe that the research conducted by mainstream liberal and positivist criminologists is designed to unmask weak, powerless members of society so they can be better dealt with by the legal system. They are particularly offended by purely empirical studies, such as those designed to show that minority group members have lower IQs than whites or that the inner city is the site of the most serious crime whereas middle-class areas are relatively crime-free.

Empirical research, however, is not considered totally incompatible with Marxist criminology, and there have been some important efforts to test its fundamental assumptions quantitatively.[49] For example, research has shown that the property crime rate reflects a change in the level of surplus value; the capitalist system's emphasis on excessive profits accounts for the need of the working class to commit property crime.[50] Nonetheless, Marxist research tends to be historical and analytical, not quantitative and empirical. Social trends are interpreted with regard to how capitalism has affected human interaction. Marxists investigate both macro-level issues, such as how the accumulation of wealth affects crime rates, and micro-level issues, such as the effect of criminal interactions on the lives of individuals living in a capitalist society. Of particular importance to Marxist critical thinkers is analyzing the historical development of capitalist social control institutions, such as criminal law, police agencies, courts, and prison systems.

Crime, the Individual, and the State Marxists devote considerable attention to the relationships among crime, victims, the criminal, and the state. Two common themes emerge: (1) Crime and its control are a function of capitalism. (2) The justice system is biased against the working class and favors upper-class interests.

Marxist analysis of the criminal justice system is designed to identify the often-hidden processes that control people's lives. It takes into account how conditions, processes, and structures evolved into what they are today. One issue considered is the process by which deviant behavior is defined as criminal or delinquent in U.S. society.[51] Another issue is the degree to which class affects the justice system's decision-making process.[52] Also subject to analysis is how power relationships help undermine any benefit the lower class receives from sentencing reforms.[53] In general, Marxist research efforts have yielded evidence linking operations of the justice system to class bias.[54] In addition, some researchers have attempted to show how capitalism intervenes across the entire spectrum of crime-related phenomena.

Historical Analysis Another type of Marxist research focuses on the historical background of commonly held institutional beliefs and practices. One goal is to show how changes in criminal law correspond to the development of the capitalist economy. The second goal is to investigate the development of modern police agencies.

To examine the changes in criminal law, historian Michael Rustigan analyzed historical records to show that law reform in nineteenth-century England was largely a response to pressure from the business community to increase punishment for property law violations in order to protect their rapidly increasing wealth.[55] Other research has focused on topics such as how the relationship between convict work and capitalism evolved during the nineteenth century. During this period, prisons became a profitable method of centralized state control over lower-class criminals, whose labor was exploited by commercial concerns. These criminals were forced to labor in order to pay off wardens and correctional administrators.[56]

Critique of Marxist Criminology

Marxist criminology has been sharply criticized by some members of the criminological mainstream, who charge that its contribution has been "hot air, heat, but no real light."[57] In turn, radicals have accused mainstream criminologists of being culprits in developing state control over individual lives and selling out their ideals for the chance to receive government funding.

Mainstream criminologists have also attacked the substance of Marxist thought. Some argue that Marxist theory simply rehashes the old tradition of helping the underdog, in which the poor steal from the rich to survive.[58] In reality, most theft is for luxury, not survival. While the wealthy do commit their share of illegal acts, these are nonviolent and leave no permanent injuries.[59] People do not live in fear of corrupt businessmen and stock traders; they fear muggers and rapists.

Other critics suggest that Marxists unfairly neglect the capitalist system's efforts to regulate itself—for example, by instituting antitrust regulations and putting violators in jail. Similarly, they ignore efforts to institute social reforms aimed at helping the poor.[60] There seems to be no logic in condemning a system that helps the poor and empowers them to take on corporate interests in a court of law. Some argue that Marxists refuse to address the problems and conflicts that exist in socialist countries, such as the gulags and purges of the Soviet Union under Stalin. Similarly, they fail to explain why some highly capitalist countries, such as Japan, have extremely low crime rates. Marxists are too quick to blame capitalism for every human vice without adequate explanation or regard for other social and environmental factors.[61] In so doing, they ignore objective reality and refuse to acknowledge that members of the lower classes tend to victimize one another. They ignore the plight of the lower classes, who must live in crime-ridden neighborhoods, while condemning the capitalist system from the security of the "ivory tower."

Marxist scholars criticize their critics for relying on "traditional" variables, such as class and poverty, in their analysis of radical thought. Although important, these do not reflect the key issues in the structural and economic process. In fact, like crime, they too may be the outcome of the capitalist system.[62] Marxists also point out that although other capitalist nations may have lower crime rates, this does not mean they are crime-free. Even Japan has significant problems with teen prostitution and organized crime. ✔ **Checkpoints**

✔ Checkpoints

✔ Marxist criminology tries to explain how the workings of the capitalist system produce inequality and crime.

✔ In this view, the state serves the interests of the ruling capitalist class. Criminal law is an instrument of economic oppression. Capitalism demands that the subordinate classes remain oppressed.

✔ Instrumental Marxists believe that the legal system supports the owners at the expense of the workers.

✔ Structural Marxists believe that the law also ensures that no capitalist becomes too powerful. The law is used to maintain the long-term interests of the capitalist system.

✔ Marxist research is designed to show how capitalism creates large groups of people who turn to crime for survival.

Emerging Forms of Social Conflict Theory

Although radical criminologists dispute criticisms, they have also responded by creating new theoretical models that innovatively incorporate Marxist ideas. The following sections discuss in detail some recent forms of radical theory.

Left Realism

left realism

Approach that sees crime as a function of relative deprivation under capitalism and favors pragmatic, community-based crime prevention and control.

preemptive deterrence

Efforts to prevent crime through community organization and youth involvement.

Preemptive deterrence is an approach that seeks to reduce crime before police involvement is required. Here, Acting Chief of Police Deborah Barrows of Hartford, Connecticut, speaks at a news conference about a federally funded gun buyback program, as HUD Assistant Secretary Cardell Cooper listens. The HUD-funded program will give a voucher worth $100 for each gun turned in to the Hartford Police Department, no questions asked.

Some radical scholars are now addressing the need for the left wing to respond to the increasing power of right-wing conservatives. They are troubled by the emergence of a strict "law and order" philosophy, which has as its centerpiece a policy of punishing juveniles severely in adult court. At the same time, they find the focus of most left-wing scholarship—the abuse of power by the ruling elite—too narrow. It is wrong, they argue, to ignore inner-city gang crime and violence, which often target indigent people.[63] The approach of scholars who share these concerns is referred to as **left realism**.[64]

Left realism is most often connected to the writings of British scholars John Lea and Jock Young. In their well-respected 1984 work, *What Is to Be Done About Law and Order?*, they reject the utopian views of "idealistic" Marxists who portray street criminals as revolutionaries.[65] They take the more "realistic" approach that street criminals prey on the poor and disenfranchised, thus making the poor doubly abused, first by the capitalist system and then by members of their own class.

Lea and Young's view of crime causation borrows from conventional sociological theory and closely resembles the relative deprivation approach, which posits that experiencing poverty in the midst of plenty creates discontent and breeds crime. As they put it, "The equation is simple: relative deprivation equals discontent; discontent plus lack of political solution equals crime."[66]

Left realists argue that crime victims in all classes need and deserve protection; crime control reflects community needs. They do not view police and the courts as inherently evil tools of capitalism whose tough tactics alienate the lower classes. In fact, they recognize that these institutions offer life-saving public services. The left realists wish, however, that police would reduce their use of force and increase their sensitivity to the public.[67]

Preemptive deterrence is an approach in which community organization efforts eliminate or reduce crime before police involvement becomes necessary. The reasoning behind this approach is that if the number of marginalized youths (those who feel they are not part of society and have nothing to lose by committing crime) could be reduced, then delinquency rates would decline.[68]

Although implementing a socialist economy might help eliminate the crime problem, left realists recognize that something must be done to control crime under the existing capitalist system. To develop crime control policies, left realists not only welcome radical ideas but also build on the work of strain theorists, social ecologists, and other mainstream views. Community-based efforts seem to hold the greatest promise of crime control.

Left realism has been criticized by radical thinkers as legitimizing the existing power structure: By supporting existing definitions of law and justice, it suggests that the "deviant" and not the capitalist system causes society's problems. Critics question whether left realists advocate the very institutions that "currently imprison us and our patterns of thought and action."[69] In rebuttal, left realists would say that it is unrealistic to speak of a socialist state lacking a police force or a system of laws and justice. They believe that the criminal code does, in fact, represent public opinion.

AP/Wide World Photos

Radical Feminist Theory

Marxist feminism

Approach that explains both victimization and criminality among women in terms of gender inequality, patriarchy, and the exploitation of women under capitalism.

patriarchal

Male-dominated.

Like so many theories in criminology, most of the efforts of radical theorists have been devoted to explaining male criminality.[70] To remedy this theoretical lapse, a number of feminist writers have attempted to explain the cause of crime, gender differences in crime rates, and the exploitation of female victims from a radical feminist perspective.

Marxist feminism views gender inequality as stemming from the unequal power of men and women in a capitalist society, which leads to the exploitation of women by fathers and husbands. Under this system, women are considered a commodity worth possessing, like land or money.[71]

The origin of gender differences can be traced to the development of private property and male domination of the laws of inheritance, which led to male control over property and power.[72] A **patriarchal** system developed in which men's work was valued and women's work was devalued. As capitalism prevailed, the division of labor by gender made women responsible for the unpaid maintenance and reproduction of the current and future labor force, which was derisively called "domestic work." Although this unpaid work done by women is crucial and profitable for capitalists, who reap these free benefits, such labor is exploitative and oppressive for women.[73] Even when women gained the right to work for pay, they were exploited as cheap labor. The dual exploitation of women within the household and in the labor market means that women produce far greater surplus value for capitalists than men.

Patriarchy, or male supremacy, has been and continues to be supported by capitalists. This system sustains female oppression at home and in the workplace.[74] Although the number of traditional patriarchal families is in steep decline, in those that still exist, a wife's economic dependence ties men more securely to wage-earning jobs, further serving the interests of capitalists by undermining potential rebellion against the system.

Patriarchy and Crime Marxist feminists link criminal behavior patterns to the gender conflict created by the economic and social struggles common in postindustrial societies. In his book *Capitalism, Patriarchy, and Crime,* James Messerschmidt argues that capitalist society is marked by both patriarchy and class conflict. Capitalists control the labor of workers, while men control women both economically and biologically.[75] This "double marginality" explains why females in a capitalist society commit fewer crimes than males. Because they are isolated in the family, they have fewer opportunities to engage in elite deviance (white-collar and economic crimes). Although powerful females as well as males will commit white-collar crimes, the female crime rate is restricted because of the patriarchal nature of the capitalist system.[76] Women are also denied access to male-dominated street crimes. Because capitalism renders lower-class women powerless, they are forced to commit less serious, nonviolent, self-destructive crimes, such as abusing drugs.

Powerlessness also increases the likelihood that women will become targets of violent acts.[77] When lower-class males are shut out of the economic opportunity structure, they try to build their self-image through acts of machismo; such acts may involve violent abuse of women. This type of reaction accounts for a significant percentage of female victims who are attacked by a spouse or intimate partner.

In *Masculinities and Crime,* Messerschmidt expands on these themes.[78] He suggests that in every culture, males try to emulate "ideal" masculine behaviors. In Western culture, this means being authoritative, in charge, combative, and controlling. Failure to adopt these roles leaves men feeling effeminate and unmanly. Their struggle to dominate women in order to prove their manliness is called "doing gender." Crime is a vehicle for men to "do gender" because it separates them from the weak and allows them to demonstrate physical bravery. Violence directed toward women is an especially economical way to demonstrate manhood. Would a weak, effeminate male ever attack a woman?

Exploitation and Criminality Radical feminists also focus on the social forces that shape women's lives and experiences to explain female criminality.[79] For example, they attempt to show how the sexual victimization of girls is a function of male socialization because so many young males learn to be aggressive and to exploit women. Males seek out same-sex peer groups for social support; these groups encourage members to exploit and sexually abuse women. On college campuses, peers encourage sexual violence against women who are considered "teasers," "bar pickups," or "loose women." These derogatory labels allow the males to justify their actions; a code of secrecy then protects the aggressors from retribution.[80]

According to the radical feminist view, exploitation triggers the onset of female delinquent and deviant behavior. When female victims run away and abuse substances, they may be reacting to abuse they have suffered at home or at school. Their attempts at survival are labeled as deviant or delinquent behavior.[81] In a sense, the female criminal is herself a victim.

Research shows that a significant number of girls who are sent to hospital emergency rooms to be treated for sexual abuse later report engaging in physical fighting as a teen or as an adult. Many of these abused girls later form romantic attachments with abusive partners. Clearly many girls involved in delinquency, crime, and violence have themselves been the victims of violence in their youth and later as adults.[82]

Radical feminist opinions differ on certain issues. For example, some feminist scholars charge that the movement focuses on the problems and viewpoints of white, middle-class, heterosexual women without taking into account the special interests of lesbians and women of color.[83]

How the Justice System Penalizes Women Radical feminists have indicted the justice system and its patriarchal hierarchy as contributing to the onset of female delinquency. Some have studied the early history of the justice system and uncovered an enduring pattern of discrimination. From its inception, the juvenile justice system has viewed most female delinquents as sexually precocious girls who have to be brought under control. Writing about the "girl problem," Ruth Alexander has described how working-class young women desiring autonomy and freedom in the 1920s were considered delinquents and placed in reformatories. Lacking the ability to protect themselves from the authorities, these young girls were considered outlaws in a male-dominated society because they flouted the very narrow rules of appropriate behavior that were applied to females. Girls who rebelled against parental authority or who engaged in sexual behavior deemed inappropriate were incarcerated in order to protect them from a career in prostitution.[84]

Mary Odem and Steven Schlossman researched the lives of young women who entered the Los Angeles Juvenile Court in 1920, and found that the majority were petitioned for either suspected sexual activity or behavior that placed them at risk of sexual relations. Despite the limited seriousness of these charges, most of the girls were detained before their trials, and while in juvenile hall, all were given a compulsory pelvic exam. Girls adjudged sexually delinquent on the basis of the exam were segregated from the merely incorrigible girls to prevent moral corruption. Those testing positive for venereal disease were usually confined in juvenile hall hospital for one to three months. More than 29 percent of these female adolescents were eventually committed to custodial institutions.[85]

A well-known feminist writer, Meda Chesney-Lind, has written extensively about the victimization of female delinquents by agents of the juvenile justice system.[86] She suggests that because female adolescents have a much narrower range of acceptable behavior than male adolescents, any sign of misbehavior in girls is seen as a substantial challenge to authority and to the viability of the double standard of sexual inequality. Female delinquency is viewed as relatively more serious than male delinquency and therefore is more likely to be severely sanctioned.

Power-Control Theory John Hagan and his associates have created a radical feminist model that uses gender differences to explain the onset of criminality.[87] Hagan's view is that crime and delinquency rates are a function of two factors: (1) class position (power) and (2) family functions (control).[88] The link between these two variables is that, within the family, parents reproduce the power relationships they hold in the workplace; a position of dominance at work is equated with control in the household. As a result, parents' work experiences and class position influence the criminality of children.

In paternalistic families, fathers assume the traditional role of breadwinners, while mothers tend to have menial jobs or remain at home to supervise domestic matters. Within the paternalistic home, mothers are expected to control the behavior of their daughters while granting greater freedom to sons. In such a home, the parent–daughter relationship can be viewed as a preparation for the "cult of domesticity," which makes girls' involvement in delinquency unlikely, whereas boys are freer to deviate because they are not subject to maternal control. Girls growing up in patriarchial families are socialized to fear legal sanctions more than are males; consequently, boys in these families exhibit more delinquent behavior than their sisters.

In egalitarian families—those in which the husband and wife share similar positions of power at home and in the workplace—daughters gain a kind of freedom that reflects reduced parental control. These families produce daughters whose law-violating behavior mirrors their brothers'. Ironically, these relationships also occur in female-headed households with absent fathers. Hagan and his associates found that when fathers and mothers hold equally valued managerial positions, the similarity between the rates of their daughters' and sons' delinquency is greatest. By implication, middle-class girls are the most likely to violate the law because they are less closely controlled than their lower-class counterparts. In homes in which both parents hold positions of power, girls are more likely to have the same expectations of career success as their brothers. Consequently, siblings of both sexes will be socialized to take risks and engage in other behavior related to delinquency.

This **power–control theory** has received a great deal of attention in the criminological community because it encourages a new approach to the study of criminality, one that includes gender differences, class position, and the structure of the family. Empirical analyis of its premises has generally been supportive. For example, Brenda Sims Blackwell's research supports a key element of power–control theory: Females in paternalistic households have learned to fear legal sanctions more than have their brothers.[89]

power–control theory

The view that gender differences in crime are a function of economic power (class position, one- versus two-earner families) and parental control (paternalistic versus egalitarian families).

Postmodern Theory

postmodernist

Approach that focuses on the use of language by those in power to define crime based on their own values and biases; also called deconstructionist.

A number of radical thinkers, referred to as **postmodernists** or **deconstructionists**, have embraced semiotics as a method of understanding all human relations, including criminal behavior. **Semiotics** refers to the use of language elements as signs or symbols beyond their literal meaning. Thus, deconstructionists critically analyze communication and language in legal codes to determine whether they contain language and content that institutionalize racism or sexism.[90]

deconstructionist

Approach that focuses on the use of language by those in power to define crime based on their own values and biases; also called postmodernist.

semiotics

The use of language elements as signs or symbols beyond their literal meaning.

peacemaking

Approach that considers punitive crime control strategies to be counterproductive and favors the use of humanistic conflict resolution to prevent and control crime.

Peacemaking Criminology

Social Conflict Theory and Social Policy

restorative justice

Using humanistic, nonpunitive strategies to right wrongs and restore social harmony.

Postmodernists rely on semiotics to conduct their research efforts. For example, the term *special needs children* is designed to describe these youngsters' learning needs, but it may also characterize the children themselves as mentally challenged, dangerous, or uncontrollable. Postmodernists believe that value-laden language can promote inequities. Truth, identity, justice, and power are all concepts whose meaning is derived from the language dictated by those in power.[91] Laws, legal skill, and justice are commodities that can be bought and sold like any other service or product.[92] For example, the O. J. Simpson case is vivid proof that the affluent can purchase a different brand of justice than the indigent.[93]

Postmodernists assert that there are different languages and ways of knowing. Those in power can use their own language to define crime and law while excluding or dismissing those who oppose their control, such as prisoners and the poor. By dismissing these oppositional languages, certain versions of how to think, feel, or act are devalued and excluded. This exclusion is seen as the source of conflict in society.[94]

One of the newer movements in radical theory is **peacemaking** criminology. To members of the peacemaking movement, the main purpose of criminology is to promote a peaceful, just society. Rather than standing on empirical analysis of data, peacemaking draws its inspiration from religious and philosophical teachings ranging from Quakerism to Zen.

Peacemakers view the efforts of the state to punish and control as crime-encouraging rather than crime-discouraging. These views were first articulated in a series of books with an anarchist theme written by criminologists Larry Tifft and Dennis Sullivan in 1980.[95] Tifft argues, "The violent punishing acts of the state and its controlling professions are of the same genre as the violent acts of individuals. In each instance these acts reflect an attempt to monopolize human interaction."[96]

Sullivan stresses the futility of correcting and punishing criminals in the context of our conflict-ridden society: "The reality we must grasp is that we live in a culture of severed relationships, where every available institution provides a form of banishment but no place or means for people to become connected, to be responsible to and for each other."[97] Sullivan suggests that mutual aid rather than coercive punishment is the key to a harmonious society.

Today, advocates of the peacemaking movement, such as Harold Pepinsky and Richard Quinney (who has shifted his theoretical orientation from conflict theory to Marxism and now to peacemaking), try to find humanist solutions to crime and other social problems.[98] Rather than punishment and prison, they advocate such policies as mediation and conflict resolution. ✔ Checkpoints

At the core of all the various branches of social conflict theory is the premise that conflict causes crime. If conflict and competition in society could somehow be reduced, crime rates would fall. Some critical theorists believe that this goal can be accomplished only by thoroughly reordering society so that capitalism is destroyed and a socialist state is created. Others call for a more practical application of conflict principles. Nowhere has this been more successful than in applying peacemaking principles in the criminal justice system.

There has been an ongoing effort to reduce the conflict created by the criminal justice system when it harshly punishes offenders, many of whom are powerless social outcasts. Rather than cast them aside, peacemakers have found a way to bring them back into the community. This peacemaking movement has applied nonviolent methods through what is known as **restorative justice**.

Springing from both academia and justice system personnel, the restorative approach relies on nonpunitive strategies to prevent and control crime.[99] The principles of restorative justice are outlined in Table 8.1.

Restoration turns the justice system into a healing process rather than a distributor of retribution and revenge. Most people involved in offender–victim relationships actually know one another or were related in some way before the crime took place. According to restorative justice advocates, instead of treating one involved party as a victim deserving sympathy and the other as a criminal deserving punishment, it is more productive to address the issues that produced conflict between these people. Rather than take sides and choose whom to isolate and punish, society should try to reconcile the parties involved in conflict.[100]

Restorative programs typically divert cases away from the formal court process. Instead, these programs encourage reconciling the conflicts between offenders and victims through victim advocacy, mediation programs, and **sentencing circles**, in which crime victims and their families are brought together with offenders and their families in an effort to formulate a sanction that addresses the needs of each party.[101]

Negotiation, mediation, consensus building, and peacemaking have been part of the dispute resolution process in European and Asian communities for centuries.[102] Native American and Native Canadian people have long used the type of community participation in the adjudication process (for example, sentencing circles, sentencing panels, and elders panels) that restorative justice advocates now embrace.[103] In some Native American communities, people accused of breaking the law will meet with community members, victims, village elders, and agents of the justice system in a sentencing circle. Each member of the circle expresses his or her feelings about the act that was committed

Table 8.1 Principles of Restorative Justice

1. Crime is fundamentally a violation of people and interpersonal relationships.
   a. Victims and the community have been harmed and need restoration. Victims include the target of the offense, family members, witnesses, and the community at large.
   b. Victims, offenders, and the affected communities are the key stakeholders in justice. The state must investigate crime and ensure safety, but it is not the center of the justice process. Victims are the key, and they must help in the search for restoration, healing, responsibility, and prevention.

2. Violations create obligations and liabilities.
   a. Offenders have the obligation to make things right as much as possible. They must understand the harm they have caused. Their participation should be as voluntary as possible; coercion is to be minimized.
   b. The community's obligations are to victims, to offenders, and to the general welfare of its members. This includes the obligation to reintegrate offenders back into the community and to ensure them the opportunity to make amends.

3. Restorative justice seeks to heal and put right the wrongs.
   a. Victims' needs are the focal concern of the justice process. Safety is a top priority, and victims should be empowered to participate in determining their needs and case outcomes.
   b. The exchange of information between victim and offender should be encouraged; when possible, face-to-face meetings might be undertaken. There should be mutual agreement over imposed outcomes.
   c. Offenders' needs and competencies need to be addressed. Healing and reintegration are emphasized; isolation and removal from the community are restricted.
   d. The justice process belongs to the community; members are encouraged to "do justice." The justice process should be sensitive to community needs and geared toward preventing similar harm in the future. Early interventions are encouraged.
   e. Justice is mindful of the outcomes, intended and unintended, of its responses to crime and victimization. It should monitor case outcome and provide necessary support and opportunity to all involved. The least restrictive intervention should be used, and overt social control should be avoided.

SOURCE: Howard Zehr and Harry Mika, "Fundamental Concepts of Restorative Justice," *Contemporary Justice Review* 1 (1998): 47–55.

Restorative justice advocates campaign against punitive measures such as the death penalty and seek nonviolent alternatives to such punishment. Is it possible to reintegrate all offenders back into society, even those who have taken another's life?

AP/Wide World Photos

sentencing circle

A peacemaking technique in which offenders, victims, and other community members are brought together in an effort to formulate a sanction that addresses the needs of all.

and raises questions or concerns. The accused can express regret about his or her actions and a desire to change the harmful behavior. People may suggest ways the offender can make things up to the community and those he or she has harmed. A treatment program such as Alcoholics Anonymous may be suggested, if appropriate. The purpose of this process is to reduce the conflict and harm and restore rather than punish.[104] The accompanying Policy and Practice in Criminology feature reviews restorative justice programs now being used in Minnesota.

Summary

Social conflict theorists view crime as a function of the conflict that exists in society. Conflict theorists suggest that crime in any society is caused by class conflict. Laws are created by those in power to protect their rights and interests.

All criminal acts have political undertones; Richard Quinney has called this the social reality of crime. Unfortunately, research efforts to validate the conflict approach have not produced significant findings. One of conflict theory's most important premises is that the justice system is biased and designed to protect the wealthy. Research has not been unanimous in supporting this point.

Marxist criminology views the competitive nature of the capitalist system as a major cause of crime. The poor commit crimes because of their frustration, anger, and need. The wealthy engage in illegal acts because they are used to competition and because they must do so to keep their positions in society. Marxist scholars have attempted to show that the law is designed to protect the wealthy and powerful and to control the poor, have-not members of society. Branches of radical theory include instrumental Marxism and structural Marxism.

During the 1990s, new forms of conflict theory emerged. Left realism takes a centrist position on crime by showing its rational, destructive nature. Feminist writers draw attention to the influence of patriarchal society on crime. Deconstructionism looks at the symbolic meaning of law and culture. Peacemaking criminology calls for humanism in criminology.

Find It on INFOTRAC
College Edition

The restorative justice movement is taking off in the United States and other nations. If you want to read about what is going on in Canada, use "restorative," "justice," and "Canada" as keywords in InfoTrac College Edition.

Policy and Practice in Criminology

Restorative Justice in the Community

A number of new and innovative community programs based on restorative justice principles are now being tested around the United States. Minnesota has been a groundbreaker in restorative justice. Its Department of Corrections created the "Restorative Justice Initiative" in 1992, hiring Kay Pranis as a full-time Restorative Justice Planner in 1994—the first such position in the country. The initiative offers training in restorative justice principles and practices, provides technical assistance to communities in designing and implementing practices, and creates networks of professionals and activists to share knowledge and provide support.

Besides promoting victim–offender mediation, family group conferencing, and neighborhood conferencing, the department has introduced sentencing circles. Citizen volunteers and criminal justice officials from Minnesota have participated in training in Canada's Yukon Territory, where peacemaking circles have been held since the late 1980s. In Minnesota, the circle process is used by the Mille Lacs Indian Reservation and by other communities in several counties.

The circle process usually has several phases. First, the Community Justice Committee conducts an intake interview with offenders who want to participate. Then, separate healing circles are held for the victim (and others who feel harmed) and the offender. The committee tries to cultivate a close personal relationship with victims and offenders and to create support networks for them. In the end, a sentencing circle, open to the community, meets to work out a sentencing plan.

In Minnesota, sentencing circles are used not only in Native American communities but also in European American rural, suburban, and African American inner-city communities. Community Justice Committees, established by citizen volunteers, handle organizational and administrative tasks and provide "keepers" who lead the discussions. Judges refer cases, and the committees make the final decision on acceptance. The agreements reached are presented to the judge as sentencing recommendations. In some cases, the judge, prosecutor, and defense attorney participate in the circle, and then the agreement becomes the final sentence.

Critical Thinking

Restorative justice may be the model that best serves alternative sanctions. How can this essentially humanistic approach be sold to the general public, which now supports more punitive sanctions? For example, would it be feasible to argue that using restoration with nonviolent offenders frees up resources for the relatively few dangerous people in the criminal population?

 InfoTrac College Edition Research

To read more about restorative justice, check out
Kent Roach, "Changing Punishment at the Turn of the Century: Restorative Justice on the Rise," *Canadian Journal of Criminology*, July 2000 v42 i3 p249

SOURCE: Leena Kurki, *Incorporating Restorative and Community Justice into American Sentencing and Corrections* (Washington, DC: National Institute of Justice, 1999).

For a summary of the various branches and forms of social conflict theory, see Table 8.2. For additional chapter links, discussions, and quizzes, see the book-specific Web site at http://www.wadsworth.com/product/0534519423s.

Thinking Like a Criminologist

An interim evaluation of Restoration House's New Hope for Families program, a community-based residential treatment program for women with dependent children, shows that 70 percent of women who complete follow-up interviews six months after treatment have maintained abstinence or reduced their drug use. The other 30 percent, however, lapse back into their old habits.

The program relies on restorative justice techniques in which community people meet with the women to discuss the harm drug use can cause and how it can damage both them and their children. The community members show their support and help the women find a niche in the community.

Table 8.2 Social Conflict Theories

THEORY	MAJOR PREMISE	STRENGTHS
Conflict theory	Crime is a function of class conflict. Law is defined by people who hold social and political power.	Accounts for class differentials in the crime rate. Shows how class conflict influences behavior.
Marxist theory	Capitalist ownership of the means of production creates class conflict. Crime is a rebellion of the lower class. The criminal justice system is an agent of class warfare.	Accounts for the associations between economic structure and crime rates.
Instrumental Marxist theory	Criminals are revolutionaries. The real crimes are sexism, racism, and profiteering.	Broadens the definition of crime and demystifies or explains the historical development of law.
Structural Marxist theory	The law is designed to sustain the capitalist economic system.	Explains the existence of white-collar crime and business control laws.
Left realism	Crime is a function of relative deprivation; criminals prey on the poor.	Represents a compromise between conflict and traditional criminology.
Radical feminist theory	The capitalist system creates patriarchy, which oppresses women.	Explains gender bias, violence against women, and repression.
Power–control theory	Girls are controlled more closely than boys in traditional male-dominated households. There is gender equity in contemporary egalitarian homes.	Explains gender differences in the crime rate as a function of class and gender conflict.
Deconstructionism	Language controls the meaning and use of the law.	Provides a critical analysis of meaning.
Peacemaking	Peace and humanism can reduce crime; conflict resolution strategies can work.	Offers a new approach to crime control through mediation.

Women who complete the Restoration House program improve their employment, reduce parenting stress, retain custody of their children, and restore their physical, mental, and emotional health. The program focuses not only on reducing drug and alcohol use but also on increasing health, safety, self-sufficiency, and positive attitudes.

As a criminologist, would you consider this program a success? What questions would have to be answered before it gets your approval? How do you think the program should handle women who do not succeed in the program? Are there any other approaches you would try with these women? If so, explain.

Key Terms

social conflict theory	instrumental Marxist	power–control theory
radical criminology	demystify	postmodernist
Marxist criminology	structural Marxist	deconstructionist
power	left realism	semiotics
social reality of crime	preemptive deterrence	peacemaking
surplus value	Marxist feminism	restorative justice
marginalization	patriarchal	sentencing circle

Discussion Questions

1. How would a conservative reply to a call for more restorative justice? How would a restorative justice advocate respond to a conservative call for more prisons?

2. Considering recent changes in American culture, how would a power–control theorist explain recent drops in the U.S. crime rate?

3. Is conflict inevitable in all cultures? If not, what can be done to reduce the level of conflict in our own society?

4. If Marx were alive today, what would he think about the prosperity enjoyed by the working class in industrial societies? Might he alter his vision of the capitalist system?

© Will Waldron/The Image Works

9 Integrated Theories: Things Change

To derive more powerful explanations of crime, some criminologists have begun integrating individual factors into complex multifactor theories. These **integrated theories** attempt to blend seemingly independent concepts into coherent explanations of criminality.

Integrated theories seek to avoid the shortcomings of single-factor theories, which focus on the onset of crime and tend to divide the world into criminals and noncriminals—those who have a crime-producing condition and those who do not. For example, people with high testosterone levels are violent; people with low levels are not.

The view that people can be classified as either criminals or noncriminals, with this status being stable for life, is now being challenged. Criminologists today are concerned not only with the onset of criminality but with its termination as well. Why do people age out of crime? If, for example, criminality is a function of lower intelligence, as some criminologists claim, why do most delinquents fail to become adult criminals? It seems unlikely that intelligence increases as young offenders mature. If the onset of criminality can be explained by low intelligence, then some other factor must explain its termination.

It has also become important to chart the natural history of a criminal career. Why do some offenders escalate their criminal activities while others decrease or limit their law violations? Why do some offenders specialize in a particular crime while others become generalists? Why do some criminals reduce criminal activity and then resume it once again? Research now shows that some offenders begin their criminal careers at a very early age, whereas others begin later. How can early- and late-onset criminality be explained?[1] This view of the nature of crime is referred to as **developmental criminology**.

Integrated theories focus attention on the chronic or persistent offender. Although the concept of chronic offenders, who begin their offending careers as children and persist into adulthood, is now an accepted fact, criminologists are still struggling to understand why this is so. They do not fully understand why, when faced with a similar set of life circumstances, such as poverty and family dysfunction, one youth becomes a chronic offender while another may commit an occasional illegal act but later desists from crime. Single-factor theories, such as social structure and social process theories, have trouble explaining why only a relatively few of the many individuals exposed to crimogenic influences in the environment actually become chronic offenders.

By integrating a variety of ecological, social, psychological, biological, and economic factors into a coherent structure, criminologists are attempting to answer these complex questions.

Recent attempts at creating integrated theories can be divided into two distinct groups. **Latent trait theories** hold that criminal behavior is controlled by a "master trait," present at birth or soon after, that remains stable and unchanging throughout a person's lifetime. Latent trait theorists believe that "people don't change, opportunities do." **Developmental theories** view criminality as a dynamic process, influenced by individual characteristics as well as social experiences. Thus, developmental theorists hope for personal change and growth. These two positions are summarized in Figure 9.1 and discussed in detail in the following sections.

Latent Trait Theories

In a popular 1985 book, *Crime and Human Nature*, two prominent social scientists, James Q. Wilson and Richard Herrnstein, argued that personal traits, such as genetic makeup, intelligence, and body build, operate in tandem with social variables such as poverty and family function. Together these factors influence people to "choose crime" over noncriminal behavioral alternatives.[2]

Figure 9.1

Latent Trait Versus Developmental Theories

Latent trait theory
- Master trait
  - Personality
  - Intelligence
  - Genetic makeup
- People do not change, criminal opportunities change; maturity brings fewer opportunities
- Early social control and proper parenting can reduce criminal propensity

- Criminal careers are a passage
- Personal and structural factors influence crime
- Change affects crime
- Personal vs. situational

Developmental theory
- Multiple traits: social, psychological, economic
- People change over the life course
- Family, job, peer influence behavior

Following their lead, David Rowe, D. Wayne Osgood, and W. Alan Nicewander proposed the concept of **latent traits**. Their model assumes that a number of people in the population have a personal attribute or characteristic that controls their inclination or propensity to commit crimes.[3] This disposition, or latent trait, is either present at birth or established early in life, and it remains stable over time. Suspected latent traits include defective intelligence, impulsive personality, genetic abnormalities, the physical-chemical functioning of the brain, and environmental influences on brain function such as drugs, chemicals, and injuries.[4] Those who carry one of these latent traits are in danger of becoming career criminals; those who lack the traits have a much lower risk. Latent traits should affect the behavioral choices of all people equally, regardless of their gender or personal characteristics.[5]

According to this emerging latent trait view, the *propensity* to commit crime is stable, but the *opportunity* to commit crime fluctuates over time. People age out of crime because, as they mature, there are simply fewer opportunities to commit crime and greater inducements to remain "straight." They may marry, have children, and obtain jobs. The former delinquents' newfound adult responsibilities leave them little time to hang with their friends, abuse substances, and get into scrapes with the law.

Assume, for example, that a stable latent trait such as low IQ causes some people to commit crime. Teenagers have more opportunity to commit crime than adults, so at every level of intelligence, adolescent crime rates will be higher. As they mature, however, teens with both high and low IQs will commit less crime because their adult responsibilities provide them with fewer criminal opportunities. Thus, latent trait theories integrate concepts usually associated with trait theories (such as personality and temperament) and concepts associated with rational choice theories (such as criminal opportunity and suitable targets).

General Theory of Crime

developmental theory

The view that criminality is a dynamic process, influenced by social experiences as well as individual characteristics.

latent trait

A stable feature, characteristic, property, or condition, such as defective intelligence or impulsive personality, that makes some people crime-prone over the life course.

general theory of crime (GTC)

A developmental theory that modifies social control theory by integrating concepts from biosocial, psychological, routine activities, and rational choice theories.

Michael Gottfredson and Travis Hirschi's **general theory of crime (GTC)** modifies and redefines some of the principles articulated in Hirschi's social control theory (Chapter 7) by integrating the concepts of control with those of biosocial, psychological, routine activities, and rational choice theories.[6]

The Act and the Offender In their general theory of crime, Gottfredson and Hirschi consider the criminal offender and the criminal act as separate concepts.

Criminal acts, such as robberies or burglaries, are illegal events or deeds that people engage in when they perceive them to be advantageous. For example, burglaries are typically committed by young males looking for cash, liquor, and entertainment; the crime provides "easy, short-term gratification."[7] Crime is rational and predictable: People commit crime when it promises rewards with minimal threat of pain. The threat of punishment can deter crime: If targets are well guarded, crime rates diminish.

Criminal offenders are individuals predisposed to commit crimes. They are not robots who commit crime without restraint; their days are also filled with conventional behaviors, such as going to school, parties, concerts, and church. But given the same set of criminal opportunities, such as having a lot of free time for mischief and living in a neighborhood with unguarded homes containing valuable merchandise, crime-prone people have a much higher probability of violating the law than do noncriminals. The propensity to commit crimes remains stable throughout a person's life. Change in the frequency of criminal activity is purely a function of change in criminal opportunity.

Figure 9.2

The General Theory of Crime

Impulsive personality
- Physical
- Insensitive
- Risk-taking
- Shortsighted
- Nonverbal

Low self-control
- Poor parenting
- Deviant parents
- Lack of supervision
- Active
- Self-centered

Weakening of social bonds
- Attachment
- Involvement
- Commitment
- Belief

Criminal opportunity
- Gangs
- Free time
- Drugs
- Suitable targets

Crime and deviance
- Delinquency
- Smoking
- Drinking
- Sex
- Crime

CONNECTIONS

In his original version of control theory, discussed in Chapter 7, Hirschi focused on the social controls that attach people to conventional society and insulate them from criminality. In this newer work, he concentrates on self-control as a stabilizing force. The two views are connected, however, because both social control (or social bonds) and self-control are acquired through early experiences with effective parenting.

By recognizing that there are stable differences in people's propensity to commit crime, the GTC adds a biosocial element to the concept of social control. The biological and psychological factors that make people impulsive and crime-prone may be inherited or may develop through incompetent or absent parenting.

What Makes People Crime-Prone? What, then, causes people to become excessively crime-prone? Gottfredson and Hirschi attribute the tendency to commit crimes to a person's level of self-control. People with limited self-control tend to be impulsive; they are insensitive to other people's feelings, physical (rather than mental), risk takers, shortsighted, and nonverbal.[8] They have a "here and now" orientation and refuse to work for distant goals; they lack diligence, tenacity, and persistence. People lacking self-control tend to be adventuresome, active, physical, and self-centered. As they mature, they often have unstable marriages, jobs, and friendships.[9] People lacking self-control are less likely to feel shame if they engage in deviant acts and are more likely to find them pleasurable.[10] They are also more likely to engage in dangerous behaviors such as drinking, smoking, and reckless driving; all of these behaviors are associated with criminality.[11] (See Figure 9.2.)

Because those with low self-control enjoy risky, exciting, or thrilling behaviors with immediate gratification, they are more likely to enjoy criminal acts, which require stealth, agility, speed, and power, than conventional acts, which demand long-term study and cognitive and verbal skills. Because they enjoy taking risks, they are more likely to get involved in accidents and suffer injuries than people who maintain self-control.[12] As Gottfredson and Hirschi put it, they derive satisfaction from "money without work, sex without courtship, revenge without court delays."[13] Many of these individuals who have a propensity for committing crime also engage in other behaviors such as smoking, drinking, gambling, and illicit sexuality.[14] Although these acts are not illegal, they too provide immediate, short-term gratification. Table 9.1 lists the elements of impulsivity, or low self-control.

Gottfredson and Hirschi trace the root cause of poor self-control to inadequate child-rearing practices. Parents who are unwilling or unable to monitor a child's behavior, to recognize deviant behavior when it occurs, and to punish that behavior will produce children who lack self-control. Children who are not attached to their parents, who are poorly supervised, and whose parents are criminal or deviant themselves are the most likely to develop poor self-control. In a sense, lack of self-control occurs naturally when steps are not taken to stop its development.[15] Low self-control develops early in life and remains stable into and through adulthood.[16]

Self-Control and Crime Gottfredson and Hirschi claim that the principles of self-control theory can explain all varieties of criminal behavior and all the social and behavioral correlates of crime. That is, such widely disparate crimes as burglary, robbery, embezzlement, drug dealing, murder, rape, and insider trading all stem from a deficiency of self-control. Likewise, gender, racial, and ecological differences in crime rates can be explained by discrepancies in self-control. Put another way, the male crime rate is higher than the female crime rate because males have lower levels of self-control.

Unlike other theoretical models that explain only narrow segments of criminal behavior (such as theories of teenage gang formation), Gottfredson and Hirschi argue that self-control applies equally to all crimes, ranging from murder to corporate theft. For example, Gottfredson and Hirschi maintain that white-collar crime rates remain low because people who lack self-control rarely attain the positions necessary to commit those crimes. However, the relatively few white-collar criminals lack self-control to the same degree and in the same

According to the general theory of crime, people who have low self-control are crime-prone even if they are born into affluent families. Here, Malissa "Lisa" Warzeka (right) and Katie Marie Dunn, both 17, enter the courtroom during their trial in Houston. Warzeka and Dunn, both affluent suburban girls, were sentenced to seven-year prison terms for committing a string of convenience store robberies over the summer vacation. Is it possible that their crime spree was a function of their impulsive personalities and low self-control?

AP/Wide World Photos

Table 9.1 The Elements of Impulsivity: Signs That a Person Has Low Self-Control

- Insensitive
- Physical
- Shortsighted
- Nonverbal
- Here-and-now orientation
- Unstable social relations
- Enjoys deviant behaviors
- Risk taker
- Refuses to work for distant goals
- Lacks diligence
- Lacks tenacity
- Adventuresome
- Self-centered
- Shameless
- Imprudent
- Lacks cognitive and verbal skills
- Enjoys danger and excitement

manner as criminals such as rapists and burglars. Although the criminal activity of individuals with low self-control also declines as those individuals mature, they maintain an offense rate that remains consistently higher than those with strong self-control.

Supporting Evidence for the GTC Following the publication of *A General Theory of Crime,* dozens of research efforts tested the validity of Gottfredson and Hirschi's theoretical views. One approach involved identifying indicators of impulsiveness and self-control to determine whether scales measuring these factors correlate with measures of criminal activity. A number of studies conducted both in the United States and abroad have successfully showed this type of association.[17] Some of the most important findings are summarized in Table 9.2.

Analyzing the GTC By integrating the concepts of socialization and criminality, Gottfredson and Hirschi help explain why some people who lack self-control can escape criminality, and, conversely, why some people who have self-control might not escape criminality. People who are at risk because they have impulsive personalities may forgo criminal careers because there are no criminal opportunities that satisfy their impulsive needs; instead they may find other outlets for their impulsive personalities. In contrast, if the opportunity is strong enough, even people with relatively strong self-control may be tempted to violate the law; the incentives to commit crime may overwhelm self-control.

Integrating criminal propensity and criminal opportunity can explain why some children enter into chronic offending while others living in similar environments are able to resist criminal activity. It can also help us understand why the corporate executive with a spotless record gets caught up in business fraud. Even a successful executive may find self-control inadequate if the potential for illegal gain is large. The driven executive, used to both academic and financial success, may find that the fear of failure can overwhelm self-control. During tough economic times, the impulsive manager who fears dismissal may be tempted to circumvent the law to improve the bottom line.[18]

Table 9.2 Empirical Evidence Supporting the General Theory of Crime

- Novice offenders, lacking in self-control, commit a garden variety of criminal acts.[1]
- More mature and experienced criminals become more specialized in their choice of crime (e.g., robbers, burglars, drug dealers).[2]
- Male and female drunk drivers are impulsive individuals who manifest low self-control.[3]
- Repeat violent offenders are more impulsive than their less violent peers.[4]
- Incarcerated youth enjoy risk-taking behavior and hold values and attitudes that suggest impulsivity.[5]
- Kids who take drugs and commit crime are impulsive and enjoy engaging in risky behaviors.[6]
- Measures of self-control can predict deviant and antisocial behavior across age groups ranging from teens to adults age 50.[7]
- People who commit white-collar and workplace crime have lower levels of self-control than nonoffenders.[8]
- Gang members have lower levels of self-control than the general population; gang members report lower levels of parental management, a factor associated with lower self-control.[9]

- Low self-control shapes perceptions of criminal opportunity and consequently conditions the decision to commit crimes.[10]
- People who lack self-control expect to commit crime in the future.[11]
- Kids whose problems develop early in life are the most resistant to change in treatment and rehabilitation programs.[12]
- Gender differences in self-control are responsible for crime rate differences. Females who lack self-control are as crime-prone as males with similar personalities.[13]
- Parents who manage their children's behavior increase their self-control, which helps reduce their delinquent activities.[14]
- Having parents (or stepparents) available to control behavior may reduce the opportunity to commit crime.[15]
- Victims have lower self-control than nonvictims. Impulsivity predicts both the likelihood that a person will engage in criminal behavior and the likelihood that the person will become a victim of crime.[16]

NOTES:

1. Xiaogang Deng and Lening Zhang, "Correlates of Self-Control: An Empirical Test of Self-Control Theory," *Journal of Crime and Justice* 21 (1998): 89–103.

2. Alex Piquero, Raymond Paternoster, Paul Mazeroole, Robert Brame, and Charles Dean, "Onset Age and Offense Specialization," *Journal of Research in Crime and Delinquency* 36 (1999): 275–299.

3. Carl Keane, Paul Maxim, and James Teevan, "Drinking and Driving, Self-Control, and Gender: Testing a General Theory of Crime," *Journal of Research in Crime and Delinquency* 30 (1993): 30–46.

4. Judith DeJong, Matti Virkkunen, and Marku Linnoila, "Factors Associated with Recidivism in a Criminal Population," *Journal of Nervous and Mental Disease* 180 (1992): 543–550.

5. David Cantor, "Drug Involvement and Offending Among Incarcerated Juveniles," paper presented at the annual meeting of the American Society of Criminology, Boston, November 1995.

6. David Brownfield and Ann Marie Sorenson, "Self-Control and Juvenile Delinquency: Theoretical Issues and an Empirical Assessment of Selected Elements of a General Theory of Crime," *Deviant Behavior* 14 (1993): 243–264; John Cochran, Peter Wood, and Bruce Arneklev, "Is the Religiosity–Delinquency Relationship Spurious? A Test of Arousal and Social Control Theories," *Journal of Research in Crime and Delinquency* 31 (1994): 92–123.

7. Velmer Burton, T. David Evans, Francis Cullen, Kathleen Olivares, and R. Gregory Dunaway, "Age, Self-Control, and Adults' Offending Behaviors: A Research Note Assessing A General Theory of Crime," *Journal of Criminal Justice* 27 (1999): 45–54; John Gibbs and Dennis Giever, "Self-Control and Its Manifestations Among University Students: An Empirical Test of Gottfredson and Hirschi's General Theory," *Justice Quarterly* 12 (1995): 231–255.

8. Carey Herbert, "The Implications of Self-Control Theory for Workplace Offending," paper presented at the annual meeting of the American Society of Criminology, San Diego, 1997.

9. Dennis Giever, Dana Lynskey, and Danette Monnet, "Gottfredson and Hirschi's General Theory of Crime and Youth Gangs: An Empirical Test on a Sample of Middle School Youth," paper presented at the annual meeting of the American Society of Criminology, San Diego, 1997.

10. Douglas Longshore, Susan Turner, and Judith Stein, "Self-Control in a Criminal Sample: An Examination of Construct Validity," *Criminology* 34 (1996): 209–228.

11. Deng and Zhang, "Correlates of Self-Control: An Empirical Test of Self-Control Theory."

12. Linda Pagani, Richard Tremblay, Frank Vitaro, and Sophie Parent, "Does Preschool Help Prevent Delinquency in Boys with a History of Perinatal Complications?" *Criminology* 36 (1998): 245–268.

13. Velmer Burton, Francis Cullen, T. David Evans, Leanne Fiftal Alarid, and R. Gregory Dunaway, "Gender, Self-Control, and Crime," *Journal of Research in Crime and Delinquency* 35 (1998): 123–147.

14. John Gibbs, Dennis Giever, and Jamie Martin, "Parental Management and Self-Control: An Empirical Test of Gottfredson and Hirschi's General Theory," *Journal of Research in Crime and Delinquency* 35 (1998): 40–70.

15. Vic Bumphus and James Anderson, "Family Structure and Race in a Sample of Offenders," *Journal of Criminal Justice* 27 (1999): 309–320.

16. Christopher Schreck, "Criminal Victimization and Low Self-Control: An Extension and Test of a General Theory of Crime," *Justice Quarterly* 16 (1999): 633–654.

Although the general theory seems persuasive, several questions and criticisms remain unanswered. Among the most important are the following:

1. *Tautological.* Some critics argue that the theory is tautological—that is, it involves circular reasoning. How do we know when people are impulsive? When they commit crimes. Are all criminals impulsive? Of course, or else they would not have broken the law![19]

2. *Personality disorder.* Saying someone lacks self-control implies a personality defect that makes him or her impulsive and rash. There is still no conclusive proof that criminals can be distinguished from noncriminals on the basis of personality alone.

3. *Ecological/individual differences.* The GTC also fails to address individual and ecological patterns in the crime rate. For example, if crime rates are higher in Los Angeles than in Albany, New York, can it be assumed that residents of Los Angeles are more impulsive than residents of Albany?

4. *Racial and gender differences.* Although distinct gender differences in the crime rate exist, there is little evidence that males are more impulsive than females (although females and males differ in many other personality traits).[20] Similarly, Gottfredson and Hirschi explain racial differences in the crime rate as a failure of child-rearing practices in the African American community.[21] In so doing, they overlook issues of institutional racism, poverty, and relative deprivation, which have been shown to have a significant impact on crime rate differentials.

5. *People change.* The general theory assumes that criminal propensity does not change; opportunities change. A number of research efforts show that factors that help control criminal behavior, such as peer relations and school performance, vary over time. Social influences, which are dominant in early adolescence, may fade and be replaced by others in adulthood.[22] This finding contradicts the GTC, which suggests that the influence of friends should be stable and unchanging.

Gottfredson and Hirschi assume that low self-control varies little with age and that low self-control is almost exclusively a product of early childhood rearing; but research shows that self-control may vary with age. As people mature, they may be better able to control their impulsive behavior.[23] These findings contradict the GTC, which assumes that levels of self-control and therefore criminal propensity are constant and independent of personal relationships. However, it is uncertain whether life changes affect the propensity to commit crime or merely the opportunity, as Gottfredson and Hirschi suggest.

6. *Modest relationship.* Some research results support the proposition that self-control is a causal factor in criminal and other forms of deviant behavior, but that the association is quite modest.[24] This would indicate that other forces influence criminal behavior and that low self-control alone cannot predict the onset of a criminal or deviant career.

7. *Cross-cultural differences.* Evidence shows that criminals in other countries do not lack self-control, indicating that the GTC may be culturally limited.[25] Behavior that may be considered imprudent in one culture may be socially acceptable in another and therefore cannot be viewed as "lack of self-control."[26]

Although questions like these remain, the strength of the general theory lies in its scope and breadth; it attempts to explain all forms of crime and deviance, from lower-class gang delinquency to sexual harassment in the business community.[27] By integrating concepts of criminal choice, criminal opportunity, socialization, and personality, Gottfredson and Hirschi make a plausible argument that all deviant behaviors may originate at the same source. Continued efforts are needed to test the GTC and establish the validity of its core concepts. It remains one of the key developments of modern criminological theory.

Control Balance Theory

control balance theory

A developmental theory that attributes deviant and criminal behaviors to imbalances between the amount of control that the individual has over others and that others have over him or her.

Charles Tittle's **control balance theory** expands on the concept of personal control as a predisposing element for criminality.[28]

According to Tittle, the concept of control has two distinct elements: the amount of control one is subject to by others and the amount of control one can exercise over others. Conformity results when these two elements are in balance; control imbalances produce deviant and criminal behaviors.

Tittle envisions control as a continuous variable (Figure 9.3), ranging from a control deficit, which occurs when a person's desires or impulses are limited by other people's ability to regulate or punish their behavior, to a control surplus, which occurs when the amount of control one can exercise over others exceeds the ability others have to control or modify one's own behavior.

People who sense a deficit of control turn to three types of behavior to restore balance: *predation, defiance,* and *submission.* Predation involves direct forms of physical violence, such as robbery or sexual assault. Defiance is designed to challenge control mechanisms but stops short of physical harm, such as vandalism, curfew violations, or unconventional sex. Submission involves passive obedience to the demands of others, such as submitting to physical or sexual abuse without response.

According to Tittle, an excess of control can also lead to deviance and crime—a contention that contradicts Hirschi and Gottfredson's view that only low control leads to crime. Those who have an excess of control engage in three types of behavior: *exploitation, plunder,* and *decadence.* Exploitation involves using others to commit crime—for example, as contract killers or drug runners. Plunder involves using power without regard for others, such as committing a hate crime or polluting the environment. Decadence involves spur-of-the-moment, irrational acts such as child molesting.

Control imbalance represents a potential to commit crime and deviance. That is, possessing deficient or excessive control increases the likelihood that when presented with situational motivations a person will react in an antisocial manner. Deviant motivations emerge when a person suffering from control imbalance believes that engaging in some antisocial act will alter his or her con-

Figure 9.3

Tittle's Control Balance Theory

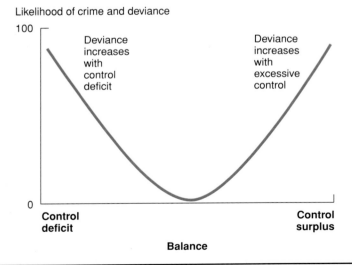

Likelihood of crime and deviance

Deviance increases with control deficit

Deviance increases with excessive control

100

0

Control deficit

Control surplus

Balance

✔ **Checkpoints**

✔ Latent trait theories assume a physical or psychological trait makes some people crime-prone.

✔ Opportunity to commit crime varies; latent traits remain stable.

✔ The general theory of crime says an impulsive personality is key.

✔ Impulsive people have low self-control, and a weak bond to society.

✔ Impulsive people often cannot resist criminal opportunities.

✔ According to Tittle, crime may be a function of efforts to maintain control and avoid restraint.

trol ratio in a favorable way. For example, when a person who has a surplus of control is insulted, he may tells his friends to attack the instigator; a student with a control deficit may vandalize a school after getting a bad grade on her report card.

Even if people are motivated to commit crime, they may be constrained by their perceptions of external forces of control. Even highly motivated individuals may be constrained if they believe that their deviant behavior is very serious and likely to be discovered by those who can exert control, such as the police. Tittle also recognizes that opportunity shapes antisocial behavior. No matter how great the motivation or how little the restraint, the actual likelihood of a crime occurring depends on the opportunity.

Tittle's view is essentially integrated because, like Hirschi and Gottfredson before him, he incorporates external or social concepts such as opportunity and restraint with internal or individual variables such as degree of control.

✔ **Checkpoints**

Developmental Theory

The second integrated approach that has emerged is developmental theory. According to this view, even as toddlers, people begin relationships and behaviors that will determine their adult life course. At first they must learn to conform to social rules and function effectively in society. Later they are expected to begin thinking about careers, leave their parental homes, find permanent relationships, and eventually marry and begin their own families.[29] These transitions are expected to take place in order, beginning with finishing school, entering the workforce, getting married, and having children.

Some individuals, however, are incapable of maturing in a reasonable and timely fashion because of family, environmental, or personal problems. In some cases transitions can occur too early—for example, when adolescents engage in precocious sex. In other cases transitions may occur too late, as when a student fails to graduate on time because of bad grades or too many incompletes. Sometimes disruption of one trajectory can harm another. For example, teenage childbirth will most likely disrupt educational and career development. Because developmental theories focus on the associations between life events and deviant behaviors, they are sometimes referred to as **life-course theories**.

life-course theory

Theory that focuses on changes in criminality over the life course; developmental theory.

Disruptions in life's major transitions can be destructive and ultimately can promote criminality. Those who are already at risk because of socioeconomic problems or family dysfunction are the most susceptible to these awkward transitions. The cumulative impact of these disruptions sustains criminality from childhood into adulthood.

Because a transition from one stage of life to another can be a bumpy ride, the propensity to commit crimes is neither stable nor constant; it is a developmental process. A positive life experience may help some criminals desist from crime for a while, whereas a negative one may cause them to resume their activities. Criminal careers are also said to be interactional because people are influenced by the behavior of those around them and, in turn, influence others' behavior. For example, a youth's antisocial behavior may turn his or her more conventional friends against him; their rejection solidifies and escalates his antisocial behavior.

Developmental theories also recognize that as people mature, the factors that influence their behavior change.[30] At first, family relations may be most influential; in later adolescence, school and peer relations predominate; in adulthood, vocational achievement and marital relations may be the most critical influences. For example, some antisocial children who are in trouble throughout their adolescence may manage to find stable work and maintain intact marriages as adults; these life events help them desist from crime. In contrast, the less fortunate adolescents who develop arrest records and get involved with the wrong crowd may find themselves limited to menial jobs and at risk for criminal careers.

Developmental theories are inherently multidimensional, suggesting that criminality has multiple roots, including maladaptive personality traits, educational failure, and dysfunctional family relations. Criminality, according to this view, cannot be attributed to a single cause, nor does it represent a single underlying tendency.[31] People are influenced by different factors as they mature. Consequently, a factor that may have an important influence at one stage of life (such as delinquent peers) may have little influence later on.[32]

The Glueck Research

One of the cornerstones of recent developmental theories has been a renewed interest in the research efforts of Sheldon and Eleanor Glueck. While at Harvard University in the 1930s, the Gluecks popularized research on the life cycle of delinquent careers. In a series of longitudinal research studies, they followed the careers of known delinquents to determine the factors that predicted persistent offending.[33] The Gluecks made extensive use of interviews and records in their elaborate comparisons of delinquents and nondelinquents.[34]

The Gluecks' research focused on early onset of delinquency as a harbinger of a criminal career: "The deeper the roots of childhood maladjustment, the smaller the chance of adult adjustment."[35] They also noted the stability of offending careers: Children who are antisocial early in life are the most likely to continue their offending careers into adulthood.

The Gluecks identified a number of personal and social factors related to persistent offending. The most important of these factors was family relations, considered in terms of quality of discipline and emotional ties with parents. The adolescent raised in a large, single-parent family of limited economic means and educational achievement was the most vulnerable to delinquency.

The Gluecks did not restrict their analysis to social variables. When they measured such biological and psychological traits as body type, intelligence, and personality, they found that physical and mental factors also played a role in determining behavior. Children with low intelligence, a background of mental disease, and a powerful (mesomorph) physique were the most likely to become persistent offenders.

Developmental Concepts

A 1990 review paper (revised in 1998) by Rolf Loeber and Marc LeBlanc was an important event in popularizing developmental theory.[36] In their landmark work, Loeber and LeBlanc proposed that criminologists should devote time and effort to understanding some basic questions about the evolution of criminal careers: Why do people begin committing antisocial acts? Why do some stop while others continue? Why do some escalate the severity of their criminality (that is, go from shoplifting to drug dealing to armed robbery) while others de-escalate and commit less serious crime as they mature? If some terminate their criminal activity, what, if anything, causes them to begin again? Why do some criminals specialize in certain types of crime, whereas others are generalists engaging in a variety of antisocial behaviors? According to Loeber and LeBlanc's developmental view, criminologists must pay attention to how a criminal career unfolds.

Consequently, a view of crime has emerged that both incorporates personal change and growth and recognizes that the factors that produce crime and delinquency at one point in the life cycle may not be relevant at another.[37] People may show a propensity to offend early in their lives, but the nature and

Table 9.3 Problem Behaviors

Social
- Family dysfunction
- Unemployment
- Educational underachievement
- School misconduct

Personal
- Substance abuse
- Suicide attempts
- Early sexuality
- Sensation seeking
- Early parenthood
- Accident-proneness
- Medical problems
- Mental disease
- Anxiety
- Eating disorders (bulimia, anorexia)

Environmental
- High-crime area
- Disorganized area
- Racism
- Exposure to poverty

problem behavior syndrome (PBS)

A cluster of antisocial behaviors that may include family dysfunction, substance abuse, smoking, precocious sexuality and early pregnancy, educational underachievement, suicide attempts, sensation seeking, and unemployment, as well as crime.

frequency of their activities are affected by outside forces beyond their control, such as the likelihood of getting arrested and being punished for crime.[38]

In this section, we review some of the more important concepts associated with the developmental perspective. In the remainder of the chapter, we discuss some prominent developmental theories.

Problem Behavior Syndrome The developmental view is that criminality can best be understood as one of many social problems faced by at-risk youth. Crime is just one among a group of antisocial behaviors that cluster together, referred to collectively as **problem behavior syndrome (PBS)**. PBS typically involves family dysfunction, substance abuse, smoking, precocious sexuality and early pregnancy, educational underachievement, suicide attempts, sensation seeking, and unemployment (see Table 9.3).[39] People who exhibit one of these conditions typically exhibit many of the others.[40] All varieties of criminal behavior, including violence, theft, and drug offenses, may be part of a generalized PBS, indicating that all forms of antisocial behavior have similar developmental patterns.[41]

Those who exhibit PBS are prone to more difficulties than the general population.[42] They face a range of personal dilemmas ranging from drug abuse, to being accident-prone, to requiring more health care and hospitalization, to becoming teenage parents. PBS has been linked to personality problems (such as rebelliousness and low ego), family problems (such as intrafamily conflict and parental mental disorder), and educational failure.[43] Multisite research has shown that PBS is not unique to any single area of the country and that children who exhibit PBS, including drug use, delinquency, and precocious sexuality, display symptoms at an early age.[44]

Pathways to Crime Developmental theorists recognize that career criminals may travel more than a single road. Some may specialize in violence and extortion; some may be involved in theft and fraud; others may engage in a variety of criminal acts. Some offenders may begin their careers early in life, whereas others are late bloomers who begin committing crime when most people desist.

Are there different pathways to crime? Using data from a longitudinal cohort study conducted in Pittsburgh, Rolf Loeber and his associates have identified three distinct paths to a criminal career (see Figure 9.4):[45]

Adolescents with multiple problems present a significant challenge for the justice system. What can be done to help them avoid more serious antisocial behavior? Some jurisdictions have developed special programs for multiproblem offenders. Here, Joey Anderson, 18, thanks his mother, Mary Sanchez, for supporting him during the Juvenile DWI/Drug Court program in Albuquerque. Anderson was placed under the no-nonsense supervision of the Drug Court team led by Children's Court Judge Geraldine Rivera. Teens qualifying for this program have had several run-ins with the law.

AP/Wide World Photos

Figure 9.4

Loeber's Pathways to Crime

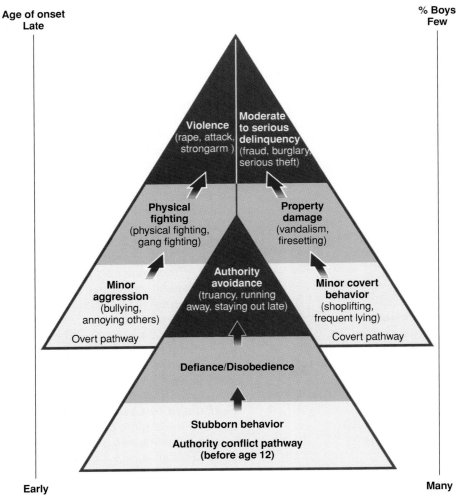

SOURCE: Barbara Tatem Kelley, Rolf Loeber, Kate Keenan, and Mary DeLamatre, "Developmental Pathways in Boys' Disruptive and Delinquent Behavior," *Juvenile Justice Bulletin* (November 1997), p. 3.

C O N N E C T I O N S

Social process theories lay the foundation for assuming that problems with peer, family, educational, and other relations, which vary over the life course, influence behaviors. See the first few sections of Chapter 7 for a review of these issues.

authority conflict pathway

Pathway to criminal deviance that begins at an early age with stubborn behavior and leads to defiance and then to authority avoidance.

1. The **authority conflict pathway** begins at an early age with stubborn behavior. This leads to defiance (doing things one's own way, disobedience) and then to authority avoidance (staying out late, truancy, running away).

2. The **covert pathway** begins with minor, underhanded behavior (lying, shoplifting) that leads to property damage (setting nuisance fires, damaging property). This behavior eventually escalates to more serious forms of criminality, ranging from joyriding, pocket picking, larceny, and fencing to passing bad checks, using stolen credit cards, stealing cars, dealing drugs, and breaking and entering.

3. The **overt pathway** escalates to aggressive acts beginning with aggression (annoying others, bullying), leading to physical (and gang) fighting and then to violence (attacking someone, forced theft).

The Loeber research indicates that each of these paths may lead to a sustained deviant career. Some people enter two or even three paths simultaneously: They are stubborn, lie to teachers and parents, are bullies, and commit petty thefts.

CONNECTIONS
- - - - - - - - - - - - - - - - - - - -
As you may recall from Chapter 2, a great deal of research has been conducted on the relationship between age and crime and the activities of chronic offenders. This scholarship has prompted interest in the life cycle of crime.

covert pathway

Pathway to a criminal career that begins with minor underhanded behavior, leads to property damage, and eventually escalates to more serious forms of theft and fraud.

overt pathway

Pathway to a criminal career that begins with minor aggression, leads to physical fighting, and eventually escalates to violent crime.

adolescent-limited

Offender who follows the most common criminal trajectory, in which antisocial behavior peaks in adolescence and then diminishes.

life-course persister

One of the small group of offenders whose criminal career continues well into adulthood.

pseudomaturity

Characteristic of life-course persisters, who tend to engage is early sexuality and drug use.

CONNECTIONS
- - - - - - - - - - - - - - - - - - - -
The contagion view is compatible with the twin studies discussed in Chapter 5, which found a high degree of concordance in the deviant behavior of twins. As twins mature, they may be more likely to influence or "infect" each other than nontwins.

These adolescents are the most likely to become persistent offenders as they mature. Although some persistent offenders may specialize in one type of behavior, others engage in varied criminal acts and antisocial behaviors as they mature. For example, they cheat on tests, bully others in the schoolyard, take drugs, commit burglary, steal a car, and then shoplift from a store.

Criminal Trajectories In addition to taking different paths to criminality, people may begin their journey at different times. Some are precocious, beginning their criminal careers early; others stay out of trouble until their teenage years. Some offenders may peak at an early age, whereas others persist into adulthood.

Research indicates a number of different classes of criminal careers that seem to reflect changes in the life course. Some adolescents maximize their offending rate at a relatively early age and then reduce their criminal activity; others persist into their 20s. Some are high-rate offenders, whereas others offend at relatively low rates.[46] According to psychologist Terrie Moffitt, although the prevalence and frequency of antisocial behavior peak in adolescence and then diminish for most offenders (she labels these **adolescent-limiteds**), a small group of **life-course persisters** offends well into adulthood.[47]

Life-course persisters combine family dysfunction with severe neurological problems that predispose them to antisocial behavior patterns. These problems can be the result of maternal drug abuse, poor nutrition, or exposure to toxic agents such as lead. Life-course persisters may have lower verbal ability, which inhibits reasoning skills, learning ability, and school achievement. They seem to mature faster and engage in early sexuality and drug use, referred to as **pseudomaturity**.[48] There may be more than one subset of life-course persisters. One group begins acting out during the preschool years; these children show signs of ADHD and do not outgrow the levels of disobedience typical of the preschool years. The second group shows few symptoms of ADHD but, from an early age, is aggressive, underhanded, and in constant opposition to authority.[49]

Adolescent-limited delinquents mimic the behavior of these more troubled teens, but reduce the frequency of their offending as they mature to around age 18.[50] They are deeply influenced by the misbehavior of their friends and peers up to around age 16, when peer group influence begins to decline. Peer influence, then, has a significant influence on their law-violating behavior.[51] This group tends to focus on a specific type of misbehavior such as drug abuse.

Why do some people enter a "path to crime" later rather than sooner? Early starters, who begin offending before age 14, follow a path from (1) poor parenting to (2) deviant behaviors and then to (3) involvement with delinquent groups. Late starters, who begin offending after age 14, follow a somewhat different path: (1) Poor parenting leads to (2) identification with delinquent groups and then to (3) deviant behaviors. By implication, adolescents who suffer poor parenting and are at risk for deviant careers can avoid criminality if they can bypass involvement with delinquent peers.[52]

Continuity of Crime Another aspect of developmental theory is the continuity of crime: The best predictor of future criminality is past criminality. Children who are repeatedly in trouble during early adolescence will generally still be antisocial in their middle and late teens and as adults.[53] Early criminal activity is likely to be sustained because these offenders seem to lack the social survival skills necessary to find work or to develop the interpersonal relationships needed to allow them to drop out of crime.[54]

One explanation for this phenomenon suggests that criminal propensity may be "contagious." Children at risk to commit crime may be located in families and neighborhoods in which they are constantly exposed to deviant behavior.

Race, Culture, Gender, and Criminology

Violent Female Criminals

Although considerable research is now being devoted to gender differences in the crime rate, little has been done to chart the life course of one subset of offenders: violent female street criminals. To correct this oversight, two studies, one by Deborah Baskin and Ira Sommers and the other by Henry Brownstein, Barry Spunt, Susan Crimmins, and Sandra Langley, have analyzed data based on samples of violent female felons in New York. These data provide considerable insight into the formation and maintenance of a criminal career.

Criminal justice scholars Baskin and Sommers used census data, analyses of political and economic changes, and direct observations and interviews to examine the career patterns of violent female offenders. They also looked at the relationships that these women have with their family members and their communities. They provide a detailed account of the criminal careers of 170 women who committed violent street crimes in New York City, describing their entry into criminal activities and their lives as persistent street criminals.

Baskin and Sommers found that about 60 percent of violent female offenders began their criminal careers at a very young age. About half reported regular fighting as early as 10 years old, and about 40 percent reported that they regularly left home carrying a weapon. In contrast, the others reported that they did not start fighting until much later, until they had left school. Because of the clear differential between when these females began their criminal careers, Baskin and Sommers independently analyzed the early- and late-onset offenders.

The women in both groups suffered from severe social and emotional problems. Most were raised in single-parent families and received little parental supervision. Both groups experienced physical and sexual abuse by a parent or guardian and were likely to have witnessed abuse between their guardians. Almost half were raised in households that relied on welfare. More than half had a parent who either was a substance abuser or had been incarcerated sometime during their childhood.

Women in the early-onset group could be distinguished by the severity of their childhood problems. They were most likely to reside in areas with high concentrations of poverty and to have family histories of psychiatric problems requiring hospitalization. They were more likely to be truant, leave school early, and associate with delinquent peers while in school. They also were more likely to be placed in a juvenile detention center.

The major distinction between the groups, however, could be found in the scale and direction of their offending careers. Although both groups used drugs, early-onset women began abusing substances two years ahead of the late-onset group. The women in the early-onset group were involved in a variety of crimes, including serious robberies, assaults, and burglaries, even before they became involved with drugs. In contrast, the women in the late-onset group were involved in mostly nonviolent crimes, such as shoplifting and prostitution, *until* they began taking drugs. The violent offending of the latter group, then, can be attributed to their drug use. In contrast, the violent

As they mature, having brothers, fathers, neighbors, and friends who engage in and support their activities reinforces their deviance.[55]

The discovery that people begin their criminal careers at different ages and follow different criminal paths and trajectories provides strong support for developmental theory. If all criminals possessed a singular latent trait that made them crime-prone, it would be unlikely that these variations in criminal careers would be observed. It is difficult to explain such concepts as late-onset and adolescent-limited behavior from the perspective of latent trait theory. The accompanying Race, Culture, Gender, and Criminology feature on violent female criminals explores this issue further. ✓ Checkpoints on page 208

Theories of Criminal Development

An ongoing effort has been made to track persistent offenders over their life course.[56] The early data seem to support what is already known about delinquent and criminal career patterns: Juvenile offenders are likely to become adult criminals; early onset predicts more lasting crime; and chronic offenders commit a significant portion of all crimes.[57] Based on these findings, criminologists have formulated a number of systematic theories that account for the onset, continuance, and desistance from crime.

behavior of the early-onset women was part of a generalized PBS.

A number of research studies support the Baskin and Sommers findings.

Henry Brownstein and his associates interviewed 215 women convicted of murder. Most of these women told a familiar story: The most violent of these women had histories of juvenile violence, drug abuse, and personal victimization. Out of a sample of 215, they found that

· 65 percent had participated in some violent activity.

· 64 percent claimed to have seriously harmed someone when they were growing up.

· 58 percent had been the victim of serious physical harm.

· 49 percent had been sexually abused.

These women had a long-term commitment to crime beginning in early childhood, which continued through adulthood and culminated in their use of deadly violence. Brownstein also focused on the behavior of 19 women who killed in the context of dealing drugs. Some of these acts were moti-

vated by economic interests, whereas others were motivated by a relationship to a man (either killing on behalf of a man who controlled them or killing a man who they feared would cause them injury).

The researchers found that there are, in fact, different pathways to crime, and that they involve both environmental and serendipitous life circumstances. These conclusions support a developmental view and repudiate the latent trait approach.

Critical Thinking

1. Crime data tell us that women are significantly less violent than men. Are the pathways to chronic offending different among violent females than among males?

2. Do you believe some conditions present at birth can control future criminal behavior?

 InfoTrac College Edition Research

There is a growing body of literature on the violent behavior of female offenders. To read more about this phenomenon, see:

Denise Hien and Nina Hien, "Women, Violence with Intimates, and Substance Abuse: Relevant Theory, Empirical Findings, and Recommendations for Future Research," *American Journal of Drug and Alcohol Abuse,* August 1998 v24 n3 p419

Karen Joe Laidler and Geoffrey Hunt, "Violence and Social Organization in Female Gangs," *Social Justice,* Winter 1997 v24 n4 p148

SOURCES: Deborah Baskin and Ira Sommers, *Casualties of Community Disorder: Women's Careers in Violent Crime* (Boulder, CO: Westview, 1998); Deborah Baskin and Ira Sommers, "Females' Initiation into Violent Street Crime," *Justice Quarterly* 10 (1993): 559–581; Henry Brownstein, Barry Spunt, Susan Crimmins, and Sandra Langley, "Women Who Kill in Drug Market Situations," *Justice Quarterly* 12 (1995): 473–498.

The Social Development Model

social development model (SDM)

A developmental theory that attributes criminal behavior patterns to childhood socialization and pro- or antisocial attachments over the life course.

In their **social development model (SDM),** Joseph Weis, Richard Catalano, J. David Hawkins, and their associates show how different factors affecting a child's social development over the life course influence criminal behavior patterns.[58] As children mature within their environment, elements of socialization control their developmental process. Children are socialized and develop bonds to their families through four distinct interactions and processes:

1. Perceived opportunities for involvement in activities and interactions with others

2. The degree of involvement and interaction with parents

3. The children's ability to participate in these interactions

4. The reinforcement (such as feedback) they perceive for their participation

prosocial bonds

Socialized attachment to conventional institutions, activities, and beliefs.

To control the risk of antisocial behavior, a child must maintain **prosocial bonds.** These are developed within the context of family life, which not only provides prosocial opportunities but reinforces them by consistent, positive feedback. Parental attachment affects a child's behavior for life, determining both school experiences and personal beliefs and values. For those with strong

According to the social development model, children must develop prosocial bonds in order to control the risk of antisocial behavior. These bonds are usually formed within the context of the family.

© Steven Rubin/The Image Works

✔ Checkpoints

✔ Pioneering criminologists Sheldon and Eleanor Glueck tracked the onset and termination of criminal careers.

✔ Developmental theories look at such issues as the onset of crime, escalation of offenses, continuity of crime, and desistance from crime.

✔ The concept of a problem behavior syndrome suggests that criminality may be just one of a cluster of social, psychological, and physical problems.

✔ There is more than one pathway to crime.

✔ Adolescent-limited offenders begin offending late and age out of crime. Life-course persisters exhibit early onset of crime that persists into adulthood.

family relationships, school will be a meaningful experience marked by academic success and commitment to education. Young people in this category are likely to develop conventional beliefs and values, become committed to conventional activities, and form attachments to conventional others.

Children's antisocial behavior also depends on the quality of their attachments to parents and other influential relations. If they remain unattached or develop attachments to deviant others, their behavior may become deviant as well. Unlike Hirschi's control theory, which assumes that all attachments are beneficial, the SDM suggests that interaction with antisocial peers and adults promotes participation in delinquency and substance abuse.[59]

As Figure 9.5 shows, the SDM differs from Hirschi's vision of how the social bond develops. Whereas Hirschi maintains that early family attachments are the key determinant of future behavior, the SDM suggests that later involvement in prosocial or antisocial behavior determines the quality of attachments. Adolescents who perceive opportunities and rewards for antisocial behavior will form deep attachments to deviant peers and will become committed to a delinquent way of life. In contrast, those who perceive opportunities for prosocial behavior will take a different path, getting involved in conventional activities and forming attachments to others who share their conventional lifestyle.

The SDM holds that commitment and attachment to conventional institutions, activities, and beliefs insulate youths from the crimogenic influences of their environment. The prosocial path inhibits deviance by strengthening bonds to prosocial others and activities. Without the proper level of bonding, adolescents can succumb to the influence of deviant others.

Interactional Theory

Terence Thornberry has proposed an age-graded view of crime that he calls **interactional theory** (see Figure 9.6).[60] He too finds that the onset of crime can be traced to a deterioration of the social bond during adolescence, marked by weakened attachment to parents, commitment to school, and belief in conventional values.

Interactional theory holds that seriously delinquent youths form belief systems that are consistent with their deviant lifestyle. They seek out the company of other adolescents who share their interests and who are likely to reinforce their beliefs about the world and support their delinquent behavior. According to inter-

Figure 9.5

The Social Development Model of Antisocial Behavior

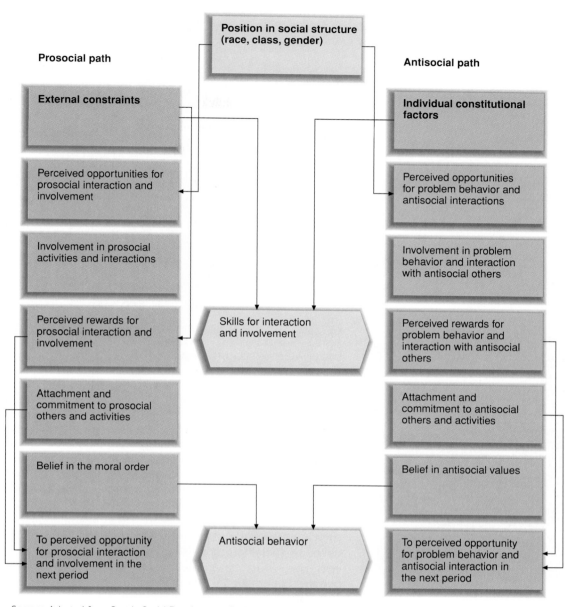

SOURCE: Adapted from Seattle Social Development Project.

interactional theory

A developmental theory that attributes criminal trajectories to mutual reinforcement between delinquents and significant others over the life course—family in early adolescence, school and friends in midadolescence, and social peers and one's own nuclear family in adulthood.

actional theory, delinquents find a criminal peer group in the same way that chess buffs look for others who share their passion for the game; hanging out with other chess players helps improve their game. Similarly, deviant peers do not turn an otherwise innocent boy into a delinquent; they support and amplify the behavior of those who have already accepted a delinquent way of life.[61]

The key idea here is that causal influences are bidirectional. Weak bonds lead children to develop friendships with deviant peers and get involved in delinquency. Frequent delinquency involvement further weakens bonds and makes it difficult to reestablish conventional ones. Delinquency-promoting factors tend to reinforce one another and sustain a chronic criminal career.

Thornberry suggests that criminality is a developmental process that takes on different meanings and forms as a person matures. According to Thornberry, the causal process is a dynamic one and develops over a person's life.[62] During

Figure 9.6

Overview of the Interactional Theory of Delinquency

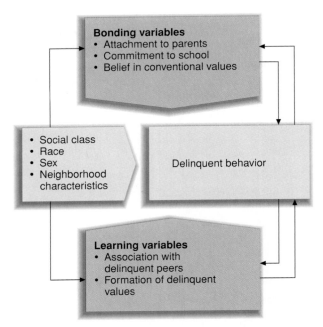

SOURCE: Terence Thornberry, Margaret Farnworth, Alan Lizotte, and Susan Stern, "A Longitudinal Examination of the Causes and Correlates of Delinquency," working paper No. 1, Rochester Youth Development Study (Albany, NY: Hindelang Criminal Justice Research Center, 1987), p. 11.

Find It on INFOTRAC
College Edition

To find more about the relationship between child-rearing techniques and social development of children, go to Info-Trac College Edition and read Bruce Bower, "Raising Trust," *Science News,* 1 July 2000 v158 i1 p8

early adolescence, attachment to the family is the single most important determinant of whether a youth will adjust to conventional society and be shielded from delinquency. By midadolescence, the influence of the family is replaced by the "world of friends, school and youth culture."[63] In adulthood, a person's behavioral choices are shaped by his or her place in conventional society and his or her own nuclear family.

In sum, interactional theory suggests that criminality is part of a dynamic social process and not just an outcome of that process. Although crime is influenced by social forces, it also influences these processes and associations to create behavioral trajectories toward increasing law violations for some people.[64] Interactional theory integrates elements of social disorganization, social control, social learning, and cognitive theories into a powerful model of the development of a criminal career.

Sampson and Laub: Age-Graded Theory

If there are various pathways to crime and delinquency, are there trails back to conformity? In an important 1993 work, *Crime in the Making,* Robert Sampson and John Laub identify **turning points** in a criminal career.[65] Reanalyzing the original Glueck data, they found that the stability of delinquent behavior can be affected by events that occur later in life, even after a chronic delinquent career has been established. They agree with Hirschi and Gottfredson that formal and informal social controls restrict criminality and that crime begins early in life and continues over the life course; they disagree that once this course is set, nothing can impede its progress.

turning points

Critical life events, such as career and marriage, that may enable adult offenders to desist from crime.

Turning Points Sampson and Laub's most important contribution is identifying the life events that enable adult offenders to desist from crime. Two critical turning points are career and marriage.

Adolescents who are at risk for crime can live conventional lives if they can find good jobs or achieve successful careers. Their success may hinge on a lucky break. Even those who have been in trouble with the law may turn from crime if employers are willing to give them a chance despite their records.

Adolescents who have had significant problems with the law are also able to desist from crime if, as adults, they become attached to a spouse who supports and sustains them even when the spouse knows they have been in trouble in the past. Happy marriages are life-sustaining, and marital quality improves over time (as people work less and have fewer parental responsibilities).[66] Spending time in marital and family activities also reduces exposure to deviant peers, which in turn reduces the opportunity to become involved in delinquent activities.[67] People who cannot sustain secure marital relations are less likely to desist from crime.

Sampson and Laub's age-graded theory is supported by research that shows that children who grow up in two-parent families are more likely to have happier marriages than children whose parents were divorced or never married.[68] This finding suggests that the marriage–crime association may be intergenerational: If people with marital problems are more crime-prone, their children will also suffer a greater long-term risk of marital failure and antisocial activity.

social capital

Positive relations with individuals and institutions, as in a successful marriage or a successful career, that support conventional behavior and inhibit deviant behavior.

Social Capital Social scientists recognize that people build **social capital**—positive relations with individuals and institutions that are life-sustaining. In the same manner that building financial capital improves the chances for economic success, building social capital supports conventional behavior and inhibits deviant behavior. A successful marriage creates social capital when it improves a person's stature, creates feelings of self-worth, and encourages others to trust the person. A successful career inhibits crime by creating a stake in conformity: Why commit crime when you are doing well at your job? The relationship is reciprocal. If people are chosen to be employees, they return the favor by doing the best job possible; if they are chosen as spouses, they blossom into devoted partners. In contrast, moving to a new city reduces social capital by closing people off from long-term relationships.[69]

Sampson and Laub's research indicates that building social capital and strong social bonds reduces the likelihood of long-term deviance. This finding suggests that, in contrast to latent trait theories, events that occur in later adolescence and adulthood do, in fact, influence the direction of delinquent and criminal careers. Life events can help either terminate or sustain deviant careers. For example, getting arrested and punished may have little direct effect on future criminality, but it can help sustain a criminal career because it reduces the chances of employment and job stability, two factors that are directly related to crime (see Figure 9.7).[70]

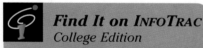

Find It on INFOTRAC
College Edition

The concept of social capital is quite complex. Use it as a subject guide in InfoTrac College Edition and find out what it actually entails.

Testing Age-Graded Theory Several indicators support the validity of age-graded theory.[71] Evidence now shows that once begun, criminal career trajectories can be reversed if life conditions improve, an outcome predicted by age-graded theory.[72] For example, employment status affects behavior. Men who are unemployed or underemployed report higher criminal participation rates than employed men. Similarly, men released from prison on parole who obtain jobs are less likely to recidivate than those who lack or lose employment.[73]

Research has been directed at identifying the sources of social capital and determining whether and how it is related to crime. For example, youths who accumulate social capital in childhood (for example, by doing well in school or having a tightly knit family) are also the most likely to maintain steady work as adults; employment may help insulate them from crime.[74] Also, people who maintain a successful marriage in their 20s and become parents themselves are

Figure 9.7

Sampson and Laub's Age-Graded Theory

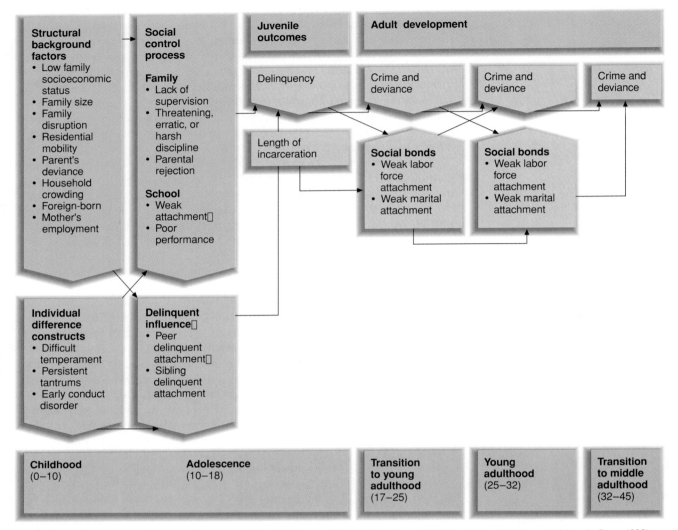

SOURCE: Robert Sampson and John Laub, *Crime in the Making: Pathways and Turning Points Through Life* (Cambridge, MA: Harvard University Press, 1993), pp. 244–245.

the most likely to mature out of crime.[75] Although it is possible that marriage stabilizes people and helps them build social capital, it is also likely that marriage may discourage crime by reducing contact with criminal peers.[76]

A number of research efforts have supported Sampson and Laub's proposed association between social capital and crime. For example, delinquents who enter the military, serve overseas, and receive veterans' benefits enhance their occupational status (social capital) while reducing criminal involvement.[77] In contrast, research shows that people who are self-centered and present-oriented are less likely to accumulate social capital and more prone to commit criminal acts.[78]

Finding the Glueck Delinquents John Laub and Robert Sampson are now conducting an important follow-up to their original research: They are finding and interviewing the survivors from the original Glueck research.[79] Sampson and Laub have located the survivors, the oldest subject being 70 years old and the youngest 62!

Their preliminary findings suggest that delinquency and other forms of antisocial conduct in childhood are strongly related to adult crime and drug and alcohol abuse. Former delinquents also suffer consequences in other areas of social life, such as school, work, and family life. For example, delinquents are far less likely to finish high school than nondelinquents and subsequently are more likely to be unemployed, receive welfare, and experience separation or divorce as adults.

In their latest research, Laub and Sampson address one of the key questions posed by developmental theories: Is it possible for former delinquents to rehabilitate themselves as adults? They find that most antisocial children do not remain antisocial as adults. Of those men who survived to age 50, 24 percent had no arrests for crimes of violence and property after age 17 (6% had no arrests for total crime); 48 percent had no arrests for these predatory crimes after age 25 (19% for total crime); 60 percent had no arrests for predatory crimes after age 31 (33% for total crime); and 79 percent had no arrests for predatory crimes after age 40 (57% for total crime). They conclude that desistance from crime is the norm and that most, if not all, serious delinquents later desist from crime.

Why Do Delinquents Desist? Their earlier research had already indicated that marriage and job, as means of building social capital, were key components of desistance from crime. In this new round of research, Laub and Sampson were able to find out more about long-term desistance by interviewing 52 men as they approached age 70. Drawing on the men's own words, they find that one important element for "going straight" is the "knifing off" of individuals from their immediate environment, offering them a new "script" for the future. Joining the military can provide this "knifing-off" effect, as does marriage and changing one's residence. One former delinquent (age 69) told them:

> I'd say the turning point was, number one, the Army. You get into an outfit, you had a sense of belonging, you made your friends. I think I became a pretty good judge of character. In the Army, you met some good ones, you met some foul balls. Then I met the wife. I'd say probably that would be the turning point. Got married, then naturally, kids come. So now you got to get a better job, you got to make more money. And that's how I got to the Navy Yard and tried to improve myself.

Former delinquents who "went straight" were able to put structure into their lives. Structure often led the men to disassociate from delinquent peers, reducing the opportunity to get into trouble. Getting married, for example, may limit the number of nights men can "hang with the guys." As one wife of a former delinquent said, "It is not how many beers you have, it's who you drink with." Even multiple offenders who had done time in prison were able to desist with the help of a stabilizing marriage.

The former delinquents who were able to turn their lives around, who had acquired a degree of maturity by taking on family and work responsibilities, and who had forged new commitments were the ones most likely to make a fresh start and find new direction and meaning in life. It seems that men who desisted changed their identity as well, and this, in turn, affected their outlook and sense

Checkpoints

✔ The social development model (SDM) integrates social control, social learning, and structural models.

✔ According to interactional theory, the causes of crime are bidirectional. Weak bonds lead to deviant peer relations and delinquency; delinquency weakens conventional bonds and strengthens relations with deviant peers.

✔ According to age-graded theory, building social capital and strong social bonds reduces the likelihood of long-term deviance.

✔ Many delinquents desist as adults. Building social capital helps people desist.

of maturity and responsibility. The ability to change did not reflect crime "specialty"; violent offenders followed the same path as property offenders.

Policy Implications Laub and Sampson find that youth problems—delinquency, substance abuse, violence, dropping out, teen pregnancy—often share common risk characteristics. Intervention strategies, therefore, should consider a broad array of antisocial, criminal, and deviant behaviors, and not limit their focus to one subgroup or crime type. Because delinquency and other social problems are linked (problem behavior syndrome), early prevention efforts that reduce crime will probably also reduce alcohol abuse, drunk driving, drug abuse, sexual promiscuity, and family violence, as well as school failure, unemployment, marital disharmony, and divorce.

The best way to achieve these goals is through four significant life-changing events: marriage, joining the military, getting a job, and changing one's environment or neighborhood. What appears to be important about these processes is that they all involve, to varying degrees, the following items: a "knifing off" of the past from the present, new situations that provide supervision and monitoring as well as new opportunities for social support and growth, and new situations that provide the opportunity for transforming identity. Prevention of crime must therefore be a policy at all times and at all stages of life. ✔ Checkpoints

Summary

Latent trait theories hold that some underlying condition present at birth or soon after controls behavior. Suspect traits include low IQ, impulsivity, and personality structure. This underlying trait explains the continuity of offending because, once present, it remains with a person throughout his or her life. The latent trait theory, developed by Gottfredson and Hirschi, integrates choice theory concepts. People with latent traits choose crime over noncrime; the opportunity for crime mediates their choice.

Developmental theories look at multiple factors derived from a number of different structural and process theories. Examples include the social development model, interactional theory, and age-graded theory. These theories suggest that events that take place over the life course influence criminal choices. The cause of crime constantly changes as people mature. At first, the nuclear family influences behavior; during adolescence, the peer group dominates; in adulthood, marriage and career are critical. There are a variety of pathways to crime: some youngsters are sneaky, others hostile, and still others defiant. Crime may be part of a variety of social problems, including health, physical, and interpersonal troubles.

For a summary of the integrated theories discussed in this chapter, see Table 9.4. For additional chapter links, discussions, and quizzes, see the book-specific Web site at http://www.wadsworth.com/product/0534519423s.

Table 9.4 Integrated Theories

THEORY	MAJOR PREMISE	STRENGTHS
Latent Trait Theories		
General theory of crime	Crime and criminality are separate concepts. People choose to commit crime when they lack self-control. People lacking in self-control will seize criminal opportunities.	Integrates choice and social control concepts. Identifies the difference between crime and criminality.
Control balance	An excess or lack of control makes people crime-prone.	Shows that control is a multidimensional concept.
Developmental Theories		
Social development model (SDM)	Weak social controls produce crime. A person's place in the structure influences his or her bond to society.	Combines elements of social structural and social process theories. Accounts for variations in the crime rate.
Interactional theory	Criminals go through lifestyle changes during their offending career.	Combines sociological and psychological theories.
Age-graded theory	As people mature, the factors that influence their propensity to commit crime change. In childhood, family factors are critical; in adulthood, marital and job factors are key.	Shows how crime is a developmental process that shifts in direction over the life course.

Thinking Like a Criminologist

Luis Francisco is the leader of the Almighty Latin Kings and Queens Nation. He was convicted of murder in 1998 and sentenced to life imprisonment plus 45 years. Luis Francisco's life has been filled with displacement, poverty, and chronic predatory crime. The son of a prostitute in Havana, at the age of 9 he was sent to prison for robbery. He had trouble in school, and teachers described him as having attention problems; he dropped out in the seventh grade. On his 19th birthday in 1980, he immigrated to the United States and soon after became a gang member in Chicago, where he joined the Latin Kings. After moving to the Bronx, he shot and killed his girlfriend in 1981. He fled to Chicago and was not apprehended until 1984. Sentenced to nine years for second-degree manslaughter, Luis Francisco ended up in a New York prison, where he started a New York prison chapter of the Latin Kings. As King Blood, Inka, First Supreme Crown, Francisco ruled the 2,000 Latin Kings in and out of prison. Disciplinary troubles erupted when some Kings were found stealing from the organization. Infuriated, King Blood wrote to his street lieutenants and ordered their termination. Federal authorities, who had been monitoring Francisco's mail, arrested 35 Latin Kings. The other 34 pled guilty; only Francisco insisted on a trial, where he was found guilty of conspiracy to commit murder.

Explain Luis's behavior patterns from a developmental perspective. How would a latent trait theorist explain his escalating criminal activities?

Key Terms

integrated theory	life-course theory	life-course persister
developmental criminology	problem behavior syndrome (PBS)	pseudomaturity
latent trait theory		social development model (SDM)
developmental theory	authority conflict pathway	prosocial bonds
latent trait	covert pathway	interactional theory
general theory of crime (GTC)	overt pathway	turning points
control balance theory	adolescent-limited	social capital

Discussion Questions

1. Do you consider yourself the holder of "social capital"? If so, what form does it take?

2. A person gets a 1600 on the SAT. Without knowing this person, what personal, family, and social characteristics must he or she have? Another person becomes a serial killer. Without knowing this person, what personal, family, and social characteristics must he or she have? If "bad behavior" is explained by multiple problems, is "good behavior" explained by multiple strengths?

3. Do you believe there is a "latent trait" that makes a person crime-prone, or is crime a function of environment and socialization?

4. Do you agree with Loeber's multiple pathway model? Do you know people who have traveled down those paths?

© Eshin-Anderson/The Image Works

Part 3

Crime Typologies

Criminologists often seek to group individual criminal offenders or behaviors so that they can be more easily studied and understood. Such groupings are referred to as offender and/or offense typologies.

Typologies can be useful in classifying large numbers of criminal offenses or offenders into easily understood categories. There are a variety of ways to construct crime typologies. Offenders may be grouped on the basis of personality, such as psychotic or economic compulsive, or by working style, such as professional versus amateur. Offenses may be grouped by legal definitions; by collective goals, objectives, and consequences; or by structural similarities, such as theft offenses.

In the next four chapters, crime patterns are clustered according to the following typology: violent crimes (Chapter 10); economic crimes involving individual-level theft (Chapter 11); economic crimes involving criminal organizations (Chapter 12); and crimes that threaten public order, such as prostitution and drug abuse (Chapter 13). This typology groups criminal behaviors on the basis of their consequences: causing physical harm to others; misappropriating other people's property; and violating laws designed to protect public morals.

© Esbin-Anderson/The Image Works

10 Violent Crime

INTRODUCTION

On Sunday, June 8, 1998, the broken body of a black man was discovered just outside the East Texas town of Jasper, population 8,000.[1] Authorities determined that James Byrd, Jr., 49, had been dragged to his death from the back of a pickup truck in a rural section of Texas known for racist and Ku Klux Klan activity. An investigation found that Byrd was picked up by three men sometime after midnight and taken to a wooded area, where he was beaten, then chained to the truck and dragged for two miles. The Jasper County district attorney called the killing "probably the most brutal I've ever seen" in 20 years as a prosecutor.

Police quickly identified three suspects, exoffenders and Klan supporters, whose bodies were covered in racist tattoos. The three had spent time in tough Texas prisons, where for their own protection they had joined inmate gangs segregated by color. Their prison experiences may have intensified preexisting racial prejudice that had been part of their boyhood culture. Two suspects were members of the Confederate Knights of America, a racist group linked to the Klan. Yet this crime was so evil and so widely condemned that Texas Klaverns have denounced it, and a small group of Klansmen applied for a permit to march not in support of the suspects but to disavow any connection with them.[2]

After the death of James Byrd, Jr., in 1998, his family pushed for a stronger hate crime law in Texas. Here, James Byrd, Sr., the victim's father, talks with reporters about the failure of the state legislature to pass a more stringent bill named after his son. Should crimes motivated by bias be punished more severely than similar acts arising from other motives, such as greed or revenge?

The Jasper killing was a shocking reminder that violence is too common in American life. "Violence is the primal problem of American history," writes social historian David Courtwright, ". . . the dark reverse of its coin of freedom and abundance."[3] Although the violent crime rate has recently declined, people are continually bombarded with news stories featuring grisly accounts of mass murder, child abuse, and serial rape. Many people have personally experienced violence or have a friend who has been victimized. Almost everyone knows someone who has been robbed, beaten, or killed. Riots and mass disturbances have ravaged urban areas; racial attacks plague schools and college campuses; assassination has claimed the lives of political, religious, and social leaders all over the world.[4]

When violence is designed to improve the financial or social position of the criminal, as in an armed robbery, it is referred to as **instrumental violence**. Crimes that vent rage, anger, or frustration are known as **expressive violence**. An extreme example of expressive violence occurred on April 20, 1999, when Eric Harris and Dylan Klebold, two students at Columbine High School in Littleton, Colorado, went on a murderous rampage that left 12 students and one teacher dead and 24 other people wounded before the boys committed suicide. Members of a cult group called the "Trenchcoat Mafia," Harris and Klebold had spent more than a year planning the attack and building homemade bombs.

This chapter surveys the nature and extent of violent crime. First, it briefly reviews some possible causes of violence. Then, it focuses on specific types of

instrumental violence

Violence designed to improve the financial or social position of the criminal.

expressive violence

Violence that vents rage, anger, or frustration.

interpersonal violence—rape, homicide, assault (including domestic violence), and robbery. Finally, it briefly examines political violence, including terrorism.

The Roots of Violence

What causes people to behave violently? A number of competing explanations have been offered for violent behavior. A few of the most prominent are discussed here.

Personal Traits

On March 13, 1995, an ex–Boy Scout leader named Thomas Hamilton took four high-powered rifles into the primary school of the peaceful Scottish town of Dunblane and slaughtered 16 children and their teacher. This horrific crime shocked the British Isles into implementing strict controls on all guns.[5]

Bizarre outbursts such as Hamilton's support a link between violence and personal traits and personality disorders. Violent offenders often display abnormal personality structures marked by psychopathic tendencies such as impulsivity, aggression, dishonesty, pathological lying, and lack of remorse.[6]

Psychologist Dorothy Otnow Lewis and her associates found that murderous youths show signs of major neurological impairment, such as abnormal EEGs, multiple psychomotor impairment, and severe seizures; low intelligence as measured on standard IQ tests; psychotic close relatives; and psychotic symptoms such as paranoia, illogical thinking, and hallucinations.[7] In her 1998 book *Guilty by Reason of Insanity,* Lewis reports that death row inmates have a history of mental impairment and intellectual dysfunction.[8] It comes as no surprise, then, that many murderers kill themselves shortly after committing their crime. Even more bizarre are the cases of people who commit murder with the expectation that they will be executed for their crimes, a form of "suicide-murder."[9]

Abnormal personality structure, including depression, borderline personality syndrome, and psychopathology, have been associated with various forms of spousal and family abuse.[10] A high proportion of serial rapists and repeat sexual offenders exhibit psychopathic personality structures.[11] Although this evidence indicates that violent offenders are more prone to psychosis than other people, no single clinical diagnosis can characterize their behavior.[12]

CONNECTIONS

As you may recall from Chapter 5, biosocial theorists link violence to a number of biological irregularities, including but not limited to genetic influences and inheritance, the action of hormones, the functioning of neurotransmitters, brain structure, and diet. Psychologists link violent behavior to observational learning from violent TV shows, traumatic childhood experiences, low intelligence, mental illness, impaired cognitive processes, and abnormal (psychopathic) personality structure.

Ineffective Families

Much research traces violence to rejecting, ineffective, or abusive parenting.[13] Absent or deviant parents, inconsistent discipline, and lack of supervision have all been linked to persistent violent offending.[14]

A number of research studies have found that children who are clinically diagnosed as abused later engage in delinquent behaviors, including violence, at a rate significantly greater than that of unabused children.[15] Samples of convicted murderers reveal a high percentage of seriously abused youth.[16] The abuse–violence association has been established in many cases in which parents have been killed by their children; sexual abuse is also a constant factor in father (patricide) and mother (matricide) killings.[17] Dorothy Otnow Lewis found in her study of juvenile death row inmates that all had long histories of intense child abuse.[18]

Evolutionary Factors/ Human Instinct

Perhaps violent responses and emotions are actually inherent in all humans, easily triggered by the right spark. Sigmund Freud believed that human aggression and violence are produced by two instinctual drives: eros, the life instinct, which drives people toward self-fulfillment and enjoyment; and thanatos, the death instinct, which produces self-destruction. Thanatos can be expressed externally (as violence and sadism) or internally (as suicide, alcoholism, or other self-destructive behaviors). Because aggression is instinctual, Freud saw little hope for its treatment.[19] A number of biologists and anthropologists have also speculated that instinctual violence-promoting traits may be common in the human species. One view is that aggression and violence are the results of instincts inborn in all animals, including human beings.[20]

Exposure to Violence

People who are constantly exposed to violence at home, at school, or in the environment may adopt violent methods themselves.[21] In a study of Chicago youth, social scientist Felton Earls found that between 30 and 40 percent of the children who reported exposure to violence also displayed significant violent behavior themselves.[22] Exposure to violence may also have an effect on adults, even police officers. Research indicates that police officers' use of deadly force is much higher in areas with high violence and murder rates. The perception of danger may contribute to the use of violent means for self-protection even among people trained in the use of force.[23]

Cultural Values

The various sources of crime statistics tell us that interpersonal violence is more common in large, urban, inner-city areas than in any other type of community.[24] It is unlikely that violent crime rates would be so high in these socially disorganized areas, however, unless other social forces encouraged violent crime.[25]

Criminologists Marvin Wolfgang and Franco Ferracuti have attributed these disproportionately high violence rates to a **subculture of violence**.[26] The norms of this subculture are separate from society's central, dominant value system. In this subculture, a potent theme of violence influences lifestyles, the socialization process, and interpersonal relationships. Its members expect that violence will be used to solve social conflicts and dilemmas, and violence is legitimized by custom and norms. It is considered appropriate behavior within culturally defined conflict situations, in which an individual who has been offended by a negative outcome in a dispute seeks reparations through violent means.[27]

subculture of violence

Norms and customs that, in contrast to society's dominant value system, legitimize and expect the use of violence to resolve social conflicts.

Substance Abuse

It has become common to link violence to substance abuse. In fact, substance abuse influences violence in three ways:[28]

1. *Psychopharmacological relationship.* Violence may be a direct consequence of ingesting mood-altering substances. Experimental evidence shows that high doses of drugs such as PCP and amphetamines may produce violent, aggressive behavior.[29] Alcohol abuse has long been associated with all forms of violence. A direct alcohol–violence link may occur because drinking reduces cognitive ability, making miscommunication more likely, while at the same time limiting the capacity for rational dialogue and compromise.[30]

2. *Economic compulsive behavior.* Drug users may resort to violence to support their habit.

3. *Systemic link.* Violence may be a function of rival gangs' battling over drug markets and territories. Drug trafficking activities can lead to personal vendettas and a perceived need for violent self-protection.[31]

CONNECTIONS

Criminal subcultures were discussed in some detail in Chapter 6. Recall that subcultural theorists portray criminals not as rebels from the normative culture, but rather as people who are in accord with the informal rules and values of their immediate culture. By adhering to cultural norms, they violate the law.

Drug testing of arrestees in major U.S. cities consistently shows that criminals are also drug abusers; in some areas, almost 75 percent of all people arrested for violent crimes test positively for drugs. Surveys of prison inmates show that a

Deputy Coroner's Investigator Pam Eacher carries the body of a small child, one of five members of a family apparently victims of a murder-suicide, who were found shot to death in a home in an unincorporated area southwest of Los Angeles. Sheriff's investigators said that Cesar Eduardo Orantes, 40, possibly upset over the breakup of his marriage, apparently shot his wife, Julia Pantiguia, 37, and their children, Douglas, 13, Jennifer, 10, and Cesar Orantes Jr., 4, before taking his own life. If handguns were banned or strictly curtailed, could such tragedies be avoided?

AP/Wide World Photos

significant majority report being under the influence of drugs or alcohol when they committed their last criminal offense.[32]

Firearm Availability

Although firearm availability does not cause violence, it is certainly a facilitating factor. A petty argument can escalate into a fatal encounter if one party has a handgun. It may not be coincidence that the United States, which has a huge surplus of guns and in which most firearms (80 percent) used in crimes are stolen or obtained through illegal or unregulated transactions, also has one of the world's highest violence rates.[33] Disturbing evidence indicates that more than 80 percent of inmates in juvenile correctional facilities owned a gun just before their confinement, and 55 percent said they carried one almost all the time.[34] The Uniform Crime Reports (UCR) indicate that more than half of all murders and 40 percent of all robberies involve firearms.[35]

Each of these factors is believed to influence violent crimes, including both traditional common-law crimes, such as rape, murder, assault, and robbery, and newly recognized problems, such as workplace violence, hate crimes, and political violence. Each of these forms of violent behavior is discussed in some detail later in this chapter.   ✔ Checkpoints on page 223

CONNECTIONS

Although it seems logical that banning the sale and ownership of firearms might help reduce violence, those in favor of gun ownership, as discussed in the feature on gun control in Chapter 2, do not agree. Some experts believe that taking guns away from citizens might endanger them from armed criminals.

Forcible Rape

rape

The carnal knowledge of a female forcibly and against her will.

Rape (from the Latin *rapere*, to take by force) is defined in common law as "the carnal knowledge of a female forcibly and against her will."[36] It is one of the most loathed, misunderstood, and frightening crimes. Under traditional common-law definitions, rape involves non-consensual sexual intercourse that a male performs against a female whom he is neither married to nor cohabitating with.

Criminologists consider rape a violent, coercive act of aggression, not a forceful expression of sexuality. There has been a national campaign to alert the public to the seriousness of rape, offer help to victims, and change legal definitions to facilitate the prosecution of rape offenders. Such efforts have made significant progress in overhauling rape laws and developing a vast social service network to aid victims.

History of Rape

Rape has been a recognized crime throughout history. It has been the subject of art, literature, film, and theater. Paintings such as the *Rape of the Sabine Women* by Nicolas Poussin, novels such as *Clarissa* by Samuel Richardson, poems such as *The Rape of Lucrece* by William Shakespeare, and films such as *The Accused* have sexual violence as their central theme.

In early civilization, rape was common. Men staked a claim of ownership on women by forcibly abducting and raping them. This practice led to males' solidification of power and their historical domination of women.[37] During the Middle Ages, it was common for ambitious men to abduct and rape wealthy women in an effort to force them into marriage. The practice of "heiress stealing" illustrates how feudal law gave little thought or protection to women and equated them with property.[38] Only in the late fifteenth century was forcible sex outlawed, and then only if the victim was of the nobility. Peasant women and married women were not considered rape victims until well into the sixteenth century.

Rape and the Military Although rape has long been associated with military conquest, Americans were still stunned when in 1996 the national media revealed the presence of a "rape ring" at the Aberdeen Proving Grounds in Maryland. Nearly 20 noncommissioned officers were accused of raping and sexually harassing 19 female trainees. The investigation prompted more than 5,000 female soldiers to call military hot lines to report similar behavior at Army bases around the country. The Army scandal was especially disturbing because it involved drill instructors, who are given almost total control over the lives of young female recruits who depend on them for support, training, and nurturing.[39]

The link between the military and rape is inescapable. Throughout recorded history, rape has been associated with armies and warfare. Soldiers of conquering armies have considered sexual possession of their enemies' women one of the spoils of war. Among the ancient Greeks, rape was socially acceptable within the rules of warfare. During the Crusades, even knights and pilgrims, ostensibly bound by vows of chivalry and Christian piety, took time to rape as they marched toward Constantinople.

The belief that women are part of the spoils of war has continued. During World War II, the Japanese army forced as many as 200,000 Korean women into frontline brothels, where they were repeatedly raped. In a 1998 Japanese ruling, the surviving Korean women were awarded the equivalent of $2,300 each in compensation.[40] The systematic rape of Bosnian and Kosovar women by Serbian army officers during the civil war in the former Yugoslavia horrified the world during the 1990s. These crimes seemed particularly atrocious because they were part of an official policy of genocide: rape was deliberately used to impregnate Bosnian women with Serbian children.[41] Human rights groups have estimated that more than 30,000 women and young girls were sexually abused in the Balkan fighting.

Incidence of Rape

According to the most recent UCR data, about 89,000 rapes or attempted rapes were reported to U.S. police in 1999, a rate of 64 per 100,000 females.[42] Although rape rates escalated throughout the 1980s, they began a decline in the 1990s, decreasing more than 12 percent between 1995 and 1999.

Population density influences the rape rate. Metropolitan areas today have rape rates significantly higher than rural areas; nonetheless, urban areas have

✔ Checkpoints

✔ There are a number of suspected causes of violence.

✔ Some violent criminals have personal traits that make them violence-prone, including mental impairment and intellectual dysfunction.

✔ Victims of severe child abuse and neglect may become violence-prone adults.

✔ Violence may have its roots in human evolution, being almost instinctual in some instances.

✔ Drug and alcohol abuse has been linked to violence, through either a psychopharmacological relationship, economic compulsive behavior, or a systemic link.

✔ Although guns do not cause violence, their presence can escalate its severity.

experienced a much greater drop in rape reports than rural areas. The police make arrests in about half of all reported rape offenses. Of the offenders arrested in 1999, about 44 percent were under 25 years of age, 61 percent were white, and 39 percent were minority group members.[43] The racial pattern of rape arrests has been fairly consistent for some time. Finally, rape is a warm-weather crime. Most incidents occur during July and August, with the lowest rates reported for December, January, and February.

These data must be interpreted with caution, because according to the National Crime Victimization Survey, rape is frequently underreported. For example, the NCVS estimates that 201,000 rapes and attempted rapes took place in 1999, suggesting that fewer than half of such incidents are reported to police.[44] Many people fail to report rapes because they are embarrassed, believe nothing can be done, or blame themselves.

Because other victim surveys indicate that at least 20 percent of adult women, 15 percent of college-age women, and 12 percent of adolescent girls have experienced sexual abuse or assault sometime during their lives, it is evident that both official and victimization statistics significantly undercount rape.[45]

Types of Rape

gang rape

Forcible sex involving multiple attackers.

acquaintance rape

Forcible sex in which offender and victim are acquainted with one another.

date rape

Forcible sex during a courting relationship.

marital rape

Forcible sex between people who are legally married to each other.

Some rapes are planned; others are spontaneous. Some focus on a particular victim; others occur almost as an afterthought during the commission of another crime, such as a burglary.[46] Some rapes involve a single offender; others, called **gang rapes**, involve multiple attackers. Compared to individual assaults, gang rapes are more likely to involve alcohol and drugs, to occur at night, and to include other types of sexual assault such as penetration with objects.[47]

Whereas some rapes involve strangers, others involve people who are acquainted with one another. Included within **acquaintance rapes** are the subcategories of **date rape**, which involves a sexual attack during a courting relationship, and **marital rape**, which is forcible sex between people who are legally married to each other. By some estimates, about 50 percent of all rapes involve acquaintances.[48]

Some rapists are one-time offenders, but others engage in multiple or serial rapes. Some serial rapists constantly increase their use of force; others do not.[49] Some rapists commit "blitz" rapes, in which they attack their victims without warning; others try to "capture" their victims by striking up a conversation or offering them a ride; still others use personal relationships to gain access to their targets.[50]

One of the best-known attempts to classify the personalities of rapists was made by psychologist A. Nicholas Groth, an expert on classifying and treating sex offenders. According to Groth, every rape encounter contains three elements: anger, power, and sexuality.[51] Consequently, rapists can be classified according to one of the dimensions described in Table 10.1. In treating rape offenders, Groth found that about 55 percent were of the power type; about 40 percent, the anger type; and about 5 percent, the sadistic type. Groth's major contribution has been his recognition that rape is generally a crime of violence, not a sexual act. In all of these circumstances, rape involves a violent criminal offense in which a predatory criminal chooses to attack a victim.[52]

Date Rape One disturbing trend is the increase in rape involving people who are in some form of courting relationship. There is no single form of date rape. Some rapes occur on first dates; others after a relationship has been developing; still others after the couple has been involved for some time. In long-term or close relationships, the male partner may feel he has invested so much time and money in his partner that he is "owed" sexual relations or that sexual intimacy is an expression that the involvement is progressing. He may make com-

Table 10.1 Varieties of Forcible Rape

Anger rape occurs when sexuality becomes a means of expressing and discharging pent-up anger and rage. The rapist uses far more brutality than would have been necessary if his real objective had been simply to have sex with his victim. His aim is to hurt his victim as much as possible; the sexual aspect of rape may be an afterthought. Often the anger rapist acts on the spur of the moment after an upsetting incident has caused him conflict, irritation, or aggravation. Surprisingly, anger rapes are less psychologically traumatic for the victim than might be expected. Because a woman is usually physically beaten during an anger rape, she is more likely to receive sympathy from her peers, relatives, and the justice system and consequently be immune from any suggestion that she complied with the attack.

Power rape involves an attacker who does not want to harm his victim as much as he wants to possess her sexually. His goal is sexual conquest, and he uses only the amount of force necessary to achieve his objective. The power rapist wants to be in control, to be able to dominate women and have them at his mercy. Yet it is not sexual gratification that drives the power rapist; in fact, he often has a consenting relationship with his wife or girlfriend. Rape is instead a way of putting personal insecurities to rest, asserting heterosexuality, and preserving a sense of manhood. The power rapist's victim usually is a woman equal in age to or younger than the rapist. The lack of physical violence may reduce the support given the victim by family and friends. Therefore, the victim's personal guilt over her rape experience is increased—perhaps, she thinks, she could have done something to get away.

Sadistic rape involves both sexuality and aggression. The sadistic rapist is bound up in ritual—he may torment his victim, bind her, or torture her. Victims are usually related, in the rapist's view, to a personal characteristic that he wants to harm or destroy. The rape experience is intensely exciting to the sadist; he gets satisfaction from abusing, degrading, or humiliating his captive. This type of rape is particularly traumatic for the victim. Victims of such crimes need psychiatric care long after their physical wounds have healed.

SOURCE: A. Nicholas Groth and Jean Birnbaum, *Men Who Rape* (New York: Plenum Press, 1979).

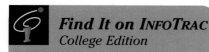

Find It on INFOTRAC
College Edition

Should date or acquaintance rape be punished less severely that stranger rape? To find out, go to InfoTrac College Edition and read

Emily C. Shanahan, "Stranger and Nonstranger Rape: One Crime, One Penalty," *American Criminal Law Review*, Fall 1999 v36 i4 p1371

marital exemption

Traditional legal doctrine that a legally married husband could not be charged with raping his wife.

parisons to other couples who have dated as long and are sexually active.[53] Males who use force in their dating relationships are more likely to be angry, jealous, and stressed, have poor communications skills, act irrationally, use alcohol, and report more efforts to control their partners than those men who never use force in dating relationships.[54]

Date rape is believed to be frequent on college campuses. It has been estimated that 15 to 20 percent of all college women are victims of rape or attempted rape. One self-report survey conducted on a Midwestern campus found that 100 percent of all rapists knew their victims beforehand.[55] The actual incidence of date rape may be even higher than surveys indicate because many victims blame themselves and do not recognize the incident as a rape, saying, for example, "I should have fought back harder" or "I shouldn't have gotten drunk."[56] Thus, despite their seriousness and prevalence, fewer than 1 in 10 date rapes may be reported to police.[57]

Marital Rape In 1978, Greta Rideout filed rape charges against her husband John. This Oregon case grabbed headlines because it was the first in which a husband was prosecuted for raping his wife while sharing a residence with her. John was acquitted, and the couple briefly reconciled; later, continued violent episodes culminated in divorce and a jail term for John.[58]

Traditionally, a legally married husband could not be charged with raping his wife; this legal doctrine was referred to as the **marital exemption**. The origin of this doctrine can be traced to the sixteenth-century pronouncement of Matthew Hale, England's chief justice, who wrote

> But the husband cannot be guilty of rape committed by himself upon his lawful wife, for by their mutual matrimonial consent and contract the wife hath given up herself in this kind unto the husband which she cannot retract.[59]

However, research indicates that many women are raped each year by their husbands as part of an overall pattern of spousal abuse. Many spousal rapes are accompanied by brutal, sadistic beatings and have little to do with normal sexual interests.[60] The marital exemption has undergone significant revision in recent years. In 1980, only three U.S. states had laws against marital rape; today, almost every state recognizes marital rape as a crime.[61] Piercing the marital exemption is not unique to U.S. courts; it has also been abolished in Canada, Israel, Scotland, and New Zealand.[62]

statutory rape

Sexual relations between an underage minor female and an adult male; though not coerced, an underage partner is considered incapable of giving informed consent.

Statutory Rape The term **statutory rape** refers to sexual relations between an underage minor female and an adult male. Although the sex is not forced or coerced, the law says that young girls are incapable of giving informed consent, so the act is legally considered nonconsensual. Typically a state's law will define an age of consent above which there can be no criminal prosecution for consensual sexual relations. Although each state is different, most evaluate the age difference between the parties in order to determine whether an offense has taken place. For example, Indiana law mandates prosecution of men aged 21 or older who have consensual sex with girls younger than 14. In some states, defendants can claim they mistakenly assumed their victims were above the age of consent, whereas in others, "mistake-of-age" defenses are ignored. A recent American Bar Association survey found that prosecution is often difficult in statutory rape cases because the young victims are reluctant to testify. Often parents have given their blessing to the relationship, and juries are reluctant to convict men involved in consensual sex with even young teenage girls.[63]

The Causes of Rape

What factors predispose some men to commit rape? Criminologists' responses to this question are almost as varied as the crime itself. However, most explanations can be grouped into a few consistent categories.

Evolutionary/Biological Factors One explanation for rape focuses on the evolutionary, biological aspects of the male sexual drive. This perspective suggests that rape may be instinctual, developed over the ages as a means of perpetuating the species. In more primitive times, forcible sexual contact may have helped spread genes and maximize offspring. Some believe that these prehistoric drives remain: Males still have a natural sexual drive that encourages them to have intimate relations with as many women as possible.[64] The evolutionary view is that the sexual urge corresponds to the unconscious need to preserve the species by spreading one's genes as widely as possible. Men who are sexually aggressive will have a reproductive edge over their more passive peers.[65]

Male Socialization In contrast to the evolutionary biological view, some researchers argue that rape is a function of modern male socialization.[66] According to this view, from an early age, boys are taught to be aggressive, forceful, tough, and dominating and are led to believe that women want to be dominated. This "virility mystique" dictates that males must separate their sexual feelings from needs for love, respect, and affection. Men are socialized to be the aggressors and expect to be sexually active with many women; consequently,

CONNECTIONS

Recall that Chapter 8 described how the need to prove masculinity helps men justify their abuse of women. Sexually violent men, the argument goes, are viewed as virile and masculine by their peers.

male virginity and sexual inexperience are shameful. Conversely, sexually aggressive women frighten some men and cause them to doubt their own masculinity. Sexual insecurity may lead some men to commit rape to bolster their self-image and masculine identity.

Hypermasculinity If rape is an expression of male anger and devaluation of women and not an act motivated by sexual desire, it follows that men who hold so-called macho attitudes will be more likely to engage in sexual violence. Hypermasculine men typically have a callous sexual attitude and believe that violence is manly. They perceive danger as exciting and are overly sensitive to insult and ridicule. They are also impulsive, more apt to brag about sexual conquests, and more likely to lose control, especially when using alcohol.[67] These men are quicker to anger and more likely to be sexually aggressive. In fact, the sexually aggressive male may view the female as a legitimate victim of sexual violence.

Violent Experiences Another view is that men learn to commit rapes much as they learn any other behavior. Groth found that 40 percent of the rapists he studied had been sexually victimized as adolescents.[68] A growing body of literature links personal sexual trauma with the desire to inflict sexual trauma on others.[69] Watching violent or pornographic films featuring women who are beaten, raped, or tortured has been linked to sexually aggressive behavior in men.[70]

Sexual Motivation NCVS data reveal that rape victims tend to be young and that rapists prefer younger, presumably more attractive victims. Data show an association between the ages of rapists and their victims, indicating that men choose rape targets of approximately the same age as consensual sex partners. And, despite the fact that younger criminals are usually the most violent, older rapists tend to harm their victims more than younger rapists. This pattern suggests that older criminals may rape for motives of power and control, whereas younger offenders may be seeking sexual gratification and may therefore be less likely to harm their victims.[71]

In sum, criminologists are still at odds over the precise cause of rape, but there is evidence that it is the product of a number of social, cultural, and

There are many different explanations of why men rape. Here, Mark A. Clark, 34, sits in a courtroom in Centerville, Tennessee, after being arrested and charged with aggravated rape, aggravated kidnapping, and aggravated robbery. Authorities said Clark was the man known as the Interstate 65 rapist, who would drive up beside a woman, tell her something was wrong with her vehicle, and offer her a ride. He would then drive to a remote area and rape his victim. Could a serial rapist such as Clark have a sexual motivation for his acts, or are they the result of a disturbed personality and troubled background?

AP/Wide World Photos

psychological forces.[72] Although some experts view it as a normal response to an abnormal environment, others view it as the product of a disturbed mind and deviant life experiences.

Rape and the Law

CONNECTIONS
- - - - - - - - - - - - - - - -
This view will be explored further in Chapter 13, where the issue of pornography and violence is analyzed in greater detail. Most research does not show a direct link between watching pornography and sexual violence, but there may be a link between sexual aggression and viewing movies with sexual violence as their theme.

Of all violent crimes, none has created such conflict in the legal system as rape. Even if women choose to report sexual assaults to police, they are often initially reluctant because of the discriminatory provisions built into rape laws. The sexist fashion in which rape victims are treated by police, prosecutors, and court personnel and the legal technicalities that authorize invasion of women's privacy when a rape case is tried in court can devastate the victim. Some police officers may be hesitant to make an arrest and testify in court when the alleged assault does not yield obvious signs of violence or struggle (presumably showing that the victim strenuously resisted the attack) or if the victim has previously known or dated her attacker.

While the prosecution of rape cases has always been a problem, police and courts are now becoming more sensitive to the plight of rape victims and are just as likely to investigate acquaintance rapes as they are aggravated rapes involving multiple offenders, weapons, and victim injuries. In some jurisdictions, the justice system takes all rape cases seriously and does not ignore those in which victim and attacker have had a prior relationship or those that did not involve serious injury.[73]

Proving Rape Proving guilt in a rape case is extremely challenging for prosecutors. Some male psychiatrists and therapists still maintain that women fantasize that a rape has occurred and therefore may falsely accuse their alleged attackers. Some judges also fear that women may charge men with rape because of jealousy, false marriage proposals, or pregnancy. In a 1996 case, as the Dallas Cowboys were preparing for the playoffs, a young woman accused star players Erik Williams and Michael Irvin of forcible rape, only to admit later that she had lied about the incident.[74] Such incidents make it more difficult for prosecutors to gain convictions in rape cases.

It is essential to prove that the attack was forced and that the victim did not give voluntary consent to her attacker. In a sense, the burden of proof is on the victim to show that her character is beyond question and that she in no way encouraged, enticed, or misled the accused rapist. Proving victim dissent is not a requirement in any other violent crime; robbery victims, for example, do not have to prove they did not entice their attackers by flaunting expensive jewelry. Yet the defense counsel in a rape case can create reasonable doubt about the woman's credibility. A common defense tactic is to introduce suspicion in the minds of the jury that the woman may have consented to the sexual act and later regretted her decision. Conversely, it is difficult for a prosecuting attorney to establish that a woman's character is so impeccable that the absence of consent is a certainty. Such distinctions are important in rape cases because male jurors may be sympathetic to the accused if the victim is portrayed as unchaste. Simply referring to the woman as "sexually liberated" or promiscuous may be enough to result in exoneration of the accused, even if violence and brutality were used in the attack.[75] Research shows that even when a defendant is found guilty in a sexual assault case, the punishment is significantly reduced if the victim is believed to have negative personal characteristics such as being a transient, hitchhiker, alone in a bar, or a drug and alcohol abuser.[76]

Reform Because of the difficulty rape victims have in obtaining justice, rape laws have been changing around the country. Reform efforts have included changing the language of statutes, dropping the condition of victim resistance, and changing the requirement of use of force to include the threat of force or injury.[77]

Most states and the federal government have developed **shield laws**, which protect women from being questioned about their sexual history unless it directly bears on the case. In some instances, these laws are quite restrictive; in others, they grant the trial judge considerable discretion to admit prior sexual conduct in evidence if it is deemed relevant for the defense. In an important 1991 case, *Michigan* v. *Lucas,* the U.S. Supreme Court upheld the validity of shield laws and ruled that excluding evidence of a prior sexual relationship between the parties did not violate the defendant's right to a fair trial.[78]

In addition to requiring evidence that consent was not given, the common law of rape required corroboration that the crime of rape actually took place. Independent evidence was required, from police officers, physicians, or witnesses, that the accused was actually the person who committed the crime, that sexual penetration took place, and that force was present and consent absent. This requirement shielded rapists from prosecution in cases where the victim delayed reporting the crime or where physical evidence had been compromised or lost. Corroboration is no longer required except under extraordinary circumstances, such as when the victim is too young to understand the crime, has had a previous sexual relationship with the defendant, or gives a version of events that is improbable and self-contradictory.[79]

The federal government may have given rape victims another source of redress when it passed the Violence Against Women Act in 1994. This statute allows rape victims to sue in federal court on the grounds that sexual violence violates their civil rights; its provisions have so far been upheld by appellate courts.[80]

Murder and Homicide

Murder is defined in common law as "the unlawful killing of a human being with malice aforethought."[81] It is the most serious of all common-law crimes and the only one that can still be punished by death. Western society's abhorrence of murderers is illustrated by the fact that there is no statute of limitations in murder cases. Whereas state laws limit prosecution of other crimes to a fixed period, usually 7 to 10 years, accused killers can be brought to justice at any time after their crimes were committed.

To legally prove that a murder has taken place, most state jurisdictions require prosecutors to show that the accused maliciously intended to kill the victim. Express or **actual malice** is the state of mind assumed to exist when someone kills another person in the absence of any apparent provocation. Implied or **constructive malice** is considered to exist when a death results from negligent or unthinking behavior. In these cases, even though the perpetrator did not wish to kill the victim, the killing resulted from an inherently dangerous act and therefore is considered murder. An unusual example of this concept is the attempted-murder conviction of Ignacio Perea, an AIDS-infected Miami man who kidnapped and raped an 11-year-old boy. Perea was sentenced to up to 25 years in prison when the jury agreed with the prosecutor's contention that the AIDS virus is a deadly weapon.[82]

Degrees of Murder

There are different levels or degrees of homicide.[83] **First-degree murder** occurs when a person kills another after premeditation and deliberation. **Premeditation** means that the killing was considered beforehand and suggests that it was motivated by more than a simple desire to engage in an act of violence. **Deliberation** means the killing was carried out after careful thought rather than carried out on impulse. The planning need not be a long process; it

---

shield laws

Legislation that protects rape victims from being questioned about their sexual history unless it bears directly on the case.

murder

The unlawful killing of a human being (homicide) with malicious intent.

actual malice

The state of mind assumed to exist when one person kills another without apparent provocation.

constructive malice

The state of mind assumed to exist when one person kills another as a result of an inherently dangerous act whose consequences could have been foreseen.

first-degree murder

The killing of another person after premeditation and deliberation.

premeditation

Prior consideration of a homicide before it occurs.

deliberation

Committing a homicide after careful thought, however brief, rather than acting on sudden impulse.

felony murder

A homicide in the context of another felony, such as robbery or rape; legally defined as first-degree murder.

second-degree murder

A homicide with malice but not premeditation or deliberation, as when a desire to inflict serious bodily harm and a wanton disregard for life result in the victim's death.

manslaughter

A homicide without malice.

voluntary manslaughter

A homicide committed in the heat of passion or during a sudden quarrel; although intent may be present, malice is not.

involuntary manslaughter

A homicide that occurs as a result of acts that are negligent and without regard for the harm they may cause others, such as driving under the influence of alcohol or drugs.

may be an almost instantaneous decision to take another's life. Also, a killing accompanying a felony, such as robbery or rape, usually constitutes first-degree murder (**felony murder**).

Second-degree murder requires the killer to have malice aforethought but not premeditation or deliberation. A second-degree murder occurs when a person's wanton disregard for the victim's life and his or her desire to inflict serious bodily harm on the victim result in the victim's death.

Homicide without malice is called **manslaughter** and is usually punished by anywhere between 1 and 15 years in prison. Nonnegligent or **voluntary manslaughter** refers to a killing committed in the heat of passion or during a sudden quarrel that provoked violence. Although intent may be present, malice is not. Negligent or **involuntary manslaughter** refers to a killing that occurs when a person's acts are negligent and without regard for the harm they may cause others. Most involuntary manslaughter cases involve motor vehicle deaths—for example, when a drunk driver kills a pedestrian.

One issue that has received national attention is whether a fetus can be a murder victim. In some instances, fetal harm involves a mother whose behavior endangers an unborn child; in other cases, feticide results from the harmful action of a third party.

Some states have prosecuted women for endangering or killing their unborn fetuses through drug or alcohol abuse. Some of these convictions have been overturned because the law applies only to a "human being who has been born and is alive."[84] At least 200 women in 30 states have been arrested and charged in connection with harming (though not necessarily killing) a fetus; appellate courts have almost universally overturned such convictions on the basis that they were without legal merit or were unconstitutional.[85]

State laws more commonly allow prosecution for murder when a third party's actions kill a fetus. Four states (Illinois, Missouri, South Dakota, and West Virginia) extend wrongful death action to the death of any fetus; the remaining states require that the fetus be viable and able to live outside the mother's body. The law extends the definition of murder to a fetus that is born alive but dies afterward as a result of injuries sustained in utero.[86]

The Nature and Extent of Murder

It is possible to track U.S. murder rate trends from 1900 to the present with the aid of coroners' reports and UCR data. The murder rate peaked in 1933, a time of high unemployment and lawlessness, and then fell until 1958. From the mid-1960s to the late 1970s, the homicide rate doubled. It peaked again in 1980, at 10.2 per 100,000 population, then fell to 7.9 per 100,000 in 1985. It rose again in the late 1980s and early 1990s, to a peak of 9.8 per 100,000 in 1991. Since then the rate has declined, to 5.7 per 100,000 by 1999. Although this decline is an extremely positive development, more than 15,500 citizens were killed in 1999.

What else do official crime statistics tell us about murder today? Murder victims tend to be males over 18 years of age. African Americans are more likely both to commit murder and to become murder victims. Murder, like rape, tends to be an intraracial crime; the great majority of victims are slain by members of their own race. People arrested for murder are generally young (under 35) and male (about 90 percent), a pattern that has proven consistent over time.

Murderous Relations

One factor that has received a great deal of attention from criminologists is the relationship between the murderer and the victim.[87] Most criminologists agree that murders can generally be separated into those involving strangers, typically stemming from a felony attempt such as a robbery or drug deal, and acquaintance homicides involving disputes between family members, friends, and acquaintances.[88] The quality of relationships and interpersonal interactions, then, may influence murder.

Acquaintance Homicide Killing someone you know or interact with is actually the most common form of murder. Social change has influenced this phenomenon. For example, the rate of homicide among married couples has declined significantly during the past two decades, a finding that can be attributed to the shift away from marriage in modern society. There are, however, significant gender differences in homicide trends among unmarried people. The number of unmarried men killed by their partners has declined (mirroring the overall trend in the murder rate), but the number of women killed by the men they live with has increased dramatically.

Research indicates that most females who kill their mates do so after suffering repeated violent attacks.[89] Perhaps the number of males killed by their partners has declined because alternatives to abusive relationships, such as battered women's shelters, are becoming more prevalent in the United States. Regions that provide greater social support for battered women and that have passed legislation to protect abuse victims also have lower rates of female-perpetrated homicide.[90]

It is possible that men kill their spouses or partners because they fear losing control and power. Because unmarried people who live together have a legally and socially more open relationship, males in such relationships may be more likely to feel loss of control and to assert their power with violence.[91]

Some people kill their mates because they find themselves involved in a love triangle.[92] Interestingly, women who kill out of jealousy aim their aggression at their partners; in contrast, men are more likely to kill their mates' suitors. Love triangles tend to become lethal when the offenders believe they have been lied to or betrayed. Lethal violence is more common when (1) the rival initiated the affair, (2) the killer knew the spouse was already in a steady relationship outside the marriage, and (3) the killer was repeatedly lied to or betrayed.[93]

Stranger Homicides Most stranger homicides occur in the aftermath of a common law crime, such as burglary or robbery. However, stranger homicides take various forms.

Thrill killing involves impulsive slaying of a stranger as an act of daring or recklessness. For example, children who drop a boulder from a highway overpass onto an oncoming car may be out for thrills or kicks.[94] Some thrill killings involve relatively stable youths who exhibit few prior symptoms of violence; others are committed by youngsters with long-standing mental or emotional problems.[95]

Gang killings involve members of teenage gangs who make violence part of their group activity. Some of these gangs fight over territory or control of the drug trade through drive-by shootings, in which enemies are killed and strangers can be caught in the cross fire. The FBI records about 1,000 gang killings each year; some cities may have close to 100 gang-related murders per year.[96]

Serial Murder According to Colombian police, Luis Alfredo Garavito is a glib predator and a "solitary sadist" who stands accused as one of the world's worst serial killers.[97] In 1999, Garavito, a 42-year-old drifter, confessed to slaying at least 140 boys, ages 8 to 16, during a five-year killing spree. Garavito would befriend the children and take them on long walks until they were tired. Then he would tie them up with nylon rope, slit their throats or behead them, and then bury their bodies. Most of Garavito's victims were street children, from poor families or separated from their parents by poverty or political violence. Authorities said it was because there was no one to notice that the children were missing or to inquire about their whereabouts that Garavito was able to go on killing for so long without being detected.

thrill killing

Impulsive slaying of a stranger as an act of daring or recklessness.

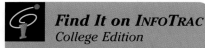

Find It on INFOTRAC
College Edition

There is evidence that serial murders were just as common in seventeenth-century England as they are today. They were less sensational in the seventeenth century, but no less horrific. The murders of seven men and women are described in *The Bloody Innkeeper* (1675). To read more about this topic, use "serial murder" as a keyword in InfoTrac College Edition.

The Criminological Enterprise

Mass Murder and Serial Killing

Criminologists Jack Levin and James Alan Fox have written extensively on two of the most frightening aspects of modern violence—mass murder and serial killing. According to Levin and Fox, it is difficult to estimate the number and extent of serial killings; but a reasoned estimate is that up to 20 serial killers are active in a given year, accounting for up to 240 killings or about 1 percent of the total number of homicides.

Why do serial murderers kill? They kill for fun. They enjoy the thrill, the sexual gratification, and the dominance they achieve over the lives of their victims. The serial killer rarely uses a gun because this method is too quick and would deprive him of his greatest pleasure, exulting in his victim's suffering. Serial killers are not insane, but "more cruel than crazy."

Fox and Levin have their own typology of serial killers, which they describe as follows:

1. *Thrill killers* strive for either sexual sadism or dominance. This is the most common type of serial murderer.
2. *Mission killers* want to reform the world or have a vision that drives them to kill.
3. *Expedience killers* are out for profit or want to protect themselves from a perceived threat.

In contrast to serial killers, mass murderers engage in a single, uncontrollable outburst. Fox and Levin define four types of mass murderers:

1. *Revenge killers* seek to get even with individuals or society at large. Their typical target is an estranged wife and "her" children or an employer and "his" employees.
2. *Love killers* are motivated by a warped sense of devotion. They are often despondent people who commit suicide and take others, such as a wife and children, with them.
3. *Profit killers* are usually trying to cover up a crime, eliminate witnesses, and carry out a criminal conspiracy.
4. *Terrorist killers* are trying to send a message. Gang killings tell rivals to watch out; cult killers may actually leave a message behind to warn society about impending doom.

Levin and Fox dispute the notion that all mass murderers and serial killers have some form of biological or psychological problems, such as genetic anomalies or schizophrenia. Even the most sadistic serial murderers are not mentally ill or driven by delusions or hallucinations. Instead, they typically exhibit a sociopathic personality with

no pangs of conscience or guilt to control their behavior. Mass murderers are typically ordinary citizens driven to extreme acts. They experience long-term frustration, blame others for their problems, and then are set off by some catastrophic loss they are unable to cope with or get help for.

Although the actions of serial killers and mass murderers may be quite different, they share some of the same motivations. These are listed and explained in Table A.

Critical Thinking

1. Are serial murderers responsible for their actions?

2. Can a mass murderer be legally sane? If not, what should be done with irrational killers?

3. Is it fair to put serial killers and mass murderers to death? Explain your response.

InfoTrac College Edition Research

Serial killers are not new to this century. To read about the history of such gruesome acts, read Bernard Capp, "Serial Killers in 17th-Century England," *History Today,* March 1996 v46 i3 p21

---

serial killer

One who kills a series of victims over a long period of time.

mass murderer

One who kills many victims in a single, violent outburst.

Serial killers operate over a long period and can be distinguished from **mass murderers**, who kill many victims in a single, violent outburst. While most are males, an estimated 10 to 15 percent of serial killers are women. Criminologists Belea Keeney and Kathleen Heide, who investigated the characteristics of a sample of 14 female serial killers, found some striking differences between the way male and female killers carried out their crimes.[98] Males were much more likely than females to use extreme violence and torture. Whereas males used a "hands-on" approach, including beating, bludgeoning, and strangling their victims, females were more likely to poison or smother their victims. Men tracked or stalked their victims, but women were more likely to lure victims to their death.

The accompanying Criminological Enterprise box discusses various types and motives of serial killers and mass murderers.

Serial killers come from diverse backgrounds. To date, law enforcement officials have been at a loss to control random killers who leave few clues, constantly move, and have little connection to their victims. Catching serial killers is

Table A Explanations for Multiple Murder

MOTIVATIONS FOR MULTIPLE MURDER	TYPE OF MULTIPLE MURDER	
	SERIAL MURDER	MASS MURDER
Power	Inspired by sadistic fantasies, a man tortures and kills a series of strangers to satisfy his need for control and dominance.	A pseudo-commando, dressed in battle fatigues and armed with a semiautomatic, turns a shopping mall into a "war zone."
Revenge	Grossly mistreated as a child, a man avenges his past by slaying women who remind him of his mother.	After being fired from his job, a gunman returns to the worksite and opens fire on his former boss and coworkers.
Loyalty	A team of killers turn murder into a ritual for proving their dedication and commitment to one another.	A depressed husband/father kills his entire family and himself to remove them from their miserable existence to a better life in the hereafter.
Profit	A woman poisons to death a series of husbands in order to collect on their life insurance.	A band of armed robbers executes the employees of a store to eliminate all witnesses to their crime.
Terror	A profoundly paranoid man commits a series of bombings to warn the world of impending doom.	A group of antigovernment extremists blows up a train to send a political message.

For more on modern serial killers, see
Jan Scott, "Serial Homicide: We Need to Explore behind the Stereotypes and Ask Why," *British Medical Journal,* 6 January 1996 v312 i7022 p2
Eugene H. Methvin, "The Face of Evil," *National Review,* 23 January 1995 v47 i1 p34(7)

SOURCES: James Alan Fox and Jack Levin, "Multiple Homicide: Patterns of Serial and Mass Murder," in *Crime and Justice: An Annual Edition,* vol. 23, ed. Michael Tonry (Chicago: University of Chicago Press, 1998): 407–455, Table A, p. 444; James Alan Fox and Jack Levin, *Overkill: Mass Murder and Serial Killing Exposed* (New York: Plenum, 1994); James Alan Fox and Jack Levin, "A Psycho-Social Analysis of Mass Murder," in *Serial and Mass Murder: Theory, Policy, and Research,* ed. Thomas O'Reilly-Fleming and Steven Egger (Toronto: University of Toronto Press, 1993); James Alan Fox and Jack Levin, "Serial Murder: A Survey," in *Serial and Mass Murder: Theory, Policy, and Research,* ed. Thomas O'Reilly-Fleming and Steven Egger (Toronto: University of Toronto Press, 1993); Jack Levin and James Alan Fox, *Mass Murder* (New York: Plenum, 1985).

battery

A physical attack that includes hitting, punching, slapping, or other offensive touching of a victim.

often a matter of luck. To help local law enforcement officials, the FBI has developed a profiling system to identify potential suspects. In addition, the Justice Department's Violent Criminal Apprehension Program (VICAP), a computerized information service, gathers information and matches offense characteristics on violent crimes around the country.[99] This program links crimes to determine if they appear to be the work of a single culprit.

Assault and Battery

Although many people mistakenly believe that the term "assault and battery" refers to a single act, they are actually two separate crimes. **Battery** requires offensive touching, such as slapping, hitting, or punching a victim. **Assault** requires no actual touching but involves either attempted battery or intentionally frightening the victim by word or deed. Although common law originally intended these twin crimes to be misdemeanors, most jurisdictions now upgrade them to felonies either when a weapon is used or when they occur during the commission of a felony

assault

An attack that may not involve physical contact; includes attempted battery or intentionally frightening the victim by word or deed.

aggravated assault

An attack on another person for the purpose of inflicting severe bodily injury.

(for example, when a person is assaulted during a robbery). In the UCR, the FBI defines serious assault, or **aggravated assault**, as "an unlawful attack by one person upon another for the purpose of inflicting severe or aggravated bodily injury"; this definition is similar to the one used in most state jurisdictions.[100]

Under common law, battery required bodily injury, such as broken limbs or wounds. However, under modern law, an assault and battery occurs if the victim suffers a temporarily painful blow, even if no injury results. Battery can also involve offensive touching, such as if a man kisses a woman against her will or puts his hands on her body.

Nature and Patterns of Assault

The pattern of criminal assault is quite similar to that of homicide; one could say that the only difference between the two is that the victim survives.[101] Assaults may be common in our society simply because of common life stresses. Motorists who assault each other have become such a familiar occurrence that the term "road rage" has been coined. There have even been frequent incidents of violent assault among frustrated airline passengers who lose control while traveling. In 1998, British Airways began issuing printed warnings to abusive passengers, giving notice that continued misbehavior could result in hefty fines and even jail sentences.[102]

In 1999, the FBI recorded about 916,000 assaults, a rate of 336 per 100,000 inhabitants. Like other crimes, assault has recently declined (down 20 percent since 1995). People arrested for assault and those identified by victims are usually young, male, and white, although the number of African Americans arrested for assault (35 percent) is disproportionate to their representation in the population. Assault victims tend to be male, but women also face a significant danger. The NCVS indicates that while about 32 males per 1,000 are victims of assault, 24 women per 1,000 are victimized. Assault rates are highest in urban areas, during the summer, and in the South and West. The weapons most commonly used in assaults are blunt instruments, hands and feet, firearms, and knives.

Assaults can thus range from a slap in the face to a stabbing, and the results can be quite serious. At last count, about 1.4 million people annually were treated for violence-related injuries in hospital emergency rooms, ranging from a nose broken in a fight to a shooting or stabbing during a robbery.[103] About 40 percent of these injuries were quite serious, resulting from rapes and sexual assaults, shootings, and stabbings; guns or knives were used in about 12 percent of the assaults.

Assault in the Home

Among the most frightening types of assault are violent attacks within the home. Criminologists recognize that intrafamily violence is an enduring social problem in the United States.

child abuse

Physical or emotional trauma to a child with no reasonable explanation such as an accident or ordinary disciplinary practices.

child neglect

Failure to provide a child with food, shelter, and basic care.

Child Abuse   One area of intrafamily violence that has received a great deal of media attention is **child abuse**.[104] This term describes any physical or emotional trauma to a child for which no reasonable explanation, such as an accident or ordinary disciplinary practices, can be found.[105]

Child abuse can result from physical beatings administered to a child by hands, feet, weapons, belts, sticks, burning, and so on. Another form of abuse results from **child neglect**—not providing a child with the care and shelter to which he or she is entitled. A third form is **sexual abuse**—the exploitation of a child through rape, incest, or molestation by a parent or other adult.

It is difficult to estimate the actual number of child abuse cases because many incidents are never reported to the police. Nonetheless, child abuse and

sexual abuse

Exploitation of a child through rape, incest, or molestation by a parent or other adult.

neglect appear to be serious social problems. The American Humane Society estimates that 3 million cases of child abuse are reported to authorities each year.[106] While it is difficult to estimate the incidence of sexual abuse, surveys of women have found that between 20 and 40 percent have experienced intra- or extrafamilial sexual abuse by the time they reach 18.[107]

Why do parents physically assault their children? Such maltreatment is a highly complex problem with neither a single cause nor a readily available solution. It cuts across ethnic, religious, and socioeconomic lines. Abusive parents cannot be categorized by sex, age, or educational level; they come from all walks of life.[108]

Three factors have been linked to abuse and neglect. First, a pattern of family violence seems to be perpetuated from one generation to the next within families. Evidence indicates that many abused and neglected children grow into adolescence and adulthood with a tendency to engage in violent behavior. The behavior of abusive parents can often be traced to negative experiences in their own childhood—physical abuse, lack of love, emotional neglect, incest, and so on. These parents become unable to separate their own childhood traumas from their relationships with their children; they also often have unrealistic perceptions of the appropriate stages of childhood development.[109]

Second, blended families, in which children live with an unrelated adult such as a stepparent or another unrelated coresident, have also been linked to abuse. For example, children who live with a mother's boyfriend are at much greater risk for abuse than children living with two genetic parents. According to sociologists Martin Daly and Margo Wilson, some stepparents do not have strong emotional ties to their nongenetic children, nor do they reap emotional benefits from the parent–child relationship.[110]

Third, parents may become abusive if they are isolated from friends, neighbors, or relatives who can help in times of crisis.[111] Many abusive and neglectful parents describe themselves as highly alienated from their families and lacking close relationships with people who could provide support in stressful situations. These people are unable to cope effectively with life crises such as divorce, financial problems, alcohol and drug abuse, or poor housing conditions, and excessive stress leads them to maltreat their children.[112]

Spouse Abuse Spouse abuse has occurred throughout recorded history. Roman men had the legal right to beat their wives for attending public games without permission, drinking wine, or walking outdoors with their faces uncovered.[113] More serious transgressions, such as adultery, were punishable by death.[114] During the early Middle Ages, a husband was expected to beat his wife for "misbehaviors" and might himself be punished by neighbors if he failed to do so.[115] Between 1400 and 1900, there was little community objection to a man's using force against his wife as long as the assaults did not exceed certain limits, usually construed as death or disfigurement. By the mid-nineteenth century, severe wife beating fell into disfavor, and accused wife beaters were subject to public ridicule. Yet the long history of husbands' domination of their wives has made physical coercion hard to control.

There is still some debate over the cause of spouse abuse. One view is that batterers are damaged individuals who suffer a variety of neuropsychological disorders and cognitive deficits; many suffered brain injuries in youth.[116] Psychologists Neil Jacobson and John Mordechai Gottman studied 200 couples and found that batterers tend to fall into one of two categories, which they call "Pit Bulls" and "Cobras."[117] Pit Bulls, whose emotions are quick to erupt, are driven by deep insecurity and a dependence on the wives and partners they abuse. They tend to become stalkers, unable to let go of relationships once they have ended. In contrast, Cobras coolly and methodically inflict pain and humiliation on their spouses. Many Cobras were physically or sexually abused in childhood and, as a consequence, see violence as an unavoidable part of life.

Some experts view spousal abuse from an evolutionary standpoint: Males are aggressive toward their mates because they have evolved with a high degree of sexual proprietariness. Men fear both losing a valued reproductive resource to a rival and making a paternal investment in a child that is not their own. Violence serves as a coercive social tool to dissuade interest in other males and to lash out in jealousy if threats are not taken seriously (that is, if the woman leaves). This explains why men often kill or injure their ex-wives; threats lose their effectiveness if they are merely a bluff.[118]

Some personal attributes and characteristics of spouse abusers are listed in Table 10.2.

It is difficult to estimate how widespread spousal abuse is today; however, some statistics show the extent of the problem. In their classic study of family violence, Richard Gelles and Murray Straus found that 16 percent of surveyed families had experienced husband–wife assaults.[119] In police departments around the country, 60 to 70 percent of evening calls involve domestic disputes. Nor is violence restricted to marriage: National surveys indicate that between 20 and 40 percent of females experience violence while dating.[120]

Table 10.2 Factors That Predict Spousal Abuse

- **Presence of alcohol.** Excessive alcohol use may turn otherwise docile husbands into wife abusers.

- **Hostility toward dependency.** Some husbands who appear docile and passive may resent their dependence on their wives and react with rage and violence; this reaction has been linked to sexual inadequacy.

- **Excessive brooding.** Obsession with a wife's behavior, however trivial, can result in violent assaults.

- **Social approval.** Some husbands believe that society approves of wife abuse and use these beliefs to justify their violent behavior.

- **Socioeconomic factors.** Men who fail as providers and are under economic stress may take their frustrations out on their wives.

- **Flashes of anger.** Research shows that a significant amount of family violence results from a sudden burst of anger after a verbal dispute.

- **Military service.** Spouse abuse among men who have served in the military service is extremely high. Similarly, those serving in the military are more likely to assault their wives than are civilian husbands. The reasons for this phenomenon may be the violence promoted by military training and the close proximity in which military families live to one another.

- **Having been battered children.** Husbands who assault their wives were generally battered as children.

- **Unpredictability.** Abusers are unpredictable, unable to be influenced by their wives, and impossible to prevent from battering once an argument has begun.

Batterers can be classified into two distinct types: men whose tempers slowly simmer until they suddenly erupt into violence, and those who strike out immediately.

SOURCES: Neil Jacobson and John Mordechai Gottman, *When Men Batter Women: New Insights into Ending Abusive Relationships* (New York: Simon and Schuster, 1998); Kenneth Leonard and Brian Quigley, "Drinking and Marital Aggression in Newlyweds: An Event-Based Analysis of Drinking and the Occurrence of Husband Marital Aggression," *Journal of Studies on Alcohol* 60 (1999): 537–541; Graeme Newman, *Understanding Violence* (New York: Lippincott, 1979).

Married women seem to be at much greater risk of domestic violence than single people who are living together. A possible cause may be that domestic relationships among single people tend to be less stable and more short-lived, insulating these couples from the pressures and conflicts that come with building longer-term marriages.[121] Nonetheless, the rate of domestic violence appears to be declining among both married couples and single cohabitants. One reason is that females now find it easier to get high-paying jobs, to obtain legal divorces, and to receive domestic violence counseling. Financial independence and emotional support allow women to leave a bad marriage before interspousal conflict leads to violence and death. And even if partners stay together in troubled relationships, newly emerging social interventions empower women to end male partner violence.[122]

Robbery

robbery

Taking or attempting to take something of value by force or threat of force and/or by putting the victim in fear.

The common-law definition of **robbery** (and the one used by the FBI) is "taking or attempting to take anything of value from the care, custody or control of a person or persons by force or threat of force or violence and/or by putting the victim in fear."[123] A robbery is considered a violent crime because it involves the use of force to obtain money or goods. Robbery is punished severely because the victim's life is put in jeopardy. In fact, the severity of punishment is based on the amount of force used during the crime, not the value of the items taken.

In 1999, about 410,000 robberies were reported to police, a rate of 150 per 100,000 population—a decrease of more than 9 percent in one year. As with other violent crimes, there was a significant reduction in the robbery rate during the 1990s. Between 1995 and 1999, the rate of robbery declined 32 percent.

The ecological pattern for robbery is similar to that of other violent crimes, with one significant exception: Northeastern states have by far the highest robbery rate. NCVS data show that robbery is more of a problem than the FBI data indicate. According to the NCVS, about 810,000 robberies were committed or attempted in 1999, indicating that about half of all robbery victims fail to report

Robbery is a crime of violence. Here, San Francisco police dust for fingerprints at a Bank of America branch where an alleged bank robber was killed and two police officers and a customer were wounded in a shootout during an attempted robbery.

AP/Wide World Photos

the crime to the police. The two data sources agree, however, on the age, race, and sexual makeup of the offenders: They are disproportionately young, male minority-group members.

Robbery is most often a street crime; that is, fewer robberies occur in the home than in public places, such as parks, streets, and alleys. The Bureau of Justice Statistics analyzed more than 14 million robbery victimizations to provide a more complete picture of the nature and extent of robbery. It found that about two-thirds of victims had property stolen, one-third were injured in the crime, and one-fourth suffered both personal injury and property loss.[124]

While most robberies involve strangers, about one-third involve acquaintances. Richard Felson and his associates found that when robbers target someone they know, they choose victims who are least likely to call police—young black males. Targets may be people with whom the robber has a preexisting grievance, so that the robbery is a form of "payback." Robbers may also have "inside information" that the victims are carrying valuables, making them a hard target to resist.[125]

Attempts have been made to classify and explain the nature and dynamics of robbery. One approach is to characterize robberies (see Table 10.3); another is to characterize types of robbers based on their specialties (see Table 10.4).

Table 10.3 Types of Robberies

Robbery of persons who, as part of their employment, are in charge of money or goods. This category includes robberies in jewelry stores, banks, offices, and other places in which money changes hands.

Robbery in an open area. These robberies include street muggings, purse snatchings, and other attacks. Street robberies are the most common type, especially in urban areas, where this type of robbery constitutes about 60 percent of reported totals. Street robbery is most closely associated with mugging or yoking, which refers to grabbing victims from behind and threatening them with a weapon. Street muggers often target unsavory characters such as drug dealers or pimps who carry large amounts of cash, because these victims would find it awkward to report the crime to the police. Most commit their robberies within a short distance of their homes.

Commercial robbery. This type of robbery occurs in businesses ranging from banks to liquor stores. Banks are among the most difficult targets to rob, usually because they have more personnel and a higher level of security.

Robbery on private premises. This type of robbery involves breaking into people's homes. FBI records indicate that this type of robbery accounts for about 10 percent of all offenses.

Robbery after a short, preliminary association. This type of robbery comes after a chance meeting—in a bar, at a party, or after a sexual encounter.

Robbery after a longer association between the victim and offender. An example of this type of robbery would be an intimate acquaintance robbing his paramour and then fleeing the jurisdiction.

Carjacking. Carjacking is a completed or attempted theft of a motor vehicle by force or threat of force. On average, there are about 49,000 completed or attempted carjackings in the United States each year.

SOURCES: Patsy Klaus, *Carjackings in the United States, 1992–96* (Washington, DC: Bureau of Justice Statistics, 1999); Peter J. van Koppen and Robert Jansen, "The Road to the Robbery: Travel Patterns in Commercial Robberies," *British Journal of Criminology* 38 (1998): 230–247; F. H. McClintock and Evelyn Gibson, *Robbery in London* (London: Macmillan, 1961), p. 15.

CONNECTIONS

Chapter 4 discussed the rationality of street robbery. Even when robbers are stealing to support a drug habit, their acts do not seem haphazard or irrational. Only the most inebriated might fail to take precautions. The fact that robbery is gender-specific is also evidence that robbers are rational decision makers.

✔ Checkpoints

✔ Forcible rape has been known throughout history and is often linked with war and violence.

✔ Types of rape include date rape, marital rape, and statutory rape; types of rapists include serial rapists and sadists.

✔ Suspected causes of rape include male socialization, hypermasculinity, and biological determinism.

✔ Murder can involve either strangers or acquaintances.

✔ Mass murder refers to the killing of numerous victims in a single outburst; serial killing involves numerous victims over an extended period of time.

✔ Patterns of assault are quite similar to those for homicide.

✔ There are millions of cases of child abuse and spouse abuse each year.

✔ Robbers use force to steal. Some are opportunists looking for ready cash; others are professionals who have a long-term commitment to crime.

Table 10.4 Types of Robbers

Professional robbers have a long-term commitment to crime as a source of livelihood. This type of robber plans and organizes crimes prior to committing them and seeks money to support a hedonistic lifestyle. Some professionals are exclusively robbers, whereas others engage in additional types of crimes. Professionals are committed to robbing because it is direct, fast, and profitable. They hold no other steady job and plan three or four "big scores" a year to support themselves. Planning and skill are the trademarks of professional robbers, who usually operate in groups with assigned roles. Professionals usually steal large amounts from commercial establishments. After a score, they may stop for a few weeks until "things cool off."

Opportunist robbers steal to obtain small amounts of money when an accessible target presents itself. They are not committed to robbery but will steal from cab drivers, drunks, the elderly, and other vulnerable persons if they need some extra spending money. Opportunists are usually young minority-group members who do not plan their crimes. Although they operate within the milieu of the juvenile gang, they are seldom organized and spend little time discussing weapon use, getaway plans, or other strategies.

Addict robbers steal to support their drug habits. They have a low commitment to robbery because of its danger but a high commitment to theft because it supplies needed funds. The addict is less likely to plan crime or use weapons than the professional robber but is more cautious than the opportunist. Addicts choose targets that present minimal risk; however, when desperate for funds, they are sometimes careless in selecting the victim and executing the crime. They rarely think in terms of the big score; they just want enough money to get their next fix.

Alcoholic robbers steal for reasons related to their excessive consumption of alcohol. Alcoholic robbers steal (1) when, in a disoriented state, they attempt to get some money to buy liquor or (2) when their condition makes them unemployable and they need funds. Alcoholic robbers have no real commitment to robbery as a way of life. They plan their crimes randomly and give little thought to their victim, circumstance, or escape. For that reason, they are the most likely to be caught.

SOURCE: John Conklin, *Robbery and the Criminal Justice System* (New York: Lippincott, 1972), pp. 1–80.

As these typologies indicate, the typical armed robber is unlikely to be a professional who carefully studies targets while planning a crime. Convenience stores, gas stations, and people walking along the street are much more likely robbery targets than banks or other highly secure environments. Robbers seem to be diverted by modest defensive measures, such as having more than one clerk in a store or locating stores in strip malls; they are more likely to try an isolated store.[126]

While most robbers may be opportunistic rather than professional, the patterns of robbery suggest that it is not merely a random act committed by an alcoholic or drug abuser. Though most crime rates are higher in the summer, robberies seem to peak during the winter months. One reason may that the cold weather allows for greater disguise. Another is that robbers may be attracted to the large amounts of cash people and merchants carry during the Christmas shopping season.[127] Robbers may also be more active during the winter because the days are shorter, affording them greater concealment in the dark.

In a recent book, Scott Decker and Richard Wright describe their interviews with active robbers in St. Louis, Missouri. Their findings are presented in the accompanying Criminological Enterprise box. ✔ Checkpoints

The Criminological Enterprise

Armed Robbers in Action

Criminologists Richard Wright and Scott Decker identified and interviewed a sample of 86 active armed robbers in St. Louis, Missouri. Their sample, primarily young African American men, helped provide an in-depth view of armed robbery that had been missing from the criminological literature.

Wright and Decker found that most armed robberies are motivated by a pressing need for cash. Many robbers careen from one financial crisis to the next, prompted by their endless quest for stimulation and thrills. Interviewees told of how they partied, gambled, drank, and abused substances until they were broke. Their partying not only provided excitement, but it helped generate a street reputation as a "hip" guy who can "make things happen." Robbers had a "here and now" mentality, which required a constant supply of cash to fuel their appetites. Those interviewed showed little long-range planning or commitment to the future. Because of their street hustler mentality, few if any of the robbers were able to obtain or keep legitimate employment, even if it was available.

Robbers show evidence of being highly rational offenders. Many choose victims who are themselves involved in illegal behavior, most often drug dealers. Ripping off a dealer kills three birds with one stone, providing both money and drugs while at the same time targeting victims who are quite unlikely to call the police. Another ideal target is a married man who is looking for illicit sexual adventures. He too is disinclined to call the police and bring attention to himself.

Others target noncriminal victims. They like to stay in their own neighborhood, relying on their intimate knowledge of streets and alleys to avoid detection. Although some range far afield seeking affluent victims, others believe that residents in the city's poorest areas are more likely to carry cash (wealthy people carry checks and credit cards). Because they realize that the risk of detection and punishment is the same whether the victim is carrying a load of cash or is penniless, experienced robbers use discretion in selecting targets. People whose clothing, jewelry, and demeanor mark them as carrying substantial amounts of cash make suitable targets; people who look like they can fight back are avoided. Some robbers station themselves at cash machines to spot targets who are flashing rolls of money.

Robbers have racial, gender, and age preferences in their selection of targets. Some African American robbers prefer white targets because they believe they are too afraid to fight back. As one interviewee put it, "White guys can be so paranoid [that] they just want to get away. . . . They're not . . . gonna argue with you." Likewise, intoxicated victims in no condition to fight back were a favored target. Others concentrate on African American victims, who are more likely to carry cash than credit cards. Some robbers tend to target women because they believe they are easy subjects; however, others avoid them for fear they will get emotionally upset and bring unwanted attention. Most agree that the elderly are less likely to put up a fuss than younger, stronger targets.

Some robbers choose commercial targets, such as convenience stores or markets, that are cash businesses open late at night. Gas stations are a favorite target. Security is of little consequence to experienced robbers, who may bring an accomplice to subdue guards.

Once they choose their targets, robbers carefully orchestrate the criminal incidents. They immediately impose their will on their chosen victim, leaving little room for the victim to maneuver and making sure the victim feels threatened enough to offer no resistance. Some approach from behind so they cannot be identified, while others approach the victim head-on, showing that they are tough and bold. By convincing victims of their impending death, the robber takes control.

Critical Thinking

1. It is unlikely that the threat of punishment can deter robbery; most robbers refuse to think about apprehension and punishment. Wright and Decker suggest that eliminating cash and relying on debit and credit cards may be the most productive method to reduce the incidence of robbery. Although this seems far-fetched, American society is becoming progressively more cashless; it is now possible to buy both gas and groceries with credit cards. Would a cashless society end the threat of robbery, or would innovative robbers find new targets?

2. Based on what you know about how robbers target victims, how can you better protect yourself from robbery?

InfoTrac College Edition Research

To learn more about robbery, see Peter J. van Koppen and Robert W. J. Jansen, "The Road to the Robbery: Travel Patterns in Commercial Robberies," *British Journal of Criminology*, Spring 1998 v38 i2 p230

D. J. Pyle and D. F. Deadman, "Crime and the Business Cycle in Post-War Britain," *British Journal of Criminology*, Summer 1994 v34 i3 p339–357

SOURCE: Richard Wright and Scott Decker, *Armed Robbers in Action: Stickups and Street Culture* (Boston, MA: Northeastern University Press, 1997).

Emerging Forms of Interpersonal Violence

Assault, rape, robbery, and murder are traditional forms of interpersonal violence. As more data become available, criminologists have recognized relatively new subcategories within these crime types, such as serial murder and date rape. Additional categories of interpersonal violence are now receiving attention in criminological literature; the following sections describe some of these newer forms of violent crime.

Stalking

In Wes Craven's popular movies *Scream 1–3*, the heroine Sydney (played by Neve Campbell) is stalked by a mysterious adversary who scares her half to death while killing off most of her peer group. While obviously extreme even by Hollywood standards, the *Scream* movies focus on a newly recognized form of long-term and repeat victimization: **stalking**.[128]

stalking

A pattern of behavior directed at a specific person that includes repeated physical or visual proximity, unwanted communications, and/or threats sufficient to cause fear in a reasonable person.

Stalking can be defined as a course of conduct directed at a specific person that involves repeated physical or visual proximity, nonconsensual communication, or verbal, written, or implied threats sufficient to cause fear in a reasonable person.

Stalking is a problem that affects about 1.4 million victims annually. It is strongly linked to the controlling behavior and physical, emotional, and sexual abuse perpetrated against women by intimate partners. About half of all female stalking victims report their victimization to the police, and about 25 percent obtain a restraining order against their assailants. In most cases stalking episodes last one year or less, but in a few cases it continues for five years or more.

Most victims know their stalker. Women are most likely to be stalked by an intimate partner—a current spouse, a former spouse, someone they lived with, or even a date. In contrast, men are typically stalked by a stranger or an acquaintance. The typical female victim is stalked because her assailant wants to

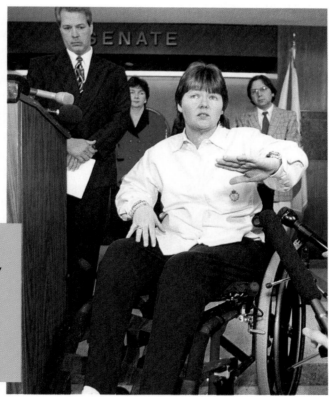

Sometimes stalkers are ex-spouses who want to "get even." Here, domestic violence survivor Kathy Haley describes to Florida state senators how she was stalked and ultimately shot and paralyzed by her husband. Sen. Richard Mitchell, shown standing, sponsored a bill that would allow victims of domestic violence to receive unemployment compensation.

AP/Wide World Photos

control her, scare her, or keep her in a relationship. Victims of both genders find that there is a clear relationship between stalking and other emotionally controlling and physically abusive behavior.

While stalkers behave in ways that induce fear, they do not always make overt threats against their victims. Many follow or spy on their victims; some threaten to kill pets; others vandalize property. However, criminologist Mary Brewster found that stalkers who make verbal threats are the ones most likely to later attack their victims.[129]

Although stalking usually stops within one to two years, victims experience its social and psychological consequences long after. About one-third seek psychological treatment, about 20 percent lose time from work, and some never return to work.

Why does stalking stop? Most often it stops when the victim moves away, the police get involved, or in some cases, the stalker meets another love interest.

Carjacking

carjacking

Theft of a car by force or threat of force.

You may have read about gunmen approaching a car and forcing the owner to give up the keys; in some cases, people have been killed when they reacted too slowly. This type of auto theft has become so common that it has its own name: **carjacking**.[130] Legally, carjacking is considered a type of robbery because it involves theft by force. It accounts for about 2 percent of all car thefts, or 35,000 per year. Carjackings are basically violent. The most recent data indicate that about 24 percent of victims suffered injuries, about 4 percent of them serious (gunshots, knifings, internal injuries, broken bones and teeth), and about 60 percent of the offenders in carjackings carried handguns.

Both victims and offenders in carjackings tend to be young black men; about half of all carjackings are committed by gangs or groups. These crimes are most likely to occur in the evening, in the central city, in an open area or parking garage.

Hate Crimes

hate crime

A violent act directed toward a particular person or group because of a discernible racial, ethnic, religious, or gender characteristic.

In the fall of 1998, Matthew Shepard, a gay college student, was kidnapped and severely beaten. He died five days after he was found unconscious on a Wyoming ranch, where he had been left tied to a fence for 18 hours in near-freezing temperatures.[131] His two killers, Aaron J. McKinney and Russell A. Henderson, 22, were sentenced to life in prison after the Shepard family granted them mercy. At McKinney's sentencing, Matthew's father, Dennis Shepard, addressed the young man:

> I would like nothing better than to see you die, McKinney. However, this is the time to begin the healing process, to show mercy to someone who refused to show any mercy. Mr. McKinney, I am going to grant you life, as hard as it is for me to do so, because of Matthew. Every time you celebrate Christmas, a birthday or the Fourth of July, remember that Matthew isn't. Every time you wake up in that prison cell, remember that you had the opportunity and the ability to stop your actions that night. You robbed me of something very precious, and I will never forgive you for that. May you live a long life and may you thank Matthew every day for it.[132]

Hate crimes or bias crimes are violent acts directed toward a particular person or members of a group merely because the targets share a discernible racial, ethnic, religious, or gender characteristic.[133] Hate crimes can include the desecration of a house of worship or cemetery, harassment of a minority-group family that has moved into a previously all-white neighborhood, or a racially motivated murder. Hate crimes usually involve convenient, vulnerable targets who are incapable of fighting back. For example, there have been numerous reported incidents of teenagers' attacking vagrants and the homeless in an effort to rid their town or neighborhood of people they consider undesirable.[134]

The Roots of Hate Why do people commit hate crimes? Research by sociologist Jack McDevitt shows that hate crimes are generally spontaneous incidents motivated by the victims' walking, driving, shopping, or socializing in an area in which their attackers believe they "do not belong."[135] Other factors that motivate bias attacks include a victim's moving into an ethnically distinct neighborhood or dating a member of a different race or ethnic group. Although hate crimes are often unplanned, McDevitt finds that most of these crimes are serious incidents that involve assaults and robberies.[136] In their book *Hate Crimes*, McDevitt and Jack Levin note that hate crimes are typically one of three types that reflect different motives:

1. *Thrill-seeking hate crimes.* In the same way some kids like to get together to shoot hoops, hate-mongers join forces to have fun by bashing minorities or destroying property. Inflicting pain on others gives them a sadistic thrill.

2. *Reactive hate crimes.* Perpetrators of these crimes rationalize their behavior as a defensive stand taken against outsiders who they believe are threatening their community or way of life. A gang of teens that attacks a new family in the neighborhood because they are the "wrong" race is committing a reactive hate crime.

3. *Mission hate crimes.* Some disturbed individuals see it as their duty to rid the world of evil. Those on a "mission"—Skinheads, the Ku Klux Klan (KKK), white supremacist groups—may seek to eliminate people who threaten their religious beliefs because they are members of a different faith or threaten "racial purity" because they are of a different race.[137]

Extent of Hate Crime Information on the extent of hate crimes is just becoming available. There is evidence that the neo-Nazi skinhead movement now contains 70,000 members worldwide in 33 countries. Germany houses about 5,000 skins, and Hungary and the Czech Republic 4,000 each.[138]

In the United States, the FBI now collects data on hate crimes as part of the Hate Crime Statistics Act of 1990. During 1999, about 8,000 bias-motivated criminal incidents were reported, involving 10,000 hate crime victims.[139] Of the reported incidents, 4,700 were motivated by racial bias, 1,400 by religious bias, 1,100 by sexual orientation bias, and 800 by ethnicity or national origin bias.

Because of the extent and seriousness of the problem, a number of legal jurisdictions have made a special effort to control the spread of hate crimes. Boston maintains the Community Disorders Unit, and the New York City police department formed the Bias Incident Investigating Unit in 1980. When a crime anywhere in the city is suspected of being motivated by bias, the unit initiates an investigation. The unit also assists victims and works with concerned organizations such as the Commission on Human Rights and the Gay and Lesbian Task Force. These agencies deal with noncriminal bias incidents through mediation, education, and other forms of prevention.[140]

Workplace Violence

Paul Calden, a former insurance company employee, walked into a Tampa cafeteria and opened fire on a table at which his former supervisors were dining. Calden shouted, "This is what you all get for firing me!" and began shooting. When he finished, three were dead and two others were wounded.[141] It has become commonplace to read of irate employees or former employees attacking coworkers or sabotaging machinery and production lines. Workplace violence is now considered the third leading cause of occupational injury or death.[142]

Who engages in workplace violence? The typical offender is a middle-aged white male who faces termination in a worsening economy. The fear of economic ruin is especially strong in agencies such as the U.S. Postal Service, where long-term employees fear job loss because of automation and reorganization. Repeated incidents have generated the term "going postal" as a synonym for a violent workplace incident. On September 1, 2000, the post office, stung by this bad publicity, was forced to issue a statement claiming that there is far less on-the-job homicide in the Postal Service than at other workplaces, and the term "going postal" is unjustified and unfair.[143]

A number of factors precipitate workplace violence. One may simply be the conflict caused by economic restructuring. As corporations cut their staffs due to recent trends such as office automation and company buyouts, long-term employees who had never thought of themselves losing a job are suddenly unemployed. There is often a correlation between sudden, unexpected layoffs and violent reactions.[144] Another trigger may be leadership styles. Some companies, including the U.S. Postal Service, have authoritarian management styles that demand performance, above all else, from employees. Unsympathetic, unsupportive managers may help trigger workplace violence.

Not all workplace violence is triggered by management-induced injustice. In some incidents, coworkers have been killed because they refused romantic relationships with the assailants or reported them for sexual harassment. Others have been killed because they got a job the assailant coveted. Irate clients and customers have also killed because of poor service or perceived slights. For example, in one Los Angeles incident, a former patient shot and critically wounded three doctors because his demands for painkillers had gone unheeded.[145]

There are a variety of responses to workplace provocations. Some people take out their anger and aggression by attacking their supervisors in an effort to punish the company that dismissed them; this is a form of murder by proxy.[146] Disgruntled employees may also attack family members or friends, misdirecting the rage and frustration caused by their work situation. Others are content with sabotaging company equipment; computer data banks are particularly vulnerable to tampering. The aggrieved party may do nothing to rectify the situation; this inaction is referred to as sufferance. Over time, the unresolved conflict may be compounded by other events that cause an eventual eruption.

The latest available data show that each year more than 2 million U.S. residents become victims of violent crime while they work. The most common type of victimization is assault, with an estimated 1.5 million simple assaults and 396,000 aggravated assaults reported annually. Each year sees 84,000 robberies, about 51,000 rapes or sexual assaults, and more than 1,000 workplace homicides.[147]

A number of efforts have been made to control workplace violence. One approach is to use third parties to mediate disputes before they escalate into violence. Another idea involves a human resources approach, with aggressive job retraining and continued medical coverage after layoffs. It is also important to hold objective, fair hearings to thwart unfair or biased terminations. Perhaps rigorous screening tests can help identify violence-prone workers so that they can be given anger management training.

Political Violence

In addition to interpersonal violence and street crime, another category of violence is politically motivated acts, including terrorism. Political crime has been with us throughout history. It is virtually impossible to find a society without political criminals, who have been described as "those craftsmen of dreams who possess a gigantic reservoir of creative energy as well as destructive force."[148]

Terrorism

terrorism

The illegal use of force against innocent people to achieve a political objective.

One aspect of political violence that greatly concerns criminologists is **terrorism.**[149] Because of its complexity, an all-encompassing definition of terrorism is difficult to formulate. However, most experts agree that it generally involves the illegal use of force against innocent people to achieve a political objective.[150]

One national commission defined terrorism as "a tactic or technique by means of which a violent act or the threat thereof is used for the prime purpose of creating overwhelming fear for coercive purposes."[151] In other words, terrorism is usually defined as a type of political crime that emphasizes violence as a mechanism to promote change. Whereas some political criminals may demonstrate, counterfeit, sell secrets, or spy, terrorists systematically murder and destroy or threaten such violence to terrorize individuals, groups, communities, or governments into conceding to the terrorists' political demands.[152] However, it may be erroneous to equate terrorism with political goals because not all terrorist actions are aimed at political change; some terrorists may try to bring about economic or social reform, for example, by attacking women wearing fur coats or sabotaging property during a labor dispute. Terrorism must also be distinguished from conventional warfare because it requires secrecy and clandestine operations to exert social control over large populations.[153]

Forms of Terrorism

Find It on INFOTRAC
College Edition

One expert claims, "Terrorism is an ambiguous danger that generates feelings of anxiety, foreboding, and a dread that anything can happen at any time and place, and that there is little anyone can do to reduce this threat." To read more, go to InfoTrac College Edition:

Lynn Kuzma, "The Polls: Trends," *Public Opinion Quarterly,* Spring 2000 v64 i1 p90

Today the term *terrorism* describes many different behaviors and goals. Some of the more common forms are briefly described here.[154]

Revolutionary Terrorists Revolutionary terrorists use violence against a regime which they consider to have unjustly taken control of their land either by force or coercion. In the Middle East, terrorist activities were first linked to Jewish groups such as the Irgun and Stern Gang, which were successful in driving the British out of Palestine in the 1940s leading to the creation of Israel, and today to Moslem groups such as Hamas and Hizballah, which seek to do the same to Israel.

Political Terrorists Political terrorism is directed at people or institutions who oppose the terrorists' political ideology. U.S. political terrorists tend to be heavily armed groups organized around such themes as white supremacy, militant tax resistance, and religious revisionism. Identified groups have included the Aryan Nation, the Posse Comitatus, and the Ku Klux Klan.

Recently, right-wing political extremists have engaged in a pattern of uncoordinated violence motivated by hate, rage, and the inability of more coordinated groups to either bring down the government or gain public support.[155] Although unlikely to topple the government, these individualistic acts of terror are difficult to predict or control. On April 19, 1995, 168 people were killed during the Oklahoma City bombing. This is the most severe example of political terrorism in the United States.

Nationalist Terrorism Nationalist terrorism promotes the interests of a minority ethnic or religious group that believes it has been persecuted under majority rule in an effort to secure a homeland within the country. In Spain, Basque terrorists have assassinated Spanish officials in order to convince the government to create a separate Basque homeland in northern Spain. In India, Sikh radicals use violence to recover what they believe to be lost homelands. On November 6, 1984, they assassinated Indian Prime Minister Indira Gandhi in retaliation for the government's storming of their Golden Temple religious shrine (and revolutionary base) in June 1984.[156]

Cause-Based Terrorism When the American embassies in Kenya and Tanzania were bombed in 1998, killing more than 250 people, Osama bin Laden's Al

genocide

The attempt by a government to wipe out a minority group within its jurisdiction.

Qaeda movement was quickly identified as the culprit. In a 1997 interview with CNN, bin Laden said his "jihad" or holy war against the United States was started because American forces were still operating in Saudi Arabia. He demanded that the United States end its "aggressive intervention against Muslims in the whole world."[157]

Bin Laden's brand of terrorist activity is one of many conducted by groups that espouse a particular social or religious cause and use violence to address their grievances.[158] For example, antiabortion groups have demonstrated at abortion clinics, and some members have attacked clients, bombed offices, and killed doctors who perform abortions. On October 23, 1998, Dr. Barnett Slepian was shot by a sniper and killed in his Buffalo, New York, home; he was one of a growing number of abortion providers believed to be the victims of terrorists who ironically claim to be "pro-life."[159]

Environmental Terrorism On October 19, 1998, several suspicious fires were set atop Vail Mountain, a luxurious ski resort in Colorado. Soon after, a militant environmental group, the Earth Liberation Front (ELF), claimed it had set the fires to stop a ski operator from expanding into animal habitats (especially that of the mountain lynx). The fires, which resulted in an estimated $12 million in damages, were the most costly of the more than 1,500 terrorist acts committed by environmental terrorists during the past two decades in an effort to slow down developers who they believe are threatening the environment or harming animals.[160] Members of such groups as the Animal Liberation Front (ALF) and Earth First! take responsibility for these attacks; they have also raided turkey farms before Thanksgiving and rabbit farms before Easter.[161]

State-Sponsored Terrorism State-sponsored terrorism occurs when a repressive governmental regime forces its citizens into obedience, oppresses minorities, and stifles political dissent.[162]

Much of what we know about state-sponsored terrorism comes from the efforts of human rights groups. London-based Amnesty International maintains that tens of thousands of people continue to become victims of security operations that result in disappearances and executions.[163] Political prisoners are now being tortured in about 100 countries; people have disappeared or are being held in secret detention in about 20; and government-sponsored death squads have been operating in more than 35. Countries known for encouraging violent control of dissidents include Brazil, Colombia, Guatemala, Honduras, Peru, Iraq, and the Sudan. When Tupac Amaru rebels seized and held hostages at the Japanese Ambassador's villa in Peru on December 17, 1996, Amnesty International charged that the action came in response to a decade-long campaign of human rights violations by national security forces and extensive abuses against opposition groups.[164]

The most extreme form of state-sponsored terrorism occurs when a government seeks to wipe out a minority group within its jurisdiction. This atrocity is referred to as **genocide**. The World War II Holocaust is the most extreme example of genocide to date, but more recent occurrences have taken place in Cambodia, Rwanda, and Bosnia.

Responses to Terrorism

Governments have tried numerous responses to terrorism. Law enforcement agencies have infiltrated terrorist groups and turned members over to police.[165] Rewards are often offered for information leading to the arrest of terrorists. "Democratic" elections have been held to discredit terrorists' complaints that the state is oppressive. Counterterrorism laws have increased penalties and decreased political rights afforded known terrorists.

In the United States, antiterrorist legislation provides jurisdiction over terrorist acts committed abroad against U.S. citizens and gives the United States the right to punish people for killing foreign officials and politically protected persons.[166] On April 24, 1996, President Clinton signed into law the Antiterrorism and Effective Death Penalty Act of 1996. Among its provisions, the legislation bans fund-raising in the United States that supports terrorist organizations. It allows U.S. officials to deport terrorists without being compelled to divulge classified information; it also bars terrorists from entering the United States.[167]

Despite U.S. efforts to control terrorism, any attempts to meet force with force are fraught with danger. Retaliation in kind could provoke increased terrorist activity—either for revenge or to gain the release of captured comrades. Of course, a weak response may be interpreted as a license for terrorists to operate with impunity. The most impressive U.S. antiterrorist action was the bombing of Libya on April 15, 1986, in an attempt to convince its leader, Muammar Gadhafi, to stop sponsoring terrorist organizations. Although this bombing made a dramatic statement, preventing terrorism has so far stymied most governments. ✓ **Checkpoints on page 246**

Summary

Although violence occurs throughout the world, the United States is an extremely violent society. Among the various explanations for violent crimes are the availability of firearms, human traits, a subculture of violence that stresses violent solutions to interpersonal problems, and family conflict.

There are many types of interpersonal violent crime. Rape, defined as the carnal knowledge of a female forcibly and against her will, has been known throughout history; however, the view of rape has evolved. Rape is an extremely difficult charge to prove in court. The victim's lack of consent must be proven; therefore, it almost seems that the victim is on trial. Consequently, changes are being made in rape law and procedure.

Murder is defined as killing a human being with malice aforethought. There are different degrees of murder, and punishments vary accordingly. One important characteristic of murder is that the victim and criminal often know each other. Assault, another serious interpersonal violent crime, often occurs in the home, including child abuse and spouse abuse. It has been estimated that almost 1 million children are abused by their parents each year, and 16 percent of families report husband–wife violence. There also appears to be a trend toward violence between dating couples.

Robbery involves theft by force, usually in a public place. Types of offenders include professional, opportunist, addict, and alcoholic robbers. Robbery is considered a violent crime because it can and often does involve violence.

Political violence is another serious problem throughout the world. Many terrorist groups exist at both the national and international levels. Hundreds of terrorist acts are reported each year in the United States alone. Terrorists may be motivated by criminal gain, psychosis, grievance against the state, or ideology.

For additional chapter links, discussions, and quizzes, see the book-specific Web site at http://www.wadsworth.com/product/0534519423s.

Thinking Like a Criminologist

The state legislature has asked you to prepare a report on statutory rape because of the growing number of underage girls who have been impregnated by adult men. Studies reveal that many teenage pregnancies result from affairs that underage girls have with older men, with age gaps ranging from 7 to 10 years. For example, the typical relationship that is prosecuted in California involves a 13-year-old girl and a 22-year-old male partner. Some outraged parents adamantly support a law that provides state grants to counties to prosecute statutory rape. These grants would allow more vigorous enforcement of the law and could result in the conviction of more than 1,500 offenders annually.

However, some critics suggest that implementing statutory rape laws to punish males who have relationships with minor girls does not solve the problems of teenage pregnancies and out-of-wedlock births. Liberals dislike the idea of using criminal law to solve social problems because it does not provide for the girls and their young children and focuses only on punishing offenders. In contrast, conservatives fear that such laws give the state power to prosecute people for victimless crimes, thereby adding to the government's ability to control people's private lives. Not all cases involve much older men, and critics ask whether we should criminalize the behavior of 17-year-old boys and their 15-year-old girlfriends. As a criminologist with expertise on rape and its effects, what would you recommend regarding implementation of the law?

Key Terms

instrumental violence	constructive malice	assault
expressive violence	first-degree murder	aggravated assault
subculture of violence	premeditation	child abuse
rape	deliberation	child neglect
gang rape	felony murder	sexual abuse
acquaintance rape	second-degree murder	robbery
date rape	manslaughter	stalking
marital rape	voluntary manslaughter	carjacking
marital exemption	involuntary manslaughter	hate crime
statutory rape	thrill killing	terrorism
shield laws	serial killer	genocide
murder	mass murderer	
actual malice	battery	

Discussion Questions

1. Would banning handguns reduce violent crime, or might it encourage the use of other weapons?

2. If robbers are in fact rational decision makers, what can potential victims do to reduce their chances of becoming targets?

3. What cultural values present in contemporary society promote violence? For example, is there a link between materialism and violence?

4. Should a violent serial child rapist be given the death penalty? If not, why not?

5. Are "terrorists" freedom fighters who lose? Were the Minutemen "nationalist terrorists" against British rule in the eighteenth century?

© Starr/Stock, Boston

11 Property Crimes

As a group, economic crimes can be defined as acts that violate criminal law and are designed to bring financial reward to an offender. The range and scope of U.S. criminal activity motivated by financial gain are tremendous. Self-report studies show that property crime is widespread among the young in every social class. National surveys of criminal behavior indicate that almost 30 million personal and household thefts occur annually; corporate and other white-collar crimes are accepted as commonplace; and political scandals, ranging from Watergate to Whitewater, indicate that even high government officials may be suspected of criminal acts.

This chapter is the first of two that review the nature and extent of economic crime in the United States. It begins with some background information on the history and nature of theft as a crime. It then discusses larceny/theft and related offenses, including shoplifting, forgery, credit card theft, auto theft, fraud, confidence games, and embezzlement. Next the discussion turns to a more serious form of theft, burglary, which involves forcible entry into a person's home or workplace for the purpose of theft. Finally, the crime of arson is discussed briefly. The next chapter is devoted to white-collar crimes and economic crimes that involve criminal organizations.

History of Theft

Theft is not unique to modern times; the theft of personal property has been known throughout recorded history. The Crusades of the eleventh century inspired peasants and downtrodden noblemen to leave the shelter of their estates to prey upon passing pilgrims.[1] Crusaders felt it within their rights to appropriate the possessions of any infidels—Greeks, Jews, or Muslims—they happened to encounter during their travels. By the thirteenth century, returning pilgrims, not content to live as serfs on feudal estates, gathered in the forests of England and the Continent to poach game that was the rightful property of their lord or king and, when possible, to steal from passing strangers. By the fourteenth century, many such highwaymen and poachers were full-time livestock thieves, stealing great numbers of cattle and sheep.[2]

The fifteenth and sixteenth centuries brought hostilities between England and France in the Hundred Years' War. Foreign mercenary troops fighting for both sides roamed the countryside; loot and pillage were viewed as a rightful part of their pay. As cities developed and a permanent class of propertyless urban poor[3] was established, theft became more professional. By the eighteenth century, three separate groups of property criminals were active:

Property crimes are not new to this century. This painting illustrates fourteenth-century thieves plundering a home in Paris.

- Skilled thieves typically worked in the larger cities, such as London and Paris. This group included pickpockets, forgers, and counterfeiters, who operated freely. They congregated in flash houses—public meeting places, often taverns, that served as headquarters for gangs. Here, deals were made, crimes were plotted, and the sale of stolen goods was negotiated.[4]
- Smugglers moved freely in sparsely populated areas and transported goods, such as spirits, gems, gold, and spices, without paying tax or duty.
- Poachers typically lived in the country and supplemented their diet and income with game that belonged to a landlord.

By the eighteenth century, professional thieves in the larger cities had banded together into gangs to protect themselves, increase the scope of their activities, and help dispose of stolen goods. Jack Wild, perhaps London's most famous thief, perfected the process of buying and selling stolen goods and gave himself the title of "Thief Taker General of Great Britain and Ireland." Before he was hanged, Wild controlled numerous gangs and dealt harshly with any thief who violated his strict code of conduct.[5]

During this period, individual theft-related crimes began to be defined by common law. The most important of these categories are still used today.

Contemporary Thieves

occasional criminals

Offenders who do not define themselves by a criminal role or view themselves as committed career criminals.

situational inducement

Short-term influence on a person's behavior, such as financial problems or peer pressure, that increases risk-taking.

professional criminals

Offenders who make a significant portion of their income from crime.

Of the millions of property and theft-related crimes that occur each year, most are committed by **occasional criminals** who do not define themselves by a criminal role or view themselves as committed career criminals. Other thefts are committed by skilled professional criminals.

Criminologists suspect that most economic crimes are the work of amateur occasional criminals, whose decision to steal is spontaneous and whose acts are unskilled, unplanned, and haphazard. Millions of thefts occur each year, and most are not reported to police agencies. Many of these theft offenses are committed by school-age youths who are unlikely to enter criminal careers and who drift between conventional and criminal behavior. Added to the pool of amateur thieves are the millions of adults whose behavior may occasionally violate the law—shoplifters, pilferers, tax cheats—but whose main source of income is conventional and whose self-identity is noncriminal. Added together, their behaviors form the bulk of theft crimes.

Occasional property crime occurs when there is an opportunity or **situational inducement** to commit crime.[6] Members of the upper class have the opportunity to engage in lucrative business-related crimes such as price-fixing, bribery, and embezzlement; lower-class individuals, lacking such opportunities, are overrepresented in street crime. Situational inducements are short-term influences on a person's behavior that increase risk-taking. They include psychological factors, such as financial problems, and social factors, such as peer pressure.

Occasional criminals may deny their criminality and instead view their transgressions as out of character. For example, they were only "borrowing" the car the police caught them with; they were going to pay for the merchandise that they stole from the store—eventually. Because of their lack of commitment to a criminal lifestyle, occasional offenders may be the most likely to respond to the general deterrent effect of the law.

In contrast to occasional criminals, **professional criminals** make a significant portion of their income from crime. Professionals do not delude themselves with the belief that their acts are impulsive, one-time efforts, nor do they use elaborate rationalizations to excuse the harmfulness of their actions ("shoplifting doesn't really hurt anyone"). Consequently, professionals pursue

Figure 11.1

Categories of Professional Theft

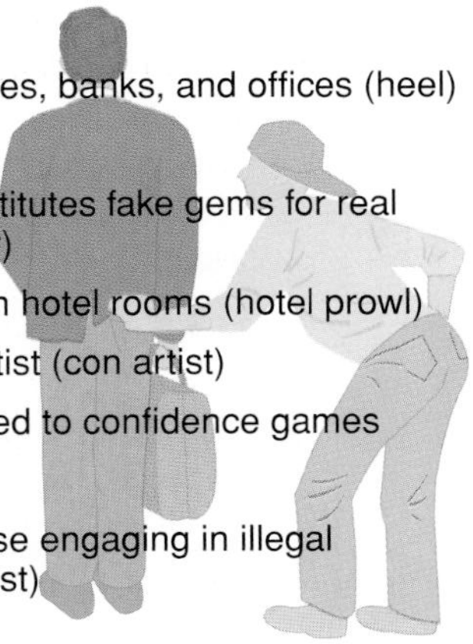

Pickpocket (cannon)

Sneak thief from stores, banks, and offices (heel)

Shoplifter (booster)

Jewel thief who substitutes fake gems for real ones (pennyweighter)

Thief who steals from hotel rooms (hotel prowl)

Confidence game artist (con artist)

Thief in rackets related to confidence games

Forger

Extortionist from those engaging in illegal acts (shakedown artist)

SOURCE: Edwin Sutherland and Chic Conwell, *The Professional Thief* (Chicago: University of Chicago Press, 1937).

their craft with vigor, attempting to learn from older, experienced criminals the techniques that will earn the most money with the least risk. Although their numbers are relatively few, professionals engage in crimes that produce the greater losses to society and perhaps cause the more significant social harm.

Professional theft traditionally refers to nonviolent forms of criminal behavior that are undertaken with a high degree of skill for monetary gain and that maximize financial opportunities and minimize the possibilities of apprehension. The most typical forms include pocket picking, burglary, shoplifting, forgery, counterfeiting, extortion, sneak theft, and confidence swindling (see Figure 11.1).[7]

The following sections discuss some of the more important contemporary theft categories in some detail. **✔ Checkpoints**

Larceny/Theft

✔ Checkpoints

✔ Theft offenses have been common throughout recorded history.

✔ During the Middle Ages, poachers stole game, smugglers avoided taxes, and thieves worked as pickpockets and forgers.

✔ Occasional thieves are opportunistic amateurs who steal because of situational inducements.

✔ Professional thieves learn their trade and develop skills that help them avoid capture.

Theft, or **larceny**, was one of the earliest common-law crimes created by English judges to define acts in which one person took for his or her own use the property of another.[8] According to common law, larceny was defined as "the trespassory taking and carrying away of the personal property of another with intent to steal."[9] Most U.S. states have incorporated the common-law crime of larceny in their legal codes. Contemporary definitions of larceny often include such familiar acts as shoplifting, passing bad checks, and other theft offenses that do not involve using force or threats on the victim or forcibly breaking into a person's home or workplace. (The former is robbery; the latter, burglary.)

As originally construed, larceny involved taking property that was in the possession of the rightful owner. For example, it would have been considered larceny for someone to sneak into a farmer's field and steal a cow. Thus, the original common-law definition required a "trespass in the taking"; that is, for an act to be considered larceny, goods must have been taken from the physical possession of the rightful owner. In creating this definition of larceny, English judges were more concerned with disturbance of the peace than with theft itself. They reasoned that if someone tried to steal property from another's possession, the act could eventually lead to a physical confrontation and possibly the death of one party or the other. Consequently, the original definition of larceny did not include crimes in which the thief had taken the property by trickery or deceit. For example, if someone entrusted with another person's property decided to keep it, it was not considered larceny.

larceny

Taking for one's own use the property of another, by means other than force or threats on the victim or forcibly breaking into a person's home or workplace; theft.

constructive possession

A legal fiction that applies to situations in which persons voluntarily give up physical custody of their property but still retain legal ownership.

petit (petty) larceny

Theft of a small amount of money or property, punished as a misdemeanor.

grand larceny

Theft of money or property of substantial value, punished as a felony.

The growth of manufacturing and the development of the free enterprise system required greater protection for private property. The pursuit of commercial enterprise often required that one person's legal property be entrusted to a second party; therefore, larceny evolved to include the theft of goods that had come into the thief's possession through legitimate means.

To get around the element of "trespass in the taking," English judges created the concept of **constructive possession**. This legal fiction applies to situations in which persons voluntarily, temporarily give up custody of their property, but still believe that the property is legally theirs. For example, if a person gives a jeweler her watch for repair, she still believes she owns the watch, although she has handed it over to the jeweler. Similarly, when a person misplaces his wallet and someone else finds it and keeps it (although identification of the owner can be plainly seen), the concept of constructive possession makes the person who has kept the wallet guilty of larceny.

Most U.S. state criminal codes separate larceny into **petit** (or **petty**) **larceny** and **grand larceny**. The former involves small amounts of money or property and is punished as a misdemeanor. Grand larceny, involving merchandise of greater value, is a felony punished by a sentence in the state prison. Each state sets its own boundary between grand larceny and petty larceny, but $50 to $100 is not unusual.

Larceny/theft is probably the most common of all crimes. Self-report studies indicate that a significant number of youths have engaged in theft. The FBI recorded almost 2 million acts of larceny in 1999, a rate of more than 2,550 per 100,000 persons. Larceny rates declined about 16 percent between 1995 and 1999.[10]

There are many different varieties of larceny. Some involve small items of little value. Many of these go unreported, especially if the victims are business owners who do not want to take the time to get involved with police; they simply write off losses as a cost of doing business. For example, hotel owners estimate that each year guests filch $100 million worth of towels, bathrobes, ashtrays, bedspreads, showerheads, flatware, and even television sets and wall paintings.[11]

Other larcenies involve complex criminal conspiracies from which no one is immune. For example, thieves stole $20.8 million worth of government equipment and supplies and another $10.4 million in personal property from General Services Administration buildings between 1992 and 1997. Nationwide, there were 41,431 reported incidents in that five-year span at 8,200 buildings. Similarly, the Department of Energy reported more than $20 million in property missing from its site in Rocky Flats, Colorado. Missing items included semitrailers, forklifts, cameras, desks, radios, and more than 1,800 pieces of computer equipment.[12]

Shoplifting

shoplifting

The taking of goods from retail stores.

Shoplifting is a common form of larceny/theft involving the taking of goods from retail stores. Usually shoplifters try to snatch goods—such as jewelry, clothes, records, and appliances—when store personnel are otherwise occupied and hide the goods on their bodies. The "five-finger discount" is an extremely common crime, and retailers lose an estimated $30 billion annually to inventory shrinkage; on average, stores small and large lose at least 2 percent of total sales to thieves.[13] Retail security measures add to the already high cost of this crime, all of which is passed on to the consumer. Shoplifting incidents have increased dramatically in the past 20 years, and retailers now expect an annual increase of from 10 to 15 percent. Some studies estimate that about one in every nine shoppers steals from department stores. Moreover, the increasingly

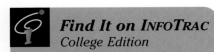

Find It on InfoTrac
College Edition

Is there a stage of life when shoplifting seems to skyrocket? To find out, go to InfoTrac College Edition and read

Janne Kivivuori, "Delinquent Phases," *British Journal of Criminology*, Autumn 1998 v38 i4 p663

booster

Professional shoplifter who steals with the intention of reselling stolen merchandise.

fence

A receiver of stolen goods.

snitch

Amateur shoplifter who does not self-identify as a thief but who systematically steals merchandise for personal use.

merchant privilege laws

Legislation that protects retailers and their employees from lawsuits if they arrest and detain a suspected shoplifter on reasonable grounds.

target removal strategy

Displaying dummy or disabled goods as a means of preventing shoplifting.

target hardening strategy

Locking goods into place or using electronic tags and sensing devices as means of preventing shoplifting.

CONNECTIONS

Situational crime prevention measures, discussed in Chapter 4, are designed to make it more difficult to commit crimes. Some stores are now using these methods—for example, placing the most valuable goods in the least vulnerable places, posting warning signs to deter potential thieves, and using closed-circuit cameras.

popular discount stores, such as Kmart, Wal-Mart, and Target, have minimal sales help and depend on highly visible merchandise displays to attract purchasers, all of which makes them particularly vulnerable to shoplifters.

The Shoplifter In the early 1960s, Mary Owen Cameron conducted a classic study of shoplifting.[14] In her pioneering effort, Cameron found that about 10 percent of all shoplifters were professionals who derived the majority of their income from shoplifting. Sometimes called **boosters**, or heels, professional shoplifters steal with the intention of reselling stolen merchandise to pawnshops or **fences** (people who buy stolen property), usually at half the original price.[15]

Cameron found that the majority of shoplifters are amateur pilferers, called **snitches** in thieves' argot. Snitches are otherwise respectable persons who do not conceive of themselves as thieves but systematically steal merchandise for their own use. They are not simply taken by an uncontrollable urge to snatch something that attracts them; they come equipped to steal. Usually snitches who are arrested have never been apprehended before. For the most part, they lack the kinds of criminal experience that suggest extensive association with a criminal subculture.

Criminologists view shoplifters as people who are likely to reform if apprehended. Cameron reasoned that because snitches are not part of a criminal subculture and do not think of themselves as criminals, they are deterred by initial contact with the law. Getting arrested traumatizes them, and they will not risk a second offense.[16] Although this argument seems plausible, some criminologists suggest that apprehension may in fact have a labeling effect that inhibits deterrence and results in repeated offending.[17]

Controlling Shoplifting Fewer than 10 percent of shoplifting incidents are detected by store employees; customers who notice boosters are unwilling to report even serious cases to managers.[18]

To encourage the arrest of shoplifters, a number of states have passed **merchant privilege laws** that are designed to protect retailers and their employees from lawsuits stemming from improper or false arrests of suspected shoplifters.[19] These laws require that arrests be made on reasonable grounds or probable cause, that detention be short, and that store employees or security guards conduct themselves reasonably.

Retail stores are now initiating a number of strategies designed to reduce or eliminate shoplifting. **Target removal strategies** involve displaying dummy or disabled goods while the "real" merchandise is locked up. For example, audio equipment is displayed with parts missing, and only after items are purchased are the necessary components installed. Some stores sell from catalogs, keeping the merchandise in stockrooms.

Target hardening strategies involve locking goods into place or having them monitored by electronic systems. Clothing stores may use racks designed to prevent large quantities of garments from being slipped off easily. Store owners also rely on electronic article surveillance (EAS) systems, featuring tags with small electronic sensors that trip alarms if not removed by employees before the item leaves the store. Security systems now feature source tagging, a process by which manufacturers embed the tag in the packaging or in the product itself. Thieves have trouble removing or defeating such tags, and retailers save on the time and labor needed to attach the tags at the store.[20] (See Figure 11.2.)

Figure 11.2

How to Stop Shoplifting

Here are some of the steps retail insurers recommend to reduce the incidence of shoplifting:

- Train employees to watch for suspicious behavior such as a shopper loitering over a trivial item. Have them keep an eye out for shoppers wearing baggy clothes, carrying their own bag, or using some other method to conceal products taken from the shelf.
- Develop a call code. When employees suspect that a customer is shoplifting, they can use the call to bring store management or security to the area.
- Because products on lower floors face the greatest risk, relocate the most tempting targets to upper floors.
- Use smaller exits, and avoid placing the most expensive merchandise near these exits.
- Design routes within stores to make theft less tempting and funnel customers toward cashiers.
- Place service departments (credit and packaging) near areas where shoplifters are likely to stash goods. Extra supervision reduces the problem.
- Avoid creating corners where there are no supervision sight lines in areas of stores favored by young males. Restrict and supervise areas where electronic tags can be removed.

SOURCE: Marcus Felson, "Preventing Retail Theft: An Application of Environmental Criminology," *Security Journal* 7 (1996): 71–75; Marc Brandeberry, "$15 Billion Lost to Shoplifting," *Today's Coverage*, a newsletter of the Grocers Insurance Group, Portland, Oregon, 1997.

Bad Checks

Another form of larceny is cashing bad checks to obtain money or property. The checks are intentionally drawn on a nonexistent or underfunded bank account. In general, for a person to be guilty of passing a bad check, the bank the check is drawn on must refuse payment and the check casher must fail to make the check good within 10 days after finding out the check was not honored.

Edwin Lemert conducted the best-known study of check forgers more than 40 years ago.[21] Lemert found that the majority of check forgers—he calls them **naive check forgers**—are amateurs who do not believe their actions will hurt anyone. Most naive check forgers come from middle-class backgrounds and have little identification with a criminal subculture. They cash bad checks because of a financial crisis that demands an immediate resolution—perhaps they have lost money at the horse track and have some pressing bills to pay. Naive check forgers are often socially isolated people who have been unsuccessful in their personal relationships. They are risk-prone when faced with a situation that is unusually stressful for them. The willingness of stores and other commercial establishments to cash checks with a minimum of fuss to promote business encourages the check forger to risk committing a criminal act.

Lemert found that a few professionals, whom he calls **systematic forgers**, make a substantial living by passing bad checks. It is difficult to estimate the number of such forgeries committed each year or the amounts involved. Stores and banks may choose not to press charges because the effort to collect the money due them is often not worth their while. It is also difficult to separate the true check forger from the neglectful shopper.

naive check forgers

Amateurs who cash bad checks because of some financial crisis but have little identification with a criminal subculture.

systematic forgers

Professionals who make a living by passing bad checks.

Credit Card Theft

The use of stolen credit cards has become a major problem in the United States. It has been estimated that fraud has caused a billion-dollar loss in the credit card industry. Most credit card abuse is the work of amateurs who acquire stolen cards through theft or mugging and then use them for two or three days. However, professional credit card rings may be getting into the act. For example, in Los Angeles, members of a credit card gang got jobs as clerks in several stores, where they collected the names and credit card numbers of customers. Gang members bought plain plastic cards and had the names and numbers of the customers embossed on them. The gang created a fictitious wholesale jewelry company and applied for and received authorization to accept credit cards from customers. The thieves then used the phony cards to charge nonexistent jewelry purchases on the accounts of the people whose names and card numbers they had collected. The banks that issued the original cards honored more than $200,000 in payments before the thieves withdrew the money from their business account and left town.[22]

To combat individual losses from credit card theft, in 1971 Congress limited a cardholder's liability to $50 per stolen card. Similarly, some states, such as California, have passed laws making it a misdemeanor to obtain property or services by means of cards that have been stolen, forged, canceled, or revoked, or whose use is for any reason unauthorized.[23]

The problem of credit card misuse is being compounded by thieves who set up bogus Internet sites to trick people into giving them their credit card numbers, which they then use for their own gain. This problem is growing so rapidly that a number of new technologies are being prepared to combat credit card number theft over the Internet. One method incorporates digital signatures into computer operating systems, which can be accessed with a digital key that comes with each computer. Owners of new systems can present three forms of identification to a notary public and trade a notarized copy of their key for a program that will sign files. The basis of the digital signature is a digital certificate, a small block of data that contains a person's "public key." This certificate is signed, in turn, by a certificate authority. The digital certificate acts like a credit card with a hologram and a photograph; it identifies the user to the distant web site.[24]

Auto Theft

Motor vehicle theft is another common larceny offense. Because of its frequency and seriousness, it is treated as a separate category in the Uniform Crime Report (UCR). The FBI recorded about 1.1 million auto thefts in 1999, accounting for a total loss of more than $7 billion. UCR projections on auto theft are similar to the projections of the National Crime Victim Survey (NCVS), probably because almost every state requires owners to insure their vehicles, and auto theft is one of the most highly reported of all major crimes (75 percent of all auto thefts are reported to police).

Types of Auto Theft A number of attempts have been made to categorize the various forms of auto theft. Typically, distinctions are made between theft for temporary personal use, for resale, and for chopping or stripping cars for parts. One of the most detailed of these typologies was developed by Charles McCaghy and his associates after examining data from police and court files in several states.[25] The researchers uncovered five categories of auto theft transactions:

1. *Joyriding.* Many car thefts are motivated by teenagers' desire to acquire the power, prestige, sexual potency, and recognition associated with an automobile. Joyriders steal cars not for profit or gain but to experience, even briefly, the benefits associated with owning an automobile.

2. *Short-term transportation.* Auto theft for short-term transportation is similar to joyriding. It involves the theft of a car simply to go from one

© Alex Quesada/Matrix

Each year millions of thefts from cars, homes, and schools are reported to police. Some are the work of professionals, while others are the spontaneous acts of occasional or amateur thieves.

place to another. In more serious cases, the thief may drive to another city or state and then steal another car to continue the journey.

3. *Long-term transportation.* Thieves who steal cars for long-term transportation intend to keep the cars for their personal use. Usually older than joyriders and from a lower-class background, these auto thieves may repaint and otherwise disguise cars to avoid detection.

4. *Profit.* Auto theft for profit is motivated by the hope of monetary gain. At one extreme are highly organized professionals who resell expensive cars after altering their identification numbers and falsifying their registration papers. At the other end of the scale are amateur auto strippers who steal batteries, tires, and wheel covers to sell them or reequip their own cars.

5. *Commission of another crime.* A few auto thieves steal cars to use in other crimes, such as robberies and thefts. This type of auto thief desires both mobility and anonymity.

At one time, joyriding was the predominant motive for auto theft, and most cars were taken by relatively affluent, white, middle-class teenagers looking for excitement.[26] There appears to be a change in this pattern: Fewer cars are being taken today, and fewer stolen cars are being recovered. Part of the reason is that there has been an increase in professional car thieves who are linked to chop shops, export rings, or both. Exporting stolen vehicles has become a global problem, and the emergence of capitalism in Eastern Europe has increased the demand for U.S-made cars.[27]

Combating Auto Theft Auto theft is a significant target of situational crime prevention efforts. One approach to theft deterrence has been to increase the risks of apprehension. Information hot lines offer rewards for information leading to the arrest of car thieves. A Michigan-based program, Operation HEAT (Help Eliminate Auto Theft), is credited with recovering more than 900 vehicles, worth $11 million, and resulting in the arrest of 647 people. Another approach has been to place fluorescent decals on windows indicating that the car is never used between 1:00 and 5:00 A.M.; if police spot a car with the decal being operated during this period, they know it is stolen.[28]

The Lojack system installs a hidden tracking device in cars; the device gives off a signal enabling the police to pinpoint its location. Research evaluating the effectiveness of this device finds that it significantly reduces crime.[29] Other prevention efforts involve making it more difficult to steal cars. Publicity campaigns have been directed at encouraging people to lock their cars. Parking lots have been equipped with theft-deterring closed-circuit TV cameras and barriers. Manufacturers have installed more sophisticated steering-column locking devices and other security systems that complicate theft.

A study by the Highway Loss Data Institute (HLDI) found that most car theft prevention methods, especially alarms, have little effect on theft rates. The most effective methods appear to be devices that immobilize a vehicle by cutting off the electrical power needed to start the engine when a theft is detected.[30]

False Pretenses/Fraud

false pretenses

Misrepresenting a fact in a way that causes a deceived victim to give money or property to the offender; fraud.

fraud

Misrepresenting a fact in a way that causes a deceived victim to give money or property to the offender; false pretenses.

The crime of **false pretenses**, or **fraud**, involves misrepresenting a fact in a way that causes a victim to willingly give his or her property to the wrongdoer, who then keeps it.[31] In 1757, the English Parliament defined false pretenses in order to cover an area of law left untouched by larceny statutes. The first false pretenses law punished people who "knowingly and designedly by false pretense or pretenses, [obtained] from any person or persons, money, goods, wares or merchandise with intent to cheat or defraud any person or persons of the same."[32]

False pretense differs from traditional larceny because the victims willingly give their possessions to the offender, and the crime does not, as does larceny, involve a "trespass in the taking." An example of false pretenses would be an unscrupulous merchant selling someone a chair by claiming it was an antique, knowing all the while that it was a cheap copy. Another example would be a phony healer selling a victim a bottle of colored sugar water as an "elixir" that would cure a disease.

Confidence Games

confidence game

A swindle, usually involving a get-rich-quick scheme, often with illegal overtones, so that the victim will be afraid or embarrassed to call the police.

Confidence games are run by swindlers who aspire to separate a victim from his or her hard-earned money. These con games usually involve getting a mark (target) interested in some get-rich-quick scheme, which may have illegal overtones. The criminal's hope is that when victims lose their money, they will be either too embarrassed or too afraid to call the police. There are hundreds of varieties of con games.

Contemporary confidence games have gone high-tech. Corrupt telemarketers contact people, typically elderly victims, over the phone in order to bilk them out of their savings. The FBI estimates that illicit telephone pitches cost Americans some $40 billion a year.[33] In one scam, a salesman tried to get $500 out of a 78-year-old woman by telling her the money was needed as a deposit to make sure she would get $50,000 she had supposedly won in a contest. In another scheme, a Las Vegas–based telephone con game used the name Feed America Inc. to defraud people out of more than $1.3 million by soliciting donations for various causes, including families of those killed in the Oklahoma City bombing. With the growth of direct-mail marketing and "900" telephone numbers that charge callers more than $2.50 per minute for conversations with what are promised to be beautiful, willing sex partners, a flood of new confidence games may be about to descend on the U.S. public. In all, about 363,000 people were arrested for fraud in 1999—most likely a very small percentage of all swindlers, scam artists, and frauds.

CONNECTIONS

Similar frauds are conducted over the Internet. These will be discussed in Chapter 12.

Embezzlement

Embezzlement goes back at least to ancient Greece; the writings of Aristotle allude to theft by road commissioners and other government officials.[34]

This crime of embezzlement was first codified into law by the English Parliament during the sixteenth century.[35] Until then, to be guilty of theft, a person had to take goods from the physical possession of another (trespass in the taking). However, as explained earlier, this definition did not cover instances in which one person trusted another and willingly gave that person temporary custody of his or her property. For example, in everyday commerce, store clerks, bank tellers, brokers, and merchants gain lawful possession but not legal ownership of other people's money. Embezzlement occurs when someone who is trusted with property fraudulently converts it—that is, keeps it for his or her own use or for the use of others. Most U.S. courts require a serious breach of trust before a person can be convicted of embezzlement. The mere act of moving property without the owner's consent, using it, or damaging it is not considered embezzlement. However, using it up, selling it, pledging it, giving it away, and holding it against the owner's will are all considered embezzlement.[36]

Although it is impossible to know how many embezzlement incidents occur annually, the FBI found that only 17,000 people were arrested for embezzlement in 1999—probably an extremely small percentage of all embezzlers. However, the number of people arrested for embezzlement has actually increased in the past two decades, indicating that (1) more employees are willing to steal from their employers, (2) more employers are willing to report instances of embezzlement, or (3) law enforcement officials are more willing to prosecute embezzlers. ✔ Checkpoints

Burglary

embezzlement

Taking and keeping the property of others, such as clients or employers, with which one has been entrusted.

burglary

Entering a home by force, threat, or deception with intent to commit a crime.

Find It on INFOTRAC
College Edition

To learn more about the definition of burglary, use it as a keyword in InfoTrac College Edition. You can also find articles on steps that can be taken to limit the risk of becoming a burglary victim.

Common law defines the crime of **burglary** as "the breaking and entering of a dwelling house of another in the nighttime with the intent to commit a felony within."[37] Burglary is considered a much more serious crime than larceny/theft because it involves entering another's home, which threatens occupants. Even though the home may be unoccupied at the time of the burglary, the potential for harm to the occupants is so significant that most state jurisdictions punish burglary as a felony.

The legal definition of burglary has undergone considerable change since its common-law origins. When first created by English judges during the late Middle Ages, laws against burglary were designed to protect people whose home might be set upon by wandering criminals. Including the phrase "breaking and entering" in the definition protected people from unwarranted intrusions; if an invited guest stole something, it would not be considered a burglary. Similarly, the requirement that the crime be committed at nighttime was added because evening was considered the time when honest people might fall prey to criminals.[38]

More recent U.S. state laws have changed the requirements of burglary, and most have discarded the necessity of forced entry. Entry through deceit (for example, by posing as a deliveryman), through threat, or through conspiracy with others such as guests and/or servants is deemed legally equivalent to breaking and is called "constructive breaking. " Many states now protect all structures, not just dwelling houses. A majority of states have also removed the nighttime element from burglary definitions. States commonly enact laws creating different degrees of burglary. The more serious, heavily punished crimes involve nighttime forced entry into the home; the least serious involve daytime entry into a nonresidential structure by an unarmed offender. Several legal gradations may be found between these extremes.

Armed burglars present a very real threat to police officers trying to make an arrest. Here, police officers follow a police dog up stairs at a house in Augusta, Michigan, as they investigate the scene where an officer was wounded and a suspect killed during a burglary investigation. The suspect, James Gregory Douglas, 20, died at the scene, and Detective Larry Napp, 49, a 28-year police veteran, was shot three times.

The Nature and Extent of Burglary

The FBI's definition of burglary is not restricted to burglary from a person's home; it includes any unlawful entry of a structure to commit theft or felony. Burglary is further categorized into three subclasses: forcible entry, unlawful entry where no force is used, and attempted forcible entry.

According to the UCR, more than 2 million burglaries occurred in 1999. The burglary rate has dropped by more than 22 percent since 1995. Both residential and commercial burglaries underwent steep declines during the 1990s; residential crimes committed at night declined more than residential daytime burglaries (Figures 11.3). Overall, the average loss for a burglary was about $1,500 per victim, for a total of about $3 billion.

The NCVS reports that about 3.6 million residential burglaries were either attempted or completed in 1999. The difference between the UCR and NCVS is explained by the fact that slightly more than half of all burglary victims reported the incident to police. However, similar to the UCR, the NCVS indicates that the number of burglaries has declined, dropping from 5.8 million in 1992 to 3.6 million in 1999.

Figure 11.3

Burglary, Residential and Nonresidential, Day and Night: Percentage Change 1995–1999

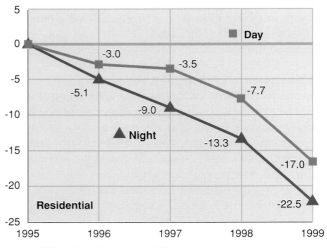

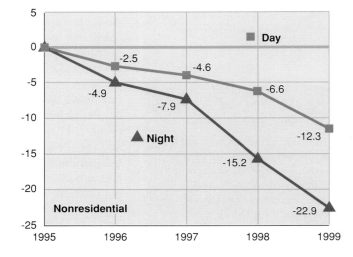

SOURCE: FBI, *Uniform Crime Report, 1999*, p. 42.

According to the NCVS, those most likely to be burglarized are relatively poor Hispanic and African American families (annual income under $7,500). Owner-occupied and single-family residences had lower burglary rates than renter-occupied and multiple-family dwellings.

Types of Burglaries

Though some burglars are crude thieves who smash a window and enter a vacant home or structure with minimal preparation, others plan a strategy. Because it involves planning, risk, and skill, burglary has long been associated with professional thieves who carefully learn their craft.[39]

Burglars must master the skills of their trade, learning to spot environmental cues that nonprofessionals fail to notice.[40] In an important book called *Burglars on the Job,* Richard Wright and Scott Decker describe the working conditions of active burglars.[41] Most are motivated by the need for cash in order to get high; they want to enjoy the good life, "keep the party going," without having to work. They approach their job in a rational, businesslike fashion; still, their lives are controlled by their culture and environment. Unskilled and uneducated, urban burglars choose crime because they have few conventional opportunities for success. (See Figure 11.4.)

Some burglars prefer to victimize commercial property rather than private homes. Of all business establishments, retail stores are the favorite target. Because they display merchandise, burglars know exactly what to look for, where it can be found, and, because the prices are also displayed, how much they can hope to gain from resale to a fence. Burglars can legitimately enter a retail store during business hours and see what the store contains and where it is stored; they can

CONNECTIONS

According to the rational choice approach discussed in Chapter 4, burglars make rational, calculating decisions before committing crimes. If circumstances and culture dictate their activities, their decisions must be considered a matter of choice.

Figure 11.4

How Burglars Approach Their "Job"

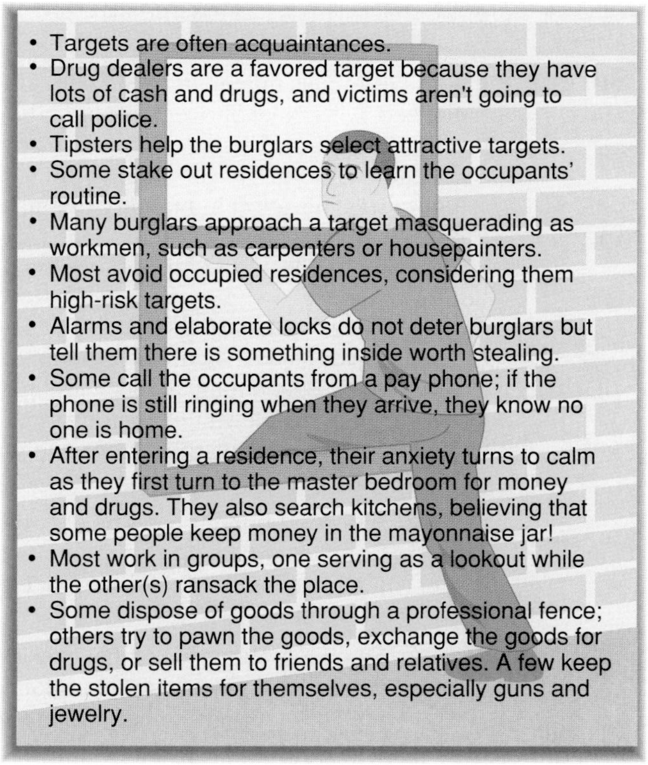

- Targets are often acquaintances.
- Drug dealers are a favored target because they have lots of cash and drugs, and victims aren't going to call police.
- Tipsters help the burglars select attractive targets.
- Some stake out residences to learn the occupants' routine.
- Many burglars approach a target masquerading as workmen, such as carpenters or housepainters.
- Most avoid occupied residences, considering them high-risk targets.
- Alarms and elaborate locks do not deter burglars but tell them there is something inside worth stealing.
- Some call the occupants from a pay phone; if the phone is still ringing when they arrive, they know no one is home.
- After entering a residence, their anxiety turns to calm as they first turn to the master bedroom for money and drugs. They also search kitchens, believing that some people keep money in the mayonnaise jar!
- Most work in groups, one serving as a lookout while the other(s) ransack the place.
- Some dispose of goods through a professional fence; others try to pawn the goods, exchange the goods for drugs, or sell them to friends and relatives. A few keep the stolen items for themselves, especially guns and jewelry.

SOURCE: Richard Wright and Scott Decker, *Burglars on the Job: Streetlife and Residential Break-ins* (Boston: Northeastern University Press, 1994).

also check for security alarms and devices. Commercial burglars perceive retail establishments as ready sources of merchandise that can be easily sold.[42]

Other commercial establishments, such as service centers, warehouses, and factories, are less attractive targets because it is more difficult to gain legitimate access to plan the theft. The burglar must use guile to scope out these places, perhaps posing as a delivery person. In addition, the merchandise is more likely to be used or more difficult to fence at a premium price. If burglars choose to attack factories, warehouses, or service centers, the most vulnerable properties are those located far from major roads and away from pedestrian traffic. In remote areas, burglar alarms are less effective because it takes police longer to respond than on more heavily patrolled thoroughfares, and an alarm is less likely to be heard by a pedestrian who would be able to call for help. Even in the most remote areas, however, burglars are wary of alarms, though their presence suggests that there is something worth stealing.

Whether residential or commercial, some burglars strike the same victim more than once.[43] Graham Farrell, Coretta Phillips, and Ken Pease have articulated some reasons why burglars might want to hit the same target more than once:

- It takes less effort to burgle a home or apartment known to be a suitable target than an unknown or unsuitable one.

- The burglar is already aware of the target's layout.

- The ease of entry of the target has probably not changed, and escape routes are known.

- The lack of protective measures and the absence of nosy neighbors, which made the first burglary a success, have probably not changed.

- Goods have been observed that could not be taken out the first time.[44]

Careers in Burglary

Some criminals make burglary their career and continually develop new specialized skills. Neal Shover has studied the careers of professional burglars and uncovered the existence of a particularly successful type—the "good burglar."[45] Characteristics of the good burglar include technical competence, personal integrity, specialization in burglary, financial success, and the ability to avoid prison sentences. Shover found that to receive recognition as good burglars, novices must develop four key requirements of the trade:

1. They must learn the many skills needed to commit lucrative burglaries. These skills may include gaining entry into homes and apartment houses; selecting targets with high potential payoffs; choosing items with a high resale value; opening safes properly without damaging their contents; and using the proper equipment, including cutting torches, electric saws, explosives, and metal bars.

2. The good burglar must be able to team up to form a criminal gang. Choosing trustworthy companions is essential if the obstacles to completing a successful job—police, alarms, secure safes—are to be overcome.

3. The good burglar must have inside information. Without knowledge of what awaits them inside, burglars can spend a tremendous amount of time and effort on empty safes and jewelry boxes.

4. The good burglar must cultivate fences or buyers for stolen wares. Once the burglar gains access to people who buy and sell stolen goods, he or she must also learn how to successfully sell these goods for a reasonable profit.

Race, Culture, Gender, and Criminology

The Female Burglar

Despite the interest shown in both the careers of residential burglars and female offenders in general, relatively little is known about female burglars. Although most burglars apprehended by police are male, about 9 percent, or 33,000, are female.

To address this issue, Scott Decker, Richard Wright, Allison Redfern Rooney, and Dietrich Smith interviewed 18 females, ranging in age from 15 to 51, who were active residential burglars. For comparison, 87 male burglars were also interviewed.

Decker and his associates found that female burglars had offending patterns quite similar to those of males. In addition to burglary, both groups engaged in other thefts, such as shoplifting and assault. The major difference was that male burglars also stole cars, but females shunned this form of larceny.

Another difference was that whereas females always worked with a partner, about 39 percent of the males said they seldom worked with others. Males also began their offending careers at an earlier age than females. About half of the females interviewed had been involved in fewer than 20 burglaries, whereas only 28 percent of the males reported as few as 20 lifetime burglaries. Because the males started earlier and committed more crimes, it is not surprising that males had a much greater chance of doing time (26 percent) than females (6 percent).

There were also many similarities between the two groups. A majority of both male and female burglars reported substance abuse problems, including cocaine, heroin, and marijuana use. About 47 percent of the females considered themselves addicts, and 72 percent said they drank alcohol before they committed crimes. Males reported less addiction, drug use, and alcohol abuse than females.

Decker and his associates found that the female burglars could be divided into two groups: "accomplices" and "partners." Accomplices committed burglaries because they were caught up in circumstances beyond their control. They felt compelled or pressured to commit crimes because of a relationship with another, more dominant person, typically a boyfriend or husband. Accomplices got into crime because they lacked legitimate employment, were drug dependent, or had alcohol problems. Accomplices exercised little control over their crimes and relied on others for planning and tactics. They commonly acted as lookouts or drivers.

In contrast, partners, who made up two-thirds of the sample, planned and carried out the crimes because they enjoyed both the reward and the excitement of burglary. In planning their crimes, partners displayed many characteristics of the rational criminal. They helped spot targets and planned entries. As one female burglar stated,

> That's one reason why we got so many youngsters in jail today. I see this, so let's go make a hit. No, no, no. If they see this and it looks good, then it's going to be there for a while. So the point is, you have to case it and make sure you know everything. I want to know what time you go to work, the time the children go to school. I know there's no one coming home for lunch. So plan it with somebody else. We'll take the new dishwasher, washing machine, and this other stuff. We just put it in the truck. Do you know when people rent a truck, nobody ever pays that any attention? They think you're moving [but] only if you rent a truck. Now if you bring it out of there and put it in the car, that's a horse of another color.

Once the burglary began, partners carried out all forms of crime-related tasks, including gaining entry, searching the house, carrying loot outside, and disposing of the stolen merchandise.

In conclusion, most female burglars maintain roles and identities similar to those of their male colleagues. Although some gender-based differences are evident, both male and female burglars actively plan crimes for many of the same reasons. The Decker research shows that for most male and female burglars, criminal careers may be a function of economic need and role equality—a finding that supports a feminist view of crime. It also illustrates that repeat criminals use rational choice in planning their activities.

Critical Thinking

1. Does the fact that so many burglars, both male and female, drink and abuse drugs conflict with a rational choice approach to crime?

2. Why are male burglars more likely to be car thieves than females are? Decker and his associates speculate that one reason may be a "strong cultural tradition linking masculinity to driving and car ownership." Can this be so?

 InfoTrac College Edition Research

To learn more about the nature of burglary and its prevention and control, see

Per Stangeland, "Other Targets or Other Locations? An Analysis of Opportunity Structures," *British Journal of Criminology,* Winter 1998 v38 p66–76
Matthew B. Robinson, "Burglary Revictimization: The Time Period of Heightened Risk," *British Journal of Criminology,* Winter 1998 v38 p78–88

SOURCE: Scott Decker, Richard Wright, Allison Redfern, and Dietrich Smith, "A Woman's Place Is in the Home: Females and Residential Burglary," *Justice Quarterly* 10 (1993): 143–163.

CONNECTIONS

Shover finds that the process of becoming a professional burglar is similar to the process described in Sutherland's theory of differential association. For more detail, refer to Chapter 7.

✔ Checkpoints

✔ Burglary is the breaking and entering of a structure in order to commit a felony, typically theft.

✔ Some burglars specialize in residential theft; others steal from commercial establishments.

✔ Some burglars repeatedly attack the same target, mainly because they are familiar with the layout and protective measures.

✔ Professional burglars have careers in which they learn the tricks of the trade from older, more experienced pros.

According to Shover, a person becomes a good burglar by learning the techniques of the trade from older, more experienced burglars. During this process, the older burglar teaches the novice how to handle such requirements of the trade as dealing with defense attorneys, bail bond agents, and other agents of the justice system. Apprentices must be known to have the appropriate character before they are accepted for training. Usually the opportunity to learn burglary comes as a reward for being a highly respected juvenile gang member; from knowing someone in the neighborhood who has made a living at burglary; or, more often, from having built a reputation for being solid while serving time in prison. Consequently, the opportunity to become a good burglar is not open to everyone.

The "good burglar" concept is supported by the interviews Paul Cromwell, James Olson, and D'Aunn Wester Avary conducted witith 30 active burglars in Texas. They found that burglars go through stages of career development, beginning as young novices who learn the trade from older, more experienced burglars, frequently siblings or relatives. Novices continue to get this tutoring as long as they can develop their own markets (fences) for stolen goods. After their education is over, novices enter the journeyman stage, characterized by forays in search of lucrative targets and by careful planning. At this point they develop reputations as experienced, reliable criminals. They become professional burglars when they have developed advanced skills and organizational abilities that give them the highest esteem among their peers.[46] Cromwell, Olson, and Avary also found that many burglars had serious drug habits and that their criminal activity was, in part, aimed at supporting their substance abuse. The accompanying Race, Culture, Gender, and Criminology describes the activities of both professional and occasional female burglars.

✔ Checkpoints

Arson

arson

The willful, malicious burning of a home, building, or vehicle.

Find It on INFOTRAC
College Edition

In the 1990s, a rash of arson against black churches terrified the nation. To read how this case was handled, use National Church Arson Task Force as a subject in InfoTrac College Edition.

Arson is the willful, malicious burning of a home, public building, vehicle, or commercial building. Arson is a young man's crime. FBI statistics for 1999 show that juveniles accounted for about half of all arson arrests; juveniles are arrested for a greater share of this crime than any other.

There are several motives for arson. Adult arsonists may be motivated by severe emotional turmoil. Some psychologists view fire starting as a function of a disturbed personality and claim that arson should be viewed as a mental health problem, not a criminal act.[47] It is alleged that arsonists often experience sexual pleasure from starting fires and then observing their destructive effects. Although some arsonists may be aroused sexually by their activities, there is little evidence that most arsonists are psychosexually motivated.[48] It is equally likely that fires are started by angry people looking for revenge against property owners or by teenagers out to vandalize property.

Juveniles, who are the most prolific firestarters, may get involved in arson for a variety of reasons as they mature. Other fires are set by professionals, who engage in arson for profit. People looking to collect insurance money, but who are afraid or unable to set the fires themselves, hire professional arsonists who know how to set fires yet make the cause seem accidental (like an electrical short). Another form is arson fraud, which involves a business owner burning his or her property, or hiring someone to do it, to escape financial problems.[49] Over the years, investigators have found that businesspeople are willing to become involved in arson to collect fire insurance or for various other reasons, such as

■ Obtaining money during a period of financial crisis

■ Getting rid of outdated or slow-moving inventory

- Destroying outmoded machines and technology
- Paying off legal and illegal debts
- Relocating or remodeling a business—for example, a theme restaurant that has not been accepted by customers
- Taking advantage of government funds available for redevelopment
- Applying for government building money, pocketing it without making repairs, and then claiming that fire destroyed the "rehabilitated" building
- Planning bankruptcies to eliminate debts after the merchandise supposedly destroyed was secretly sold before the fire
- Eliminating business competition by burning out rivals
- Employing extortion schemes that demand that victims pay up or the rest of their holdings will be burned
- Solving labor–management problems (this type of arson may be committed by a disgruntled employee)
- Concealing another crime, such as embezzlement

During the past decade, hundreds of jurisdictions across the nation have established programs to address the growing concern about juvenile firesetting. Housed primarily within the fire service, these programs are designed to identify, evaluate, and treat juvenile firesetters to prevent the recurrence of firesetting behaviors.

Summary

Economic crimes are designed to financially reward the offender. Opportunistic amateurs commit the majority of economic crimes. However, economic crime has also attracted professional criminals. Professionals earn most of their income from crime, view themselves as criminals, and possess skills that aid them in their law-breaking behavior. A good example of the professional criminal is the fence who buys and sells stolen merchandise.

Common theft offenses include larceny, fraud, and embezzlement. These are common-law crimes, defined by English judges, to meet social needs. Larceny involves taking the legal possessions of another. Petty larceny is typically theft of amounts under $100; grand larceny usually refers to amounts over $100. The crime of false pretenses, or fraud, is similar to larceny in that it involves the theft of goods or money; it differs in that the criminal tricks victims into voluntarily giving up their possessions. Embezzlement involves people taking something that was temporarily entrusted to them, such as bank tellers taking money out of the cash drawer and keeping it for themselves. Most U.S. states have codified these common-law crimes in their legal codes. New larceny crimes have also been defined to keep abreast of changing social conditions: shoplifting, passing bad checks, stealing or illegally using credit cards, and stealing automobiles.

Burglary, a more serious theft offense, was defined in common law as the "breaking and entering of a dwelling house of another in the nighttime with the intent to commit a felony within." This definition has also evolved over time. Today most states have modified their definitions of burglary to include theft from any structure at any time of day. Because burglary involves planning and risk, it attracts professional thieves. The most competent have technical competence and personal integrity, specialize in burglary, are financially successful, and avoid prison sentences.

Arson is another serious property crime. Although most arsonists are teenage vandals, there are professional arsonists who specialize in burning commercial buildings for profit.

For additional chapter links, discussions, and quizzes, see the book-specific Web site at http://www.wadsworth.com/product/0534519423s.

Thinking Like a Criminologist

To reduce the risk of loss during the Christmas holidays, the Security Industry Association (SIA) suggests that you do not display presents where they can be seen from a window or doorway, and put gifts in a safe place before leaving the house or taking a trip. Closing drapes or blinds during even short trips away from home is a good habit.

It is important to trick burglars into believing someone is home. If you are away, the SIA suggests having lights on timers, stopping mail and newspaper delivery, and arranging, if possible, to have the walkways shoveled and have a car parked in the driveway as additional security measures. Other suggestions include installing a good dead-bolt lock with at least a one-inch throat into a solid wood or steel door that fits securely into a sturdy frame, keeping doors locked, putting a chain-link fence around a yard, getting a dog, and having police inspect the house for security. Also, buy a weighted safe deposit box to secure items that cannot be replaced, and engrave your driver's license number and state of residence on your property to give police a way to contact you if your home is burglarized and the stolen items are later found.

Con artists may take advantage of people's generosity during the holidays by making appeals for nonexistent charities. The SIA suggests that you always ask for identification from solicitors.

As a criminologist, can you come up with any new ideas that the Security Industry Association failed to cover?

Key Terms

occasional criminal	booster	false pretenses
situational inducement	fence	fraud
professional criminal	snitch	confidence game
larceny	merchant privilege laws	embezzlement
constructive possession	target removal strategy	burglary
petit (petty) larceny	target hardening strategy	arson
grand larceny	naive check forgers	
shoplifting	systematic forgers	

Discussion Questions

1. Differentiate between an occasional and professional criminal. Which one would be more likely to resort to violence?

2. What crime occurs when a person who owns an antique store sells a client an "original" Tiffany lamp that they know is a fake? Would it still be a crime if they were not aware that the lamp was a copy? Should antique dealers have a duty to determine the authenticity of the products they sell?

3. What is the difference between a booster and a snitch? If caught, should they receive different punishments? What about naive and systematic check forgers?

4. What are the characteristics of the "good burglar"? Can you compare them to any other professionals?

Reuters/Joe Traver/Archive Photos

12 White-Collar and Organized Crime

The Nature of White-Collar Crime
Components of White-Collar Crime
   Stings and Swindles
   Chiseling
   Individual Exploitation of Institutional Position
   Influence Peddling and Bribery
   Embezzlement and Employee Fraud
   Client Fraud
   Corporate Crime
   High-Tech Crime
The Cause of White-Collar Crime
Controlling White-Collar Crime
   Compliance Strategies

Deterrence Strategies
POLICY AND PRACTICE IN CRIMINOLOGY
   Can Corporations Commit Murder?
Organized Crime
   Characteristics of Organized Crime
   Activities of Organized Crime
   The Concept of Organized Crime
   Controlling Organized Crime
   The Future of Organized Crime
Summary
Thinking Like a Criminologist
Key Terms
Discussion Questions

INTRODUCTION

In August 2000, Firestone, one of the world's most respected tire manufacturers, announced that it was recalling more than 14 million tires in the aftermath of numerous accidents caused by manufacturing defects. As reports began pouring in, it became clear than more than 80 people had died in vehicles, mainly Ford Explorers, equipped with Firestones whose tread and belts separated under normal usage. This was not the first time Firestone tires had to be recalled because they were linked to numerous auto fatalities. In 1978, 14.5 million Firestone 500 tires were recalled after they resulted in hundreds of crashes and dozens of deaths. At that time, the U.S. Congress and federal regulators made a series of proposals to tighten tire standards, but because the auto industry was undergoing financial problems, the suggested standards were never implemented. Had they been, it is possible that this recent spate of accidents and fatalities may have been avoided.[1]

Should the deaths of so many people be considered a tragic accident, a product of negligent manufacturing techniques, or a criminal offense? Would it be a crime if the manufacturer knew that the tires were dangerous and continued to sell them to the public? But in a giant corporation like Firestone, who should take the blame? The president and CEO? The people running the manufacturing plant that produced the tires? Or even the shareholders who gained income from the sale of faulty tires? Surely none of these people intended to harm anyone, and they may not even have been aware that the tires caused harm. (At the time of this writing, a congressional committee is investigating the case.)

The Firestone tire recall illustrates the fine line between business-based criminality and innocent, albeit shoddy, professional practices. In some cases, the law treats these incidents as civil matters, in others as criminal. Making that decision is quite difficult. What may appear to some as an innocent exercise of misjudgment may be considered a heinous crime by others.

Typically, business-related crimes involve efforts to bend the rules of enterprise and commerce in order to make a profit or gain an illegal advantage over competitors. In this chapter, we divide these crimes of illicit entrepreneurship into two distinct categories: white-collar crime and organized crime. **White-collar crime** involves illegal activities of people and institutions whose acknowledged purpose is profit through legitimate business transactions. **Organized crime** involves illegal activities of people and organizations whose acknowledged purpose is profit through illegitimate business enterprise. Organized crime and white-collar crime are linked together here because **enterprise**, not crime, is the governing characteristic of both phenomena. They are not inherently evil but are considered criminal because of an externally imposed evaluation by those who control the legal system.[2]

According to criminologist Dwight Smith, business enterprise can be viewed as flowing through a spectrum of acts ranging from the most "saintly" to the most "sinful."[3] Although "sinful" organizational practices may be desirable to many consumers (such as the sale of narcotics) or an efficient way of doing business (such as the dumping of hazardous wastes), society has regulated or outlawed these behaviors. Organized crime and business crimes are the results

white-collar crime

Illegal acts that capitalize on a person's status in the marketplace. White-collar crimes may include theft, embezzlement, fraud, market manipulation, restraint of trade, and false advertising.

organized crime

Illegal activities of people and organizations whose acknowledged purpose is profit through illegitimate business enterprise.

enterprise

Taking risks for profit in the marketplace.

of a process by which "political, value-based constraints are based on economic activity."[4]

White-collar and organized crime share some striking similarities. Mark Haller has coined the phrase "illegal enterprise crimes" to signify the sale of illegal goods and services to customers who know they are illegal. Haller's analysis also shows the overlap between criminal and business enterprise. For example, he compares the Mafia crime family to a chamber of commerce, as an association of businesspeople who join to further their business careers. Joining a crime syndicate allows one to cultivate contacts and be in a position to take advantage of good deals offered by more experienced players. The criminal group settles disputes between members, who, after all, cannot take their problems to court.[5]

Both organized crime and white-collar crime taint and corrupt the free market system; they involve all phases of illegal entrepreneurial activity. Organized crime involves individuals or groups whose marketing techniques (threat, extortion, smuggling) and product lines (drugs, sex, gambling, loan-sharking) have been outlawed. White-collar crimes include the use of illegal business practices (embezzlement, price-fixing, bribery) to merchandise what are ordinarily legitimate commercial products.

Surprisingly to some, both forms of crime can involve violence. Although the use of force and coercion by organized crime members has been popularized in the media and therefore comes as no shock, that white-collar crimes may inflict pain and suffering seems more astonishing. Yet experts claim that more than 200,000 occupational deaths occur each year and that "corporate violence" annually kills and injures more people than all street crimes combined.[6]

It is also possible to link organized and white-collar crime because some criminal enterprises involve both forms of activity. Organized criminals may seek legitimate enterprises to launder money, diversify their source of income, increase their power and influence, and gain and enhance respectability.[7] Otherwise legitimate businesspeople may turn to organized criminals to help them with economic problems (such as breaking up a strike or dumping hazardous waste products), stifle or threaten competition, and increase their influence. The distinction between organized crime and white-collar criminals may often become blurred.[8]

Some forms of white-collar crime may be more like organized crime than others.[9] Whereas some corporate executives cheat to improve their company's position in the business world, others are motivated purely for personal gain. It is this latter group, people who engage in ongoing criminal conspiracies for their own profit, that most resembles organized crime.[10]

The Nature of White-Collar Crime

In the late 1930s, the distinguished criminologist Edwin Sutherland first used the phrase "white-collar crime" to describe the criminal activities of the rich and powerful. He defined white-collar crime as "a crime committed by a person of respectability and high social status in the course of his occupation."[11] As Sutherland saw it, white-collar crime involved conspiracies by members of the wealthy classes to use their position in commerce and industry for personal gain without regard to the law. Often these actions were handled by civil courts, because injured parties were more concerned with recovering their losses than seeing the offenders punished criminally. Yet the cost of white-collar crime is probably several times greater than all the crimes that are customarily regarded as the "crime problem." And, in contrast to street crimes, white-collar offenses breed distrust in economic and social institutions, lowering public morale and undermining faith in business and government.[12]

Although Sutherland's work is considered a milestone in criminological history, his focus was on corporate criminality, including the crimes of the rich and powerful. Contemporary definitions of white-collar crime are typically much broader, including both middle-income Americans and corporate titans who use the marketplace for their criminal activity.[13] Included within recent views of white-collar crime are such middle-class acts as income tax evasion, credit card fraud, and bankruptcy fraud. Other white-collar criminals use their positions of trust in business or government to commit crimes. Their activities might include pilfering, soliciting bribes or kickbacks, and embezzlement. Some white-collar criminals set up business for the sole purpose of victimizing the general public. They engage in land swindles (for example, representing swamps as choice building sites), securities theft, medical fraud, and so on.

In addition to acting as individuals, some white-collar criminals become involved in criminal conspiracies designed to improve the market share or profitability of their corporations. This type of white-collar crime, which includes antitrust violations, price-fixing, and false advertising, is known as **corporate crime**.[14]

It is difficult to estimate the extent and influence of white-collar crime on victims because all too often those who suffer the consequences of white-collar crime are ignored by victimologists.[15] Some experts place its total monetary value in the hundreds of billions of dollars, far outstripping the expense of any other type of crime. For example, in the United States, the loss due to employee theft from businesses alone amounts to $90 billion per year.[16] Beyond their monetary cost, white-collar crimes often damage property and kill people. Violations of safety standards, pollution of the environment, and industrial accidents due to negligence can be classified as corporate violence. It is possible that corporate crime annually results in 20 million serious injuries, including 110,000 people who become permanently disabled and 30,000 deaths.[17] White-collar crime also destroys confidence, saps the integrity of commercial life, and has the potential for devastating destruction. Think of the possible results if nuclear regulatory rules are flouted or if toxic wastes are dumped into a community's drinking water supply.[18]

Nor is white-collar crime a uniquely U.S. phenomenon. It occurs in other countries, as well, often in the form of corruption by government agents. In China, corruption by public officials accounts for a high percentage of all cases of economic crime, despite the fact that the penalty for corruption is death.[19] China is not alone in experiencing organizational crimes. In Thailand, crime and corruption are skyrocketing; top executives of the Bangkok Bank of Commerce are believed to have absconded with billions of dollars worth of depositors' money.[20] U.S. companies are also the targets of white-collar criminals. Agents have been inserted into U.S. companies abroad to steal trade secrets and confidential procedures, including intellectual property such as computer programs and technology. The cost is somewhere between a conservative $50 billion and an astounding $240 billion a year.[21] ✓ **Checkpoints**

corporate crime

A legal offense, such as price fixing, restraint of trade, or hazardous waste dumping, committed by a corporate entity to improve its market share or profitability.

✔ Checkpoints

✔ White-collar crime involves the illegal distribution of legal material.

✔ Organized crime involves the illegal distribution of illegal material.

✔ White-collar and organized crime are linked together because they involve entrepreneurship.

✔ The definition of white-collar crime has expanded to include all forms of corrupt business practices by individuals as well as corporations.

✔ Losses from white-collar crime may far outstrip any other type of crime.

Components of White-Collar Crime

White-collar crimes today represent a range of behaviors involving individuals acting alone and within the context of a business structure. The victims of white-collar crime can be the general public, the organization that employs the offender, or a competing organization. Numerous attempts have been made to create subcategories or typologies of white-collar criminality.[22]

This text adopts a typology created by criminologist Mark Moore to organize the analysis of white-collar crime.[23] Moore's typology contains seven elements, ranging from an individual's using a business enterprise to commit theft-related crimes, to an individual's using his or her place within a business enterprise for

In 1993, New York City empowered the Mollen Commission to investigate corruption among city police. The commission found that a relatively small number (compared to the pervasive corruption found earlier by the Knapp Commission) of rogue cops were immersed in a pattern of violence, coercion, theft, and drug dealing. Testifying before the commission to gain a reduced sentence on a narcotics charge, one officer told of shaking down drug dealers, brutalizing innocent citizens, and intimidating fellow officers to force their silence. Protected by the "blue curtain"—the police officer code of secrecy—rogue cops were able to purchase luxury homes and cars with the profits from their illegal thefts, extortion, and drug sales.[43]

Even the high visibility given the Mollen Commission has failed to completely eliminate corruption. In 1998, New Yorkers awoke to front-page headlines describing police involvement with a midtown brothel. More than 20 officers were alleged to have been patrons of prostitutes working at 335 West 39th Street and a nearby massage parlor; some officers were filmed demanding sex. In the days following the story, 21 officers and one sergeant were stripped of their guns and badges and placed on modified duty.[44]

Influence Peddling in Business Politicians and government officials are not the only ones accused of bribery; business has had its share of scandals. The 1970s witnessed revelations that multinational corporations regularly made payoffs to foreign officials and businesspeople to secure business contracts. Gulf Oil executives admitted paying $4 million to the South Korean ruling party; Burroughs Corporation admitted paying $1.5 million to foreign officials; and Lockheed Aircraft admitted paying $202 million. McDonnell–Douglas Aircraft Corporation was indicted for paying $1 million in bribes to officials of Pakistani International Airlines to secure orders.[45]

In response to these revelations, Congress in 1977 passed the Foreign Corrupt Practices Act (FCPA), which makes it a criminal offense to bribe foreign officials or to make other questionable overseas payments. Violations of the FCPA draw strict penalties for both the defendant company and its officers.[46] For example, for violating the antibribery provisions of the FCPA, a domestic corporation can be fined up to $1 million. Moreover, all fines imposed on corporate officers are paid by them, not absorbed by the company. Despite the penalties imposed by the FCPA, corporations that deal in foreign trade have continued to give bribes to secure favorable trade agreements.[47] In 1995, for example, several former executives of the Lockheed Aircraft Corporation pleaded guilty to bribery in the sale of transport aircraft to the Egyptian government.[48]

Embezzlement and Employee Fraud

The fifth type of white-collar crime involves individuals' use of their positions to embezzle company funds or appropriate company property for themselves. Here the company or organization that employs the criminal, rather than an outsider, is the victim of white-collar crime. Employee theft can reach all levels of the organizational structure.

Blue-collar employees have been involved in systematic theft of company property, commonly called **pilferage**.[49] Employee theft is most accurately explained by factors relevant to the work setting, such as job dissatisfaction and the workers' belief that they are being exploited by employers or supervisors; economic problems play a relatively small role in the decision to pilfer. Although employers attribute employee fraud to economic conditions and declining personal values, workers themselves say they steal because of strain and conflict. It is difficult to determine the value of goods taken by employees, but it has been estimated that pilferage accounts for 30 to 75 percent of all shrinkage and amounts to losses of up to $10 billion annually.[50]

pilferage

Employee theft of company property.

Blue-collar workers are not the only employees who commit corporate theft. Management-level fraud is also quite common. Such acts include (1) converting company assets for personal benefit; (2) fraudulently receiving increases in compensation (such as raises or bonuses); (3) fraudulently increasing personal holdings of company stock; (4) retaining one's present position within the company by manipulating accounts; and (5) concealing unacceptable performance from stockholders.[51]

Client Fraud

A sixth component of white-collar crime is theft from an organization that advances credit to its clients or reimburses them for services rendered. These offenses are linked together because they involve cheating an organization (such as a government agency or insurance company) with many individual clients that the organization supports financially (such as welfare clients), reimburses for services provided (such as health care providers), covers losses of (such as insurance policyholders), or extends credit to (such as bank clients or taxpayers). Included in this category are insurance fraud, credit card fraud, fraud related to welfare and Medicare programs, and tax evasion.

Health Care Fraud Client fraud may be common even among upper-income people.[52] Some physicians have been caught cheating the federal government out of Medicare or Medicaid payments. Abusive practices include such techniques as "ping-ponging" (referring patients to other physicians in the same office), "gang visits" (billing for multiple services), and "steering" (directing patients to particular pharmacies). Doctors who abuse their Medicaid or Medicare patients in this way are liable to civil suits and even criminal penalties. For example, in 1997, the Baptist Medical Center in Kansas City, Missouri, agreed to pay the government $17.5 million to settle claims that it bribed doctors to send it Medicare patients for treatment; the doctors had received more than a million dollars in kickbacks.[53]

In addition to individual physicians, some large health care providers have been accused of routinely violating the law in order to obtain millions in illegal

Health care fraud is a common form of white-collar crime. Here, Vince Coyle, a special investigations manager for Progressive Insurance, points to a chart detailing an alleged medical fraud scam by a group of New York doctors. According to a civil suit filed by Progressive, Allstate, GEICO, and New York Central Mutual, the physicians allegedly sold the use of their names and medical licenses to chiropractors and laypeople for the purpose of forming 40 phony medical corporations, which they used as fronts to improperly bill patients and fraudulently bill insurance companies.

AP/Wide World Photos

payments. In 1998, the federal government filed suit against two of the nation's largest hospital chains, Columbia/HCA Healthcare Corporation (320 hospitals) and Quorum Health Group (250 hospitals), alleging that they routinely over-stated expenses in order to bilk Medicare.[54] It has been estimated that $100 billion spent annually on federal health care is lost to fraudulent practices.[55] Despite the magnitude of this abuse, the state and federal governments have been reluctant to prosecute Medicaid fraud.[56]

In light of these and other health care scandals, the government has attempted to tighten control over the industry. New regulations restrict the opportunity for physicians to commit fraud. For example, in 1993, Congress passed what are known as the Stark Amendments,[57] which prohibit physicians from making a referral to a health care provider that accepts Medicare patients if that physician or a family member holds a financial interest.

Bank Fraud Bank fraud can encompass such diverse schemes as check kiting, check forgery, false statements on loan applications, sale of stolen checks, bank credit card fraud, unauthorized use of automatic teller machines (ATMs), auto title fraud, and illegal transactions with offshore banks.[58] To be found guilty of **bank fraud**, one must knowingly execute or attempt to execute a scheme to fraudulently obtain money or property from a financial institution. For example, a car dealer would commit bank fraud by securing loans on titles to cars it no longer owned. A real estate owner would be guilty of bank fraud if he or she obtained a false appraisal on a piece of property with the intention of obtaining a bank loan in excess of the property's real worth. Penalties for bank fraud include a maximum fine of $1 million and up to 30 years in prison.

Tax Evasion Another important aspect of client fraud is tax evasion. Here the victim, the government, is cheated by one of its clients, the errant taxpayer to whom it has extended credit by allowing the taxpayer to delay paying taxes on money he or she has already earned. Tax fraud is a particularly challenging area for criminological study because (1) so many U.S. citizens regularly underreport their income, and (2) it is often difficult to separate honest error from deliberate tax evasion. The basic law on tax evasion is contained in the U.S. Internal Revenue Code, section 7201, which states:

> Any person who willfully attempts in any manner to evade or defeat any tax imposed by this title or the payment thereof shall, in addition to other penalties provided by law, be guilty of a felony and, upon conviction thereof, shall be fined not more than $100,000 or imprisoned not more than 5 years, or both, together with the costs of prosecution.

To prove tax fraud, the government must find that the taxpayer either underreported his or her income or did not report taxable income. No minimum dollar amount is stated before fraud exists, but the government can take legal action when there is a "substantial underpayment of tax." A second element of tax fraud is "willfulness" on the part of the tax evader, defined as a "voluntary, intentional violation of a known legal duty and not the careless disregard for the truth."[59] Finally, to prove tax fraud, the government must show that the taxpayer has purposely attempted to evade or defeat a tax payment. **Passive neglect**, a misdemeanor, means simply not paying taxes, not reporting income, or not paying taxes when due. On the other hand, **affirmative tax evasion**, such as keeping double books, making false entries, destroying books or records, concealing assets, or covering up sources of income, is a felony.

---

bank fraud

To obtain money or property from a financial institution by false pretenses, as by forgery or misrepresentation.

---

passive neglect

Failure to report income or pay taxes when due; a misdemeanor.

---

affirmative tax evasion

Willful and intentional nonpayment of taxes, as by concealing assets or income, making false entries, or destroying records; a felony.

Corporate Crime

organizational crime

A legal offense, such as price fixing, restraint of trade, or hazardous waste dumping, committed by an institution or its representatives; corporate crime.

Yet another component of white-collar crime involves situations in which powerful institutions or their representatives willfully violate the laws that restrain these institutions from doing social harm or require them to do social good. This is also known as corporate or **organizational crime**.

Corporate crimes are socially injurious acts committed by people who control companies to further their business interests. The target of their crimes can be the general public, the environment, or even their companies' workers. What makes these crimes unique is that the perpetrator is a legal fiction—a corporation—and not an individual. In reality, it is company employees or owners who commit corporate crimes and who ultimately benefit through career advancement or greater profits.

For a corporation to be held criminally liable, the employee committing the crime must be acting within the scope of his or her employment and must have actual or apparent authority to engage in the particular act in question. Actual authority occurs when a corporation knowingly gives authority to an employee; apparent authority is satisfied if a third party, such as a customer, reasonably believes that the agent has the authority to perform the act in question. Courts have ruled that actual authority may occur even when the illegal behavior is not condoned by the corporation but is nonetheless within the scope of the employee's authority.[60]

Some of the acts included within corporate crime are price-fixing and illegal restraint of trade, false advertising, and the use of company practices that violate environmental protection statutes. The variety of crimes contained within this category is great, and they cause vast damage. The following subsections examine some of the most important offenses.

restraint of trade

A contract or conspiracy designed to stifle competition, create a monopoly, artificially maintain prices, or otherwise interfere with free market competition.

Illegal Restraint of Trade and Price-Fixing   A **restraint of trade** involves a contract or conspiracy designed to stifle competition, create a monopoly, artificially maintain prices, or otherwise interfere with free market competition. The control of restraint of trade violations has its legal basis in the Sherman Antitrust Act, which subjects to criminal or civil sanctions any person "who shall make any contract or engage in any combination or conspiracy" in restraint of interstate commerce.[61] For violations of its provisions, this federal law created criminal penalties of up to three years' imprisonment and $100,000 in fines for individuals and $10 million in fines for corporations.[62] The act outlaws conspiracies between corporations designed to control the marketplace.

In most instances, the act lets the presiding court judge whether corporations have conspired to "unreasonably restrain competition." However, four types of market conditions are considered so inherently anticompetitive that federal courts, through the Sherman Antitrust Act, have defined them as illegal per se, without regard to the facts or circumstances of the case. The first is division of markets; here firms divide a region into territories, and each firm agrees not to compete in the others' territories.[63] The second is the tying arrangement, in which a corporation requires customers of one of its services to use other services it offers. For example, it would be an illegal restraint of trade if a railroad required that companies doing business with it or supplying it with materials ship all goods they produce on trains owned by the rail line.[64] A third type of absolute Sherman Act violation is **group boycotts**, in which an organization or company boycotts retail stores that do not comply with its rules or desires. Finally, **price-fixing**—a conspiracy to set and control the price of a necessary commodity—is considered an absolute violation of the act.

group boycott

A company's refusal to do business with retail stores that do not comply with its rules or desires.

price-fixing

A conspiracy to set and control the price of a necessary commodity.

Deceptive Pricing   Even the largest U.S. corporations commonly use deceptive pricing schemes when they respond to contract solicitations. Deceptive pricing occurs when contractors provide the government or other corporations with incomplete or misleading information on how much it will actually cost to fulfill the contracts they are bidding on or use mischarges once the contracts are signed.[65] For example, defense contractors have been prosecuted for charging the government for costs incurred on work they are doing for private firms or shifting the costs on fixed-price contracts to ones in which the government reimburses the contractor for all expenses ("cost-plus" contracts).

False Claims and Advertising Executives in even the largest corporations sometimes face stockholders' expectations of ever-increasing company profits, which seem to demand that sales be increased at any cost. Executives sometimes respond to this challenge by making claims about their products that cannot be justified by actual performance. However, the line between clever, aggressive sales techniques and fraudulent claims is a fine one. It is traditional to show a product in its best light, even if that involves resorting to fantasy. It is not fraudulent to show a delivery service vehicle taking off into outer space or to imply that taking one sip of iced tea will make people feel they have just jumped into a swimming pool. However, it is illegal to knowingly and purposely advertise a product as possessing qualities that the manufacturer realizes it does not have.

Charges stemming from false and misleading claims have been common in several U.S. industries. For example, the Federal Trade Commission reviewed and disallowed advertising by the three major U.S. car companies that alleged that new cars got higher gas mileage than buyers actually could expect. The Warner–Lambert drug company was prohibited from claiming that Listerine mouthwash could prevent or cure colds. Sterling Drug was prohibited from claiming that Lysol disinfectant killed germs associated with colds and flu. An administrative judge ruled that the American Home Products Company falsely advertised Anacin as a tension reliever. The list seems endless.[66]

Environmental Crimes Much attention has been paid to intentional or negligent environmental pollution caused by many large corporations. The numerous allegations in this area involve almost every aspect of U.S. business.

There are many different types of environmental crimes. Some corporations have endangered the lives of their own workers by maintaining unsafe conditions in their plants and mines. It has been estimated that 21 million workers have been exposed to hazardous materials while on the job. The National

The remains of one of the many migratory fowl that rely on the playa lakes in southeastern New Mexico. The chalky white material covering most of the bird is the result of salt toxicity caused by potash wastewater, according to the group Forest Guardians. The environmental group has sued two southeastern New Mexico mining companies it claims are killing thousands of migratory waterfowl by illegally dumping tons of pollutants into shallow lakes on which the birds depend.

AP/Wide World Photos

Table 12.1 Federal Laws That Regulate the Environment

- The Clean Air Act provides sanctions for companies that do not comply with the air quality standards established by the Environmental Protection Agency (EPA). The act can impose penalties on any person or institution that, for example, knowingly violates EPA plan requirements or emission standards, tampers with EPA monitoring devices, or makes false statements to EPA officials. The Clean Air Act was amended in 1990 to toughen standards for emissions of many air pollutants. 42 U.S.C. 7401–7642 (1988), amended 1990, 104 Stat. 2399 (1990).

- The Federal Water Pollution Control Act, more commonly called the Clean Water Act, punishes the knowing or negligent discharge of a pollutant into navigable waters. According to the act, a pollutant is any "man-made or man-induced alteration of the chemical, physical, biological, and radiological integrity of the water." 33 U.S.C. 1251–1387 (1988).

- The Rivers and Harbors Act of 1899 (Refuse Act) punishes any discharge of waste materials that damages natural water quality. 33 U.S.C. 407 (1988).

- The Resource Conservation and Recovery Act of 1976 provides criminal penalties for four acts involving the illegal treatment of solid wastes: (1) the knowing transportation of any hazardous waste to a facility that does not have a legal permit for hazardous waste disposal; (2) the knowing treatment, storage, or disposal of any hazardous waste without a government permit or in violation of the provision of the permit; (3) the deliberate making of any false statement or representation in a report filed in compliance with the act; and (4) the destruction or alteration of records required to be maintained by the act. 42 U.S.C. 6901–6992 (k) (1988).

- The Toxic Substance Control Act addresses the manufacture, processing, or distributing of chemical mixtures or substances in a manner not in accordance with established testing or manufacturing requirements; commercial use of a chemical substance or mixture that the commercial user knew was manufactured, processed, or distributed in violation of the act's requirements; and noncompliance with the reporting and inspection requirements of the act. 15 U.S.C. 2601–2629 (1988).

- The Federal Insecticide, Fungicide, and Rodenticide Act regulates the manufacture and distribution of toxic pesticides. 7 U.S.C. 136 (1988).

- The Comprehensive Environmental Response, Compensation, and Liability Act, also referred to as the "Superfund," requires the cleanup of hazardous waste at contaminated sites. 42 U.S.C. 9601–9675 (1988).

Institute of Occupational Safety and Health has estimated that it would cost about $40 million just to alert these workers to the danger of their exposure to hazardous waste and $54 billion to track whether they develop occupationally related disease.[67]

Some industries have been hit particularly hard by complaints and allegations. The asbestos industry was inundated with lawsuits after environmental scientists found a close association between exposure to asbestos and the development of cancer. More than 250,000 people have filed 12,000 lawsuits against 260 asbestos manufacturers. In all, some insurance company officials estimate that asbestos-related lawsuits could amount to as much as $150 billion. Similarly, some 100,000 cotton mill workers suffer from some form of respiratory disease linked to prolonged exposure to cotton dust. About one-third of the workers are seriously disabled by brown lung disease, an illness similar to emphysema.[68]

The control of workers' safety has been the province of the Occupational Safety and Health Administration (OSHA). OSHA sets industry standards for the proper use of such chemicals as benzene, arsenic, lead, and coke. Intentional violation of OSHA standards can result in criminal penalties.

The nature and scope of environmental crimes have prompted the federal government to pass a series of control measures designed to outlaw the worst abuses. These measures are summarized in Table 12.1.

High-Tech Crime

High-tech crimes are a new breed of white-collar offenses that can be singular or ongoing and typically involve the theft of information, resources, or funds. High-tech crimes cost consumers billions of dollars each year and will most likely increase dramatically in the years to come. What are some of these emerging forms of white-collar crime?

Internet Crimes On October 27, 1998, the SEC announced that it had filed charges against 44 stock promoters for fraudulently recommending more than 235 small companies on the Internet. The alleged fraud occurred when Internet stock newsletters touted investments in small companies without notifying investors that they were being paid by the companies whose shares they were promoting. The promoters not only profited from the fees but were able to sell shares they personally owned when the stock prices jumped as a result of their involvement. The promoters posted messages on web sites, flooded the Internet with junk e-mail, were paid more than $6.2 million in cash, and were given 1.8 million shares of stock or stock options for their work.[69]

Millions of people use the Internet daily in the United States and Canada alone, and the number entering cyberspace is growing rapidly. Criminal entrepreneurs view this vast pool as a target for high-tech crimes. In a number of highly publicized cases, adults have solicited teenagers in Internet "chat rooms." Others have used the Internet to sell and distribute obscene material, prompting some service providers to censor or control sexually explicit material.

Selling pornographic material on the Internet is just one method of its illegal use. Bogus get-rich-quick schemes, weight-loss scams, and investment swindles have been pitched on the Internet. In some cases, these fraudulent acts can actually be dangerous to clients. For example, in a 1995 case, a Minnesota woman advertised the health benefits of "germanium" on an Internet provider, claiming that it could cure AIDS, cancer, and other diseases. Germanium products have been banned because they cause irreversible kidney damage.[70]

There are also cases of fraud involving Internet auction sites. In some instances, counterfeit or fake items are sold as originals; in other cases, stolen items are peddled using the Internet as a "fencing" portal. The FBI's Internet Fraud Complaint Center currently receives upward of 1,000 consumer complaints a week and expects that number soon to reach 1,000 complaints a day when it is more fully automated and linked to such major web portals as America Online and Yahoo.[71]

Controlling Internet Crime Enforcing the law on the Internet can fall to a number of different agencies. The Securities and Exchange Commission, Federal Trade Commission, Secret Service, and state attorneys general have all assigned personnel to be "cybercops." In 1996, the federal government passed the Communications Decency Act, which proscribes the use of a computer to provide minors with "indecent material" as well as the knowing use of a computer to intentionally harass the recipient of communication.[72] Some civil liberty groups consider this law tantamount to censorship, and suits have been filed in federal court requesting clarification of its provisions; so far the Justice Department has suspended enforcement until the cases have been settled.[73]

Computer Crimes Computer-related thefts are a new trend in employee theft and embezzlement. The widespread use of computers to record business transactions has encouraged some people to use them for illegal purposes.

Computer crimes generally fall into one of five categories:[74]

1. Theft of services, in which the criminal uses the computer for unauthorized purposes or an unauthorized user penetrates the computer system. Included within this category is the theft of processing time and services to which an employee is not entitled.

2. Use of data in a computer system for personal gain.

3. Unauthorized use of computers employed for various types of financial processing to obtain assets.

4. Theft of property by computer for personal use or conversion to profit.

5. Making the computer itself the subject of a crime—for example, by infecting it with a virus to destroy data.

Although most of these types of crime involve using computers for personal gain, the last category typically involves activities that are motivated more by malice than by profit. When computers themselves are the target, criminals are typically motivated by revenge for some perceived wrong, a need to exhibit their technical prowess and superiority, a wish to highlight the vulnerability of computer security systems, a desire to spy on other peoples' private financial and personal information ("computer voyeurism"), or a philosophy of open access to all systems and programs.[75]

Computer criminals use several common techniques. In fact, computer theft has become so common that experts have created their own jargon to describe theft styles and methods:

- *The Trojan horse.* One computer is used to reprogram another for illicit purposes. In one incident, two high school–age computer users reprogrammed the computer at DePaul University, preventing that institution from using its own processing facilities. The youths were convicted of a misdemeanor.

- *The salami slice.* An employee sets up a dummy account in the company's computerized records. A small amount—even a few pennies—is subtracted from each customer's account and added to the thief's account. Even if they detect the loss, the customers don't complain, because a few cents is an insignificant amount to them. The pennies picked up here and there eventually amount to thousands of dollars in losses.

- *"Super-zapping."* Most computer programs used in business have built-in antitheft safeguards. However, employees can use a repair or maintenance program to supersede the antitheft program. Some tinkering with the program is required, but the "super-zapper" is soon able to order the system to issue checks to the thief's private account.

- *The logic bomb.* A program is secretly attached to the company's computer system. The new program monitors the company's work and waits for a sign of error to appear, some illogic that was designed for the computer to follow. Illogic causes the logic bomb to kick into action and exploit the weakness. The way the thief exploits the situation depends on his or her original intent—theft of money or defense secrets, sabotage, or whatever.

- *Impersonation.* An unauthorized person uses the identity of an authorized computer user to access the computer system.

- *Data leakage.* A person illegally obtains data from a computer system by leaking it out in small amounts.

A different type of computer crime involves installing a virus in a computer system. A **virus** is a program that disrupts or destroys existing programs and networks.[76] All too often, this high-tech vandalism is the work of hackers, who consider their efforts to be pranks.

An accurate accounting of computer crime will probably never be made because so many offenses go unreported. Sometimes company managers refuse to report the crime to police lest they display their incompetence and vulnerability to stockholders and competitors.[77] In other instances, computer

---

✔ Checkpoints

✔ White-collar crime has a number of different subcategories.

✔ Stings and swindles involve long-term efforts to cheat people out of their money.

✔ Chiseling involves regular cheating of an organization or its customers.

✔ People who engage in exploitation demand that victims pay for services they are entitled to by threatening consequences if they refuse. The victim here is the client.

✔ Influence peddling and bribery occur when a person in authority demands payment for a service to which the payer is clearly not entitled. The victim here is the organization.

✔ Embezzlement and employee fraud occur when a person uses a position of trust to steal from an organization.

✔ Client fraud invoves theft from an organization that advances credit, covers losses, or reimburses for services.

✔ Corporate crime involves various illegal business practices such as price-fixing, restraint of trade, and false advertising.

✔ High-tech crimes are a new form of white-collar crime involving computer and Internet fraud.

---

virus

A computer program that disrupts or destroys existing programs and networks.

Find It on InfoTrac
College Edition

In addition to hacker and virus attacks, the continued growth of the Internet and network computing is breeding new categories of peril. Information theft and access violations threaten companies worldwide. To read how business leaders are fighting back, go to InfoTrac College Edition and read

Luis Ramiro Hernandez, "Integrated Risk Management in the Internet Age," *Risk Management*, June 2000 v47 i6 p29

crimes go unreported because they involve low-visibility acts such as copying computer software in violation of copyright laws.[78]

Controlling Computer Crime As computer applications become more varied, so will the use of computers for illegal purposes. The growth of computer-related crimes prompted Congress to enact the Counterfeit Active Device and Computer Fraud and Abuse Act (amended in 1986).[79] This statute makes it a felony for a person to illegally enter a computer to gain $5,000, to cause another to lose $5,000, or to access data affecting the national interest. Violating this act can bring up to 10 years in prison and a $10,000 fine. Repeat offenders can receive 20-year prison sentences and $100,000 fines. In 1994, the Computer Abuse Amendments Act was passed to update federal enforcement efforts.[80] This statute addresses six areas of computer-related abuses, including obtaining information related to national defense or financial records, or using a "federal interest computer" to defraud, obtain something of value, or destroy data. The 1994 Act criminalizes "reckless conduct," which means that hackers who plant viruses will now violate federal law.

In addition to the Computer Abuse Act, people who illegally copy software violate the Criminal Copyright Infringement Act, which punishes copying and distribution of software for financial gain or advantage.[81] Computer crime may also be controlled by other federal statutes, including the Electronic Communications Privacy Act of 1986, which prohibits unauthorized interception of computer communications and prohibits obtaining, altering, or preventing authorized access to data through intentional unauthorized access to the stored data.[82] The act is designed to prevent hackers from intercepting computer communications and invading the privacy of computer users.[83] ✔ Checkpoints on page 282

The Cause of White-Collar Crime

When Wall Street financial whiz Ivan Boesky pleaded guilty to one count of securities fraud, he agreed to pay a civil fine of $100 million, the largest at that time in SEC history. Boesky's fine was later surpassed by financier Michael Milken's fine of more than $1 billion. How, people asked, can people with so much disposable wealth get involved in a risky scheme to produce even more?

There probably are as many explanations for white-collar crime as there are white-collar crimes. Many offenders feel free to engage in business crime because they can easily rationalize its effects; they are convinced that their actions are not really crimes because the acts involved do not resemble street crimes. For example, a banker who uses his position of trust to lend his institution's assets to a company he secretly controls may see himself as a shrewd businessman, not as a criminal. Some businesspeople feel justified in committing white-collar crime because they believe that government regulators do not really understand the business world or the problems of competing in the free enterprise system. Even when caught, many white-collar criminals cannot see the error of their ways. For example, one offender convicted in a major electrical industry price-fixing conspiracy categorically denied the illegality of his actions. "We did not fix prices," he said; "I am telling you that all we did was recover costs."[84] Some white-collar criminals believe that everyone violates business laws, so it is not so bad if they do so themselves. Rationalizing greed is a common trait of white-collar criminals.

Greed is not the only motivation for white-collar crime; need also plays an important role. Executives may tamper with company books because they feel the need to keep or improve their jobs, satisfy their egos, or support their children. Blue-collar workers may pilfer because they need to keep pace with inflation or buy a new car.[85]

C O N N E C T I O N S

As you may recall from Chapter 9, Hirschi and Gottfredson's general theory of crime holds that criminals lack self-control; the motivation and pressure to commit white-collar crime may be the same as for any other form of crime.

corporate culture view

The view that some business organizations promote white-collar crime by maintaining a business climate that stresses profit over fair play.

self-control view

The view that white-collar crime, like all crime, is a product of low self-control.

A well-known study of embezzlers by Donald Cressey illustrates the important role need plays in white-collar crime.[86] According to Cressey, embezzlement is caused by what he calls a "nonshareable financial problem." This condition may be the result of offenders' living beyond their means, perhaps piling up gambling debts; offenders feel they cannot let anyone know about such financial problems without ruining their reputations. Cressey claims that the door to solving personal financial problems through criminal means is opened by the rationalizations society has developed for white-collar crime: "Some of our most respectable citizens got their start in life by using other people's money temporarily"; "in the real estate business, there is nothing wrong about using deposits before the deal is closed"; "all people steal when they get in a tight spot."[87] Offenders use these and other rationalizations to resolve the conflict they experience over engaging in illegal behavior. Rationalizations allow offenders' financial needs to be met without compromising their values.

There are a number of more formal theories of white-collar crime. The **corporate culture view** is that some business organizations promote white-collar criminality in the same way that lower-class culture encourages the development of juvenile gangs and street crime. According to this view, some business enterprises cause crime by placing excessive demands on employees while at the same time maintaining a business climate tolerant of employee deviance. New employees acquire the attitudes and techniques needed to commit white-collar crime from their business peers through a learning process. Those holding the corporate culture view would see the savings and loan and insider trading scandals as prime examples of what happens when people work in organizations whose cultural values stress profit over fair play, in which government scrutiny is limited and regulators are viewed as the enemy, and in which senior members encourage newcomers to believe that "greed is good."

According to the **self-control view**, the motives that produce white-collar crimes are the same as those that produce any other criminal behaviors: "the desire for relatively quick, relatively certain benefit, with minimal effort."[88] According to this view, white-collar criminals have low self-control and are inclined to follow momentary impulses without considering the long-term costs of such behavior.[89] White-collar crime is relatively rare because, as a matter of course, business executives tend to hire people with self-control, thereby limiting the number of potential white-collar criminals.

Controlling White-Collar Crime

On the federal level, detection of white-collar crime is primarily in the hands of administrative departments and agencies.[90] Usually the decision to pursue criminal rather than civil violations is based on the seriousness of the case and the perpetrator's intent, actions to conceal the violation, and prior record. Any evidence of criminal activity is then sent to the Department of Justice or the FBI for investigation. Some other federal agencies, such as the Securities and Exchange Commission and the U.S. Postal Service, have their own investigative arms. Usually enforcement is reactive (generated by complaints) rather than proactive (involving ongoing investigations or the monitoring of activities). Investigations are carried out by the various federal agencies and the FBI.

The FBI has made enforcement of white-collar criminal law one of its three top priorities (along with combating foreign counterintelligence and organized crime). If criminal prosecution is called for, the case will be handled by attorneys from the criminal, tax, antitrust, and civil rights divisions of the Justice Department. If insufficient evidence is available to warrant a criminal prosecution, the case will be handled civilly or administratively by some other federal agency. For example, the Federal Trade Commission can issue a cease and desist order in antitrust or merchandising fraud cases.

On the state and local levels, enforcement of white-collar criminal law is often disorganized and inefficient. Confusion may exist over the jurisdiction of the state attorney general and local prosecutors. The technical expertise of the federal government is often lacking on the state level. However, local and state law enforcement officials have made progress in a number of areas, such as controlling consumer fraud. The Environmental Crimes Strike Force in Los Angeles County, California, is considered a model for the control of illegal dumping and pollution.[91] The number of state-funded technical assistance offices to help local prosecutors has increased significantly; more than 40 states offer such services.

Local prosecutors pursue white-collar criminals more vigorously if they are part of a team effort involving a network of law enforcement agencies.[92] National surveys of local prosecutors find that many do not consider white-collar crimes particularly serious problems. They are more willing to prosecute cases if the offense causes substantial harm and if other agencies fail to act. Relatively few prosecutors participate in interagency task forces designed to investigate white-collar criminal activity.[93]

The prevailing wisdom is that unlike lower-class street criminals, white-collar criminals are rarely prosecuted and, when convicted, receive relatively light sentences. In years past, it was rare for a corporate or white-collar criminal to receive a serious criminal penalty.[94]

What efforts have been made to bring violators of the public trust to justice? White-collar criminal enforcement typically involves two strategies designed to control organizational deviance: compliance and deterrence.[95]

Compliance Strategies

compliance strategies

Fostering law conformity, cooperation, and self-policing in the business community through the use of economic incentives and administrative agencies.

Compliance strategies aim for law conformity without the necessity of detecting, processing, or penalizing individual violators. At a minimum, they ask for cooperation and self-policing from the business community. Compliance systems attempt to create conformity by giving companies economic incentives to obey the law. They rely on administrative efforts to prevent unwanted conditions before they occur. Compliance systems depend on the threat of economic sanctions or civil penalties to control corporate violators.

One method of compliance is to set up administrative agencies to oversee business activity. For example, the Securities and Exchange Commission regulates Wall Street activities, and the Food and Drug Administration regulates drugs, cosmetics, medical devices, meats, and other foods. The legislation creating these agencies usually spells out the penalties for violating regulatory standards.

This approach has been used to control environmental crimes, for example, by levying heavy fines based on the quantity and quality of pollution released into the environment.[96] For example, after the FMC Corporation was fined $11.8 million in 1998 for violating federal hazardous waste laws at its southeastern Idaho plant, it agreed to spend $158 million over the next four years to upgrade air and hazardous waste treatment operations at the plant, located on the Shoshone–Bannock Indian reservation.[97] It is easier and less costly to be in compliance, the theory goes, than to pay costly fines and risk criminal prosecution for repeat violations. Moreover, the federal government bars people and businesses from receiving government contracts if they have engaged in repeated business law violations. Compliance strategies avoid stigmatizing and shaming businesspeople by focusing on the act, rather than the actor, in white-collar crime.[98]

Deterrence Strategies

deterrence strategies

Detecting criminal violations, determining who is responsible, and penalizing the offenders to deter future violations.

Deterrence strategies involve detecting criminal violations, determining who is responsible, and penalizing the offenders to deter future violations.[99] Deterrence systems are oriented toward apprehending violators and punishing them rather than creating conditions that induce conformity to the law.

Policy and Practice in Criminology

Can Corporations Commit Murder?

One of the most controversial issues surrounding the punishment of white-collar criminals involves prosecuting corporate executives who work for companies that manufacture products believed to have killed workers or consumers. Are the executives guilty of manslaughter, or even murder? This issue is especially relevant when we consider that more than 80 people have been killed by defective Firestone tires. How should corporate executives whose products cause death or whose business practices result in fatal harm to their employees be treated?

Federal Law

The Occupational Safety and Health Act makes employers criminally liable if their willful violation of a safety rule causes the death of an employee. In one case, for example, corporate officers of a Massachusetts asbestos firm were indicted when they made false statements to Occupational Safety and Health Administration (OSHA) officials about the safety of worker respirators

when in reality the safety and fit of the devices had not been tested.

Although OSHA officials can bring criminal charges, critics maintain that they rarely do, preferring to punish even serious crimes with fines. For example, they negotiated a $10 million fine with IMC Fertilizer and Angus Chemical following a 1991 plant explosion that killed eight workers. They also fined Firestone Tire Company $7.5 million in 1994 after determining that the company had violated OSHA standards by failing to properly use locks and lockout procedures when servicing equipment, resulting in the death of a maintenance worker.

State Enforcement

States may also bring criminal charges for deaths. More than 20 years ago, a local prosecutor failed in an attempt to convict Ford Motor Company executives on charges of homicide in crashes involving Pintos, where deaths were due to known dangers in the car's design. The Pinto had a gas tank that burst into flame when involved in

a low-velocity, rear-end collision. Although the design defect could have been corrected for about $20 per car, the company failed to take prompt action. When three people were killed in crashes, an Indiana prosecutor brought murder charges against Ford executives. However, they were acquitted because the jury did not find sufficient evidence that they intended the deaths to occur.

The question of whether corporate executives could be successfully prosecuted for murder was answered on June 16, 1985, when an Illinois judge found three officials of the Film Recovery Systems Corporation guilty of murder in the death of a worker. The employee died after inhaling cyanide under "totally unsafe" work conditions. During the trial, evidence was presented showing that employees were not warned that they were working with dangerous substances, that company officials ignored complaints of illness, and that safety precautions had been deliberately ignored. The murder convictions were later overturned on appeal.

Find It on INFOTRAC
College Edition

Research shows that there is wide disparity among courts in the way white-collar criminals are punished. Some federal courts are quite likely to send convicted white-collar criminals to prison, while others seem reluctant to use incarceration. To read a news report on this phenomenon, go to Info-Trac College Edition and read "Wide Disparity in White-Collar Sentences," *USA Today (Magazine),* April 2000 v128 i2659 p11

Deterrence strategies should work—and they have—because white-collar crime by its nature is a rational act whose perpetrators are extremely sensitive to the threat of criminal sanctions. Perceptions of detection and punishment for white-collar crimes appear to be a powerful deterrent to future law violations.[100] There are numerous instances in which prison sentences for corporate crimes have produced a significant decline in white-collar criminal activity.[101]

Although deterrence strategies may prove effective, federal agencies have traditionally been reluctant to throw corporate executives in jail. For example, the courts have not hesitated to enforce the Sherman Antitrust Act in civil actions, but they have limited application of the criminal sanctions. Similarly, the government seeks criminal indictments in corporate violations only in "instances of outrageous conduct of undoubted illegality," such as price-fixing.[102] The government has also been lenient with companies and individuals that cooperate voluntarily after an investigation has begun; leniency is not given as part of a confession or plea arrangement. Those who comply with the leniency policy are charged criminally for the activity reported.[103]

Despite years of neglect, there is growing evidence that white-collar crime deterrence strategies have become increasingly common. The federal government has created sentencing guidelines that control punishment for convicted

The Pinto and Film Recovery cases opened the door for prosecuting corporate executives on violent crime charges stemming from unsafe products or working conditions. There is little question that corporate liability may be increasing. As Nancy Frank points out, a number of states have adopted the concept of unintended murder in their legal codes. This means that persons can be charged and convicted of murder if their acts, although essentially unintended, are imminently dangerous to another or have a strong probability of causing death or great bodily harm. This legal theory would include corporate executives who knew about the dangers of their products but chose to do nothing, either because correction would lower profits or because they simply did not care about consumers or workers.

A case illustrating this legal doctrine involved a fire on September 3, 1991, at Imperial Food Products, Inc., a North Carolina chicken-processing plant. The fire, which claimed 25 lives, was deadly because the plant had no sprinkler system, windows, or escape routes. Company executives had locked exit doors to prevent employee pilferage. Emmett Roe, the firm's owner, was convicted of involuntary manslaughter and received a 19-year prison sentence. In this case and others around the country, local prosecutors are taking the initiative to prosecute corporate executives as violent criminals.

Critical Thinking

1. If Ford executives knew they had a dangerous car, should they have been found guilty of murder, even though the deaths were the result of collisions?
2. Is it fair to blame a single executive for the activities of a company that has thousands of employees?

InfoTrac College Edition Research

To learn more about work-related dangers, read
Barbra Marcus, Sarah Minifie, Raj Natarajan, and Joseph D. Wilson, "Employment-Related Crimes (Twelfth Survey of White-Collar Crime)," *American Criminal Law Review,* Winter 1997 v34 i2 p457–490

Anton Foek, "Sweatshop Barbie: Exploitation of Third World Labor," *The Humanist,* January–February 1997 v57 i1 p9
Dana Wilkie, "The Uphill Struggle for Workplace Health," *State Legislatures,* June 1997 v23 i6 p27

SOURCES: David B. Darden, Susannah Merritt, and Robyn J. Greenburg, "Employment-Related Crimes," *American Criminal Law Review* 35 (1998): 561–596; Occupational Safety and Health Act, 29 U.S.C. sections 651–678 (1994); John Wright, Francis Cullen, and Michael Blankenship, "The Social Construction of Corporate Violence: Media Coverage of the Imperial Food Products Fire," paper presented at the annual meeting of the American Society of Criminology, Phoenix, Arizona, November 1993; Nancy Frank, "Unintended Murder and Corporate Risk-Taking: Defining the Concept of Justifiability," *Journal of Criminal Justice* 16 (1988): 17–24; Francis Cullen, William Maakestad, and Gray Cavender, "The Ford Pinto Case and Beyond: Corporate Crime, Moral Boundaries, and the Criminal Sanction," in *Corporations as Criminals,* ed. Ellen Hochstedler (Beverly Hills, CA: Sage, 1984), pp. 107–130.

✔ Checkpoints

✔ There are numerous explanations for white-collar crime.

✔ Some offenders are motivated by greed; others offend due to personal problems.

✔ Corporate culture theory suggests that some businesses actually encourage employees to cheat or cut corners.

✔ The self-control view is that white-collar criminals are like any other law violators: impulsive people who lack self-control.

✔ White-collar enforcement may encourage self-regulation. Organizations that violate the law are given civil fines.

✔ Deterrence systems punish individuals with prison sentences.

criminals. Prosecutors can now control the length and type of sentence through their handling of the charging process. The guidelines also create mandatory minimum prison sentences that must be served for some crimes; judicial clemency can no longer be counted on.[104] This new get-tough deterrence approach appears to be affecting all classes of white-collar criminals. Although many people believe that affluent corporate executives usually avoid serious punishment, public displeasure with highly publicized white-collar crimes may be producing a backlash that is resulting in more frequent use of prison sentences.[105] Some commentators now argue that the government may actually be going overboard in its efforts to punish white-collar criminals, especially for crimes that are the result of negligent business practices rather than intentional criminal conspiracy.[106]

Because white-collar crime is rarely a one-time event, the identification of white-collar criminals is certainly less difficult than it is for street criminals.[107] Deterrence strategies have gone so far as charging business executives with murder in incidents where employees have died because of business-related injuries or illness. This issue is disussed in the accompanying Policy and Practice in Criminology. ✔ Checkpoints

Organized Crime

The second branch of organizational criminality involves organized crime—the ongoing criminal enterprise groups whose ultimate purpose is personal economic gain through illegitimate means. Here, a structured enterprise system is set up to supply consumers with merchandise and services banned by criminal law but for which a ready market exists: prostitution, pornography, gambling, and narcotics. The system may resemble a legitimate business run by an ambitious chief executive officer, his or her assistants, staff attorneys, and accountants, with thorough, efficient accounts receivable and complaint departments.[108]

Because of its secrecy, power, and fabulous wealth, a great mystique has grown up about organized crime. Its legendary leaders—Al Capone, Meyer Lansky, Lucky Luciano—have been the subjects of books and films. The famous *Godfather* films popularized and humanized organized crime figures; the media often glamorize organized crime figures.[109] Most citizens believe that organized criminals are capable of taking over legitimate business enterprises if given the opportunity. Almost everyone is familiar with such terms as *mob, underworld, Mafia, wise guys, syndicate,* or *La Cosa Nostra,* all of which refer to organized crime. Although most of us have neither met nor seen members of organized crime families, we feel sure that they exist, and we fear them. This section briefly defines organized crime, reviews its activities, and discusses its economic effect and control.

Characteristics of Organized Crime

A precise description of the characteristics of organized crime is difficult to formulate, but here are some of its general traits:[110]

- Organized crime is a conspiratorial activity, involving the coordination of numerous persons in the planning and execution of illegal acts or in the pursuit of a legitimate objective by unlawful means (for example, threatening a legitimate business to get a stake in it). Organized crime involves continuous commitment by primary members, although individuals with specialized skills may be brought in as needed. Organized crime is usually structured along hierarchical lines—a chieftain supported by close advisers, several ranks of subordinates, and so on.

- Organized crime has economic gain as its primary goal, although power and status may also be motivating factors. Economic gain is achieved through maintenance of a near-monopoly on illegal goods and services, including drugs, gambling, pornography, and prostitution.

- Organized crime activities are not limited to providing illicit services. They include such sophisticated activities as laundering illegal money through legitimate businesses, land fraud, and computer crimes.

- Organized crime employs predatory tactics, such as intimidation, violence, and corruption. It appeals to greed to accomplish its objectives and preserve its gains.

- By experience, custom, and practice, organized crime's conspiratorial groups are usually very quick and effective in controlling and disciplining their members, associates, and victims. The individuals involved know that any deviation from the rules of the organization will evoke a prompt response from the other participants. This response may range from a reduction in rank and responsibility to a death sentence.

- Organized crime is not synonymous with the Mafia—the most experienced, most diversified, and possibly best-disciplined of these groups. The Mafia is actually a common stereotype of organized crime. Although several families in the organization called the Mafia are important components of organized crime activities, they do not hold a monopoly on underworld activities.

- Organized crime does not include terrorists dedicated to political change. Although violent acts are a major tactic of organized crime, the use of violence does not mean that a group is part of a confederacy of organized criminals.

Activities of Organized Crime

What are the main activities of organized crime? The traditional sources of income are providing illicit materials and using force to enter into and maximize profits in legitimate businesses.[111] Annual gross income from criminal activity is at least $50 billion, more than 1 percent of the gross national product; some estimates put gross earnings as high as $90 billion, outranking most major industries in the United States.[112]

Most organized crime income comes from narcotics distribution (more than $30 billion annually), loan-sharking (lending money at illegal rates, $7 billion), and prostitution ($3 billion). However, additional billions come from gambling, theft rings, and other illegal enterprises. For example, the Attorney General's Commission on Pornography has concluded that organized crime figures exert substantial influence and control over the pornography industry.[113]

Organized criminals have infiltrated labor unions, taking control of their pension funds and dues. Alan Block has described mob control of the New York waterfront and its influence on the use of union funds to buy insurance, health care, and so on from mob-controlled companies.[114] Hijacking of shipments and cargo theft are other sources of income. One study found that the annual losses from theft of air cargo amount to $400 million; rail cargo, $600 million; trucking, $1.2 billion; and maritime shipments, $300 million.[115] Underworld figures fence high-value items and maintain international sales territories. In recent years, they have branched into computer crime and other white-collar activities. Organized crime figures have also kept up with the information age by using computers and the Internet to sell illegal material such as pornography.

The Concept of Organized Crime

Mafia

A criminal society that originated in Sicily, Italy, and is believed to control racketeering in the United States.

alien conspiracy theory

The view that organized crime in the United States is controlled by the Mafia, centrally coordinated by a national committee that settles disputes, dictates policy, and assigns territory.

La Cosa Nostra

A national syndicate of 25 or so Italian-dominated crime families who control crime in distinct geographic areas.

One view of organized crime is that it is a direct offshoot of a criminal society—the **Mafia**—that first originated in Sicily, Italy, and now controls racketeering in major U.S. cities. A major premise of this **alien conspiracy theory** is that the Mafia is centrally coordinated by a national committee that settles disputes, dictates policy, and assigns territory.[116] According to the alien conspiracy theory, organized crime is made up of a national syndicate of 25 or so Italian-dominated crime families that call themselves **La Cosa Nostra**. The major families have a total membership of about 1,700 "made men," who have been inducted into organized crime families, and another 17,000 "associates," who are criminally involved with syndicate members.[117] The families control crime in distinct geographic areas. New York City, the most important organized crime area, alone contains five families—the Gambino, Columbo, Lucchese, Bonnano, and Genovese families—named after their founding "godfathers"; in contrast, Chicago contains a single mob organization called the "outfit," which also influences racketeering in such cities as Milwaukee, Kansas City, and Phoenix (see Figure 12.1).

Not all criminologists believe in this narrow concept of organized crime, and many view the alien conspiracy theory as a figment of the media's imagination.[118] Their view depicts organized crime as a group of ethnically diverse gangs or groups who compete for profit in the sale of illegal goods and services or who use force and violence to extort money from legitimate enterprises. These groups are not bound by a central national organization but act independently

Figure 12.1

Traditional Organization of the Mafia "Family"

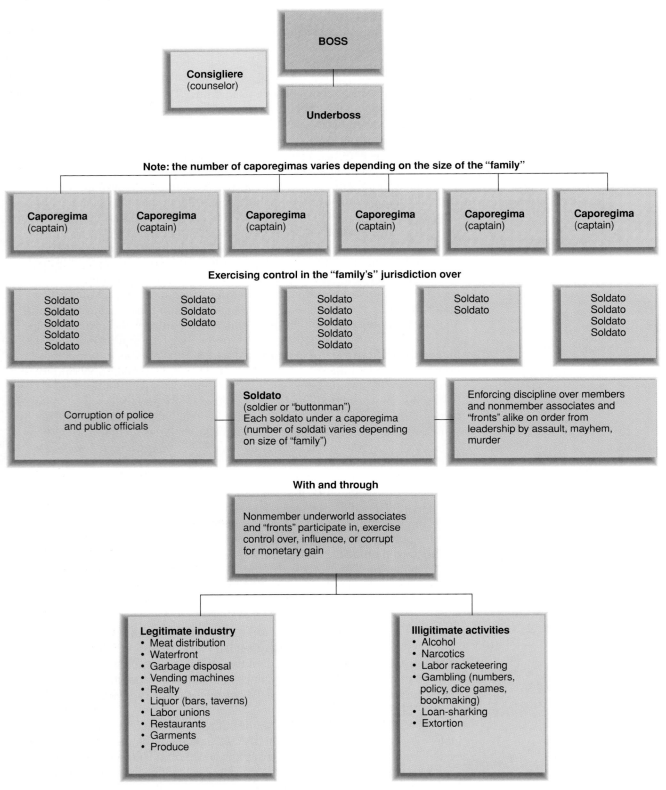

SOURCE: U.S. Senate, Permanent Subcommittee on Investigations, Committee on Government Affairs, *Hearings on Organized Crime and Use of Violence*, 96th Cong., 2d Sess., April 1980, p. 117.

AP/Wide World Photos

John "Junior" Gotti (left), son of imprisoned Mafia boss John Gotti, Sr., moves through a crowd after drawing a 77-month sentence for bribery, extortion, gambling, and fraud. Gotti's fall illustrates the pressure being put on the "mob" by state and federal law enforcers.

on their own turf. For example, Philip Jenkins and Gary Potter studied organized crime in Philadelphia and found little evidence that this supposed "Mafia stronghold" was controlled by an Italian-dominated crime family.[119]

Sociologist Alan Block finds that independent crime organizations can be characterized as either "enterprise syndicates" or "power syndicates."[120] The former are involved in providing services; they include madams, drug distributors, bookmakers, and and the like—"workers in the world of illegal enterprise." In contrast, power syndicates perform no set task except to extort or terrorize. Their leaders can operate against legitimate business or against fellow criminals who operate enterprise syndicates. Through coercion, buyouts, and other means, power syndicates graft themselves onto enterprise systems, legitimate businesses, and trade unions.

Even such devoted alien conspiracy advocates as the U.S. Justice Department now view organized crime as a loose confederation of ethnic and regional crime groups, bound together by a commonality of economic and political objectives.[121] Some of these groups are located in fixed geographical areas. For example, the so-called Dixie Mafia operates in the South. Chicano crime families are found in areas with significant Hispanic populations, such as California and Arizona. White-ethnic crime organizations are found across the nation. Some Italian and Cuban groups operate internationally. Some have preserved their past identity, whereas others are constantly changing organizations.

One important recent change in organized crime is the interweaving of ethnic groups into the traditional structure. African American, Hispanic, and Asian racketeers now compete with the more traditional groups, overseeing the distribution of drugs, prostitution, and gambling in a symbiotic relationship with old-line racketeers. Since 1970, Russian and Eastern European groups have been operating on U.S. soil. As many as 2,500 Russian immigrants are believed to be involved in criminal activity, primarily in Russian enclaves in New York City. Beyond extortion from immigrants, Russian organized crime groups have cooperated with Mafia families in narcotics trafficking, fencing stolen property, money laundering, and other traditional organized crime schemes.[122]

As law enforcement pressure has been put on traditional organized crime figures, these newer groups have filled the vacuum. For example, the Hell's

Find It on INFOTRAC
College Edition

Some experts believe that Russian crime families, thanks to their control of gasoline terminals and distributorships in the New York metropolitan area, evade as much as $5 billion a year in state and federal taxes. Some of that money then goes to pay off their allies, the Italian Mafia. To find out more, use "Russian organized crime" as a subject in InfoTrac College Edition. Also read

Sherry Ricchiardi, "The Best Investigative Reporter You've Never Heard Of," *American Journalism Review,* January 2000 v22 i1 p44

Angels motorcycle club is now one of the leading distributors of narcotics in the United States. Similarly, Chinese criminal gangs have taken over the dominant role in New York City's heroin market from the traditional Italian-run syndicates.[123]

Have these newly emerging groups achieved the same level of control as traditional crime families? Some experts argue that minority gangs will have a tough time developing the network of organized corruption that involves working with government officials and unions, which traditional crime families have enjoyed.[124]

In sum, most experts now agree that it is simplistic to view organized crime in the United States as a national syndicate that controls all illegitimate rackets in an orderly fashion. This view seems to ignore the variety of gangs and groups, their membership, and their relationship to the outside world.[125] Mafia-type groups may play a major role in organized crime, but they are by no means the only ones that can be considered organized criminals.[126]

Controlling Organized Crime

Racketeer Influenced and Corrupt Organization Act (RICO)

Part of the federal Organized Crime Control Act of 1970, which defines racketeering and provides penalties including prison, fine, and forfeiture of business assets.

Federal and state governments actually did little to combat organized crime until fairly recently. One of the first measures aimed directly at organized crime was the Interstate and Foreign Travel or Transportation in Aid of Racketeering Enterprises Act (Travel Act).[127] The Travel Act prohibits travel in interstate commerce or use of interstate facilities with the intent to promote, manage, establish, carry on, or facilitate an unlawful activity; it also prohibits the actual or attempted engagement in these activities. In 1970, Congress passed the Organized Crime Control Act. Title IX of that act, probably its most effective measure, has been called the **Racketeer Influenced and Corrupt Organization Act (RICO)**.[128]

RICO did not create new categories of crimes but rather new categories of offenses in racketeering activity, which it defined as involvement in two or more acts prohibited by 24 existing federal and 8 state statutes. The offenses listed in RICO include both state-defined crimes, such as murder, kidnapping, gambling, arson, robbery, bribery, extortion, and narcotics violations, and federally defined crimes, such as bribery, counterfeiting, transmission of gambling information, prostitution, and mail fraud. RICO is designed to limit patterns of organized criminal activity by prohibiting involvement in acts intended to

- Derive income from racketeering or the unlawful collection of debts and use or invest such income.
- Acquire through racketeering an interest in or control over any enterprise engaged in interstate or foreign commerce.
- Conduct business through a pattern of racketeering.
- Conspire to use racketeering as a means of making income, collecting loans, or conducting business.

An individual convicted under RICO is subject to 20 years in prison and a $25,000 fine. Additionally, the accused must forfeit to the U.S. government any interest in a business in violation of RICO. These penalties are much more potent than simple conviction and imprisonment.

To enforce these policy initiatives, the federal government created the Strike Force Program. This program, operating in 18 cities, brings together various state and federal law enforcement officers and prosecutors to work as a team against racketeering. Several states, including New York, Illinois, New Jersey, and New Mexico, have created their own special investigative teams devoted to organized criminal activity.

The Future of Organized Crime

Indications exist that the traditional organized crime syndicates are in decline. Law enforcement officials in Philadelphia, New Jersey, New England, New Orleans, Kansas City, Detroit, and Milwaukee all report that years of federal and state interventions have severely eroded the Mafia organizations in their areas.[129]

What has caused this alleged erosion of Mafia power? First, a number of the reigning family heads are quite old, in their 70s and 80s, prompting some law enforcement officials to dub them "the Geritol gang."[130] A younger generation of mob leaders is stepping in to take control of the families, and they seem to lack the skill and leadership of the older bosses. In addition, active government enforcement policies have halved what the estimated made membership was 20 years ago; a number of the highest-ranking leaders have been imprisoned. Additional pressure comes from newly emerging ethnic gangs that want to muscle in on traditional syndicate activities, such as drug sales and gambling. For example, Chinese Triad gangs have been active in New York and California in the drug trade, loan-sharking, and labor racketeering. Other ethnic crime groups include black and Colombian drug cartels and the Sicilian Mafia, which operates independently of U.S. groups.

The Mafia has also been hurt by changing values in U.S. society. White-ethnic inner-city neighborhoods, which were the locus of Mafia power, have been shrinking as families move to the suburbs. Organized crime groups have consequently lost their political and social base of operations. In addition, the code of silence that protected Mafia leaders is now broken regularly by younger members who turn informer rather than face prison terms. It is also possible that their very success has hurt organized crime families: Younger members are better educated than their forebears and better equipped to seek their fortunes through legitimate enterprise.[131]

Summary

White-collar and organized criminals are similar in that both use ongoing business enterprises to make personal profits.

There are various types of white-collar crime. Stings and swindles involve the use of deception to bilk people out of their money. Chiseling customers, businesses, or the government is a second common type of white-collar crime. Surprisingly, many professionals engage in chiseling offenses. Other white-collar criminals use their positions in business and the marketplace to commit economic crimes. Their crimes include exploitation of position in a company or the government to secure illegal payments; influence peddling and bribery; embezzlement and employee pilferage and fraud; and client fraud. Further, corporate officers sometimes violate the law to improve the position and profitability of their businesses. Their crimes include price-fixing, false advertising, and environmental offenses.

So far, little has been done to combat white-collar crime. Most offenders do not view themselves as criminals and therefore do not seem to be deterred by criminal statutes. Although thousands of white-collar criminals are prosecuted each year, their numbers are insignificant compared with the magnitude of the problem. The government has used various law enforcement strategies to combat white-collar crime. Some involve compliance strategies, which create economic incentives to obey the law. Others involve deterrence, which uses punishment to frighten potential offenders.

The demand for illegal goods and services has produced a symbiotic relationship between the public and an organized criminal network. Organized crime supplies drugs, gambling, prostitutes, and pornography to the public. It has traditionally been immune from prosecution because of public apathy and because of its own strong political connections. Organized criminals used to be white ethnics—Jews, Italians, and Irish—but today African Americans, Hispanics, and other groups have become included in organized crime activities. The old-line "families" are now more likely to use their criminal wealth and power to buy into legitimate businesses.

There is debate over the control of organized crime. Some experts believe a national crime cartel controls all activities. Others view organized crime as a group of disorganized, competing gangs dedicated to extortion or to providing illegal goods and services. Efforts to control organized crime have been stepped up. The federal government has used antiracketeering statutes to arrest syndicate leaders. But as long as huge profits can be made, illegal enterprises should continue to flourish.

For additional chapter links, discussions, and quizzes, see the book-specific Web site at http://www.wadsworth.com/product/0534519423s.

Thinking Like a Criminologist

People who commit computer crime are found in every segment of society. They range in age from 10 to 60, and their skill levels run from novice to professional. They are otherwise average people, not supercriminals possessing unique abilities and talents. Any person of any age with even a little skill is a potential computer criminal.

Most studies indicate that employees represent the greatest threat to computers. Almost 90 percent of computer crimes against businesses are inside jobs. Ironically, as advances continue in remote data processing, the threat from external sources will probably increase.

With the networking of systems and the adoption of more user-friendly software, the sociological profile of the computer offender may change. For example, computer criminals may soon be members of organized crime syndicates. They will use computer systems to monitor law enforcement activities. To become a "made man" in the twenty-first-century organized crime family, the recruit will have to develop knowledge of the equipment used for audio surveillance of law enforcement communications: computers with sound card or microphone, modems, and software programs for the remote operation of the systems.

Which theories of criminal behavior best explain the actions of computer criminals, and which theories fail to account for computer crime?

Key Terms

white-collar crime	pilferage	corporate culture view
organized crime	bank fraud	self-control view
enterprise	passive neglect	compliance strategies
corporate crime	affirmative tax evasion	deterrence strategies
chiseling	organizational crime	Mafia
churning	restraint of trade	alien conspiracy theory
front running	group boycott	La Cosa Nostra
bucketing	price-fixing	Racketeer Influenced and Corrupt Organization Act (RICO)
insider trading	virus	

Discussion Questions

1. How would you punish corporate executives whose product killed people, if they themselves had no knowledge that the product was potentially lethal? What if they did know?

2. Is organized crime inevitable as long as immigrant groups seek to become part of the "American Dream"?

3. Do the media glamorize organized crime? Do they paint an inaccurate picture of noble crime lords fighting to protect their families?

© Todd Yates/Black Star

13 Public Order Crimes

In the fall of 1999, New York City Mayor Rudolph W. Giuliani took on Arnold Lehman, director of the Brooklyn Museum of Art, over *Sensations,* a controversial art exhibition he had scheduled.[1] The show contained the work of avant-garde British artists such as Damien Hirst, whose art depicts a pair of sliced-up cows suspended in a tank of formaldehyde. While the exhibit contained many controversial works, the focus was on a dung-stained portrait of the Virgin Mary, surrounded by cutouts of female sex organs, by Chris Ofili, a British artist of Nigerian descent. British art is "sick stuff," claimed Giuliani, while the museum administrators claimed they were showing works with "diverse artistic visions." In an effort to force removal of the work he found offensive, the mayor threatened to withhold the museum's funding and evict it from the city-owned building. Museum supporters countercharged that the mayor was playing politics. While the case was in federal court, the prestigious *New York Times* ran an article suggesting that the show's backers had a heavy financial interest in the paintings and may have been motivated by profit and not art. Then, on November 1, 1999, a federal judge ruled that Mayor Giuliani had violated the First Amendment when he cut city financing and began eviction proceedings against the museum.

The flap over the *Sensations* exhibit became a national sensation. Should politicians such as Mayor Giuliani have the right to censor public art exhibitions they find offensive or immoral? After all, many of the great works of Western art depict nude

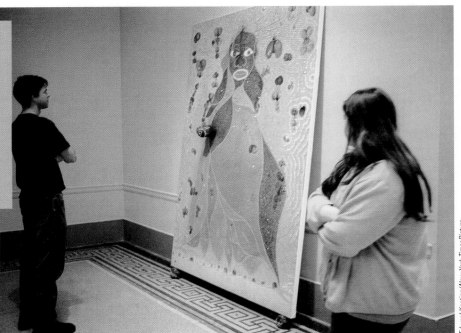

Viewers ponder *The Holy Virgin Mary,* a painting by Chris Ofili, a British artist of Nigerian descent, at the Brooklyn Museum in New York City. Declaring that British art is "sick stuff," Mayor Rudolph Giuliani threatened to withhold the museum's funding and evict it from its city-owned building. Should a politician's moral values dictate what can be shown at a metropolitan museum? Who is to say what is offensive and what is "art"?

Edward Keating/*New York Times* Picture

males and females, some quite young. Should a politician be able to ban Michelangelo's *David*, one of the world's most famous sculptures, because he or she considers the nude statue "pornographic"? And does the fact that a show's backers stand to profit from the notoriety make it fair game for political censors?

public order crime

Behavior that is outlawed because it threatens the general well-being of society and challenges its accepted moral principles.

Societies have long banned or limited behaviors that are believed to run contrary to social norms, customs, and values. These behaviors are often referred to as **public order crimes** or victimless crimes, although the latter term can be misleading.[2] Public order crimes involve acts that interfere with the operations of society and the ability of people to function efficiently. Put another way, whereas such common-law crimes as rape or robbery are considered inherently wrong and damaging, other behaviors are outlawed because they conflict with social policy, prevailing moral rules, and current public opinion.

Statutes designed to uphold public order usually prohibit the manufacture and distribution of morally questionable goods and services such as erotic material, commercial sex, and mood-altering drugs. They may also ban acts that a few people holding political power consider morally tinged, such as homosexual contact. Statutes like these are controversial in part because millions of otherwise law-abiding citizens often engage in these outlawed activities and consequently become criminal. These statutes are also controversial because they selectively prohibit desired goods, services, and behaviors; in other words, they outlaw sin and vice.

This chapter covers these public order crimes. It first briefly discusses the relationship between law and morality. Next the chapter addresses public order crimes of a sexual nature: pornography, prostitution, deviant sex, and homosexual acts. The chapter concludes by focusing on the abuse of drugs and alcohol.

Law and Morality

Legislation of moral issues has continually frustrated lawmakers. There is little debate that the purpose of criminal law is to protect society and reduce social harm. When a store is robbed or a child assaulted, it is relatively easy to see and condemn the harm done the victim. It is, however, more difficult to sympathize with or even identify the victims of immoral acts, such as pornography or prostitution, where the parties involved may be willing participants. If there is no victim, can there be a crime? Should acts be made illegal merely because they violate prevailing moral standards? If so, who defines morality?

victimless crime

Public order crime that violates the moral order but has no specific victim other than society as a whole.

To answer these questions, we might first consider whether there is actually a victim in so-called **victimless crimes**. Some participants may have been coerced into their acts; if so, then they are victims. Opponents of pornography, such as Andrea Dworkin, charge that women involved in adult films, far from being highly paid stars, are "dehumanized—turned into objects and commodities."[3] Research on prostitution shows that many young runaways and abandoned children are coerced into a life on the streets, where they are cruelly treated and held as virtual captives.[4]

Some scholars argue that pornography, prostitution, and drug use erode the moral fabric of society and therefore should be prohibited and punished. They are crimes, according to the great legal scholar Morris Cohen, because "it is one of the functions of the criminal law to give expression to the collective feeling of revulsion toward certain acts, even when they are not very dangerous."[5]

According to this view, so-called victimless crimes are prohibited because one of the functions of criminal law is to express a shared sense of public morality.[6] However, basing criminal definitions on moral beliefs is often an impossible task. Who defines morality? Are we not punishing differences rather than social harm? As U.S. Supreme Court Justice William O. Douglas so succinctly put it, "What may be trash to me may be prized by others."[7] Would not any attempt to control or limit "objectionable" material eventually lead to the suppression of free speech and political dissent? Is this not a veiled form of censorship? Not so, according to social commentator Irving Kristol:

> If we start censoring pornography and obscenity, shall we not inevitably end up censoring political opinion? A lot of people seem to think this would be the case—which only shows the power of doctrinaire thinking over reality. We had censorship of pornography and obscenity for 150 years, until almost yesterday, and I am not aware that freedom of opinion in this country was in any way diminished as a consequence of this fact.[8]

Criminal or Immoral?

Acts that most of us deem highly immoral are not criminal. There is no law against lust, gluttony, avarice, spite, or envy, although they are considered some of the "seven deadly sins." Nor is it a crime in most jurisdictions to ignore the pleas of a drowning person, even though such callous behavior is surely immoral.

Some acts that seem both well-intentioned and moral are nonetheless considered criminal. It is a crime (euthanasia) to kill a loved one who is suffering from an incurable disease to spare him or her further pain. Stealing a rich person's money to feed a poor family is considered larceny. Marrying more than one woman is considered a crime (bigamy), even though multiple marriage may conform to religious beliefs.[9] As legal experts Wayne LaFave and Austin Scott, Jr., state, "A good motive will not normally prevent what is otherwise criminal from being a crime."[10]

Generally, immoral acts can be distinguished from crimes on the basis of the social harm they cause: Acts that harm the public are usually outlawed. Yet this perspective does not always hold sway. Some acts that cause enormous amounts of social harm are perfectly legal. All of us are aware of the illness and death associated with the consumption of tobacco and alcohol, but they remain legal to produce and sell. Manufacturers continue to sell sports cars and motorcycles that can accelerate to more than 100 mph, although the legal speed limit is usually 65. More people die each year from alcohol-, tobacco-, and auto-related deaths than from all illegal drugs combined. Should drugs be legalized and fast cars outlawed?

> ### C O N N E C T I O N S
> Moral entrepreneurs are likely to use the interactionist definition of crime discussed in Chapter 1. Acts are illegal because they violate the moral standards of those in power and/or those who try to shape public opinion.

Moral Crusaders

moral entrepreneur

A person who creates moral rules, which thus reflect the values of those in power rather than any objective, universal standards of right and wrong.

Public order crimes often trace their origin to moral crusaders who seek to shape the law toward their own way of thinking; Howard Becker calls them **moral entrepreneurs**. These rule creators, argues Becker, operate with an absolute certainty that their way is right and that any means are justified to get their way; "the crusader is fervent and righteous, often self-righteous."[11] Today's moral crusaders take on such issues as prayer in school, the right to legal abortions, and the distribution of sexually explicit books and magazines.

Moral crusades are often directed against people clearly defined as evil by one segment of the population, even though they may be admired by others. For example, antismut campaigns may attempt to ban the books of a popular author from the school library or prevent a controversial figure from speaking at the local college. One way for moral crusaders to accomplish their goal is to prove to all who will listen that some unseen or hidden trait makes their target truly evil and unworthy of a public audience—for example, the Bible condemns their behavior. This polarization of good and evil creates a climate

Moral crusaders seek to rid society of people whose behavior falls outside their personal standards of right and wrong. Sometimes their vocation gets them in trouble. Here, Parkrose (Oregon) School Board member Jennifer Young, accused of pepper-spraying a teenager she mistook for a prostitute, leaves court in Portland after assault charges against her were dropped. Young had been crusading against prostitution in her neighborhood for the past four years, earning her a reputation as a vigilante.

AP/Wide World Photos

✔ Checkpoints

✔ Societies can ban behaviors that lawmakers consider offensive. Critics question whether this amounts to censorship.

✔ The line between behaviors that are merely immoral and those that are criminal is often blurred.

✔ People who seek to control or criminalize deviant behaviors are called moral entrepreneurs.

where those categorized as "good" are deified while the "bad" are demonized and become objects suitable for control.

The public order crimes discussed in this chapter are divided into two broad areas. The first relates to what conventional society considers deviant sexual practices: homosexual acts, paraphilias, prostitution, and pornography. The second area concerns the use of substances that have been outlawed or controlled because of the alleged harm they cause: drugs and alcohol.

✔ Checkpoints

Homosexuality

It may be surprising that a section on homosexuality is still included in a criminology text, but even as a new millennium arrives, homosexuals not only face archaic legal restrictions but are targeted for so many violent hate crimes that a specific term, **gay bashing**, has been coined to describe violent acts directed at people because of their sexual orientation.

Homosexuality (the word derives from the Greek *homos,* meaning "same") refers to erotic interest in members of one's own sex, one "who is motivated in adult life by a definite preferential erotic attraction to members of the same sex and who usually (but not necessarily) engages in overt sexual relations with them."[12]

gay bashing

Violent hate crimes directed toward people because of their sexual orientation.

Attitudes Toward Homosexuality

Homosexual behavior has existed in most societies. Records of it can be found in prehistoric art and hieroglyphics.[13] Nonetheless, throughout much of Western history, homosexuals have been subject to discrimination, sanction, and violence. The Bible implies that God destroyed the ancient cities of Sodom and Gomorrah because of their residents' deviant behavior, presumably homosexuality; Sodom is the source of the term **sodomy** (deviant intercourse). The Bible expressly forbids homosexuality—in Leviticus in the Old Testament; Paul's Epistles, Romans, and Corinthians in the New Testament—and this prohibition has been the basis for repressing homosexual behavior.[14] Gays were brutalized and

homosexuality

Erotic interest in members of one's own sex.

sodomy

Illegal forms of sexual intercourse, as defined by statute.

homophobia

Extremely negative overreaction to homosexuals.

CONNECTIONS

As you may recall from Chapter 10, gay men and women are still subject to thousands of incidents of violence and other hate crimes each year.

killed by the ancient Hebrews, a practice continued by the Christians who ruled Western Europe. Laws providing the death penalty for homosexuals existed until 1791 in France, until 1861 in England, and until 1889 in Scotland. Until the Revolution, some American colonies punished homosexuality with death. In Hitler's Germany, 50,000 homosexuals were put in concentration camps; up to 400,000 more from occupied countries were killed. In 1996, conservative Christian groups in the United States began a national campaign aimed at counteracting legislative victories won by gay rights groups in the area of discrimination and civil rights.[15] Some groups have taken out ads in local newspapers showing "former homosexuals" who "overcame" their sexual orientation through prayer and the help of Christian "ex-gay ministries."

Today, many reasons are given for the extremely negative overreaction to homosexuals referred to as **homophobia**.[16] Some ultrareligious people believe that the Bible condemns same-sex relations and that this behavior is therefore a sin. Others are ignorant about the lifestyle of gays and fear that homosexuality is a contagious disease or that homosexuals will seduce their children.[17] Research shows that some males who express homophobic attitudes are also likely to become aroused by erotic images of homosexual behavior. Homophobia, then, may be associated with homosexual arousal that the homophobe is either unaware of or denies.[18]

There are constant reminders of antigay sentiments. In 2000, for example, the United States Supreme Court upheld the right of the Boy Scouts to reject gay scout masters; in 1998, Maine voters repealed a law protecting gays from discrimination; also in 1998, the Presbyterian Church in Atlanta banned sexually active gays from its pulpits.[19]

Homosexuality and the Law

Homosexuality, considered a legal and moral crime throughout most of Western history, is no longer a crime in the United States. In the case of *Robinson* v. *California,* the U.S. Supreme Court determined that people could not be criminally prosecuted because of their status (such as drug addict or homosexual).[20] Despite this protection, most states and the federal government criminalize the lifestyle and activities of homosexuals. For example, aside from Vermont (which has civil unions), no state or locality allows any form of same-sex marriage, and homosexuals cannot obtain a marriage license to legitimize their relationship. In 1996, Congress passed the Defense of Marriage Act, which declared that states are not obligated to recognize same-sex marriages performed in other states.[21]

Despite long-standing biases, it is illegal to deprive gay men and women of due process of law. In a 1996 Colorado case, *Romer* v. *Evans,* the U.S. Supreme Court said that gay people cannot be stripped of legal protection and made "strangers to the law."[22] Nonetheless, the Supreme Court let stand a Cincinnati city charter amendment barring protective legislation for gay people; this amendment prevented homosexuals from obtaining special civil protections such as affirmative action.[23]

Oral and anal sex and all other forms of intercourse that are not heterosexual and genital are banned in about half the U.S. states under statutes prohibiting sodomy, deviant sexuality, or buggery. Maximum penalties range from three years to life in prison, with 10 years being the most common sentence.[24] In 1986, the Supreme Court, in *Bowers* v. *Hardwick,* upheld a Georgia statute making it a crime to engage in consensual sodomy, even within one's own home.[25] The Court disregarded Bowers's claim that homosexuals have a fundamental right to engage in sexual activity and that consensual, voluntary sex between adults in the home is a private matter that should not be controlled by law. If all sex within the home were a private matter, Justice Byron White argued for the majority, then such crimes as incest and adultery could not be prosecuted.[26]

Prestigious legal bodies such as the American Law Institute (ALI) have called for the abolition of statutes prohibiting homosexual sex unless force or coercion is used.[27] About 25 states, including Illinois, Connecticut, and Nebraska, have adopted the ALI's Model Penal Code policy of legalizing any private, consensual sexual behavior between adults; however, the remaining states still treat sodomy as a felony.[28] Consider the Massachusetts statute:

> *Chapter 272: Section 34. Crime against nature.*
> Whoever commits the abominable and detestable crime against nature, either with mankind or with a beast, shall be punished by imprisonment in the state prison for not more than twenty years.

The U.S. military bans openly gay people from serving but has compromised with a "don't ask, don't tell" policy. The military does not ask about sexual orientation, and gay people can serve as long as their sexuality remains secret. In 1996, the U.S. Supreme Court tacitly approved this policy by declining to hear a case brought by Navy Lieutenant Paul Thomasson, who was discharged in 1994 for openly declaring himself homosexual.[29] In January 1998, a federal judge barred the U.S. Navy from dismissing Chief Petty Officer Timothy McVeigh, who had posted sexually oriented material on the Internet. The judge ruled that the Navy had violated McVeigh's privacy when it asked America Online to divulge his identity; in so doing, the Navy violated the spirit of the "don't ask, don't tell" policy.[30] Gays have also lost custody of their children because of their sexual orientation, although more courts are now refusing to consider a gay lifestyle alone as evidence of parental unfitness.[31]

Is the Tide Turning?

Although the unenlightened may still hold negative attitudes toward gays, there seems to be a long overdue increase in social tolerance. A recent survey published by the National Gay and Lesbian Task Force shows that strong majorities of Americans now support gays in the military and equality in employment, housing, inheritance rights, and social security benefits for same-sex couples.[32] Changing public attitudes are reflected in legal change. In 1998, more than 20 years after one of the country's first gay rights ordinances was repealed in Miami, Florida, the Miami–Dade County commission voted again to ban discrimination based on sexual orientation, a position adopted in more than 136 other cities nationwide.[33] Ironically, in November 1998, by a vote of 6–1, the Georgia Supreme Court struck down the state's 182-year-old sodomy law that was the basis for the *Bowers* v. *Hardwick* decision. The court ruled that the law violated the right to privacy guaranteed by the state's constitution. "We cannot think of any other activity that reasonable persons would rank as more private and more deserving of protection from governmental interference than consensual, private, adult sexual activity," wrote Chief Justice Robert Benham in his majority opinion.[34]

Find It on INFOTRAC
College Edition

Like other crimes, assaults on homosexuals are adjudicated in the criminal courts. How have victims fared when they seek damages in civil courts? To find out, go to InfoTrac College Edition and read

Lisa Gelhaus, "Gay-Bashing Victims Overcome Prejudice to Win Civil Settlements," *Trial,* February 1999 v35 i2 p14(1)

Paraphilias

In October 1996, more than 250,000 Belgians took to the streets to protest what they considered the government's inept handling of a case involving the deaths of four children allegedly killed by a pedophile ring led by convicted rapist Marc Dutroix. Two of the victims (8-year-old girls) had been imprisoned and molested for months in Dutroix's home. They starved to death when he was arrested and sent to jail on an unrelated charge. Other children had been kidnapped, raped, tortured, and allegedly sold into sexual slavery by the ring that many believe enjoyed high-level protection from prosecution.[35]

Demonstrators in Belgium protest the killing of young girls by pedophile Marc Dutroix. Belgian police had failed to discover two young girls held captive by Dutroix in his basement, even though they had him under arrest. The girls starved to death in a crime that shocked an entire nation.

paraphilia

Bizarre or abnormal sexual practices that may involve nonhuman objects, humiliation, or children.

The case of pedophile Marc Dutroix is an extreme example of sexual abnormality referred to as **paraphilia**, from the Greek *para*, "to the side of," and *philos*, "loving." Paraphilias are bizarre or abnormal sexual practices involving recurrent sexual urges focused on (1) nonhuman objects (such as underwear, shoes, or leather), (2) humiliation or the experience of receiving or giving pain (as in sadomasochism or bondage), or (3) children or others who cannot grant consent.[36] Paraphilias have existed and been recorded for thousands of years. Buddhist texts more than 2000 years old contain references to sexually deviant behaviors among monastic communities, including sexual activity with animals and sexual interest in corpses. Richard von Krafft-Ebing's *Psychopathia Sexualis*, first published in 1887, was the first text to discuss such paraphilias as sadism, bestiality, and incest.[37]

Some paraphilias, such as wearing clothes normally worn by the opposite sex (transvestite fetishism), can be engaged in by adults in the privacy of their homes and do not involve a third party; these are usually outside the law's reach. Others, however, risk social harm and are subject to criminal penalties. This group of outlawed sexual behavior includes

- *Frotteurism*—rubbing against or touching a nonconsenting person in a crowd, elevator, or other public area.

- *Voyeurism*—obtaining sexual pleasure from spying on a stranger while he or she disrobes or engages in sexual behavior with another.

- *Exhibitionism*—deriving sexual pleasure from exposing the genitals to surprise or shock a stranger.

- *Sadomasochism*—deriving pleasure from receiving pain or inflicting pain on another.

- *Pedophilia*—attaining sexual pleasure through sexual activity with prepubescent children. Research indicates that more than 20 percent of males report sexual attraction to at least one child, although the rate of sexual fantasies and the potential for sexual contacts are much lower.[38]

In their extreme, paraphilias can lead to sexual assaults in which the victims suffer severe harm.

Prostitution

prostitution

The granting of nonmarital sexual access for remuneration.

Prostitution has been known for thousands of years. The term derives from the Latin *prostituere,* which means "to cause to stand in front of." The prostitute is viewed as publicly offering his or her body for sale. The earliest record of prostitution appears in ancient Mesopotamia, where priests engaged in sex to promote fertility in the community. All women were required to do temple duty, and passing strangers were expected to make donations to the temple after enjoying its services.[39]

Modern commercial sex appears to have its roots in ancient Greece, where Solon established licensed brothels in 500 B.C. The earnings of Greek prostitutes helped pay for the temple of Aphrodite. Famous men openly went to prostitutes to enjoy intellectual, aesthetic, and sexual stimulation; prostitutes, however, were prevented from marrying.[40]

Today **prostitution** can be defined as the granting of nonmarital sexual access, established by mutual agreement of the prostitutes, their clients, and their employers, for remuneration. This definition is sexually neutral because prostitutes can be straight or gay and male or female. A recent analysis has amplified the definition of prostitution by describing the conditions usually present in a commercial sexual transaction:

- *Activity that has sexual significance for the customer.* This includes the entire range of sexual behavior, from sexual intercourse to exhibitionism, sadomasochism, oral sex, and so on.

- *Economic transaction.* Something of economic value, not necessarily money, is exchanged for the activity.

- *Emotional indifference.* The sexual exchange is simply for economic consideration. Although the participants may know one another, their interaction has nothing to do with affection for one another.[41]

When interviewing a prostitute's clients, sociologist Monica Prasad found that while their decision to employ a prostitute was shaped by sexuality, it was also influenced by pressure from friends to try something different and exciting, the wish for a sexual exchange free from obligations, and curiosity about the world of prostitution. Prasad found that most customers who became "regulars" began to view prostitution as a service occupation not different from other service occupations.[42]

Incidence of Prostitution

It is difficult to assess the number of prostitutes operating in the United States. Fifty years ago, about two-thirds of non-college-educated men and one-quarter of college-educated men had visited a prostitute.[43] It is likely that the number of men who hire prostitutes has declined sharply since then. The number of arrests for prostitution has remained stable for the past two decades, while the population has increased.[44]

How can these changes be accounted for? Changing sexual mores, brought about by the so-called sexual revolution, have liberalized sexuality. Men are less likely to use prostitutes because legitimate alternatives for sexuality are more open to them. In addition, the prevalence of sexually transmitted diseases has caused many men to avoid visiting prostitutes for fear of irreversible health hazards.[45]

Despite such changes, the Uniform Crime Reports (UCR) indicate that about 90,000 prostitution arrests are made annually, with the gender ratio being about 3 males:4 females.[46] More alarming is the fact that about 900 arrests are of minors under 18. In 1999, 126 recorded arrests were of children age 15 and under; 108 were children under 14, including 18 who were under 10 years of age. Arguments that criminal law should not interfere with sexual transactions because no one is harmed are undermined by these disturbing statistics.

Types of Prostitutes Several different types of prostitutes operate in the United States.

Streetwalkers Prostitutes who work the streets in plain sight of police, citizens, and customers are referred to as hustlers, hookers, or streetwalkers. Although glamorized by the Julia Roberts character in the film *Pretty Woman* (who winds up with multimillionaire Richard Gere), streetwalkers are considered the least attractive, lowest paid, most vulnerable men and women in the profession. Streetwalkers wear bright clothing, makeup, and jewelry to attract customers; they take their customers to hotels. The term *hooker*, however, is not derived from the ability of streetwalkers to hook clients on their charms. It actually stems from the popular name given women who followed Union General "Fighting Joe" Hooker's army during the Civil War.[47] Studies indicate they are most likely to be impoverished members of ethnic or racial minorities. Many are young runaways who gravitate to major cities to find a new, exciting life and escape from sexual and physical abuse at home.[48] Of all prostitutes, streetwalkers have the highest incidence of drug abuse.[49]

Bar Girls B-girls, as they are also called, spend their time in bars, drinking and waiting to be picked up by customers. Although alcoholism may be a problem, B-girls usually work out an arrangement with the bartender so they are served diluted drinks or water colored with dye or tea, for which the customer is charged an exorbitant price. In some bars, the B-girl is given a credit for each drink she gets the customer to buy. It is common to find B-girls in towns with military bases and large transient populations.[50]

Brothel Prostitutes Also called bordellos, cathouses, sporting houses, and houses of ill repute, brothels flourished in the nineteenth and early twentieth centuries. They were large establishments, usually run by madams, that housed several prostitutes. A madam is a woman who employs prostitutes, supervises their behavior, and receives a fee for her services; her cut is usually 40 to 60 percent of the prostitutes' earnings. The madam's role may include recruiting women into prostitution and socializing them in the trade.[51]

Brothels declined in importance following World War II. The closing of the last brothel in Texas is chronicled in the play and movie *The Best Little Whorehouse in Texas*. Today the best-known brothels exist in Nevada, where prostitution is legal outside large population centers.

Call Girls The aristocrats of prostitution are call girls. They charge customers up to $1,500 per night and may net more than $100,000 per year. Some gain clients through employment in escort services, while others develop independent customer lists. Many call girls come from middle-class backgrounds and service upper-class customers. Attempting to dispel the notion that their service is simply sex for money, they concentrate on making their clients feel important and attractive. Working exclusively via telephone "dates," call girls get their clients by word of mouth or by making arrangements with bellhops, cab drivers, and so on. They either entertain clients in their own apartments or visit clients' hotels and apartments. Upon retiring, a call girl can sell her datebook listing client names and sexual preferences for thousands of dollars. Despite the lucrative nature of their business, call girls suffer considerable risk by being alone and unprotected with strangers. They often request the business cards of their clients to make sure they are dealing with "upstanding citizens."

Escort Services/Call Houses Some escort services are fronts for prostitution rings. Both male and female sex workers can be sent out after the client calls an ad in the yellow pages. In Las Vegas, 134 pages in the phone book are dedicated to such services.[52] A relatively new phenomenon, the call house, combines elements of the brothel and call-girl rings. A madam receives a call from a prospective customer, and if she finds the client acceptable, she arranges a meeting between the caller and a prostitute in her service. The madam maintains a list of prostitutes who are on call rather than living together in a house. The call house insulates the madam from arrest because she never meets the client or receives direct payment.[53]

Circuit Travelers Prostitutes known as circuit travelers move around in groups of two or three to lumber, labor, and agricultural camps. They ask the foreman for permission to ply their trade, service the whole crew in an evening, and then move on. Some circuit travelers seek clients at truck stops and rest areas.

Sometimes young girls are forced to become circuit travelers by unscrupulous pimps. In 1998, 16 people were charged with enslaving at least 20 women, some as young as 14, and forcing them to work for months as prostitutes in agricultural migrant camps in Florida and South Carolina. The young women were lured from Mexico with offers of jobs in landscaping, health care, housecleaning, and restaurants. During their captivity, the young women were raped, beaten, and forced to have abortions. Those who tried to escape were tracked down, brought back, beaten, and raped.[54]

Becoming a Prostitute

Why does someone turn to prostitution? Both male and female prostitutes often come from troubled homes marked by extreme conflict and hostility and from poor urban areas or rural communities. Divorce, separation, or death splits the family; most prostitutes grew up in homes without fathers.[55] Many prostitutes were initiated into sex by family members at ages as young as 10 to 12 years; they have long histories of sexual exploitation and abuse.[56] The early experiences with sex help teach them that their bodies have value and that sexual encounters can be used to obtain affection, power, or money. Lower-class girls who get into "the life" report conflict with school authorities, poor grades, and an overly regimented school experience.[57] Drug abuse, including heroin and cocaine addiction, is often a factor in the prostitute's life.[58] However, there is no actual evidence that people become prostitutes because of psychological problems or personality disturbances. Money, drugs, and survival seem to be greater motivations.

Research indicates that few girls are forced into prostitution by a pimp. Pimps may convince girls by flattery, support, promises, and affection, but relatively few kidnap or coerce kids into prostitution. There is more evidence that both males and females enter prostitution voluntarily because they dislike the discipline of conventional work.[59] Women who are socialized to view themselves as sex objects may easily step over the line of propriety and accept money for their favors.[60] These women view their bodies as salable commodities, and most prostitution does in fact pay better than other occupations available to women with limited education.

Legalize Prostitution?

Feminists have staked out conflicting views of prostitution. One position is that women must become emancipated from male oppression and reach sexual equality. The sexual equality view considers the prostitute a victim of male dominance. In patriarchal societies, male power is predicated on female subjugation, and prostitution is a clear example of this gender exploitation.[61] In contrast, for some feminists, the fight for equality depends on controlling all attempts by men or women to impose their will on women. The free choice view is that prostitution, if freely chosen, expresses women's equality and is not a symptom of subjugation.[62]

Advocates of both positions argue that the penalties for prostitution should be reduced (decriminalized), but neither side advocates outright legalization. Decriminalization would relieve already desperate women of the additional burden of severe legal punishment. However, legalization might be coupled with regulation by male-dominated justice agencies. For example, required medical examinations would mean increased male control over women's bodies. Although both sides advocate change in the criminal status of prostitution, few communities, except San Francisco, have openly debated or voted on its legalization.

Pornography

pornography

Sexually explicit books, magazines, films, or tapes intended to provide sexual titillation and excitement for paying customers.

obscenity

Material that violates community standards of morality or decency and has no redeeming social value.

The term **pornography** derives from the Greek *porne,* meaning "prostitute," and *graphein,* meaning "to write." In the heart of many major cities are stores that display and sell books, magazines, and films explicitly depicting every imaginable sex act. Suburban video stores also rent and sell sexually explicit tapes, which make up 15 to 30 percent of the home rental market. The purpose of this material is to provide sexual titillation and excitement for paying customers. Although material depicting nudity and sex is typically legal, protected by the First Amendment's provision limiting government control of speech, most criminal codes prohibit the production, display, and sale of obscene material.

Obscenity, derived from the Latin *caenum* for "filth," is defined by Webster's dictionary as "deeply offensive to morality or decency . . . designed to incite to lust or depravity."[63] The problem of controlling pornography centers on this definition of obscenity. Police and law enforcement officials can legally seize only material that is judged obscene. "But who," critics ask, "is to judge what is obscene?" At one time, such novels as *Tropic of Cancer* by Henry Miller, *Ulysses* by James Joyce, and *Lady Chatterley's Lover* by D. H. Lawrence were prohibited because they were considered obscene; today they are considered works of great literary value. Thus, what is obscene today may be considered socially acceptable at a future time. After all, *Playboy* and *Penthouse* magazines, sold openly on most college campuses, display nude models in all kinds of sexually explicit poses. The uncertainty surrounding this issue is illustrated by Supreme Court Justice Potter Stewart's famous 1964 statement on how he defined obscenity: "I know it when I see it." Because of this legal and moral ambiguity, the sex trade is booming around the United States.

Is Pornography Harmful?

Opponents of pornography argue that it degrades both the people who are photographed and members of the public who are sometimes forced to see obscene material. Pornographers exploit their models, who often include underage children. The Attorney General's Commission on Pornography, set up by the Reagan administration to review the sale and distribution of sexually explicit material, concluded that many performers and models are victims of physical and psychological coercion.[64]

One uncontested danger of pornography is "kiddie porn." Each year more than a million children are believed to be used in pornography or prostitution, many of them runaways whose plight is exploited by adults.[65] Ann Wolbert Burgess studied 55 child pornography rings and found that they typically contain between 3 and 11 children, predominantly males, some of nursery school age. The adults who control the ring use positions of trust to recruit the children and then continue to exploit them through a combination of material and psychological rewards. Burgess found different types of child pornography rings. Solo sex rings involve several children and a single adult, usually male, who uses a position of trust (counselor, teacher, Boy Scout leader) to recruit children into sexual activity. Transition rings are impromptu groups set up to sell and trade photos and sex. Syndicated rings are well-structured organizations that re-cruit children and create extensive networks of customers who desire sexual services.[66] Sexual exploitation by these rings can devastate the child victims. Exploited children are prone to such acting-out behavior as setting fires and be-coming sexually focused in the use of language, dress, and mannerisms. In cases of extreme, prolonged victimization, children may lock onto the sex group's behavior and become prone to further victimization or even become victimizers themselves.

Does Pornography Cause Violence?

An issue critical to the debate over pornography is whether viewing it produces sexual violence or assaultive behavior. This debate was given added interest when serial killer Ted Bundy claimed his murderous rampage was fueled by reading pornography.

Some evidence exists that viewing sexually explicit material actually has little effect on behavior. In 1970, the National Commission on Obscenity and Pornography reviewed all available material on the effects of pornography and found no clear relationship between pornography and violence.[67] Almost 20 years later, the highly controversial Attorney General's Commission on Pornography, sponsored by the conservative Reagan administration, called for legal attacks on hard-core pornography and condemned all sexually related material—but also found little evidence that obscenity causes antisocial behavior.[68]

How might we account for this surprisingly insignificant association? It is possible that viewing erotic material may act as a safety valve for those whose impulses might otherwise lead them to violence.[69] Convicted rapists and sex offenders report less exposure to pornography than control groups of nonoffenders.[70]

Viewing prurient material may have the unintended side effect of satisfying erotic impulses that otherwise might result in more sexually aggressive behavior. This issue is far from settled. A number of criminologists believe that the positive relationship between pornography consumption and rape rates in various countries, including the United States, is evidence that obscenity may powerfully influence criminality.[71] Nonetheless, the weight of the evidence shows little relationship between violence and pornography per se.

Although there is little or no documentation of a correlation between pornography and violent crime, there is stronger evidence that people exposed to material that portrays violence, sadism, and women enjoying being raped and degraded are likely to be sexually aggressive toward female victims.[72] Laboratory experiments conducted by a number of leading authorities have found that men exposed to violent pornography are more likely to act aggressively toward women.[73] The evidence suggests that violence and sexual aggression are not linked to erotic or pornographic films per se but that erotic films depicting violence, rape, brutality, and aggression may evoke similar feelings in viewers. This finding is especially distressing because it is common for adult books and films to have sexually violent themes such as rape, bondage, and mutilation.[74]

Find It on INFOTRAC
College Edition

Prior to the nineteenth century, pornography essentially involved the written word. During the 1880s and 1890s, the photographic image began to replace older forms of pornography. The content stayed remarkably similar: Visual pornography continued to focus on women as the objects of sexual desire. To read more about the history of pornography, go to InfoTrac College Edition and read

Lisa Z. Sigel, "Filth in the Wrong People's Hands: Postcards and the Expansion of Pornography in Britain and the Atlantic World, 1880–1914," *Journal of Social History*, Summer 2000 v33 i4 p859

Pornography and the Law

The First Amendment of the U.S. Constitution protects free speech and prohibits police agencies from limiting the public's right of free expression. However, the Supreme Court held in the twin cases of *Roth* v. *United States* and *Alberts* v. *California* that although the First Amendment protects all "ideas with even the slightest redeeming social importance—unorthodox ideas, controversial ideas, even ideas hateful to the prevailing climate of opinion . . . implicit in the history of the First Amendment is the rejection of obscenity as utterly without redeeming social importance."[75] These decisions left unclear how obscenity is defined.

The technology revolution represented by the Internet poses a major obstacle for people who want to control or limit sex-related entertainment. Here, Ashley West, one of the roommates on the VoyeurDorm.com web site, poses in front of a new recreational vehicle owned by the site, while Faith Gardner demonstrates the real-time video being shot inside. Clients pay a monthly fee to watch the girls 24 hours a day. Should such activities be criminalized? Or are they legitimate and harmless business transactions between consenting adults?

If a highly erotic movie tells a "moral tale," must it be judged legal even if 95 percent of its content is objectionable? A spate of movies made after the *Roth* decision claimed that they were educational or warned the viewer about sexual depravity, so they could not be said to lack redeeming social importance. Many state obscenity cases were appealed to federal courts so judges could decide whether the films totally lacked redeeming social importance. To rectify the situation, the Supreme Court redefined its concept of obscenity in the case of *Miller* v. *California:*

> The basic guidelines for the trier of fact must be (a) whether the average person applying contemporary community standards would find that the work taken as a whole appeals to the prurient interest; (b) whether the work depicts or describes, in a patently offensive way, sexual conduct specifically defined by the applicable state law, and (c) whether the work, taken as a whole, lacks serious literary, artistic, political or scientific value.[76]

To convict a person of obscenity under the *Miller doctrine,* the state or local jurisdiction must specifically define obscene conduct in its statute, and the pornographer must engage in that behavior. The Court gave some examples of what is considered obscene: "patently offensive representations or descriptions of masturbation, excretory functions and lewd exhibition of the genitals."[77] Obviously a plebiscite cannot be held to determine the community's attitude for every trial concerning the sale of pornography. Works that are considered obscene in Omaha might be considered routine in New York, but how can we be sure? To resolve this dilemma, the Supreme Court articulated in *Pope* v. *Illinois* a reasonableness doctrine: A work is obscene if a reasonable person applying objective (national) standards would find the material lacking in any social value.[78]

Controlling Sex for Profit

Sex for profit predates Western civilization. Considering its longevity, there seems to be little evidence that it can be controlled or eliminated by legal means alone. Recent reports indicate that the sex business is currently booming and now amounts to $10 billion per year.[79] There has been a concerted effort by the federal government to prosecute adult movie distributors.[80]

Although politically appealing, law enforcement crusades may not necessarily obtain the desired effect. A get-tough policy could make sex-related goods and services scarce, driving up prices and making their sale even more desirable and profitable. Going after national distributors may help decentralize the adult movie and photo business and encourage local rings to expand their activities, for example, by making and marketing videos as well as still photos or distributing them through computer networks.

An alternative approach has been to restrict the sale of pornography within acceptable boundaries. For example, New York City has enacted zoning that seeks to break up the concentration of peep shows, topless bars, and X-rated businesses in several neighborhoods, particularly in Times Square.[81] The law forbids sex-oriented businesses within 500 feet of residential zones, schools, churches, or day-care centers. Sex shops cannot be located within 500 feet of each other, so concentrated "red light" districts must be dispersed. Rather than close their doors, sex shops got around the law by adding products such as luggage, cameras, T-shirts, and classic films. The courts have upheld the law, ruling that stores can stay in business if no more than 40 percent of their floor space and inventory are dedicated to adult entertainment.[82] Ironically, zoning statutes may not be needed as skyrocketing downtown real estate prices make sex clubs and stores relatively unprofitable. New York's Times Square area has been redeveloped as land values skyrocket and Disney theme stores replace strip joints.

Technological Change

A 1993 letter to advice columnist Ann Landers gave this cry for help:

> Dear Ann Landers,
> . . . several months ago, I caught my husband making calls to a 900-sex number. After a week of denial, he admitted that for several years he had been hooked on porn magazines, porn movies, peep shows, strippers, and phone sex. This addiction can start early in life. With my husband it began at age 12 with just one simple, "harmless" magazine. By the time he was 19, it had become completely out of control. . . . For years my husband hated himself, and it affected his entire life.[83]

A 1998 letter updates the problem:

> Dear Ann Landers,
> My husband and I have had a fabulous marriage. We have two wonderful children, ages 22 and 25. . . . Here's the problem. Phil has become obsessed with porn on the Internet. . . . Recently, when I returned from an evening out, I noticed Phil appeared quite nervous and upset. I looked at the computer, and sure enough, he had been looking at some unbelievably raunchy stuff. He said he was sincere when he promised to give it up, but he just couldn't stay away from it. I now believe he is obsessed and self-destructive.[84]

Technological change will provide the greatest challenge to those seeking to control the sex-for-profit industry. Adult movie theaters are closing as people are able to buy or rent tapes in their local video stores and play them in the privacy of their homes.[85] Adult CD-ROMs are now a staple of the computer industry. Internet sex services include live, interactive stripping and sexual activities.[86]

To control the spread of Internet pornography, Congress passed the Communications Decency Act (CDA), which made all Internet service providers, commercial on-line services, bulletin board systems, and electronic mail providers criminally liable whenever their services are used to transmit any material

✔ Checkpoints

✔ It is illegal to engage in homosexual acts in about half the U.S. states. Many organizations, including the Boy Scouts and the U.S. military, limit gay participation.

✔ Paraphilias are deviant sexual acts such as exhibitionism and voyeurism. Many are considered crimes.

✔ Prostitution has been common throughout recorded history. There are many kinds of prostitutes, including streetwalkers, bar girls, call girls, brothel prostitutes, and circuit travelers.

✔ It is feared that some girls are forced or tricked into prostitution against their will.

(continued)

✔ **Checkpoints**

✔ Pornography is a billion-dollar industry that is growing through technological advances such as the Internet.

✔ There is great debate whether obscene materials are harmful and are related to violence.

✔ The Supreme Court has ruled that material is obscene if it has prurient sexual content and is devoid of social value.

considered "obscene, lewd, lascivious, filthy, or indecent" (S 314, 1996). These acts were punishable by fines of up to $100,000 and two years in prison. Civil libertarians decried this effort to regulate Internet content, and the American Civil Liberties Union (ACLU) filed suit questioning the constitutionality of the CDA on the grounds that it violated the First Amendment right to free speech. In *Reno* v. *ACLU* (1997), the Supreme Court upheld the ACLU's claim, ruling that the CDA unconstitutionally restricted free speech.[87] In a landmark 7–2 decision written by Justice Stevens, the Court ruled that the CDA places an "unacceptably heavy burden on protected speech" that "threatens to torch a large segment of the Internet community." Despite this setback, lawmakers are seeking other means of controlling Internet pornography.[88] For example, a more recent law, the Child Online Protection Act (H.R. 3783), would ban web postings of material deemed "harmful to minors." The act, signed into law by President Clinton in October 1998, will not take effect while it is undergoing legal challenges.[89]

Despite these efforts, the popularity of pornography on the Internet, on CD-ROMs, and in satellite broadcasts may overwhelm law enforcement efforts and spur the growth of sex-related materials. ✔ **Checkpoints**

Substance Abuse

The problem of substance abuse stretches across the United States. Large urban areas are beset by drug-dealing gangs, drug users who engage in crime to support their habits, and alcohol-related violence. Rural areas are important staging centers for the shipment of drugs across the country and are often the production sites for synthetic drugs and marijuana farming.[90] Nor is the United States alone in experiencing a problem with substance abuse. In Australia, 19 percent of youths in detention centers and 40 percent of adult prisoners report having used heroin at least once; in Canada, cocaine and crack are considered serious urban problems; South Africa reports increased cocaine and heroin abuse; Thailand has a serious heroin and methamphetamine problem; and British police have found a major increase in heroin abuse.[91]

Another indication of the concern about drugs has been the increasing number of drug-related visits to hospital emergency rooms. For example, marijuana-related visits to hospital emergency departments (EDs) have risen from an estimated 16,000 visits in 1991 to 76,870 in 1998. Heroin-related visits increased from about 35,000 to more than 77,009, while cocaine continues to be the illicit drug responsible for the most emergency department visits, accounting for more than 150,000 visits in 1999 (see Figure 13.1).[92]

Despite the scope of the drug problem, some still view it as another type of victimless public order crime. There is great debate over the legalization of drugs and the control of alcohol. Some consider drug use a private matter and drug control another example of government intrusion into people's private lives. Furthermore, legalization could reduce the profit of selling illegal substances and drive suppliers out of the market.[93] Others see these substances as dangerous, believing that the criminal activity of users makes the term "victimless" nonsensical. Still another position is that the possession and use of all drugs and alcohol should be legalized but the sale and distribution of drugs should be heavily penalized. This would punish those profiting from drugs while enabling users to be helped without fear of criminal punishment.

When Did Drug Use Begin?

The use of chemical substances to change reality and provide stimulation, relief, or relaxation has gone on for thousands of years. Mesopotamian writings indicate that opium was used 4,000 years ago—it was known as the "plant of joy."[94] The ancient Greeks knew and understood the problem of drug use. At the time of the Crusades, the Arabs were using marijuana. In the Western Hemi-

Figure 13.1

Estimated Number of Emergency Department Drug Mentions, 1991–1999

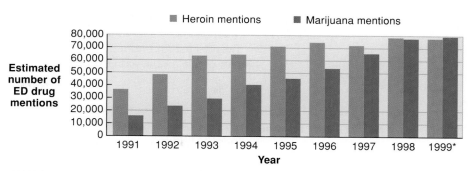

*1999 figures are projected based on estimates from the first half of 1999.

NOTES: A drug mention is defined as a substance that was mentioned in a drug-related episode. In addition to alcohol-in-combination, up to 4 substances can be reported for each drug-related episode. A drug-related episode is an emergency department visit that was induced by or related to the use of an illegal drug(s) or the nonmedical use of a legal drug for patients age 6 years and older. These estimates are based on a representative sample of non-Federal, short-stay hospitals with 24-hour emergency departments in the coterminous U.S.

SOURCE: Adapted by Center for Substance Abuse Research from data from Substance Abuse and Mental Health Services Administration (SAMHSA), *Mid-Year 1999 Preliminary Emergency Data from the Drug Abuse Warning Network,* March 2000, Rockville, MD: SAMHSA.

sphere, natives of Mexico and South America chewed coca leaves and used "magic mushrooms" in their religious ceremonies.[95] Drug use was also accepted in Europe well into the twentieth century. Recently uncovered pharmacy records circa 1900 to 1920 showed sales of cocaine and heroin solutions to members of the British royal family; records from 1912 show that Winston Churchill, then a member of Parliament, was sold a cocaine solution while staying in Scotland.[96]

In the early years of the United States, opium and its derivatives were easily obtained. Opium-based drugs were used in various patent medicine cure-alls. Morphine was used extensively to relieve the pain of wounded soldiers in the Civil War. By the turn of the century, an estimated 1 million U.S. citizens were opiate users.[97]

Alcohol and Its Prohibition

temperance movement

The drive to prohibit the sale of alcohol in the United States, culminating in ratification of the Eighteenth Amendment in 1919.

Prohibition

The period from 1919 until 1933, when the Eighteenth Amendment to the U.S. Constitution outlawed the sale of alcohol; also known as the "noble experiment."

The history of alcohol and the law in the United States has also been controversial and dramatic. At the turn of the century, a drive was mustered to prohibit the sale of alcohol. This **temperance movement** was fueled by the belief that the purity of the U.S. agrarian culture was being destroyed by the growth of cities. Urbanism was viewed as a threat to the lifestyle of the majority of the nation's population, then living on farms and in villages. The forces behind the temperance movement were such lobbying groups as the Anti-Saloon League led by Carrie Nation, the Women's Temperance Union, and the Protestant clergy of the Baptist, Methodist, and Congregationalist faiths.[98] They viewed the growing city, filled with newly arriving Irish, Italian, and Eastern European immigrants, as centers of degradation and wickedness. Ratification of the Eighteenth Amendment in 1919, prohibiting the sale of alcoholic beverages, was viewed as a triumph of the morality of middle- and upper-class Americans over the threat posed to their culture by the "new Americans."[99]

Prohibition failed. It was enforced by the Volstead Act, which defined intoxicating beverages as those containing one-half of 1 percent, or more, alcohol.[100] What doomed Prohibition? One factor was the use of organized crime to supply illicit liquor. Also, the law made it illegal only to sell alcohol, not to purchase it, which reduced the deterrent effect. Finally, despite the work of Elliot

Ness and his "Untouchables," law enforcement agencies were inadequate, and officials were likely to be corrupted by wealthy bootleggers.[101] In 1933, the Twenty-First Amendment to the Constitution repealed Prohibition, signaling the end of the "noble experiment."

The Extent of Substance Abuse

Despite continuing efforts at control, the use of mood-altering substances persists in the United States. What is the extent of the substance abuse problem today? Despite the media attention devoted to drug abuse, there is actually significant controversy over its nature and extent. The media assume that drug use is a pervasive, growing menace that threatens to destroy the American way of life. This view is countered by national surveys showing that drug use is now less common than it was two decades ago.

A number of national surveys attempt to chart trends in drug abuse in the general population. One important source of information on drug use is the annual self-report survey of drug abuse among high school students conducted by the Institute of Social Research (ISR) at the University of Michigan.[102] This survey is based on the self-report responses of about 17,000 high school seniors, 15,500 tenth-graders, and 18,800 eighth-graders in hundreds of schools around the United States.

As Figure 13.2 shows, drug use among the general population declined from a high point around 1980 until 1990, when it began to increase once again. Usage rates for most drugs reached peak levels in the mid-1990s—inhalants in 1995; hallucinogens, including LSD and PCP, in 1996; and marijuana and am-

Figure 13.2

Trends in Annual Prevalence of an Illicit Drug Use Index: Eighth, Tenth, and Twelfth Graders

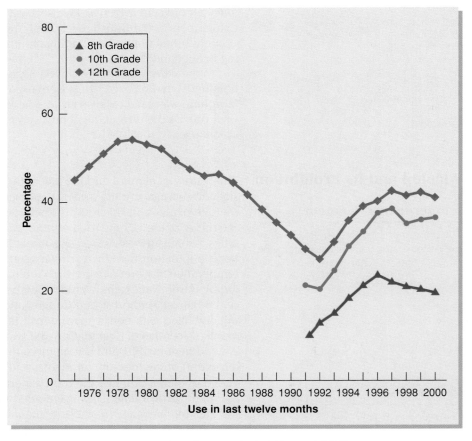

SOURCE: *Monitoring the Future* (Ann Arbor, MI: Institute for Social Research, 2000).

Figure 13.3

Percentage of U.S. High School Seniors Reporting Drug Use in the Past 30 Days, by Drug Type, 2000

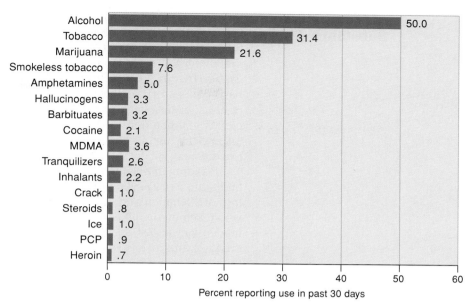

SOURCE: *Monitoring the Future* (Ann Arbor, MI: Institute for Social Research, 2000).

phetamines in 1996 or 1997. Since then, drug use has stabilized or receded. In 2000, there were some positive trends in drug use: a significant drop in the use of cigarettes, smokeless tobacco, LSD, crystal methamphetamine, and Rohypnol (the "date rape" drug); crack cocaine use has also been in decline. One trouble spot has been an uptick in the use of "Ecstasy" (MDMA). As Figure 13.3 shows, more than half of all high school seniors report drinking during the past month, more than a third have used tobacco, and almost a quarter have smoked marijuana.

How can the trends in drug use be explained? These data indicate that although general usage is lower than it was 20 years ago, the drug problem has not gone away and the use of some drugs, such as Ecstasy, may be increasing among high school youth. Why has drug use remained a major social problem? When drug use declined in the 1980s, one reason may have been changing perceptions about the harmfulness of drugs such as cocaine and marijuana; as people come to view these drugs as harmful, they tend to use them less. Because of widespread publicity linking drug use, needle sharing, and the AIDS virus, people began to see drug taking as dangerous and risky. Today, the perceived risk of drugs has declined. For example, the ISR reports that 80 percent of high school seniors in 1991 thought they ran a great risk if they were regular marijuana users; today only about 60 percent view regular marijuana use as risky.

In addition, when drug use declined, youths reported greater disapproval of drug use among their friends, and peer pressure may help account for lower use rates. The number of youths disapproving of drugs has declined significantly in the past decade (although a majority still disapproves); with lower disapproval has come increased usage.

It also appears that it is easier to obtain drugs, especially for younger adolescents. For example, the ISR survey found that in 1992 about 42 percent of eighth-graders said it was easy to obtain pot; today about 47 percent say that it is easy to get that drug. So, despite a decade-long "war on drugs," it may be easier to get drugs today than 10 years ago. Finally, parents may now be unwilling or reluctant to educate their children about the dangers of substance abuse because as baby boomers they were drug abusers themselves in the 1960s and 1970s.

The Causes of Substance Abuse

What causes people to abuse substances? Although there are many different views on the cause of drug use, most can be characterized as seeing the onset of an addictive career as either an environmental or a personal matter.

Subcultural View Those who view drug abuse as having an environmental basis concentrate on lower-class addiction. Because a disproportionate number of drug abusers are poor, the onset of drug use can be tied to such factors as racial prejudice, devalued identities, low self-esteem, poor socioeconomic status, and the high level of mistrust, negativism, and defiance found in impoverished areas.

Residing in a deteriorated inner-city slum area is often correlated with entry into a drug subculture. Youths living in these depressed areas, where feelings of alienation and hopelessness run high, often meet established drug users, who teach them that narcotics provide an answer to their feelings of personal inadequacy and stress.[103] The youths may join peers to learn the techniques of drug use and receive social support for their habit. Research shows that peer influence is a significant predictor of drug careers that actually grows stronger as people mature.[104] Shared feelings and a sense of intimacy lead the youths to become fully enmeshed in what has been described as the "drug-use subculture."[105] Some join gangs and enter into a career of using and distributing illegal substances while also committing property and violent crimes.[106]

Psychodynamic View Not all drug abusers reside in lower-class slum areas; the problem of middle-class substance abuse is very real. Consequently, some experts have linked substance abuse to personality disturbance and emotional problems that can strike people in any economic class. Psychodynamic explanations of substance abuse suggest that drugs help youths control or express unconscious needs and impulses. Drinking alcohol may reflect an oral fixation that is associated with other nonfunctional behaviors, such as dependence and depression.[107] A young teen may resort to drug abuse to remain dependent on an overprotective mother, to reduce the emotional turmoil of adolescence, or to cope with troubling impulses.[108]

Personality testing of known users suggests that a significant percentage suffer from psychotic disorders, including various levels of schizophrenia. Surveys show that youngsters with serious behavioral problems were more than seven times more likely than those with less serious problems to report that they were dependent on alcohol or illicit drugs. Youths with serious emotional problems were nearly four times more likely to report dependence on drugs than those without such issues.[109]

These views have been substantiated by research involving a sample of more than 20,291 people in five large U.S. cities. The results of this first large-scale study on the personality characteristics of abusers indicate a significant association between mental illness and drug abuse: About 53 percent of drug abusers and 37 percent of alcohol abusers have at least one serious mental illness. Conversely, 29 percent of the diagnosed mentally ill people in the survey have substance abuse problems.[110]

Genetic Factors It is also possible that substance abuse may have a genetic basis. For example, the biological children of alcoholics reared by nonalcoholic adoptive parents develop alcohol problems more often than the biological children of the adoptive parents.[111] In a similar vein, a number of studies comparing alcoholism among identical twins and fraternal twins have found that the degree of concordance (both siblings behaving identically) is twice as high among the identical twin groups. These inferences are still inconclusive because identical twins are more likely to be treated similarly than fraternal twins and are therefore more likely to be influenced by environmental conditions.

Nonetheless, most children of abusing parents do not become drug dependent themselves, suggesting that even if drug abuse is heritable, environment and socialization must play some role in the onset of abuse.[112]

Social Learning Social psychologists suggest that drug abuse may also result from observing parental drug use. Parental drug abuse begins to have a damaging effect on children as young as 2 years old, especially when parents manifest drug-related personality problems such as depression or poor impulse control.[113] Children whose parents abuse drugs are more likely to have persistent abuse problems than the children of nonabusers.[114]

People who learn that drugs provide pleasurable sensations may be the most likely to experiment with illegal substances; a habit may develop if the user experiences lower anxiety, fear, and tension levels.[115] Having a history of family drug and alcohol abuse has been found to be a characteristic of violent teenage sexual abusers.[116] Heroin abusers report an unhappy childhood that included harsh physical punishment and parental neglect and rejection.[117]

According to the social learning view, drug involvement begins with using tobacco and drinking alcohol at an early age, which progresses to experimentation with marijuana and hashish and finally to cocaine and even heroin. Although most recreational users do not progress to "hard stuff," few addicts begin their involvement with narcotics without first experimenting with recreational drugs. By implication, if teen smoking and drinking could be reduced, the gateway to hard drugs would be narrowed.

Problem Behavior Syndrome (PBS) For many people, substance abuse is just one of many problem behaviors. Longitudinal studies show that drug abusers are maladjusted, alienated, and emotionally distressed and that their drug use is one among many social problems.[118] Having a deviant lifestyle begins early in life and is punctuated with criminal relationships, family history of substance abuse, educational failure, and alienation. People who abuse drugs lack commitment to religious values, disdain education, and spend most of their time in peer activities. A recent analysis of PBS by sociologist John Donovan found robust support for the interconnection of problem drinking and drug abuse, delinquency, precocious sexual behavior, school failure, family conflict, and other similar social problems.[119]

Rational Choice Not all people who abuse drugs do so because of personal pathology. Some may use drugs and alcohol because they want to enjoy their effects: get high, relax, improve creativity, escape reality, and increase sexual responsiveness. Research indicates that adolescent alcohol abusers believe that getting high will make them powerful, increase their sexual performance, and facilitate their social behavior; they care little about negative future consequences.[120]

Substance abuse, then, may be a function of the rational but mistaken belief that drugs can benefit the user. The decision to use drugs involves evaluations of personal consequences (such as addiction, disease, and legal punishment) and the expected benefits of drug use (such as peer approval, positive affective states, heightened awareness, and relaxation). Adolescents may begin using drugs because they believe their peers expect them to do so.[121]

Is There a Single "Cause" of Drug Abuse? There are many different views of why people take drugs, and no one theory has proved adequate to explain all forms of substance abuse. Recent research efforts show that drug users suffer a variety of family and socialization difficulties, have addiction-prone personalities, and are generally at risk for many other social problems.[122] And although it is popular to believe that addicts progress along a continuum from using so-called gateway drugs to using ever more potent substances, that view may also be misleading. Research by Andrew Golub and Bruce Johnson shows that many hard-core drug abusers have never smoked or used alcohol. Examining a sample of more than 130,000 hard drug–using arrestees, Golub and Johnson found that the proportion who used marijuana before trying heroin and cocaine shifted significantly over time. The pathways may be different at various times and in different locales.[123]

In sum, there may be no single cause of substance abuse. People may try and continue to use illegal substances for a variety of reasons. As sociologist James Inciardi points out,

> There are as many reasons people use drugs as there are individuals who use drugs. For some, it may be a function of family disorganization, or cultural learning, or maladjusted personality, or an "addiction-prone" personality. . . . For others, heroin use may be no more than a normal response to the world in which they live.[124]

Drugs and Crime

One of the main reasons for the criminalization of particular substances is the significant association believed to exist between drug abuse and crime. Research suggests that many criminal offenders have extensive experience with alcohol and drug use and that abusers commit an enormous amount of crime.[125] Almost 40 percent of violent crimes involve alcohol, and about 4 in 10 criminal offenders report that they were using alcohol at the time of their offenses.[126]

Substance abuse appears to be an important precipitating factor in domestic assault, armed robbery, and homicide cases.[127] Table 13.1 shows the findings of a study of 136 domestic violence cases reported to the authorities. Note that 94 percent of those arrested used substances before the assault; almost half the victims were users also. The accompanying Criminological Enterprise box explores this issue further.

Although the drug–crime connection is powerful, the relationship is still uncertain because many users had a history of criminal activity before the onset of their substance abuse.[128] Nonetheless, if drug use does not turn otherwise law-abiding citizens into criminals, it certainly amplifies the extent of their criminal activities.[129] And as addiction levels increase, so do the frequency and seriousness of criminality.[130]

An important source of data on the drug abuse–crime connection is the federally sponsored Arrestee Drug Abuse Monitoring Program (ADAM). Ar-

---

Table 13.1 Substance Use by Assailants and Victims Prior to Domestic Assault (as reported by participants and/or family members) (n = 136)

SUBSTANCE	PERCENTAGE OF ASSAILANTS USING SUBSTANCE PRIOR TO ASSAULT	PERCENTAGE OF VICTIMS USING SUBSTANCE PRIOR TO ASSAULT
Cocaine and alcohol	47% ⎱ 67%	8% ⎱ 15%
Cocaine, marijuana, and alcohol	20% ⎰	7% ⎰
Alcohol alone	17%	14%
Marijuana and alcohol	8%	6%
Other drugs/combinations	2%	8%
Any alcohol or other drug use	94%	43%

SOURCE: Daniel Brookoff, "Drug Use and Domestic Violence," National Institute of Justice Research in Progress Seminar Series (prepared by the Center for Substance Abuse Research, January 27, 1997).

The Criminological Enterprise

How Substance Abuse Provokes Violence

Jeffrey Fagan and his fellow researchers at Columbia University's Center for Violence Research and Prevention are conducting a multistage study on adolescent violence in order to construct a situational framework for understanding violent behavior. The research design includes three samples of young men, ages 16 to 24, with histories of involvement in violent activities and currently (or, if incarcerated, formerly) residing in two of New York City's neighborhoods with the highest rates of youth homicide—East New York (Brooklyn) and Mott Haven (South Bronx). The criminal justice sample includes young men convicted on gun-related charges and incarcerated in the Rikers Island Correctional Facility and facilities under the auspices of the New York State Division for Youth Facilities. The second sample consists of victims of violence identified in the emergency rooms of two hospitals, one near each of the two neighborhoods. The community sample consists of young men who are involved in violence but have avoided both the criminal justice system and the emergency room.

The study has found that alcohol and drugs can influence social interactions in two ways that may lead to violence. First, alcohol can shape the dynamics, decisions, and strategies in a violent or near-violent episode. That is, interactions in which one or both individuals have been drinking will turn out differently than those in which one or both are sober. Second, the context in which drinking occurs independently affects how violent or near-violent events unfold. The young men reported that intoxication increased the likelihood that a person's language would become provocative and boastful, turning minor disputes into violent encounters. Alcohol exaggerated the sense of outrage over perceived transgressions of personal codes, resulting in violence to exert control or exact retribution. Some drinkers acted on bystanders' provocations to fight more seriously; others felt invincible and started fights that they then lost. In addition, certain bars were frequent scenes of violence, regardless of who was present or how much alcohol had been consumed; being in the wrong place at the wrong time resulted in injuries, including gunshot wounds, to a number of respondents.

Interestingly, the effects of drugs on violence were much less clear. Marijuana made some subjects less prone to violence, whereas other users sought out victims to exploit or dominate. Another type of user became paranoid and either avoided human contact or became hostile and prone to defensive violence. Yet, if a fight broke out, even the most relaxed, "mellow" individual would immediately snap out of his stupor to defend himself.

Not all of the young men who were interviewed blamed their violent behavior on alcohol or drugs. A number of young men used alcohol or drugs after violent events as a form of self-medication. And some youths, even under the influence of alcohol, were able to walk away from violence. Researchers repeatedly heard stories of "graceful," strategic retreats from violence. However, making a careful, controlled exit in a threatening situation takes verbal skills and mental agility, two cognitive abilities that not everyone possesses.

Critical Thinking

The Fagan research shows how substance abuse can facilitate violent episodes. Interestingly, alcohol seems to have a greater influence on violent behavior than other drugs. Some drugs, like marijuana, may even help regulate violence if they provide a sense of euphoria that reduces conflict. Could this be used as an argument for drug legalization?

 InfoTrac College Edition Research

Treating alcohol abusers is a major social goal. To research current treatment programs, see
Deborah Pappas, Chudley E. Werch, and Joan M. Carlson, "Recruitment and Retention in an Alcohol Prevention Program of Two Inner-City Middle Schools," *Journal of School Health*, August 1998 v68 i6 p231(6)
John P. Allen, "Project MATCH: A Clarification," *Behavioral Health Management*, July–August 1998 v18 i4 p42(2)

SOURCE: Jeffrey Fagan, *Adolescent Violence: A View from the Street*, NIJ Research Preview (Washington, DC: National Institute of Justice, 1998).

restees in 34 cities around the country are tested for drug use.[131] The most recent ADAM data released in 2000 shows that most sites report overall drug use rates of 50–77 percent or greater among arrestees; in 27 of the 34 sites measured, more than 60 percent of the arrestees tested positive for drugs. Data are collected on female arrestees in 32 cities; in 22 of them, more than 60 percent of all women tested reported positive. In all, about two-thirds of both male and female arrestees test positive for drug usage.

It is of course possible that most criminals are not actually drug users but that police are more likely to apprehend muddle-headed substance abusers than clear-thinking abstainers. A second, and probably more plausible, interpretation

Though drug use per se may not be a cause of crime, it does involve people in highly risky behaviors and increases the frequency of offending. Here, investigators inspect a charred vehicle containing the remains of Jeremy Lindsey and Joseph Clayton. According to police, the men had driven from Erie to Pittsburgh so that one of them could buy $7,000 worth of marijuana, but the drug dealers robbed and killed them before lighting their car and bodies on fire.

AP/Wide World Photos

is that most criminals are in fact substance abusers. Drug use interferes with maturation and socialization. Drug abusers are more likely to drop out of school, be underemployed, engage in premarital sex, and become unmarried parents. These factors have been linked to a weakening of the social bond that leads to antisocial behaviors.[132] Typically, as Table 13.2 shows, the drug–crime relationship may be explained in one of three possible ways.

In sum, research testing both the criminality of known narcotics users and the narcotics use of known criminals produces a very strong association between drug use and crime. Even if the crime rate of drug users were actually half that reported in the research literature, users would be responsible for a significant portion of the total criminal activity in the United States.

✔ **Checkpoints on page 319**

Drugs and the Law

narcotic

A drug that produces sleep and relieves pain, such as heroin, morphine, and opium; a habit-forming drug.

The federal government first initiated legal action to curtail the use of some drugs early in the twentieth century.[133] In 1906, the Pure Food and Drug Act required manufacturers to list the amounts of habit-forming drugs in products on the labels but did not restrict their use. However, the act prohibited the importation and sale of opiates except for medicinal purposes. In 1914, the Harrison Narcotics Act restricted the importation, manufacture, sale, and dispensing of narcotics. It defined **narcotic** as any drug that produces sleep and relieves pain, such as heroin, morphine, and opium. The act was revised in 1922 to allow importation of opium and coca (cocaine) leaves for qualified medical practitioners. The Marijuana Tax Act of 1937 required registration and payment of a tax by all persons who imported, sold, or manufactured marijuana. Because marijuana was classified as a narcotic, those registering would also be subject to criminal penalty.

In later years, other federal laws were passed to clarify existing drug statutes and revise penalties. For example, the Boggs Act of 1951 provided mandatory sentences for violating federal drug laws. The Durham–Humphrey Act of 1951 made it illegal to dispense barbiturates and amphetamines without a prescription. The Narcotic Control Act of 1956 increased penalties for drug offenders. In 1965, the Drug Abuse Control Act set up stringent guidelines for the legal use and sale of mood-modifying drugs, such as barbiturates, amphetamines, LSD, and any other "dangerous drugs," except narcotics prescribed by doctors and

Table 13.2 Summary of Drug–Crime Relationship

DRUGS AND CRIME RELATIONSHIP	DEFINITION	EXAMPLES
Drug-defined offenses	Violations of laws prohibiting or regulating the possession, use, distribution, or manufacture of illegal drugs	Drug possession or use; marijuana cultivation; methamphetamine production; cocaine, heroin, or marijuana sales
Drug-related offenses	Offenses in which a drug's pharmacologic effects contribute; offenses motivated by the user's need for money to support continued use; and offenses connected to drug distribution itself	Violent behavior resulting from drug effects; stealing to get money to buy drugs; violence against rival drug dealers
Drug-using lifestyle	Drug use and crime are common aspects of a deviant lifestyle. The likelihood and frequency of involvement in illegal activity is increased because drug users may not participate in the legitimate economy and are exposed to situations that encourage crime.	A life orientation with an emphasis on short-term goals supported by illegal activities; opportunities to offend resulting from contacts with offenders and illegal markets; criminal skills learned from other offenders

SOURCE: White House Office of National Drug Control Policy, *Fact Sheet: Drug-Related Crime* (Washington, DC, 1997).

✔ Checkpoints

✔ Substance abuse is an ancient practice dating back more than 4,000 years.

✔ There is a wide variety of drugs in use today; alcohol is a major problem.

✔ Drug use in the general population has stabilized, but about half of all high school seniors have tried illegal drugs at least once.

✔ There is no single cause of substance abuse. Some people may use drugs because they are predisposed to abuse.

✔ There is a strong link between drug abuse and crime. People who become addicts may increase their illegal activities to support their habits. Others engage in violence as part of their drug-dealing activities.

pharmacists. Illegal possession was punished as a misdemeanor and manufacture or sale as a felony. And in 1970, the Comprehensive Drug Abuse Prevention and Control Act set up unified categories of illegal drugs and attached specific penalties to their sale, manufacture, or possession. The law gave the U.S. attorney general discretion to decide in which category to place any new drug.

Since then, various federal laws have attempted to increase penalties imposed on drug smugglers and limit the manufacture and sale of newly developed substances. For example, the 1984 Controlled Substances Act set new, stringent penalties for drug dealers and created five categories of narcotic and nonnarcotic substances subject to federal laws.[134] The Anti–Drug Abuse Act of 1986 again set new standards for minimum and maximum sentences for drug offenders, increased penalties for most offenses, and created a new drug penalty classification for large-scale offenses (such as trafficking in more than one kilogram of heroin), for which the penalty for a first offense was 10 years to life in prison.[135] With then-President George Bush's endorsement, Congress passed the Anti–Drug Abuse Act of 1988, which created a coordinated national drug policy under a "drug czar," set treatment and prevention priorities, and, symbolizing the government's hard-line stance against drug dealing, imposed the death penalty for drug-related killings.[136]

For the most part, state laws mirror federal statutes. Some, such as New York's, apply extremely heavy penalties for selling or distributing dangerous drugs, involving long prison sentences of up to 25 years.

State legislatures have also acted to control alcohol-related crimes. Spurred by such groups as Mothers Against Drunk Drivers, state legislatures are beginning to create more stringent penalties for drunk driving. In California, a drunk driver faces a maximum of six months in jail, a $500 fine, the suspension of his or her operator's license for six months, and impoundment of the vehicle. As a minimum penalty, a first offender could get (1) four days in jail, a $375 fine, and loss of license for six months or (2) three years' probation, a $375 fine, and either two days in jail or restricted driving privileges for 90 days.[137] In New York, persons arrested for drunk driving now risk having their automobiles seized by the government under the state's new Civil Forfeiture Law. Originally designed to combat drug trafficking and racketeering, the new law allows state prosecutors to confiscate cars involved in felony drunk-driving cases, sell them at auction, and give the proceeds to the victims of the crime.[138] More than 30 jurisdictions have passed laws providing severe penalties for drunk drivers, including mandatory jail sentences.

Drug Control Strategies

Substance abuse remains a major social problem in the United States. Politicians looking for a safe campaign issue can take advantage of the public's fear of drug addiction by calling for a war on drugs. These wars have been declared even when drug usage is stable or in decline.[139] Can these efforts pay off? Can illegal drug use be eliminated or controlled?

A number of different drug control strategies have been tried, with varying degrees of success. Some aim to deter drug use by stopping the flow of drugs into the country, apprehending and punishing dealers, and cracking down on street-level drug deals. Others focus on preventing drug use by educating potential users to the dangers of substance abuse (convincing them to "say no to drugs") and by organizing community groups to work with the at-risk population in their area. Still another approach is to treat known users so they can control their addictions. Some of these efforts are discussed here.

Source Control One approach to drug control is to deter the sale and importation of drugs through the systematic apprehension of large-volume drug dealers, coupled with the enforcement of strict drug laws that carry heavy penalties. This approach is designed to capture and punish known international drug dealers and deter those who are considering entering the drug trade. A major effort has been made to cut off supplies of drugs by destroying overseas crops and arresting members of drug cartels in Central and South America, Asia, and the Middle East, where many drugs are grown and manufactured. The federal government has been in the vanguard of encouraging exporting nations to step up efforts to destroy drug crops and prosecute dealers. Three South American nations, Peru, Bolivia, and Colombia, have agreed with the United States to coordinate control efforts. However, translating words into deeds is a formidable task. Drug lords are willing and able to fight back through intimidation, violence, and corruption when necessary. The Colombian drug cartels do not hesitate to use violence and assassination to protect their interests.

The amount of narcotics grown each year is so vast that even if three-quarters of the opium crop were destroyed, the U.S. market would still require only 10 percent of the remainder to sustain the drug trade.

Adding to control problems is the fact that the drug trade is an important source of foreign revenue for Third World nations, and destroying the drug trade undermines their economies. More than 1 million people in Peru, Bolivia, Colombia, Thailand, Laos, and other developing nations depend on the cultivating and processing of illegal substances. The federal government estimates that U.S. citizens spend more than $40 billion annually on illegal drugs, and much of this money is funneled overseas. Even if the government of one nation were willing to cooperate in vigorous drug suppression efforts, suppliers in other nations, eager to cash in on the seller's market, would be encouraged to turn more acreage over to coca or poppy production. For example, between 1994 and 1999, enforcement efforts in Peru and Bolivia were so successful that they altered cocaine cultivation patterns. As a consequence, Colombia became the premier coca-cultivating country because the local drug cartels encouraged local growers to cultivate coca plants. When the Colombian government mounted an effective eradication campaign in the traditional growing areas, the cartels linked up with rebel groups in remote parts of the country for their drug supply.[140] Neighbors expressed fear when, in August 2000, the U.S. announced $1.3 billion in military aid to fight Columbia's rural drug dealers/rebels. Ecuador's foreign minister, Heinz Moeller, told reporters, "Our worry is that the removal of this cancerous tumor will cause it to metastasize into Ecuador."[141]

Interdiction Strategies Law enforcement efforts have also been directed at intercepting drug supplies as they enter the country. Border patrols and military personnel using sophisticated hardware have been involved in massive interdiction efforts; many impressive multimillion-dollar seizures have been made. Yet the U.S. borders are so vast and unprotected that meaningful interdiction is impossible. And even if all importation were shut down, homegrown marijuana and laboratory-made drugs, such as "ice," LSD, and PCP, could become the drugs of choice. Even now, their easy availability and relatively low cost are increasing their popularity among the at-risk population.

Law Enforcement Strategies Local, state, and federal law enforcement agencies have been actively fighting against drugs. One approach is to direct efforts at large-scale drug rings. The long-term consequence has been to decentralize drug dealing and encourage young independent dealers to become major suppliers. Ironically, it has proven easier for federal agents to infiltrate and prosecute traditional organized crime groups than to take on drug-dealing gangs. Consequently, some nontraditional groups have broken into the drug trade. Police can also target, intimidate, and arrest street-level dealers and users in an effort to make drug use so much of a hassle that consumption is cut back and the crime rate reduced. Approaches that have been tried include reverse stings, in which undercover agents pose as dealers to arrest users who approach them for a buy. Police have attacked fortified crack houses with heavy equipment to breach their defenses. They have used racketeering laws to seize the assets of known dealers. Special task forces of local and state police have used undercover operations and drug sweeps to discourage both dealers and users.[142]

Although some street-level enforcement efforts have succeeded, others are considered failures. Drug sweeps have clogged courts and correctional facilities with petty offenders while draining police resources. There are also suspicions that a displacement effect occurs: Stepped-up efforts to curb drug dealing in one area or city simply encourage dealers to seek out friendlier territory.[143]

Punishment Strategies Even if law enforcement efforts cannot produce a general deterrent effect, the courts may achieve the required result by severely punishing known drug dealers and traffickers. A number of initiatives have made the prosecution and punishment of drug offenders a top priority. State prosecutors have expanded their investigations into drug importation and distribution and created special prosecutors to focus on drug dealers. The fact that drugs such as crack are considered a serious problem may have convinced judges and prosecutors to expedite substance abuse cases. Research by the federal government shows that the average sentence for drug offenders sent to federal prison is about six years.[144]

However, these efforts often have their downside. Defense attorneys consider delay tactics sound legal maneuvering in drug-related cases. Courts are so backlogged that prosecutors are anxious to plea-bargain. The consequence of this legal maneuvering is that about 25 percent of people convicted on federal drug charges are granted probation or some other form of community release.[145] Even so, prisons have become jammed with inmates, many of whom were involved in drug-related cases. Many drug offenders sent to prison do not serve their entire sentences because they are released in an effort to relieve prison overcrowding.[146]

Community Strategies Another type of drug control effort relies on the involvement of local community groups to lead the fight against drugs. Representatives of various local government agencies, churches, civic organizations, and similar institutions are being brought together to create drug prevention and awareness programs.

Citizen-sponsored programs attempt to restore a sense of community in drug-infested areas, reduce fear, and promote conventional norms and values.[147] These efforts can be classified into one of four distinct categories.[148] The first involves law enforcement–type efforts, which may include block watches, cooperative police–community efforts, and citizen patrols. Some of these citizen groups are nonconfrontational: They simply observe or photograph dealers, write down their license plate numbers, and then notify police.

A second tactic is to use the civil justice system to harass offenders. Landlords have been sued for owning properties that house drug dealers; neighborhood groups have scrutinized drug houses for building code violations. Information acquired from these various sources is turned over to local authorities, such as police and housing agencies, for more formal action.

A third approach is through community-based treatment efforts in which citizen volunteers participate in self-help support programs, such as Narcotics Anonymous or Cocaine Anonymous, which have more than 1,000 chapters nationally. Other programs provide youths with martial arts training, dancing, and social events as alternatives to the drug life.

A fourth type of community-level drug prevention effort is designed to enhance the quality of life, improve interpersonal relationships, and upgrade the neighborhood's physical environment. Activities might include the creation of drug-free school zones (which encourage police to keep drug dealers away from the vicinity of schools). Consciousness-raising efforts include demonstrations and marches to publicize the drug problem and build solidarity among participants.

Drug Education and Prevention Strategies Prevention strategies are aimed at convincing youths not to get involved in drug abuse; heavy reliance is placed on educational programs that teach kids to say no to drugs. The most widely used program is Drug Abuse Resistance Education (DARE), an elementary school course designed to give students the skills for resisting peer pressure to experiment with tobacco, drugs, and alcohol. It is unique in that it employs uniformed police officers to carry the antidrug message to the students before they enter junior high school. The program has five major focus areas:

- Providing accurate information about tobacco, alcohol, and drugs
- Teaching students techniques to resist peer pressure
- Teaching students respect for the law and law enforcers
- Giving students ideas for alternatives to drug use
- Building the self-esteem of students

DARE is based on the concept that young students need specific analytical and social skills to resist peer pressure and refuse drugs.[149] However, evaluations show that the program does little to reduce drug use or convince abusers that drugs are harmful.[150] Although there are indications that DARE may be effective with some subsets of the population, such as female and Hispanic students, overall success appears problematic at best.[151]

Drug-Testing Programs   Drug testing of private employees, government workers, and criminal offenders is believed to deter substance abuse. In the workplace, employees are tested to enhance on-the-job safety and productivity. In some industries, such as mining and transportation, drug testing is considered essential because abuse can pose a threat to the public.[152] Business leaders have been enlisted in the fight against drugs. Mandatory drug-testing programs in government and industry are common; more than 40 percent of the country's largest companies, including IBM and AT&T, have drug-testing programs. The federal government requires employee testing in regulated industries such as nuclear energy and defense contracting. About 4 million transportation workers are subject to testing.

Criminal defendants are now routinely tested at all stages of the justice system, from arrest to parole. The goal is to reduce criminal behavior by detecting current users and curbing their abuse. Can such programs reduce criminal activity? Two evaluations of pretrial drug-testing programs found little evidence that monitoring defendants' drug use influenced their behavior.[153]

Treatment Strategies   A number of approaches are taken to treat known users, getting them clean of drugs and alcohol and thereby reducing the at-risk population. One approach rests on the assumption that users have low self-esteem and treatment efforts must focus on building a sense of self. For example, users have been placed in worthwhile programs of outdoor activities and wilderness training to create self-reliance and a sense of accomplishment.[154] More intensive efforts use group therapy approaches, relying on group leaders who have been substance abusers; through such sessions, users get the skills and support to help them reject social pressure to use drugs. These programs are based on the Alcoholics Anonymous approach, which holds that users must find within themselves the strength to stay clean and that peer support from those who understand their experiences can help them achieve a drug-free life.

There are also residential programs for the more heavily involved, and a large network of drug treatment centers has been developed. Some detoxification units use medical procedures to wean patients from the more addicting drugs to others, such as methadone, that can be more easily regulated. Methadone is a drug similar to heroin, and addicts can be treated at clinics where they receive methadone under controlled conditions. However, methadone programs have been undermined because some users sell their methadone in the black market, and others supplement their dosages with illegally obtained heroin.

Other therapeutic programs attempt to deal with the psychological causes of drug use. Hypnosis, aversion therapy (getting users to associate drugs with unpleasant sensations, such as nausea), counseling, biofeedback, and other techniques are often used.

The long-term effects of treatment on drug abuse are still uncertain. Critics charge that a stay in a residential program can help stigmatize people as addicts even if they never used hard drugs; and in treatment they may be introduced to hard-core users with whom they will associate after release. Users do not often enter these programs voluntarily and have little motivation to change.[155] Supporters of treatment argue that many addicts are helped by intensive inpatient and outpatient treatment, and the cost saving is considerable.[156] Moreover, it is estimated that less than half of the 5 million people who need drug treatment actually get it, so that treatment strategies have not been given a fair trial. And despite efforts to eradicate drug use, the percentage of people receiving treatment has remained stable over the past several years (Figure 13.4).

Find It on INFOTRAC
College Edition

Did you know that the State of New York is implementing sweeping new drug court reforms that will increase the number of nonviolent drug-addicted offenders who go into court-mandated substance abuse treatment? To read more, go to InfoTrac College Edition and read

"New York Drug Reforms Call for Drug Treatment, Not Incarceration," *Alcoholism & Drug Abuse Weekly,* 3 July 2000 v12 i27 p1

Figure 13.4

Estimated Number of Persons Needing Treatment for Severe Drug Abuse Problems and the Percentage Who Received Treatment, 1991–1998

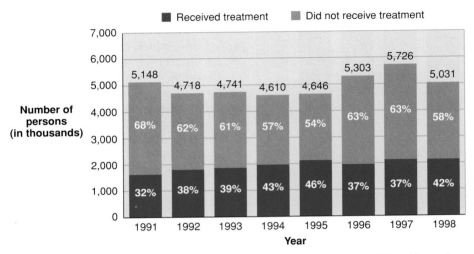

SOURCE: Office of National Drug Control Policy, "National Drug Control Strategy: 2000 Annual Report," 2000. Available online at http://www.whitehousedrugpolicy.gov/policy/ndcs.html

Employment Programs Research indicates that drug abusers who obtain and keep employment will end or reduce the incidence of their substance abuse.[157] Not surprisingly, then, there have been a number of efforts to provide vocational rehabilitation for drug abusers. One approach is the supported work program, which typically involves job-site training, ongoing assessment, and job-site intervention. Rather than teach work skills in a classroom, support programs rely on helping drug abusers deal with real work settings. Other programs provide training to overcome barriers to employment, including help with motivation, education, experience, the job market, job-seeking skills, and personal issues. For example, female abusers may be unaware of child-care resources that would enable them to seek employment opportunities while caring for their children. Another approach is to help addicts improve their interviewing skills so that once a job opportunity can be identified, they are equipped to convince potential employers of their commitment and reliability.

Legalization Considering these problems, some commentators have called for the legalization or decriminalization of restricted drugs. The so-called war on drugs is expensive, costing more than $500 billion over the past 20 years—money that could have been spent on education and economic development. Drug enforcement now costs federal, state, and local governments more than $30 billion per year.[158] And effectiveness is questionable. Two decades ago, a kilogram of cocaine sold for a wholesale price of $40,000; today it goes for $20,000 to $25,000. Translated into consumer prices, a gram of cocaine costs $50 today, compared to $100 in 1990. Declining prices suggest that the supply of cocaine is rising despite the billions spent to prevent its importation.[159]

Legalization is warranted, according to drug expert Ethan Nadelmann, because the use of mood-altering substances is customary in almost all human societies; people have always wanted, and will find ways of obtaining, psychoactive drugs.[160] Banning drugs creates networks of manufacturers and distributors, many of whom use violence as part of their standard operating procedures. Although some believe that drug use is immoral, Nadelmann questions whether it is any worse than the unrestricted use of alcohol and cigarettes, both of which are addicting and unhealthful. Far more people die each year because they abuse these legal substances than are killed in drug wars or from abusing illegal substances.[161]

Nadelmann also states that just as Prohibition failed to stop the flow of alcohol in the 1920s while it increased the power of organized crime, the policy of prohibiting drugs is similarly doomed to failure. When drugs were legal and freely available earlier in this century, the proportion of Americans using drugs was not much greater than today. Most users led normal lives, most likely because of the legal status of their drug use.[162]

If drugs were legalized, the argument goes, price and distribution could be controlled by the government. This would reduce addicts' cash requirements, so crime rates would drop, because users would no longer need the same cash flow to support their habits. Drug-related deaths would decline because government control would reduce needle sharing and the spread of AIDS. Legalization would also destroy the drug-importing cartels and gangs. Because drugs would be bought and sold openly, the government would reap a tax windfall both from taxes on the sale of drugs and from income taxes paid by drug dealers on profits that have been part of the hidden economy. Of course, as with alcohol, drug distribution would be regulated, keeping drugs away from adolescents, public servants such as police and airline pilots, and known felons. Those who favor legalization point to the Netherlands as a country that has legalized drugs and remains relatively crime-free.[163]

This approach might have the short-term effect of reducing the association between drug use and crime, but it might also have grave social consequences. Legalization might increase the nation's rate of drug usage, creating an even larger group of nonproductive, drug-dependent people who must be cared for by the rest of society.[164] In countries such as Iran and Thailand, where drugs are cheap and readily available, the rate of narcotics use is quite high. Historically, the availability of cheap narcotics has preceded drug use epidemics, as was the case when British and American merchants sold opium in nineteenth-century China.

If juveniles, criminals, and members of other at-risk groups were forbidden to buy drugs, who would be the customers? Noncriminal, nonabusing middle-aged adults? And would not those prohibited from legally buying drugs create an underground market almost as vast as the current one? If the government tried to raise money by taxing legal drugs, as it now does with liquor and cigarettes, that might encourage drug smuggling to avoid tax payments; these "illegal" drugs might then fall into the hands of adolescents.

Decriminalization or legalization of controlled substances is unlikely in the near term, but further study is warranted. What effect would a policy of partial decriminalization (for example, legalizing small amounts of marijuana) have on drug use rates? Would a get-tough policy help to "widen the net" of the justice system and actually deepen some youths' involvement in substance abuse? Can society provide alternatives to drugs that will reduce teenage drug dependency?[165] The answers to these questions have proven elusive.

Summary

Public order crimes are acts considered illegal because they conflict with social policy, accepted moral rules, and public opinion. There is usually great debate over public order crimes. Some charge that they are not really crimes at all and that it is foolish to legislate morality. Others view such morally tinged acts as prostitution, gambling, and drug abuse as harmful and therefore subject to public control.

Many public order crimes are sex-related. Although homosexuality is not a crime, homosexual acts are subject to legal control. Some states still follow the archaic custom of legislating long prison terms for consensual homosexual sex.

Prostitution is another sex-related public order crime. Although prostitution has been practiced for thousands of years and is legal in some areas, most states outlaw commercial sex. There are a variety of prostitutes, including streetwalkers, B-girls, and call girls. Studies indicate that prostitutes came from poor, troubled families and have abusive parents. However, there is little evidence that prostitutes are emotionally disturbed, addicted to drugs, or sexually abnormal. Although prostitution is illegal, some cities have set up adult entertainment areas where commercial sex is tolerated by law enforcement agents.

Pornography involves the sale of sexually explicit material intended to sexually excite paying customers. The depiction of sex and nudity is not illegal, but it does violate the law when it is judged obscene. Obscenity is a legal term that today is defined as material offensive to community standards. Thus, each local jurisdiction must decide what pornographic material is obscene. A growing problem is the exploitation of children in obscene materials (kiddie porn). The Supreme Court has ruled that local communities can pass statutes outlawing any sexually explicit material. There is no hard evidence that pornography is related to crime or aggression, but data suggest that sexual material with a violent theme is related to sexual violence by those who view it.

Substance abuse is another type of public order crime. Most states and the federal government outlaw a wide variety of drugs they consider harmful, including narcotics, amphetamines, barbiturates, cocaine, hallucinogens, and marijuana. One of the main reasons for the continued ban on drugs is their relationship to crime. Numerous studies have found that drug addicts commit enormous amounts of property crime.

Alcohol is another commonly abused substance. Although alcohol is legal to possess, it too has been linked to crime. Drunk driving and deaths caused by drunk drivers are growing national problems.

There are many different strategies to control substance abuse, ranging from source control to treatment. So far, no single method seems effective. Although legalization is debated, the fact that so many people already take drugs and the association of drug abuse with crime make legalization unlikely in the near term.

For additional chapter links, discussions, and quizzes, see the book-specific Web site at http://www.wadsworth.com/product/0534519423s.

Thinking Like a Criminologist

According to data from a 2000 national school survey, high school boys who have been physically or sexually abused are at least twice as likely as nonabused boys to drink, smoke, or use drugs. The survey was an in-class questionnaire completed by 3,162 boys in grades 5–12 at a nationally representative sample of 265 public, private, and parochial schools from December 1999 to June 2000. The survey included roughly equal samples of adolescent boys in grades 5–8 and 9–12. Of those in grades 9–12, 13 percent said that they had been physically or sexually abused. Of these abused boys, 30 percent reported that they drank frequently and 34 percent reported that they had used drugs in the past month, compared to 16 percent and 15 percent, respectively, of nonabused boys. Abused boys were also nearly three times more likely to smoke frequently (27 percent versus 10 percent).

As a criminologist, what would be your interpretation of these data? What is the possible association between child abuse and substance abuse?

Key Terms

public order crime	sodomy	obscenity
victimless crime	homophobia	temperance movement
moral entrepreneur	paraphilia	Prohibition
gay bashing	prostitution	narcotic
homosexuality	pornography	

Discussion Questions

1. Why do you think people take drugs? Do you know anyone with an addiction-prone personality, or do you believe that is a myth?

2. What policy might be the best strategy to reduce teenage drug use: source control? reliance on treatment? national education efforts? community-level enforcement?

3. Under what circumstances, if any, might the legalization or decriminalization of sexually related material be beneficial to society?

4. Do you consider alcohol a drug? Should greater control be placed on the sale of alcohol?

5. Is prostitution really a crime? Should men or women have the right to sell sexual favors if they so choose?

Part 4

The Criminal Justice System

The text's final section reviews the agencies and the process of justice designed to exert social control over criminal offenders. Chapter 14 provides an overview of the justice system and describes its major institutions and processes. This vast array of people and institutions is beset by conflicting goals and values. Some view the justice system as a mammoth agency of social control; others see it as a great social agency dispensing therapy to those who cannot fit within the boundaries of society.

Consequently, a major goal of justice system policymakers is to formulate and disseminate effective models of crime prevention and control. Efforts are now being undertaken at all levels of the justice system to improve information flow, experiment with new program concepts, and evaluate current operating procedures.

14 The Criminal Justice System

During his lifetime, Michael Riggs had been convicted eight times in California for such offenses as car theft and robbery. In 1996, he was once again in trouble, this time for shoplifting a $20 bottle of vitamins. Riggs was sentenced to a term of 25 years to life under California's "three strikes" law, which mandates a life sentence for anyone convicted of a third offense. The law requires a trial judge to treat a defendant's third offense, even a petty crime such as shoplifting, as if it were a felony for purposes of applying the law's mandatory sentencing provisions. Riggs must serve a minimum of 20.8 years before parole eligibility. Without the "three strikes" law, he would ordinarily have earned a maximum sentence of six months; if he had been convicted of murder, he would have had to serve only 17 years. Riggs appealed his conviction to the Supreme Court in 1999, but the justices refused to rule on the case, letting his sentence stand.[1]

criminal justice system

The agencies of government—police, courts, and corrections—responsible for apprehending, adjudicating, sanctioning, and treating criminal offenders.

The Riggs case symbolizes the dilemmas faced by the component agencies of the **criminal justice system**—police, courts, and corrections—that have been established to apprehend, adjudicate, sanction, and treat criminal offenders. These government institutions are charged by law with dispensing fair, equal justice to all who come before them; maintaining the rule of law in a society beset by racial and social injustice and conflict; deterring crime; and treating both offenders and victims in a just, evenhanded manner. Questions are still being asked about the general direction the justice system should take, how the problem of crime control should be approached, and what is the most effective method of dealing with known criminal offenders.

This chapter reviews the various components and processes of criminal justice and then discusses the legal constraints on criminal justice agencies. Some of the philosophical concepts that dominate the system will be mentioned and explained.

The Concept of a Criminal Justice System

Although firmly entrenched in our culture, common criminal justice agencies have existed for only 150 years or so. At first these institutions operated independently, with little recognition that their functions could be coordinated or share common ground.

In 1931, President Herbert Hoover appointed the National Commission of Law Observance and Enforcement, commonly known today as the Wickersham Commission. This national study group analyzed the American justice system in detail and helped usher in the era of treatment and rehabilitation. It showed the complex rules and regulations that govern the system and exposed how difficult it was for justice personnel to keep track of its legal and administrative complexity.

The modern era of criminal justice study began with a series of explorations of the criminal justice process conducted under the auspices of the American Bar Foundation.[2] As a group, the Bar Foundation studies brought to light some of the hidden or low-visibility processes that were at the heart of justice system operations. They showed how informal decision making and the use of personal discretion were essential ingredients of the justice process.

Another milestone occurred in 1967, when the President's Commission on Law Enforcement and the Administration of Justice (the Crime Commission), appointed by President Lyndon Johnson, published its final report, *The Challenge of Crime in a Free Society.*[3] This group of practitioners, educators, and attorneys had been charged with creating a comprehensive view of the criminal justice process and offering recommendations for its reform. Its efforts resulted in passage of the Safe Streets and Crime Control Act of 1968, which provided federal funds for state and local crime control efforts. This legislation helped launch a massive campaign to restructure the justice system by funding the Law Enforcement Assistance Administration (LEAA), an agency that provided hundreds of millions of dollars in aid to local and state justice agencies. Federal intervention through the LEAA ushered in a new era in research and development in criminal justice and established the concept that its component agencies actually make up a system.[4]

Though the LEAA is no longer in operation, its efforts helped identify the concept of a unified system of criminal justice. Rather than viewing police, courts, and correctional agencies as thousands of independent institutions, it has become common to see them as components of a large, integrated, people-processing system that manages law violators from the time of their arrest through trial, punishment, and release.

What Is the Criminal Justice System?

Criminal justice refers to the agencies of government charged with enforcing law, adjudicating crime, and correcting criminal conduct. The criminal justice system is essentially an instrument of social control: Society considers some behaviors so dangerous and destructive that it either strictly controls their occurrence or outlaws them outright. It is the job of the agencies of justice to prevent these behaviors by apprehending and punishing transgressors and deterring their future occurrence. Although society maintains other forms of social control, such as the family, school, and church, they are designed to deal with moral, not legal, misbehavior. Only the criminal justice system has the power to control crime and punish criminals. The contemporary U.S. criminal justice system is huge, costing taxpayers well over $100 billion per year, including almost $50 billion for police, $25 billion for the courts and legal system, and $40 billion for corrections. And as Figure 14.1 shows, these costs have been rising dramatically.

The justice system today employs close to 2 million people, including more than 900,000 in law enforcement, 400,000 in the courts, and 650,000 in correc-

Figure 14.1

Direct Expenditure by Criminal Justice Function, 1982–1996

Direct expenditure for each of the major criminal justice functions (police, corrections, judicial) has been increasing dramatically.

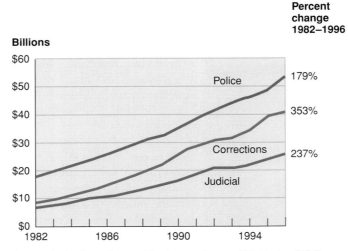

SOURCE: *Justice Expenditure and Employment Extracts* (Washington, DC: Bureau of Justice Statistics, 2000).

tions.[5] It consists of more than 55,000 public agencies, including approximately 17,000 police agencies, nearly 17,000 courts, more than 8,000 prosecutorial agencies, about 6,000 correctional institutions, and more than 3,500 probation and parole departments. There are also capital costs. State jurisdictions are now conducting a massive correctional building campaign, adding tens of thousands of prison cells. It costs about $70,000 to build a prison cell and about $25,000 dollars per year to keep an inmate in prison; juvenile institutions cost about $30,000 per year per resident. And beyond the direct costs of funding police, courts, and corrections, federal, state, and local governments incur many additional crime-related expenses.

The system is so big because it must process, treat, and care for millions of people each year. Although the crime rate has been in decline, about 15 million people are still being arrested each year, including almost 3 million for serious felony offenses.[6] In addition, about 1.5 million juveniles are handled by the juvenile courts.[7] State courts annually convict more than 870,000 adults of felonies.[8]

Considering the enormous number of people processed each year, it comes as no surprise that the correctional system population is at an all-time high. More than 6 million people are now under the control of the correctional system, with close to 2 million men and women in the nation's jails and prisons. About 4 million adult men and women are being supervised in the community while on probation or parole, a number that has been increasing by more than 3 percent each year since 1990.[9]

The major components of this immense system—the police, courts, and correctional agencies—are described in the sections that follow. What are their duties? What are the major stages in the formal criminal justice process, and how are decisions made at these critical junctures? What is the informal justice process, and how does it operate? These important questions are addressed next.

Find It on INFOTRAC
College Edition

Despite its size and cost, some critics believe that the criminal justice system does not work very well. To read one such critique, go to InfoTrac College Edition and look at
Barbara Dority, "The U.S. Criminal Injustice System," *The Humanist*, May 2000 v60 i3 p33

Police and Law Enforcement

Approximately 17,000 law enforcement agencies operate in the United States. Most are municipal, general-purpose police forces, numbering about 12,000 in all. In addition, local jurisdictions maintain more than 1,000 special police units, including park rangers, harbor police, transit police, and campus security agencies at local universities. At the county level, there are approximately 3,000 sheriff's departments, which, depending on the jurisdiction, provide police protection in unincorporated areas of a county, perform judicial functions such as serving subpoenas, and maintain the county jail and detention facilities. Every state except Hawaii maintains a state police force. The federal government has its own law enforcement agencies, including the FBI and the Secret Service.

Law enforcement agencies have been charged with peacekeeping, deterring potential criminals, and apprehending law violators.[10] The traditional police role involved maintaining order through patrolling public streets and highways, responding to calls for assistance, investigating crimes, and identifying criminal suspects. The police role has gradually expanded to include a variety of human service functions, including preventing youth crime and diverting juvenile offenders from the criminal justice system, resolving family conflicts, facilitating the movement of people and vehicles, preserving civil order during emergencies, providing emergency medical care, and improving police–community relations.[11]

Police are the most visible agents of the justice process. Their reactions to victims and offenders are carefully scrutinized in the news media. Police have been criticized for being too harsh or too lenient, too violent or too passive. Police response to minority groups, youths, political dissidents, protesters, and union workers has been publicly debated.

AP/Wide World Photos

It is said that the police are the most visible agents of the justice system. Here, Maurice Price, age 6, pets a police horse in Fresno, California. Officers Al Hernandez (left) and Tom Hardin were in a southwest Fresno neighborhood looking for a parolee.

Find It on INFOTRAC
College Edition

Are the community police officers of today similar to the small-town doctor of yesteryear who knew every patient on a personal level and made house calls? To find out, go to InfoTrac College Edition and read

Joseph A. Harpold, "A Medical Model for Community Policing," *FBI Law Enforcement Bulletin,* June 2000 v69 i6 p23

Compounding the problem is the tremendous discretion afforded police officers, who determine when a domestic dispute becomes disorderly conduct or criminal assault, whether it is appropriate to arrest juveniles or refer them to a social agency, and when to assume that probable cause exists to arrest a suspect for a crime.[12] At the same time, police agencies have been criticized for such problems as internal corruption, inefficiency, lack of effectiveness, brutality, and discriminatory hiring.[13] Widely publicized cases of police brutality, such as the Rodney King beating in Los Angeles, have prompted calls for the investigation and prosecution of police officers. Consequently, police at all levels of government have traditionally been defensive toward and suspicious of the public, resistant to change, and secretive in their activities.

In recent years, police departments have experimented with new forms of law enforcement, including community policing and problem-oriented policing. Rather than respond to crime, police officers have taken on the role of community change agents, working with citizens to prevent crimes before they occur. Community programs involve police in such activities as citizen crime patrols and councils that identify crime problems. Community policing often involves decentralized units that operate on the neighborhood level in order to be more sensitive to the particular concerns of the public. Table 14.1 shows what one expert considers the most notable changes in policing since 1960.

The Criminal Court System

The criminal courts are considered by many to be the core element in the administration of criminal justice. The court is a complex social agency with many independent but interrelated subsystems—clerk, prosecutor, defense attorney, judge, and probation department—each having a role in the court's operation.

Table 14.1 The Most Notable Achievements of American Police, 1960–Present

1. The intellectual caliber of the police has risen dramatically. American police today at all ranks are smarter, better informed, and more sophisticated than police in the 1960s.

2. Senior police managers are more ambitious for their organizations than they used to be. Chiefs and their deputies want to leave their own distinctive stamp on their organizations. Many recognize that management is an important specialized skill that must be developed.

3. An explicit scientific mindset has taken hold in American policing that involves an appreciation of the importance of evaluation and the timely availability of information.

4. The standards of police conduct have risen. Despite recent well-publicized incidents of brutality and corruption, American police today treat the public more fairly, more equitably, and less venally than police did 30 years ago.

5. Police are remarkably more diverse in terms of race and gender than a generation ago. This amounts to a revolution in American policing, changing both its appearance and, more slowly, its behavior.

6. Police work has become intellectually more demanding, requiring an array of new specialized knowledge about technology, forensic analysis, and crime. This has had profound effects on recruitment, notably civilianization, organizational structure, career patterns, and operational coordination.

7. Civilian review of police discipline has gradually become accepted by police. Although the struggle is not yet over, expansion is inevitable as more senior police executives see that civilian review reassures the public and validates their own favorable opinion of the overall quality of police performance.

SOURCE: David H. Bayley, "Policing in America," *Society* 36 (December 1998): 16–20.

It is also the scene of many important elements of criminal justice decision making—detention, jury selection, trial, and sentencing. Ideally, the judiciary process operates with absolute fairness and equality. The entire process—from filing the initial complaint to final sentencing of the defendant—is governed by precise rules of law designed to ensure fairness. No defendant tried before a U.S. court should suffer or benefit because of his or her personal characteristics, beliefs, or affiliations.

discretion

The use of personal decision making by those carrying out police, judicial, and sanctioning functions within the criminal justice system.

However, U.S. criminal justice can be selective. **Discretion** accompanies defendants through every step of the process, determining what will happen to them and how their cases will be resolved. Discretion means that two people committing similar crimes may receive highly dissimilar treatment. For example, most people convicted of homicide receive a prison sentence, but about 5 percent receive probation as a sole sentence; more murderers get probation than the death penalty.[14]

Court Structure The typical state court structure is illustrated in Figure 14.2. Most states employ a multitiered court structure. Lower courts try misdemeanors and conduct the preliminary processing of felony offenses. Superior trial courts try felony cases. Appellate courts review the criminal procedures of trial courts to determine whether the offenders were treated fairly. Superior appellate courts or state supreme courts, used in about half the states, review lower appellate court decisions.

The independent federal court system has three tiers, as shown in Figure 14.3. The U.S. district courts are the trial courts of the system; they have jurisdiction over cases involving violations of federal law, such as interstate transportation of

Figure 14.2

Structure of a State Judicial System

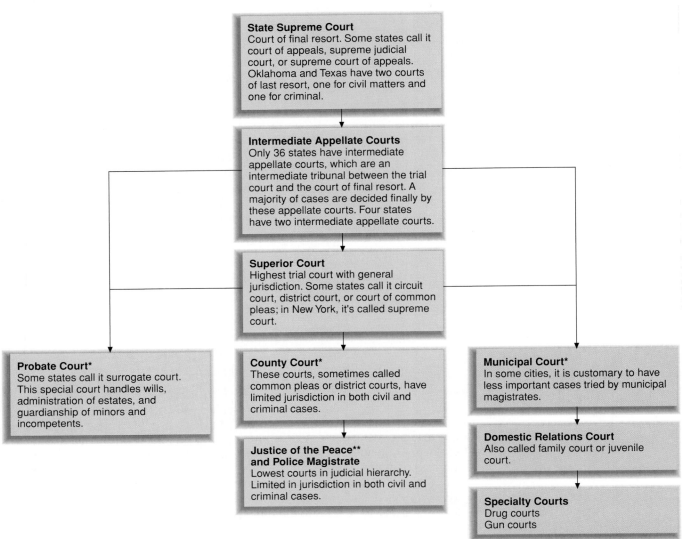

*Courts of special jurisdiction, such as probate, family, or juvenile courts, and the so-called inferior courts, such as common pleas or municipal courts, may be separate courts or part of the trial court of general jurisdiction.

**Justices of the peace do not exist in all states. Where they do exist, their jurisdictions vary greatly from state to state.

SOURCE: American Bar Association, *Law and the Courts* (Chicago: ABA, 1974), 20. Updated information provided by West Publishing, St. Paul, Minnesota.

stolen vehicles and racketeering. Appeals from the district court are heard in one of the intermediate federal courts of appeal. The highest federal appeals court, the U.S. Supreme Court, is the court of last resort for all cases tried in the various federal and state courts.

The Supreme Court The U.S. Supreme Court is composed of nine members, appointed for lifetime terms by the president with the approval of Congress. In general, the Court hears only cases it deems important and ap-

Figure 14.3

The Federal Judicial System

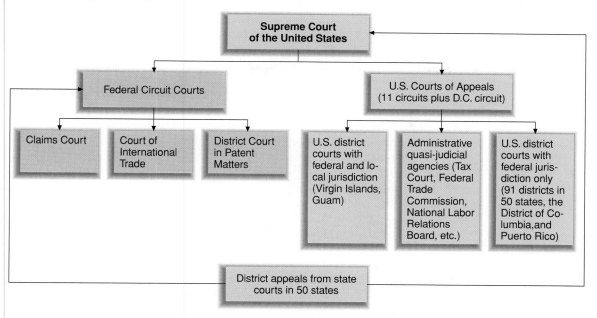

SOURCE: American Bar Association, *Law and the Courts* (Chicago: ABA, 1974), 21. Updated information provided by the Federal Courts Improvement Act of 1982 and West Publishing, St. Paul, Minnesota.

landmark decision

A ruling by the U.S. Supreme Court that serves as a precedent for similar legal issues; often influences the everyday operating procedures of police agencies, trial courts, and corrections institutions.

adversary system

U.S. method of criminal adjudication in which prosecution (the state) and defense (the accused) each try to bring forward evidence and arguments, with guilt or innocence ultimately decided by an impartial judge or jury.

prosecutor

Public official who represents the government in criminal proceedings, presenting the case against the accused.

defendant

In criminal proceedings, the person accused of violating the law.

propriate. When the Court decides to hear a case, it usually grants a writ of certiorari, requesting a transcript of the case proceedings for review.

The Supreme Court can word a decision so that it becomes a precedent that must be honored by all lower courts. For example, if the Court grants a particular litigant the right to counsel at a police lineup, then all people in similar situations must be given the same right. This type of ruling is usually referred to as a **landmark decision**. The use of precedent in the legal system gives the Supreme Court power to influence and mold the everyday operating procedures of police agencies, trial courts, and corrections institutions.

Prosecution and Defense Within the structure of the court system, the prosecutor and the defense attorney are opponents in what is known as the **adversary system**. These two parties oppose each other in a hotly disputed contest—the criminal trial—in accordance with rules of law and procedure. In every criminal case, the state acts against the defendant and the defense attorney acts for the defendant before an impartial judge or jury, with each side trying to bring forward evidence and arguments to advance its case. Theoretically, the ultimate objective of the adversary system is to seek the truth, determining the guilt or innocence of the defendant from the formal evidence presented at the trial. The adversary system is designed to ensure that the defendant is given a fair trial, that the relevant facts of a given case emerge, and that an impartial decision is reached.

Criminal Prosecution The **prosecutor** is the public official who represents the government and presents its case against the **defendant**, who is charged with a violation of the criminal law. Traditionally, the prosecutor is a local attorney whose area of jurisdictional responsibility is limited to a particular county or city. The prosecutor is known variously as a district attorney or a prosecuting attorney and is either an elected or an appointed official. On the state level, the prosecutor may be referred to as the attorney general, while in the federal jurisdiction, the title is United States attorney.

The prosecutor is responsible not only for charging the defendant with the crime but also for bringing the case to trial and to a final conclusion. The prosecutor's authority ranges from determining the nature of the charge to reducing the charge by negotiation or recommending that the complaint be dismissed. The prosecutor also participates in bail hearings, presents cases before a grand jury, and appears for the state at arraignments. In sum, the prosecutor is responsible for presenting the state's case from the time of the defendant's arrest through conviction and sentencing in the criminal court.

The prosecutor, like the police officer, exercises a great deal of discretion; he or she can decide initially whether to file a criminal charge, determine what charge to bring, or explore the availability of noncriminal dispositions. Prosecutorial discretion would not be as important as it is were it desirable to prosecute all violations of the law. However, full enforcement of every law is not practical, since police officers and prosecutors ordinarily lack sufficient resources, staff, and support services to carry out that goal. Therefore, it makes sense to screen out cases where the accused is obviously innocent, where the evidence is negligible, or where criminal sanctions may seem inappropriate. Instead of total or automatic law enforcement, a process of selective or discretionary enforcement exists; as a result, the prosecutor must make many decisions that significantly influence police operations and control the actual number of cases processed through the court and correctional systems.

defense attorney

The person responsible for protecting the constitutional rights of the accused and presenting the best possible legal defense; represents a defendant from initial arrest through trial, sentencing, and any appeal.

Criminal Defense The defense attorney is responsible for providing legal representation of the defendant. This role involves two major functions:

1. Protecting the constitutional rights of the accused
2. Presenting the best possible legal defense for the defendant

The defense attorney represents a client from initial arrest through the trial stage, during the sentencing hearing, and, if needed, through the process of appeal. The defense attorney is also expected to enter into plea negotiations and obtain for the defendant the most suitable bargain regarding type and length of sentence.

right to counsel

The right of a person accused of crime to have the assistance of a defense attorney in all criminal prosecutions.

public defender

An attorney employed by the state whose job is to provide free legal counsel to indigent defendants.

pro bono

The provision of free legal counsel to indigent defendants by private attorneys as a service to the profession and the community.

Any person accused of a crime can obtain the services of a private attorney if he or she can afford to do so. One of the most critical questions in the criminal justice system has been whether an indigent (poor) defendant has a right to counsel. The federal court system has long provided counsel to the indigent on the basis of the Sixth Amendment of the U.S. Constitution, which gives the accused the right to have the assistance of defense counsel. Through a series of landmark U.S. Supreme Court decisions, beginning with *Powell v. Alabama* in 1932 and continuing with *Gideon v. Wainwright* in 1963 and *Argersinger v. Hamlin* in 1972, the right of a criminal defendant to have counsel has become fundamental to the U.S. system of criminal justice.[15] Today, state courts must provide counsel to indigent defendants who are charged with criminal offenses where the possibility of incarceration exists. Consequently, more than 1,000 public defender agencies have been set up around the United States to provide free legal counsel to indigent defendants. In other jurisdictions, defense lawyers volunteer their services, referred to as working pro bono, and are assigned to criminal defendants. A few rural counties have defense lawyers under contract who handle all criminal matters.

Corrections

probation

The conditional release of a convicted offender into the community under the supervision of a probation officer and subject to certain conditions.

incarceration

Confinement in jail or prison.

jail

Institution, usually run by the county, for short-term detention of those convicted of misdemeanors and those awaiting trial or other judicial proceedings.

prison

State or federally operated facility for the incarceration of felony offenders sentenced by the criminal courts; penitentiary.

penitentiary

State or federally operated facility for the incarceration of felony offenders sentenced by the criminal courts; prison.

parole

A conditional early release from prison, with the offender serving the remainder of the sentence in the community under the supervision of a parole officer.

✔ Checkpoints

✔ The concept of a criminal justice sytem is relatively new.

✔ The system is vast, costing taxpayers about $100 billion a year.

✔ The police are the largest component of the system. They identify law violators, keep the peace, and provide emergency services.

✔ The court system dispenses fair and even-handed justice.

✔ Prosecutors bring the criminal charge, and defense attorneys represent the accused.

✔ Correctional agencies incarcerate and treat millions of convicted offenders.

✔ Included within corrections are closed institutions, such as prisons and jails, and community correctional efforts, such as probation.

After conviction and sentencing, the offender enters the correctional system. Correctional agencies administer the postjudicatory care given to offenders, which, depending on the seriousness of the crime and the individual needs of the offender, can range from casual monitoring in the community to solitary confinement in a maximum-security prison.

The most common correctional treatment, **probation**, is a legal disposition that allows the convicted offender to remain in the community, subject to conditions imposed by court order under the supervision of a probation officer. This lets the offender continue working and avoid the crippling effects of **incarceration**.

A person given a sentence involving incarceration is ordinarily confined to a correctional institution for a specified period. Different types of institutions are used to hold offenders. **Jails** or houses of correction hold those convicted of misdemeanors and those awaiting trial or involved in other proceedings, such as grand jury deliberations, arraignments, or preliminary hearings. Many of these institutions for short-term detention are administered by county governments. Little is done to treat inmates because the personnel and institutions lack the qualifications, services, and resources.

State and federally operated facilities that receive felony offenders sentenced by the criminal courts are called **prisons** or **penitentiaries**. They may be minimum-, medium-, or maximum-security institutions. Prison facilities vary throughout the country. Some have high walls, cells, and large, heterogeneous inmate populations; others offer much freedom, good correctional programs, and small, homogeneous populations.

Most new inmates are first sent to a reception and classification center, where they are given diagnostic evaluations and assigned to institutions that meet their individual needs as much as possible within the system's resources. The diagnostic process in the reception center may range from a physical examination and a single interview to an extensive series of psychiatric tests, orientation sessions, and numerous personal interviews. Classification is a way of evaluating inmates and assigning them to appropriate placements and activities within the state institutional system.

Because the gap between what correctional programs promise to deliver and their actual performance is often significant, many jurisdictions have instituted community-based correctional facilities. These programs emphasize the use of small neighborhood residential centers, halfway houses, prerelease centers, and work release and home furlough programs. Experts believe that only a small percentage of prison inmates require maximum security and that most can be more effectively rehabilitated in community-based facilities. Rather than totally confining offenders in an impersonal, harsh prison, such programs offer them the opportunity to maintain normal family and social relationships while providing rehabilitative services and resources at a lower cost to taxpayers.

The last segment of the corrections system, **parole**, is a process whereby an inmate is selected for early release and serves the remainder of the sentence in the community under the supervision of a parole officer. The main purpose of parole is to help the ex-inmate bridge the gap between institutional confinement and a positive adjustment within the community. All parolees must adhere to a set of rules of behavior while they are "on the outside." If these rules are violated, the parole privilege can be terminated (revoked), and the parolee will be sent back to the institution to serve the remainder of the sentence.

Other ways an offender may be released from an institution include mandatory release upon completion of the sentence and the pardon, a form of executive clemency. ✔ Checkpoints

The Process of Justice

In addition to viewing the criminal justice system as a collection of agencies, it is possible to see it as a series of decision points through which offenders flow. This process, illustrated in Figure 14.4, begins with initial contact with police and ends with the offender's reentry into society. At any point in the process, a decision may be made to drop further proceedings and allow the accused back into society without further penalty.

In a classic statement, political scientist Herbert Packer described this process as follows:

> The image that comes to mind is an assembly line conveyor belt down which moves an endless stream of cases, never stopping, carrying them to workers who stand at fixed stations and who perform on each case as it comes by the same small but essential operation that brings it one step closer to being a finished product, or to exchange the metaphor for the reality, a closed file. The criminal process is seen as a screening process in which each successive stage—pre-arrest investigation, arrest, post-arrest investigation, preparation for trial, or entry of plea, conviction, disposition—involves a series of routinized operations whose success is gauged primarily by their tendency to pass the case along to a successful conclusion.[16]

Although each jurisdiction is somewhat different, a comprehensive view of the processing of a felony offender would probably contain the following decision points:

1. *Initial contact.* The initial contact an offender has with the justice system occurs when police officers observe a criminal act during their patrol of city streets, parks, or highways. They may also find out about a crime through a citizen or victim complaint. Similarly, an informer may alert them about criminal activity in return for financial or other consideration. Sometimes political officials, such as the mayor or city council, ask police to look into ongoing criminal activity, such as gambling, and during their subsequent investigations police officers encounter an illegal act.

2. *Investigation.* Regardless of whether the police observe, hear of, or receive a complaint about a crime, they may investigate to gather sufficient facts, or evidence, to identify the perpetrator, justify an arrest, and bring the offender to trial. An investigation may take a few minutes, as when patrol officers see a burglary in progress and apprehend the burglar at the scene of the crime. An investigation may also take years to complete and involve numerous investigators. For example, when federal agents tracked and captured Theodore Kaczinski (known as the Unabomber) in 1996, it completed an investigation that had lasted more than a decade.

arrest

The taking into police custody of an individual suspected of a crime.

probable cause

Evidence of a crime, and of a suspect's involvement in it, sufficient to warrant an arrest.

3. *Arrest.* An **arrest** occurs when the police take a person into custody for allegedly committing a criminal act. An arrest is legal when all of the following conditions exist: (a) the officer believes there is sufficient evidence (**probable cause**) that a crime is being or has been committed and that the suspect committed the crime; (b) the officer deprives the individual of freedom; and (c) the suspect believes that he or she is in the custody of a police officer and cannot voluntarily leave. The police officer is not required to use the word "arrest" or any similar word to initiate an arrest; nor does the officer first have to bring the suspect to the police station. For all practical purposes, a person who has been deprived of liberty is under arrest. Arrests can be made at the scene of a crime or after a warrant is issued by a magistrate.

4. *Custody.* After arrest, the suspect remains in police custody. The person may be taken to the police station to be fingerprinted and photographed and to

Figure 14.4

The Critical Stages in the Justice Process

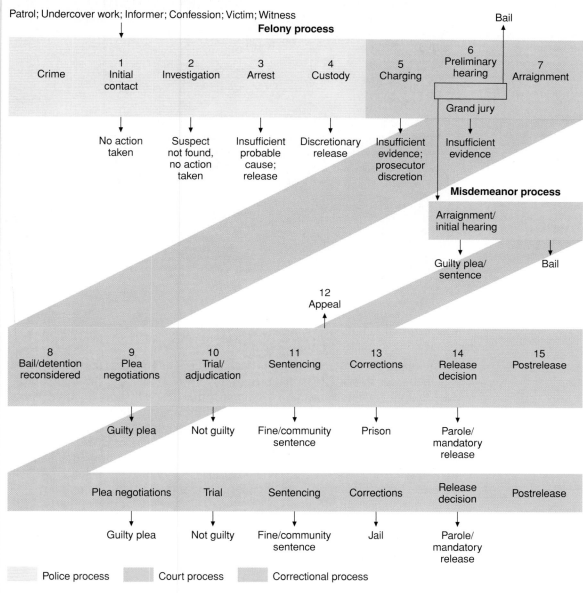

| Police process | Court process | Correctional process |

---

booking

Fingerprinting, photographing, and recording of personal information of a suspect in police custody.

interrogation

The questioning of a suspect in police custody.

have personal information recorded—a procedure popularly referred to as **booking**. Witnesses may be brought in to view the suspect (in a lineup), and further evidence may be gathered on the case. Suspects may be interrogated by police officers to get their side of the story, they may be asked to sign a confession of guilt, or they may be asked to identify others involved in the crime. The law allows suspects to have their lawyer present when police conduct an in-custody **interrogation**.

5. *Complaint/charging.* After police turn the evidence in a case over to the prosecutor, who represents the state at any criminal proceedings, a decision will be made whether to file a complaint, information, or bill of indictment with the

Indianapolis Police Department officer Mark Fagan and his partner Raider, a Dutch shepherd, examine a car for possible narcotics during a 1998 roadblock set up to look for illegal drugs. Lawyers for motorists delayed by the roadblock asked the Supreme Court to ban the practice, calling it risky and heavy-handed. The city of Indianapolis argued that such roadblocks were a simple and effective way to stem drug trafficking in high-crime neighborhoods and were no more intrusive than random checks for drunk drivers or illegal immigrants. The Supreme Court disagreed and in the case of *Indianapolis v. Edmond* (2000) ruled the practice unlawful.

AP/Wide World Photos

indictment

A written accusation returned by a grand jury charging an individual with a specified crime, based on the prosecutor's presentation of probable cause.

grand jury

A group of citizens chosen to hear testimony in secret and to issue formal criminal accusations (indictments).

preliminary hearing

Alternative to a grand jury, in which an impartial lower-court judge decides whether there is probable cause sufficient for a trial.

arraignment

The step in the criminal justice process when the accused is brought before the trial judge, formal charges are read, defendants are informed of their rights, a plea is entered, bail is considered, and a trial date is set.

bail

A money bond intended to ensure that the accused will return for trial.

recognizance

Pledge by the accused to return for trial, which may be accepted in lieu of bail.

court having jurisdiction over the case. Complaints are used in misdemeanors; information and indictment are employed in felonies. Each is a charging document asking the court to bring a case forward to be tried.

6. *Preliminary hearing/grand jury.* Because it is a tremendous personal and financial burden to stand trial for a serious felony crime, the U.S. Constitution provides that the state must first prove to an impartial hearing board that there is probable cause that the accused committed the crime and, therefore, that there is sufficient reason to try the person as charged. In about half the states and in the federal system, the decision of whether to bring a suspect to trial (**indictment**) is made by a group of citizens brought together to form a **grand jury**. The grand jury considers the case in a closed hearing, in which only the prosecutor presents evidence. In the remaining states, an information is filed before an impartial lower-court judge, who decides whether the case should go forward. This is known as a **preliminary hearing** or probable cause hearing. The defendant may appear at a preliminary hearing and dispute the prosecutor's charges. During either procedure, if the prosecution's evidence is accepted as factual and sufficient, the suspect is called to stand trial for the crime. These procedures are not used for misdemeanors because of their lesser importance and seriousness.

7. *Arraignment.* An **arraignment** brings the accused before the court that will actually try the case. The formal charges are read, and defendants are informed of their constitutional rights (such as the right to legal counsel). Bail is considered, and a trial date is set.

8. *Bail or detention.* If the bail decision has not been considered previously, it is evaluated at arraignment. **Bail** is a money bond, the amount of which is set by judicial authority; it is intended to ensure the presence of suspects at trial while allowing them their freedom until that time. Suspects who do not show up for trial forfeit their bail. Suspects who cannot afford bail or whose cases are so serious that a judge refuses them bail (usually restricted to capital cases) must remain in detention until trial. In most instances, this means an extended stay in the county jail. Many jurisdictions allow defendants awaiting trial to be released on their own **recognizance**, without bail, if they are stable members of the community.

plea bargain

An agreement between prosecution and defense in which the accused pleads guilty in return for a reduction of charges, a more lenient sentence, or some other consideration.

hung jury

A jury that is unable to agree on a decision, thus leaving the case unresolved and open for a possible retrial.

disposition

Sentencing of a defendant who has been found guilty; usually involves a fine, probation, and/or incarceration.

appeal

Taking a criminal case to a higher court on the grounds that the defendant was found guilty because of legal error or violation of consitutional rights; a successful appeal may result in a new trial.

9. *Plea bargaining.* After arraignment, it is common for the prosecutor to meet with the defendant and his or her attorney to discuss a possible **plea bargain**. If a bargain can be struck, the accused pleads guilty as charged, thus ending the criminal trial process. In return for the plea, the prosecutor may reduce charges, request a lenient sentence, or grant the defendant some other consideration.

10. *Adjudication.* If a plea bargain cannot be arranged, a criminal trial takes place. This involves a full-scale inquiry into the facts of the case before a judge, a jury, or both. The defendant can be found guilty or not guilty, or the jury can fail to reach a decision (**hung jury**), thereby leaving the case unresolved and open for a possible retrial.

11. *Disposition.* After a criminal trial, a defendant who is found guilty as charged is sentenced by the presiding judge. **Disposition** usually involves a fine, a term of community supervision (probation), a period of incarceration in a penal institution, or some combination of these penalties. In the most serious capital cases, it is possible to sentence the offender to death. Dispositions are usually made after a presentencing investigation is conducted by the court's probation staff. Sentencing is a complex process; Table 14.2 shows how people are currently sentenced in the United States. After disposition, the defendant may appeal the conviction to a higher court.

12. *Postconviction remedies.* After conviction, if the defendant believes he or she was not treated fairly by the justice system, the individual may **appeal** the conviction. An appellate court reviews trial procedures in order to determine whether an error was made. It considers such questions as whether evidence was used properly, whether the judge conducted the trial in an approved fashion,

---

Table 14.2 How Are People Sentenced?

What sentences do people actually receive for their criminal behavior? According to the latest (1996) survey conducted by the federal government, state and federal courts convicted a combined total of more than 1 million adults of felonies. Of these, 997,970 were state convictions and 43,839 were federal.

- About 69 percent of all convicted felons were sentenced to a period of confinement—38 percent to state prisons and 31 percent to local jails. Jail sentences are for short-term confinement (usually a year or less) in a county or city facility; prison sentences are for long-term confinement (usually more than a year) in a state facility.

- Felons sentenced to a state prison in 1996 had an average sentence of five years but were likely to serve less than half (45%) of that sentence—or just over 2 years—before release.

- The average sentence to local jail was six months. The average probation sentence was about 3½ years.

- Besides being sentenced to incarceration or probation, 32 percent or more of convicted felons were also ordered to pay a fine, pay victim restitution, receive treatment, perform community service, or comply with some other additional penalty. A fine was imposed on at least 20 percent of convicted felons.

- The proportion of felons sentenced to prison in 1996 (38%) was lower than in any previous year (1988, 44%; 1990, 46%; 1992, 44%; 1994, 45%).

- Prison sentences imposed by state courts are becoming shorter on average. In 1992, the average prison sentence length was 79 months; in 1996, it was 62 months.

SOURCE: David J. Levin, Patrick A. Langan, and Jodi M. Brown, *State Court Sentencing of Convicted Felons, 1996* (Washington, DC: Bureau of Justice Statistics, 2000).

whether the jury was representative, and whether the attorneys in the case acted appropriately. If the court rules that the appeal has merit, it can hold that the defendant be given a new trial or, in some instances, order his or her outright release. Outright release can be ordered when the state prosecuted the case in violation of the double jeopardy clause of the U.S. Constitution or when it violated the defendant's right to a speedy trial.

13. *Correctional treatment.* Offenders who are found guilty and are formally sentenced come under the jurisdiction of correctional authorities. They may serve a term of community supervision under control of the county probation department; they may have a term in a community correctional center; or they may be incarcerated in a large penal institution.

14. *Release.* At the end of the correctional sentence, the offender is released into the community. Most incarcerated offenders are granted parole before the expiration of the maximum term given them by the court and therefore finish their prison sentences in the community under supervision of the parole department. Offenders sentenced to community supervision, if successful, simply finish their terms and resume their lives unsupervised by court authorities.

15. *Postrelease/aftercare.* After termination of correctional treatment, the offender must successfully return to the community. This adjustment is usually aided by corrections department staff members, who attempt to counsel the offender through the period of reentry into society. The offender may be asked to spend some time in a community correctional center, which acts as a bridge between a secure treatment facility and absolute freedom. Offenders may find that their conviction has cost them some personal privileges, such as the right to hold certain kinds of jobs. These privileges may be returned by court order once the offenders have proven their trustworthiness and willingness to adjust to society's rules. Successful completion of the postrelease period marks the end of the criminal justice process.

At every stage of the criminal justice process, a decision is made by an agency of criminal justice whether to send the case farther down the line or "kick it" from the system. For example, an investigation is pursued for a few days, and if a suspect is not identified, the case is dropped. A prosecutor decides not to charge a person in police custody because he or she believes there is insufficient evidence to sustain a finding of guilt. A grand jury fails to hand down an indictment because it finds that the prosecutor presented insufficient evidence. A jury fails to convict the accused because it doubts his or her guilt. A parole board decides to release one inmate but denies another's request for early release. These decisions transform the identity of the individual passing through the system from an accused to a defendant, convicted criminal, inmate, and ex-con. Conversely, if decision makers take no action, people accused of crime can return to their daily lives with minimal interference in their lives or identities. Their friends and neighbors may not even know that they were once the subject of criminal investigation. Decision making and discretion mark each stage of the system.

Thus, the criminal justice system acts like a funnel in which a great majority of cases are screened out before trial. As Figure 14.5 shows, cases are dismissed at each stage of the system, and relatively few actually reach trial. Those that do are more likely to be handled with a plea bargain than with a criminal trial. The funnel indicates that the justice system does not treat all felonies alike; only the relatively few serious cases make it through to the end of the formal process.[17]

Public perceptions about criminal justice are often formed on the basis of what happens in a few celebrated cases that receive widespread media attention.

Figure 14.5

The Criminal Justice "Funnel"

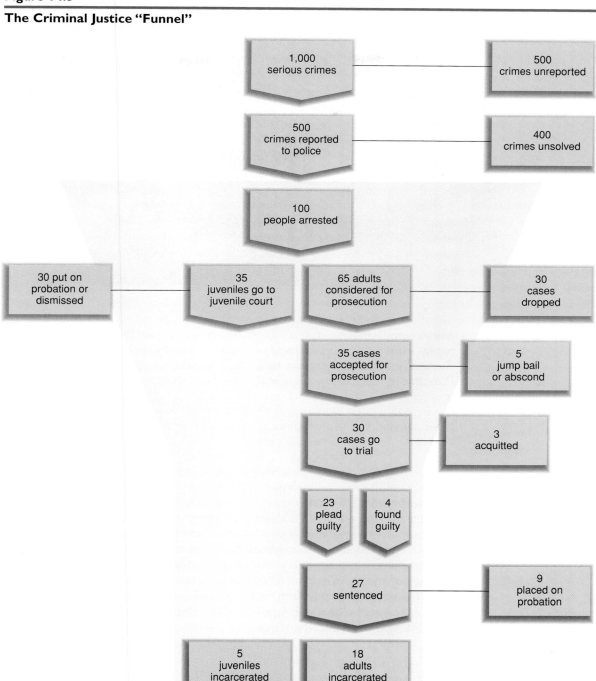

SOURCE: Brian Reaves and Pheny Smith, *Felony Defendants in Large Urban Counties, 1992* (Washington, DC: Bureau of Justice Statistics, 1995).

Some involve wealthy clients who can afford to be represented by high-powered attorneys who can hire the best experts to convince the jury that their client is innocent. The O. J. Simpson case is the best example of the celebrity defendant. Other defendants become celebrities when they are accused of particularly heinous or notorius crimes and draw the attention of both the press

The courtroom work group seeks to hammer out deals and plea bargains in even the most serious and heinous crimes. Here, Lawrence Michael Hensley, with his family behind him, awaits sentencing in a Sidney, Ohio, courtroom. To avoid a possible death sentence, Hensley pled guilty to aggravated murder, attempted aggravated murder, and kidnapping. He received a life sentence for killing three teenage girls and a Bible studies teacher.

AP/Wide World Photos

and accomplished defense attorneys. The trial of Louise Woodward, the British nanny who in 1998 was accused of killing young Matthew Eappen, the child she was hired to care for, is an example of the notorious media spectacle. (Woodward was found guilty, but the trial judge reduced the verdict and she was set free.)

In reality, these celebrity cases are few and far between. Most defendants are indigent people who cannot afford a comprehensive defense. The system is actually dominated by judges, prosecutors, and public defenders who work in concert to get cases processed quickly and efficiently. Trials are rare; most cases are handled with a quick plea bargain and sentencing. This pattern of cooperation is referred to as the **courtroom work group**. By working together in a cooperative fashion, the prosecution and defense make sure that the cases flowing through the justice system proceed in an orderly and effective manner. Such "bargain justice" is estimated to occur in more than 90 percent of all criminal cases. If each defendant were afforded the full measure of constitutional rights, including a jury trial, the system would quickly become overloaded. Court dockets are too crowded and funds too scarce to grant each defendant a full share of justice.[18] Although the criminal court system is founded on the concept of equality before the law, poor and wealthy citizens receive unquestionably different treatment when they are accused of crimes.

courtroom work group

Prosecution, defense, and judges working together to resolve criminal cases quickly and efficiently through plea bargaining.

Criminal Justice and the Rule of Law

For many years, U.S. courts exercised little control over the operations of criminal justice agencies, believing that their actions were not an area of judicial concern. This policy is referred to as the hands-off doctrine. However, in the 1960s, under the guidance of Chief Justice Earl Warren, the U.S. Supreme Court became more active in the affairs of the justice system. Today, each component of the justice system is closely supervised by state and federal courts through the **law of criminal procedure**, which sets out and guarantees citizens certain rights and privileges when they are accused of crime. Procedural laws control the actions of the agencies of justice and define the rights of criminal defendants. They first come into play when people are suspected of committing crimes and the police wish

law of criminal procedure

Judicial precedents that define and guarantee the rights of criminal defendants and control the various components of the criminal justice system.

Bill of Rights

The first 10 amendments to the U.S. Constitution, including guarantees against unreasonable search and seizure, self-incrimination, and cruel punishment.

✔ Checkpoints

✔ The criminal justice process can be best understood as a series of decision points.

✔ At each stage of the system, a decision is reached whether to process an offender to the next stage or terminate the case.

✔ While a few celebrity cases receive the full range of justice procedures, most cases are handled in a cursory fashion and settled with a plea bargain.

✔ The justice system is bound by the rule of law, which ensures that criminal defendants are protected from violations of their civil rights.

to investigate them, search their property, or interrogate them. Here the law dictates, for example, whether police can search the homes of or interrogate unwilling suspects. If a formal charge is filed, procedural laws guide pretrial and trial activities; for example, they determine when and if people can obtain state-financed attorneys and when they can be released on bail. If a person is found guilty of committing a criminal offense, procedural laws guide the posttrial and correctional processes; for example, they determine when a conviction can be appealed.

Procedural laws have several different sources. Most important are the first 10 amendments to the U.S. Constitution, ratified in 1791 and generally called the **Bill of Rights**. Included within these amendments are the right of the people to be secure in their homes from unwarranted intrusion by government agents, to be free from self-incrimination, and to be protected against cruel punishments, such as torture.

The guarantees of freedom contained in the Bill of Rights initially applied only to the federal government and did not affect the individual states. In 1868, the Fourteenth Amendment made the first 10 amendments to the Constitution binding on the state governments. However, it has remained the duty of state and federal court systems to interpret constitutional law and develop a body of case law that spells out the exact procedural rights to which a person is entitled. Thus, it is the U.S. Supreme Court that interprets the Constitution and sets out the procedural laws that must be followed by the lower federal and state courts. If the Supreme Court has not ruled on a procedural issue, then the lower courts are free to interpret the Constitution as they see fit.

Today, procedural rights protect defendants from illegal searches and seizures and overly aggressive police interrogations. According to the *exclusionary rule*, such illegally seized evidence cannot be used during a trial. ✔ Checkpoints

Concepts of Justice

Many justice system operations are controlled by the rule of law, but they are also influenced by the various philosophies or viewpoints held by its practitioners and policymakers. These, in turn, have been influenced by criminological theory and research. Knowledge about crime, its causes, and its control has significantly affected perceptions of how criminal justice should be managed.

Not surprisingly, many competing views of justice exist simultaneously in U.S. culture. Those in favor of one position or another try to win public opinion to their side, hoping to influence legislative, judicial, or administrative decision making. Over the years, different philosophical viewpoints tend to predominate, only to fall into disfavor as programs based on their principles fail to prove effective.

The remainder of this chapter briefly discusses the most important concepts of criminal justice.

Crime Control Model

crime control model

View that the overriding purpose of the justice system is to protect the public, deter criminal behavior, and incapacitate known criminals; favors speedy, efficient justice and punishment.

Those espousing the **crime control model** believe that the overriding purpose of the justice system is to protect the public, deter criminal behavior, and incapacitate known criminals. Those who embrace its principles view the justice system as a barrier between destructive criminal elements and conventional society. Speedy, efficient justice, unencumbered by legal red tape and followed by punishment designed to fit the crime, is the goal of advocates of the crime control model. Its disciples promote such policies as increasing the size of police forces, maximizing the use of discretion, building more prisons, using the death penalty, and reducing legal controls on the justice system. They

Penal Harm: The No-Frills Movement

Research indicates that the general public still wants rehabilitation as an integral part of correctional policy. A majority of citizens still express support for a treatment approach to rehabilitation of prisoners. There is little question that some treatment does work and that the quest for offender rehabilitation should not be abandoned. Yet, in line with the crime control perspective, some correctional administrators and politicians believe that prisons should be places of punishment only and that all inmate privileges and treatment programs should be curtailed. Inmates in some states have suffered reduced visiting hours, removal of televisions and exercise gear, and substitution of cold sandwiches for hot meals.

In some county jurisdictions, the old inmate "chain gangs" have been reintroduced, but instead of inmates' being shackled to prevent flight, they are forced to wear "stun belts." After detonation, the belts give fleeing inmates an eight-second, 50,000-volt jolt of electricity, which renders them helpless for up to 10 minutes. The practice has been condemned by human rights watch agency Amnesty International. In a telephone survey conducted in January 1999, 20 state Departments of Corrections told Amnesty International that they currently authorize the use of stun belts. Amnesty International has asked Congress to ban the belts, in part because they can be used for torture. Amnesty charges that the belts are "cruel, inhumane, and degrading."

Advocates of the no-frills or "penal harm" movement claim to be responding to the public's desire to get tough on crime. They are tired of hearing that some prison inmates get free education, watch cable television, or get special educational programs. Some of the efforts to restrict inmates' rights include the following:

- The Alabama Department of Corrections (DOC) introduced no-frills chain gangs in each of the state's three prisons in 1994. Inmates in the gangs do not have telephone or visitation privileges, and recreation is limited to basketball on the weekends. Chain gang members include primarily parole violators and repeat offenders, especially former gang members. After six months of good behavior, chain gang members return to the general population and are given standard inmate privileges.

- The Arizona DOC, supplementing the legislature's ban on weightlifting equipment, reduced the amount of property and clothing inmates may keep in their cells, the number of items for sale in the store, the number and types of movies and television programs they may watch, and the frequency of telephone calls.

- The Kansas DOC introduced a formal incentive program in which incoming inmates have to earn a range of privileges, including television, handicrafts, use of outside funds, canteen expenditures, personal property, and visitation. Under a three-level system, new inmates must spend their first 120 days (Incentive Level 1) without disciplinary reports and participate in educational programs or work

Miranda rights

Rights of criminal defendants, including the right against self-incrimination and right to counsel, spelled out in the case of *Miranda v. Arizona*.

exclusionary rule

The rule that evidence against a defendant may not be presented in court if it was obtained in violation of the defendant's rights.

point to evidence showing that as many as 30,000 violent criminals, 62,000 drunk drivers, 46,000 drug dealers, and several hundred thousand other criminals go free every year in cases dropped because police believe they have violated the suspects' **Miranda rights**.[19] They lobby for abolition of the **exclusionary rule** and applaud when the Supreme Court hands down rulings that increase police power.

The crime control philosophy emphasizes protecting society and compensating victims. The criminal is responsible for his or her actions, has broken faith with society, and has chosen to violate the law for reasons such as anger, greed, or revenge. Therefore, money spent should be directed not at making criminals more comfortable but at increasing the efficiency of police in apprehending them and the courts in trying them effectively. As David Garland suggests, criminal punishment has only a limited ability to change the wicked; instead, it can enforce cultural values and express the conviction that crime will not be tolerated. Punishment symbolizes the legitimate social order and the power societies have to regulate behavior and punish those who break social rules.[20]

The crime control philosophy has become a dominant force in American justice. Fear of crime in the 1960s and 1970s was coupled with a growing skepticism about the effectiveness of rehabilitation efforts. A number of important reassignments to earn increased privileges (Incentive Level II). After another 120 days of similar behavior, additional privileges are made available (Incentive Level III). Inmates are reduced one level for misbehavior. Furloughs were banned permanently for all inmates.

- Complementing the action of his governor, the commissioner of corrections in Wisconsin reduced the amount of personal property inmates may own, established limits on the amount of personal clothing and electronic equipment they may keep, and introduced monitoring of telephone calls.

- A number of sheriffs have eliminated privileges in their jails. Seven sheriffs in Florida have eliminated television and weightlifting; seven jails in Los Angeles County have also eliminated weightlifting equipment; the Niagara County, New York, sheriff eliminated free coffee; and the sheriff of Maricopa County (Phoenix) eliminated "girlie" magazines, hot lunches, most hot breakfasts, and coffee, and reduced recreation time, television programming,

visitation, and the number of items in the commissary.

- The Federal Bureau of Prisons ordered—and federal legislation now requires—wardens to stop purchasing or repairing televisions for individual cells.

Although many politicians embrace the no-frills prison idea to appeal to their more conservative constituents, wardens and prison administrators are more wary of a policy that restricts inmate activities, increases boredom, and threatens their control over inmates. One approach is to limit privileges at first but return them as rewards for good behavior. Whether the no-frills approach is a political fad or a long-term correctional policy trend remains to be seen.

Critical Thinking

Do you believe that inmates should be "harmed" by their prison experience to shock them into conformity? The penal harm movement is the antithesis of the rehabilitation ideal. By "harming" inmates and taking away privileges, are

correctional administrators giving up on the prison as a place of reform?

 InfoTrac College Edition Research

To read a critical review of stun belts, check out Anne-Marie Cusac, "Shock Value: U.S. Stun Devices Pose Human-Rights Risk," *The Progressive,* September 1997 v61 i9 p28(4)

SOURCES: Amnesty International, "Cruelty in Control? The Stun Belt and Other Electro-Shock Equipment in Law Enforcement," June 1999; Peter Finn, "No-Frills Prisons and Jails: A Movement in Flux," *Federal Probation* 60 (1996): 35–49; W. Wesley Johnson, Katherine Bennett, and Timothy Flanagan, "Getting Tough on Prisoners: Results from the National Corrections Executive Survey, 1995," *Crime and Delinquency* 43 (1997): 24–41; Peter Kilborn, "Revival of Chain Gangs Takes a Twist," *New York Times,* 11 March 1997, p. A18; Brandon K. Applegate, Francis Cullen, and Bonnie Fisher, "Public Support for Correctional Treatment: The Continuing Appeal of the Rehabilitative Ideal," *Prison Journal* 77 (1997): 237–259.

CONNECTIONS

The crime control model is rooted in choice theory, discussed in Chapter 4. Fear of criminal sanctions is viewed as the primary deterrent to crime. Because criminals are rational and choose to commit crime, it stands to reason that their activities can be controlled if the costs of crime become too high. Swift, sure, and efficient justice is considered an essential element of an orderly society.

views claimed that treatment and rehabilitation efforts directed at known criminals just did not work.[21] The lack of clear evidence that criminals can be successfully treated has produced a climate in which conservative, hard-line solutions to the crime problem are being sought. The results of this swing can be seen in such phenomena as the increasing use of the death penalty, erosion of the exclusionary rule, prison overcrowding, and attacks on the insanity defense. In the past few years, a number of states, including Tennessee, Utah, Iowa, Ohio, and West Virginia, have changed their juvenile codes, making it easier to try juveniles as adults. Other states have expanded their control over ex-offenders, as by requiring registration of sex offenders. New York has passed a death penalty statute, and other states, including Delaware and South Dakota, have expanded the circumstances under which a person may be eligible for the death penalty.[22] And, as the accompanying Policy and Practice in Criminology shows, some correctional authorities are using a get-tough stance with inmates.

Can such measures deter crime? There is some evidence that strict crime control measures can in fact have a deterrent effect.[23] For example, research indicates that people arrested for domestic violence violations who receive more severe sentences (such as jail) are less likely to repeat their offenses than those who receive more lenient treatment (such as probation).[24] Similarly, a study by the National Center for Policy Analysis uncovered a direct correlation between the probability of imprisonment for a particular crime and a subsequent decline in the rate of that crime.[25] The probability of going to prison for murder increased 17 percent between 1993 and 1997, and the murder rate dropped 23 percent during that period; robbery declined 21 percent as the probability of prison increased 14 percent. These data support the crime control model.

Justice Model

justice model

View that emphasizes fairness and equal treatment in criminal procedures and sentencing.

According to the **justice model**, it is futile to rehabilitate criminals, both because treatment programs are ineffective and because they deny people equal protection under the law.[26] It is unfair if two people commit the same crime but receive different sentences because only one is receptive to treatment. The consequence is a sense of injustice in the criminal justice system.

Beyond these problems, justice model advocates question the crime control perspective's reliance on deterrence. Is it fair to punish or incarcerate based on predictions of what offenders will do in the future or on whether others will be deterred by their punishment? Justice model advocates are also concerned with unfairness in the system, such as racism and discrimination, that causes sentencing disparity and unequal treatment before the law.[27]

As an alternative, the justice model calls for fairness in criminal procedure. This would require **determinate sentencing**, in which all offenders in a particular crime category would receive the same sentence. Prisons would be viewed as places of just, evenhanded punishment, not rehabilitation. Parole would be abolished to avoid the discretionary unfairness associated with that mechanism of early release.

determinate sentencing

Principle that all offenders who commit the same crime should receive the same sentence.

The justice model has had an important influence on criminal justice policy. Some states have adopted flat sentencing statutes and have limited the use of parole. There is a trend toward giving prison sentences because people deserve punishment rather than because the sentences will deter or rehabilitate them. Such measures as sentencing guidelines, which are aimed at reducing sentencing disparity, are a direct offshoot of the justice model.

Due Process Model

due process model

View that focuses on protecting the civil rights of those accused of crime.

In *The Limits of the Criminal Sanction,* Herbert Packer contrasted the crime control model with an opposing view that he referred to as the **due process model**.[28] According to Packer, the due process model combines elements of liberal/positivist criminology with the legal concept of procedural fairness for the accused. Those who adhere to due process principles believe in individualized justice, treatment, and rehabilitation of offenders. If discretion exists in the criminal justice system, it should be used to evaluate the treatment needs of offenders. Most important, the civil rights of the accused should be protected at all costs. This emphasis calls for strict scrutiny of police search and interrogation procedures, review of sentencing policies, and development of prisoners' rights.

Advocates of the due process model have demanded that competent defense counsel, jury trials, and other procedural safeguards be offered to every criminal defendant. They have also called for making public the operations of the justice system and placing controls over its discretionary power.

Due process advocates see themselves as protectors of civil rights. They view overzealous police as violators of basic constitutional rights. Similarly, they are skeptical about the intentions of meddling social workers, whose treatments often entail greater confinement and penalties than punishment does. Their concern is magnified by data showing that the poor and minority group members are often maltreated in the criminal justice system. In some jurisdictions, such as Washington, D.C., almost half of all African American young men are under the control of the justice system. Is it possible that this reflects racism, dis-

Find It on INFOTRAC
College Edition

The concept of due process is one of the most complex issues in the criminal justice system. It is guaranteed by the Fifth and Fourteenth Amendments to the U.S. Constitution. To read more on this topic, use "due process" as a keyword in InfoTrac College Edition.

crimination, and a violation of their civil rights?[29] Research shows that in at least some states, African Americans are more likely to be sent to prison than European Americans; these racial differences in the incarceration rate cannot be explained the the fact that blacks are arrested more often than whites.[30] The accompanying Race, Culture, Gender, and Criminology explores the issue of racial discrimination in the sentencing process.

Due process exists to protect citizens—both from those who wish to punish them and from those who wish to treat them without regard for legal and civil rights. Due process model advocates worry about the government's expanding ability to use computers to intrude into people's private lives. In 1996, for example, the federal government announced plans for a computerized registry of sex offenders; there are plans for nationwide computer-based mug shot and fingerprint systems. Background and fingerprint checks on employees in sensitive areas such as airports will soon become routine. These measures can harm privacy and civil liberties, although research shows that they may have relatively little impact on controlling crime.[31]

Advocates of the due process orientation are quick to point out that the justice system remains an adversary process that pits the forces of an all-powerful state against those of a solitary individual accused of crime. If an overriding concern for justice and fairness did not exist, the defendant who lacked resources could easily be overwhelmed. They point to miscarriages of justice such as the case of Jeffrey Blake, who went to prison for a double murder in 1991 and spent seven years behind bars before his conviction was overturned in 1998. The prosecution's star witness conceded that he had lied on the stand, forcing Blake to spend a quarter of his life in prison for a crime he did not commit.[32] His wrongful conviction would have been even more tragic if he had been executed for his alleged crime. The Institute for Law and Justice, a Virginia-based research firm, found that at least 28 cases of sexual assault have been overturned because DNA evidence proved that the convicted men could not have committed the crimes; the inmates averaged seven years in prison before their release.[33] Because such mistakes can happen, even the most apparently guilty offender deserves all the protection the justice system can offer.

The due process orientation has not fared well in recent years. The movement to grant greater civil rights protections to criminal defendants has been undermined by Supreme Court decisions expanding police ability to search and seize evidence and to question suspects. Similarly, the movement between 1960 and 1980 to grant prison inmates an ever-increasing share of constitutional protections has been curtailed. There is growing evidence that the desire to protect the public has overshadowed concerns for the rights of criminal defendants. Although the most important legal rights won by criminal defendants in the 1960s and 1970s remain untouched (for example, the right to a fair and impartial jury of one's peers), there was little urgency to increase the scope of civil rights in the more conservative 1990s.

Rehabilitation Model

rehabilitation model

View that sees criminals as victims of social injustice, poverty, and racism and suggests that appropriate treatment can change them into productive, law-abiding citizens.

The **rehabilitation model** embraces the notion that given the proper care and treatment, criminals can be changed into productive, law-abiding citizens. Influenced by positivist criminology, the rehabilitation school suggests that people commit crimes through no fault of their own. Instead, criminals themselves are the victims of social injustice, poverty, and racism; their acts are a response to a society that has betrayed them. And because of their disturbed and impoverished upbringing, they may be suffering psychological problems and personality disturbances that further enhance their crime-committing capabilities. Although the general public wants protection from crime, the argument goes, it also favors programs designed to help unfortunate people who commit crime because of emotional or social problems.[34]

Race, Culture, Gender, and Criminology

Race and Sentencing

Due process advocates believe that the justice system must carefully scrutinize decision making in order to avoid civil rights abuses. No area is more critical than the sentencing of those convicted of crime. As you may recall, about one-third of convicted offenders are sent to prison, while another third are given a sentence of probation to be served in the community. Considering the significant difference in this outcome, it is critical that sentencing decisions be examined for any taint of racial bias.

Racial disparity in sentencing has been suspected because of the disproportionate number of minority inmates in state prisons and on death row. Research efforts show that minority defendants suffer discrimination in a variety of court actions. They are more likely than whites to be detained before trial and, upon conviction, are more likely to receive jail sentences rather than fines. Prosecutors are less likely to divert minorities from the legal system than whites who commit the same crimes, and minorities are less likely than whites to win appeals.

The relationship between race and sentencing may be difficult to establish because their association may not be linear. While minority defendants may be punished more severely for some crimes under some circumstances, they are treated more leniently for others. Sociologist Darnell Hawkins explains this phenomenon as a matter of "appropriateness":

> Certain crime types are considered less "appropriate" for blacks than for whites. Blacks who are charged with committing these offenses will be treated more severely than blacks who commit crimes that are considered more "appropriate." Included in the former category are various white-collar offenses and crimes against political and social structures of authority. The latter groups of offenses would include various forms of victimless crimes associated with lower social status (e.g., prostitution, minor drug use, or drunkenness). This may also include various crimes against the person, especially those involving black victims.

Race may affect sentencing because some race-specific crimes are punished more harshly than others. African Americans receive longer sentences for drug crimes than European Americans because (a) they are more likely to be arrested for crack possession and sales and (b) state and federal laws punish crack dealing more severely than other drug crimes. Because whites are more likely to use marijuana and methamphetamines, prosecutors are more willing to plea-bargain and offer shorter jail terms.

Racial bias has also been linked to victim status. Minority defendants are sanctioned more severely if their victim is white than if their target is a fellow minority-group member. Judges may base sentencing decisions on the race of the victim and not the race of the defendant. Research shows that African American defendants are more likely to be prosecuted under habitual offender statutes if they commit crimes in which the victim is likely to be white, such as larceny and burglary, than if they commit violent crimes in which the victim is typically black. Where there is a perceived "racial threat," punishments are enhanced.

Sentencing disparity may also reflect race-based differences in criminal justice practices and policies. Presentence probation reports may favor white over minority defendants, causing judges to award whites probation more often than minorities. Defendants who can afford bail receive more lenient sentences than those who remain in pretrial detention; minority defendants are less likely to make bail because they suffer a higher degree of

CONNECTIONS

The rehabilitation model is linked to social structure and social process theories because it assumes that if lifestyle and socialization could be improved, crime rates would decline. See Chapters 6 and 7 for more on these theories.

Dealing effectively with crime requires attacking its root causes. Funds must be devoted to equalizing access to conventional means of success. This requires supporting such programs as public assistance, educational opportunity, and job training. If individuals run afoul of the law, efforts should be made to treat them, not punish them, by emphasizing counseling and psychological care in community-based treatment programs. Whenever possible, offenders should be placed on probation in halfway houses or in other rehabilitation-oriented programs.

This view of the justice system portrays it as a method for dispensing "treatment" to needy "patients." Also known as the medical model, it portrays offenders as people who, because they have failed to exercise self-control, need the help of the state. The medical model rejects the crime control philosophy on the ground that it ignores the needs of offenders, who are people whom society has failed to help.

Research evidence suggests that correctional treatment can have an important influence on offenders.[35] Programs that teach interpersonal skills and use income inequality. Sentencing outcome is also affected by the defendant's ability to afford a private attorney and to put on a vigorous legal defense that makes use of high-paid expert witnesses. These factors place the poor and minority-group members at a disadvantage in the sentencing process and result in sentencing disparity. And while considerations of prior record may be legitimate in forming sentencing decisions, there is evidence that minorities are more likely to have prior records because of organizational and individual bias on the part of police.

In a thorough review of sentencing disparity, Samuel Walker, Cassia Spohn and Miriam Delone identify what they call "contextual discrimination"—the tendency of some judges to impose harsher sentences on African Americans who victimize whites or to give racial minorities prison sentences in "borderline" cases in which whites would get probation. This subtle racial bias in the criminal justice system encourages due process advocates to be vigilant and to call for reforms to eliminate all traces of disparity.

Critical Thinking

Do you believe that sentences should be influenced by the fact that one ethnic or racial group is more likely to commit a particular crime? For example, critics have called for changing drug policies that punish crack possession more heavily than powdered cocaine possession because African Americans are more likely to use crack and European Americans to use powdered cocaine. Do you approve of such a change?

InfoTrac College Edition Research

To read a critical analysis of race, criminal justice, and sentencing policies, see Carolyn Wolpert, "Considering Race and Crime: Distilling Non-partisan Policy from Opposing Theories," *American Criminal Law Review,* v36 (1999) p. 265.

Sources: Travis Pratt, "Race and Sentencing: A Meta-Analysis of Conflicting Empirical Research Results," *Journal of Criminal Justice* 26 (1998): 513–525; Charles Crawford, Ted Chiricos, and Gary Kleck, "Race, Racial Threat, and Sentencing of Habitual Offenders," *Criminology* 36 (1998): 481–511; Jon'a Meyer and Tara Gray, "Drunk Drivers in the Courts: Legal and Extra-Legal Factors Affecting Pleas and Sentences," *Journal of Criminal Justice* 25 (1997): 155–163; Alexander Alvarez and Ronet Bachman, "American Indians and Sentencing Disparity: An Arizona Test," *Journal of Criminal Justice* 24 (1996): 549–561; Carole Wolff Barnes and Rodney Kingsnorth, "Race, Drug, and Criminal Sentencing: Hidden Effects of the Criminal Law," *Journal of Criminal Justice* 24 (1996): 39–55; Samuel Walker, Cassia Spohn, and Miriam DeLone, *The Color of Justice: Race, Ethnicity and Crime in America* (Belmont,

CA: Wadsworth, 1996), pp. 145–146; Jo Dixon, "The Organizational Context of Sentencing," *American Journal of Sociology* 100 (1995): 1157–1198; Alfred Blumstein, "On the Racial Disproportionality of the United States Prison Population," *Journal of Criminal Law and Criminology* 73 (1982); Celesta Albonetti and John Hepburn, "Prosecutorial Discretion to Defer Criminalization: The Effects of Defendant's Ascribed and Achieved Status Characteristics," *Journal of Quantitative Criminology* 12 (1996): 63–81; Jimmy Williams, "Race of Appellant, Sentencing Guidelines, and Decision Making in Criminal Appeals: A Research Note," *Journal of Criminal Justice* 23 (1995); Joan Petersilia, *Racial Disparities in the Criminal Justice System* (Santa Monica, CA: Rand Corporation, 1983); Darnell Hawkins, "Race, Crime Type and Imprisonment," *Justice Quarterly* 3 (1986): 251–269; James Nelson, "A Dollar or a Day: Sentencing Misdemeanants in New York State," *Journal of Research in Crime and Delinquency* 31 (1994): 183–201; Robert Crutchfield, George Bridges, and Susan Pitchford, "Analytical and Aggregation Biases in Analyses of Imprisonment: Reconciling Discrepancies in Studies of Racial Disparity," *Journal of Research in Crime and Delinquency* 31 (1994): 166–182.

individual counseling and behavioral modification techniques have produced positive results both in the community and within correctional institutions.[36] And while some politicians call for a strict law-and-order approach, the general public is quite supportive of treatment programs such as early childhood intervention and services for at-risk children.[37]

Nonintervention Model

In the late 1960s and 1970s, both the rehabilitation ideal and the due process movement were viewed suspiciously by experts concerned by the stigmatization of offenders. Regardless of the purpose, the more the government intervenes in the lives of people, the greater the harm done to their future behavior patterns. Once arrested and labeled, the offender is placed at a disadvantage at home, at school, and in the job market.[38] Rather than deter crime, the stigma of a criminal label erodes social capital and jeopardizes future success and achievement.

It is common for prisons to employ a variety of rehabilitation and counseling programs. Here, Nita Arndt (left) and Jennifer Wilen, both inmates of the women's prison in Pierre, South Dakota, use role-playing to practice their parenting skills, as prison activities director Aaron Miller looks on. Both women praised the parenting classes, which have been required of inmates since December 1998.

noninterventionist model

The view that arresting and labeling offenders does more harm than good, that youthful offenders in particular should be diverted into informal treatment programs, and that minor offenses should be decriminalized.

The **noninterventionist model** calls for limiting government intrusion into the lives of people, especially minors, who run afoul of the law.[39] Noninterventionists advocate deinstitutionalization of nonserious offenders, diversion from formal court processes into informal treatment programs, and decriminalization of nonserious offenses, such as possessing small amounts of marijuana. Under this concept, the justice system should interact as little as possible with offenders. Police, courts, and correctional agencies would concentrate their efforts on diverting law violators out of the formal justice system, thereby helping them avoid the stigma of formal labels such as "delinquent" or "ex-con." Programs instituted under this model include mediation (instead of trial), diversion (instead of formal processing), and community-based corrections (instead of secure corrections).

Nonintervention advocates are also skeptical about the creation of laws that criminalize acts that were previously legal, thus expanding the reach of justice and creating new classes of offenders. For example, it has become popular to expand control over youthful offenders by passing local curfew laws that make it a crime for young people to be out at night after a certain hour, such as 11 P.M. An adolescent who was formerly a night owl is now a criminal![40]

There are many examples of nonintervention ideas in practice. For example, the juvenile justice system has made a major effort to remove youths from adult jails and reduce the use of pretrial detention. Mediation programs have proven successful alternatives to the formal trial process.[41] In the adult system, pretrial release programs (alternatives to bail) are now the norm instead of an experimental innovation. And, although the prison population is rising, probation and community treatment have become the most common forms of criminal sanction.

There has also been criticism of the noninterventionist philosophy. There is little evidence that alternative programs actually reduce recidivism rates. Some critics charge that alternative programs actually result in "widening the net."[42] That is, efforts to remove people from the justice system actually enmesh them further within it by ordering them to spend more time in treatment than they would have had to spend in the formal legal process.

In the future, the nonintervention philosophy will be aided by the rising cost of justice. Although low-impact, nonintrusive programs may work no better than prison, they are certainly cheaper; program costs may receive greater consideration than program effectiveness.

Restorative Justice Model

restorative justice model

View that emphasizes the promotion of a peaceful, just society through reconciliation and reintegration of the offender into society.

A number of liberal and left-oriented scholars have devised the concept of restorative justice. They believe that the true purpose of the criminal justice system is to promote a peaceful, just society; they advocate peacemaking, not punishment.[43]

The **restorative justice model** draws its inspiration from religious and philosophical teachings ranging from Quakerism to Zen. Advocates of restorative justice say that state efforts to punish and control encourage crime. The violent punishing acts of the state, they claim, are not dissimilar from the violent acts of individuals.[44] Whereas crime control advocates associate lower crime rates with increased punishment, restorative justice advocates counter that studies show that punitive methods of correction (such as jail) are no more effective than more humanitarian efforts (such as probation with treatment).[45] Therefore, mutual aid rather than coercive punishment is the key to a harmonious society. Without the capacity to restore damaged social relations, society's response to crime has been almost exclusively punitive.

Restorative justice is guided by three essential principles: community "ownership" of conflict (including crime); material and symbolic reparation for crime victims; and social reintegration of the offender. Maintaining ownership, or jurisdiction, over the conflict means that the conflict between criminal and victim should be resolved in the community in which it originated, not in some faraway prison. The victim should be given a chance to voice his or her story, and the offender should help compensate the victim financially or by providing some service. The goal is to enable the offender to appreciate the damage caused, to make amends, and to be reintegrated into society.

Restorative justice programs are geared to these principles. The ability of police officers to mediate disputes rather than resort to formal arrest has long been recognized; it is an essential element of community policing.[46] Mediation and conflict resolution programs are now common. Financial and community-service restitution programs as an alternative to imprisonment have been in operation for more than two decades.

Although restorative justice has become an important perspective in recent years, questions are now being raised about its effectiveness. Is it possible that restorative programs actually help widen the net, helping to label clients as criminal or deviant? Might clients be coerced into programs to escape harsher forms of punishment? What happens to clients who fail to meet the terms of a restorative justice program? Will they be incarcerated or similarly punished? And, finally, can restorative justice programs actually reduce or control crime rates? So far, restorative justice programs do not provide a blueprint for crime control; they rely on untested principles and beliefs.[47]

CONNECTIONS

The basis of restorative justice was reviewed in Chapter 8, on social conflict theory.

Concepts of Justice Today

The various philosophies of justice compete today for dominance in the criminal justice system (see Figure 14.6). Each has supporters who lobby diligently for their positions. At the time of this writing, it seems that the crime control and justice models have captured the support of legislators and the general public. There is a growing emphasis on protecting the public by increasing criminal sentences and swelling prison populations. Yet advocates of the rehabilitation model claim that the recent imprisonment binge may be a false panacea. For

Figure 14.6

Perspectives on Justice: Key Concerns and Concepts

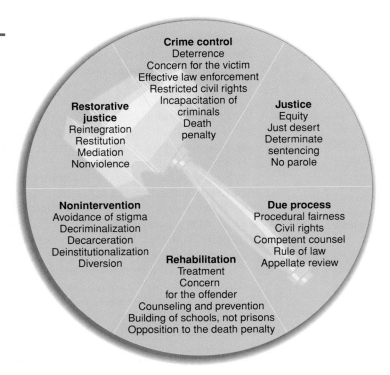

Crime control
Deterrence
Concern for the victim
Effective law enforcement
Restricted civil rights
Incapacitation of criminals
Death penalty

Restorative justice
Reintegration
Restitution
Mediation
Nonviolence

Justice
Equity
Just desert
Determinate sentencing
No parole

Nonintervention
Avoidance of stigma
Decriminalization
Decarceration
Deinstitutionalization
Diversion

Due process
Procedural fairness
Civil rights
Competent counsel
Rule of law
Appellate review

Rehabilitation
Treatment
Concern for the offender
Counseling and prevention
Building of schools, not prisons
Opposition to the death penalty

example, in his 1998 book *Crime and Punishment in America,* liberal scholar Elliott Currie concedes that the crime rate has declined as the incarceration rate has increased.[48] Nonetheless, he claims that the association may be misleading because the crime rate is undergoing a natural revision from the abnormally high, unprecedented increases brought about by the crack cocaine epidemic in the 1980s. He claims that punitive, incarceration-based models of justice are doomed to fail in the long run. Most offenders eventually return to society, and if the justice system does not help inmates achieve a productive lifestyle, a steadily increasing cohort of ex-offenders with limited life chances will be on the street. Their chances of success in the legitimate world have, if anything, been severely diminished by their prison experiences. Punishment may produce short-term reductions in the crime rate, but only rehabilitation and treatment can produce long-term gains.

So, despite the demand for punishing serious, chronic offenders, the door to treatment for nonviolent, nonchronic offenders has not been closed. The number of noninterventionist and restorative justice programs featuring restitution and nonpunitive sanctions is growing. As the cost of justice skyrockets and the correctional system becomes increasingly overcrowded, alternatives such as house arrest, electronic monitoring, intensive probation supervision, and other cost-effective programs have come to the forefront.

Summary

Criminal justice refers to the formal processes and institutions that have been established to apprehend, try, punish, and treat law violators. The major components of the criminal justice system are the police, courts, and correctional agencies. Police maintain public order, deter crime, and apprehend law violators. The courts determine the criminal liability of accused offenders brought before them and dispense sanctions to those found guilty of crime. Corrections agencies provide postjudicatory care to offenders who are sentenced by the courts to confinement or community supervision. Dissatisfaction with traditional forms of corrections has spurred the development of community-based facilities and work-release and work-furlough programs.

Justice can also be conceived of as a process through which offenders flow. The justice process begins with initial contact by a police agency and proceeds through investigation and custody, trial stages, and correctional system processing. At any stage of the process, the offender may be excused because evidence is lacking, the case is trivial, or a decision maker simply decides to discontinue interest in the case.

Procedures, policies, and practices employed within the criminal justice system are scrutinized by the courts to make sure they do not violate the guidelines in the first 10 amendments to the U.S. Constitution. If a violation occurs, the defendant can appeal the case and seek to overturn the conviction. Among the rights that must be honored are freedom from illegal searches and seizures and treatment with overall fairness and due process.

Several different philosophies or perspectives dominate the justice process. The crime control model asserts that the goals of justice are protection of the public and incapacitation of known offenders. The justice model calls for fair, equal treatment for all offenders. The due process model emphasizes liberal principles, such as legal rights and procedural fairness for the offender. The rehabilitation model views the justice system as a wise and caring parent. The noninterventionist perspective calls for minimal interference in offenders' lives. The restorative justice model seeks nonpunitive, humane solutions to the conflict inherent in crime and victimization.

For additional chapter links, discussions, and quizzes, see the book-specific Web site at http://www.wadsworth.com/product/0534519423s.

Thinking Like a Criminologist

You have been appointed assistant to the president's drug czar, who is in charge of coordinating the nation's drug control policy. She has asked you to develop a plan to reduce drug abuse by 25 percent within three years.

You realize that multiple perspectives of justice exist and that the agencies of the criminal justice system can use a number of strategies to reduce drug trafficking and the use of drugs. It might be possible to control the drug trade through a strict crime control effort, for example, using law enforcement officers to cut off supplies of drugs by destroying crops and arresting members of drug cartels in drug-producing countries. Border patrols and military personnel using sophisticated hardware could also help prevent drugs from entering the country. According to the justice model, if drug violations were punished with criminal sentences commensurate with their harm, then the rational drug trafficker might look for a new line of employment. The adoption of mandatory sentences for drug crimes to ensure that all offenders receive similar punishment for their acts might reduce crime. The rehabilitation model suggests that strategies should be aimed at reducing the desire to use drugs and increasing incentives for users to eliminate substance abuse. A noninterventionist strategy calls for the legalization of drugs so distribution could be controlled by the government. Crime rates would be cut because drug users would no longer need the same cash flow to support their habit.

Considering these different approaches, how would you shape drug control strategies?

Key Terms

criminal justice system	penitentiary	disposition
discretion	parole	appeal
landmark decision	arrest	courtroom work group
adversary system	probable cause	law of criminal procedure
prosecutor	booking	Bill of Rights
defendant	interrogation	crime control model
defense attorney	indictment	Miranda rights
right to counsel	grand jury	exclusionary rule
public defender	preliminary hearing	justice model
pro bono	arraignment	determinate sentencing
probation	bail	due process model
incarceration	recognizance	rehabilitation model
jail	plea bargain	noninterventionist model
prison	hung jury	restorative justice model

Discussion Questions

1. Describe the differences between the formal and informal justice systems. Is it fair to treat some offenders informally?

2. What are the basic elements of each model or perspective on justice? Which best represents your own point of view?

3. How would each perspective on criminal justice consider the use of the death penalty as a sanction for first-degree murder? In your opinion, does the death penalty serve as a deterrent to murder? If not, why not?

4. Discuss the trends that will influence policing during the coming decade.

5. Why does the problem of sentencing disparity exist? Do programs exist that can reduce disparate sentences? If so, what are they?

6. Should all people who commit the same crime receive the same sentence?

NOTES

Chapter 1

1. "Al Koski Trial Starts for Michigan Boy Charged with Murder," *Reuters Internet News,* October 11, 1999; L. L. Brasier and Desiree Cooper, "Abraham Jury Is Seated," *Detroit Free Press,* 29 October 1999, p. 1.
2. Keith Bradsher, "Boy Who Killed Gets 7 Years," *New York Times,* 14 January 2000, p. 1.
3. John Hagan and Alberto Palloni, "Sociological Criminology and the Mythology of Hispanic Immigration and Crime," *Social Problems* 46 (1999): 617–632.
4. Eugene Weber, *A Modern History of Europe* (New York: W. W. Norton, 1971), p. 398.
5. Marvin Wolfgang, *Patterns in Criminal Homicide* (Philadelphia: University of Pennsylvania Press, 1958).
6. Described in David Lykken, "Psychopathy, Sociopathy, and Crime," *Society* 34 (1996): 29–38.
7. See Peter Scott, "Henry Maudsley," in *Pioneers in Criminology,* ed. Hermann Mannheim (Montclair, NJ: Prentice-Hall, 1981).
8. Nicole Hahn Rafter, "Criminal Anthropology in the United States," *Criminology* 30 (1992): 525–547.
9. Rafter, "Criminal Anthropology," p. 535.
10. See, generally, Robert Nisbet, *The Sociology of Emile Durkheim* (New York: Oxford University Press, 1974).
11. L.A.J. Quetelet, *A Treatise on Man and the Development of His Faculties* (Gainesville, FL: Scholars' Facsimiles and Reprints, 1969), pp. 82–96.
12. Quetelet, *A Treatise on Man,* p. 85.
13. Emile Durkheim, *Rules of the Sociological Method,* reprint ed., trans. W. D. Halls (New York: Free Press, 1982).
14. Emile Durkheim, *The Division of Labor in Society,* reprint ed. (New York: Free Press, 1997).
15. Robert Park and Ernest Burgess, *The City* (Chicago: University of Chicago Press, 1925).
16. Karl Marx and Friedrich Engels, *Capital: A Critique of Political Economy,* trans. E. Aveling (Chicago: Charles Kern, 1906); Karl Marx, *Selected Writings in Sociology and Social Philosophy,* trans. P. B. Bottomore (New York: McGraw-Hill, 1956). For a general discussion of Marxist thought, see Michael Lynch and W. Byron Groves, *A Primer in Radical Criminology* (New York: Harrow and Heston, 1986), pp. 6–26.
17. Marvin Wolfgang and Franco Ferracuti, *The Subculture of Violence* (London: Social Science Paperbacks, 1967), p. 20.
18. Associated Press, "Michigan Senate Acts to Outlaw Aiding Suicides," *Boston Globe,* 20 March 1994, p. 22.
19. Marvin Wolfgang, *Patterns in Criminal Homicide* (Philadelphia: University of Pennsylvania Press, 1958).
20. Hans von Hentig, *The Criminal and His Victim* (New Haven: Yale University Press, 1948); Stephen Schafer, *The Victim and His Criminal* (New York: Random House, 1968).
21. Charles McCaghy, *Deviant Behavior* (New York: Macmillan, 1976), pp. 2–3.
22. Edwin Sutherland and Donald Cressey, *Criminology,* 8th ed. (Philadelphia: J. B. Lippincott, 1960), p. 8.
23. Eugene Doleschal and Nora Klapmuts, "Toward a New Criminology," *Crime and Delinquency* 5 (1973): 607.
24. Michael Lynch and W. Byron Groves, *A Primer in Radical Criminology* (Albany, NY: Harrow and Heston, 1989).
25. Howard Becker, *Outsiders: Studies in the Sociology of Deviance* (New York: Free Press, 1963), p. 9.
26. Ibid.
27. Oliver Wendell Holmes, *The Common Law,* ed. Mark De Wolf (Boston: Little, Brown, 1881), p. 36.
28. 320 U.S. 277 (1943).
29. Marvin Zalman, John Strate, Denis Hunter, and James Sellars, "Michigan Assisted Suicide Three Ring Circus: The Intersection of Law and Politics," *Ohio Northern Law Review* 23 (1997): 112–138.
30. 1992 P.A. 270 as amended by 1993 P.A. 3, M.C.L. ss. 752.1021 to 752.1027.
31. National Institute of Justice, *Project to Develop a Model Anti-Stalking Statute* (Washington, DC: National Institute of Justice, 1994).
32. "Clinton Signs Tougher 'Megan's Law,'" *CNN News Service,* 17 May 1996.
33. Associated Press, "Judge Upholds State's Sexual Predator Law," *Bakersfield Californian,* 2 October 1996.
34. Michael Gottfredson and Travis Hirschi, "The Methodological Adequacy of Longitudinal Research on Crime," *Criminology* 25 (1987): 581–614.
35. The most recent version available at the time of this writing is Federal Bureau of Investigation, *Crime in the United States, 1999* (Washington, DC: U.S. Government Printing Office, 2000).
36. Claire Sterk, "Just for Fun? Cocaine Use Among Middle-Class Women," *Journal of Drug Issues* 26 (1996): 63–76.
37. Ibid., p. 63.
38. William F. Whyte, *Street Corner Society* (Chicago: University of Chicago Press, 1955).
39. Herman Schwendinger and Julia Schwendinger, *Adolescent Subcultures and Delinquency* (New York: Praeger, 1985).
40. For a review of these studies, see L. Rowell Huesmann and Neil Malamuth, "Media Violence and Antisocial Behavior," *Journal of Social Issues* 42 (1986): 31–53.
41. See, for example, Michael Hindelang and Travis Hirschi, "Intelligence and Delinquency: A Revisionist Review," *American Sociological Review* 42 (1977): 471–486.
42. Richard Herrnstein and Charles Murray, *The Bell Curve* (New York: Free Press, 1994).
43. Anthony Petrosino, Carolyn Turpin-Petrosino, and James Finckenauer, "Well-Meaning Programs Can Have Harmful Effects! Lessons from Experiments of Programs Such as Scared Straight," *Crime and Delinquency* 46 (2000): 354–379.
44. Victor Boruch, Timothy Victor, and Joe Cecil, "Resolving Ethical and Legal Problems in Randomized Experiments," *Crime and Delinquency* 46 (2000): 330–353.

Chapter 2

1. Fox Butterfield, "A Fatality: Parental Violence and Youth Sports," *New York Times,* 11 July 2000, p. 1.
2. Federal Bureau of Investigation, *Crime in the United States, 1999* (Washington, DC: U.S. Government Printing Office, 2000). Herein cited in notes as FBI, Uniform Crime Report, and referred to in text as Uniform Crime Report or UCR.
3. Callie Marie Rennison, *Criminal Victimization 1999: Changes 1998–99 with Trends 1993–98* (Washington, DC: Bureau of Justice Statistics, 2000).
4. Duncan Chappell, Gilbert Geis, Stephen Schafer, and Larry Siegel, "Forcible Rape: A Comparative Study of Offenses Known to the Police in Boston and Los Angeles," in *Studies in the Sociology of Sex,* ed. James Henslin (New York: Appleton Century Crofts, 1971), pp. 169–193.
5. David Seidman and Michael Couzens, "Getting the Crime Rate Down: Political Pressure and Crime Reporting," *Law and Society Review* 8 (1974): 457.
6. Robert O'Brien, "Police Productivity and Crime Rates: 1973–1992," *Criminology* 34 (1996): 183–207.
7. FBI, *UCR Handbook* (Washington, DC: U.S. Government Printing Office, 1998), p. 33.
8. Rennison, *Criminal Victimization 1999.*
9. L. Edward Wells and Joseph Rankin, "Juvenile Victimization: Convergent Validation of Alternative Measurements," *Journal of Research in Crime and Delinquency* 32 (1995): 287–307.
10. A pioneering effort in self-report research is A. L. Porterfield, *Youth in Trouble* (Fort Worth, TX: Leo Potishman Foundation, 1946); for a review, see Robert Hardt and George Bodine, *Development of Self-Report Instruments in Delinquency Research: A Conference Report* (Syracuse, NY: Syracuse University Youth Development Center, 1965). See also Fred Murphy, Mary Shirley, and Helen Witner, "The Incidence of Hidden Delinquency," *American Journal of Orthopsychology* 16 (1946): 686–696.
11. See, for example, John Paul Wright and Francis Cullen, "Juvenile Involvement in Occupational Delinquency," *Criminology* 38 (2000): 863–896.
12. For example, the following studies have noted the great discrepancy between official statistics and self-report studies: Martin Gold, "Undetected Delinquent Behavior," *Journal of Research in Crime and Delinquency* 3 (1966): 27–46; James Short and F. Ivan Nye, "Extent of Undetected Delinquency: Tentative Conclusions," *Journal of Criminal Law, Criminology and Police Science* 49 (1958): 296–302; Michael Hindelang, "Causes of Delinquency: A Partial Replication and Extension," *Social Problems* 20 (1973): 471–487.
13. D. Wayne Osgood, Lloyd Johnston, Patrick O'Malley, and Jerald Bachman, "The Generality of Deviance in Late Adolescence and Early Adulthood," *American Sociological Review* 53 (1988): 81–93.
14. Lloyd Johnston, Patrick O'Malley, and Jerald Bachman, *Monitoring the Future, 1990* (Ann Arbor, MI: Institute for Social Research, 1991); Timothy Flanagan and Kathleen Maguire, *Sourcebook of Criminal Justice Statistics, 1989* (Washington, DC: U.S. Government Printing Office, 1990), pp. 290–291.
15. Leonore Simon, "Validity and Reliability of Violent Juveniles: A Comparison of Juvenile Self-Reports with Adult Self-Reports Incarcerated in Adult Prisons," paper presented at the annual meeting of the American Society of Criminology, Boston, November 1995, p. 26.
16. Stephen Cernkovich, Peggy Giordano, and Meredith Pugh, "Chronic Offenders: The Missing Cases in Self-Report Delinquency Research," *Journal of Criminal Law and Criminology* 76 (1985): 705–732.
17. Terence Thornberry, Beth Bjerregaard, and William Miles, "The Consequences of Respondent Attrition in Panel Studies: A Simulation Based on the Rochester Youth Development Study," *Journal of Quantitative Criminology* 9 (1993): 127–158.
18. Alfred Blumstein, Jacqueline Cohen, and Richard Rosenfeld, "Trend and Deviation in Crime Rates: A Comparison of UCR and NCVS Data for Burglary and Robbery," *Criminology* 29 (1991): 237–248. See also Michael Hindelang, Travis Hirschi, and Joseph Weis, *Measuring Delinquency* (Beverly Hills, CA: Sage, 1981).
19. Clarence Schrag, *Crime and Justice: American Style* (Washington, DC: U.S. Government Printing Office, 1971), p. 17.
20. Thomas Bernard, "Juvenile Crime and the Transformation of Juvenile Justice: Is There a Juvenile Crime Wave?" *Justice Quarterly* 16 (1999): 336–356.
21. James A. Fox, *Trends in Juvenile Violence: A Report to the United States Attorney General on Current and Future Rates of Juvenile Offending* (Boston: Northeastern University, 1996).
22. Steven Levitt, "The Limited Role of Changing Age Structure in Explaining Aggregate Crime Rates," *Criminology* 37 (1999): 581–599.

23. Ralph Weisheit and L. Edward Wells, "The Future of Crime in Rural America," *Journal of Crime and Justice* 22 (1999): 1–22.

24. Peter Van Koppen and Robert Jansen, "The Time to Rob: Variations in Time of Number of Commercial Robberies," *Journal of Research in Crime and Delinquency* 36 (1999): 7–29.

25. Ellen Cohn, "The Effect of Weather and Temporal Variations on Calls for Police Service," *American Journal of Police* 15 (1996): 23–43.

26. R. A. Baron, "Aggression as a Function of Ambient Temperature and Prior Anger Arousal," *Journal of Personality and Social Psychology* 21 (1972): 183–189.

27. Ellen Cohn, "The Prediction of Police Calls for Service: The Influence of Weather and Temporal Variables on Rape and Domestic Violence," *Journal of Environmental Psychology* 13 (1993): 71–83.

28. See, generally, Franklin Zimring and Gordon Hawkins, *Crime Is Not the Problem: Lethal Violence in America* (New York: Oxford University Press, 1997).

29. Ibid., p. 36.

30. Robert Nash Parker, "Bringing 'Booze' Back In: The Relationship Between Alcohol and Homicide," *Journal of Research in Crime and Delinquency* 32 (1995): 3–38.

31. Victoria Brewer and M. Dwayne Smith, "Gender Inequality and Rates of Female Homicide Victimization Across U.S. Cities," *Journal of Research in Crime and Delinquency* 32 (1995): 175–190.

32. R. Gregory Dunaway, Francis Cullen, Velmer Burton, and T. David Evans, "The Myth of Social Class and Crime Revisited: An Examination of Class and Adult Criminality," *Criminology* 38 (2000): 589–632.

33. Ivan Nye, James Short, and Virgil Olsen, "Socioeconomic Status and Delinquent Behavior," *American Journal of Sociology* 63 (1958): 381–389; Robert Dentler and Lawrence Monroe, "Social Correlates of Early Adolescent Theft," *American Sociological Review* 63 (1961): 733–743. See also Terence Thornberry and Margaret Farnworth, "Social Correlates of Criminal Involvement: Further Evidence on the Relationship Between Social Status and Criminal Behavior," *American Sociological Review* 47 (1982): 505–518.

34. Charles Tittle, Wayne Villemez, and Douglas Smith, "The Myth of Social Class and Criminality: An Empirical Assessment of the Empirical Evidence," *American Sociological Review* 43 (1978): 643–656. See also Charles Tittle and Robert Meier, "Specifying the SES/Delinquency Relationship," *Criminology* 28 (1990): 271–301.

35. Delbert Elliott and Suzanne Ageton, "Reconciling Race and Class Differences in Self-Reported and Official Estimates of Delinquency," *American Sociological Review* 45 (1980): 95–110.

36. See also Delbert Elliott and David Huizinga, "Social Class and Delinquent Behavior in a National Youth Panel: 1976–1980," *Criminology* 21 (1983): 149–177. For a similar view, see John Braithwaite, "The Myth of Social Class and Criminality Reconsidered," *American Sociological Review* 46 (1981): 35–58; Hindelang, Hirschi, and Weis, *Measuring Delinquency*, p. 196.

37. Dunaway, Cullen, Burton, and Evans, "The Myth of Social Class and Crime Revisited."

38. Judith Blau and Peter Blau, "The Cost of Inequality: Metropolitan Structure and Violent Crime," *American Sociological Review* 147 (1982): 114–129; Richard Block, "Community Environment and Violent Crime," *Criminology* 17 (1979): 46–57; Robert Sampson, "Structural Sources of Variation in Race-Age-Specific Rates of Offending Across Major U.S. Cities," *Criminology* 23 (1985): 647–673.

39. Chin-Chi Hsieh and M. D. Pugh, "Poverty, Income Inequality, and Violent Crime: A Meta-Analysis of Recent Aggregate Data Studies," *Criminal Justice Review* 18 (1993): 182–199.

40. Robert Agnew, "A General Strain Theory of Community Differences in Crime Rates," *Journal of Research in Crime and Delinquency* 36 (1999): 123–155.

41. Bonita Veysey and Steven Messner, "Further Testing of Social Disorganization Theory: An Elaboration of Sampson and Groves's 'Community Structure and Crime,'" *Journal of Research in Crime and Delinquency* 36 (1999): 156–174.

42. Lance Hannon and James Defronzo, "Welfare and Property Crime," *Justice Quarterly* 15 (1998): 273–288.

43. Alan Lizotte, Terence Thornberry, Marvin Krohn, Deborah Chard-Wierschem, and David Mc-Dowall, "Neighborhood Context and Delinquency: A Longitudinal Analysis," in *Cross National Longitudinal Research on Human Development and Criminal Behavior*, ed. E. M. Weitekamp and H. J. Kerner (Stavernstr, Netherlands: Kluwer, 1994), pp. 217–227.

44. Travis Hirschi and Michael Gottfredson, "Age and the Explanation of Crime," *American Journal of Sociology* 89 (1983): 552–584, at p. 581.

45. Darrell Steffensmeier and Cathy Streifel, "Age, Gender, and Crime Across Three Historical Periods: 1935, 1960 and 1985," *Social Forces* 69 (1991): 869–894.

46. For a comprehensive review of crime and the elderly, see Kyle Kercher, "Causes and Correlates of Crime Committed by the Elderly," in *Critical Issues in Aging Policy*, ed. E. Borgatta and R. Montgomery (Beverly Hills, CA: Sage, 1987), pp. 254–306; Darrell Steffensmeier, "The Invention of the 'New' Senior Citizen Criminal," *Research on Aging* 9 (1987): 281–311.

47. Margo Wilson and Martin Daly, "Life Expectancy, Economic Inequality, Homicide, and Reproductive Timing in Chicago Neighbourhoods," *British Journal of Medicine* 314 (1997): 1271–1274.

48. Edward Mulvey and John LaRosa, "Delinquency Cessation and Adolescent Development: Preliminary Data," *American Journal of Orthopsychiatry* 56 (1986): 212–224.

49. Gordon Trasler, "Cautions for a Biological Approach to Crime," in *The Causes of Crime: New Biological Approaches*, ed. Sarnoff Mednick, Terrie Moffitt, and Susan Stack (Cambridge: Cambridge University Press, 1987), pp. 7–25.

50. James Q. Wilson and Richard Herrnstein, *Crime and Human Nature* (New York: Simon and Schuster, 1985), pp. 126–147.

51. Wilson and Herrnstein, *Crime and Human Nature*, p. 219.

52. Timothy Brezina, "Delinquent Problem-solving: An Interpretive Framework for Criminological Theory and Research," *Journal of Research in Crime and Delinquency* 37 (2000): 3–30.

53. Walter Gove, "The Effect of Age and Gender on Deviant Behavior: A Biopsychosocial Perspective," in *Gender and the Life Course*, ed. A. Ross (Chicago: Aldine, 1985), p. 131.

54. Cesare Lombroso, *The Female Offender* (New York: Appleton Publishers, 1920), p. 122.

55. Lombroso, *The Female Offender*.

56. Alan Booth and D. Wayne Osgood, "The Influence of Testosterone on Deviance in Adulthood: Assessing and Explaining the Relationship," *Criminology* 31 (1993): 93–118.

57. Gisela Konopka, *The Adolescent Girl in Conflict* (Englewood Cliffs, NJ: Prentice-Hall, 1966); Clyde Vedder and Dora Somerville, *The Delinquent Girl* (Springfield, IL: Charles C. Thomas, 1970).

58. Robert Hoge, D. A. Andrews, and Alan Leschied, "Tests of Three Hypotheses Regarding the Predictors of Delinquency," *Journal of Abnormal Child Psychology* 22 (1994): 547–559.

59. Rita James Simon, *The Contemporary Woman and Crime* (Washington, DC: U.S. Government Printing Office, 1975).

60. David Rowe, Alexander Vazsonyi, and Daniel Flannery, "Sex Differences in Crime: Do Mean and Within-Sex Variation Have Similar Causes?" *Journal of Research in Crime and Delinquency* 32 (1995): 84–100; Michael Hindelang, "Age, Sex, and the Versatility of Delinquency Involvements," *Social Forces* 14 (1971): 525–534; Martin Gold, *Delinquent Behavior in an American City* (Belmont, CA: Brooks/Cole, 1970); Gary Jensen and Raymond Eve, "Sex Differences in Delinquency: An Examination of Popular Sociological Explanations," *Criminology* 13 (1976): 427–448.

61. UCR, 1997, p. 215.

62. David Huizinga and Delbert Elliott, "Juvenile Offenders: Prevalence, Offender Incidence, and Arrest Rates by Race," *Crime and Delinquency* 33 (1987): 206–223. See also Dale Dannefer and Russell Schutt, "Race and Juvenile Justice Processing in Court and Police Agencies," *American Journal of Sociology* 87 (1982): 1113–1132.

63. Paul Tracy, "Race and Class Differences in Official and Self-Reported Delinquency," in *From Boy to Man, from Delinquency to Crime*, ed. Marvin Wolfgang, Terence Thornberry, and Robert Figlio (Chicago: University of Chicago Press, 1987), p. 120.

64. Phillipe Rushton, "Race and Crime: An International Dilemma," *Society* 32 (1995): 37–42; for a rebuttal, see Jerome Neapolitan, "Cross-National Variation in Homicides: Is Race a Factor?" *Criminology* 36 (1998): 139–156.

65. Miriam Sealock and Sally Simpson, "Unraveling Bias in Arrest Decisions: The Role of Juvenile Offender Type-scripts," *Justice Quarterly* 15 (1998): 427–457.

66. "Law Enforcement Seeks Answers to 'Racial Profiling' Complaints," *Criminal Justice Newsletter* 29 (1998): 5.

67. Daniel Georges-Abeyie, "Definitional Issues: Race, Ethnicity and Official Crime/Victimization Rates," in *The Criminal Justice System and Blacks*, ed. D. Georges-Abeyie (New York: Clark Boardman, 1984), p. 12; Robert Sampson, "Race and Criminal Violence: A Demographically Disaggregated Analysis of Urban Homicide," *Crime and Delinquency* 31 (1985): 47–82.

68. Barry Sample and Michael Philip, "Perspectives on Race and Crime in Research and Planning," in *The Criminal Justice System and Blacks*, ed. D. Georges-Abeyie (New York: Clark Boardman, 1984), pp. 21–36.

69. Candace Kruttschnitt, "Violence by and Against Women: A Comparative and Cross-National Analysis," *Violence and Victims* 8 (1994): 1–28, at p. 4.

70. Fox Butterfield, *All God's Children: The Bosket Family and the American Tradition of Violence* (New York: Avon, 1996).

71. Michael Leiber and Jayne Stairs, "Race, Contexts and the Use of Intake Diversion," *Journal of Research in Crime and Delinquency* 36 (1999): 56–86; Darrell Steffensmeier, Jeffery Ulmer, and John Kramer, "The Interaction of Race, Gender, and Age in Criminal Sentencing: The Punishment Cost of Being Young, Black, and Male," *Criminology* 36 (1998): 763–798.

72. Tracy Nobiling, Cassia Spohn, and Miriam DeLone, "A Tale of Two Counties: Unemployment and Sentence Severity," *Justice Quarterly* 15 (1998): 459–486.

73. Alexander Weiss and Steven Chermak, "The News Value of African-American Victims: An Examination of the Media's Presentation of Homicide," *Journal of Crime and Justice* 21 (1998): 71–84.

74. Roy Austin, "Progress Toward Racial Equality and Reduction of Black Criminal Violence," *Journal of Criminal Justice* 15 (1987): 437–459.

75. Reynolds Farley and William Frey, "Changes in the Segregation of Whites from Blacks During the 1980s: Small Steps Toward a More Integrated Society," *American Sociological Review* 59 (1994): 23–45.

76. Marvin Wolfgang, Robert Figlio, and Thorsten Sellin, *Delinquency in a Birth Cohort* (Chicago: University of Chicago Press, 1972).

77. Lyle Shannon, *Criminal Career Opportunity* (New York: Human Sciences Press, 1988); D. J. West and David P. Farrington, *The Delinquent Way of Life* (London: Heinemann, 1977).

Chapter 3

1. Ben Fox, "Jury Recommends Death for Convicted Child Killer," *Boston Globe* 6 October 1999, p. 3.
2. Federal Bureau of Investigation, *Crime in the United States, 1999* (Washington, DC: U.S. Government Printing Office, 2000), p. 210. Hereinafter cited as FBI, Uniform Crime Report, 1999.
3. Ted Miller, Mark Cohen, and Brian Wiersema, *The Extent and Costs of Crime Victimization: A New Look* (Washington, DC: National Institute of Justice, 1996).
4. George Rengert, *The Geography of Illegal Drugs* (Boulder, CO: Westview Press, 1996), p. 5.
5. Ross Macmillan, "Adolescent Victimization and Income Deficits in Adulthood: Rethinking the Costs of Criminal Violence from a Life-Course Perspective," *Criminology* 38 (2000): 553–588.
6. Rebecca Campbell and Sheela Raja, "Secondary Victimization of Rape Victims: Insights from Mental Health Professionals Who Treat Survivors of Violence," *Violence and Victims* 14 (1999): 261–274.
7. Peter Finn, *Victims* (Washington, DC: Bureau of Justice Statistics, 1988), p. 1.
8. Michael Wiederman, Randy Sansone, and Lori Sansone, "History of Trauma and Attempted Suicide Among Women in a Primary Care Setting," *Violence and Victims* 13 (1998): 3–11; Susan Leslie Bryant and Lillian Range, "Suicidality in College Women Who Were Sexually and Physically Abused and Physically Punished by Parents," *Violence and Victims* 10 (1995): 195–215; William Downs and Brenda Miller, "Relationships Between Experiences of Parental Violence During Childhood and Women's Self-Esteem," *Violence and Victims* 13 (1998): 63–78; Sally Davies-Netley, Michael Hurlburt, and Richard Hough, "Childhood Abuse as a Precursor to Homelessness for Homeless Women with Severe Mental Illness," *Violence and Victims* 11 (1996): 129–142.
9. Jeanne Kaufman and Cathy Spatz Widom, "Childhood Victimization, Running Away, and Delinquency," *Journal of Research in Crime and Delinquency* 36 (1999): 347–370.
10. Dina Vivian and Jean Malone, "Relationship Factors and Depressive Symptomology Associated with Mild and Severe Husband-to-Wife Physical Aggression," *Violence and Victims* 12 (1997): 19–37; Walter Gleason, "Mental Disorders in Battered Women," *Violence and Victims* 8 (1993): 53–66. Daniel Saunders, "Posttraumatic Stress Symptom Profiles of Battered Women: A Comparison of Survivors in Two Settings," *Violence and Victims* 9 (1994): 31–43.
11. K. Daniel O'Leary, "Psycholgocial Abuse: A Variable Deserving Critical Attention in Domestic Violence," *Violence and Victims* 14 (1999): 1–21.
12. James Anderson, Terry Grandison, and Laronistine Dyson, "Victims of Random Violence and the Public Health Implication: A Health Care or Criminal Justice Issue," *Journal of Criminal Justice* 24 (1996): 379–393.
13. Susan Popkin, Victoria Gwlasda, Dennis Rosenbaum, Jean Amendolla, Wendell Johnson, and Lynn Olson, "Combating Crime in Public Housing: A Qualitative and Quantitative Longitudinal Analysis of the Chicago Housing Authority's Anti-drug Initiative," *Justice Quarterly* 16 (1999): 519–557.
14. Pamela Wilcox Rountree, "A Reexamination of the Crime–Fear Linkage," *Journal of Research in Crime and Delinquency* 35 (1998): 341–372.
15. Robert Davis, Bruce Taylor, and Arthur Lurigio, "Adjusting to Criminal Victimization: The Correlates of Postcrime Distress," *Violence and Victimization* 11 (1996): 21–34.
16. Timothy Ireland and Cathy Spatz Widom, *Childhood Victimization and Risk for Alcohol and Drug Arrests* (Washington, DC: National Institute of Justice, 1995).
17. Brigette Erwin, Elana Newman, Robert McMackin, Carlo Morrissey, and Danny Kaloupek, "PTSD, Malevolent Environment, and Criminality Among Criminally Involved Male Adolescents," *Criminal Justice and Behavior* 27 (2000): 196–215.
18. Cathy Spatz Widom, *The Cycle of Violence* (Washington, DC: National Institute of Justice, 1992), p. 1.
19. Steve Spaccarelli, J. Douglas Coatsworth, and Blake Sperry Bowden, "Exposure to Serious Family Violence Among Incarcerated Boys: Its Association with Violent Offending and Potential Mediating Variables," *Violence and Victims* 10 (1995): 163–180; Jerome Kolbo, "Risk and Resilience Among Children Exposed to Family Violence," *Violence and Victims* 11 (1996): 113–127.
20. Victim data used in these sections is from Callie Marie Rennison, *Criminal Victimization 1999* (Washington, DC: Bureau of Justice Statistics, 2000).
21. Ronet Bachman, *Violence Against Women* (Washington, DC: Bureau of Justice Statistics, 1994).
22. U.S. Centers for Disease Control, "Homicide Among Young Black Males: United States, 1978–1987," *Morbidity and Mortality Weekly Report* 39 (7 December 1990): 869–873.
23. Karin Wittebrood and Paul Nieuwbeerta, "Criminal Victimization During One's Life Course: The Effects of Previous Victimization and Patterns of Routine Activities," *Journal of Research in Crime and Delinquency* 37 (2000): 91–122; Janet Lauritsen and Kenna Davis Quinet, "Repeat Victimizations Among Adolescents and Young Adults," *Journal of Quantitative Criminology* 11 (1995): 143–163.
24. Denise Osborn, Dan Ellingworth, Tim Hope, and Alan Trickett, "Are Repeatedly Victimized Households Different?" *Journal of Quantitative Criminology* 12 (1996): 223–245.
25. Graham Farrell, "Predicting and Preventing Revictimization," in *Crime and Justice: An Annual Review of Research,* Michael Tonry and David Farrington, eds., vol. 20 (Chicago: University of Chicago Press, 1995), pp. 61–126.
26. Ibid., p. 61.
27. David Finkelhor and Nancy Asigian, "Risk Factors for Youth Victimization: Beyond a Lifestyles/Routine Activities Theory Approach," *Violence and Victimization* 11 (1996): 3–19.
28. Graham Farrell, Coretta Phillips, and Ken Pease, "Like Taking Candy: Why Does Repeat Victimization Occur?" *British Journal of Criminology* 35 (1995): 384–399.
29. Christopher Innes and Lawrence Greenfeld, *Violent State Prisoners and Their Victims* (Washington, DC: Bureau of Justice Statistics, 1990).
30. Hans Von Hentig, *The Criminal and His Victim: Studies in the Sociobiology of Crime* (New Haven, CT: Yale University Press, 1948), p. 384.
31. Marvin Wolfgang, *Patterns of Criminal Homicide* (Philadelphia: University of Pennsylvania Press, 1958).
32. Menachem Amir, *Patterns in Forcible Rape* (Chicago: University of Chicago Press, 1971).
33. Susan Estrich, *Real Rape* (Cambridge, MA: Harvard University Press, 1987).
34. Edem Avakame, "Female's Labor Force Participation and Intimate Femicide: An Empirical Assessment of the Backlash Hypothesis," *Violence and Victims* 14 (1999): 277–283.
35. Martin Daly and Margo Wilson, *Homicide* (New York: Aldine de Gruyter, 1988).
36. Rosemary Gartner and Bill McCarthy, "The Social Distribution of Femicide in Urban Canada, 1921–1988," *Law and Society Review* 25 (1991): 287–311.
37. Dan Hoyt, Kimberly Ryan, and Mari Cauce, "Personal Victimizaton in a High-Risk Environment: Homeless and Runaway Adolescents," *Journal of Research in Crime and Delinquency* 36 (1999): 371–392.
38. See, generally, Gary Gottfredson and Denise Gottfredson, *Victimization in Schools* (New York: Plenum Press, 1985).
39. Gary Jensen and David Brownfield, "Gender, Lifestyles, and Victimization: Beyond Routine Activity Theory," *Violence and Victims* 1 (1986): 85–99.
40. Rolf Loeber, Mary DeLamatre, George Tita, Jacqueline Cohen, Magda Stouthamer-Loeber, and David Farrington, "Gun Injury and Mortality: The Delinquent Backgrounds of Juvenile Offenders," *Violence and Victims* 14 (1999): 339–351.
41. Bonnie Fisher, John Sloan, Francis Cullen, and Chunmeng Lu, "Crime in the Ivory Tower: The Level and Sources of Student Victimization," *Criminology* 36 (1998): 671–710.
42. James Garofalo, "Reassessing the Lifestyle Model of Criminal Victimization," in *Positive Criminology,* ed. Michael Gottfredson and Travis Hirschi (Newbury Park, CA: Sage, 1987), pp. 23–42.
43. Terance Miethe and David McDowall, "Contextual Effects in Models of Criminal Victimization," *Social Forces* 71 (1993): 741–759.
44. Rodney Stark, "Deviant Places: A Theory of the Ecology of Crime," *Criminology* 25 (1987): 893–911.
45. Ibid., p. 902.
46. Pamela Wilcox Rountree, Kenneth Land, and Terance Miethe, "Macro–Micro Integration in the Study of Victimization: A Hierarchical Logistic Model Analysis Across Seattle Neighborhoods," paper presented at the annual meeting of the American Society of Criminology, Phoenix, Arizona, November 1993.
47. Lawrence Cohen and Marcus Felson, "Social Change and Crime Rate Trends: A Routine Activities Approach," *American Sociological Review* 44 (1979): 588–608.
48. For a review, see James LeBeau and Thomas Castellano, "The Routine Activities Approach: An Inventory and Critique," unpublished paper, Center for the Studies of Crime, Delinquency, and Corrections, Southern Illinois University, Carbondale, 1987.
49. Teresa LaGrange, "The Impact of Neighborhoods, Schools, and Malls on the Spatial Distribution of Property Damage," *Journal of Research in Crime and Delinquency* 36 (1999): 393–422.
50. Lawrence Cohen, Marcus Felson, and Kenneth Land, "Property Crime Rates in the United States: A Macrodynamic Analysis, 1947–1977, with Ex-ante Forecasts for the Mid-1980s," *American Journal of Sociology* 86 (1980): 90–118.
51. Terence Miethe and Robert Meier, *Crime and Its Social Context: Toward an Integrated Theory of Offenders, Victims, and Situations* (Albany: State University of New York Press, 1994).
52. Richard Felson, "Routine Activities and Involvement in Violence as Actor, Witness, or Target," *Violence and Victimization* 12 (1997): 209–223.
53. Georgina Hammock and Deborah Richardson, "Perceptions of Rape: The Influence of Closeness of Relationship, Intoxication, and Sex of Participant," *Violence and Victimization* 12 (1997): 237–247.
54. Karin Wittebrood and Paul Nieuwbeerta, "Criminal Victimization During One's Life Course," pp. 112–113.
55. Patricia Resnick, "Psychological Effects of Victimization: Implications for the Criminal Justice System," *Crime and Delinquency* 33 (1987): 468–478.
56. Dean Kilpatrick, Benjamin Saunders, Lois Veronen, Connie Best, and Judith Von, "Criminal Victimization: Lifetime Prevalence, Reporting to Police, and Psychological Impact," *Crime and Delinquency* 33 (1987): 479–489.
57. U.S. Department of Justice, *Report of the President's Task Force on Victims of Crime* (Washington, DC: U.S. Government Printing Office, 1983).
58. Ibid., pp. 2–10; "Review on Victims: Witnesses of Crime," *Massachusetts Lawyers Weekly,* 25 April 1983, p. 26.
59. Robert Davis, *Crime Victims: Learning How to Help Them* (Washington, DC: National Institute of Justice, 1987).
60. Peter Finn and Beverly Lee, *Establishing a Victim–Witness Assistance Program* (Washington, DC: U.S. Government Printing Office, 1988).

61. This section leans heavily on Albert Roberts, "Delivery of Services to Crime Victims: A National Survey," *American Journal of Orthopsychiatry* 6 (1991): 128–137; see also Albert Roberts, *Helping Crime Victims: Research, Policy, and Practice* (Newbury Park, CA: Sage, 1990).

62. Randall Schmidt, "Crime Victim Compensation Legislation: A Comparative Study," *Victimology* 5 (1980): 428–437.

63. Ibid.

64. Pater Jaffe, Marlies Sudermann, Deborah Reitzel, and Steve Killip, "An Evaluation of a Secondary School Primary Prevention Program on Violence in Intimate Relationships," *Violence and Victims* 7 (1992): 129–145.

65. Andrew Karmen, "Victim–Offender Reconciliation Programs: Pro and Con," *Perspectives of the American Probation and Parole Association* 20 (1996): 11–14.

66. See Frank Carrington, "Victim's Rights Litigation: A Wave of the Future," in *Perspectives on Crime Victims*, ed. Burt Galaway and Joe Hudson (St. Louis: Mosby, 1981).

67. Andrew Karmen, "Toward the Institutionalization of a New Kind of Justice Professional: The Victim Advocate," *Justice Professional* 9 (1995): 2–15.

68. Ibid., pp. 9–10.

69. Sara Flaherty and Austin Flaherty, *Victims and Victims' Risk* (New York: Chelsea House, 1998).

70. Pamela Wilcox Rountree and Kenneth Land, "Burglary Victimization, Perceptions of Crime Risk, and Routine Activities: A Multilevel Analysis Across Seattle Neighborhoods and Census Tracts," *Journal of Research in Crime and Delinquency* 33 (1996): 1147–1180.

71. Leslie Kennedy, "Going It Alone: Unreported Crime and Individual Self-Help," *Journal of Criminal Justice* 16 (1988): 403–413.

72. Ronald Clarke, "Situational Crime Prevention: Its Theoretical Basis and Practical Scope," in *Annual Review of Criminal Justice Research*, ed. Michael Tonry and Norval Morris (Chicago: University of Chicago Press, 1983).

73. See, generally, Dennis P. Rosenbaum, Arthur J. Lurigio, and Robert C. Davis, *The Prevention of Crime: Social and Situational Strategies* (Belmont, CA: Wadsworth, 1998).

74. Andrew Buck, Simon Hakim, and George Rengert, "Burglar Alarms and the Choice Behavior of Burglars," *Journal of Criminal Justice* 21 (1993): 497–507; for an opposing view, see James Lynch and David Cantor, "Ecological and Behavioral Influences on Property Victimization at Home: Implications for Opportunity Theory," *Journal of Research in Crime and Delinquency* 29 (1992): 335–362.

75. James Garofalo and Maureen McLeod, *Improving the Use and Effectiveness of Neighborhood Watch Programs* (Washington, DC: National Institute of Justice, 1988).

76. Peter Finn, *Block Watches Help Crime Victims in Philadelphia* (Washington, DC: National Institute of Justice, 1986).

77. Ibid.

Chapter 4

1. John Tagliabue, "Russian Racket Linked to New York Bank," *New York Times*, 28 September 1999, p. 1.

2. Bob Roshier, *Controlling Crime* (Chicago: Lyceum Books, 1989), p. 10.

3. James Q. Wilson, *Thinking About Crime*, rev. ed. (New York: Vintage Books, 1983), p. 260.

4. See, generally, Derek Cornish and Ronald Clarke, eds. *The Reasoning Criminal: Rational Choice Perspectives on Offending* (New York: Springer Verlag, 1986); Philip Cook, "The Demand and Supply of Criminal Opportunities," in *Crime and Justice*, vol. 7, ed. Michael Tonry and Norval Morris (Chicago: University of Chicago Press, 1986), pp. 1–28; Ronald Clarke and Derek Cornish, "Modeling Offenders' Decisions: A Framework for Research and Policy," in *Crime and Justice*, vol. 6, ed. Michael Tonry and Norval Morris

(Chicago: University of Chicago Press, 1985), pp. 147–187; Morgan Reynolds, *Crime by Choice: An Economic Analysis* (Dallas: Fisher Institute, 1985).

5. George Rengert and John Wasilchick, *Suburban Burglary: A Time and Place for Everything* (Springfield, IL: Charles Thomas, 1985).

6. John McIver, "Criminal Mobility: A Review of Empirical Studies," in *Crime Spillover*, ed. Simon Hakim and George Rengert (Beverly Hills, CA: Sage, 1981), pp. 110–121; Carol Kohfeld and John Sprague, "Demography, Police Behavior, and Deterrence," *Criminology* 28 (1990): 111–136.

7. Derek Cornish and Ronald Clarke, "Understanding Crime Displacement: An Application of Rational Choice Theory," *Criminology* 25 (1987): 933–947.

8. Lloyd Phillips and Harold Votey, "The Influence of Police Interventions and Alternative Income Sources on the Dynamic Process of Choosing Crime as a Career," *Journal of Quantitative Criminology* 3 (1987): 251–274.

9. Michael Gottfredson and Travis Hirschi, *A General Theory of Crime* (Stanford, CA: Stanford University Press, 1990).

10. Liliana Pezzin, "Earnings Prospects, Matching Effects, and the Decision to Terminate a Criminal Career," *Journal of Quantitative Criminology* 11 (1995): 29–50.

11. Pierre Tremblay and Carlo Morselli, "Patterns in Criminal Achievement: Wilson and Abrahmse Revisited," *Criminology* 38 (2000): 633–660.

12. Ronald Akers, "Rational Choice, Deterrence and Social Learning Theory in Criminology: The Path Not Taken," *Journal of Criminal Law and Criminology* 81 (1990): 653–676.

13. Neal Shover, *Aging Criminals* (Beverly Hills, CA: Sage, 1985).

14. Robert Agnew, "Determinism, Indeterminism, and Crime: An Empirical Exploration," *Criminology* 33 (1995): 83–109.

15. Ibid., pp. 103–104.

16. Bruce Jacobs, "Crack Dealers' Apprehension Avoidance Techniques: A Case of Restrictive Deterrence," *Justice Quarterly* 13 (1996): 359–381.

17. Ibid., p. 367.

18. Ibid., p. 372.

19. Michael Rand, *Crime and the Nation's Households, 1989* (Washington, DC: Bureau of Justice Statistics, 1990), p. 4.

20. Paul Cromwell, James Olson, and D'Aunn Wester Avary, *Breaking and Entering: An Ethnographic Analysis of Burglary* (Newbury Park, CA: Sage, 1989), p. 24.

21. Ibid., pp. 30–32.

22. George Rengert and John Wasilchick, *Space, Time, and Crime: Ethnographic Insights into Residential Burglary* (Washington, DC: National Institute of Justice, 1989); see also Rengert and Wasilchick, *Suburban Burglary.*

23. Matthew Robinson, "Lifestyles, Routine Activities, and Residential Burglary Victimization," *Journal of Criminal Justice* 22 (1999): 27–52.

24. Patrick Donnelly and Charles Kimble, "Community Organizing, Environmental Change, and Neighborhood Crime," *Crime and Delinquency* 43 (1997): 493–511.

25. Leanne Fiftal Alarid, James Marquart, Velmer Burton, Francis Cullen, and Steven Cuvelier, "Women's Roles in Serious Offenses: A Study of Adult Felons," *Justice Quarterly* 13 (1996): 431–454 at p. 448.

26. Ronald Clarke and Marcus Felson, "Introduction: Criminology, Routine Activity and Rational Choice," in *Routine Activity and Rational Choice* (New Brunswick, NJ: Transaction Publishers, 1993), pp. 1–14.

27. Associated Press, "Thrift Hearings Resume Today in Senate," *Boston Globe*, 2 January 1991, p. 10.

28. Ronald Clarke and Patricia Harris, "Auto Theft and Its Prevention," in *Crime and Justice: An Annual Edition*, ed. Michael Tonry and Norval Morris (Chicago: University of Chicago Press, 1992), pp. 1–54, at pp. 20–21.

29. William Smith, Sharon Glave Frazee, and Elizabeth Davison, "Furthering the Integration of Routine Activity and Social Disorganization Theories: Small Units of Analysis and the Study of Street Robbery as a Diffusion Process," *Criminology* 38 (2000): 489–521,

30. Paul Bellair, "Informal Surveillance and Street Crime: A Complex Relationship," *Criminology* 38 (2000): 137–167.

31. John Gibbs and Peggy Shelly, "Life in the Fast Lane: A Retrospective View by Commercial Thieves," *Journal of Research in Crime and Delinquency* 19 (1982): 229–230.

32. Gordon Knowles, "Deception, Detection, and Evasion: A Trade Craft Analysis of Honolulu, Hawaii's Street Crack Cocaine Traffickers," *Journal of Criminal Justice* 27 (1999): 443–455.

33. John Petraitis, Brian Flay, and Todd Miller, "Reviewing Theories of Adolescent Substance Use: Organizing Pieces in the Puzzle," *Psychological Bulletin* 117 (1995): 67–86.

34. George Rengert, *The Geography of Illegal Drugs* (Boulder, CO: Westview Press, 1996).

35. Jacobs, "Crack Dealers' Apprehension Avoidance Techniques."

36. Ibid., p. 367.

37. Richard Felson and Steven Messner, "To Kill or Not to Kill? Lethal Outcomes in Injurious Attacks," *Criminology* 34 (1996): 519–545, at p. 541.

38. Richard Wright and Scott Decker, *Armed Robbers in Action: Stickups and Street Culture* (Boston, MA: Northeastern University Press, 1997).

39. Ibid., p. 52.

40. James Wright and Peter Rossi, *Armed and Considered Dangerous: A Survey of Felons and Their Firearms* (Hawthorne, NY: Aldine De Gruyter, 1983), pp. 141–159.

41. Scott Decker, "Deviant Homicide: A New Look at the Role of Motives and Victim–Offender Relationships," *Journal of Research in Crime and Delinquency* 33 (1996): 427–449.

42. Felson and Messner, "To Kill or Not to Kill?"

43. Peter Wood, Walter Gove, James Wilson, and John Cochran, "Nonsocial Reinforcement and Habitual Criminal Conduct: An Extension of Learning," *Criminology* 35 (1997): 335–366.

44. Jeff Ferrell, "Criminological Verstehen: Inside the Immediacy of Crime," *Justice Quarterly* 14 (1997): 3–23, at p. 12.

45. Jack Katz, *Seductions of Crime* (New York: Basic Books, 1988).

46. Bill McCarthy, "Not Just 'For the Thrill of It': An Instrumentalist Elaboration of Katz's Explanation of Sneaky Thrill Property Crime," *Criminology* 33 (1995): 519–539.

47. George Rengert, "Spatial Justice and Criminal Victimization," *Justice Quarterly* 6 (1989): 543–564.

48. Ronald Clarke, *Situational Crime Prevention: Successful Case Studies* (Albany, NY: Harrow and Heston, 1992).

49. Nancy LaVigne, "Gasoline Drive-Offs: Designing a Less Convenient Environment," in *Crime Prevention Studies*, vol. 2, ed. Ronald Clarke (Monsey, NY: Criminal Justice Press, 1994), pp. 91–114.

50. Barry Webb, "Steering Column Locks and Motor Vehicle Theft: Evaluations for Three Countries," in *Crime Prevention Studies*, vol. 2, ed. Ronald Clarke (Monsey, NY: Criminal Justice Press, 1994), pp. 71–89.

51. Barbara Morse and Delbert Elliott, "Effects of Ignition Interlock Devices on DUI Recidivism: Findings from a Longitudinal Study in Hamilton County, Ohio," *Crime and Delinquency* 38 (1992): 131–157.

52. Ronald Clarke, "Deterring Obscene Phone Callers: The New Jersey Experience," in *Situational Crime Prevention*, ed. Ronald Clarke (Albany, NY: Harrow and Heston, 1992), pp. 124–132.

53. Robert Barr and Ken Pease, "Crime Placement, Displacement, and Deflection," in *Crime and Justice, A Review of Research*, vol. 12, ed. Michael Tonry and Norval Morris (Chicago: University of Chicago Press, 1990), pp. 277–319.

54. Clarke, *Situational Crime Prevention,* p. 27.

55. Ibid., p. 35.

56. Ronald Clarke and David Weisburd, "Diffusion of Crime Control Benefits: Observations of the Reverse of Displacement," in *Crime Prevention Studies,* vol. 2, ed. Ronald Clarke (New York: Criminal Justice Press, 1994).

57. David Weisburd and Lorraine Green, "Policing Drug Hot Spots: The Jersey City Drug Market Analysis Experiment," *Justice Quarterly* 12 (1995): 711–734.

58. Ian Ayres and Steven D. Levitt, "Measuring Positive Externalities from Unobservable Victim Precaution: An Empirical Analysis of Lojack," *Quarterly Journal of Economics* 113 (1998): 43–78.

59. R. Steven Daniels, Lorin Baumhover, William Formby, and Carolyn Clark-Daniels, "Police Discretion and Elder Mistreatment: A Nested Model of Observation, Reporting, and Satisfaction," *Journal of Criminal Justice* 27 (1999): 209–225.

60. R. Yeaman, *The Deterrent Effectiveness of Criminal Justice Sanction Strategies: Summary Report* (Washington, DC: U.S. Government Printing Office, 1972). See, generally, Jack Gibbs, "Crime Punishment and Deterrence," *Social Science Quarterly* 48 (1968): 515–530.

61. Robert Bursik, Harold Grasmick, and Mitchell Chamlin, "The Effect of Longitudinal Arrest Patterns on the Development of Robbery Trends at the Neighborhood Level," *Criminology* 28 (1990): 431–450; Theodore Chiricos and Gordon Waldo, "Punishment and Crime: An Examination of Some Empirical Evidence," *Social Problems* 18 (1970): 200–217.

62. Stewart D'Alessio and Lisa Stolzenberg, "Crime, Arrests, and Pretrial Jail Incarceration: An Examination of the Deterrence Thesis," paper presented at the annual meeting of the American Society of Criminology, San Diego, November 1997.

63. Jiang Wu and Allen Liska, "The Certainty of Punishment: A Reference Group Effect and Its Functional Form," *Criminology* 31 (1993): 447–464.

64. Edwin Zedlewski, "Deterrence Findings and Data Sources: A Comparison of the Uniform Crime Rates and the National Crime Surveys," *Journal of Research in Crime and Delinquency* 20 (1983): 262–276.

65. David Bayley, *Policing for the Future* (New York: Oxford, 1994).

66. For a review, see Thomas Marvell and Carlisle Moody, "Specification Problems, Police Levels, and Crime Rates," *Criminology* 34 (1996): 609–646.

67. Charles Tittle and Alan Rowe, "Certainty of Arrest and Crime Rates: A Further Test of the Deterrence Hypothesis," *Social Forces* 52 (1974): 455–462.

68. Kenneth Novak, Jennifer Hartman, Alexander Holsinger, and Michael Turner, "The Effects of Aggressive Policing of Disorder on Serious Crime," *Policing* 22 (1999): 171–190.

69. Lawrence Sherman, "Police Crackdowns," *NIJ Reports* (March/April 1990): 2–6, at p. 2.

70. Anthony Braga, David Weisburd, Elin Waring, Lorraine Green Mazerolle, William Spelman, and Francis Gajewski, "Problem-Oriented Policing in Violent Crime Places: A Randomized Controlled Experiment," *Criminology* 37 (1999): 541–580.

71. Eric Fritsch, Tory Caeti, and Robert Taylor, "Gang Suppression Through Saturation Patrol, Aggressive Curfew, and Truancy Enforcement: A Quasi-Experimental Test of the Dallas Anti-Gang Initiative," *Crime and Delinquency* 45 (1999): 122–139.

72. Ed Stevens and Brian Payne, "Applying Deterrence Theory in the Context of Corporate Wrongdoing: Limitations on Punitive Damages," *Journal of Criminal Justice* 27 (1999): 195–209; Jeffrey Roth, *Firearms and Violence* (Washington, DC: National Institute of Justice, 1994); and Thomas Marvell and Carlisle Moody, "The Impact of Enhanced Prison Terms for Felonies Committed with Guns," *Criminology* 33 (1995): 247–281; Gary Green, "General Deterrence and Television

Cable Crime: A Field Experiment in Social Crime," *Criminology* 23 (1986): 629–645.

73. H. Laurence Ross, "Implications of Drinking-and-Driving Law Studies for Deterrence Research," in *Critique and Explanation: Essays in Honor of Gwynne Nettler,* ed. Timothy Hartnagel and Robert Silverman (New Brunswick, NJ: Transaction Books, 1986), pp. 159–171; H. Laurence Ross, Richard McCleary, and Gary LaFree, "Can Mandatory Jail Laws Deter Drunk Driving? The Arizona Case," *Journal of Criminal Law and Criminology* 81 (1990): 156–167.

74. For a review, see Jeffrey Roth, *Firearms and Violence* (Washington, DC: National Institute of Justice, 1994); and Thomas Marvell and Carlisle Moody, "The Impact of Enhanced Prison Terms for Felonies Committed with Guns," *Criminology* 33 (1995): 247–281.

75. Robert Dann, "The Deterrent Effect of Capital Punishment," *Friends Social Service Series* 29 (1935).

76. William Bowers and Glenn Pierce, "Deterrence or Brutalization: What Is the Effect of Executions?" *Crime and Delinquency* 26 (1980): 453–484.

77. John Cochran, Mitchell Chamlin, and Mark Seth, "Deterrence or Brutalization? An Impact Assessment of Oklahoma's Return to Capital Punishment," *Criminology* 32 (1994): 107–134.

78. David Phillips, "The Deterrent Effect of Capital Punishment," *American Journal of Sociology* 86 (1980): 139–148; Hans Zeisel, "A Comment on 'The Deterrent Effect of Capital Punishment' by Phillips," *American Journal of Sociology* 88 (1982): 167–169; see also Sam McFarland, "Is Capital Punishment a Short-Term Deterrent to Homicide? A Study of the Effects of Four Recent American Executions," *Journal of Criminal Law and Criminology* 74 (1984): 1014–1032.

79. Steven Stack, "Publicized Executions and Homicide, 1950–1980," *American Sociological Review* 52 (1987): 532–540; for a study challenging Stack's methods, see William Bailey and Ruth Peterson, "Murder and Capital Punishment: A Monthly Time-Series Analysis of Execution Publicity," *American Sociological Review* 54 (1989): 722–743.

80. Karl Schuessler, "The Deterrent Influence of the Death Penalty," *Annals of the Academy of Political and Social Sciences* 284 (1952): 54–62.

81. Thorsten Sellin, *The Death Penalty* (Philadelphia: American Law Institute, 1959); Walter Reckless, "Use of the Death Penalty," *Crime and Delinquency* 15 (1969): 43–51.

82. Richard Lempert, "The Effect of Executions on Homicides: A New Look in an Old Light," *Crime and Delinquency* 29 (1983): 88–115.

83. Derral Cheatwood, "Capital Punishment and the Deterrence of Violent Crime in Comparable Counties," *Criminal Justice Review* 18 (1993): 165–181.

84. Dane Archer, Rosemary Gartner, and Marc Beitel, "Homicide and the Death Penalty: A Cross-National Test of a Deterrence Hypothesis," *Journal of Criminal Law and Criminology* 74 (1983): 991–1014.

85. Isaac Ehrlich, "The Deterrent Effect of Capital Punishment: A Question of Life and Death," *American Economic Review* 65 (1975): 397–417.

86. James Fox and Michael Radelet, "Persistent Flaws in Econometric Studies of the Deterrent Effect of the Death Penalty," *Loyola of Los Angeles Law Review* 23 (1987): 29–44; William B. Bowers and Glenn Pierce, "The Illusion of Deterrence in Isaac Ehrlich's Research on Capital Punishment," *Yale Law Journal* 85 (1975): 187–208.

87. Jon Sorenson, Robert Wrinkle, Victoria Brewer, and James Marquart, "Capital Punishment and Deterrence: Examining the Effect of Executions on Murder in Texas," *Crime and Delinquency* 45 (1999): 481–493.

88. William Bailey, "Disaggregation in Deterrence and Death Penalty Research: The Case of Murder

in Chicago," *Journal of Criminal Law and Criminology* 74 (1986): 827–859.

89. Steven Messner and Kenneth Tardiff, "Economic Inequality and Level of Homicide: An Analysis of Urban Neighborhoods," *Criminology* 24 (1986): 297–317.

90. Donald Green, "Past Behavior as a Measure of Actual Future Behavior: An Unresolved Issue in Perceptual Deterrence Research," *Journal of Criminal Law and Criminology* 80 (1989): 781–804.

91. Donna Bishop, "Deterrence: A Panel Analysis," *Justice Quarterly* 1 (1984): 311–328; Julie Horney and Ineke Haen Marshall, "Risk Perceptions Among Serious Offenders: The Role of Crime and Punishment," *Criminology* 30 (1992): 575–594.

92. Wanda Foglia, "Perceptual Deterrence and the Mediating Effect of Internalized Norms Among Inner-City Teenagers," *Journal of Research in Crime and Delinquency* 34 (1997): 414–442; Raymond Paternoster, "Decisions to Participate in and Desist from Four Types of Common Delinquency: Deterrence and the Rational Choice Perspective," *Law and Society Review* 23 (1989): 7–29; Raymond Paternoster, "Examining Three-Wave Deterrence Models: A Question of Temporal Order and Specification," *Journal of Criminal Law and Criminology* 79 (1988): 135–163; Raymond Paternoster, Linda Saltzman, Gordon Waldo, and Theodore Chiricos, "Estimating Perceptual Stability and Deterrent Effects: The Role of Perceived Legal Punishment in the Inhibition of Criminal Involvement," *Journal of Criminal Law and Criminology* 74 (1983): 270–297; M. William Minor and Joseph Harry, "Deterrent and Experiential Effects in Perceptual Deterrence Research: A Replication and Extension," *Journal of Research in Crime and Delinquency* 19 (1982): 190–203; Lonn Lanza-Kaduce, "Perceptual Deterrence and Drinking and Driving Among College Students," *Criminology* 26 (1988): 321–341.

93. Steven Klepper and Daniel Nagin, "The Deterrent Effect of Perceived Certainty and Severity of Punishment Revisited," *Criminology* 27 (1989): 721–746; Scott Decker, Richard Wright, and Robert Logie, "Perceptual Deterrence Among Active Residential Burglars: A Research Note," *Criminology* 31 (1993): 135–147.

94. Alex Piquero and George Rengert, "Studying Deterrence with Active Residential Burglars," *Justice Quarterly* 16 (1999): 451–462.

95. Foglia, "Perceptual Deterrence and the Mediating Effect of Internalized Norms Among Inner-City Teenagers," pp. 414–442.

96. Harold Grasmick, Robert Bursik, and Karyl Kinsey, "Shame and Embarrassment as Deterrents to Noncompliance with the Law: The Case of an Anti-Littering Campaign," paper presented at the annual meeting of the American Society of Criminology, Baltimore, November 1990, p. 3.

97. Charles Tittle, *Sanctions and Social Deviance* (New York: Praeger, 1980).

98. Green, "Past Behavior as a Measure of Actual Future Behavior," p. 803; Matthew Silberman, "Toward a Theory of Criminal Deterrence," *American Sociological Review* 41 (1976): 442–461; Linda Anderson, Theodore Chiricos, and Gordon Waldo, "Formal and Informal Sanctions: A Comparison of Deterrent Effects," *Social Problems* 25 (1977): 103–114. See also Maynard Erickson and Jack Gibbs, "Objective and Perceptual Properties of Legal Punishment and Deterrence Doctrine," *Social Problems* 25 (1978): 253–264; Daniel Nagin and Raymond Paternoster, "Enduring Individual Differences and Rational Choice Theories of Crime," *Law and Society Review* 27 (1993): 467–485.

99. Harold Grasmick and Robert Bursik, "Conscience, Significant Others, and Rational Choice: Extending the Deterrence Model," *Law and Society Review* 24 (1900): 837–861, at p. 854.

100. Grasmick, Bursik, and Kinsey, "Shame and Embarrassment as Deterrents to Noncompliance

with the Law"; Harold Grasmick, Robert Bursik, and Bruce Arneklev, "Reduction in Drunk Driving as a Response to Increased Threats of Shame, Embarrassment, and Legal Sanctions," *Criminology* 31 (1993): 41–69.

101. Harold Grasmick, Brenda Sims Blackwell, and Robert Bursik, "Changes in the Sex Patterning of Perceived Threats of Sanctions," *Law and Society Review* 27 (1993): 679–699.

102. Thomas Peete, Trudie Milner, and Michael Welch, "Levels of Social Integration in Group Contexts and the Effects of Informal Sanction Threat on Deviance," *Criminology* 32 (1994): 85–105.

103. Ernest Van Den Haag, "The Criminal Law as a Threat System," *Journal of Criminal Law and Criminology* 73 (1982): 709–785.

104. David Lykken, "Psychopathy, Sociopathy, and Crime," *Society* 34 (1996): 30–38.

105. George Lowenstein, Daniel Nagin, and Raymond Paternoster, "The Effect of Sexual Arousal on Expectations of Sexual Forcefulness," *Journal of Research in Crime and Delinquency* 34 (1997): 443–473.

106. David Klinger, "Policing Spousal Assault," *Journal of Research in Crime and Delinquency* 32 (1995): 308–324.

107. James Williams and Daniel Rodeheaver, "Processing of Criminal Homicide Cases in a Large Southern City," *Sociology and Social Research* 75 (1991): 80–88.

108. James Q. Wilson, *Thinking About Crime* (New York: Basic Books, 1975).

109. James Q. Wilson and Richard Herrnstein, *Crime and Human Nature* (New York: Simon and Schuster, 1985), p. 494.

110. Christina Dejong, "Survival Analysis and Specific Deterrence: Integrating Theoretical and Empirical Models of Recidivism," *Criminology* 35 (1997): 561–576; Paul Tracy and Kimberly Kempf-Leonard, *Continuity and Discontinuity in Criminal Careers* (New York: Plenum Press, 1996).

111. Allen Beck and Bernard Shipley, *Recidivism of Prisoners Released in 1983* (Washington, DC: Bureau of Justice Statistics, 1989).

112. Dejong, "Survival Analysis and Specific Deterrence," p. 573.

113. David Weisburd, Elin Waring, and Ellen Chayet, "Specific Deterrence in a Sample of Offenders Convicted of White-Collar Crimes," *Criminology* 33 (1995): 587–607.

114. Dejong, "Survival Analysis and Specific Deterrence"; Raymond Paternoster and Alex Piquero, "Reconceptualizing Deterrence: An Empirical Test of Personal and Vicarious Experiences," *Journal of Research in Crime and Delinquency* 32 (1995): 251–258.

115. John Braithwaite, *Crime, Shame, and Reintegration* (Melbourne, Australia: Cambridge University Press, 1989).

116. Anthony Petrosino and Carolyn Petrosino, "The Public Safety Potential of Megan's Law in Massachusetts: An Assessment from a Sample of Criminal Sexual Psychopaths," *Crime and Delinquency* 45 (1999): 140–158.

117. See, generally, Raymond Paternoster, "Absolute and Restrictive Deterrence in a Panel of Youth: Explaining the Onset, Persistence/Desistance, and Frequency of Delinquent Offending," *Social Problems* 36 (1989): 289–307; Raymond Paternoster, "The Deterrent Effect of Perceived Severity of Punishment: A Review of the Evidence and Issues," *Justice Quarterly* 42 (1987): 173–217.

118. Isaac Ehrlich, "Participation in Illegitimate Activities: An Economic Analysis," *Journal of Political Economy* 81 (1973): 521–567; Lee Bowker, "Crime and the Use of Prisons in the United States: A Time Series Analysis," *Crime and Delinquency* 27 (1981): 206–212.

119. David Greenberg, "The Incapacitative Effects of Imprisonment: Some Estimates," *Law and Society Review* 9 (1975): 541–580.

120. Ibid., p. 558.

121. Reuel Shinnar and Shlomo Shinnar, "The Effects of the Criminal Justice System on the Control of Crime: A Quantitative Approach," *Law and Society Review* 9 (1975): 581–611.

122. Thomas Marvell and Carlisle Moody, "The Impact of Out-of-State Prison Population on State Homicide Rates: Displacement and Free-Rider Effects," *Criminology* 36 (1998): 513–538; Thomas Marvell and Carlisle Moody, "The Impact of Prison Growth on Homicide," *Homicide Studies* 1 (1997): 205–233.

123. David Greenberg and Nancy Larkin, "The Incapacitation of Criminal Opiate Users," *Crime and Delinquency* 44 (1998): 205–228.

124. John Wallerstedt, *Returning to Prison: Bureau of Justice Statistics Special Report* (Washington, DC: U.S. Department of Justice, 1984).

125. James Marquart, Victoria Brewer, Janet Mullings, and Ben Crouch, "The Implications of Crime Control Policy on HIV/AIDS-Related Risk Among Women Prisoners," *Crime and Delinquency* 45 (1999): 82–98.

126. Jose Canela-Cacho, Alfred Blumstein, and Jacqueline Cohen, "Relationship Between the Offending Frequency of Imprisoned and Free Offenders," *Criminology* 35 (1997): 133–171.

127. Kate King and Patricia Bass, "Southern Prisons and Elderly Inmates: Taking a Look Inside," paper presented at the annual meeting of the American Society of Criminology, San Diego, November 1997.

128. Marc Mauer, testimony before the U.S. Congress, House Judiciary Committee, on "Three Strikes and You're Out," 1 March 1994.

129. Canela-Cacho, Blumstein, and Cohen, "Relationship Between the Offending Frequency of Imprisoned and Free Offenders."

130. Stephen Markman and Paul Cassell, "Protecting the Innocent: A Response to the Bedeau-Radelet Study," *Stanford Law Review* 41 (1988): 121–170, at p. 153.

131. James Stephan and Tracy Snell, *Capital Punishment, 1994* (Washington, DC: Bureau of Justice Statistics, 1996), p. 8.

132. Andrew Von Hirsch, *Doing Justice* (New York: Hill and Wang, 1976).

133. Ibid., pp. 15–16.

134. Ibid.

Chapter 5

1. Based on James Brooke, Pam Belluck, and John Kifner, and written by James Brooke, "Man Hospitalized in 1996 for Writing Ominous Letters," *New York Times,* 26 July 1998, p. 1.

2. Lee Ellis, "A Discipline in Peril: Sociology's Future Hinges on Curing Biophobia," *American Sociologist* 27 (1996): 21–41.

3. Edmund O. Wilson, *Sociobiology* (Cambridge, MA: Harvard University Press, 1975).

4. Per-Olof Wikstrom and Rolf Loeber, "Do Disadvantaged Neighborhoods Cause Well-Adjusted Children to Become Adolescent Delinquents?" *Criminology* (in press).

5. See, generally, Lee Ellis, *Theories of Rape* (New York: Hemisphere Publications, 1989).

6. Dalton Conley and Neil Bennett, "Is Biology Destiny? Birth Weight and Life Chances," *American Sociological Review* 654 (2000): 458-467.

7. Anthony Walsh and Lee Ellis, "Shoring Up the Big Three: Improving Criminological Theories with Biosocial Concepts," paper presented at the annual meeting of the Society of Criminology, San Diego, November 1997, p. 16.

8. Israel Nachshon, "Neurological Bases of Crime, Psychopathy and Aggression," in *Crime in Biological, Social and Moral Contexts,* ed. Lee Ellis and Harry Hoffman (New York: Praeger, 1990), p. 199.

9. *Time,* 28 May 1979, p. 57.

10. Michael Krassner, "Diet and Brain Function," *Nutrition Reviews* 44 (1986): 12–15.

11. Leonard Hippchen, ed., *Ecologic-Biochemical Approaches to Treatment of Delinquents and Criminals* (New York: Van Nostrand Reinhold, 1978).

12. J. Kershner and W. Hawke, "Megavitamins and Learning Disorders: A Controlled Double-Blind Experiment," *Journal of Nutrition* 109 (1979): 819–826.

13. Stephen Schoenthaler and Walter Doraz, "Types of Offenses Which Can Be Reduced in an Institutional Setting Using Nutritional Intervention," *International Journal of Biosocial Research* 4 (1983): 74–84; Stephen Schoenthaler and Walter Doraz, "Diet and Crime," *International Journal of Biosocial Research* 4 (1983): 74–84. See also A. G. Schauss, "Differential Outcomes Among Probationers Comparing Orthomolecular Approaches to Conventional Casework Counseling," paper presented at the annual meeting of the American Society of Criminology, Dallas, November 1978; A. Schauss and C. Simonsen, "A Critical Analysis of the Diets of Chronic Juvenile Offenders: Part I," *Journal of Orthomolecular Psychiatry* 8 (1979): 222–226; A. Hoffer, "Children with Learning and Behavioral Disorders," *Journal of Orthomolecular Psychiatry* 5 (1976): 229.

14. H. Bruce Ferguson, Clare Stoddart, and Jovan Simeon, "Double-Blind Challenge Studies of Behavioral and Cognitive Effects of Sucrose-Aspartame Ingestion in Normal Children," *Nutrition Reviews Supplement* 44 (1986): 144–158; Gregory Gray, "Diet, Crime and Delinquency: A Critique," *Nutrition Reviews Supplement* 44 (1986): 89–94.

15. Mark Wolraich, Scott Lindgren, Phyllis Stumbo, Lewis Stegink, Mark Appelbaum, and Mary Kiritsy, "Effects of Diets High in Sucrose or Aspartame on the Behavior and Cognitive Performance of Children," *New England Journal of Medicine* 330 (1994): 303–306.

16. Dian Gans, "Sucrose and Unusual Childhood Behavior," *Nutrition Today* 26 (1991): 8–14.

17. Diana Fishbein, "Neuropsychological Function, Drug Abuse, and Violence: A Conceptual Framework," *Criminal Justice and Behavior* 27 (2000): 139–159.

18. D. Hill and W. Sargent, "A Case of Matricide," *Lancet* 244 (1943): 526–527.

19. E. Podolsky, "The Chemistry of Murder," *Pakistan Medical Journal* 15 (1964): 9–14.

20. J. A. Yaryura-Tobias and F. Neziroglu, "Violent Behavior, Brain Dysrhythmia and Glucose Dysfunction: A New Syndrome," *Journal of Orthopsychiatry* 4 (1975): 182–188.

21. Matti Virkkunen, "Reactive Hypoglycemic Tendency Among Habitually Violent Offenders," *Nutrition Reviews Supplement* 44 (1986): 94–103.

22. James Q. Wilson, *The Moral Sense* (New York: Free Press, 1993).

23. Lee Ellis, "Evolutionary and Neurochemical Causes of Sex Differences in Victimizing Behavior: Toward a Unified Theory of Criminal Behavior and Social Stratification," *Social Science Information* 28 (1989): 605–636.

24. Lee Ellis and Phyllis Coontz, "Androgens, Brain Functioning, and Criminality: The Neurohormonal Foundations of Antisociality," in *Crime in Biological, Social and Moral Contexts,* ed. Lee Ellis and Harry Hoffman (New York: Praeger, 1990), pp. 162–193, at p. 181.

25. Alan Booth and D. Wayne Osgood, "The Influence of Testosterone on Deviance in Adulthood: Assessing and Explaining the Relationship," *Criminology* 31 (1993): 93–118.

26. Ibid.

27. Christy Miller Buchanan, Jacquelynne Eccles, and Jill Becker, "Are Adolescents the Victims of Raging Hormones? Evidence for Activational Effects of Hormones on Moods and Behavior at Adolescence," *Psychological Bulletin* 111 (1992): 62–107.

28. Booth and Osgood, "The Influence of Testosterone on Deviance in Adulthood."

29. Albert Reiss and Jeffrey Roth, eds., *Understanding and Preventing Violence* (Washington, DC: National Academy Press, 1993), p. 118.

30. Anthony Walsh, "Genetic and Cytogenetic Intersex Anomalies," *International Journal of Offender*

Therapy and Comparative Criminology (in press).

31. Walter Gove, "The Effect of Age and Gender on Deviant Behavior: A Biopsychosocial Perspective," in *Gender and the Life Course,* ed. A. S. Rossi (New York: Aldine, 1985), pp. 115–144.

32. For a review of this concept, see Anne E. Figert, "The Three Faces of PMS: The Professional, Gendered, and Scientific Structuring of a Psychiatric Disorder," *Social Problems* 42 (1995): 56–72.

33. Katharina Dalton, *The Premenstrual Syndrome* (Springfield, IL: Charles C. Thomas, 1971).

34. Julie Horney, "Menstrual Cycles and Criminal Responsibility," *Law and Human Nature* 2 (1978): 25–36.

35. Diana Fishbein, "Selected Studies on the Biology of Antisocial Behavior," in *New Perspectives in Criminology,* ed. John Conklin (Needham Heights, MA: Allyn and Bacon, 1996), pp. 26–38.

36. Ibid.; Karen Paige, "Effects of Oral Contraceptives on Affective Fluctuations Associated with the Menstrual Cycle," *Psychosomatic Medicine* 33 (1971): 515–537.

37. Alexander Schauss, *Diet, Crime and Delinquency* (Berkeley, CA: Parker House, 1980).

38. C. Hawley and R. E. Buckley, "Food Dyes and Hyperkinetic Children," *Academy Therapy* 10 (1974): 27–32.

39. John Ott, "The Effects of Light and Radiation on Human Health and Behavior," in *Ecologic-Biochemical Approaches to Treatment of Delinquents and Criminals,* ed. Leonard Hippchen (New York: Van Nostrand Reinhold, 1978), pp. 105–183. See also A. Kreuger and S. Sigel, "Ions in the Air," *Human Nature* (July 1978): 46–47; Harry Wohlfarth, "The Effect of Color Psychodynamic Environmental Modification on Discipline Incidents in Elementary Schools over One School Year: A Controlled Study," *International Journal of Biosocial Research* 6 (1984): 44–53.

40. Oliver David, Stanley Hoffman, Jeffrey Sverd, Julian Clark, and Kytja Voeller, "Lead and Hyperactivity, Behavior Response to Chelation: A Pilot Study," *American Journal of Psychiatry* 133 (1976): 1155–1158.

41. Deborah Denno, "Considering Lead Poisoning as a Criminal Defense," *Fordham Urban Law Journal* 20 (1993): 377–400.

42. Terrie Moffitt, "The Neuropsychology of Juvenile Delinquency: A Critical Review," in *Crime and Justice: An Annual Review,* vol. 12, ed. Norval Morris and Michael Tonry (Chicago: University of Chicago Press, 1990), pp. 99–169.

43. Terrie Moffitt, Donald Lynam, and Phil Silva, "Neuropsychological Tests Predicting Persistent Male Delinquency," *Criminology* 32 (1994): 277–300; Elizabeth Kandel and Sarnoff Mednick, "Perinatal Complications Predict Violent Offending," *Criminology* 29 (1991): 519–529; Sarnoff Mednick, Ricardo Machon, Matti Virkkunen, and Douglas Bonett, "Adult Schizophrenia Following Prenatal Exposure to an Influenza Epidemic," *Archives of General Psychiatry* 44 (1987): 35–46; C. A. Fogel, S. A. Mednick, and N. Michelson, "Hyperactive Behavior and Minor Physical Anomalies," *Acta Psychiatrica Scandinavia* 72 (1985): 551–556.

44. R. Johnson, *Aggression in Man and Animals* (Philadelphia: Saunders, 1972), p. 79.

45. Jean Seguin, Robert Pihl, Philip Harden, Richard Tremblay, and Bernard Boulerice, "Cognitive and Neuropsychological Characteristics of Physically Aggressive Boys," *Journal of Abnormal Psychology* 104 (1995): 614–624; Deborah Denno, "Gender, Crime and the Criminal Law Defenses," *Journal of Criminal Law and Criminology* 85 (1994): 80–180.

46. Adrian Raine, Patricia Brennan, Brigitte Mednick, and Sarnoff Mednick, "High Rates of Violence, Crime, Academic Problems, and Behavioral Problems in Males with Both Early Neuromotor Deficits and Unstable Family Environments," *Archives of General Psychiatry* 53 (1996): 544–549; Deborah Denno, *Biology, Crime and Violence: New Evidence* (Cambridge: Cambridge University Press, 1989).

47. Diana Fishbein and Robert Thatcher, "New Diagnostic Methods in Criminology: Assessing Organic Sources of Behavioral Disorders," *Journal of Research in Crime and Delinquency* 23 (1986): 240–267.

48. Lorne Yeudall, "A Neuropsychosocial Perspective on Persistent Juvenile Delinquency and Criminal Behavior," paper presented at the New York Academy of Sciences, 26 September 1979.

49. See, generally, Jan Volavka, "Electroencephalogram Among Criminals," in *The Causes of Crime: New Biological Approaches,* ed. Sarnoff Mednick, Terrie Moffitt, and Susan Stack (Cambridge: Cambridge University Press, 1987), pp. 137–145; Z. A. Zayed, S. A. Lewis, and R. P. Britain, "An Encephalographic and Psychiatric Study of 32 Insane Murderers," *British Journal of Psychiatry* 115 (1969): 1115–1124.

50. Nathaniel Pallone and James Hennessy, "Brain Dysfunction and Criminal Violence," *Society* 35 (1998): 21–27; P. F. Goyer, P. J. Andreason, and W. E. Semple, "Positronic Emission Tomography and Personality Disorders," *Neuropsychopharmacology* 10 (1994): 21–28.

51. Diana Fishbein, "Neuropsychological Function, Drug Abuse, and Violence"; Adrian Raine, Monte Buchsbaum, and Lori LaCasse, "Brain Abnormalities in Murderers Indicated by Positron Emission Tomography," *Biological Psychiatry* 42 (1997): 495–508.

52. Pallone and Hennessy, "Brain Dysfunction and Criminal Violence," p. 25.

53. D. R. Robin, R. M. Starles, T. J. Kenney, B. J. Reynolds, and F. P. Heald, "Adolescents Who Attempt Suicide," *Journal of Pediatrics* 90 (1977): 636–638.

54. Raine, Buchsbaum, and LaCasse, "Brain Abnormalities in Murderers Indicated by Positron Emission Tomography."

55. Leonore Simon, "Does Criminal Offender Treatment Work?" *Applied and Preventive Psychology* (Summer 1998); Stephen Faraone et al., "Intellectual Performance and School Failure in Children with Attention Deficit Hyperactivity Disorder and in Their Siblings," *Journal of Abnormal Psychology* 102 (1993): 616–623.

56. Simon, "Does Criminal Offender Treatment Work?"

57. Ibid.

58. Terrie Moffitt and Phil Silva, "Self-Reported Delinquency, Neuropsychological Deficit, and History of Attention Deficit Disorder," *Journal of Abnormal Child Psychology* 16 (1988): 553–569.

59. Elizabeth Hart et al., "Developmental Change in Attention-Deficit Hyperactivity Disorder in Boys: A Four-Year Longitudinal Study," *Journal of Consulting and Clinical Psychology* 62 (1994): 472–491.

60. Eugene Maguin, Rolf Loeber, and Paul LeMahieu, "Does the Relationship Between Poor Reading and Delinquency Hold for Males of Different Ages and Ethnic Groups?" *Journal of Emotional and Behavioral Disorders* 1 (1993): 88–100.

61. Reiss and Roth, *Understanding and Preventing Violence,* p. 119.

62. Matti Virkkunen, David Goldman, and Markku Linnoila, "Serotonin in Alcoholic Violent Offenders," *The Ciba Foundation Symposium: Genetics of Criminal and Antisocial Behavior* (Chichester, England: Wiley, 1995).

63. Lee Ellis, "Left- and Mixed-Handedness and Criminality: Explanations for a Probable Relationship," in *Left-Handedness: Behavioral Implications and Anomalies,* ed. S. Coren (Amsterdam: Elsevier, 1990): 485–507.

64. Lee Ellis, "Monoamine Oxidase and Criminality: Identifying an Apparent Biological Marker for Antisocial Behavior," *Journal of Research in Crime and Delinquency* 28 (1991): 227–251.

65. Lee Ellis, "Arousal Theory and the Religiosity–Criminality Relationship," in *Contemporary Criminological Theory,* ed. Peter Cordella and Larry Siegel (Boston, MA: Northeastern University, 1996), pp. 65–84.

66. Adrian Raine, Peter Venables, and Sarnoff Mednick, "Low Resting Heart Rate at Age 3 Years Predisposes to Aggression at Age 11 Years: Evidence from the Mauritius Child Health Project," *Journal of the American Academy of Adolescent Psychiatry* 36 (1997): 1457–1464.

67. David Rowe, "As the Twig Is Bent: The Myth of Child-Rearing Influences on Personality Development," *Journal of Counseling and Development* 68 (1990): 606–611; David Rowe, Joseph Rogers, and Sylvia Meseck-Bushey, "Sibling Delinquency and the Family Environment: Shared and Unshared Influences," *Child Development* 63 (1992): 59–67; Gregory Carey and David DiLalla, "Personality and Psychopathology: Genetic Perspectives," *Journal of Abnormal Psychology* 103 (1994): 32–43.

68. T. R. Sarbin and L. E. Miller, "Demonism Revisited: The XYY Chromosome Anomaly," *Issues in Criminology* 5 (1970): 195–207.

69. Sarnoff Mednick and Jan Volavka, "Biology and Crime," in *Crime and Justice,* ed. Norval Morris and Michael Tonry (Chicago: University of Chicago Press, 1980), pp. 85–159, at p. 93.

70. For an early review, see Barbara Wooton, *Social Science and Social Pathology* (London: Allen and Unwin, 1959); John Laub and Robert Sampson, "Unraveling Families and Delinquency: A Reanalysis of the Gluecks' Data," *Criminology* 26 (1988): 355–380.

71. D. J. West and D. P. Farrington, "Who Becomes Delinquent?" in *The Delinquent Way of Life,* ed. D. J. West and D. P. Farrington (London: Heinemann, 1977), pp. 1–28; D. J. West, *Delinquency: Its Roots, Careers, and Prospects* (Cambridge, MA: Harvard University Press, 1982).

72. West, *Delinquency,* p. 114.

73. David Farrington, "Understanding and Preventing Bullying," in *Crime and Justice,* vol. 17, ed. Michael Tonry (Chicago: University of Chicago Press, 1993), pp. 381–457.

74. David Rowe and David Farrington, "The Familial Transmission of Criminal Convictions," *Criminology* 35 (1997): 177–201.

75. Mednick and Volavka, "Biology and Crime," p. 94.

76. Ibid., p. 95.

77. David Rowe, "Genetic and Environmental Components of Antisocial Behavior: A Study of 265 Twin Pairs," *Criminology* 24 (1986): 513–532; David Rowe and D. Wayne Osgood, "Heredity and Sociological Theories of Delinquency: A Reconsideration," *American Sociological Review* 49 (1984): 526–540.

78. Edwin J. C. G. van den Oord, Frank Verhulst, and Dorret Boomsma, "A Genetic Study of Maternal and Paternal Ratings of Problem Behaviors in 3-Year-Old Twins," *Journal of Abnormal Psychology* 105 (1996): 349–357.

79. Michael Lyons, "A Twin Study of Self-Reported Criminal Behavior," and Judy Silberg, Joanne Meyer, Andrew Pickles, Emily Simonoff, Lindon Eaves, John Hewitt, Hermine Maes, and Michael Rutter, "Heterogeneity Among Juvenile Antisocial Behaviors: Findings from the Virginia Twin Study of Adolescent Behavioral Development," in The Ciba Foundation Symposium, *Genetics of Criminal and Antisocial Behavior* (Chichester, England: Wiley), 1995.

80. Gregory Carey, "Twin Imitation for Antisocial Behavior: Implications for Genetic and Family Environment Research," *Journal of Abnormal Psychology* 101 (1992): 18–25; David Rowe and Joseph Rogers, "The Ohio Twin Project and ADSEX Studies: Behavior Genetic Approaches to Understanding Antisocial Behavior," paper presented at the annual meeting of the American Society of Criminology, Montreal, November 1987.

81. David Rowe, *The Limits of Family Influence: Genes, Experiences and Behavior* (New York: Guilford Press, 1995), p. 64.

82. R. J. Cadoret, C. Cain, and R. R. Crowe, "Evidence for a Gene–Environment Interaction in the Development of Adolescent Antisocial Behavior," *Behavior Genetics* 13 (1983): 301–310.

83. Barry Hutchings and Sarnoff A. Mednick, "Criminality in Adoptees and Their Adoptive and Biological Parents: A Pilot Study," in *Biological Bases in Criminal Behavior,* ed. S. A. Mednick and K. O. Christiansen (New York: Gardner Press, 1977).

84. For similar results, see Sarnoff Mednick, Terrie Moffitt, William Gabrielli, and Barry Hutchings, "Genetic Factors in Criminal Behavior: A Review," *Development of Antisocial and Prosocial Behavior* (New York: Academic Press, 1986), pp. 3–50; Sarnoff Mednick, William Gabrielli, and Barry Hutchings, "Genetic Influences in Criminal Behavior: Evidence from an Adoption Cohort," in *Perspective Studies of Crime and Delinquency,* ed. Katherine Teilmann Van Dusen and Sarnoff Mednick (Boston: Kluwer-Nijhoff, 1983), pp. 39–57.

85. Glenn Walters, "A Meta-Analysis of the Gene–Crime Relationship," *Criminology* 30 (1992): 595–613.

86. Lawrence Cohen and Richard Machalek, "A General Theory of Expropriative Crime: An Evolutionary Ecological Approach," *American Journal of Sociology* 94 (1988): 465–501.

87. For a general review, see Martin Daly and Margo Wilson, "Crime and Conflict: Homicide in Evolutionary Psychological Theory," in *Crime and Justice: An Annual Edition,* ed. Michael Tonry (Chicago: University of Chicago Press, 1997), pp. 51–100.

88. Lee Ellis, "The Evolution of Violent Criminal Behavior and Its Nonlegal Equivalent," in *Crime in Biological, Social and Moral Contexts,* ed. Lee Ellis and Harry Hoffman (New York: Praeger, 1990), pp. 63–65.

89. David Rowe, Alexander Vazsonyi, and Aurelio Jose Figuerdo, "Mating-Effort in Adolescence: A Conditional Alternative Strategy," *Personal Individual Differences* 23 (1997): 105–115.

90. Ibid., p. 101.

91. Margo Wilson, Holly Johnson, and Martin Daly, "Lethal and Nonlethal Violence Against Wives," *Canadian Journal of Criminology* 37 (1995): 331–361.

92. Lee Ellis and Anthony Walsh, "Gene-Based Evolutionary Theories of Criminology," *Criminology* 35 (1997): 229–276.

93. Byron Roth, "Crime and Child Rearing," *Society* 34 (1994): 39–45.

94. Deborah Denno, "Sociological and Human Developmental Explanations of Crime: Conflict or Consensus," *Criminology* 23 (1985): 711–741.

95. Glenn Walters and Thomas White, "Heredity and Crime: Bad Genes or Bad Research?" *Criminology* 27 (1989): 455–486, at p. 478.

96. Edwin Driver, "Charles Buckman Goring," in *Pioneers in Criminology,* ed. Hermann Mannheim (Montclair, NJ: Patterson Smith, 1970), p. 440.

97. Gabriel Tarde, *Penal Philosophy,* trans. R. Howell (Boston: Little, Brown, 1912).

98. See, generally, Donn Byrne and Kathryn Kelly, *An Introduction to Personality* (Englewood Cliffs, NJ: Prentice-Hall, 1981).

99. David Abrahamsen, *Crime and the Human Mind* (New York: Columbia University Press, 1944), p. 137; also see, generally, Fritz Redl and Hans Toch, "The Psychoanalytic Perspective," in *Psychology of Crime and Criminal Justice,* ed. Hans Toch (New York: Holt, Rinehart and Winston, 1979), pp. 193–195.

100. August Aichorn, *Wayward Youth* (New York: Viking Press, 1935).

101. See, generally, D. A. Andrews and James Bonta, *The Psychology of Criminal Conduct* (Cincinnati: Anderson, 1994), pp. 72–75.

102. Paige Crosby Ouimette, "Psychopathology and Sexual Aggression in Nonincarcerated Men," *Violence and Victimization* 12 (1997): 389–397.

103. Robert Krueger, Avshalom Caspi, Phil Silva, and Rob McGee, "Personality Traits Are Differentially Linked to Mental Disorders: A Multitrait–Multidiagnosis Study of an Adolescent Birth Cohort," *Journal of Abnormal Psychology* 105 (1996): 299–312.

104. Seymour Halleck, *Psychiatry and the Dilemmas of Crime* (Berkeley: University of California Press, 1971).

105. Richard Rosner, "Adolescents Accused of Murder and Manslaughter: A Five-Year Descriptive Study," *Bulletin of the American Academy of Psychiatry and the Law* 7 (1979): 342–351.

106. Richard Famularo, Robert Kinscherff, and Terence Fenton, "Psychiatric Diagnoses of Abusive Mothers: A Preliminary Report," *Journal of Nervous and Mental Disease* 180 (1992): 658–660.

107. Bruce Link, Howard Andrews, and Francis Cullen, "The Violent and Illegal Behavior of Mental Patients Reconsidered," *American Sociological Review* 57 (1992): 275–292; Ellen Hochstedler Steury, "Criminal Defendants with Psychiatric Impairment: Prevalence, Probabilities and Rates," *Journal of Criminal Law and Criminology* 84 (1993): 354–374.

108. Marc Hillbrand, John Krystal, Kimberly Sharpe, and Hilliard Foster, "Clinical Predictors of Self-Mutilation in Hospitalized Patients," *Journal of Nervous and Mental Disease* 182 (1994): 9–13.

109. Carmen Cirincione, Henry Steadman, Pamela Clark Robbins, and John Monahan, *Mental Illness as a Factor in Criminality: A Study of Prisoners and Mental Patients* (Delmar, NY: Policy Research Associates, 1991); see also Carmen Cirincione, Henry Steadman, Pamela Clark Robbins, and John Monahan, *Schizophrenia as a Contingent Risk Factor for Criminal Violence* (Delmar, NY: Policy Research Associates, 1991).

110. John Monahan, *Mental Illness and Violent Crime* (Washington, DC: National Institute of Justice, 1996).

111. Ibid.

112. This discussion is based on three works by Albert Bandura: *Aggression: A Social Learning Analysis* (Englewood Cliffs, NJ: Prentice-Hall, 1973); *Social Learning Theory* (Englewood Cliffs, NJ: Prentice-Hall, 1977); and "The Social Learning Perspective: Mechanisms of Aggression," in *Psychology of Crime and Criminal Justice,* ed. Hans Toch (New York: Holt, Rinehart and Winston, 1979), pp. 198–236.

113. David Phillips, "The Impact of Mass Media Violence on U.S. Homicides," *American Sociological Review* 48 (1983): 560–568.

114. K. A. Dodge, "A Social Information Processing Model of Social Competence in Children," in *Minnesota Symposium in Child Psychology,* vol. 18, ed. M. Perlmutter (Hillsdale, NJ: Erlbaum, 1986), pp. 77–125.

115. Adrian Raine, Peter Venables, and Mark Williams, "Better Autonomic Conditioning and Faster Electrodermal Half-Recovery Time at Age 15 Years as Possible Protective Factors Against Crime at Age 29 Years," *Developmental Psychology* 32 (1996): 624–630.

116. L. Huesmann and L. Eron, "Individual Differences and the Trait of Aggression," *European Journal of Personality* 3 (1989): 95–106.

117. Rolf Loeber and Dale Hay, "Key Issues in the Development of Aggression and Violence from Childhood to Early Adulthood," *Annual Review of Psychology* 48 (1997): 371–410.

118. D. Lipton, E. C. McDonel, and R. McFall, "Heterosocial Perception in Rapists," *Journal of Consulting and Clinical Psychology* 55 (1987): 17–21.

119. See, generally, Walter Mischel, *Introduction to Personality,* 4th ed. (New York: Holt, Rinehart and Winston, 1986).

120. See, generally, Hans Eysenck, *Personality and Crime* (London: Routledge and Kegan Paul, 1977).

121. Edelyn Verona and Joyce Carbonell, "Female Violence and Personality," *Criminal Justice and Behavior* 27 (2000): 176–195.

122. Hans Eysenck and M. W. Eysenck, *Personality and Individual Differences* (New York: Plenum, 1985).

123. David Farrington, "Psychobiological Factors in the Explanation and Reduction of Delinquency," *Today's Delinquent* (1988): 37–51.

124. Laurie Frost, Terrie Moffitt, and Rob McGee, "Neuropsychological Correlates of Psychopathology in an Unselected Cohort of Young Adolescents," *Journal of Abnormal Psychology* 98 (1989): 307–313.

125. David Lykken, "Psychopathy, Sociopathy, and Crime," *Society* 34 (1996): 30–38.

126. Avshalom Caspi, Terrie Moffitt, Phil Silva, Magda Stouthamer-Loeber, Robert Krueger, and Pamela Schmutte, "Are Some People Crime-Prone? Replications of the Personality–Crime Relationship Across Countries, Genders, Races and Methods," *Criminology* 32 (1994): 163–195.

127. Henry Goddard, *Efficiency and Levels of Intelligence* (Princeton, NJ: Princeton University Press, 1920); Edwin Sutherland, "Mental Deficiency and Crime," in *Social Attitudes,* ed. Kimball Young (New York: Henry Holt, 1931), chap. 15.

128. William Healy and Augusta Bronner, *Delinquency and Criminals: Their Making and Unmaking* (New York: McMillan, 1926).

129. Joseph Lee Rogers, H. Harrington Cleveland, Edwin van den Oord, and David Rowe, "Resolving the Debate Over Birth Order, Family Size and Intelligence," *American Psychologist* 55 (2000): 599–612.

130. Sutherland, "Mental Deficiency and Crime."

131. Travis Hirschi and Michael Hindelang, "Intelligence and Delinquency: A Revisionist Review," *American Sociological Review* 42 (1977): 471–586.

132. Deborah Denno, "Sociological and Human Developmental Explanations of Crime: Conflict or Consensus," *Criminology* 23 (1985): 711–741; Christine Ward and Richard McFall, "Further Validation of the Problem Inventory for Adolescent Girls: Comparing Caucasian and Black Delinquents and Nondelinquents," *Journal of Consulting and Clinical Psychology* 54 (1986): 732–733; L. Hubble and M. Groff, "Magnitude and Direction of WISC-R Verbal Performance IQ Discrepancies Among Adjudicated Male Delinquents," *Journal of Youth and Adolescence* 10 (1981): 179–183; Robert Gordon, "IQ Commensurability of Black–White Differences in Crime and Delinquency," paper presented at the annual meeting of the American Psychological Association, Washington, DC, August 1986; Robert Gordon, "Two Illustrations of the IQ-Surrogate Hypothesis: IQ Versus Parental Education and Occupational Status in the Race–IQ–Delinquency Model," paper presented at the annual meeting of the American Society of Criminology, Montreal, November 1987.

133. James Q. Wilson and Richard Herrnstein, *Crime and Human Nature* (New York: Simon and Schuster, 1985), p. 148.

134. Ibid., p. 171.

135. Richard Herrnstein and Charles Murray, *The Bell Curve: Intelligence and Class Structure in American Life* (New York: Free Press, 1994).

136. H. D. Day, J. M. Franklin, and D. D. Marshall, "Predictors of Aggression in Hospitalized Adolescents," *Journal of Psychology* 132 (1998): 427–435; Scott Menard and Barbara Morse, "A Structuralist Critique of the IQ–Delinquency Hypothesis: Theory and Evidence," *American Journal of Sociology* 89 (1984): 1347–1378; Denno, "Sociological and Human Developmental Explanations of Crime."

137. Ulric Neisser et al., "Intelligence: Knowns and Unknowns," *American Psychologist* 51 (1996): 77–101, at p. 83.

138. Susan Pease and Craig T. Love, "Optimal Methods and Issues in Nutrition Research in the Correctional Setting," *Nutrition Reviews Supplement* 44 (1986): 122–131.

139. Mark O'Callaghan and Douglas Carroll, "The Role of Psychosurgical Studies in the Control of Antisocial Behavior," in *The Causes of Crime: New Biological Approaches,* ed. Sarnoff Med-

nick, Terrie Moffitt, and Susan Stack (Cambridge: Cambridge University Press, 1987), pp. 312–328.

140. Reiss and Roth, *Understanding and Preventing Violence,* p. 389.

141. Kathleen Cirillo, B. E. Pruitt, Brian Colwell, Paul M. Kingery, Robert S. Hurley, and Danny Ballard, "School Violence: Prevalence and Intervention Strategies for At-Risk Adolescents," *Adolescence* 33 (1998): 319–331.

Chapter 6

1. Associated Press, "3 Arrested in Killing of London Boy," *New York Times,* 3 December 2000, p. A3.
2. Steven Messner and Richard Rosenfeld, *Crime and the American Dream* (Belmont, CA: Wadsworth, 1994), p. 11.
3. Edwin Lemert, *Human Deviance, Social Problems and Social Control* (Englewood Cliffs, NJ: Prentice-Hall, 1967).
4. Based on William Julius Wilson, "Studying Inner-City Social Dislocations: The Challenge of Public Agenda Research," *American Sociological Review* 56 (1991): 1–14, at p. 3.
5. Jeanne Brooks-Gunn and Greg J. Duncan, "The Effects of Poverty on Children," *Future of Children* 7 (1997): 34–39.
6. Greg Duncan, W. Jean Yeung, Jeanne Brooks-Gunn, and Judith Smith, "How Much Does Childhood Poverty Affect the Life Chances of Children?" *American Sociological Review* 63 (1998): 406–423.
7. Ibid., p. 409.
8. Brooks-Gunn and Duncan, "The Effects of Poverty on Children."
9. Jonathan Crane, "The Epidemic Theory of Ghettos and Neighborhood Effects on Dropping Out and Teenage Childbearing," *American Journal of Sociology* 96 (1991): 1226–1259; see also Rodrick Wallace, "Expanding Coupled Shock Fronts of Urban Decay and Criminal Behavior: How U.S. Cities Are Becoming 'Hollowed Out,' " *Journal of Quantitative Criminology* 7 (1991): 333–355.
10. Oscar Lewis, "The Culture of Poverty," *Scientific American* 215 (1966): 19–25.
11. Gunnar Myrdal, *The Challenge of World Poverty* (New York: Vintage Books, 1970).
12. Children's Defense Fund, *The State of America's Children, 1999* (Washington, DC: Children's Defense Fund, 2000); U.S. Department of Census Data, *Race and Income* (Washington, DC: Census Bureau, 1998).
13. James Ainsworth-Darnell and Douglas Downey, "Assessing the Oppositional Culture Explanation for Racial/Ethnic Differences in School Performances," *American Sociological Review* 63 (1998): 536–553.
14. Eric Lotke, "Hobbling a Generation: Young African-American Men in Washington, D.C.'s Criminal Justice System—Five Years Later," *Crime and Delinquency* 44 (1998): 355–366.
15. Laurence Lynn and Michael G. H. McGeary, eds., *Inner-City Poverty in the United States* (Washington, DC: National Academy Press, 1990), p. 3.
16. William Julius Wilson, *The Truly Disadvantaged* (Chicago: University of Chicago Press, 1987).
17. Cynthia Rexroat, *Declining Economic Status of Black Children: Examining the Change* (Washington, DC: Joint Center for Political and Economic Studies, 1990), p. 1.
18. See Charles Tittle and Robert Meier, "Specifying the SES/Delinquency Relationship," *Criminology* 28 (1990): 271–295, at p. 293.
19. See Ruth Kornhauser, *Social Sources of Delinquency* (Chicago: University of Chicago Press, 1978), p. 75.
20. Clifford R. Shaw and Henry D. McKay, *Juvenile Delinquency and Urban Areas,* rev. ed. (Chicago: University of Chicago Press, 1972).
21. Ibid., p. 52.
22. Ibid., p. 171.
23. The best-known of these critiques is Kornhauser, *Social Sources of Delinquency.*

24. For a general review, see James Byrne and Robert Sampson, eds., *The Social Ecology of Crime* (New York: Springer Verlag, 1985).
25. See, generally, Robert Bursik, "Social Disorganization and Theories of Crime and Delinquency: Problems and Prospects," *Criminology* 26 (1988): 521–539.
26. D. Wayne Osgood and Jeff Chambers, "Social Disorganization Outside the Metropolis: An Analysis of Rural Youth Violence," *Criminology* 38 (2000): 81–117.
27. William Spelman, "Abandoned Buildings: Magnets for Crime?" *Journal of Criminal Justice* 21 (1993): 481–493.
28. Keith Harries and Andrea Powell, "Juvenile Gun Crime and Social Stress: Baltimore, 1980–1990," *Urban Geography* 15 (1994): 45–63.
29. Ellen Kurtz, Barbara Koons, and Ralph Taylor, "Land Use, Physical Deterioration, Resident-Based Control, and Calls for Service on Urban Streetblocks," *Justice Quarterly* 15 (1998): 121–149.
30. Steven Messner and Kenneth Tardiff, "Economic Inequality and Levels of Homicide: An Analysis of Urban Neighborhoods," *Criminology* 24 (1986): 297–317.
31. G. David Curry and Irving Spergel, "Gang Homicide, Delinquency, and Community," *Criminology* 26 (1988): 381–407.
32. Darrell Steffensmeier and Dana Haynie, "Gender, Structural Disadvantage, and Urban Crime: Do Macrosocial Variables Also Explain Female Offending Rates?" *Criminology* 38 (2000): 403–438.
33. Bursik, "Social Disorganization and Theories of Crime and Delinquency," p. 520.
34. Richard McGahey, "Economic Conditions, Organization, and Urban Crime," in *Communities and Crime,* ed. Albert Reiss and Michael Tonry (Chicago: University of Chicago Press, 1986), pp. 231–270.
35. Scott Menard and Delbert Elliott, "Self-Reported Offending, Maturational Reform, and the Easterlin Hypothesis," *Journal of Quantitative Criminology* 6 (1990): 237–268.
36. Elijah Anderson, *Streetwise: Race, Class and Change in an Urban Community* (Chicago: University of Chicago Press, 1990), pp. 243–244.
37. Pamela Wilcox Rountree and Kenneth Land, "Burglary Victimization, Perceptions of Crime Risk, and Routine Activities: A Multilevel Analysis Across Seattle Neighborhoods and Census Tracts," *Journal of Research in Crime and Delinquency* 33 (1996): 147–180.
38. Randy LaGrange, Kenneth Ferraro, and Michael Supancic, "Perceived Risk and Fear of Crime: Role of Social and Physical Incivilities," *Journal of Research in Crime and Delinquency* 29 (1992): 311–334.
39. Wesley Skogan, "Fear of Crime and Neighborhood Change," in *Communities and Crime,* ed. Albert Reiss and Michael Tonry (Chicago: University of Chicago Press, 1986), pp. 191–232.
40. Stephanie Greenberg, "Fear and Its Relationship to Crime, Neighborhood Deterioration, and Informal Social Control," in *The Social Ecology of Crime,* ed. James Byrne and Robert Sampson (New York: Springer Verlag, 1985), pp. 47–62.
41. Skogan, "Fear of Crime and Neighborhood Change."
42. Ibid.
43. Finn Aage-Esbensen and David Huizinga, "Community Structure and Drug Use: From a Social Disorganization Perspective," *Justice Quarterly* 7 (1990): 691–709.
44. Allen Liska and Paul Bellair, "Violent-Crime Rates and Racial Composition: Convergence over Time," *American Journal of Sociology* 101 (1995): 578–610.
45. Wesley Skogan, *Disorder and Decline: Crime and the Spiral of Decay in American Neighborhoods* (New York: Free Press, 1990), pp. 15–35.
46. Ralph Taylor and Jeanette Covington, "Neighborhood Changes in Ecology and Violence," *Criminology* 26 (1988): 553–589.

47. Leo Scheurman and Solomon Kobrin, "Community Careers in Crime," in *Communities and Crime,* ed. Albert Reiss and Michael Tonry (Chicago: University of Chicago Press, 1986), pp. 67–100.
48. Ibid.
49. Wilson, *The Truly Disadvantaged.*
50. Barbara Warner and Glenn Pierce, "Reexamining Social Disorganization Theory Using Calls to the Police as a Measure of Crime," *Criminology* 31 (1993): 493–519.
51. Karen Parker and Matthew Pruitt, "Poverty, Poverty Concentration, and Homicide," *Social Science Quarterly* 81 (2000): 555–582.
52. Carolyn Rebecca Block and Richard Block, *Street Gang Crime in Chicago* (Washington, DC: National Institute of Justice, 1993), p. 7.
53. Felton Earls, *Linking Community Factors and Individual Development* (Washington, DC: National Institute of Justice, 1998).
54. Donald Black, "Social Control as a Dependent Variable," in *Toward a General Theory of Social Control,* ed. D. Black (Orlando: Academic Press, 1990).
55. Robert Bursik and Harold Grasmick, "The Multiple Layers of Social Disorganization," paper presented at the annual meeting of the American Society of Criminology, New Orleans, November 1992.
56. David Klinger, "Negotiating Order in Patrol Work: An Ecological Theory of Police Response to Deviance," *Criminology* 35 (1997): 277–306.
57. Rodney Stark, "Deviant Places: A Theory of the Ecology of Crime," *Criminology* 25 (1987): 893–911.
58. Delbert Elliott, William Julius Wilson, David Huizinga, Robert Sampson, Amanda Elliott, and Bruce Rankin, "The Effects of Neighborhood Disadvantage on Adolescent Development," *Journal of Research in Crime and Delinquency* 33 (1996): 389–426.
59. Ibid., p. 414.
60. Robert Bursik and Harold Grasmick, "Economic Deprivation and Neighborhood Crime Rates, 1960–1980," *Law and Society Review* 27 (1993): 263–278.
61. Robert Sampson and W. Byron Groves, "Community Structure and Crime: Testing Social Disorganization Theory," *American Journal of Sociology* 94 (1989): 774–802; Denise Gottfredson, Richard McNeill, and Gary Gottfredson, "Social Area Influences on Delinquency: A Multilevel Analysis," *Journal of Research in Crime and Delinquency* 28 (1991): 197–206.
62. Ruth Peterson, Lauren Krivo, and Mark Harris, "Disadvantage and Neighborhood Violent Crime: Do Local Institutions Matter?" *Journal of Research in Crime and Delinquency* 37 (2000): 31–63.
63. Ralph Taylor, "Social Order and Disorder of Street Blocks and Neighborhoods: Ecology, Microecology, and the Systemic Model of Social Disorganization," *Journal of Research in Crime and Delinquency* 34 (1997): 113–155.
64. James DeFronzo, "Welfare and Homicide," *Journal of Research in Crime and Delinquency* 34 (1997): 395–406.
65. Robert Merton, *Social Theory and Social Structure,* enlarged ed. (New York: Free Press, 1968).
66. Albert Cohen, "The Sociology of the Deviant Act: Anomie Theory and Beyond," *American Sociological Review* 30 (1965): 5–14.
67. Steven Messner and Richard Rosenfeld, *Crime and the American Dream* (Belmont, CA: Wadsworth, 1994).
68. John Hagan, Gerd Hefler, Gabriele Classen, Klaus Boehnke, and Hans Merkens, "Subterranean Sources of Subcultural Delinquency Beyond the American Dream," *Criminology* 36 (1998): 309–340.
69. John Braithwaite, "Poverty Power, White-Collar Crime and the Paradoxes of Criminological Theory," *Australian and New Zealand Journal of Criminology* 24 (1991): 40–58.

70. Margo Wilson and Martin Daly, "Life Expectancy, Economic Inequality, Homicide, and Reproductive Timing in Chicago Neighbourhoods," *British Journal of Medicine* 314 (1997): 1271–1274.

71. Judith Blau and Peter Blau, "The Cost of Inequality: Metropolitan Structure and Violent Crime," *American Sociological Review* 147 (1982): 114–129.

72. Tomislav Kovandzic, Lynne Vieraitis, and Mark Yeisley, "The Structural Covariates of Urban Homicide: Reassessing the Impact of Income Inequality and Poverty in the Post-Reagan Era," *Criminology* 36 (1998): 569–600.

73. Scott South and Steven Messner, "Structural Determinants of Intergroup Association," *American Journal of Sociology* 91 (1986): 1409–1430; Steven Messner and Scott South, "Economic Deprivation, Opportunity Structure, and Robbery Victimization," *Social Forces* 64 (1986): 975–991.

74. Richard Fowles and Mary Merva, "Wage Inequality and Criminal Activity: An Extreme Bounds Analysis for the United States 1975–1990," *Criminology* 34 (1996): 163–182.

75. Beverly Stiles, Xiaoru Liu, and Howard Kaplan, "Relative Deprivation and Deviant Adaptations: The Mediating Effects of Negative Self Feelings," *Journal of Research in Crime and Delinquency* 37 (2000): 64–90.

76. Robert Agnew, "Foundation for a General Strain Theory of Crime and Delinquency," *Criminology* 30 (1992): 47–87.

77. Ibid., p. 57.

78. Timothy Brezina, "Adolescent Maltreatment and Delinquency: The Question of Intervening Processes," *Journal of Research in Crime and Delinquency* 35 (1998): 71–99.

79. Robert Agnew, "Stability and Change in Crime over the Life Course: A Strain Theory Explanation," in *Advances in Criminological Theory: Vol. 7. Developmental Theories of Crime and Delinquency,* ed. Terence Thornberry (New Brunswick, NJ: Transaction Books, 1995), pp. 113–137.

80. Lawrence Wu, "Effects of Family Instability, Income, and Income Instability on the Risk of Premarital Birth," *American Sociological Review* 61 (1996): 386–406.

81. Robert Agnew and Helene Raskin White, "An Empirical Test of General Strain Theory," *Criminology* 30 (1992): 475–499.

82. John Hoffman and Alan Miller, "A Latent Variable Analysis of General Strain Theory," *Journal of Quantitative Criminology* 13 (1997): 111–113; Raymond Paternoster and Paul Mazerolle, "General Strain Theory and Delinquency: A Replication and Extension," *Journal of Research in Crime and Delinquency* 31 (1994): 235–263; G. Roger Jarjoura, "The Conditional Effect of Social Class on the Dropout–Delinquency Relationship," *Journal of Research in Crime and Delinquency* 33 (1996): 232–255.

83. Paul Mazerolle, Velmer Burton, Francis Cullen, T. David Evans, and Gary Payne, "Strain, Anger, and Delinquent Adaptations: Specifying General Strain Theory," *Journal of Criminal Justice* 28 (2000): 89–101.

84. Timothy Brezina, "Adapting to Strain: An Examination of Delinquent Coping Responses," *Criminology* 34 (1996): 39–61.

85. Stephen Cernkovich, Peggy Giordano, and Jennifer Rudolph, "Race, Crime and the American Dream," *Journal of Research in Crime and Delinquency* 37 (2000): 131–170.

86. Walter Miller, "Lower-Class Culture as a Generating Milieu of Gang Delinquency," *Journal of Social Issues* 14 (1958): 5–19.

87. Ibid., pp. 14–17.

88. Fred Markowitz and Richard Felson, "Social-Demographic Attitudes and Violence," *Criminology* 36 (1998): 117–138.

89. Jeffrey Fagan, *Adolescent Violence: A View from the Street,* NIJ Research Preview (Washington, DC: National Institute of Justice, 1998).

90. Albert Cohen, *Delinquent Boys* (New York: Free Press, 1955).

91. Ibid., p. 25.

92. Ibid., p. 28.

93. Ibid.

94. Ibid., p. 30.

95. Ibid., p. 133.

96. Richard Cloward and Lloyd Ohlin, *Delinquency and Opportunity* (New York: Free Press, 1960).

97. Ibid., p. 171.

98. Ibid., p. 73.

99. James DeFronzo, "Welfare and Burglary," *Crime and Delinquency* 42 (1996): 223–230.

Chapter 7

1. Charles Tittle and Robert Meier, "Specifying the SES/Delinquency Relationship," *Criminology* 28 (1990): 271–299, at p. 274.

2. Sheldon Glueck and Eleanor Glueck, *Unraveling Juvenile Delinquency* (Cambridge, MA: Harvard University Press, 1950); Ashley Weeks, "Predicting Juvenile Delinquency," *American Sociological Review* 8 (1943): 40–46.

3. Denise Kandel, "The Parental and Peer Contexts of Adolescent Deviance: An Algebra of Interpersonal Influences," *Journal of Drug Issues* 26 (1996): 289–315; Ann Goetting, "The Parenting–Crime Connection," *Journal of Primary Prevention* 14 (1994): 167–184.

4. For general reviews of the relationship between families and delinquency, see Alan Jay Lincoln and Murray Straus, *Crime and the Family* (Springfield, IL: Charles C. Thomas, 1985); Rolf Loeber and Magda Stouthamer-Loeber, "Family Factors as Correlates and Predictors of Juvenile Conduct Problems and Delinquency," in *Crime and Justice: An Annual Review of Research,* vol. 7, ed. Michael Tonry and Norval Morris (Chicago: University of Chicago Press, 1986), pp. 29–151; Goetting, "The Parenting–Crime Connection."

5. Joseph Weis, Katherine Worsley, and Carol Zeiss, *The Family and Delinquency: Organizing the Conceptual Chaos* (Monograph, Center for Law and Justice, University of Washington, 1982).

6. Susan Stern and Carolyn Smith, "Family Processes and Delinquency in an Ecological Context," *Social Service Review* 37 (1995): 707–731.

7. Lawrence Rosen and Kathleen Neilson, "Broken Homes," in *Contemporary Criminology,* ed. Leonard Savitz and Norman Johnston (New York: Wiley, 1982), pp. 126–132.

8. James Q. Wilson and Richard Herrnstein, *Crime and Human Nature* (New York: Simon and Schuster, 1985), p. 249.

9. L. Edward Wells and Joseph Rankin, "Families and Delinquency: A Meta-Analysis of the Impact of Broken Homes," *Social Problems* 38 (1991): 71–90.

10. Nan Marie Astone and Sara McLanahan, "Family Structure, Parental Practices and High School Completion," *American Sociological Review* 56 (1991): 309–320.

11. Joseph Rankin and L. Edward Wells, "The Effect of Parental Attachments and Direct Controls on Delinquency," *Journal of Research in Crime and Delinquency* 27 (1990): 140–165.

12. Ronald Simons, Chyi-In Wu, Kuei-Hsiu Lin, Leslie Gordon, and Rand Conger, "A Cross-Cultural Examination of the Link Between Corporal Punishment and Adolescent Antisocial Behavior," *Criminology* 38 (2000): 47–79.

13. Robert Roberts and Vern Bengston, "Affective Ties to Parents in Early Adulthood and Self-Esteem Across 20 Years," *Social Psychology Quarterly* 59 (1996): 96–106.

14. Robert Johnson, S. Susan Su, Dean Gerstein, Hee-Choon Shin, and John Hoffman, "Parental Influences on Deviant Behavior in Early Adolescence: A Logistic Response Analysis of Age- and Gender-Differentiated Effects," *Journal of Quantitative Criminology* 11 (1995): 167–192.

15. Judith Brook and Li-Jung Tseng, "Influences of Parental Drug Use, Personality, and Child Rearing on the Toddler's Anger and Negativity," *Genetic, Social and General Psychology Monographs* 122 (1996): 107–128.

16. Thomas Ashby Wills, Donato Vaccaro, Grace McNamara, and A. Elizabeth Hirky, "Escalated Substance Use: A Longitudinal Grouping Analysis from Early to Middle Adolescence," *Journal of Abnormal Psychology* 105 (1996): 166–180.

17. Carolyn Smith and Terence Thornberry, "The Relationship Between Childhood Maltreatment and Adolescent Involvement in Delinquency," *Criminology* 33 (1995): 451–479.

18. Murray A. Straus, "Spanking and the Making of a Violent Society: The Short- and Long-Term Consequences of Corporal Punishment," *Pediatrics* 98 (1996): 837–843.

19. *The Forgotten Half: Pathways to Success for America's Youth and Young Families* (Washington, DC: William T. Grant Foundation, 1988); Lee Jussim, "Teacher Expectations: Self-Fulfilling Prophecies, Perceptual Biases, and Accuracy," *Journal of Personality and Social Psychology* 57 (1989): 469–480.

20. Eugene Maguin and Rolf Loeber, "Academic Performance and Delinquency," in *Crime and Justice: A Review of Research,* vol. 20, ed. Michael Tonry (Chicago: University of Chicago Press, 1995), pp. 145–264.

21. Jeannie Oakes, *Keeping Track: How Schools Structure Inequality* (New Haven, CT: Yale University Press, 1985); Marc LeBlanc, Evelyne Valliere, and Pierre McDuff, "Adolescents' School Experience and Self-Reported Offending: A Longitudinal Test of Social Control Theory," paper presented at the annual meeting of the American Society of Criminology, Baltimore, November 1990.

22. G. Roger Jarjoura, "Does Dropping Out of School Enhance Delinquent Involvement? Results from a Large-Scale National Probability Sample," *Criminology* 31 (1993): 149–172; Terence Thornberry, Melanie Moore, and R. L. Christenson, "The Effect of Dropping Out of High School on Subsequent Criminal Behavior," *Criminology* 23 (1985): 3–18.

23. Irving Janis, *Groupthink: Psychological Studies of Policy Decisions and Fiascoes* (Boston: Houghton Mifflin, 1982).

24. Delbert Elliott, David Huizinga, and Suzanne Ageton, *Explaining Delinquency and Drug Use* (Beverly Hills, CA: Sage, 1985); Helene Raskin White, Robert Padina, and Randy LaGrange, "Longitudinal Predictors of Serious Substance Use and Delinquency," *Criminology* 6 (1987): 715–740.

25. Robert Agnew and Timothy Brezina, "Relational Problems with Peers, Gender and Delinquency," *Youth and Society* 29 (1997): 84–111.

26. Scott Menard, "Demographic and Theoretical Variables in the Age-Period Cohort Analysis of Illegal Behavior," *Journal of Research in Crime and Delinquency* 29 (1992): 178–199.

27. Patrick Jackson, "Theories and Findings About Youth Gangs," *Criminal Justice Abstracts* (June 1989): 313–327.

28. Marvin Krohn and Terence Thornberry, "Network Theory: A Model for Understanding Drug Abuse Among African-American and Hispanic Youth," in *Drug Abuse Among Minority Youth: Advances in Research and Methodology,* ed. Mario De La Rosa and Juan-Luis Recio Adrados (Washington, DC: U.S. Department of Health and Human Services, 1993), pp. 29–46.

29. D. Wayne Osgood, Janet Wilson, Patrick O'Malley, Jerald Bachman, and Lloyd Johnston, "Routine Activities and Individual Deviant Behavior," *American Sociological Review* 61 (1996): 635–655.

30. Mark Warr, "Age, Peers, and Delinquency," *Criminology* 31 (1993): 17–40.

31. Sara Battin, Karl Hill, Robert Abbott, Richard Catalano, and J. David Hawkins, "The Contribution of Gang Membership to Delinquency Beyond Delinquent Friends," *Criminology* 36 (1998): 93–116.

32. Terence Thornberry, Alan Lizotte, Marvin Krohn, Margaret Farnworth, and Sung Joon Jang, "Delinquent Peers, Beliefs, and Delinquent Behavior: A Longitudinal Test of Interactional Theory," Working Paper no. 6, rev. (Albany, NY: Rochester Youth Development Study, Hindelang Criminal Justice Research Center, 1992), pp. 8–30.

33. Warr, "Age, Peers, and Delinquency."

34. David Fergusson, L. John Horwood, and Daniel Nagin, "Offending Trajectories in a New Zealand Birth Cohort," *Criminology* 38 (2000): 525–551.

35. Travis Hirschi and Rodney Stark, "Hellfire and Delinquency," *Social Problems* 17 (1969): 202–213.

36. T. David Evans, Francis Cullen, R. Gregory Dunaway, and Velmer Burton, Jr., "Religion and Crime Reexamined: The Impact of Religion, Secular Controls, and Social Ecology on Adult Criminality," *Criminology* 33 (1995): 195–224.

37. Lee Ellis and James Patterson, "Crime and Religion: An International Comparison Among Thirteen Industrial Nations," *Personal Individual Differences* 20 (1996): 761–768.

38. Edwin H. Sutherland, *Principles of Criminology* (Philadelphia: Lippincott, 1939).

39. See, for example, Edwin Sutherland, "White-Collar Criminality," *American Sociological Review* 5 (1940): 2–10.

40. See Edwin Sutherland and Donald Cressey, *Criminology*, 8th ed. (Philadelphia: Lippincott, 1970), pp. 77–79.

41. Sandra Brown, Vicki Creamer, and Barbara Stetson, "Adolescent Alcohol Expectancies in Relation to Personal and Parental Drinking Patterns," *Journal of Abnormal Psychology* 96 (1987): 117–121.

42. Leanne Fiftal Alarid, Velmer Burton, and Francis Cullen, "Gender and Crime Among Felony Offenders: Assessing the Generality of Social Control and Differential Association Theory," *Journal of Research in Crime and Delinquency* 37 (2000): 171–199.

43. Denise Kandel and Mark Davies, "Friendship Networks, Intimacy, and Illicit Drug Use in Young Adulthood: A Comparison of Two Competing Theories," *Criminology* 29 (1991): 441–467.

44. Krohn and Thornberry, "Network Theory," pp. 123–124.

45. Matthew Ploeger, "Youth Employment and Delinquency: Reconsidering a Problematic Relationship," *Criminology* 35 (1997): 659–675.

46. Warr, "Age, Peers, and Delinquency."

47. Craig Reinerman and Jeffrey Fagan, "Social Organization and Differential Association: A Research Note from a Longitudinal Study of Violent Juvenile Offenders," *Crime and Delinquency* 34 (1988): 307–327.

48. Sue Titus Reed, *Crime and Criminology*, 2d ed. (New York: Holt, Rinehart & Winston, 1979), p. 234.

49. Gresham Sykes and David Matza, "Techniques of Neutralization: A Theory of Delinquency," *American Sociological Review* 22 (1957): 664–670; David Matza, *Delinquency and Drift* (New York: John Wiley, 1964).

50. Matza, *Delinquency and Drift*, p. 51.

51. Sykes and Matza, "Techniques of Neutralization"; see also David Matza, "Subterranean Traditions of Youths," *Annals of the American Academy of Political and Social Science* 378 (1961): 116.

52. Sykes and Matza, "Techniques of Neutralization."

53. Ibid.

54. Ian Shields and George Whitehall, "Neutralization and Delinquency Among Teenagers," *Criminal Justice and Behavior* 21 (1994): 223–235; Robert A. Ball, "An Empirical Exploration of Neutralization Theory," *Criminologica* 4 (1966): 22–32. See also M. William Minor, "The Neutralization of Criminal Offense," *Criminology* 18 (1980): 103–120; Robert Gordon, James Short, Desmond Cartwright, and Fred Strodtbeck, "Values and Gang Delinquency: A Study of Street Corner Groups," *American Journal of Sociology* 69 (1963): 109–128.

55. Michael Hindelang, "The Commitment of Delinquents to Their Misdeeds: Do Delinquents Drift?" *Social Problems* 17 (1970): 500–509; Robert Regoli and Eric Poole, "The Commitment of Delinquents to Their Misdeeds: A Reexamination," *Journal of Criminal Justice* 6 (1978): 261–269.

56. Larry Siegel, Spencer Rathus, and Carol Ruppert, "Values and Delinquent Youth: An Empirical Reexamination of Theories of Delinquency," *British Journal of Criminology* 13 (1973): 237–244.

57. Robert Agnew, "The Techniques of Neutralization and Violence," *Criminology* 32 (1994): 555–580.

58. Jeffrey Fagan, *Adolescent Violence: A View From the Street*, NIJ Research Preview (Washington, DC: National Institute of Justice, 1998).

59. Eric Wish, *Drug Use Forecasting 1990* (Washington, DC: National Institute of Justice, 1991).

60. Scott Briar and Irving Piliavin, "Delinquency: Situational Inducements and Commitment to Conformity," *Social Problems* 13 (1965–1966): 35–45.

61. Lawrence Sherman and Douglas Smith, with Janell Schmidt and Dennis Rogan, "Crime, Punishment, and Stake in Conformity: Legal and Informal Control of Domestic Violence," *American Sociological Review* 57 (1992): 680–690.

62. Albert Reiss, "Delinquency as the Failure of Personal and Social Controls," *American Sociological Review* 16 (1951): 196–207.

63. Briar and Piliavin, "Delinquency."

64. Walter Reckless, *The Crime Problem* (New York: Appleton-Century Crofts, 1967), pp. 469–483.

65. Among the many research reports by Reckless and his colleagues are Walter Reckless, Simon Dinitz, and Ellen Murray, "Self-Concept as an Insulator Against Delinquency," *American Sociological Review* 21 (1956): 744–746; Walter Reckless, Simon Dinitz, and Barbara Kay, "The Self-Component in Potential Delinquency and Potential Non-Delinquency," *American Sociological Review* 22 (1957): 566–570; Walter Reckless, Simon Dinitz, and Ellen Murray, "The Good Boy in a High Delinquency Area," *Journal of Criminal Law, Criminology, and Police Science* 48 (1957): 12–26; Frank Scarpitti, Ellen Murray, Simon Dinitz, and Walter Reckless, "The Good Boy in a High Delinquency Area: Four Years Later," *American Sociological Review* 23 (1960): 555–558; Walter Reckless and Simon Dinitz, "Pioneering with Self-Concept as a Vulnerability Factor in Delinquency," *Journal of Criminal Law, Criminology, and Police Science* 58 (1967): 515–523.

66. Travis Hirschi, *Causes of Delinquency* (Berkeley: University of California Press, 1969).

67. Ibid., p. 231.

68. Ibid., pp. 66–74.

69. Michael Wiatroski, David Griswold, and Mary K. Roberts, "Social Control Theory and Delinquency," *American Sociological Review* 46 (1981): 525–541.

70. Patricia Van Voorhis, Francis Cullen, Richard Mathers, and Connie Chenoweth Garner, "The Impact of Family Structure and Quality on Delinquency: A Comparative Assessment of Structural and Functional Factors," *Criminology* 26 (1988): 235–261.

71. Bobbi Jo Anderson, Malcolm Holmes, and Erik Ostresh, "Male and Female Delinquent's Attachments and Effects of Attachments on Severity of Self-Reported Delinquency," *Criminal Justice and Behavior* 26 (1999): 435–452.

72. Patricia Jenkins, "School Delinquency and the School Social Bond," *Journal of Research in Crime and Delinquency* 34 (1997): 337–367.

73. For a review of exciting research, see Kimberly Kempf, "The Empirical Status of Hirschi's Control Theory," in *Advances in Criminological Theory*, ed. Bill Laufer and Freda Adler (New Brunswick, NJ: Transaction Publishers, 1992), pp. 111–129.

74. Peggy Giordano, Stephen Cernkovich, and M. D. Pugh, "Friendships and Delinquency," *American Journal of Sociology* 91 (1986): 1170–1202.

75. Denise Kandel and Mark Davies, "Friendship Networks, Intimacy, and Illicit Drug Use in Young

Adulthood: A Comparison of Two Competing Theories," *Criminology* 29 (1991): 441–467.

76. Stephen Cernkovich, Peggy Giordano, and Jennifer Rudolph, "Race, Crime and the American Dream," *Journal of Research in Crime and Delinquency* 37 (2000): 131–170.

77. Velmer Burton, Francis Cullen, T. David Evans, R. Gregory Dunaway, Sesha Kethineni, and Gary Payne, "The Impact of Parental Controls on Delinquency," *Journal of Criminal Justice* 23 (1995): 111–126.

78. Michael Hindelang, "Causes of Delinquency: A Partial Replication and Extension," *Social Problems* 21 (1973): 471–487.

79. Gary Jensen and David Brownfield, "Parents and Drugs," *Criminology* 21 (1983): 543–554. See also M. Wiatrowski, D. Griswold, and M. Roberts, "Social Control Theory and Delinquency," *American Sociological Review* 46 (1981): 525–541.

80. Leslie Samuelson, Timothy Hartnagel, and Harvey Krahn, "Crime and Social Control Among High School Dropouts," *Journal of Crime and Justice* 18 (1990): 129–161.

81. Alan E. Liska and M. D. Reed, "Ties to Conventional Institutions and Delinquency: Estimating Reciprocal Effects," *American Sociological Review* 50 (1985): 547–560.

82. Michael Wiatrowski, David Griswold, and Mary K. Roberts, "Social Control Theory and Delinquency," *American Sociological Review* 46 (1981): 525–541.

83. Linda Jackson, John Hunter, and Carole Hodge, "Physical Attractiveness and Intellectual Competence: A Meta-Analytic Review," *Social Psychology Quarterly* 58 (1995): 108–122.

84. President's Commission on Law Enforcement and the Administration of Youth Crime, *Task Force Report: Juvenile Delinquency and Youth* (Washington, DC: U.S. Government Printing Office, 1967), p. 43.

85. Howard Becker, *Outsiders: Studies in the Sociology of Deviance* (New York: Macmillan, 1963), p. 9.

86. Laurie Goodstein, "The Architect of the 'Gay Conversion' Campaign," *New York Times*, 13 August 1998, p. A10.

87. Christy Visher, "Gender, Police Arrest Decision, and Notions of Chivalry," *Criminology* 21 (1983): 5–28.

88. Marjorie Zatz, "Race, Ethnicity and Determinate Sentencing," *Criminology* 22 (1984): 147–171.

89. Christina DeJong and Kenneth Jackson, "Putting Race into Context: Race, Juvenile Justice Processing, and Urbanization," *Justice Quarterly* 15 (1998): 487–504.

90. Joan Petersilia, "Racial Disparities in the Criminal Justice System: A Summary," *Crime and Delinquency* 31 (1985): 15–34.

91. Harold Garfinkle, "Conditions of Successful Degradation Ceremonies," *American Journal of Sociology* 61 (1956): 420–424.

92. Karen Heimer and Ross Matsueda, "Role-Taking, Role-Commitment and Delinquency: A Theory of Differential Social Control," *American Sociological Review* 59 (1994): 400–437.

93. Karen Heimer, "Gender, Race, and the Pathways to Delinquency: An Interactionist Explanation," in *Crime and Inequality*, ed. John Hagan and Ruth Peterson (Stanford, CA: Stanford University Press, 1995), pp. 32–57.

94. Heimer and Matsueda, "Role-Taking, Role-Commitment and Delinquency."

95. See, for example, Howard Kaplan and Hiroshi Fukurai, "Negative Social Sanctions, Self-Rejection, and Drug Use," *Youth and Society* 23 (1992): 275–298; Howard Kaplan and Robert Johnson, "Negative Social Sanctions and Juvenile Delinquency: Effects of Labeling in a Model of Deviant Behavior," *Social Science Quarterly* 72 (1991): 98–122; Howard Kaplan, Robert Johnson, and Carol Bailey, "Deviant Peers and Deviant Behavior: Further Elaboration of a Model," *Social Psychology Quarterly* 30 (1987): 277–284.

96. John Lofland, *Deviance and Identity* (Englewood Cliffs, NJ: Prentice-Hall, 1969).

97. Frank Tannenbaum, *Crime and the Community* (New York: Columbia University Press, 1938), pp. 19–20.

98. Edwin Lemert, *Social Pathology* (New York: McGraw-Hill, 1951).

99. Ibid., p. 75.

100. Carl Pope and William Feyerherm, "Minority Status and Juvenile Justice Processing," *Criminal Justice Abstracts* 22 (1990): 327–336. See also Carl Pope, "Race and Crime Revisited," *Crime and Delinquency* 25 (1979): 347–357; National Minority Council on Criminal Justice, *The Inequality of Justice* (Washington, DC: National Minority Advisory Council on Criminal Justice, 1981), p. 200.

101. Samuel Walker, Cassia Spohn, and Miriam DeLone, *The Color of Justice: Race, Ethnicity and Crime in America* (Belmont, CA: Wadsworth, 1996), pp. 145–146.

102. Howard Kaplan and Robert Johnson, "Negative Social Sanctions and Juvenile Justice: Effects of Labeling in a Model of Deviant Behavior," *Social Science Quarterly* 72 (1991): 98–122.

103. Ruth Triplett, "The Conflict Perspective, Symbolic Interactionism, and the Status Characteristics Hypothesis," *Justice Quarterly* 10 (1993): 540–558.

104. Ross Matsueda, "Reflected Appraisals: Parental Labeling, and Delinquency: Specifying a Symbolic Interactionist Theory," *American Journal of Sociology* 97 (1992): 1577–1611.

105. Suzanne Ageton and Delbert Elliott, *The Effect of Legal Processing on Self-Concept* (Boulder, CO: Institute of Behavioral Science, 1973).

106. Christine Bowditch, "Getting Rid of Troublemakers: High School Disciplinary Procedures and the Production of Dropouts," *Social Problems* 40 (1993): 493–507.

107. Melvin Ray and William Downs, "An Empirical Test of Labeling Theory Using Longitudinal Data," *Journal of Research in Crime and Delinquency* 23 (1986): 169–194.

108. Sherman and Smith, with Schmidt and Rogan, "Crime, Punishment, and Stake in Conformity."

109. Charles Tittle, "Two Empirical Regularities (Maybe) in Search of an Explanation: Commentary on the Age/Crime Debate," *Criminology* 26 (1988): 75–85.

110. Robert Sampson and John Laub, "A Life-Course Theory of Cumulative Disadvantage and the Stability of Delinquency," in *Developmental Theories of Crime and Delinquency*, ed. Terence Thornberry (New Brunswick, NJ: Transaction Press, 1997): 133–161; Douglas Smith and Robert Brame, "On the Initiation and Continuation of Delinquency," *Criminology* 4 (1994): 607–630.

111. Raymond Paternoster and Leeann Iovanni, "The Labeling Perspective and Delinquency: An Elaboration of the Theory and an Assessment of the Evidence," *Justice Quarterly* 6 (1989): 358–394.

Chapter 8

1. Michael Lynch, "Rediscovering Criminology: Lessons from the Marxist Tradition," in *Marxist Sociology: Surveys of Contemporary Theory and Research*, ed. Donald McQuarie and Patrick McGuire (New York: General Hall Press, 1994).

2. Michael Lynch and W. Byron Groves, *A Primer in Radical Criminology*, 2d ed. (Albany, NY: Harrow and Heston, 1989), pp. 32–33.

3. Ibid., p. 4.

4. James Short and F. Ivan Nye, "Extent of Undetected Delinquency: Tentative Conclusions," *Journal of Criminal Law, Criminology, and Police Science* 49 (1958): 296–302.

5. See, generally, Robert Meier, "The New Criminology: Continuity in Criminological Theory," *Journal of Criminal Law and Criminology* 67 (1977): 461–469.

6. David Greenberg, ed., *Crime and Capitalism* (Palo Alto, CA: Mayfield, 1981), p. 3.

7. William Chambliss and Robert Seidman, *Law, Order, and Power* (Reading, MA: Addison-Wesley, 1971), p. 503.

8. John Braithwaite, "Retributivism, Punishment, and Privilege," in *Punishment and Privilege*, ed. W. Byron Groves and Graeme Newman (Albany, NY: Harrow and Heston, 1986), pp. 55–66.

9. John Hagan and Celesta Albonetti, "Race, Class, and the Perception of Criminal Injustice in America," *American Journal of Sociology* 88 (1982): 329–355.

10. Austin Turk, *Criminality and Legal Order* (Chicago: Rand McNally, 1969), p. 58.

11. Lynch and Groves, *A Primer in Radical Criminology*, p. 38.

12. David McDowall, "Poverty and Homicide in Detroit, 1926–1978," *Victims and Violence* 1 (1986): 23–34; David McDowall and Sandra Norris, "Poverty and Homicide in Baltimore, Cleveland, and Memphis, 1937–1980," paper presented at the annual meeting of the American Society of Criminology, Montreal, November 1987.

13. Judith Blau and Peter Blau, "The Cost of Inequality: Metropolitan Structure and Violent Crime," *American Sociological Review* 147 (1982): 114–129; Richard Block, "Community Environment and Violent Crime," *Criminology* 17 (1979): 46–57; Robert Sampson, "Structural Sources of Variation in Race-Age-Specific Rates of Offending Across Major U.S. Cities," *Criminology* 23 (1985): 647–673.

14. David Jacobs and David Britt, "Inequality and Police Use of Deadly Force: An Empirical Assessment of a Conflict Hypothesis," *Social Problems* 26 (1979): 403–412.

15. Malcolm Homes, "Minority Threat and Police Brutality: Determinants of Civil Rights Criminal Complaints in U.S. Municipalities," *Criminology* 38 (2000): 343–368.

16. Alan Lizotte, "Extra-Legal Factors in Chicago's Criminal Courts: Testing the Conflict Model of Criminal Justice," *Social Problems* 25 (1978): 564–580.

17. Terance Miethe and Charles Moore, "Racial Differences in Criminal Processing: The Consequences of Model Selection on Conclusions About Differential Treatment," *Sociological Quarterly* 27 (1987): 217–237.

18. Tracy Nobiling, Cassia Spohn, and Miriam DeLone, "A Tale of Two Counties: Unemployment and Sentence Severity," *Justice Quarterly* 15 (1998): 459–485.

19. Nancy Wonders, "Determinate Sentencing: A Feminist and Postmodern Story," *Justice Quarterly* 13 (1996): 610–648; Douglas Smith, Christy Visher, and Laura Davidson, "Equity and Discretionary Justice: The Influence of Race on Police Arrest Decisions," *Journal of Criminal Law and Criminology* 75 (1984): 234–249.

20. Thomas Arvanites, "Increasing Imprisonment: A Function of Crime or Socioeconomic Factors?" *American Journal of Criminal Justice* 17 (1992): 19–38.

21. Michael Leiber, Anne Woodrick, and E. Michele Roudebush, "Religion, Discriminatory Attitudes, and the Orientations of Juvenile Justice Personnel: A Research Note," *Criminology* 33 (1995): 431–447; Michael Leiber and Katherine Jamieson, "Race and Decision Making Within Juvenile Justice: The Importance of Context," *Journal of Quantitative Criminology* 11 (1995): 363–388.

22. Dragan Milovanovic, "Postmodern Criminology: Mapping the Terrain," *Justice Quarterly* 13 (1996): 567–610.

23. Ian Taylor, Paul Walton, and Jock Young, *The New Criminology: For a Social Theory of Deviance* (London: Routledge and Kegan Paul, 1973).

24. Barry Krisberg, *Crime and Privilege: Toward a New Criminology* (Englewood Cliffs, NJ: Prentice-Hall, 1975), p. 167.

25. David Friedrichs, "Critical Criminology and Critical Legal Studies," *Critical Criminologist* 1 (1989): 7.

26. See, for example, Larry Tifft and Dennis Sullivan, *The Struggle to Be Human: Crime, Criminology, and Anarchism* (Over-the-Water-Sanday, Scotland: Cienfuegos Press, 1979); Dennis Sullivan, *The Mask of Love* (Port Washington, NY: Kennikat Press, 1980).

27. Lynch and Groves, *A Primer in Radical Criminology*, p. 6.

28. This section borrows heavily from Richard Sparks, "A Critique of Marxist Criminology," in *Crime and Justice*, vol. 2, ed. Norval Morris and Michael Tonry (Chicago: University of Chicago Press, 1980), pp. 159–208.

29. Barbara Sims, "Crime, Punishment, and the American Dream: Toward a Marxist Integration," *Journal of Research in Crime and Delinquency* 34 (1997): 5–24.

30. Jeffery Reiman, *The Rich Get Richer and the Poor Get Prison* (New York: Wiley, 1984), pp. 43–44.

31. For a general review of Marxist criminology, see Lynch and Groves, *A Primer in Radical Criminology*.

32. Sims, "Crime, Punishment, and the American Dream."

33. Robert Bohm, "Radical Criminology: Back to the Basics," paper presented at the annual meeting of the American Society of Criminology, Phoenix, Arizona, November 1993, p. 2.

34. Ibid., p. 4.

35. Lynch and Groves, *A Primer in Radical Criminology*, p. 7.

36. W. Byron Groves and Robert Sampson, "Critical Theory and Criminology," *Social Problems* 33 (1986): 58–80.

37. Gregg Barak, "'Crimes of the Homeless' or the 'Crime of Homelessness': A Self-Reflexive, New-Marxist Analysis of Crime and Social Control," paper presented at the annual meeting of the American Society of Criminology, Montreal, November 1987.

38. Michael Lynch, "Assessing the State of Radical Criminology: Toward the Year 2000," paper presented at the annual meeting of the American Society of Criminology, Phoenix, Arizona, November 1993.

39. Steven Box, *Recession, Crime, and Unemployment* (London: MacMillan, 1987).

40. David Barlow, Melissa Hickman-Barlow, and W. Wesley Johnson, "The Political Economy of Criminal Justice Policy: A Time-Series Analysis of Economic Conditions, Crime, and Federal Criminal Justice Legislation, 1948–1987," *Justice Quarterly* 13 (1996): 223–241.

41. Mahesh Nalla, Michael Lynch, and Michael Leiber, "Determinants of Police Growth in Phoenix, 1950–1988," *Justice Quarterly* 14 (1997): 144–163.

42. Gresham Sykes, "The Rise of Critical Criminology," *Journal of Criminal Law and Criminology* 65 (1974): 211–229.

43. David Jacobs, "Corporate Economic Power and the State: A Longitudinal Assessment of Two Explanations," *American Journal of Sociology* 93 (1988): 852–881.

44. Deanna Alexander, "Victims of the L.A. Riots: A Theoretical Consideration," paper presented at the annual meeting of the American Society of Criminology, Phoenix, Arizona, November 1993.

45. Richard Quinney, "Crime Control in Capitalist Society," in *Critical Criminology*, ed. Ian Taylor, Paul Walton, and Jock Young (London: Routledge and Kegan Paul, 1975), p. 199.

46. Ibid.

47. John Hagan, *Structural Criminology* (New Brunswick, NJ: Rutgers University Press, 1989), pp. 110–119.

48. Roy Bhaskar, "Empiricism," in *A Dictionary of Marxist Thought*, ed. T. Bottomore (Cambridge, MA: Harvard University Press, 1983), pp. 149–150.

49. Byron Groves, "Marxism and Positivism," *Crime and Social Justice* 23 (1985): 129–150; Michael Lynch, "Quantitative Analysis and Marxist Criminology: Some Old Answers to a Dilemma in

Marxist Criminology," *Crime and Social Justice* 29 (1987): 110–117.

50. Alan Lizotte, James Mercy, and Eric Monkkonen, "Crime and Police Strength in an Urban Setting: Chicago, 1947–1970," in *Quantitative Criminology,* ed. John Hagan (Beverly Hills, CA: Sage, 1982), pp. 129–148.

51. William Chambliss, "The State, the Law, and the Definition of Behavior as Criminal or Delinquent," in *Handbook of Criminology,* ed. D. Glazer (Chicago: Rand McNally, 1974), pp. 7–44.

52. Timothy Carter and Donald Clelland, "A Neo-Marxian Critique, Formulation, and Test of Juvenile Dispositions as a Function of Social Class," *Social Problems* 27 (1979): 96–108.

53. David Greenberg, "Socio-Economic Status and Criminal Sentences: Is There an Association?" *American Sociological Review* 42 (1977): 174–175; David Greenberg and Drew Humphries, "The Co-optation of Fixed Sentencing Reform," *Crime and Delinquency* 26 (1980): 206–225.

54. Steven Box, *Power, Crime and Mystification* (London: Tavistock, 1984); Gregg Barak, *In Defense of Whom? A Critique of Criminal Justice Reform* (Cincinnati: Anderson, 1980). For an opposing view, see Franklin Williams, "Conflict Theory and Differential Processing: An Analysis of the Research Literature," in *Radical Criminology: The Coming Crisis,* ed. J. Inciardi (Beverly Hills, CA: Sage, 1980), pp. 213–231.

55. Michael Rustigan, "A Reinterpretation of Criminal Law Reform in Nineteenth-Century England," in *Crime and Capitalism,* ed. D. Greenberg (Palo Alto, CA: Mayfield, 1981), pp. 255–278.

56. Rosalind Petchesky, "At Hard Labor: Penal Confinement and Production in Nineteenth-Century America," in *Crime and Capitalism,* ed. D. Greenberg (Palo Alto, CA: Mayfield, 1981), pp. 341–357; Paul Takagi, "The Walnut Street Jail: A Penal Reform to Centralize the Powers of the State," *Federal Probation* 49 (1975): 18–26.

57. Jack Gibbs, "An Incorrigible Positivist," *Criminologist* 12 (1987): 2–3.

58. Jackson Toby, "The New Criminology Is the Old Sentimentality," *Criminology* 16 (1979): 513–526.

59. Richard Sparks, "A Critique of Marxist Criminology," in *Crime and Justice,* vol. 2, ed. Norval Morris and Michael Tonry (Chicago: University of Chicago Press, 1980), pp. 159–208.

60. Carl Klockars, "The Contemporary Crises of Marxist Criminology," in *Radical Criminology: The Coming Crisis,* ed. J. Inciardi (Beverly Hills, CA: Sage, 1980), pp. 92–123.

61. Ibid.

62. Michael Lynch, W. Byron Groves, and Alan Lizotte, "The Rate of Surplus Value and Crime: A Theoretical and Empirical Examination of Marxian Economic Theory and Criminology," *Crime, Law, and Social Change* 18 (1994): 1–11.

63. Anthony Platt, "Criminology in the 1980s: Progressive Alternatives to 'Law and Order,' " *Crime and Social Justice* 21–22 (1985): 191–199.

64. See, generally, Roger Matthews and Jock Young, eds., *Confronting Crime* (London: Sage, 1986); for a thorough review of left realism, see Martin Schwartz and Walter DeKeseredy, "Left Realist Criminology: Strengths, Weaknesses, and the Feminist Critique," *Crime, Law, and Social Change* 15 (1991): 51–72.

65. John Lea and Jock Young, *What Is to Be Done About Law and Order?* (Harmondsworth, England: Penguin, 1984).

66. Ibid., p. 88.

67. Richard Kinsey, John Lea, and Jock Young, *Losing the Fight Against Crime* (London: Blackwell, 1986).

68. Martin Schwartz and Walter DeKeseredy, *Contemporary Criminology* (Belmont, CA: Wadsworth, 1993), p. 249.

69. Schwartz and DeKeseredy, "Left Realist Criminology."

70. For a general review of this issue, see Kathleen Daly and Meda Chesney-Lind, "Feminism and Criminology," *Justice Quarterly* 5 (1988): 497–538;

Douglas Smith and Raymond Paternoster, "The Gender Gap in Theories of Deviance: Issues and Evidence," *Journal of Research in Crime and Delinquency* 24 (1987): 140–172; and Pat Carlen, "Women, Crime, Feminism, and Realism," *Social Justice* 17 (1990): 106–123.

71. Herman Schwendinger and Julia Schwendinger, *Rape and Inequality* (Newbury Park, CA: Sage, 1983).

72. Daly and Chesney-Lind, "Feminism and Criminology."

73. Janet Saltzman Chafetz, "Feminist Theory and Sociology: Underutilized Contributions for Mainstream Theory," *Annual Review of Sociology* 23 (1997): 97–121.

74. Ibid.

75. James Messerschmidt, *Capitalism, Patriarchy, and Crime* (Totowa, NJ: Rowman and Littlefield, 1986); for a critique of this work, see Herman Schwendinger and Julia Schwendinger, "The World According to James Messerschmidt," *Social Justice* 15 (1988): 123–145.

76. Kathleen Daly, "Gender and Varieties of White-Collar Crime," *Criminology* 27 (1989): 769–793.

77. Jane Roberts Chapman, "Violence Against Women as a Violation of Human Rights," *Social Justice* 17 (1990): 54–71.

78. James Messerschmidt, *Masculinities and Crime: Critique and Reconceptualization of Theory* (Lanham, MD: Rowman and Littlefield, 1993).

79. Suzie Dod Thomas and Nancy Stein, "Criminality, Imprisonment, and Women's Rights in the 1990s," *Social Justice* 17 (1990): 1–5.

80. Walter DeKeseredy and Martin Schwartz, "Male Peer Support and Woman Abuse: An Expansion of DeKeseredy's Model," *Sociological Spectrum* 13 (1993): 393–413.

81. Daly and Chesney-Lind, "Feminism and Criminology." See also Drew Humphries and Susan Caringella-MacDonald, "Murdered Mothers, Missing Wives: Reconsidering Female Victimization," *Social Justice* 17 (1990): 71–78.

82. Jane Siegel and Linda Meyer Williams, "Aggressive Behavior Among Women Sexually Abused as Children," paper presented at the annual meeting of the American Society of Criminology, Phoenix, Arizona, 1993, revised version.

83. Susan Ehrlich Martin and Nancy Jurik, *Doing Justice, Doing Gender* (Thousand Oaks, CA: Sage, 1996), p. 27.

84. Ruth Alexander, *The "Girl Problem": Female Sexual Delinquency in New York, 1900–1930* (Ithaca, NY: Cornell University Press, 1995).

85. Mary Odem and Steven Schlossman, "Guardians of Virtue: The Juvenile Court and Female Delinquency in Early 20th-Century Los Angeles," *Crime and Delinquency* 37 (1991): 186–203.

86. Meda Chesney-Lind, "Judicial Enforcement of the Female Sex Role: The Family Court and the Female Delinquent," *Issues in Criminology* 8 (1973): 51–69. See also Meda Chesney-Lind, "Women and Crime: The Female Offender," *Signs: Journal of Women in Culture and Society* 12 (1986): 78–96; "Female Offenders: Paternalism Reexamined," in *Women, the Courts, and Equality,* ed. Laura L. Crites and Winifred L. Hepperle (Newbury Park, CA: Sage, 1987): 114–139; "Girls' Crime and a Woman's Place: Toward a Feminist Model of Female Delinquency," paper presented at the annual meeting of the American Society of Criminology, Montreal, 1987.

87. Hagan, *Structural Criminology.*

88. John Hagan, A. R. Gillis, and John Simpson, "The Class Structure and Delinquency: Toward a Power-Control Theory of Common Delinquent Behavior," *American Journal of Sociology* 90 (1985): 1151–1178; John Hagan, John Simpson, and A. R. Gillis, "Class in the Household: A Power-Control Theory of Gender and Delinquency," *American Journal of Sociology* 92 (1987): 788–816.

89. Brenda Sims Blackwell, "Perceived Sanction Threats, Gender, and Crime: A Test and Elabora-

tion of Power-Control Theory," *Criminology* 38 (2000): 439–488.

90. See, generally, Lynch, "Rediscovering Criminology," pp. 27–28.

91. See, generally, Stuart Henry and Dragan Milovanovic, *Constitutive Criminology: Beyond Postmodernism* (London: Sage, 1996).

92. Dragan Milovanovic, *A Primer in the Sociology of Law* (Albany, NY: Harrow and Heston, 1988), pp. 127–128.

93. See, generally, Henry and Milovanovic, *Constitutive Criminology.*

94. Bruce Arrigo and Thomas Bernard, "Postmodern Criminology in Relation to Radical and Conflict Criminology," *Critical Criminology* 8 (1997): 39–60.

95. See, for example, Tifft and Sullivan, *The Struggle to Be Human*; Sullivan, *The Mask of Love.*

96. Larry Tifft, "Foreword," in Sullivan, *The Mask of Love,* p. 6.

97. Sullivan, *The Mask of Love,* p. 141.

98. Richard Quinney, "The Way of Peace: On Crime, Suffering, and Service," in *Criminology as Peacemaking,* ed. Harold Pepinsky and Richard Quinney (Bloomington: Indiana University Press, 1991), pp. 8–9.

99. Kathleen Daly and Russ Immarigeon, "The Past, Present, and Future of Restorative Justice: Some Critical Reflections," *Contemporary Justice Review* 1 (1998): 21–45.

100. Gene Stephens, "The Future of Policing: From a War Model to a Peace Model," in *The Past, Present and Future of American Criminal Justice,* ed. Brendan Maguire and Polly Radosh (Dix Hills, NY: General Hall, 1996), pp. 77–93.

101. Daly and Immarigeon, "The Past, Present, and Future of Restorative Justice," p. 26.

102. Kay Pranis, "Peacemaking Circles: Restorative Justice in Practice Allows Victims and Offenders to Begin Repairing the Harm," *Corrections Today* 59 (1997): 74.

103. Carol LaPrairie, "The 'New' Justice: Some Implications for Aboriginal Communities," *Canadian Journal of Criminology* 40 (1998): 61–79.

104. Adapted from Kay Pranis, "Peacemaking Circles."

Chapter 9

1. Gerald Patterson and Karen Yoerger, "Developmental Models for Delinquent Behavior," in *Mental Disorder and Crime,* ed. Sheilagh Hodgins (Newbury Park, CA: Sage, 1993), pp. 150–159.

2. James Q. Wilson and Richard Herrnstein, *Crime and Human Nature* (New York: Simon and Schuster, 1985).

3. David Rowe, D. Wayne Osgood, and W. Alan Nicewander, "A Latent Trait Approach to Unifying Criminal Careers," *Criminology* 28 (1990): 237–270.

4. Lee Ellis, "Neurohormonal Bases of Varying Tendencies to Learn Delinquent and Criminal Behavior," in *Behavioral Approaches to Crime and Delinquency,* ed. E. Morris and C. Braukmann (New York: Plenum, 1988), pp. 499–518.

5. David Rowe, Alexander Vazsonyi, and Daniel Flannery, "Sex Differences in Crime: Do Means and Within-Sex Variation Have Similar Causes?" *Journal of Research in Crime and Delinquency* 32 (1995): 84–100.

6. Michael Gottfredson and Travis Hirschi, *A General Theory of Crime* (Stanford, CA: Stanford University Press, 1990).

7. Ibid., p. 27.

8. Ibid., p. 90.

9. Ibid., p. 89.

10. Alex Piquero and Stephen Tibbetts, "Specifying the Direct and Indirect Effects of Low Self-Control and Situational Factors in Offenders' Decision Making: Toward a More Complete Model of Rational Offending," *Justice Quarterly* 13 (1996): 481–508.

11. David Forde and Leslie Kennedy, "Risky Lifestyles, Routine Activities, and the General Theory of Crime," *Justice Quarterly* 14 (1997): 265–294.

12. Marianne Junger and Richard Tremblay, "Self-Control, Accidents, and Crime," *Criminal Justice and Behavior* 26 (1999): 485–501.

13. Gottfredson and Hirschi, *A General Theory of Crime*, p. 112.

14. Ibid.

15. Dennis Giever, "An Empirical Assessment of the Core Elements of Gottfredson and Hirschi's General Theory of Crime," paper presented at the annual meeting of the American Society of Criminology, Boston, November 1995.

16. Robert Agnew, "The Contribution of Social-Psychological Strain Theory to the Explanation of Crime and Delinquency," *Advances in Criminological Theory* 6 (1994): 211–213.

17. David Brownfield and Ann Marie Sorenson, "Self-Control and Juvenile Delinquency: Theoretical Issues and an Empirical Assessment of Selected Elements of a General Theory of Crime," *Deviant Behavior* 14 (1993): 243–264; Harold Grasmick, Charles Tittle, Robert Bursik, and Bruce Arneklev, "Testing the Core Empirical Implications of Gottfredson and Hirschi's General Theory of Crime," *Journal of Research in Crime and Delinquency* 30 (1993): 5–29; John Cochran, Peter Wood, and Bruce Arneklev, "Is the Religiosity–Delinquency Relationship Spurious? A Test of Arousal and Social Control Theories," *Journal of Research in Crime and Delinquency* 31 (1994): 92–123; Marc LeBlanc, Marc Ouimet, and Richard Tremblay, "An Integrative Control Theory of Delinquent Behavior: A Validation 1976–1985," *Psychiatry* 51 (1988): 164–176.

18. Michael Benson and Elizabeth Moore, "Are White-Collar and Common Offenders the Same? An Empirical and Theoretical Critique of a Recently Proposed General Theory of Crime," *Journal of Research in Crime and Delinquency* 29 (1992): 251–272.

19. Ronald Akers, "Self-Control as a General Theory of Crime," *Journal of Quantitative Criminology* 7 (1991): 201–211.

20. Alan Feingold, "Gender Differences in Personality: A Meta Analysis," *Psychological Bulletin* 116 (1994): 429–456.

21. Gottfredson and Hirschi, *A General Theory of Crime*, p. 153.

22. Scott Menard, Delbert Elliott, and Sharon Wofford, "Social Control Theories in Developmental Perspective," *Studies on Crime and Crime Prevention* 2 (1993): 69–87.

23. Charles R. Tittle and Harold G. Grasmick, "Criminal Behavior and Age: A Test of Three Provocative Hypotheses," *Journal of Criminal Law and Criminology* 88 (1997): 309–342.

24. Douglas Longshore, "Self-Control and Criminal Opportunity: A Prospective Test of the General Theory of Crime," *Social Problems* 45 (1998): 102–114.

25. Otwin Marenin and Michael Resig, "A General Theory of Crime and Patterns of Crime in Nigeria: An Exploration of Methodological Assumptions," *Journal of Criminal Justice* 23 (1995): 501–518.

26. Bruce Arneklev, Harold Grasmick, Charles Tittle, and Robert Bursik, "Low Self-Control and Imprudent Behavior," *Journal of Quantitative Criminology* 9 (1993): 225–246.

27. Kevin Thompson, "Sexual Harassment and Low Self-Control: An Application of Gottfredson and Hirschi's General Theory of Crime," paper presented at the annual meeting of the American Society of Criminology, Phoenix, Arizona, November 1993.

28. Charles Tittle, *Control Balance: Toward a General Theory of Deviance* (Boulder, CO: Westview, 1995).

29. Marvin Krohn, Alan Lizotte, and Cynthia Perez, "The Interrelationship Between Substance Use and Precocious Transitions to Adult Sexuality," *Journal of Health and Social Behavior* 38 (1997): 87–103, at p. 88.

30. G. R. Patterson, Barbara DeBaryshe, and Elizabeth Ramsey, "A Developmental Perspective on Antisocial Behavior," *American Psychologist* 44 (1989): 329–335.

31. Joan McCord, "Family Relationships, Juvenile Delinquency, and Adult Criminality," *Criminology* 29 (1991): 397–417.

32. Paul Mazerolle, "Delinquent Definitions and Participation Age: Assessing the Invariance Hypothesis," *Studies on Crime and Crime Prevention* 6 (1997): 151–168.

33. See, generally, Sheldon Glueck and Eleanor Glueck, *500 Criminal Careers* (New York: Knopf, 1930); Sheldon Glueck and Eleanor Glueck, *One Thousand Juvenile Delinquents* (Cambridge, MA: Harvard University Press, 1934); Sheldon Glueck and Eleanor Glueck, *Predicting Delinquency and Crime* (Cambridge, MA: Harvard University Press, 1967), pp. 82–83.

34. Sheldon Glueck and Eleanor Glueck, *Unraveling Juvenile Delinquency* (Cambridge, MA: Harvard University Press, 1950).

35. Ibid., p. 48.

36. Rolf Loeber and Marc LeBlanc, "Toward a Developmental Criminology," in *Crime and Justice*, vol. 12, ed. Norval Morris and Michael Tonry (Chicago: University of Chicago Press, 1990), pp. 375–473; Rolf Loeber and Marc LeBlanc, "Developmental Criminology Updated," in *Crime and Justice*, vol. 23, ed. Michael Tonry (Chicago: University of Chicago Press, 1998), pp. 115–198.

37. G. R. Patterson, L. Crosby, and S. Vuchinich, "Predicting Risk for Early Police Arrest," *Journal of Quantitative Criminology* 8 (1992): 335–355; Rolf Loeber, Magda Stouthamer-Loeber, Welmoet Van Kammen, and David Farrington, "Initiation, Escalation, and Desistance in Juvenile Offending and Their Correlates," *Journal of Criminal Law and Criminology* 82 (1991): 36–82.

38. Raymond Paternoster, Charles Dean, Alex Piquero, Paul Mazerolle, and Robert Brame, "Generality, Continuity, and Change in Offending," *Journal of Quantitative Criminology* 13 (1997): 231–266.

39. Magda Stouthamer-Loeber and Evelyn Wei, "The Precursors of Young Fatherhood and Its Effect on Delinquency of Teenage Males," *Journal of Adolescent Health* 22 (1998): 56–65; Richard Jessor, John Donovan, and Francis Costa, *Beyond Adolescence: Problem Behavior and Young Adult Development* (New York: Cambridge University Press, 1991).

40. Marvin Krohn, Alan Lizotte, and Cynthia Perez, "The Interrelationship Between Substance Use and Precocious Transitions to Adult Sexuality," *Journal of Health and Social Behavior* 38 (1997): 87–103, at p. 88; Richard Jessor, "Risk Behavior in Adolescence: A Psychosocial Framework for Understanding and Action," in *Adolescents at Risk: Medical and Social Perspectives*, ed. D. E. Rogers and E. Ginzburg (Boulder, CO: Westview, 1992).

41. Deborah Capaldi and Gerald Patterson, "Can Violent Offenders Be Distinguished from Frequent Offenders: Prediction from Childhood to Adolescence," *Journal of Research in Crime and Delinquency* 33 (1996): 206–231; D. Wayne Osgood, "The Covariation Among Adolescent Problem Behaviors," paper presented at the annual meeting of the American Society of Criminology, Baltimore, November 1990.

42. Terence Thornberry, Carolyn Smith, and Gregory Howard, "Risk Factors for Teenage Fatherhood," *Journal of Marriage and the Family* 59 (1997): 505–522; Todd Miller, Timothy Smith, Charles Turner, Margarita Guijarro, and Amanda Hallet, "A Meta-Analytic Review of Research on Hostility and Physical Health," *Psychological Bulletin* 119 (1996): 322–348; Marianne Junger, "Accidents and Crime," in *The Generality of Deviance*, ed. T. Hirschi and M. Gottfredson (New Brunswick, NJ: Transaction Press, 1993).

43. Robert Johnson, S. Susan Su, Dean Gerstein, Hee-Choon Shin, and John Hoffman, "Parental Influences on Deviant Behavior in Early Adolescence: A Logistic Response Analysis of Age- and Gender-Differentiated Effects," *Journal of Quantitative Criminology* 11 (1995): 167–192; Judith Brooks, Martin Whiteman, and Patricia Cohen, "Stage of Drug Use, Aggression, and Theft/Vandalism," in *Drugs, Crime and Other Deviant Adaptations: Longitudinal Studies*, ed. Howard Kaplan (New York: Plenum, 1995), pp. 83–96; Robert Hoge, D. A. Andrews, and Alan Leschied, "Tests of Three Hypotheses Regarding the Predictors of Delinquency," *Journal of Abnormal Child Psychology* 22 (1994): 547–559.

44. David Huizinga, Rolf Loeber, and Terence Thornberry, "Longitudinal Study of Delinquency, Drug Use, Sexual Activity, and Pregnancy Among Children and Youth in Three Cities," *Public Health Reports* 108 (1993): 90–96.

45. Rolf Loeber, Phen Wung, Kate Keenan, Bruce Giroux, Magda Stouthamer-Loeber, Wemoet Van Kammen, and Barbara Maughan, "Developmental Pathways in Disruptive Behavior," *Development and Psychopathology* (1993): 12–48.

46. Amy D'Unger, Kenneth Land, Patricia McCall, and Daniel Nagin, "How Many Latent Classes of Delinquent/Criminal Careers? Results from Mixed Poisson Regression Analyses," *American Journal of Sociology* 103 (1998): 1593–1630.

47. Terrie Moffitt, "Natural Histories of Delinquency," in *Cross-National Longitudinal Research on Human Development and Criminal Behavior*, ed. Elmar Weitekamp and Hans-Jurgen Kerner (Dordrecht, Netherlands: Kluwer, 1994), pp. 3–65.

48. Michael Newcomb, "Pseudomaturity Among Adolescents: Construct Validation, Sex Differences, and Associations in Adulthood," *Journal of Drug Issues* 26 (1996): 477–504.

49. Rolf Loeber and Magda Stouthamer-Loeber, "Development of Juvenile Aggression and Violence," *American Psychologist* 53 (1998): 242–259.

50. Terrie Moffitt, "Adolescence-Limited and Life-Course-Persistent Antisocial Behavior: A Developmental Taxonomy," *Psychological Review* 100 (1993): 674–701.

51. David Fergusson, L. John Horwood, and Daniel Nagin, "Offending Trajectories in a New Zealand Birth Cohort," *Criminology* 38 (2000): 525–551.

52. Ronald Simons, Chyi-In Wu, Rand Conger, and Frederick Lorenz, "Two Routes to Delinquency: Differences Between Early and Later Starters in the Impact of Parenting and Deviant Careers," *Criminology* 32 (1994): 247–275.

53. Mark Lipsey and James Derzon, "Predictors of Violent or Serious Delinquency in Adolescence and Early Adulthood: A Synthesis of Longitudinal Research," in *Serious and Violent Juvenile Offenders: Risk Factors and Successful Interventions*, ed. Rolf Loeber and David Farrington (Thousand Oaks, CA: Sage, 1998).

54. G. R. Patterson and Karen Yoerger, "Differentiating Outcomes and Histories for Early and Late Onset Arrests," paper presented at the annual meeting of the American Society of Criminology, Phoenix, Arizona, November 1993.

55. Marshall Jones and Donald Jones, "The Contagious Nature of Antisocial Behavior," *Criminology* 38 (2000): 25–46.

56. See, for example, the Rochester Youth Development Study, Hindelang Criminal Justice Research Center, 135 Western Avenue, Albany, New York 12222.

57. David Farrington, "The Development of Offending and Antisocial Behavior from Childhood to Adulthood," paper presented at the Congress on Rethinking Delinquency, University of Minho, Braga, Portugal, July 1992.

58. Joseph Weis and J. David Hawkins, *Reports of the National Juvenile Assessment Centers: Preventing Delinquency* (Washington, DC: U.S. Department of Justice, 1981); Joseph Weis and John Sederstrom, *Reports of the National Juvenile Justice Assessment Centers: The Prevention of Serious Delinquency: What to Do* (Washington, DC: U.S. Department of Justice, 1981).

59. Julie O'Donnell, J. David Hawkins, and Robert Abbott, "Predicting Serious Delinquency and Substance Use Among Aggressive Boys," *Journal*

of Consulting and Clinical Psychology 63 (1995): 529–537.

60. Terence Thornberry, "Toward an Interactional Theory of Delinquency," *Criminology* 25 (1987): 863–891.

61. Ross Matsueda and Kathleen Anderson, "The Dynamics of Delinquent Peers and Delinquent Behavior," *Criminology* 36 (1998): 269–308.

62. Thornberry, "Toward an Interactional Theory of Delinquency."

63. Ibid., p. 863.

64. Terrence Thornberry, Alan Lizotte, Marvin Krohn, Margaret Farnworth, and Sung Joon Jang, *Delinquent Peers, Beliefs, and Delinquent Behavior: A Longitudinal Test of Interactional Theory,* working paper no. 6, rev., Rochester Youth Development Study (Albany, NY: Hindelang Criminal Justice Research Center, 1992), pp. 628–629.

65. Robert Sampson and John Laub, *Crime in the Making: Pathways and Turning Points Through Life* (Cambridge, MA: Harvard University Press, 1993); John Laub and Robert Sampson, "Turning Points in the Life Course: Why Change Matters to the Study of Crime," paper presented at the annual meeting of the American Society of Criminology, New Orleans, November 1992.

66. Terri Orbuch, James House, Richard Mero, and Pamela Webster, "Marital Quality Over the Life Course," *Social Psychology Quarterly* 59 (1996): 162–171; Lee Lillard and Linda Waite, " 'Til Death Do Us Part: Marital Disruption and Mortality," *American Journal of Sociology* 100 (1995): 1131–1156.

67. Mark Warr, "Life-Course Transitions and Desistance from Crime," *Criminology* 36 (1998): 183–216.

68. Pamela Webster, Terri Orbuch, and James House, "Effects of Childhood Family Background on Adult Marital Quality and Perceived Stability," *American Journal of Sociology* 101 (1995): 404–432.

69. John Hagan, Ross MacMillan, and Blair Wheaton, "New Kid in Town: Social Capital and the Life Course Effects of Family Migration on Children," *American Sociological Review* 61 (1996): 368–385.

70. Sampson and Laub, *Crime in the Making,* p. 249.

71. Raymond Paternoster and Robert Brame, "Multiple Routes to Delinquency? A Test of Developmental and General Theories of Crime," *Criminology* 35 (1997): 49–84.

72. Robert Hoge, D. A. Andrews, and Alan Leschied, "An Investigation of Risk and Protective Factors in a Sample of Youthful Offenders," *Journal of Child Psychology and Psychiatry* 37 (1996): 419–424.

73. Candace Kruttschnitt, Christopher Uggen, and Kelly Shelton, "Individual Variability in Sex Offending and Its Relationship to Informal and Formal Social Controls," paper presented at the annual meeting of the American Society of Criminology, San Diego, 1997; Mark Collins and Don Weatherburn, "Unemployment and the Dynamics of Offender Populations," *Journal of Quantitative Criminology* 11 (1995): 231–245.

74. Avshalom Caspi, Terrie Moffitt, Bradley Entner Wright, and Phil Silva, "Early Failure in the Labor Market: Childhood and Adolescent Predictors of Unemployment in the Transition to Adulthood," *American Sociological Review* 63 (1998): 424–451.

75. Erich Labouvie, "Maturing Out of Substance Use: Selection and Self-Correction," *Journal of Drug Issues* 26 (1996): 457–474.

76. Mark Warr, "Life-Course Transitions and Desistance from Crime," *Criminology* 36 (1998): 502–535.

77. Robert Sampson and John Laub, "Socioeconomic Achievement in the Life Course of Disadvantaged Men: Military Service as a Turning Point, circa 1940–1965," *American Sociological Review* 61 (1996): 347–367.

78. Daniel Nagin and Raymond Paternoster, "Personal Capital and Social Control: The Deterrence Implications of a Theory of Criminal Offending," *Criminology* 32 (1994): 581–606.

79. John Laub, "Crime Over the Life Course," *Poverty Research News,* Newsletter of the Northwestern University/University of Chicago Joint Center for Poverty Research, Vol. 4, No. 3, May–June 2000.

Chapter 10

1. Carol Marie Cropper, "3 Whites Charged in Brutal Killing of Black," *New York Times,* 10 June 1998.

2. Rick Bragg, "Unfathomable Crime, Unlikely Figure in Jasper, Texas," *New York Times,* 17 June 1998.

3. David Courtwright, "Violence in America," *American Heritage* 47 (1996): 36.

4. Hans Toch, *Violent Men* (Chicago: Aldine, 1969), p. 1.

5. Stryker McGuire, "The Dunblane Effect," *Newsweek,* 28 October 1996, p. 46.

6. Richard Rogers, Randall Salekin, Kenneth Sewell, and Keith Cruise, "Prototypical Analysis of Antisocial Personality Disorder," *Criminal Justice and Behavior* 27 (2000): 234–255.

7. Dorothy Otnow Lewis, Ernest Moy, Lori Jackson, Robert Aaronson, Nicholas Restifo, Susan Serra, and Alexander Simos, "Biopsychosocial Characteristics of Children Who Later Murder," *American Journal of Psychiatry* 142 (1985): 1161–1167.

8. Dorothy Otnow Lewis, *Guilty by Reason of Insanity* (New York: Fawcett Columbine, 1998).

9. Katherine Van Wormer and Chuk Odiah, "The Psychology of Suicide-Murder and the Death Penalty," *Journal of Criminal Justice* 27 (1999): 361–370.

10. Amy Holtzworth-Munroe and Gregory Stuart, "Typologies of Male Batterers: Three Subtypes and the Differences Among Them," *Psychological Bulletin* 116 (1994): 476–497.

11. Stephen Porter, David Fairweather, Jeff Drugge, Huues Herve, Angela Birt, and Douglas Boer, "Profiles of Psychopathy in Incarcerated Sexual Offenders," *Criminal Justice and Behavior* 27 (2000): 216–233.

12. Albert Reiss and Jeffrey Roth, *Understanding and Preventing Violence* (Washington, DC: National Academy Press, 1993), pp. 112–113.

13. Robert Marcus and Lewis Gray, Jr., "Close Relationships of Violent and Nonviolent African American Delinquents," *Violence and Victimization* 13 (1998): 31–42.

14. Pamela Lattimore, Christy Visher, and Richard Linster, "Predicting Rearrest for Violence Among Serious Youthful Offenders," *Journal of Research in Crime and Delinquency* 32 (1995): 54–83.

15. Robert Scudder, William Blount, Kathleen Heide, and Ira Silverman, "Important Links Between Child Abuse, Neglect, and Delinquency," *International Journal of Offender Therapy* 37 (1993): 315–323.

16. Dorothy Lewis et al., "Neuropsychiatric, Psychoeducational, and Family Characteristics of 14 Juveniles Condemned to Death in the United States," *American Journal of Psychiatry* 145 (1988): 584–588.

17. Charles Patrick Ewing, *When Children Kill* (Lexington, MA: Lexington Books, 1990), p. 22.

18. Lewis, *Guilty by Reason of Insanity,* pp. 11–35.

19. Sigmund Freud, *Beyond the Pleasure Principle* (London: Inter-Psychoanalytic Press, 1922).

20. Konrad Lorenz, *On Aggression* (New York: Harcourt Brace Jovanovich, 1966).

21. Graham Ousey, "Homicide, Structural Factors and the Racial Invariance Assumption," *Criminology* 37 (1999): 405–425.

22. Michael Greene, "Chronic Exposure to Violence and Poverty: Interventions That Work for Youth," *Crime and Delinquency* 39 (1993): 106–124.

23. John MacDonald, Geoffrey Alpert, and Abraham Tennenbaum, "Justifiable Homicide by Police and Criminal Homicide: A Research Note," *Journal of Crime and Justice* 22 (1999): 153–164.

24. Paul Joubert and Craig Forsyth, "A Macro View of Two Decades of Violence in America," *American Journal of Criminal Justice* 13 (1988): 10–25.

25. M. Dwayne Smith and Victoria Brewer, "A Sex-Specific Analysis of Correlates of Homicide Victimization in United States Cities," *Violence and Victims* 7 (1992): 279–285.

26. Marvin Wolfgang and Franco Ferracuti, *The Subculture of Violence* (London: Tavistock, 1967).

27. David Luckenbill and Daniel Doyle, "Structural Position and Violence: Developing a Cultural Explanation," *Criminology* 27 (1989): 419–436.

28. Paul Goldstein, Henry Brownstein, and Patrick Ryan, "Drug-Related Homicide in New York: 1984–1988," *Crime and Delinquency* 38 (1992): 459–476.

29. Reiss and Roth, *Understanding and Preventing Violence,* pp. 193–194.

30. James Collins and Pamela Messerschmidt, "Epidemiology of Alcohol-Related Violence," *Alcohol Health and Research World* 17 (1993): 93–100.

31. James Howell, "Youth Gang Homicides: A Literature Review," *Crime and Delinquency* 45 (1999): 208–241.

32. Christopher Innes, *Profile of State Prison Inmates 1986* (Washington, DC: Bureau of Justice Statistics, 1988).

33. Reiss and Roth, *Understanding and Preventing Violence,* p. 19.

34. Joseph Sheley and James Wright, *Gun Acquisition and Possession in Selected Juvenile Samples* (Washington, DC: National Institute of Justice, 1993).

35. Federal Bureau of Investigation, *Crime in the United States, 1999* (Washington, DC: U.S. Government Printing Office, 2000).

36. William Green, *Rape* (Lexington, MA: Lexington Books, 1988), p. 5.

37. Susan Brownmiller, *Against Our Will: Men, Women and Rape* (New York: Simon and Schuster, 1975).

38. Green, *Rape,* p. 6.

39. Gregory Vistica, "Rape in the Ranks," *Newsweek,* 25 November 1996, pp. 29–31.

40. Yuri Kageyama, "Court Orders Japan to Pay Sex Slaves," *Boston Globe,* 28 April 1998, p. A2.

41. Marlise Simons, "Bosnian Serb Pleads Guilty to Rape Charge Before War Crimes Tribunal," *New York Times,* 10 March 1998, p. A8.

42. FBI, *Uniform Crime Report, 1999,* pp. 25–28.

43. FBI, *Uniform Crime Report, 1999.*

44. Callie Marie Rennison, *Criminal Victimization 1999: Changes 1998–99 with Trends 1993–99* (Washington, DC: Bureau of Justice Statistics, 2000).

45. Angela Browne, "Violence Against Women: Relevance for Medical Practitioners," *Journal of the American Medical Association* 267 (1992): 3184–3189.

46. Mark Warr, "Rape, Burglary and Opportunity," *Journal of Quantitative Criminology* 4 (1988): 275–288.

47. Sarah Ullman, "A Comparison of Gang and Individual Rape Incidents," *Violence and Victims* 14 (1999): 123–134.

48. Julie Allison and Lawrence Wrightsman, *Rape: The Misunderstood Crime* (Newbury Park, CA: Sage, 1993), p. 51.

49. Janet Warren, Roland Reboussin, Robert Hazlewood, Natalie Gibbs, Susan Trumbetta, and Andrea Cummings, "Crime Scene Analysis and the Escalation of Violence in Serial Rape," *Forensic Science International* 2 (1998): 56–62.

50. James LeBeau, "Patterns of Stranger and Serial Rape Offending Factors Distinguishing Apprehended and At-Large Offenders," *Journal of Criminal Law and Delinquency* 78 (1987): 309–326.

51. A. Nicholas Groth and Jean Birnbaum, *Men Who Rape* (New York: Plenum, 1979).

52. For another typology, see Raymond Knight, "Validation of a Typology of Rapists," in *Sex Offender Research and Treatment: State-of-the-Art in North America and Europe,* ed. W. L. Marshall and

J. Frenken (Newbury Park, CA: Sage, 1997), pp. 58–75.

53. R. Lance Shotland, "A Model of the Causes of Date Rape in Developing and Close Relationships," in *Close Relationships*, ed. C. Hendrick (Newbury Park, CA: Sage, 1989), pp. 247–270.

54. Diane Follingstad, Rebekah Bradley, James Laughlin, and Leslie Burke, "Risk Factors and Correlates of Dating Violence: The Relevance of Examining Frequency and Severity Levels in a College Sample," *Violence and Victims* 14 (1999): 365–378.

55. Thomas Meyer, "Date Rape: A Serious Campus Problem That Few Talk About," *Chronicle of Higher Education* 29 (5 December 1984): 15.

56. Allison and Wrightsman, *Rape*, p. 64.

57. Martin Schwartz, "Humanist Sociology and Date Rape on the College Campus," *Humanity and Society* 15 (1991): 304–316.

58. Allison and Wrightsman, *Rape*, pp. 85–87.

59. Cited in Diana Russell, "Wife Rape," in *Acquaintance Rape: The Hidden Crime*, ed. A. Parrot and L. Bechhofer (New York: Wiley, 1991), pp. 129–139, at p. 129.

60. David Finkelhor and K. Yllo, *License to Rape: Sexual Abuse of Wives* (New York: Holt, Rinehart and Winston, 1985).

61. Allison and Wrightsman, *Rape*, p. 89.

62. Associated Press, "British Court Rejects Precedent, Finds a Man Guilty of Raping Wife," *Boston Globe*, 15 March 1991, p. A8.

63. Sharon Elstein and Roy Davis, *Sexual Relationships Between Adult Males and Young Teen Girls: Exploring the Legal and Social Responses* (Chicago: American Bar Association, 1997).

64. Donald Symons, *The Evolution of Human Sexuality* (Oxford: Oxford University Press, 1979).

65. Lee Ellis, "A Synthesized (Biosocial) Theory of Rape," *Journal of Consulting and Clinical Psychology* 39 (1991): 631–642.

66. Diana Russell, *The Politics of Rape* (New York: Stein and Day, 1975).

67. Kala Downs and Steven Gold, "The Role of Blame, Distress, and Anger in the Hypermasculine Man," *Violence and Victims* 12 (1997): 19–36.

68. Groth and Birnbaum, *Men Who Rape*, p. 101.

69. See, generally, Edward Donnerstein, Daniel Linz, and Steven Penrod, *The Question of Pornography* (New York: Free Press, 1987); Diana Russell, *Sexual Exploitation* (Beverly Hills, CA: Sage, 1985), pp. 115–116.

70. Neil Malamuth and John Briere, "Sexual Violence in the Media: Indirect Effects on Aggression Against Women," *Journal of Social Issues* 42 (1986): 75–92.

71. Richard Felson and Marvin Krohn, "Motives for Rape," *Journal of Research in Crime and Delinquency* 27 (1990): 222–242.

72. Larry Baron and Murray Straus, "Four Theories of Rape: A Macrosociological Analysis," *Social Problems* 34 (1987): 467–489.

73. Julie Horney and Cassia Spohn, "The Influence of Blame and Believability Factors on the Processing of Simple Versus Aggravated Rape Cases," *Criminology* 34 (1996): 135–163.

74. Associated Press, "Apology Is Aired for Lie About Rape," *Boston Globe*, 6 September 1990, p. A12.

75. Associated Press, "Jury Stirs Furor by Citing Dress in Rape Acquittal," *Boston Globe*, 6 October 1989, p. A12.

76. Rodney Kingsworth, Randall MacIntosh, and Jennifer Wentworth, "Sexual Assault: The Role of Prior Relationship and Victim Characteristics in Case Processing," *Justice Quarterly* 16 (1999): 276–302.

77. Susan Estrich, *Real Rape* (Cambridge, MA: Harvard University Press, 1987), pp. 58–59.

78. *Michigan* v. *Lucas* 90-149 (1991); Comment, "The Rape Shield Paradox: Complainant Protection Amidst Oscillating Trends of State Judicial Interpretation," *Journal of Criminal Law and Criminology* 78 (1987): 644–698.

79. Andrew Karmen, *Crime Victims* (Pacific Grove, CA: Brooks/Cole, 1990), p. 252.

80. "Court Upholds Civil Rights Portion of Violence Against Women Act," *Criminal Justice Newsletter* 28 (1 December 1997), p. 3.

81. Donald Lunde, *Murder and Madness* (San Francisco: San Francisco Book, 1977), p. 3.

82. Lisa Baertlein, "HIV Ruled Deadly Weapon in Rape Case," *Boston Globe*, 2 March 1994, p. 3.

83. The legal principles here come from Wayne LaFave and Austin Scott, *Criminal Law* (St. Paul, MN: West Publishing, 1986; updated, 1993). The definitions and discussion of legal principles used in this chapter lean heavily on this work.

84. Pauline Arrillaga, "Jurors Give Drunk Driver 16 Years in Fetus's Death," *Manchester Union Leader*, 22 October 1996, p. B20.

85. Center for Reproductive Law and Policy, *Punishing Women for their Behavior During Pregnancy* (New York: Center for Reproductive Law and Policy, 1996), pp. 1–2.

86. Janet Kreps, *Feticide and Wrongful Death Laws* (New York: Center For Reproductive Law and Policy, 1996), pp. 1–2.

87. See, generally, Marc Reidel and Margaret Zahn, *The Nature and Pattern of American Homicide* (Washington, DC: U.S. Government Printing Office, 1985).

88. James L. Williams, "A Discriminant Analysis of Urban Homicide Patterns," paper presented at the annual meeting of the American Society of Criminology, Baltimore, November 1990.

89. Linda Saltzman and James Mercy, "Assaults Between Intimates: The Range of Relationships Involved," in *Homicide: The Victim/Offender Connection*, ed. Anna Victoria Wilson (Cincinnati: Anderson Publishing, 1993), pp. 65–74.

90. Angela Browne and Kirk Williams, "Exploring the Effect of Resource Availability and the Likelihood of Female-Perpetrated Homicides," *Law and Society Review* 23 (1989): 75–94.

91. Angela Browne and Kirk Williams, "Gender, Intimacy, and Lethal Violence: Trends from 1976 Through 1987," *Gender and Society* 7 (1993): 78–98.

92. Richard Felson, "Anger, Aggression, and Violence in Love Triangles," *Violence and Victimization* 12 (1997): 345–363.

93. Ibid., p. 361.

94. Associated Press, "Parents Forgive Teenager Convicted of Toddler's Death," *Boston Globe*, 22 January 1987, p. A2.

95. Charles Ewing, *When Children Kill* (Lexington, MA: Lexington Books, 1990), p. 64.

96. Carolyn Rebecca Block and Richard Block, *Street Gang Crime in Chicago* (Washington, DC: National Institute of Justice, 1993), p. 2.

97. Larry Rohter, "In the Chaos of Colombia, the Makings of a Mass Killer," *New York Times*, 1 November 1999, p. A3.

98. Belea Keeney and Kathleen Heide, "Gender Differences in Serial Murderers: A Preliminary Analysis," *Journal of Interpersonal Violence* 9 (1994): 37–56.

99. Jennifer Browdy, "VI-CAP System to Be Operational This Summer," *Law Enforcement News*, 21 May 1984, p. 1.

100. FBI, *Crime in the United States, 1997*, p. 33.

101. Keith Harries, "Homicide and Assault: A Comparative Analysis of Attributes in Dallas Neighborhoods, 1981–1985," *Professional Geographer* 41 (1989): 29–38.

102. Laurence Zuckerman, "The Air-Rage Rage: Taking a Cold Look at a Hot Topic," *New York Times*, 4 October 1998, p. A3.

103. Michael Rand, *Violence-Related Injuries Treated in Hospital Emergency Departments* (Washington, DC: Bureau of Justice Statistics, 1997).

104. See, generally, Joel Milner, ed., "Special Issue: Physical Child Abuse," *Criminal Justice and Behavior* 18 (1991).

105. See, generally, Ruth S. Kempe and C. Henry Kempe, *Child Abuse* (Cambridge, MA: Harvard University Press, 1978).

106. *Current Trends in Child Abuse Reporting and Fatalities: The Results of the 1998 Annual Fifty-State Survey* (Chicago: National Committee to Prevent Child Abuse, 1999).

107. Diana Russell, "The Incidence and Prevalence of Intrafamilial and Extrafamilial Sexual Abuse of Female Children," *Child Abuse and Neglect* 7 (1983): 133–146. See also David Finkelhor, *Sexually Victimized Children* (New York: Free Press, 1979), p. 88; Jeanne Hernandez, "Eating Disorders and Sexual Abuse in Adolescents," paper presented at the annual meeting of the American Psychosomatic Society, Charleston, South Carolina, March 1993; Glenn Wolfner and Richard Gelles, "A Profile of Violence Toward Children: A National Study," *Child Abuse and Neglect* 17 (1993): 197–212.

108. Wolfner and Gelles, "A Profile of Violence Toward Children."

109. Ruth Inglis, *Sins of the Fathers: A Study of the Physical and Emotional Abuse of Children* (New York: St. Martin's Press, 1978), p. 68.

110. Martin Daly and Margo Wilson, "Violence Against Step Children," *Current Directions in Psychological Science* 5 (1996): 77–81.

111. Inglis, *Sins of the Fathers*, p. 53.

112. Brandt Steele, "Violence Within the Family," in *Child Abuse and Neglect: The Family and the Community*, ed. R. Helfer and C. H. Kempe (Cambridge, MA: Ballinger, 1976), p. 12.

113. R. Emerson Dobash and Russell Dobash, *Violence Against Wives* (New York: Free Press, 1979).

114. Julia O'Faolain and Laura Martines, eds., *Not in God's Image: Women in History* (Glasgow: Fontana/Collins, 1974).

115. Dobash and Dobash, *Violence Against Wives*, p. 46.

116. Ronald Cohen, Alan Rosenbaum, Robert Kane, William Warneken, and Sheldon Benjamin, "Neuropsychological Correlates of Domestic Violence," *Violence and Victims* 15 (2000): 397–410.

117. Neil Jacobson and John Mordechai Gottman, *When Men Batter Women: New Insights into Ending Abusive Relationships* (New York: Simon and Schuster, 1998).

118. Margo Wilson and Martin Daly, "Male Sexual Proprietariness and Violence Against Wives," *Current Directions in Psychological Science* 5 (1996): 2–7.

119. Richard Gelles and Murray Straus, "Violence in the American Family," *Journal of Social Issues* 35 (1979): 15–39.

120. Miguel Schwartz, Susan O'Leary, and Kimberly Kendziora, "Dating Aggression Among High School Students," *Violence and Victimization* 12 (1997): 295–307; James Makepeace, "Social Factor and Victim-Offender Differences in Courtship Violence," *Family Relations* 33 (1987): 87–91.

121. Richard Rosenfeld, "Changing Relationships Between Men and Women: A Note on the Decline in Intimate Partner Homicide," *Homicide Studies* 1 (1997): 72–83.

122. Desmond Ellis and Lori Wright, "Estrangement, Interventions, and Male Violence Toward Female Partners," *Violence and Victims* 12 (1997): 51–68.

123. FBI, *Crime in the United States, 1997*, p. 28.

124. Caroline Wolf Harlow, *Robbery Victims* (Washington, DC: Bureau of Justice Statistics, 1989), pp. 1–5.

125. Richard Felson, Eric Baumer, and Steven Messner, "Acquaintance Robbery," *Journal of Research in Crime and Delinquency* 37 (2000): 284–305.

126. James Calder and John Bauer, "Convenience Store Robberies: Security Measures and Store Robbery Incidents," *Journal of Criminal Justice* 20 (1992): 553–566.

127. Peter Van Koppen and Robert Jansen, "The Time to Rob: Variations in Time and Number of Commercial Robberies," *Journal of Research in Crime and Delinquency* 36 (1999): 7–29.

128. The following sections rely heavily on Patricia Tjaden, *The Crime of Stalking: How Big Is the Problem?* (Washington, DC: National Institute of Justice, 1997). See also Robert M. Emerson, Kerry

O. Ferris, and Carol Brooks Gardner, "On Being Stalked," *Social Problems* 45 (1998): 289–298.

129. Mary Brewster, "Stalking by Former Intimates: Verbal Threats and Other Predictors of Physical Violence," *Violence and Victims* 15 (2000): 41–51.

130. Michael Rand, *Carjacking* (Washington, DC: Bureau of Justice Statistics, 1994), p. 1.

131. James Brooke, "Gay Student Who Was Kidnapped and Beaten Dies," *New York Times*, 13 October 1998, p. A1.

132. Michael Janofsky, "Wyoming Man Gets Life Term in Gay's Death," *New York Times*, 5 November 1999, p. A1.

133. James Garofalo, "Bias and Non-Bias Crimes in New York City: Preliminary Findings," paper presented at the annual meeting of the American Society of Criminology, Baltimore, November 1990.

134. "Boy Gets 18 Years in Fatal Park Beating of Transient," *Los Angeles Times*, 24 December 1987, p. B9.

135. Jack McDevitt, "The Study of the Character of Civil Rights Crimes in Massachusetts (1983–1987)," paper presented at the annual meeting of the American Society of Criminology, Reno, Nevada, November 1989.

136. Ibid., p. 8.

137. Jack Levin and Jack McDevitt, *Hate Crimes: The Rising Tide of Bigotry and Bloodshed* (New York: Plenum, 1993).

138. "ADL Survey Analyzes Neo-Nazi Skinhead Menace and International Connections," *CJ International* 12 (1996): 7.

139. FBI, *Crime in the United States, 1999*, p. 60.

140. Garofalo, "Bias and Non-Bias Crimes in New York City," p. 3.

141. Carl Weiser, "This Is What You Get for Firing Me," *USA Today*, 28 January 1993, p. A3.

142. James Alan Fox and Jack Levin, "Firing Back: The Growing Threat of Workplace Homicide," *Annals* 536 (1994): 16–30.

143. Hubert Herring, "The Good News About 'Going Postal,'" *New York Times*, 3 September 2000, p. A3.

144. John King, "Workplace Violence: A Conceptual Framework," paper presented at the annual meeting of the American Society of Criminology, Phoenix, Arizona, November 1993.

145. Associated Press, "Gunman Wounds 3 Doctors in L.A. Hospital," *Cleveland Plain Dealer*, 9 February 1993, p. B1.

146. Fox and Levin, "Firing Back," p. 5.

147. Greg Warchol, *Workplace Violence, 1992–96* (Washington, DC: Bureau of Justice Statistics, 1998).

148. Stephen Schafer, *The Political Criminal* (New York: Free Press, 1974), p. 1.

149. Robert Friedlander, *Terrorism* (Dobbs Ferry, NY: Oceana, 1979).

150. Walter Laquer, *The Age of Terrorism* (Boston: Little, Brown, 1987), p. 72.

151. National Advisory Commission on Criminal Justice Standards and Goals, *Report of the Task Force on Disorders and Terrorism* (Washington, DC: U.S. Government Printing Office, 1976), p. 3.

152. Paul Wilkinson, *Terrorism and the Liberal State* (New York: Wiley, 1977), p. 49.

153. Jack Gibbs, "Conceptualization of Terrorism," *American Sociological Review* 54 (1989): 329–340, at p. 330.

154. For a general view, see Jonathan White, *Terrorism* (Pacific Grove, CA: Brooks/Cole, 1991).

155. Michael Barkun, "Leaderless Resistance and Phineas Priests: Strategies of Uncoordinated Violence on the Far Right," paper presented at the annual meeting of the American Society of Criminology, San Diego, November 1997.

156. William Smith, "Libya's Ministry of Fear," *Time*, 30 April 1984, pp. 36–38.

157. Stephen Engelberg, "Terrorism's New (and Very Old) Face," *New York Times*, 12 September 1998, p. A5.

158. Bruce Hoffman, *Inside Terrorism* (New York: Columbia University Press, 1998).

159. Joseph Berger, "Murdered Doctor Remembered as Conscientious and Courageous," *New York Times*, 26 October 1998, p. A1.

160. Associated Press, "Colorado Resort Fires Breed Fear of Ecologically Inspired Terrorism," *Boston Globe*, 23 October 1998, p. A21; David Johnston, "Vail Fires Were Arson, Federal Experts Say," *New York Times*, 23 October 1998, p. B1.

161. Charles Hillsinger and Mark Stein, "Militant Vegetarians Tied to Attacks on Livestock Industry," *Boston Globe*, 23 November 1989, p. A34.

162. Ted Robert Gurr, "Political Terrorism in the United States: Historical Antecedents and Contemporary Trends," in *The Politics of Terrorism*, ed. Michael Stohl (New York: Dekker, 1988).

163. Amnesty International, *Annual Report, 1992* (Washington, DC: July 1993).

164. This report on state action in Peru can be obtained on the Amnesty International web site at http://www.amnesty.org/ailib/aipub/1996/AMR/2460396.htm.

165. Brent Smith and Gregory Orvis, "America's Response to Terrorism: An Empirical Analysis of Federal Intervention Strategies During the 1980s," *Justice Quarterly* 10 (1993): 660–681.

166. 18 USC 113a; 18 USC 51, 1166.

167. U.S. State Department news release, 25 April 1996.

Chapter 11

1. Andrew McCall, *The Medieval Underworld* (London: Hamish Hamilton, 1979), p. 86.

2. Ibid., p. 104.

3. J. J. Tobias, *Crime and Police in England, 1700–1900* (London: Gill and Macmillan, 1979).

4. Ibid., p. 9.

5. Marilyn Walsh, *The Fence* (Westport, CT: Greenwood Press, 1977), pp. 18–25.

6. John Hepburn, "Occasional Criminals," in *Major Forms of Crime*, ed. Robert Meier (Beverly Hills, CA: Sage, 1984), pp. 73–94.

7. James Inciardi, "Professional Crime," in *Major Forms of Crime*, ed. Robert Meier (Beverly Hills, CA: Sage, 1984), p. 223.

8. This section depends heavily on a classic book: Wayne La Fave and Austin Scott, *Handbook on Criminal Law* (St. Paul, MN: West Publishing, 1972).

9. La Fave and Scott, *Handbook on Criminal Law*, p. 622.

10. FBI, *Crime in the United States, 1999* (Washington, DC: U.S. Government Printing Office, 2000).

11. Margaret Loftus, "Gone: One TV," *U.S. News & World Report*, 14 July 1997, p. 61.

12. Timothy W. Maier, "Uncle Sam Gets Rolled," *Insight on the News*, 10 March 1997, p. 13.

13. Jill Jordan Siedfer, "To Catch a Thief, Try This: Peddling High-Tech Solutions to Shoplifting," *U.S. News & World Report*, 23 September 1996, p. 71.

14. Mary Owen Cameron, *The Booster and the Snitch* (New York: Free Press, 1964).

15. Ibid., p. 57.

16. Lawrence Cohen and Rodney Stark, "Discriminatory Labeling and the Five-Finger Discount: An Empirical Analysis of Differential Shoplifting Dispositions," *Journal of Research on Crime and Delinquency* 11 (1974): 25–35.

17. Lloyd Klemke, "Does Apprehension for Shoplifting Amplify or Terminate Shoplifting Activity?" *Law and Society Review* 12 (1978): 390–403.

18. Erhard Blankenburg, "The Selectivity of Legal Sanctions: An Empirical Investigation of Shoplifting," *Law and Society Review* 11 (1976): 109–129.

19. George Keckeisen, *Retail Security Versus the Shoplifter* (Springfield, IL: Charles Thomas, 1993), pp. 31–32.

20. Siedfer, "To Catch a Thief, Try This."

21. Edwin Lemert, "An Isolation and Closure Theory of Naive Check Forgery," *Journal of Criminal Law, Criminology and Police Science* 44 (1953): 297–298.

22. "Credit Card Fraud Toll 1 Billion," *Omaha World Herald*, 16 March 1982, p. 1.

23. La Fave and Scott, *Handbook on Criminal Law*, p. 672.

24. Peter Wayner, "Bogus Web Sites Troll for Credit Card Numbers," *New York Times*, 12 February 1997, p. A18.

25. Charles McCaghy, Peggy Giordano, and Trudy Knicely Henson, "Auto Theft," *Criminology* 15 (1977): 367–381.

26. Donald Gibbons, *Society, Crime and Criminal Careers* (Englewood Cliffs, NJ: Prentice-Hall, 1977), p. 310.

27. Kim Hazelbaker, "Insurance Industry Analyses and the Prevention of Motor Vehicle Theft," in *Business and Crime Prevention*, ed. Marcus Felson and Ronald Clarke (Monsey, NY: Criminal Justice Press, 1997), pp. 283–293.

28. Ronald Clarke and Patricia Harris, "Auto Theft and Its Prevention," in *Crime and Justice: An Annual Review*, ed. N. Morris and M. Tonry (Chicago: Chicago University Press, 1992).

29. Ian Ayres and Steven D. Levitt, "Measuring Positive Externalities from Unobservable Victim Precaution: An Empirical Analysis of Lojack," *Quarterly Journal of Economics* 113 (1998): 43–78.

30. Hazelbaker, "Insurance Industry Analyses and the Prevention of Motor Vehicle Theft," p. 289.

31. La Fave and Scott, *Handbook on Criminal Law*, p. 655.

32. 30 Geo. III, C.24 (1975).

33. Susan Gembrowski and Tim Dahlberg, "Over 100 Here Indicted After Telemarketing Fraud Probe Around the U.S.," *San Diego Daily Transcript Online*, 8 December 1995. http://www.sddt.com/files/library/95headlines/DN951208/DN95120802.html

34. Jerome Hall, *Theft, Law and Society* (Indianapolis: Bobbs-Merrill, 1952), p. 36.

35. La Fave and Scott, *Handbook on Criminal Law*, p. 644.

36. Ibid., p. 649.

37. Ibid., p. 708.

38. E. Blackstone, *Commentaries on the Laws of England* (London: 1769), p. 224.

39. Frank Hoheimer, *The Home Invaders: Confessions of a Cat Burglar* (Chicago: Chicago Review, 1975).

40. Richard Wright, Robert Logie, and Scott Decker, "Criminal Expertise and Offender Decision Making: An Experimental Study of the Target Selection Process in Residential Burglary," *Journal of Research in Crime and Delinquency* 32 (1995): 39–53.

41. Richard Wright and Scott Decker, *Burglars on the Job: Streetlife and Residential Break-ins* (Boston, MA: Northeastern University Press, 1994).

42. Simon Hakim and Yochanan Shachmurove, "Spatial and Temporal Patterns of Commercial Burglaries," *American Journal of Economics and Sociology* 55 (1996): 443–457.

43. Roger Litton, "Crime Prevention and the Insurance Industry," in *Business and Crime Prevention*, ed. Marcus Felson and Ronald Clarke (Monsey, NY: Criminal Justice Press, 1997), p. 162.

44. Graham Farrell, Coretta Phillips, and Ken Pease, "Like Taking Candy: Why Does Repeat Victimization Occur?" *British Journal of Criminology* 35 (1995): 384–399, at p. 391.

45. See, generally, Neal Shover, "Structures and Careers in Burglary," *Journal of Criminal Law, Criminology and Police Science* 63 (1972): 540–549.

46. Paul Cromwell, James Olson, and D'Aunn Wester Avary, *Breaking and Entering: An Ethnographic Analysis of Burglary* (Newbury Park, CA: Sage, 1991), pp. 48–51.

47. Nancy Webb, George Sakheim, Luz Towns-Miranda, and Charles Wagner, "Collaborative Treatment of Juvenile Firestarters: Assessment and Outreach," *American Journal of Orthopsychiatry* 60 (1990): 305–310.

48. Vernon Quinsey, Terry Chaplin, and Douglas Unfold, "Arsonists and Sexual Arousal to Fire Setting: Correlations Unsupported," *Journal of Be-*

havior Therapy and Experimental Psychiatry 20 (1989): 203–209.

49. Leigh Edward Somers, *Economic Crimes* (New York: Clark Boardman, 1984), pp. 158–168.

Chapter 12

1. Keith Bradsher, "Stricter Rules for Tire Safety Were Scrapped by Reagan," *New York Times,* 4 September 2000, p. C4.

2. Dwight C. Smith, Jr., "White-Collar Crime, Organized Crime and the Business Establishment: Resolving a Crisis in Criminological Theory," in *White-Collar and Economic Crime: A Multidisciplinary and Crossnational Perspective,* ed. P. Wickman and T. Dailey (Lexington, MA: Lexington Books, 1982), p. 53.

3. See, generally, Dwight C. Smith, Jr., "Organized Crime and Entrepreneurship," *International Journal of Criminology and Penology* 6 (1978): 161–177; Dwight C. Smith, Jr., "Paragons, Pariahs, and Pirates: A Spectrum-Based Theory of Enterprise," *Crime and Delinquency* 26 (1980): 358–386; Dwight C. Smith, Jr., and Richard S. Alba, "Organized Crime and American Life," *Society* 16 (1979): 32–38.

4. Smith, "White-Collar Crime, Organized Crime and the Business Establishment," p. 33.

5. Mark Haller, "Illegal Enterprise: A Theoretical and Historical Interpretation," *Criminology* 28 (1990): 207–235.

6. Nancy Frank and Michael Lynch, *Corporate Crime, Corporate Violence* (Albany, NY: Harrow and Heston, 1992), p. 7.

7. Nikos Passas and David Nelken, "The Thin Line Between Legitimate and Criminal Enterprises: Subsidy Frauds in the European Community," *Crime, Law and Social Change* 19 (1993): 223–243.

8. Ibid., p. 238.

9. For a thorough review, see David Friedrichs, *Trusted Criminals* (Belmont, CA: Wadsworth, 1996).

10. Kitty Calavita and Henry Pontell, "Savings and Loan Fraud as Organized Crime: Toward a Conceptual Typology of Corporate Illegality," *Criminology* 31 (1993): 519–548.

11. Edwin Sutherland, *White-Collar Crime: The Uncut Version* (New Haven, CT: Yale University Press, 1983).

12. Edwin Sutherland, "White-Collar Criminality," *American Sociological Review* 5 (1940): 2–10.

13. David Weisburd and Kip Schlegel, "Returning to the Mainstream," in *White-Collar Crime Reconsidered,* ed. Kip Schlegel and David Weisburd (Boston: Northeastern University Press, 1992), pp. 352–365.

14. Ronald Kramer and Raymond Michalowski, "State-Corporate Crime," paper presented at the annual meeting of the American Society of Criminology, Baltimore, November 1990.

15. Elizabeth Moore and Michael Mills, "The Neglected Victims and Unexamined Costs of White-Collar Crime," *Crime and Delinquency* 36 (1990): 408–418.

16. Stuart Traub, "Battling Employee Crime: A Review of Corporate Strategies and Programs," *Crime and Delinquency* 42 (1996): 244–256.

17. Laura Schrager and James Short, "Toward a Sociology of Organizational Crime," *Social Problems* 25 (1978): 415–425.

18. Gilbert Geis, "White-Collar and Corporate Crime," in *Major Forms of Crime,* ed. Robert Meier (Beverly Hills, CA: Sage, 1984), p. 145.

19. Xie Baogue, "The Function of the Chinese Procuratorial Organ in Combat Against Corruption," *Police Studies* 11 (1988): 38–43.

20. Jim Moran, "Thailand: Crime and Corruption Become Increasing Threat," *CJ International* 12 (1996): 5.

21. Sam Perry, "Economic Espionage and Corporate Responsibility," *CJ International* 11 (1995): 3–4.

22. Marshall Clinard and Richard Quinney, *Criminal Behavior Systems: A Typology* (New York: Holt, Rinehart and Winston, 1973), p. 117.

23. Mark Moore, "Notes Toward a National Strategy to Deal with White-Collar Crime," in *A National Strategy for Containing White-Collar Crime,* ed. Herbert Edelhertz and Charles Rogovin (Lexington, MA: Lexington Books, 1980), pp. 32–44.

24. For a general review, see John Braithwaite, "White Collar Crime," *Annual Review* 11 (1985): 1–25.

25. Nikos Passas, "Structural Sources of International Crime: Policy Lessons from the BCCI Affair," *Crime, Law and Social Change* 19 (1994): 223–231.

26. Nikos Passas, "Accounting for Fraud: Auditors' Ethical Dilemmas in the BCCI Affair," in *The Ethics of Accounting and Finance,* ed. W. Michael Hoffman, Judith Brown Kamm, Robert Frederick, and Edward Petry (Westport, CT: Quorum, 1996), pp. 85–99.

27. Mike Schneider, "In Florida, Man Suspected of a Religious Scam," *Boston Globe,* 27 October 1998, p. B1.

28. Earl Gottschalk, "Churchgoers Are the Prey as Scams Rise," *Wall Street Journal,* 7 August 1989, p. C1.

29. Associated Press, "NYC Cab Scam Warning Given," *Boston Globe,* 19 September 1997, p. 13.

30. Richard Quinney, "Occupational Structure and Criminal Behavior: Prescription Violation of Retail Pharmacists," *Social Problems* 11 (1963): 179–185; see also John Braithwaite, *Corporate Crime in the Pharmaceutical Industry* (London: Routledge and Kegan Paul, 1984).

31. Amy Dockser Marcus, "Thievery by Lawyers Is on the Increase, with Duped Clients Losing Bigger Sums," *Wall Street Journal,* 26 November 1990, p. B1.

32. Ibid.

33. James Armstrong et al., "Securities Fraud," *American Criminal Law Review* 33 (1995): 973–1016.

34. Scott McMurray, "Futures Pit Trader Goes to Trial," *Wall Street Journal,* 8 May 1990, p. C1; Scott McMurray, "Chicago Pits' Dazzling Growth Permitted a Free-for-All Mecca," *Wall Street Journal,* 3 August 1989, p. A4.

35. Associated Press, "12 Westchester Stockbrokers Indicted in $100 Million Telephone-Sales Fraud," *New York Times,* 3 October 1998, p. B1.

36. *Carpenter* v. *United States* 484 U.S. 19 (1987); also see John Boland, "The SEC Trims the First Amendment," *Wall Street Journal,* 4 December 1986, p. 28.

37. Kevin Sack, "49ers Owner Pleads Guilty in Louisiana Casino Case," *New York Times,* 7 October 1998, p. 1.

38. Charles V. Bagli, "Kickback Investigation Extends to Middle-Class Buildings in New York," *New York Times,* 14 October 1998, p. A19.

39. Discussed in Friedrichs, *Trusted Criminals,* p. 147.

40. Larry Tye, "A Tide of State Corruption Sweeps from Coast to Coast," *Boston Globe,* 25 March 1991, p. 1.

41. Maureen Kline, "Italian Magistrates Query Montedison Former Chairman," *Wall Street Journal,* 19 July 1993, p. A6.

42. *The Knapp Commission Report on Police Corruption* (New York: George Braziller, 1973), pp. 1–3, 170–182.

43. Michael Rezendes, "N.Y. Hears of Police Corrupted," *Boston Globe,* 10 October 1993, p. 1.

44. David Kocieniewski and David M. Halbfinger, "New York's Most Respected Officers Led Precinct Where Sex Scandal Festered," *New York Times,* 20 July 1998, p. 1.

45. Cited in Hugh Barlow, *Introduction to Criminology,* 2d ed. (Boston: Little, Brown, 1984).

46. Pub. L. No. 95-213, 101-104, 91 Stat. 1494.

47. Thomas Burton, "The More Baxter Hides Its Israeli Boycott Role, the More Flak It Gets," *Wall Street Journal,* 25 April 1991, p. 1.

48. "Newsbreaks," *Aviation Week and Space Technology,* 10 July 1995, p. 19.

49. Charles McCaghy, *Deviant Behavior* (New York: Macmillan, 1976), p. 178.

50. Associated Press, "Business Fraud Prevails, May Worsen, Study Says," *Wall Street Journal,* 17 August 1993, p. A4.

51. J. Sorenson, H. Grove, and T. Sorenson, "Detecting Management Fraud: The Role of the Independent Auditor," in *White-Collar Crime: Theory and Research,* ed. G. Geis and E. Stotland (Beverly Hills, CA: Sage, 1980), pp. 221–251.

52. See Kristine DeBry, Bonny Harbinger, and Susan Rotkis, "Health Care Fraud," *American Criminal Law Review* 33 (1995): 818–838.

53. Associated Press, "Hospital Settles Bribe Allegation," *Boston Globe,* 19 September 1997, p. 13.

54. Kurt Eichenwald, "Hospital Chain Cheated U.S. on Expenses, Documents Show," *New York Times,* 18 December 1997, p. B1.

55. Laura Johannes and Wendy Bounds, "Corning Agrees to Pay $6.8 Million to Settle Medicare Billing Charges," *Wall Street Journal,* 22 February 1996, p. B2.

56. Ibid.

57. 42 U.S.C. section 1395nn (1993).

58. 18 U.S.C. section 1344 (1994).

59. *United States* v. *Bishop,* 412 U.S. 346 (1973).

60. Joseph S. Hall, "Corporate Criminal Liability," *American Criminal Law Review* 35 (1998): 549–560.

61. 15 U.S.C. [sections] 1 (1994).

62. 15 U.S.C. 1–7 (1976).

63. See *United States* v. *Sealy, Inc.,* 383 U.S. 350.

64. *Northern Pacific Railways* v. *United States,* 356 U.S. 1 (1958).

65. Tim Carrington, "Federal Probes of Contractors Rise for Year," *Wall Street Journal,* 23 February 1987, p. 50.

66. Marshall Clinard and Peter Yeager, *Corporate Crime* (New York: Free Press, 1980).

67. "Econotes," *Environmental Action* 13 (October 1981): 7.

68. "Econotes," *Environmental Action* 13 (September 1981): 5.

69. David Barboza, "S.E.C. Accuses 44 Stock Promoters of Internet Fraud," *New York Times,* 29 October 1998, p. A1.

70. Roger Fillion, "Cracking Down on Internet Crime," *Boston Globe,* 28 December 1995, p. 65.

71. Noelle Knox, "Online Auctions Top List of Internet Fraud: 1,000 Complaints a Week Lodged," *USA Today,* 29 August 2000, p. B1.

72. Pub. L. No. 104-104, Title V sections 501–551 (1996).

73. Xan Raskin and Jeannie Schaldach-Paiva, "Computer Crimes," *American Criminal Law Review* 33 (1995): 541–573.

74. M. Swanson and J. Territo, "Computer Crime: Dimensions, Types, Causes and Investigations," *Journal of Political Science and Administration* 8 (1980): 305–306; see also Donn Parker, "Computer-Related White-Collar Crime," in *White Collar Crime: Theory and Research,* ed. G. Geis and E. Stotland (Beverly Hills, CA: Sage, 1980), pp. 199–220.

75. Anne Branscomb, "Rogue Computer Programs and Computer Rogues: Tailoring Punishment to Fit the Crime," *Rutgers Computer and Technology Law Journal* 16 (1990): 24–26.

76. Carl Benson, Andrew Jablon, Paul Kaplan, and Mara Elena Rosenthal, "Computer Crimes," *American Criminal Law Review* 34 (1997): 409–443.

77. Erik Larson, "Computers Turn Out to Be Valuable Aid in Employee Crime," *Wall Street Journal,* 14 January 1985, p. 1.

78. Clyde Wilson, "Software Piracy: Uncovering Mutiny on the Cyberseas," *Trial* 32 (1996): 24–31.

79. Comprehensive Crime Control Act of 1984, Pub. L. No. 98-473, 2101-03, 98 Stat. 1837, 2190 (1984), adding 18 USC 1030 (1984). Amended by Pub. L. No. 99-474, 100 Stat. 1213 (1986) codified at 18 U.S.C. 1030 (Supp. V 1987).

80. 18 U.S.C. section 1030 (1994).

81. Copyright Infringement Act 17 U.S.C. section 506(a) 1994.

82. 18 U.S.C. 2510–2520 (1988 and Supp. II 1990).

83. "Project: Eighth Survey of White-Collar Crime," *American Criminal Law Review* 30 (1993): 501.

84. Herbert Edelhertz and Charles Rogovin, eds., *A National Strategy for Containing White-Collar Crime* (Lexington, MA: Lexington Books, 1980), Appendix A, pp. 122–123.

85. Kathleen Daly, "Gender and Varieties of White-Collar Crime," *Criminology* 27 (1989): 769–793.

86. Donald Cressey, *Other People's Money: A Study of the Social Psychology of Embezzlement* (Glencoe, IL: Free Press, 1973).

87. Ibid., p. 96.

88. Travis Hirschi and Michael Gottfredson, "Causes of White-Collar Crime," *Criminology* 25 (1987): 949–974.

89. Michael Gottfredson and Travis Hirschi, *A General Theory of Crime* (Stanford, CA: Stanford University Press, 1990), p. 191.

90. This section relies heavily on Daniel Skoler, "White-Collar Crime and the Criminal Justice System: Problems and Challenges," in *A National Strategy for Containing White-Collar Crime*, ed. Herbert Edelhertz and Charles Rogovin (Lexington, MA: Lexington Books, 1980), pp. 57–76.

91. Theodore Hammett and Joel Epstein, *Prosecuting Environmental Crime: Los Angeles County* (Washington, DC: National Institute of Justice, 1993).

92. Michael Benson, Francis Cullen, and William Maakestad, "Local Prosecutors and Corporate Crime," *Crime and Delinquency* 36 (1990): 356–372.

93. Ibid., pp. 369–370.

94. David Simon and D. Stanley Eitzen, *Elite Deviance* (Boston: Allyn and Bacon, 1982), p. 28.

95. This section relies heavily on Albert Reiss, Jr., "Selecting Strategies of Social Control over Organizational Life," in *Enforcing Regulation*, ed. Keith Hawkins and John M. Thomas (Boston: Klowver, 1984), pp. 25–37.

96. John Braithwaite, "The Limits of Economism in Controlling Harmful Corporate Conduct," *Law and Society Review* 16 (1981–1982): 481–504.

97. Associated Press, "Idaho Plant to Pay $11.8M Fine," *New York Times,* 17 October 1998, p. C2.

98. Michael Benson, "Emotions and Adjudication: Status Degradation Among White-Collar Criminals," *Justice Quarterly* 7 (1990): 515–528; John Braithwaite, *Crime, Shame and Reintegration* (Sydney: Cambridge University Press, 1989).

99. Raymond Michalowski and Ronald Kramer, "The Space Between Laws: The Problem of Corporate Crime in a Transnational Context," *Social Problems* 34 (1987): 34–53.

100. Steven Klepper and Daniel Nagin, "The Deterrent Effect of Perceived Certainty and Severity of Punishment Revisited," *Criminology* 27 (1989): 721–746.

101. Geis, "White-Collar and Corporate Crime," p. 154.

102. Christopher M. Brown and Nikhil S. Singhvi, "Antitrust Violations," *American Criminal Law Review* 35 (1998): 467–501.

103. Howard Adler, "Current Trends in Criminal Antitrust Enforcement," *Business Crimes Bulletin* (April 1996): 1.

104. Robert Bennett, "Foreword," Eighth Survey of White-Collar Crime, *American Criminal Law Review* 30 (1993).

105. David Weisburd, Elin Waring, and Stanton Wheeler, "Class, Status, and the Punishment of White-Collar Criminals," *Law and Social Inquiry* 15 (1990): 223–243.

106. Mark Cohen, "Environmental Crime and Punishment: Legal/Economic Theory and Empirical Evidence on Enforcement of Federal Environmental Statutes," *Journal of Criminal Law and Criminology* 82 (1992): 1054–1109.

107. Frank Pearce and Steve Tombs, "Hazards, Law and Class: Contextualizing the Regulation of Corporate Crime," *Social and Legal Studies* 6 (1997): 79–107, at p. 92.

108. See, generally, President's Commission on Organized Crime, Report to the President and the Attorney General, *The Impact: Organized Crime Today* (Washington, DC: U.S. Government Printing Office, 1986). Hereafter cited as *Organized Crime Today.*

109. Frederick Martens and Michele Cunningham-Niederer, "Media Magic, Mafia Mania," *Federal Probation* 49 (1985): 60–68.

110. *Organized Crime Today,* pp. 7–8.

111. Alan Block and William Chambliss, *Organizing Crime* (New York: Elsevier, 1981).

112. *Organized Crime Today,* p. 462.

113. Attorney General's Commission on Pornography, *Final Report* (Washington, DC: U.S. Government Printing Office, 1986), p. 1053.

114. Alan Block, *East Side/West Side* (New Brunswick, NJ: Transaction Books, 1983), pp. vii, 10–11.

115. G. R. Blakey and M. Goldsmith, "Criminal Redistribution of Stolen Property: The Need for Law Reform," *Michigan Law Review* 81 (August 1976): 45–46.

116. Donald Cressey, *Theft of the Nation* (New York: Harper and Row, 1969).

117. *Organized Crime Today,* p. 489.

118. Dwight Smith, *The Mafia Mystique* (New York: Basic Books, 1975).

119. Philip Jenkins and Gary Potter, "The Politics and Mythology of Organized Crime: A Philadelphia Case Study," *Journal of Criminal Justice* 15 (1987): 473–484.

120. Block, *East Side/West Side.*

121. *Organized Crime Today,* p. 11.

122. Omar Bartos, "Growth of Russian Organized Crime Poses Serious Threat," *CJ International* 11 (1995): 8–9.

123. Peter Kerr, "Chinese Now Dominate New York Heroin Trade," *New York Times,* 9 August 1987, p. 1.

124. Robert Kelly and Rufus Schatzberg, "Types of Minority Organized Crime: Some Considerations," paper presented at the annual meeting of the American Society of Criminology, Montreal, November 1987.

125. Jenkins and Potter, "The Politics and Mythology of Organized Crime."

126. William Chambliss, *On the Take* (Bloomington: Indiana University Press, 1978).

127. 18 U.S.C. 1952 (1976).

128. Pub. L. No. 91-452, Title IX, 84 Stat. 922 (1970) (codified at 18 U.S.C. 1961–68, 1976).

129. Selwyn Raab, "A Battered and Ailing Mafia Is Losing Its Grip on America," *New York Times,* 22 October 1990, p. B1.

130. Ibid.

131. Ibid., p. B7.

Chapter 13

1. Dan Barry and Carol Cogel, "Giuliani Vows to Cut Subsidy Over Art He Calls Offensive," *New York Times,* 23 September 1999, p. 1; David Barstow, "Brooklyn Museum Official Discussed Removing an Offending Work," *New York Times,* 28 September 1999, p. 1; David Barstow, "Exhibit Was Heavily Financed by Those with Much to Gain," *New York Times,* 31 October 1999, p. 1; David Barstow, "Giuliani Is Ordered to Halt Attacks Against Museum," *New York Times,* 2 November 1999, p. 1.

2. Edwin Schur, *Crimes Without Victims* (Englewood Cliffs, NJ: Prentice-Hall, 1965).

3. Andrea Dworkin, quoted in "Where Do We Stand on Pornography?" *Ms* (January–February 1994), p. 34.

4. Jennifer Williard, *Juvenile Prostitution* (Washington, DC: National Victim Resource Center, 1991).

5. Morris Cohen, "Moral Aspects of the Criminal Law," *Yale Law Journal* 49 (1940): 1017.

6. See Joel Feinberg, *Social Philosophy* (Englewood Cliffs, NJ: Prentice-Hall, 1973), chap. 2, 3.

7. *United States* v. *12 200-ft Reels of Super 8mm Film,* 413 U.S. 123 (1973) at 137.

8. Irving Kristol, "Liberal Censorship and the Common Culture," *Society* 36 (September 1999): 5.

9. Wayne La Fave and Austin Scott, Jr., *Criminal Law* (St. Paul, MN: West, 1986), p. 12.

10. Ibid.

11. Howard Becker, *Outsiders* (New York: Macmillan, 1963), pp. 13–14.

12. Judd Marmor, "The Multiple Roots of Homosexual Behavior," in *Homosexual Behavior,* ed. J. Marmor (New York: Basic Books, 1980), p. 5.

13. J. Money, "Sin, Sickness, or Status? Homosexual Gender Identity and Psychoneuroendocrinology," *American Psychologist* 42 (1987): 384–399.

14. J. McNeil, *The Church and the Homosexual* (Kansas City, MO: Sheed, Andrews, and McNeel, 1976).

15. Laurie Goodstein, "The Architect of the 'Gay Conversion' Campaign," *New York Times,* 13 August 1998, p. A10.

16. Marmor, "The Multiple Roots of Homosexual Behavior," pp. 18–19.

17. Ibid., p. 19.

18. Henry Adams, Lester Wright, and Bethany Lohr, "Is Homophobia Associated with Homosexual Arousal?" *Journal of Abnormal Psychology* 105 (1996): 440–445.

19. Elsa Arnett, "Efforts Grow to Cap Gay-Rights Gains," *Boston Globe,* 12 April 1998, p. A10.

20. 376 U.S. 660; 82 S.Ct. 1417; 8 L.Ed.2d 758 (1962).

21. Arnett, "Efforts Grow to Cap Gay-Rights Gains."

22. *Romer* v. *Evans,* 517 U.S. 620 (1996).

23. *Equality Foundation of Greater Cincinnati* v. *City of Cincinnati,* No. 97–1795, 1998.

24. F. Inbau, J. Thompson, and J. Zagel, *Criminal Law and Its Administration* (Mineola, NY: Foundation Press, 1974), p. 287.

25. *Bowers* v. *Hardwick,* 106 S.Ct. 2841 (1986); reh. den. 107 S.Ct. 29 (1986).

26. Georgia Code Ann. 16–6–2 (1984).

27. American Law Institute, Model Penal Code, Section 207.5.

28. Gary Caplan, "Fourteenth Amendment—The Supreme Court Limits the Right to Privacy," *Journal of Criminal Law and Criminology* 77 (1986): 894–930.

29. John Biskupic, "Justice Let Stand 'Don't Ask, Don't Tell' Policy," *Boston Globe,* 22 October 1996, p. A6.

30. Michael Joseph Gross, "A Problem with Privacy, and with Openness," *Boston Globe,* 15 February 1998, p. C3.

31. Associated Press, "Court Gives Sons Back to Gay Father," *Boston Globe,* 16 October 1996, p. A5.

32. National Gay and Lesbian Task Force, "Eye on Equality: Pride and Public Opinion," press release, 5 July 1998.

33. Mireya Navarro, "Miami Restores Gay Rights Law," *New York Times,* 2 December 1998, p. B1.

34. American Civil Liberties Union, press release, 23 November 1998.

35. Reuters, "Belgians Promise to Clean Up Courts," *Boston Globe,* 22 October 1996, p. A17.

36. See, generally, Spencer Rathus and Jeffery Nevid, *Abnormal Psychology* (Englewood Cliffs, NJ: Prentice-Hall, 1991), pp. 373–411.

37. W. P. de Silva, "Sexual Variations," *British Medical Journal* 318 (1999): 654–655.

38. Kathy Smiljanich and John Briere, "Self-Reported Sexual Interest in Children: Sex Differences and Psychosocial Correlates in a University Sample," *Violence and Victims* 11 (1996): 39–50.

39. See, generally, V. Bullogh, *Sexual Variance in Society and History* (Chicago: University of Chicago Press, 1958), pp. 143–144.

40. Spencer Rathus, *Human Sexuality* (New York: Holt, Rinehart and Winston, 1983), p. 463.

41. Charles McCaghy, *Deviant Behavior* (New York: Macmillan, 1976), pp. 348–349.

42. Monica Prasad, "The Morality of Market Exchange: Love, Money, and Contractual Justice," *Sociological Perspectives* 42 (1999): 181–187.

43. Cited in McCaghy, *Deviant Behavior.*

44. FBI, *Crime in the United States, 1997,* p. 222.

45. Michael Waldholz, "HTLV–I Virus Found in Blood of Prostitutes," *Wall Street Journal,* 5 January 1990, p. B2.

46. FBI, *Crime in the United States, 1992,* p. 172.

47. Charles Winick and Paul Kinsie, *The Lively Commerce* (Chicago: Quadrangle, 1971), p. 58.

48. Mark-David Janus, Barbara Scanlon, and Virginia Price, "Youth Prostitution," in *Child Pornography and Sex Rings*, ed. Ann Wolbert Burgess (Lexington, MA: Lexington Books, 1989), pp. 127–146.

49. Jennifer James, "Prostitutes and Prostitution," in *Deviants: Voluntary Action in a Hostile World*, ed. E. Sagarin and F. Montanino (New York: Scott, Foresman, 1977), p. 384.

50. Winick and Kinsie, *The Lively Commerce*, pp. 172–173.

51. Paul Goldstein, "Occupational Mobility in the World of Prostitution: Becoming a Madam," *Deviant Behavior* 4 (1983): 267–279.

52. Associated Press, "Mob Seen in Las Vegas Sex Trade," *New York Times*, 17 October 1998, p. A7.

53. Goldstein, "Occupational Mobility in the World of Prostitution," pp. 267–270.

54. Mireya Navarro, "Group Forced Illegal Aliens into Prostitution, U.S. Says," *New York Times*, 24 April 1998, p. A10.

55. D. Kelly Weisberg, *Children of the Night: A Study of Adolescent Prostitution* (Lexington, MA: Lexington Books, 1985), pp. 44–55.

56. Gerald Hotaling and David Finkelhor, *The Sexual Exploitation of Missing Children* (Washington, DC: U.S. Department of Justice, 1988).

57. N. Jackman, Richard O'Toole, and Gilbert Geis, "The Self-Image of the Prostitute," in *Sexual Deviance*, ed. J. Gagnon and W. Simon (New York: Harper and Row, 1967), pp. 152–153.

58. Weisberg, *Children of the Night*, p. 98.

59. Paul Gebhard, "Misconceptions about Female Prostitutes," *Medical Aspects of Human Sexuality* 3 (July 1969): 28–30.

60. James, "Prostitutes and Prostitution," pp. 388–389.

61. Andrea Dworkin, *Pornography* (New York: Dutton, 1989).

62. Annette Jolin, "On the Backs of Working Prostitutes: Feminist Theory and Prostitution Policy," *Crime and Delinquency* 40 (1994): 60–83, at pp. 76–77.

63. *Merriam-Webster Dictionary* (New York: Pocket Books, 1974), p. 484.

64. Attorney General's Commission, Report on Pornography, *Final Report* (Washington, DC: U.S. Government Printing Office, 1986), pp. 837–901. Hereafter cited as Pornography Commission.

65. John Hurst, "Children—A Big Profit Item for the Smut Peddlers," *Los Angeles Times*, 26 May 1977, cited in *Take Back the Night*, ed. Laura Lederer (New York: William Morrow, 1980), pp. 77–78.

66. Albert Belanger et al., "Typology of Sex Rings Exploiting Children," in *Child Pornography and Sex Rings*, ed. Ann Wolbert Burgess (Lexington, MA: Lexington Books, 1984), pp. 51–81.

67. *Report of the Commission on Obscenity and Pornography* (Washington, DC: U.S. Government Printing Office, 1970).

68. Pornography Commission, pp. 837–902.

69. Berl Kutchinsky, "The Effect of Easy Availability of Pornography on the Incidence of Sex Crimes," *Journal of Social Issues* 29 (1973): 95–112.

70. Michael Goldstein, "Exposure to Erotic Stimuli and Sexual Deviance," *Journal of Social Issues* 29 (1973): 197–219.

71. John Court, "Sex and Violence: A Ripple Effect," *Pornography and Aggression*, ed. Neal Malamuth and Edward Donnerstein (Orlando, FL: Academic Press, 1984).

72. See Edward Donnerstein, Daniel Linz, and Steven Penrod, *The Question of Pornography* (New York: Free Press, 1987).

73. Edward Donnerstein, "Pornography and Violence Against Women," *Annals of the New York Academy of Science* 347 (1980): 277–288; E. Donnerstein and J. Hallam, "Facilitating Effects of Erotica on Aggression Against Women," *Journal of Personality and Social Psychology* 36 (1977): 1270–1277; Seymour Fishbach and Neil Malamuth, "Sex and Aggression: Proving the Link," *Psychology Today* 12 (1978): 111–122.

74. Don Smith, "Sexual Aggression in American Pornography: The Stereotype of Rape," paper presented at the annual meeting of the American Sociological Association, Salt Lake City, August 1976.

75. 354 U.S. 476; 77 S.Ct. 1304 (1957).

76. 413 U.S. 15 (1973).

77. R. George Wright, "Defining Obscenity: The Criterion of Value," *New England Law Review* 22 (1987): 315–341.

78. *Pope v. Illinois*, 107 S.Ct. 1918 (1987).

79. Anthony Flint, "Skin Trade Spreading Across U.S.," *Boston Globe*, 1 December 1996, pp. 1, 36–37.

80. Bob Cohn, "The Trials of Adam and Eve," *Newsweek*, 7 January 1991, p. 48.

81. Thomas J. Lueck, "At Sex Shops, Fear That Ruling Means the End Is Near," *New York Times*, 25 February 1998, p. 1.

82. David Rohde, "In Giuliani's Crackdown on Porn Shops, Court Ruling Is a Setback," *New York Times*, 29 August 1998, p. A11.

83. Ann Landers, "Pornography Can Be an Addiction," *Boston Globe*, 19 July 1993, p. D36.

84. Ann Landers, "Husband Is Obsessed with Internet Porn," *Boston Globe*, 22 May 1998, p. D12.

85. Joseph Scott, "Violence and Erotic Material: The Relationship Between Adult Entertainment and Rape," paper presented at the annual meeting of the American Association for the Advancement of Science, Los Angeles, 1985.

86. Flint, "Skin Trade Spreading Across U.S."

87. ACLU, *Reno v. ACLU*, No. 96–511.

88. ACLU, "Supreme Court Rules: Cyberspace Will be Free! ACLU Hails Victory in Internet Censorship Challenge," news release, 26 June 1997.

89. ACLU, "*ACLU v. Reno*, Round 2: Broad Coalition Files Challenge to New Federal Net Censorship Law," news release, 22 October 1998.

90. Ralph Weisheit, "Studying Drugs in Rural Areas: Notes from the Field," *Journal of Research in Crime and Delinquency* 30 (1993): 213–232.

91. "British Officials Report Skyrocketing Heroin Use," *Alcoholism & Drug Abuse Weekly* 10 (17 August 1998): 7; National Institute on Drug Abuse, Community Epidemiology Work Group, *Epidemiological Trends in Drug Abuse, Advance Report* (Washington, DC: National Institute on Drug Abuse, 1997).

92. Substance Abuse and Mental Health Services Administration (SAMHSA), *Mid-Year 1999 Preliminary Emergency Data from the Drug Abuse Warning Network* (Rockville, MD: SAMHSA, March 2000).

93. Arnold Trebach, *The Heroin Solution* (New Haven, CT: Yale University Press, 1982).

94. James Inciardi, *The War on Drugs* (Palo Alto, CA: Mayfield, 1986), p. 2.

95. See, generally, David Pittman, "Drug Addiction and Crime," in *Handbook of Criminology*, ed. D. Glazer (Chicago: Rand McNally, 1974), pp. 209–232; Board of Directors, National Council on Crime and Delinquency, "Drug Addiction: A Medical, Not a Law Enforcement, Problem," *Crime and Delinquency* 20 (1974): 4–9.

96. Associated Press, "Records Detail Royals' Turn-of-Century Drug Use," *Boston Globe*, 29 August 1993, p. 13.

97. See Edwin Brecher, *Licit and Illicit Drugs* (Boston: Little, Brown, 1972).

98. James Inciardi, *Reflections on Crime* (New York: Holt, Rinehart and Winston, 1978), pp. 8–10; see also A. Greeley, William McCready, and Gary Theisen, *Ethnic Drinking Subcultures* (New York: Praeger, 1980).

99. Joseph Gusfield, *Symbolic Crusade* (Urbana: University of Illinois Press, 1963), chap. 3.

100. McCaghy, *Deviant Behavior*, p. 280.

101. McCaghy, *Deviant Behavior*.

102. The annual survey is conducted by Lloyd Johnston, Jerald Bachman, and Patrick O'Malley of the Institute of Social Research, University of Michigan, Ann Arbor.

103. C. Bowden, "Determinants of Initial Use of Opioids," *Comprehensive Psychiatry* 12 (1971): 136–140.

104. Marvin Krohn, Alan Lizotte, Terence Thornberry, Carolyn Smith, and David McDowall, "Reciprocal Causal Relationships Among Drug Use, Peers, and Beliefs: A Five-Wave Panel Model," *Journal of Drug Issues* 26 (1996): 205–228.

105. R. Cloward and L. Ohlin, *Delinquency and Opportunity: A Theory of Delinquent Gangs* (Glencoe, IL: Free Press, 1960).

106. Lening Zhang, John Welte, and William Wieczorek, "Youth Gangs, Drug Use and Delinquency," *Journal of Criminal Justice* 27 (1999): 101–109.

107. Rathus and Nevid, *Abnormal Psychology*, p. 361.

108. Spencer Rathus, *Psychology* (New York: Harcourt Brace Jovanovich, 1986), p. 158.

109. Substance Abuse and Mental Health Services Administration, Office of Applied Studies, "The Relationship Between Mental Health and Substance Abuse Among Adolescents," Analytic Series: A-9, 1999.

110. Alison Bass, "Mental Ills, Drug Abuse Linked," *Boston Globe*, 21 November 1990, p. 3.

111. D. W. Goodwin, "Alcoholism and Genetics," *Archives of General Psychiatry* 42 (1985): 171–174.

112. For a thorough review of this issue, see John Petraitis, Brian Flay, and Todd Miller, "Reviewing Theories of Adolescent Substance Use: Organizing Pieces in the Puzzle," *Psychological Bulletin* 117 (1995): 67–86.

113. Judith Brooks and Li-Jung Tseng, "Influences of Parental Drug Use, Personality, and Child Rearing on the Toddler's Anger and Negativity," *Genetic, Social and General Psychology Monographs* 122 (1996): 107–128.

114. Thomas Ashby Wills, Donato Vaccaro, Grace McNamara, and A. Elizabeth Hirky, "Escalated Substance Use: A Longitudinal Grouping Analysis from Early to Middle Adolescence," *Journal of Abnormal Psychology* 105 (1996): 166–180.

115. Denise Kandel and Mark Davies, "Friendship Networks, Intimacy, and Illicit Drug Use in Young Adulthood: A Comparison of Two Competing Theories," *Criminology* 29 (1991): 441–471.

116. J. S. Mio, G. Nanjundappa, D. E. Verlur, and M. D. DeRios, "Drug Abuse and the Adolescent Sex Offender: A Preliminary Analysis," *Journal of Psychoactive Drugs* 18 (1986): 65–72.

117. D. Baer and J. Corrado, "Heroin Addict Relationships with Parents During Childhood and Early Adolescent Years," *Journal of Genetic Psychology* 124 (1974): 99–103.

118. John Wallace and Jerald Bachman, "Explaining Racial/Ethnic Differences in Adolescent Drug Use: The Impact of Background and Lifestyle," *Social Problems* 38 (1991): 333–357.

119. John Donovan, "Problem-Behavior Theory and the Explanation of Adolescent Marijuana Use," *Journal of Drug Issues* 26 (1996): 379–404.

120. A. Christiansen, G. T. Smith, P. V. Roehling, and M. S. Goldman, "Using Alcohol Expectancies to Predict Adolescent Drinking Behavior After One Year," *Journal of Counseling and Clinical Psychology* 57 (1989): 93–99.

121. Icek Ajzen, *Attitudes, Personality and Behavior* (Homewood, IL: Dorsey Press, 1988).

122. Judith Brook, Martin Whiteman, Elinor Balka, and Beatrix Hamburg, "African-American and Puerto Rican Drug Use: Personality, Familial, and Other Environmental Risk Factors," *Genetic, Social, and General Psychology Monographs* 118 (1992): 419–438.

123. Andrew Golub and Bruce Johnson, "The Multiple Paths Through Alcohol, Tobacco and Marijuana to Hard Drug Use Among Arrestees," paper presented at the annual meeting of the American Society of Criminology, San Diego, November 1997.

124. Inciardi, *The War on Drugs*, p. 60.

125. Marvin Dawkins, "Drug Use and Violent Crime Among Adolescents," *Adolescence* 32 (1997): 395–406.

126. U.S. Department of Justice, "Four in Ten Criminal Offenders Report Alcohol as a Factor in Violence," press release, 5 April 1998.

127. Eric Baumer, Janet Lauritsen, Richard Rosenfeld, and Richard Wright, "The Influence of Crack Cocaine on Robbery, Burglary, and Homicide Rates: A Cross-City, Longitudinal Analysis," *Journal of Research in Crime and Delinquency* 35 (1998): 316–340; Carolyn Rebecca Block and Antigone Christakos, "Intimate Partner Homicide in Chicago over 29 Years," *Crime and Delinquency* 41 (1995): 496–526.

128. George Speckart and M. Douglas Anglin, "Narcotics Use and Crime: An Overview of Recent Research Advances," *Contemporary Drug Problems* 13 (1986): 741–769; Charles Faupel and Carl Klockars, "Drugs–Crime Connections: Elaborations from the Life Histories of Hard-Core Heroin Addicts," *Social Problems* 34 (1987): 54–68.

129. M. Douglas Anglin, Elizabeth Piper Deschenes, and George Speckart, "The Effect of Legal Supervision on Narcotic Addiction and Criminal Behavior," paper presented at the annual meeting of the American Society of Criminology, Montreal, November 1987, p. 2.

130. Speckart and Anglin, "Narcotics Use and Crime," p. 752.

131. Arrestee Drug Abuse Monitoring Program (ADAM), *1999 Annual Report on Drug Use Among Adult and Juvenile Arrestees* (Washington, DC: National Institute of Justice, 2000).

132. Paul Goldstein, "The Drugs–Violence Nexus: A Tripartite Conceptual Framework," *Journal of Drug Issues* 15 (1985): 493–506; Marvin Krohn, Alan Lizotte, and Cynthia Perez, "The Interrelationship Between Substance Use and Precocious Transitions to Adult Sexuality," *Journal of Health and Social Behavior* 38 (1997): 87–103, at p. 88; Richard Jessor, "Risk Behavior in Adolescence: A Psychosocial Framework for Understanding and Action," in *Adolescents at Risk: Medical and Social Perspectives*, ed. D. E. Rogers and E. Ginzburg (Boulder, CO: Westview, 1992).

133. See Kenneth Jones, Louis Shainberg, and Carter Byer, *Drugs and Alcohol* (New York: Harper and Row, 1979) pp. 137–146.

134. Controlled Substance Act, 21 U.S.C. 848 (1984).

135. Anti–Drug Abuse Act of 1986, Pub. L. No. 99-570, U.S.C. 841 (1986).

136. Anti–Drug Abuse Act of 1988, Pub. L. No. 100-690; 21 U.S.C. 1501; Subtitle A—Death Penalty, Sec. 7001, Amending the Controlled Substances Abuse Act, 21 U.S.C. 848.

137. "New Drunken Driver Law Shows Results in California," *Omaha World Herald*, 26 May 1982, p. 34.

138. Faye Silas, "Gimme the Keys," *ABA Journal* 71 (1985): 36.

139. Eric Jensen, Jurg Gerber, and Ginna Babcock, "The New War on Drugs: Grass Roots Movement or Political Construction?" *Journal of Drug Issues* 21 (1991): 651–667.

140. U.S. Department of State, *1998 International Narcotics Control Strategy Report*, February 1999.

141. Clifford Krauss, "Neighbors Worry About Colombian Aid," *New York Times*, 25 August 2000, p. A3.

142. David Hayeslip, "Local-Level Drug Enforcement: New Strategies," *NIJ Reports* (March/April 1989): 1.

143. Mark Moore, *Drug Trafficking* (Washington, DC: National Institute of Justice, 1988).

144. Carol Kaplan, *Sentencing and Time Served* (Washington, DC: Bureau of Justice Statistics, 1987).

145. Ibid., p. 2.

146. Peter Rossi, Richard Berk, and Alec Campbell, "Just Punishments: Guideline Sentences and Normative Consensus," *Journal of Quantitative Criminology* 13 (1997): 267–283.

147. Robert Davis, Arthur Lurigio, and Dennis Rosenbaum, eds., *Drugs and the Community* (Springfield, IL: Charles Thomas, 1993), pp. xii–xv.

148. Saul Weingart, "A Typology of Community Responses to Drugs," in *Drugs and the Community*, ed. Robert Davis, Arthur Lurigio, and Dennis Rosenbaum (Springfield, IL: Charles Thomas, 1993), pp. 85–105.

149. Earl Wyson, Richard Aniskiewicz, and David Wright, "Truth and DARE: Tracking Drug Education to Graduation as Symbolic Politics," *Social Problems* 41 (1994): 448–471.

150. Ibid.

151. Dennis Rosenbaum, Robert Flewelling, Susan Bailey, Chris Ringwalt, and Deanna Wilkinson, "Cops in the Classroom: A Longitudinal Evaluation of Drug Abuse Resistance Education (DARE)," *Journal of Research in Crime and Delinquency* 31 (1994): 3–31.

152. Mareanne Zawitz, *Drugs, Crime, and the Justice System* (Washington, DC: U.S. Government Printing Office, 1992), pp. 115–122.

153. John Goldkamp and Peter Jones, "Pretrial Drug-Testing Experiments in Milwaukee and Prince George's County: The Context of Implementation," *Journal of Research in Crime and Delinquency* 29 (1992): 430–465; Chester Britt, Michael Gottfredson, and John Goldkamp, "Drug Testing and Pretrial Misconduct: An Experiment on the Specific Deterrent Effects of Drug Monitoring Defendants on Pretrial Release," *Journal of Research in Crime and Delinquency* 29 (1992): 62–78.

154. See, generally, Peter Greenwood and Franklin Zimring, *One More Chance* (Santa Monica, CA: Rand Corporation, 1985).

155. Eli Ginzberg, Howard Berliner, and Miriam Ostrow, *Young People at Risk: Is Prevention Possible?* (Boulder, CO: Westview, 1988), p. 99.

156. Michael French, H. J. Jeanne Salome, Jody Sindelar, and A. Thomas McLellan, "Benefit–Cost Analysis of Ancillary Social Services in Publicly Supported Addiction Treatment," 1 February 1999, data supplied by the Center for Substance Abuse Research (CESAR), College Park, MD 20740.

157. The following section is based on material found in Jerome Platt, "Vocational Rehabilitation of Drug Abusers," *Psychological Bulletin* 117 (1995): 416–433.

158. Ernest Drucker, "Drug Prohibition and Public Health: 25 Years of Evidence," *Public Health Reports* 114 (1999): 14–15.

159. Charlie LeDuff, "Cocaine Quietly Reclaims Its Hold as Good Times Return," *New York Times*, 21 August 2000, p. A1.

160. Ethan Nadelmann, "America's Drug Problem," *Bulletin of the American Academy of Arts and Sciences* 65 (1991): 24–40.

161. Ibid., p. 24.

162. Ethan Nadelmann, "Should We Legalize Drugs? History Answers Yes," *American Heritage* (February/March 1993): 41–56.

163. See, generally, Ralph Weisheit, *Drugs, Crime and the Criminal Justice System* (Cincinnati: Anderson, 1990).

164. David Courtwright, "Should We Legalize Drugs? History Answers No," *American Heritage* (February/March 1993): 43–56.

165. Kathryn Ann Farr, "Revitalizing the Drug Decriminalization Debate," *Crime and Delinquency* 36 (1990): 223–237.

Chapter 14

1. *Riggs* v. *California*, No. 98–5021 (1999).

2. For a detailed analysis of this work, see Samuel Walker, "Origins of the Contemporary Criminal Justice Paradigm: The American Bar Foundation Survey, 1953–1969," *Justice Quarterly* 9 (1992): 47–76.

3. President's Commission on Law Enforcement and the Administration of Justice, *The Challenge of Crime in a Free Society* (Washington, DC: U.S. Government Printing Office, 1967).

4. See Public Law 90-351, Title I—Omnibus Crime Control Safe Streets Act of 1968, 90th Congress, June 19, 1968.

5. Lea S. Gifford, *Justice Expenditure and Employment in the United States, 1995* (Washington, DC: Bureau of Justice Statistics, November 1999).

6. Federal Bureau of Investigation, *Crime in the United States, 1995* (Washington, DC: U.S. Government Printing Office, 1996), p. 208.

7. Jeffrey Butts, *Offenders in Juvenile Court, 1994* (Washington, DC: Office of Juvenile Justice and Delinquency Prevention, 1996).

8. Patrick A. Langan and Jodi M. Brown, *Felony Sentences in State Courts, 1994* (Washington, DC: Bureau of Justice Statistics, 1997).

9. U.S. Department of Justice, "Nation's Probation and Parole Population Reached New High Last Year," press release, 16 August 1998.

10. See Albert Reiss, *Police and the Public* (New Haven, CT: Yale University Press, 1972).

11. American Bar Association, *Standards Relating to the Urban Police Function* (New York: Institute of Judicial Administration, 1973), Standard 2.2, p. 9.

12. Kenneth L. Davis, *Police Discretion* (St. Paul, MN: West, 1975).

13. See Peter Manning and John Van Maanen, eds., *Policing: A View from the Streets* (Santa Monica, CA: Goodyear, 1978).

14. Patrick A. Langan and Jodi M. Brown, *Felony Sentences in State Courts, 1994* (Washington, DC: Bureau of Justice Statistics, 1997).

15. *Powell* v. *Alabama*, 287 U.S. 45, 53 S.Ct. 55, 77 L.Ed. 158 (1932); *Gideon* v. *Wainwright*, 372 U.S. 335, 83 S.Ct. 792, 9 L.Ed. 2d 799 (1963); *Argersinger* v. *Hamlin*, 407 U.S. 25, 92 S.Ct. 2006, 32 L.Ed. 2d 530 (1972).

16. Herbert L. Packer, *The Limits of the Criminal Sanction* (Stanford, CA: Stanford University Press, 1968), p. 159.

17. Barbara Boland, Catherine Conly, Paul Mahanna, Lynn Warner, and Ronald Sones, *The Prosecution of Felony Arrests, 1987* (Washington, DC: Bureau of Justice Statistics, 1990), p. 3.

18. See Donald Newman, *Conviction: The Determination of Guilt or Innocence without Trial* (Boston: Little, Brown, 1966).

19. Paul Cassell, "How Many Criminals Has Miranda Set Free?" *Wall Street Journal*, 1 March 1995, p. A15.

20. David Garland, *Punishment and Modern Society* (Chicago: University of Chicago Press, 1990).

21. The most often cited of these is Douglas Lipton, Robert Martinson, and Judith Wilks, *The Effectiveness of Correctional Treatment: A Survey of Treatment Evaluation Studies* (New York: Praeger, 1975).

22. "Many State Legislatures Focused on Crime in 1995, Study Finds," *Criminal Justice Newsletter*, 17 January 1996, pp. 1–2.

23. Daniel Nagin, "Criminal Deterrence Research: A Review of the Evidence and a Research Agenda for the Outset of the 21st Century," in *Crime and Justice: An Annual Review*, ed. Michael Tonry (Chicago: University of Chicago Press, 1997), pp. 126–158.

24. Amy Thistlewaite, John Wooldredge, and David Gibbs, "Severity of Dispositions and Domestic Violence Recidivism," *Crime and Delinquency* 44 (1998): 388–398.

25. "Crime and Punishment in America: 1997 Update," National Center for Policy Analysis, Dallas, 1997.

26. David Fogel, *We Are the Living Proof* (Cincinnati: Anderson, 1975). See also David Fogel, *Justice as Fairness* (Cincinnati: Anderson, 1980).

27. Travis Pratt, "Race and Sentencing: A Meta-Analysis of Conflicting Empirical Research Results," *Journal of Criminal Justice* 26 (1998): 513–525.

28. Packer, *The Limits of the Criminal Sanction*.

29. Eric Lotke, "Hobbling a Generation: Young African-American Men in Washington, D.C.'s Criminal Justice System—Five Years Later," *Crime and Delinquency* 44 (1998): 355–366.

30. Roy Austin and Mark Allen, "Racial Disparity in Arrest Rates as an Explanation of Racial Disparity in Commitment to Pennsylvania's Prisons," *Journal of Research in Crime and Delinquency* 37 (2000): 200–220.

31. Anthony Petrosino and Carolyn Petrosino, "The Public Safety Potential of Megan's Law in Massachusetts: An Assessment from a Sample of Criminal Sexual Psychopaths," *Crime and Delinquency* 43 (1999): 140–158; "New Laws Said to Raise Demands on Justice Information Systems," *Criminal Justice Newsletter*, 17 September 1996, pp. 3–4.

32. Jim Yardley, "Convicted in Murder Case, Man Cleared 7 Years Later," *New York Times*, 29 October 1998, p. 11.

33. "DNA Testing Has Exonerated 28 Prison Inmates, Study Finds," *Criminal Justice Newsletter*, 17 June 1996, p. 2.

34. Richard McCorkle, "Research Note: Punish and Rehabilitate? Public Attitudes Toward Six Common Crimes," *Crime and Delinquency* 39 (1993): 240–252.

35. For example, see D. A. Andrews, Ivan Zinger, R. D. Hoge, James Bonta, Paul Gendreau, and Francis Cullen, "Does Correctional Treatment Work? A Clinically-Relevant and Psychologically-Informed Meta-Analysis," *Criminology* 28 (1990): 369–404; Carol Garrett, "Effects of Residential Treatment on Adjudicated Delinquents: A Meta-Analysis," *Journal of Research in Crime and Delinquency* 22 (1985): 287–308.

36. Mark Lipsey and David Wilson, "Effective Intervention for Serious Juvenile Offenders: A Synthesis of Research," in *Serious and Violent Juvenile Offenders: Risk Factors and Successful Interventions*, ed. Rolf Loeber and David Farrington (Thousand Oaks, CA: Sage, 1998), pp. 39–53.

37. Francis Cullen, John Paul Wright, Shayna Brown, Melissa Moon, Michael Blankenship, and Brandon Applegate, "Public Support for Early Intervention Programs: Implications for a Progressive Policy Agenda," *Crime and Delinquency* 44 (1998): 187–204.

38. Shawn Bushway, "The Impact of an Arrest on the Job Stability of Young White American Men," *Journal of Research in Crime and Delinquency* 35 (1998): 454–479.

39. Edwin M. Lemert, "The Juvenile Court—Quest and Realities," in President's Commission on Law Enforcement and the Administration of Justice, *Task Force Report: Juvenile Delinquency and Youth Crime* (Washington, DC: U.S. Government Printing Office, 1967).

40. Craig Hemmens and Katherine Bennett, "Juvenile Curfews and the Courts: Judicial Response to a Not-So-New Crime Control Strategy," *Crime and Delinquency* 45 (1999): 99–121.

41. Mark Umbreit and Robert Coates, "Cross-Site Analysis of Victim–Offender Mediation in Four States," *Crime and Delinquency* 39 (1993): 565–585.

42. James Austin and Barry Krisberg, "The Unmet Promise of Alternatives to Incarceration," *Crime and Delinquency* 28 (1982): 3–19. For an alternative view, see Arnold Binder and Gilbert Geis, "Ad Populum Argumentation in Criminology: Juvenile Diversion as Rhetoric," *Criminology* 30 (1984): 309–333.

43. Herbert Bianchi, *Justice as Sanctuary* (Bloomington: Indiana University Press, 1994); Nils Christie, "Conflicts as Property," *British Journal of Criminology* 17 (1977) 1–15; L. Hulsman, "Critical Criminology and the Concept of Crime," *Contemporary Crises* 10 (1986): 63–80.

44. Larry Tifft, "Foreword," in Dennis Sullivan, *The Mask of Love* (Port Washington, NY: Kennikat Press, 1980), p. 6.

45. Robert Davis, Barbara Smith, and Laura Nickles, "The Deterrent Effect of Prosecuting Domestic Violence Misdemeanors," *Crime and Delinquency* 44 (1998): 434–442.

46. Christopher Cooper, "Patrol Police Officer Conflict Resolution Processes," *Journal of Criminal Justice* 25 (1997): 87–101.

47. Sharon Levrant, Francis Cullen, Betsy Fulton, and John Wozniak, "Reconsidering Restorative Justice: The Corruption of Benevolence Revisited," *Crime and Delinquency* 45 (1999): 3–27.

48. Elliott Currie, *Crime and Punishment in America* (New York: Henry Holt, 1998). See also Elliott Currie, *Confronting Crime: An American Challenge* (New York: Pantheon, 1985); Elliott Currie, *Reckoning: Drugs, the Cities, and the American Future* (New York: Hill and Wang, 1993).

GLOSSARY

acquaintance rape Forcible sex in which offender and victim are acquainted with one another.

active precipitation Aggressive or provocative behavior of victims that results in their victimization.

actual malice The state of mind assumed to exist when one person kills another without apparent provocation.

actus reus An illegal or "guilty" act. It may be an affirmative act, such as killing, or a failure to act when legally required to do so.

adolescent-limited Offender who follows the most common criminal trajectory, in which antisocial behavior peaks in adolescence and then diminishes.

adversary system U.S. method of criminal adjudication in which prosecution (the state) and defense (the accused) each try to bring forward evidence and arguments, with guilt or innocence ultimately decided by an impartial judge or jury.

affirmative tax evasion Willful and intentional nonpayment of taxes, as by concealing assets or income, making false entries, or destroying records; a felony.

aggravated assault An attack on another person for the purpose of inflicting severe bodily injury.

aging out (desistance) The fact that people commit less crime as they mature.

alien conspiracy theory The view that organized crime in the United States is controlled by the Mafia, centrally coordinated by a national committee that settles disputes, dictates policy, and assigns territory.

American Dream The goal of accumulating material goods and wealth through individual competition; the process of being socialized to pursue material success and to believe it is achievable.

androgens Male sex hormones.

anomie A lack of norms or clear social standards. Because of rapidly shifting moral values, the individual has few guides to what is socially acceptable.

anomie theory View that anomie results when socially defined goals (such as wealth and power) are universally mandated but access to legitimate means (such as education and job opportunities) is stratified by class and status.

antisocial personality Combination of traits, such as hyperactivity, impulsivity, hedonism, and inability to empathize with others, that make a person prone to deviant behavior and violence; also referred to as sociopathic or psychopathic personality.

appeal Taking a criminal case to a higher court on the grounds that the defendant was found guilty because of legal error or violation of consitutional rights; a successful appeal may result in a new trial.

appellate court Court that reviews trial court procedures to determine whether they have complied with accepted rules and constitutional doctrines.

arousal theory The view that people seek to maintain a preferred level of arousal, but vary in how they process sensory input. A need for high levels of environmental stimulation may lead to aggressive, violent behavior patterns.

arraignment The step in the criminal justice process when the accused is brought before the trial judge, formal charges are read, defendants are informed of their rights, a plea is entered, bail is considered, and a trial date is set.

arrest The taking into police custody of an individual suspected of a crime.

arson The willful, malicious burning of a home, building, or vehicle.

assault An attack that may not involve physical contact; includes attempted battery or intentionally frightening the victim by word or deed.

attention deficit/hyperactivity disorder (ADHD) A developmentally inappropriate lack of attention, along with impulsivity and hyperactivity.

authority conflict pathway Pathway to criminal deviance that begins at an early age with stubborn behavior and leads to defiance and then to authority avoidance.

bail A money bond intended to ensure that the accused will return for trial.

bank fraud To obtain money or property from a financial institution by false pretenses, as by forgery or misrepresentation.

battery A physical attack that includes hitting, punching, slapping, or other offensive touching of a victim.

behavior modeling Process of learning behavior (notably aggression) by observing others. Aggressive models may be par-ents, criminals in the neighborhood, or characters on television or in movies.

behavior theory The view that all human behavior is learned through a process of social reinforcement (rewards and punishment).

Bill of Rights The first 10 amendments to the U.S. Constitution, including guarantees against unreasonable search and seizure, self-incrimination, and cruel punishment.

biosocial theory Approach to criminology that focuses on the interaction between biological and social factors as they relate to crime.

bipolar disorder An emotional disturbance in which moods alternate between periods of wild elation and deep depression.

booking Fingerprinting, photographing, and recording of personal information of a suspect in police custody.

booster Professional shoplifter who steals with the intention of reselling stolen merchandise.

Brady law Federal law that imposes a five-day waiting period for gun purchases and provides an instant check on whether a prospective buyer is prohibited from purchasing a weapon.

brutalization effect The belief that capital punishment creates an atmosphere of brutality that enhances rather than deters the level of violence in society.

bucketing A form of stockbroker chiseling in which brokers skim customer trading profits by falsifying trade information.

burglary Entering a home by force, threat, or deception with intent to commit a crime.

capable guardians Effective deterrents to crime, such as police or watchful neighbors.

capital punishment The execution of criminal offenders; the death penalty.

carjacking Theft of a car by force or threat of force.

cheater theory A theory suggesting that a subpopulation of men has evolved with genes that incline them toward extremely low parental involvement. Sexually aggressive, they use deceit for sexual conquest of as many females as possible.

Chicago School Group of urban sociologists who studied the relation between environmental conditions and crime.

child abuse Physical or emotional trauma to a child with no reasonable explanation such as an accident or ordinary disciplinary practices.

child neglect Failure to provide a child with food, shelter, and basic care.

chiseling Regularly cheating an organization, its consumers, or both.

choice theory The school of thought holding that people choose to engage in delinquent and criminal behavior after weighing the consequences and benefits of their actions.

chronic offenders A small group of persistent offenders who account for a majority of all criminal offenses.

churning A form of stockbroker chiseling involving repeated, excessive, and unnecessary buying and selling of stock.

classical criminology The theoretical perspective suggesting that (1) people have free will to choose criminal or conventional behaviors; (2) people choose to commit crime for reasons of greed or personal need; and (3) crime can be controlled only by the fear of criminal sanctions.

Code of Hammurabi The first written criminal code, developed in Babylonia about 2000 B.C.

coercion External restraint.

cognitive theory Psychological perspective that focuses on mental processes: how people perceive and mentally represent the world around them and solve problems.

cohort A group of subjects that is studied over time.

collective efficacy Social control exerted by cohesive communities, based on mutual trust, including intervention in the supervision of children and maintenance of public order.

commitment to conformity A strong personal investment in conventional institutions, individuals, and processes that prevents people from engaging in behavior that might jeopardize their reputation and achievements.

common law Early English law, developed by judges, that became the standardized law of the land in England and eventually formed the basis of the criminal law in the United States.

compensation Financial aid awarded to crime victims to repay them for their loss and injuries; may cover medical bills, loss of wages, loss of future earnings, and/or counseling.

compliance strategies Fostering law conformity, cooperation, and self-policing in the business community through the use of economic incentives and administrative agencies.

concentration effect As working- and middle-class families flee inner-city poverty areas, the most disadvantaged population is consolidated in urban ghettos.

confidence game A swindle, usually involving a get-rich-quick scheme, often with illegal overtones, so that the victim will be afraid or embarrassed to call the police.

conflict theory The view that human behavior is shaped by interpersonal conflict and that those who maintain social power will use it to further their own ends.

conflict view The belief that criminal behavior is defined by those in a position of power to protect and advance their own self-interest.

consensus view The belief that the majority of citizens in a society share common values and agree on what behaviors should be defined as criminal.

constructive malice The state of mind assumed to exist when one person kills another as a result of an inherently dangerous act whose consequences could have been foreseen.

constructive possession A legal fiction that applies to situations in which persons voluntarily give up physical custody of their property but still retain legal ownership.

contextual discrimination A practice in which African Americans receive harsher punishments in some instances (as when they victimize whites) but not in others (as when they victimize other blacks).

control balance theory A developmental theory that attributes deviant and criminal behaviors to imbalances between the amount of control that the individual has over others and that others have over him or her.

corporate crime A legal offense, such as price fixing, restraint of trade, or hazardous waste dumping, committed by a corporate entity to improve its market share or profitability.

corporate culture view The view that some business organizations promote white-collar crime by maintaining a business climate that stresses profit over fair play.

courtroom work group Prosecution, defense, and judges working together to resolve criminal cases quickly and efficiently through plea bargaining.

covert pathway Pathway to a criminal career that begins with minor underhanded behavior, leads to property damage, and eventually escalates to more serious forms of theft and fraud.

crackdown The concentration of police resources on a particular problem area to eradicate or displace criminal activity.

crime An act, deemed socially harmful or dangerous, that is specifically defined, prohibited, and punished under the criminal law.

crime control model View that the overriding purpose of the justice system is to protect the public, deter criminal behavior, and incapacitate known criminals; favors speedy, efficient justice and punishment.

criminal justice system The agencies of government—police, courts, and corrections—responsible for apprehending, adjudicating, sanctioning, and treating criminal offenders.

criminal law The written code that defines crimes and their punishments.

criminology The scientific study of the nature, extent, cause, and control of criminal behavior.

crisis intervention Emergency counseling for crime victims.

cross-sectional research Interviewing or questioning a diverse sample of subjects, representing a cross-section of a community, at the same point in time.

cultural deviance theory Branch of social structure theory that sees strain and social disorganization together resulting in a unique lower-class culture that conflicts with conventional social norms.

cultural transmission Process whereby values, beliefs, and traditions are handed down from one generation to the next.

culture conflict Result of exposure to opposing norms, attitudes, and definitions of right and wrong, moral and immoral.

culture of poverty A separate lower-class culture, characterized by apathy, cynicism, helplessness, and mistrust of social institutions such as schools, government agencies, and the police, that is passed from one generation to the next.

cycle of violence Victims of crime, especially childhood abuse, are more likely to commit crime themselves.

date rape Forcible sex during a courting relationship.

deconstructionist Approach that focuses on the use of language by those in power to define crime based on their own values and biases; also called postmodernist.

defendant In criminal proceedings, the person accused of violating the law.

defense attorney The person responsible for protecting the constitutional rights of the accused and presenting the best possible legal defense; represents a defendant from initial arrest through trial, sentencing, and any appeal.

defensible space The principle that crime can be prevented or displaced by modifying the physical environment to reduce the opportunity individuals have to commit crime.

deliberation Planning a homicide after careful thought, however brief, rather than acting on sudden impulse.

delinquent subculture A value system adopted by lower-class youths that is directly opposed to that of the larger society.

demystify To unmask the true purpose of law, justice, or other social institutions.

determinate sentencing Principle that all offenders who commit the same crime should receive the same sentence.

deterrence strategies Detecting criminal violations, determining who is responsible, and penalizing the offenders to deter future violations.

developmental criminology A branch of criminology that examines changes in criminal careers over the life course.

developmental theory The view that criminality is a dynamic process, influenced by social experiences as well as individual characteristics.

deviance Behavior that departs from the social norm, but is not necessarily criminal.

deviance amplification Process whereby secondary deviance pushes offenders out of mainstream of society and locks them into an escalating cycle of deviance, apprehension, labeling, and criminal self-identity.

deviant place theory The view that victimization is primarily a function of where people live.

differential association theory The view that people commit crime when their social learning leads them to perceive more definitions favoring crime than favoring conventional behavior.

differential coercion theory A developmental theory that sees criminal behavior patterns as a function of the amount, type, and consistency of coercion that people experience.

differential opportunity The view that lower-class youths, whose legitimate opportunities are limited, join gangs and pursue criminal careers as alternative means to achieve universal success goals.

diffusion of benefits An effect that occurs when efforts to prevent one crime unintentionally prevent another, or when crime control efforts in one locale reduce crime in other nontarget areas.

discouragement An effect that occurs when limiting access to one target reduces other types of crime as well.

discretion The use of personal decision making by those carrying out police, judicial, and sanctioning functions within the criminal justice system.

disorder Any type of psychological problem (formerly labeled neurotic or psychotic), such as anxiety disorders, mood disorders, and conduct disorders.

displacement An effect of crime prevention efforts in which efforts to control crime in one area shift illegal activities to another.

disposition Sentencing of a defendant who has been found guilty; usually involves a fine, probation, and/or incarceration.

diversion programs Programs of rehabilitation that remove offenders from the normal channels of the criminal justice process, thus avoiding the stigma of a criminal label.

dizygotic (DZ) twins Fraternal (nonidentical) twins.

drift Movement in and out of delinquency, shifting between conventional and deviant values.

due process model View that focuses on protecting the civil rights of those accused of crime.

edgework The excitement or exhilaration of successfully executing illegal activities in dangerous situations.

ego The part of the personality, developed in early childhood, that helps con-

trol the id and keep people's actions within the boundaries of social convention.

embezzlement Taking and keeping the property of others, such as clients or employers, with which one has been entrusted.

enterprise Taking risks for profit in the marketplace.

equipotentiality The view that all humans are born with equal potential to learn and achieve.

exclusionary rule The rule that evidence against a defendant may not be presented in court if it was obtained in violation of the defendant's rights.

excuse defense Criminal defense based on a lack of criminal intent (*mens rea*). Excuse defenses include insanity, intoxication, and ignorance.

experimental research Manipulating or intervening in the lives of subjects to observe the outcome or effect of a specific intervention. True experiments usually include (1) random selection of subjects, (2) a control or comparison group, and (3) an experimental condition.

expressive crimes Offenses committed not for profit or gain but to vent rage, anger, or frustration.

expressive violence Violence that vents rage, anger, or frustration.

extinction The phenomenon in which a crime prevention effort has an immediate impact that then dissipates as criminals adjust to new conditions.

false pretenses Misrepresenting a fact in a way that causes a deceived victim to give money or property to the offender; fraud.

felony A serious offense that carries a penalty of imprisonment, usually for one year or more, and may entail loss of political rights.

felony murder A homicide in the context of another felony, such as robbery or rape; legally defined as first-degree murder.

fence A receiver of stolen goods.

first-degree murder The killing of another person after premeditation and deliberation.

focal concerns Values, such as toughness and street smarts, that have evolved specifically to fit conditions in lower-class environments.

fraud Misrepresenting a fact in a way that causes a deceived victim to give money or property to the offender; false pretenses.

front running A form of stockbroker chiseling in which brokers place personal orders ahead of a large customer's order to profit from the market effects of the trade.

gang rape Forcible sex involving multiple attackers.

gay bashing Violent hate crimes directed toward people because of their sexual orientation.

general deterrence A crime control policy that depends on the fear of criminal penalties, convincing the potential law violator that the pains associated with crime outweigh its benefits.

general strain theory (GST) The view that multiple sources of strain interact with an individual's emotional traits and responses to produce criminality.

general theory of crime (GTC) A developmental theory that modifies social control theory by integrating concepts from biosocial, psychological, routine activities, and rational choice theories.

genocide The attempt by a government to wipe out a minority group within its jurisdiction.

grand jury A group of citizens chosen to hear testimony in secret and to issue formal criminal accusations (indictments).

grand larceny Theft of money or property of substantial value, punished as a felony.

group boycott A company's refusal to do business with retail stores that do not comply with its rules or desires.

hate crime A violent act directed toward a particular person or group because of a discernible racial, ethnic, religious, or gender characteristic.

homophobia Extremely negative overreaction to homosexuals.

homosexuality Erotic interest in members of one's own sex.

hung jury A jury that is unable to agree on a decision, thus leaving the case unresolved and open for a possible retrial.

hypoglycemia A condition that occurs when glucose (sugar) in the blood falls below levels necessary for normal and efficient brain functioning.

id The primitive part of people's mental makeup, present at birth, that represents unconscious biological drives for food, sex, and other life-sustaining necessities. The id seeks instant gratification without concern for the rights of others.

impersonal coercion Pressures beyond individual control, such as economic and social pressure caused by unemployment, poverty, or business competition.

incapacitation effect The idea that keeping offenders in confinement will eliminate the risk of their committing further offenses.

incarceration Confinement in jail or prison.

index crimes The eight most serious offenses included in the UCR: murder, rape, assault, robbery, burglary, arson, larceny, and motor vehicle theft.

indictment A written accusation returned by a grand jury charging an individual with a specified crime, based on the prosecutor's presentation of probable cause.

informal sanctions Disapproval, stigma, or anger directed toward an offender by significant others (parents, peers, neighbors, teachers), resulting in shame, embarrassment, and loss of respect.

information-processing theory Theory that focuses on how people process, store, encode, retrieve, and manipulate information to make decisions and solve problems.

insider trading Buying and selling securities based on business information derived from a position of trust and not available to the general public.

institutional anomie theory The view that anomie pervades U.S. culture because the drive for material wealth dominates and undermines social and community values.

instrumental crimes Offenses designed to improve the financial or social position of the criminal.

instrumental Marxist One who sees criminal law and the criminal justice system as capitalist instruments for controlling the lower class.

instrumental violence Violence designed to improve the financial or social position of the criminal.

integrated theory A complex, multifactor theory that attempts to blend seemingly independent concepts into a coherent explanation of criminality.

interactional theory A developmental theory that attributes criminal trajectories to mutual reinforcement between delinquents and significant others over the life course—family in early adolescence, school and friends in midadolescence, and social peers and one's own nuclear family in adulthood.

interactionist view The belief that those with social power are able to impose their values on society as a whole, and these values then define criminal behavior.

interdisciplinary Involving two or more academic fields.

interpersonal coercion The use of force, threat of force, or intimidation by parents, peers, or significant others.

interrogation The questioning of a suspect in police custody.

involuntary manslaughter A homicide that occurs as a result of acts that are negligent and without regard for the harm they may cause others, such as driving under the influence of alcohol or drugs.

jail Institution, usually run by the county, for short-term detention of those convicted of misdemeanors and those awaiting trial or other judicial proceedings.

just desert The principle that those who violate the rights of others deserve punishment commensurate with the seriousness of the crime, without regard to their personal characteristics or circumstances.

justice model View that emphasizes fairness and equal treatment in criminal procedures and sentencing.

justification defense Criminal defense that claims an illegal action was justified by circumstances and therefore not criminal. Justification defenses include necessity, duress, self-defense, and entrapment.

La Cosa Nostra A national syndicate of 25 or so Italian-dominated crime families who control crime in distinct geographic areas.

landmark decision A ruling by the U.S. Supreme Court that serves as a precedent for similar legal issues; often influences the everyday operating procedures of police agencies, trial courts, and corrections institutions.

larceny Taking for one's own use the property of another, by means other than force or threats on the victim or forcibly breaking into a person's home or workplace; theft.

latent delinquency A psychological predisposition to commit antisocial acts because of an id-dominated personality that renders an individual incapable of controlling impulsive, pleasure-seeking drives.

latent trait A stable feature, characteristic, property, or condition, such as defective intelligence or impulsive personality, that makes some people crime-prone over the life course.

latent trait theory The view that criminal behavior is controlled by a "master trait," present at birth or soon after, that remains stable and unchanging throughout a person's lifetime.

law of criminal procedure Judicial precedents that define and guarantee the rights of criminal defendants and control the various components of the criminal justice system.

left realism Approach that sees crime as a function of relative deprivation under capitalism and favors pragmatic, community-based crime prevention and control.

life-course persister One of the small group of offenders whose criminal career continues well into adulthood.

life-course theory Theory that focuses on changes in criminality over the life course; developmental theory.

lifestyle theories The view that people become crime victims because of lifestyles that increase their exposure to criminal offenders.

longitudinal research Tracking the development of the same group of subjects over time.

Mafia A criminal society that originated in Sicily, Italy, and is believed to control racketeering in the United States.

mandatory sentences A statutory requirement that a certain penalty shall be carried out in all cases of conviction for a specified offense or series of offenses.

manslaughter A homicide without malice.

marginalization Displacement of workers, pushing them outside the economic and social mainstream.

marital exemption Traditional legal doctrine that a legally married husband could not be charged with raping his wife.

marital rape Forcible sex between people who are legally married to each other.

Marxist criminology The view that crime is a product of the capitalist system; radical criminology.

Marxist feminism Approach that explains both victimization and criminality among women in terms of gender inequality, patriarchy, and the exploitation of women under capitalism.

masculinity hypothesis The view that women who commit crimes have biological and psychological traits similar to those of men.

mass murderer One who kills many victims in a single, violent outburst.

mens rea A "guilty mind"; the intent to commit a criminal act.

merchant privilege laws Legislation that protects retailers and their employees from lawsuits if they arrest and detain a suspected shoplifter on reasonable grounds.

middle-class measuring rods The standards by which authority figures, such as teachers and employers, evaluate lowerclass youngsters and often prejudge them negatively.

minimal brain dysfunction (MBD) An abruptly appearing, maladaptive behavior, such as episodic periods of explosive rage.

Miranda rights Rights of criminal defendants, including the right against selfincrimination and right to counsel, spelled out in the case of *Miranda* v. *Arizona*.

misdemeanor A minor crime usually punished by a short jail term and/or a fine.

monozygotic (MZ) twins Identical twins.

moral entrepreneur A person who creates moral rules, which thus reflect the values of those in power rather than any objective, universal standards of right and wrong.

Mosaic Code The laws of the ancient Israelites, found in the Old Testament of the Judeo-Christian Bible.

motivated offenders People willing and able to commit crimes.

murder The unlawful killing of a human being (homicide) with malicious intent.

naive check forgers Amateurs who cash bad checks because of some financial crisis but have little identification with a criminal subculture.

narcotic A drug that produces sleep and relieves pain, such as heroin, morphine, and opium; a habit-forming drug.

National Crime Victimization Survey (NCVS) The ongoing victimization study conducted jointly by the Justice Department and the U.S. Census Bureau that surveys victims about their experiences with law violation.

nature theory The view that intelligence is largely determined genetically and that low intelligence is linked to criminal behavior.

negative affective states Anger, frustration, and adverse emotions produced by a variety of sources of strain.

neurophysiology The study of brain activity.

neurotic In Freudian psychology, a personality marked by mental anguish and feared loss of control.

neurotransmitters Chemical compounds that influence or activate brain functions.

neutralization techniques Methods of rationalizing deviant behavior, such as denying responsibility or blaming the victim.

neutralization theory The view that law violators learn to neutralize conventional values and attitudes, enabling them to drift back and forth between criminal and conventional behavior.

noninterventionist model The view that arresting and labeling offenders does more harm than good, that youthful offenders in particular should be diverted into informal treatment programs, and that minor offenses should be decriminalized.

nurture theory The view that intelligence is not inherited, but is largely a product of environment. Low IQ scores do not cause crime, but may result from the same environmental factors.

obscenity Material that violates community standards of morality or decency and has no redeeming social value.

occasional criminals Offenders who do not define themselves by a criminal role or view themselves as committed career criminals.

offender-specific The idea that offenders evaluate their skills, motives, needs, and fears before deciding to commit crime.

offense-specific The idea that offenders react selectively to the characteristics of particular crimes.

organizational crime A legal offense, such as price fixing, restraint of trade, or hazardous waste dumping, committed by an institution or its representatives; corporate crime.

organized crime Illegal activities of people and organizations whose acknowledged purpose is profit through illegitimate business enterprise.

overt pathway Pathway to a criminal career that begins with minor aggression, leads to physical fighting, and eventually escalates to violent crime.

paraphilia Bizarre or abnormal sexual practices that may involve nonhuman objects, humiliation, or children.

parole A conditional early release from prison, with the offender serving the remainder of the sentence in the community under the supervision of a parole officer.

passive neglect Failure to report income or pay taxes when due; a misdemeanor.

passive precipitation Personal or social characteristics of victims that make them "attractive" targets for criminals; such victims may unknowingly either threaten or encourage their attackers.

patriarchal Male-dominated.

peacemaking Approach that considers punitive crime control strategies to be counterproductive and favors the use of humanistic conflict resolution to prevent and control crime.

penitentiary State or federally operated facility for the incarceration of felony offenders sentenced by the criminal courts; prison.

penology Subarea of criminology that focuses on the correction and control of criminal offenders.

personality The reasonably stable patterns of behavior, including thoughts and emotions, that distinguish one person from another.

petit (petty) larceny Theft of a small amount of money or property, punished as a misdemeanor.

pilferage Employee theft of company property.

plea bargain An agreement between prosecution and defense in which the accused pleads guilty in return for a reduction of charges, a more lenient sentence, or some other consideration.

population All people who share a particular characteristic, such as all high school students or all police officers.

pornography Sexually explicit books, magazines, films, or tapes intended to provide sexual titillation and excitement for paying customers.

positivism The branch of social science that uses the scientific method of the natural sciences and suggests that human behavior is a product of social, biological, psychological, or economic forces.

postmodernist Approach that focuses on the use of language by those in power to define crime based on their own values and biases; also called deconstructionist.

posttraumatic stress disorder Psychological reaction to a highly stressful event; symptoms may include depression, anxiety, flashbacks, and recurring nightmares.

power The ability of persons and groups to control the behavior of others, to shape public opinion, and to define deviance.

power–control theory The view that gender differences in crime are a function of economic power (class position, one-versus two-earner families) and parental control (paternalistic versus egalitarian families).

precedent A rule derived from previous judicial decisions and applied to future cases; the basis of common law.

preemptive deterrence Efforts to prevent crime through community organization and youth involvement.

preliminary hearing Alternative to a grand jury, in which an impartial lower-court judge decides whether there is probable cause sufficient for a trial.

premeditation Consideration of a homicide before it occurs.

premenstrual syndrome (PMS) The idea that several days prior to and during menstruation, excessive amounts of female sex hormones stimulate antisocial, aggressive behavior.

preventive detention The practice of holding dangerous suspects before trial without bail.

price-fixing A conspiracy to set and control the price of a necessary commodity.

primary deviance A norm violation or crime with little or no long-term influence on the violator.

primary prevention programs Programs, such as substance abuse clinics and mental health associations, that seek to treat personal problems before they manifest themselves as crime.

prison State or federally operated facility for the incarceration of felony offenders sentenced by the criminal courts; penitentiary.

probable cause Evidence of a crime, and of a suspect's involvement in it, sufficient to warrant an arrest.

probation The conditional release of a convicted offender into the community under the supervision of a probation officer and subject to certain conditions.

problem behavior syndrome (PBS) A cluster of antisocial behaviors that may include family dysfunction, substance abuse, smoking, precocious sexuality and early pregnancy, educational underachievement, suicide attempts, sensation seeking, and unemployment, as well as crime.

pro bono The provision of free legal counsel to indigent defendants by private attorneys as a service to the profession and the community.

professional criminals Offenders who make a significant portion of their income from crime.

Prohibition The period from 1919 until 1933, when the Eighteenth Amendment to the U.S. Constitution outlawed the sale of alcohol; also known as the "noble experiment."

prosecutor Public official who represents the government in criminal proceedings, presenting the case against the accused.

prosocial bonds Socialized attachment to conventional institutions, activities, and beliefs.

prostitution The granting of nonmarital sexual access for remuneration.

pseudomaturity Characteristic of life-course persisters, who tend to engage in early sexuality and drug use.

psychodynamic (psychoanalytic) Theory originated by Freud that the human personality is controlled by unconscious mental processes developed early in childhood, involving the interaction of id, ego, and superego.

psychotic In Freudian psychology, a personality marked by complete loss of control over the id, characterized by delusions, hallucinations, and sudden mood shifts.

public defender An attorney employed by the state whose job is to provide free legal counsel to indigent defendants.

public order crime Behavior that is outlawed because it threatens the general well-being of society and challenges its accepted moral principles.

Racketeer Influenced and Corrupt Organization Act (RICO) Part of the federal Organized Crime Control Act of 1970, which defines racketeering and provides penalties including prison, fine, and forfeiture of business assets.

radical criminology The view that crime is a product of the capitalist system; Marxist criminology.

rape The carnal knowledge of a female forcibly and against her will.

rational choice theory The view that crime is a function of a decision-making process in which the potential offender weighs the potential costs and benefits of an illegal act.

reaction formation Irrational hostility evidenced by young delinquents, who adopt norms directly opposed to middle-class goals and standards that seem impossible to achieve.

recidivism Repetition of criminal behavior.

recognizance Pledge by the accused to return for trial, which may be accepted in lieu of bail.

reflective role-taking Assuming an identity based on the actual or perceived appraisals of others.

rehabilitation Treatment of criminal offenders aimed at preventing future criminal behavior.

rehabilitation model View that sees criminals as victims of social injustice, poverty, and racism and suggests that appropriate treatment can change them into productive, law-abiding citizens.

reintegrative shaming Brief and controlled shaming that is followed by forgiveness, apology, repentance, and reconnection with the community.

relative deprivation Envy, mistrust, and aggression resulting from perceptions of economic and social inequality.

reliable Producing consistent results from one measurement to another.

restitution Permitting an offender to repay the victim or do useful work in the community rather than face the stigma of a formal trial and a court-ordered sentence.

restorative justice Using humanistic, nonpunitive strategies to right wrongs and restore social harmony.

restorative justice model View that emphasizes the promotion of a peaceful, just society through reconciliation and reintegration of the offender into society.

restraint of trade A contract or conspiracy designed to stifle competition, create a monopoly, artificially maintain prices, or otherwise interfere with free market competition.

retrospective reading The reassessment of a person's past to fit a current generalized label.

right to counsel The right of a person accused of crime to have the assistance of a defense attorney in all criminal prosecutions.

robbery Taking or attempting to take something of value by force or threat of force and/or by putting the victim in fear.

routine activities theory The view that victimization results from the interaction of three everyday factors: the availability of suitable targets, the absence of capable guardians, and the presence of motivated offenders.

sampling Selecting a limited number of people for study as representative of a larger group.

schizophrenia A severe disorder marked by hearing nonexistent voices, seeing hallucinations, and exhibiting inappropriate responses.

secondary deviance A norm violation or crime that comes to the attention of significant others or social control agents, who apply a negative label with long-term consequences for the violator's self-identity and social interactions.

secondary prevention programs Programs that provide treatment such as psychological counseling to youths and adults after they have violated the law.

second-degree murder A homicide with malice but not premeditation or deliberation, as when a desire to inflict serious bodily harm and a wanton disregard for life result in the victim's death.

seductions of crime The situational inducements or immediate benefits that draw offenders into law violations.

self-control A strong moral sense that renders a person incapable of hurting others or violating social norms.

self-control view The view that white-collar crime, like all crime, is a product of low self-control.

self-report surveys A research approach that requires subjects to reveal their own participation in delinquent or criminal acts.

semiotics The use of language elements as signs or symbols beyond their literal meaning.

sentencing circle A peacemaking technique in which offenders, victims, and other community members are brought together in an effort to formulate a sanction that addresses the needs of all.

serial killer One who kills a series of victims over a long period of time.

sexual abuse Exploitation of a child through rape, incest, or molestation by a parent or other adult.

shield laws Legislation that protects rape victims from being questioned about their sexual history unless it bears directly on the case.

shoplifting The taking of goods from retail stores.

situational crime prevention A method of crime prevention that seeks to eliminate or reduce particular crimes in narrow settings.

situational inducement Short-term influence on a person's behavior, such as financial problems or peer pressure, that increases risk-taking.

snitch Amateur shoplifter who does not self-identify as a thief but who systematically steals merchandise for personal use.

social altruism Voluntary mutual support systems, such as neighborhood associations and self-help groups, that reinforce moral and social obligations.

social bond The ties that bind people to society, including relationships with friends, family, neighbors, teachers, and employers. Elements of the social bond include commitment, attachment, involvement, and belief.

social capital Positive relations with individuals and institutions, as in a successful marriage or a successful career, that support conventional behavior and inhibit deviant behavior.

social class Segment of the population whose members are at a relatively similar economic level and who share attitudes, values, norms, and an identifiable lifestyle.

social conflict theory The view that crime is a function of class conflict and power relations. Laws are created and enforced by those in power to protect their own interests.

social control theory The view that people commit crime when the forces that bind them to society are weakened or broken.

social development model (SDM) A developmental theory that attributes criminal behavior patterns to childhood socialization and pro- or antisocial attachments over the life course.

social disorganization theory Branch of social structure theory that focuses on the breakdown of institutions such as the family, school, and employment in inner-city neighborhoods.

socialization Process of human development and enculturation. Socialization is influenced by key social processes and institutions.

social learning theory The view that people learn to be aggressive by observing others acting aggressively to achieve some goal or being rewarded for violent acts.

social process theory The view that criminality is a function of people's interactions with various organizations, institutions, and processes in society.

social reaction theory (labeling theory) The view that people become criminals when significant members of society label them as such and they accept those labels as a personal identity.

social reality of crime The main purpose of criminology is to promote a peaceful, just society.

social structure theory The view that disadvantaged economic class position is a primary cause of crime.

sociobiology View that human behavior is motivated by inborn biological urges to survive and preserve the species.

sociological criminology Approach to criminology, based on the work of Quertelet and Durkheim, that focuses on the relationship between social factors and crime.

sodomy Illegal forms of sexual intercourse, as defined by statute.

specific deterrence The view that criminal sanctions should be so powerful that offenders will never repeat their criminal acts.

stalking A pattern of behavior directed at a specific person that includes repeated physical or visual proximity, unwanted communications, and/or threats sufficient to cause fear in a reasonable person.

status frustration A form of culture conflict experienced by lower-class youths because social conditions prevent them from achieving success as defined by the larger society.

statutory crimes Crimes defined by legislative bodies in response to changing social conditions, public opinion, and custom.

statutory rape Sexual relations between an underage minor female and an adult male; though not coerced, an underage partner is considered incapable of giving informed consent.

stigmatization Ongoing degradation or humiliation, in which the offender is branded as an evil person and cast out of society.

stigmatize To apply negative labeling with enduring effects on a person's self-image and social interactions.

strain The anger, frustration, and resentment experienced by people who believe they cannot achieve their goals through legitimate means.

strain theory Branch of social structure theory that sees crime as a function of the conflict between people's goals and the means available to obtain them.

stratified Grouped according to economic or social class; characterized by the unequal distribution of wealth, power, and prestige.

strict liability crimes Illegal acts in which guilt does not depend on intent. They are usually acts that endanger the public welfare, such as violations of health and safety regulations.

structural Marxist One who sees criminal law and the criminal justice system as means of defending and preserving the capitalist system.

subculture A set of values, beliefs, and traditions unique to a particular social class or group within a larger society.

subculture of violence Norms and customs that, in contrast to society's dominant value system, legitimize and expect the use of violence to resolve social conflicts.

suitable targets Objects of crime (persons or property) that are attractive and readily available.

superego Incorporation within the personality of the moral standards and values of parents, community, and significant others.

surplus value The difference between what workers produce and what they are paid, which goes to business owners as profits.

systematic forgers Professionals who make a living by passing bad checks.

target hardening Making one's home or business crime-proof through the use of locks, bars, alarms, and other devices.

target hardening strategy Locking goods into place or using electronic tags and sensing devices as means of preventing shoplifting.

target removal strategy Displaying dummy or disabled goods as a means of preventing shoplifting.

temperance movement The drive to prohibit the sale of alcohol in the United States, culminating in ratification of the Eighteenth Amendment in 1919.

terrorism The illegal use of force against innocent people to achieve a political objective.

testosterone The principal male sex hormone.

three strikes and you're out Policy whereby people convicted of three felony offenses receive a mandatory life sentence.

thrill killing Impulsive slaying of a stranger as an act of daring or recklessness.

trait theory The view that criminality is a product of abnormal biological and/or psychological traits.

transitional neighborhood An area undergoing a shift in population and structure, usually from middle-class residential to lower-class mixed use.

truly disadvantaged The lowest level of the underclass; urban, inner-city, socially isolated people who occupy the bottom rung of the social ladder and are the victims of discrimination.

turning points Critical life events, such as career and marriage, that may enable adult offenders to desist from crime.

underclass The lowest social stratum in any country, whose members lack the education and skills needed to function successfully in modern society.

Uniform Crime Report (UCR) Large database, compiled by the Federal Bureau of Investigation (FBI), of crimes reported and arrests made each year throughout the United States.

utilitarianism The view that people's behavior is motivated by the pursuit of pleasure and the avoidance of pain.

valid Actually measuring what one intends to measure; relevant.

victimless crime Public order crime that violates the moral order but has no specific victim other than society as a whole.

victim–offender reconciliation programs Mediated face-to-face encounters between victims and their attackers, designed to produce restitution agreements and, if possible, reconciliation.

victimologists Criminologists who focus on the victims of crime.

victimology The study of the victim's role in criminal events.

victim precipitation theory The view that victims may initiate, either actively or passively, the confrontation that leads to their victimization.

victim–witness assistance programs Government programs that help crime victims and witnesses; may include compensation, court services, and/or crisis intervention.

virus A computer program that disrupts or destroys existing programs and networks.

voluntary manslaughter A homicide committed in the heat of passion or during a sudden quarrel; although intent may be present, malice is not.

white-collar crime Illegal acts that capitalize on a person's status in the marketplace. White-collar crimes may include theft, embezzlement, fraud, market manipulation, restraint of trade, and false advertising.

NAME INDEX

SUBJECT INDEX

PHOTO CREDITS

Page v: A. C. Cooper Ltd.; by permission of The Inner Temple   vii: AP/Wide World Photos   x: © Esbin-Anderson/The Image Works   xiii: AP/Wide World Photos

Chapter 1.   1: A. C. Cooper Ltd; by permission of The Inner Temple, London   2: A. C. Cooper Ltd; by permission of The Inner Temple, London   3: AP/Wide World Photos   5: The Image Works   11: © Scott Houston/Corbis Sygma   18: AP/Wide World Photos

Chapter 2.   26: © Topham/The Image Works   27: AP/Wide World Photos   36: © Rodolfo Gonzalez/*Rocky Mountain News*/Corbis-Sygma   43: © Deborah Copaken/Liaison Agency

Chapter 3.   48: © The Register-Guard/Corbis-Sygma   49: AP/Wide World Photos   51: © Albany Times Union/The Image Works   57: AP/Wide World Photos   61: AP/Wide World Photos

Chapter 4.   67: AP/Wide World Photos   68: AP/Wide World Photos   73: © John T. Barr/Liaison Agency   79: The Granger Collection, New York, NY   86: AP/Wide World Photos

Chapter 5.   91: © Sovereign/PhotoTake   92: AP/Wide World Photos   100: Dr. Alan Zametkin/Clinical Brain Imaging, Courtesy of Office of Scientific Information, NIMH   108: AP/Wide World Photos

Chapter 6.   117: © Lee Snider/The Image Works   126: AP/Wide World Photos   129: AP/Wide World Photos   139 © Stephen Shames/Matrix

Chapter 7.   145: © Anthony P. Gutierez/Liaison Agency   150: AP/Wide World Photos   158: © Deborah Copaken/Liaison Agency   160: AP/Wide World Photos   167: AP/Wide World Photos

Chapter 8.   171: © Paul Joseph Brown/Seattle Post Intelligencer   175: © Andrew Lichtenstein/Corbis-Sygma   179: © Jana Birchum/The Image Works   183: AP/Wide World Photos   189: AP/Wide World Photos

Chapter 9.   193: © Will Waldron/The Image Works   197: AP/Wide World Photos   203: AP/Wide World Photos   208: © Steven Rubin/The Image Works

Chapter 10.   217 and 218: © Esbin-Anderson/The Image Works   219: AP/Wide World Photos   222: AP/Wide World Photos   227: AP/Wide World Photos   237: AP/Wide World Photos   241: AP/Wide World Photos

Chapter 11.   249: © Starr/Stock, Boston   250: Roy 20 CVii f. 41v British Library/Bridgeman Art Library   257: © Alex Quesada/Matrix   260: AP/Wide World Photos

Chapter 12.   267: Reuters/Joe Traver/Archive Photos   271: AP/Wide World Photos   276: AP/Wide World Photos   279: AP/Wide World Photos   291: AP/Wide World Photos

Chapter 13.   295: © Todd Yates/ Black Star   296: Edward Keating/New York Times Picture   299: AP/Wide World Photos   302: © Lebraun/Photo Agency News/Liaison Agency   308: AP/Wide World Photos   318: AP/Wide World Photos

Chapter 14.   329: AP/Wide World Photos   330: AP/Wide World Photos   334: AP/Wide World Photos   342: AP/Wide World Photos   346: AP/Wide World Photos   354: AP/Wide World Photos